MANUAL OF
DWARF CONIFERS

HUMPHREY J. WELCH

MANUAL OF
DWARF CONIFERS

THEOPHRASTUS   1979

15 14 13 12 11 10 9 8 7 6 5 4 3 2 1

Library of Congress Cataloging in Publication Data

Welch, Humphrey James.
  Manual of dwarf conifers.

  Bibliography: p.
  Includes index.
  1. Dwarf conifers. I. Title.
SB428.W42   635.9'775'2   79–675
ISBN 0–913728–07–1

Published by
Theophrastus Publishers/Garland STPM Press
A division of Garland Publishing, Inc.
545 Madison Avenue, New York, New York   10022

Printed in the United States of America

CONTENTS

AUTHOR'S INTRODUCTION

When my earlier book on dwarf conifers appeared, although it was loosed onto an unsuspecting public with only a publisher's usual warning, it did not lack introduction—and that of the most unimpeachable authority—because Mr. J. S. L. Gilmour, then Director of the University Botanic Garden, Cambridge, and (amongst other things) Chairman of the International Commission for the Nomenclature of Cultivated Plants, the body responsible for producing the *International Code of Nomenclature of Cultivated Plants,* without whose help the book could not have been written, kindly agreed to write a Foreword for it. I have no doubt that some of Mr. Gilmour's well intentioned, albeit incautious remarks in its favour helped a great deal in the kindly reception of the book by the public, extending to a second edition two years later, but now that, much amplified, it appears as a new book I cannot pretend that it any longer needs introduction in the same sense as it did at the first, so I feel the time has come to stand on my own feet and write my own introduction.

This at once poses a question: 'What am I to say?' Introductions by authors are seldom read, for the simple reason that they are frequently long and consisting mainly of remarks of so general a nature that the author could not decide which chapter to put them in. To avoid this I shall deal only with two points.

The first point is simple—I have tried this time to make it better as a reference book by including many new forms and by adding authorities and synonymies.

My second point—acknowledgments of help received—is not simple at all. Previously I did not attempt any acknowledgment of help received, partly for fear of damaging reputations should my book make a flop. But so much extra help from so many others has gone into this new book that here again I feel I am come to the moment of truth.

To begin compiling a list of those who should be included was simple enough. Names flooded into the mind—those of nurserymen, for instance, from both hemispheres and worlds old and new, some famous, some obscure, some who shared my native tongue, some who were multi-lingual, and some who spoke no word of English. There were the botanists at the Royal Botanical Gardens at Kew and Edinburgh and at The British Museum, and the patient librarians at those institutions and at the Royal Horticultural Society. And then there were the Instituut voor de Veredeling van Tuinbouwgewassen at Wageningen in Holland, the Arnold Arboretum in the United States, and many other establishments in that country and others throughout the world—nor can I ever forget the antiquarian booksellers in several countries of the world who worked so hard and with such great profit to build up my own conifer library.

But where was I to stop? What about the amateurs and dwarf conifer enthusiasts and the many knowledgeable visitors to the Pygmy Pinetum? And where do I begin in time? Do notes of conversations with, say, the late A. H. Nisbet of Gosport 18 years ago come in, and if so what about scraps of information recorded in those early days which turned out to be wrong yet undoubtedly contributed to the building up of the knowledge I drew on in the end in preparing the present work?

Inevitably, in the circumstances, even a reasonably complete list of merited acknowledgments would be so little short of a horticultural *'Who's Who?'* that, reluctantly, I cannot undertake it. Anyone who has ever attempted to compile a work of reference of this kind will forgive me for making exceptions in order to acknowledge the patient enthusiasm of my secretary, Mrs. V. A. Hayward, and the patient tolerance of my wife Elaine. These apart, there must be very few persons interested in dwarf conifers who cannot trace their own contribution to the book somewhere in its pages.

I can only say to everyone 'Thank you all very much!'

H. J. Welch

LIST OF ILLUSTRATIONS

CHAPTER ONE
GENERAL INTRODUCTION

When the first edition of my earlier book appeared in 1966 there had been no major work on dwarf conifers published during the 28 years that had elapsed since the second edition of the late Murray Hornibrook's classical work on the subject *Dwarf and Slow-Growing Conifers* was issued in 1938.

When Hornibrook produced his first edition in 1923 he found that the classification and nomenclature of this interesting group of plants was in considerable confusion. He very largely, although not entirely, sorted things out, but 28 years is too long for any group of cultivated plants to lack its own literature, so when I took up the study of dwarf conifers I found that in the intervening years confusion had once again reared its head—might even have been said to be reigning—and I felt that continuity had been largely lost and that whilst Hornibrook's valuable work on this group would always have to be the basis of any new contribution, yet in a very real sense I was having to make a fresh start. In my previous book I wrote: 'If we have all been helped to identify our plants by means of this book and its illustrations . . . my principal object in writing it will have been realized. Most of the present almost hopeless confusion will have been dissipated if in this matter we follow the injunction of St. Paul in another connection and "all speak the same thing" '. I have, privately, been much gratified by the success of that book in this particular direction.

History has also repeated itself in another way. The appearance of Hornibrook's book gave rise to a lot of interest in the planting of dwarf conifers and many new forms were evidently brought to his notice and so he wrote his second edition from much fuller knowledge and was able to correct certain earlier mistakes and add much more material. I now find myself in a similarly fortunate position.

The dwarf conifers form a valuable group of garden plants which is enjoying a revival of interest nowadays after some decades of partial neglect. In North America they are becoming increasingly popular whilst in several European countries and in the British Isles the gardening public seem to have discovered the dwarf conifer, to judge from the increase in the demand for these plants.

I believe that there is much more in this than a passing craze, since in these days of ever more diminutive gardens no group of plants is more successful in producing, in scale with the reduced surroundings, that sense of maturity and serenity which their full size counterparts have always brought to the spacious landscape gardening of the past. And when, as nowadays, all the emphasis is on the saving of labour in the garden I can understand their increasing popularity, since they are (I dare not, of course, use the word fool-proof) most accommodating as to soil and—within limits—climate, and are singularly free from pests and diseases. Once established they are permanent, evergreen and require the minimum attention. Indeed, I believe that, taking the year round, no type of planting will give more pleasure over the years than a well chosen group of dwarf conifers.

The term conifer is one of those words which we commonly use and suppose that we understand, but which give rise to difficulties as soon as we try to define them. It includes of course the true cone-bearing trees such as the Pines, Spruces and Larch, also Cupressus and Thuja. After that the purists may argue about the inclusion of this genus or that, but for most of us it includes the Junipers and Yews and similar tree-like groups which rely for their garden value upon having evergreen foliage rather than a display of flowers. But if we can happily leave a definition of the word conifer to the pundits we are all in trouble over the question 'What is a dwarf conifer?'

To avoid any misunderstanding, perhaps I should explain straight away that throughout this book the term dwarf conifer relates to plants that are naturally dwarf, whether they be species, variety or cultivar, and I have nothing to say about Bonsai trees; i.e., artificially dwarfed plants (they may or may not be conifers) which owe their size to root pruning or other cultural practices. The plants I am dealing with are all natural dwarfs—healthy garden plants in their own right. A dwarf conifer may either be of a species which (although truly a conifer and even perhaps tree-like in habit) reaches its maturity when only a few feet high, or it may be a specimen of a normally tree-like species which as a result of one of Nature's pranks (of which more below) shews much less than the normal rate of growth and so can only achieve, even in maturity, a much smaller plant than the species normally produces.

The use of dwarf conifers had quite a vogue in the middle years of the last century, in the days when horticultural keeping up with the Joneses meant the possession of a better arboretum than Lord So-and-so's in the next county. The few such plantings of those expansive days that still survive remain as proof (or otherwise) of their claim to be dwarf forms, but with the decline in the number and spending power of those large establishments the demand for the dwarf forms virtually disappeared, and many recorded varieties seem to have been lost to cultivation by the end of the century.

With the rise in the vogue for alpine gardening and of rock garden construction based on the aim of simulating nature as closely as possible, a new and altogether happier use for these conifer microforms was found and the demand increased. Apart, however, from occasional references in gardening journals and in general textbooks on conifers there was no literature on the dwarf forms and so when the late Murray Hornibrook published the first edition of his work *Dwarf and Slow-Growing Conifers* in 1923 he was breaking new ground.

In that book he described and listed about 250 varieties. In 1938 he was able to increase the number to about 530, some of which have since been lost to cultivation. On the other hand, many new forms have been introduced. I now

1. Masterly use of one rock and a single dwarf conifer in an area of greensward.

have lists of most of the principal collections throughout the world. It is difficult to be precise, because of duplication of names, but I estimate that if all the forms were combined into one grand global list this would come out at round about the fifteen hundred mark.

Ever since I became interested in dwarf conifers and their nomenclature I have advocated the formation of a national (or even world-wide) reference collection but so far without success. At the Pygmy Pinetum at Devizes, Wiltshire, England, there is now probably the most representative collection of dwarf conifers ever gathered together in one place. It embraces about 1200 varieties and more are constantly being added by exchanges with other collections throughout the world. This collection is open to inspection by visitors during all normal working hours, and as my small contribution to horticulture, is available to all botanic gardens, herbaria and nurserymen anywhere as a source of material for study or propagation.

At this point may I make a suggestion for consideration by members of park authorities of all kinds and their advisers; i.e., that an attraction of local or even regional interest could be made in less space and at less cost of public money by a good collection of dwarf conifers than perhaps in any other way.

The widest range listed by any nursery today is I believe about 200 varieties. A careful search might bring to light in other nurseries a further 50 or so. After that, the hunt would be on. But the average gardener has no interest in astronomical figures; he needs advice in making the best of his own garden. Hardly a garden exists that would not benefit from the presence of some dwarf conifers, and when he first becomes dwarf conifer conscious the garden owner is mainly concerned with how many he should introduce (and, of course, which ones) so as to secure the greatest improvement in his garden without altering its character.

The builder of the tiniest trough garden knows he must have his one or two pygmy trees to give his miniature world scale and an air of permanence and maturity, and the garden or rockery is small indeed that cannot make good use of a half-dozen suitably chosen specimens. A large garden could accommodate 100 or more dwarf conifers without their becoming at all obtrusive. Most gardens will lie between these two extremes, and the planting plan for the average suburban garden might very well find good use for anything from a dozen dwarf conifers upwards.

The best way to purchase dwarf conifers is to go to a nursery which specialises in them. Most local nurseries with a general trade will from time to time buy in a mixed parcel and these will be planted out in some odd corner to await the advent of the occasional customer asking for dwarf conifers. Even if when he arrives he is fortunate enough to find the labels still legible he is unlikely to find in that type of nursery anyone able or willing to answer his invariable question 'How big will it grow?'

The fact is that there is not, nor ever can be, an absolute answer to this apparently simple question. Apart from the fact that the combined influences of locality, climate, nutrition, water supply and so on (from a sheltered valley in Cornwall at one extreme to years of semi-starvation and neglect in its original pot at the other) can affect the rate of growth in the ratio of quite ten to one, trees (whether dwarf or not) unlike animals, do not grow quickly to maturity and then stop. They go on quietly growing for 200 years or more, so clearly any forecast of the probable size of any particular dwarf conifer after five years' growth will look pretty silly 50 years later. Because of this, any advice on ultimate size must be a compromise and therefore the choice of a conifer for a particular situation must be a compromise too. Those magnificent plantings of lofty conifers which we so much admire today will have looked very feeble during the lifetime of those who planted them and perhaps that of their sons as well. Because of this we must, when planting conifers (especially the dwarf forms), abandon the instinctive idea that we are planting for posterity and in its place accept what I call the *useful life* concept.

This means that where we need a conifer of a certain size to give us the particular garden effect we wish to achieve, instead of choosing a very dwarf form and either (a) putting in a tiny plant and waiting for many years for the effect we want, or (b) scouring the country for a large and ancient specimen and paying the high price rightly asked for such a thing (if we can find one), we select a somewhat stronger-growing form that we know will outgrow the situation we have to fill, purchase a plant large enough to give us a worthwhile immediate effect (yet at reasonable cost), enjoy it as it grows for five to ten years knowing all the time that its days are numbered, and replace it with a fresh young specimen when we feel it has outgrown its welcome.

In other words we accept that that conifer will have a useful life of five to ten years *in that particular spot*. Lifting and replanting any tree every second or

2. Good use of upright-growing forms to give a strong foreground interest in the Royal Botanic Garden, Edinburgh.

3. Another view in the same garden.

4. Dwarf conifers used to give interest and emphasis to a house approach. Mixed planting at the residence of H. J. Draijer at Heemstede, Holland.

5. *Picea abies* 'Microsperma' flanking the late H. J. Hohman's front door at Kingsville Nursery, Kingsville, Maryland, U.S.A.

third year will slow down its rate of growth much more effectively than heavy pruning can ever do, and in this way we put off the evil day when replacement of the tree can no longer be deferred. Not only this, a tree thus treated will have developed a dense, fibrous root system ideal for facing yet another move. So it need not be destroyed. If we ourselves have neither room elsewhere in the garden to set it out permanently where it will have room to develop to maturity, nor a neighbour who has, almost certainly the local parks or highway authority will be only too glad to make use of it.

Many gardeners will choose trees the appearance of which at a show or in a nursery appeals to them, caring little or nothing whether they are labelled correctly or at all, but for the keen plantsman who must have his plants correctly named I would say 'Go to the nurseries that make a specialty of dwarf conifers'. There are not many of these, but their number is on the increase. There even is one nowadays which grows nothing but dwarf conifers.

So far as possible get plants that are 'on their own roots'. This means simply that they have been propagated from cuttings (less commonly by layering) and not by grafting. There is actually no inherent objection to grafted plants. Pinus, Cedrus, Pseudotsuga, Larix, some of the Picea and a few varieties of some other genera are impossible to propagate economically from cuttings so these must be increased by grafting and the resulting plants are healthy and long-lived. But conifers respond to rootstock vigour just as much as do fruit trees. As is well known, an apple variety worked on the dwarfing stock EM IX remains small and suitable for use as a cordon or dwarf bush whereas the same variety worked on a vigorous stock such as EM XVI will soon become a large tree. Similarly, a dwarf conifer grafted on to a strong-growing seedling of an arboreal species will make much stronger growth than we want and may even lose character entirely. Unfortunately, producers of nursery stock whose normal aim is, of course, to produce a good, vigorous and healthy looking plant, tend to overlook the different requirements when it comes to dwarf forms and this has brought all grafted plants of dwarf conifers under a cloud of suspicion. It is always possible to detect a grafted plant—the healed-over but still discernible remains of the graft will be found on the trunk an inch or so above the soil, but it is impossible to tell with certainty what rootstock has been used. Some estimate of the vigour of the plant can be formed by a careful inspection of the amount of annual growth it has been making in the nursery, but the safest course is to avoid grafted plants whenever possible. This is specially the case if you are buying the real pygmy forms for a trough garden or window box.

A word of warning is needed as to the figures for annual rates of growth given by writers on dwarf forms. Where these have been measured on plants growing in pots or on recently transplanted specimens they will bear no reference whatever to the growth of a healthy, well established plant in the open ground.

There is another important but seldom mentioned advantage in buying dwarf conifers from a specialist nurseryman in this country who raises his own stock, since the importation of conifers in several genera is prohibited under the *Importation of Forest Trees (Prohibition) Orders*. Nurseries dependent upon obtaining

6. Dwarf conifers planted in a formal grouping at the National Botanic Garden, Glasnevin, Dublin.

7. Dwarf conifers grouped informally in a corner of the Pygmy Pinetum at Devizes, Wiltshire, England.

supplies from abroad will consequently be unable to supply Abies, Larix, Picea, Pinus, Pseudotsuga, Sequoia, Tsuga or Thuja, and many of our choicest dwarf forms are found in these genera.

I should have liked to finish this chapter for the benefit of my scientifically-minded readers with a learned account of how dwarf forms originate but it would appear that little is known of the mechanism giving rise to nature's freaks and oddities amongst which (let us admit it) our cherished dwarf forms have to be classed. At the practical level of the average gardener's mind, however, sufficient is known to enable us to group the dwarf forms to our own satisfaction, the advantage of so doing being the knowledge it brings us of the probable behaviour of our plants, especially with regard to their likelihood of reversion. A gardener's classification is as follows:

SEEDLING MUTATIONS

From time to time a seedling will appear showing some distinct variation from the rest. This may be a peculiarity in vigour (in this way arise giant and dwarf forms), in colour (presenting us with golden and glaucous forms), in habit (fastigiate, weeping and globose forms) or in foliage (thread-like, congested and monstrous forms). These seedling mutations are very uncommon. It is possible that dwarf seedling forms arise more frequently than we suppose but the chances of survival in the wild or in a forestry nursery (where the culling of the runts is normal practice) are very small indeed, and the probability of raising a new dwarf form from a packet of conifer seed is of the order of millions to one against. Occasionally one such plant has been rescued from destruction by someone with an eye to its value as a garden plant, and by subsequent vegetative propagation it has found its way into our gardens as a named dwarf form. These seedling forms as a class are stable and show no tendency to revert to the typical arboreal form, although there is a tendency for the peculiarity to become less pronounced with age; i.e., golden forms become greener, congestion of foliage gets less noticeable, dwarf forms develop more vigour and so forth.

Examples of seedling mutations are most cultivars of *Chamaecyparis lawsoniana* and *C. obtusa*, *Chamaecyparis pisifera* 'Nana', *Picea abies* 'Clanbrassiliana' (probably) and most if not all the cultivars of *Thuja occidentalis*. Unfortunately for us, a trick Nature has done once she can do again, so at any time a seedling may turn up showing the same peculiarity or combination of peculiarities as an already established cultivar in anything from a broadly similar to an indistinguishably identical manner. At either end of the range the situation is clear enough. Where there are marked differences from all existing cultivars and the new seedling is felt after prolonged trial to have some distinctive garden value it can be propagated and given a new cultivar name, as has been done in the case of all the various globose forms of *Thuja occidentalis* that have been named. At the other end of the range a seedling so like an existing cultivar as to be indistinguishable from it even in old age may sometimes get propagated in its place and no harm will have been done. In any intermediate situation on the other hand, in cases where small differences from existing clones are discernible (or are found to develop as the new seedling ages) the possibility of confusion arises in two ways. The plant may stray into cultivation under an existing cultivar name and so give it a reputation for being variable (this is the probable explanation in the *Chamaecyparis lawsoniana* forms 'Forsteckensis' and 'Tamariscifolia', where in both cases I believe there are several clones in cultivation) or it may be enthusiastically named by its excited and impatient owner, only to turn out in the end to be for all practical purposes identical with an existing cultivar. In every case the exercise of caution and restraint on the part of the raiser is necessary and no attempt should ever be made to introduce a new cultivar until the mother plant has been allowed to grow freely for some years so as to have outgrown any merely juvenile tendencies, and even then the opinion of some authority should be sought on whether the new form is worth introducing. I return to this subject below in Chapter IV.

In this connection it might be well to point out that unless and until a new form is propagated and distributed it is not a cultivar within the definition given in Article 11 of the *Cultivated Code,* and if it is necessary to distinguish it during its period of trial I would suggest that it be grown under a number, or a name containing a number, to avoid any confusion. 'A/40' or 'Bill's No. 1' will define a plant as well as any name and its temporary nature will be self-evident, for such number-names are frowned on heavily in Recommendation 31A of the *Code.*

We are told that Nature preserves her species by making her freaks sterile, so, as we should expect, most of the seedling mutations we have in our gardens do not set seed. But once in a while Nature relaxes her vigilance and lets one get by and in that event it is usually found that the resulting seedlings or most of them have reverted to the typical, arboreal habit of the species, but occasionally a seedling will arise in which the peculiarity of its mother is accentuated. In Chapter V I retell the story of how the pygmy forms of *Chamaecyparis obtusa* arose from seeds developing on the usually sterile dwarf form *Chamaecyparis obtusa* 'Nana Gracilis'. In recent years *Chamaecyparis lawsoniana* 'Fletcheri' has been seeding freely and a few pygmy seedlings have been reported. I hope we are not in for another collection of named forms almost impossible to tell apart after a few years, and that raisers of these interesting plants will exercise patience and restraint.

The true weeping forms are of the seedling mutation class and so this peculiarity is stable. These forms will need to be grafted on to a stem as is done with standard roses or be trained up to a cane in their nursery days unless they are to remain for ever a sprawling victim of their own congenital inability to lift their branches off the ground. Left to grow like this they are usually more curious than beautiful, but where a bold rock face is to be clothed they can be very effective. Plants in this group are *Picea abies* 'Inversa' and 'Reflexa' and *Cedrus libani* 'Sargentii'.

JUVENILE FIXATIONS

This might be considered a sub-form of the previous class.

All seedling conifers commence life with a type of foliage quite unlike the adult foliage which the plant develops later. Occasionally a seedling can continue to carry only juvenile foliage all its life. These fixed juvenile forms may grow into trees (see Chapter V for remarks on the special case represented by the Junipers) and may even set seed on juvenile foliage, but in the majority of cases they also show much reduced vigour, so are amongst us as dwarf forms. Several of them are excellent garden plants.

The juvenile foliage of all conifers is very similar in general appearance and these longer and more freely held leaves were once thought to give a plant something of the appearance of heather. As a result, most of these forms have been given the cultivar name 'Ericoides' so it is not surprising that there is much uncertainty in gardens as to the correct labelling of these forms. At one time two botanists named Siebold and Zuccarini supposed that they were all species of a distinct genus which they named *"Retinospora"*, but the occasional development of adult foliage dispels this notion and these juvenile forms have been distributed, not without difficulty, amongst the species to which they each belong. The name *"Retinospora"* survives on many old labels and, incredibly enough, in a few nurseries (where often it is not even spelt correctly) although it has been officially abandoned by botanists for more than a quarter of a century. 'This nuisance must now cease' fits the case and will be the case if and when the public refuse to purchase any plant labelled *"Retinospora"* or *"Retinispora"*.

In some species there are also forms with foliage intermediate between the juvenile and the adult form. A familiar case is *Chamaecyparis pisifera* in which the juvenile forms are given the name 'Squarrosa' and the intermediate forms the name 'Plumosa'. As might be expected in the circumstances these forms are often variable and sometimes unstable. A few (e.g., *Chamaecyparis pisifera* 'Squarrosa Minima') may suddenly throw up strong adult growth which soon takes over if not removed. Others may show plumose growth on squarrose forms and *vice versa*, and even the stablest of the juvenile forms may occasionally throw a small spray of the typical, adult foliage. This, by revealing to us the specific loyalty of our plant, is very interesting, but any tendency of the plant to extend this habit should be cut away immediately.

BUD MUTATIONS

This is the usual origin of variegated forms. These have arisen as sporting branches shewing this peculiarity on a normal green plant. It can be argued that any departure from the normal in plant life must represent in some degree a loss of perfect health and this may be the reason why these variegated forms are often lacking in vigour although apparently healthy in other respects. As this

8. Dwarf conifers in a formal layout at Castlewellan, Saintfield, Northern Ireland, home of a fine conifer collection.

loss of vigour makes them slow-growing it can be an advantage from the gardener's point of view.

Several genera of conifer are prone to sudden and so far unexplained mutations. These can occur within a growth bud or at any point along a shoot and they invariably result in a change in vigour. Local stands of trees of exceptionally vigorous growth, of great interest to foresters, may possibly have originated in a mutation which resulted in an increased rate of growth, but the phenomenon is usually only taken notice of where a decrease in vigour results in a dense mass of foliage popularly referred to as a witch's broom. Forms of abnormal and congested growth are found on many kinds of plants, but whereas these are always otherwise associated with parasites or other pathological causes, within the conifers often no causal mechanism can be found. Frequently the reduction in rate of growth and leaf size is not accompanied by a reduced number of buds and where this occurs the broom may get so dense that its interior becomes a mass of dead tissue and where the rest of the tree has continued to grow normally the whole broom will eventually perish through lack of light.

Except for this the growth is quite healthy and it has been found that cuttings or grafts taken from the broom develop into dwarf plants with a quaint charm all of their own and many of our most sought-after dwarf conifers have arisen in this way, *Picea abies* 'Pygmaea' being a typical example. A characteristic of bud mutations is a tendency to revert to the normal colour, type of foliage or habit, as the case may be. The gardener in his practical but unscientific way thinks of some sort of virus having entered the plant to cause the brooming and explains that the reversion is due to the plant's success in 'throwing off the virus'. However that may be, we must keep a close watch on variegated forms and these witch's broom plants and at once cut out any undesirable growth that appears.

Although in most cases the broom growth never develops male strobili or sets cones, these latter have been recorded on several genera including Spruce, Pine and Douglas fir. Invariably the broom cones have been smaller than normal, in scale with the broom growth on which they appear and they carry very small seeds. These are, however, often fertile and accounts of the progeny resulting from the sowing of such seeds have been published from time to time by several writers, references being given below.[1] The general finding has been that whilst about half of the seedlings turned out to be quite normal in habit and rate of growth, the others shewed definite inherited dwarfism in various degrees and gave rise to compact or prostrate little plants. Since these trials have often been conducted by research workers whose main interest has lain in forestry or genetics they have been regarded as of academic interest only and the potential garden value of these dwarf plants has not been explored. Now, however, selections from the plants raised by Alfred Fordham at the Arnold Arboretum of Harvard University, The Arborway, Jamaica Plain, Massachusetts, U.S.A., and Albert G. Johnson et al., at the School of Forestry of the University of Minnesota, St. Paul, Minnesota, U.S.A., in *Pinus banksiana, P. resinosa, P. rigida, P. strobus* and *P. virginiana* have been named and particulars will be found in Chapter V under these species. I have also recently seen a very interesting collection of seedlings showing the same genetic dwarfism in *P. sylvestris* by an experimenter in this country.

If seeds collected from brooms are viable, dwarf plants developed from naturally sown seed must be expected to occur as well. Because of their slowness of growth the survival rate of these dwarf forms must be very low, but it is highly probable that many of the dwarf plants found in the wild have originated in this way, and where a small and very local population of similarly dwarfed plants has been found (as in the well known cases of *Picea glauca* 'Albertiana Conica' and *Tsuga canadensis* 'Minuta') this almost certainly was the case.

[1] 1927 *Hexenbesen: ihre Morphologie, Anatomie und Entstehung.* Liernur, A. G. M., Rotterdam, Nijgh and Van Ditmar, 57 pp. Contains a full Bibliography. (German and Dutch).

1933 'Das Problem der Hexenbesen'. Tubeuf, C. von, *Z. PflKrankh., PflPath. Pflschutz.* **43:** 194–242. (German.)

1933 'Verebung der Hexenbesenbildung bei der Kiefer.' Liese, J., *Z. Forst- u. Jagdw.* **65:** 541–4. (German.)

1936 'Unexplained brooming of Douglas Fir and other conifers in British Columbia and Alberta'. Buckland, D. C. and Kulit, J., *For. Sci.* **3:** 236-242.

1965 'Dwarf Seedlings from Witches' Brooms in Jack Pine'. Johnson, A. G. *et al.* in *Sci. Journ. Ser. Paper No. 5618, Univ. of Minn. Agr. Exp. Sta.,* St. Paul 1, Minnesota. (2 pp) 15th Jan. 1965, and *Paper No. 5758* (2 pp.) 15th April 1965.

1966 'Dwarf seedlings from Broomed Douglas Fir'. Duffield, J. W. and Wheat, J. G., *Silvae Genetica.* **4:** 129–133.

1967 'Dwarf Conifers from Witches' Brooms'. Fordham, A. J., *Arnoldia.* **27:** 29–50.

1967 'Witches' Brooms and Dwarf Conifers'. Corley, R. S., *Gar. Chron.* **161,** 20.

1975 'Witches'-brooms. Sources of New and Interesting Dwarf Forms of Picea, Pinus and Tsuga Species'. Waxman, S., *Acta Horticulturae.* **54.** 25.

Whether or not all variations turning up in the seed beds are due in the first place to a bud mutation is doubtless an interesting speculation for geneticists, but it does seem certain that those forms known to have come to us as seedlings prove to be much more stable in cultivation than those that have been propagated vegetatively from an actual witch's broom. So far as I have been able to ascertain only female cones occur on these brooms, so all the progeny must needs be open pollinated, but another interesting speculation is whether the tiny forms of *Chamaecyparis obtusa* raised by the late G. Gardener, and again more recently by Joel W. Spingarn (see below in Chapter V), were self-pollinated.

ALPINE FORMS

Several species of conifer whose range includes an area of high mountains, although normally of tree-like habit, have developed stunted, shrubby or even prostrate forms, many of which make excellent garden plants. As these are established in the wild and have a natural habitat they are given varietal rank by the botanists so they will have names of Latin form such as *Abies balsamea* var. *hudsonia,* even although they have been brought into garden cultivation. Because they are botanical varieties we find them more or less variable and in a few cases an outstanding clone has been given a cultivar name.

Because of their origin these alpine or mountain forms (the word alpine is commonly used with a wider meaning than its true sense of 'from the Alps') are indestructibly hardy and within the life-span of a single plant seldom revert to the lowland habit of the species and so they are a very useful group. Many are appropriate subjects for Bonsai specimens or, with less rigorous attention, for trough gardens.

CULTIVARIANTS

This is the word I use to describe a class of plant which is not at present recognised by the *Cultivated Code,* although the plants in question are distinguished by characters which are sufficiently stable when reproduced asexually for the plants to fill a distinct place in our planting schemes and consequently to be called for by the gardening public.

In this class there are two distinct groups, although they both arise from the deliberate selection of propagating material. The first group was drawn attention to by the late Murray Hornibrook in his classic work on the dwarf conifers where in his remarks on *Chamaecyparis lawsoniana* 'Fletcheri' he points out the possibility of securing diminutive and often bun-shaped plants from this and certain other upright varieties by the selection of cutting wood from weak-growing shoots low down on the plant.

Our hypothetical gardener friend will come up here with one of his pseudo-scientific theories in explanation. This time he will talk in terms of a mysterious substance (he will probably call it a hormone) which collects at the growing tips

9. Dwarf conifers can be equally well used—in the grand manner.

10. In a small garden corner.

of plants and controls their growth. An upright or pyramidal habit, according to him, is caused by the plant sharply differentiating between the central leader and all other growing tips in its distribution of this substance; a globose habit on the other hand results from its even distribution. The cutting away of the leading shoot or shoots compels the plants to step up the supply to the remaining shoots, causing them to break in the expected manner. A plant that can mobilize its remaining stocks of the hormone to initiate new growth buds when the whole plant has been cut hard back survives, one that cannot do this dies under such hard treatment, and so on.

According to this theory, weak-growing shoots low down on the plant will be so far down the plant's scale of priorities for a ration of this growth substance that they will be so poorly endowed with it (even to the point of its being entirely absent) that when used for cuttings they will produce plants with little or even no ability ever to throw up leader growth. There are some obviously thin places in this theory but it does delightfully cover the known facts. These are that the slow-growing dense foliaged forms often put on the market as 'var. *nana*' frequently romp away quite suddenly after years maybe of very slow growth, as though the plant had suddenly learned how to use its meagre stock of the growth hormone (or perhaps had found out how to make some for itself) yet that it is undeniably possible to obtain in this way pygmy forms which remain so indefinitely and retain their character when propagated. In the Pygmy Pinetum there is a plant *Chamaecyparis lawsoniana* 'Ellwoods Pygmy', obviously a very old plant, which measures 45 cm high by 60 cm across. Rooted cuttings are indistinguishable from the normal 'Ellwoodii' but if (as has happened on occasion) I get the two varieties muddled they are unmistakably distinct after one year's growth.

The other group of cultivariants consists of the low-growing forms frequently listed as 'var. *prostrata*', which have been produced by appropriate selection of grafting wood. If an Abies be examined (Picea and Taxus are much the same) it will be found to carry two types of shoot, leader growth on which the foliage is radial, and side growth on which it is not. The nurseryman knows that the best trees are always produced by the use of leader growth as grafts, but unfortunately there is never enough of this and so he has to use side growth as well, in spite of the additional trouble he knows he will have to take with the resulting plants by careful staking and other professional knowhow to induce it to form the symmetrical, upright plant which most of his customers demand. Left to itself a graft from side wood tends to maintain this horizontal habit however large the plant grows. A large prostrate specimen so produced of any of the good forms of the beautiful blue spruce *Picea pungens,* or of any other of the more spectacular Abies or Picea, tumbling down over the rocks for a dozen or more feet from where it was planted can be a magnificent sight and it is amusing to recollect that most of such plants started life as a graft intended for sale in the normal upright form which was accidentally left (nurserymen are busy folk) until it had become too late to take its training in hand.

Because of this reluctance of side growth to change its habit, plants of these genera are very liable to lose their symmetry if the leader becomes damaged or

11. Dwarf conifers quite at home at one of England's stately homes.

12. Dwarf conifers equally at home in a suburban front garden.

destroyed. To meet this situation Nature has endowed them with the ability to throw up new leader growth from what I believe botanists call a plastic bud. This can on occasion have curious results. Sometimes several such buds will develop, producing a small clump of leader shoots from which one will eventually assume the mastery and become the tree's new leader. Rarely, one fails to appear on or near the trunk (or it may have been neatly removed by a passing cow) but one will develop at the end of a horizontal branch following stimulation from later damage. The resulting tree, looking like half a swastika, is usually too unsightly to be left and so this effect is rarely seen, but the fact that it does happen gives us a clue to the reputed instability of these pseudo-prostrate forms. The fact probably is that they are completely and indefinitely stable, subject to the aptitude the plant has for initiating leader growth from a plastic bud following damage. I know of several of these prostrate blue spruces (there is one at Kew, another at Edinburgh) where this has happened and whenever it does occur the tree always loses its grace and becomes something of a monstrosity, so it behoves us (ourselves, our offspring and our cattle) not to walk about on such plants and to prune them as little as possible. If pruning is necessary it would probably be worth while to watch closely for the appearance of unwanted leader growth the following spring and literally to nip it in the bud.

CHAPTER TWO
THE USES OF
DWARF CONIFERS

The late Murray Hornibrook, who in his early days might very well have had a paragraph all to himself in Burke's *Landed Gentry of Ireland,* obtained much of his information from the large estates around him in some of which extensive plantings of dwarf conifers had been made.

Now, alas, many of these fine gardens are no more. They are either uninhabited, like Kilmacurragh; or, like Curragh Grange and Rostrevor, are occupied by new owners with different interests, and very few indeed of the collections mentioned in his book *Dwarf and Slow-growing Conifers* still survive. And in England, where the social changes of our day have proceeded with perhaps less turbulence than in Hornibrook's native land, many of the stately homes now manage to run the garden with two men and a rotavator whereas at one time they needed twenty men and several boys.

During the same period enormous numbers of smaller houses have been built in every town and village and with them that worthy character the owner/occupier (who, together with the local Council's Parks Department, is the mainstay of the nursery trade these days) has been increasing in his millions.

And it is in these small gardens of today that the dwarf conifer has come into its own. Gone are the days of Capability Brown, the eighteenth century landscape architect and his famous stock remark, 'Your estate has great capabilities, my lord'. The new landed proprietor, when he has ejected the brick ends, cement bags and other debris left by the builder, has to set to work to get his landscape effects in a fraction (often a small fraction) of an acre. The centre of gravity of gardening has shifted from the great estate to the suburban plot, and the obvious plant to reproduce on the new scale the effect of serenity and restful maturity produced on the grand scale by plantations of majestic conifers is, of course, the dwarf conifer.

The garden uses of dwarf conifers are many. Perhaps the most obvious place for them is on the rock garden or around the garden pool. The habit of growth of many of the forms suggest at once their garden value. The prostrate, mat-forming forms of the Junipers, for example, are useful ground cover plants, excellent for draping a bank or an old tree root, whilst certain of the conical or even the globose forms make excellent specimens for isolation on a small lawn or in tubs on the terrace.

I should like to see a national (or, better still, an international) collection of dwarf conifers under the control of a suitable public authority in some place readily accessible to the public where not only would each plant be labelled

13. Part of the dwarf conifer collection in the Dortmund-Brunninghausen Botanic Garden, West Germany.

14. A corner of the Pygmy Pinetum at Devizes, Wiltshire.

with unimpeachable accuracy so as to be in practice the end of all controversy on questions of identification or nomenclature, but where the potential value of the different forms would have been developed and exploited so that lovers of gardens of all sizes (the gardens I mean) could gather inspiration and ideas for use at home.

Pending some such development I am doing the best that I, as an individual can do, to fill the gap here in Devizes. The Pygmy Pinetum has been planted on an open hillside which has lent itself to the construction of a rock garden on a bold scale in which the large blocks of stone that were available could be used to simulate rocky outcrops. As well as taking great pains to get my labelling correct I have tried to exploit the various potential uses of the differing forms, colours, textures and habits of the dwarf conifers and their association with other plants.

In my planting I have observed few rules, believing that in this as in every form of art to look right is to be right. But certain conclusions have formed in my mind as the result of some of my experiments and experience here, particularly as to the most effective use to be made of certain varieties, and these I refer to in Chapter V under the names of the plants concerned.

There is, however, one basic and inescapable rule, I believe, for the use of dwarf conifers (along with miniature plants of any kind, no doubt) and that is, ALWAYS PLANT THEM IN THE OPEN AWAY FROM OTHER LARGE PLANT MASSES. The dwarf conifers are serious, dignified little plants and they resent being made to look ridiculous. Our object must be to use dwarf conifers to set the scale of the miniature garden picture and not let them become out of scale by the overtowering presence of larger plants.

The key word in the use of dwarf conifers is *scale* and from this arises another useful principle, which is to plant dwarf conifers wherever possible together in groups. This is more of a recommendation than a rule as there are clear exceptions, but in a general way it can be said that dwarf conifers usually look best together. Planted in this way they are in scale with each other. If dwarf conifers are used in the traditional way, on a rockery, they thereby automatically achieve this grouping more or less, but there are many other ways of using them and if your space (or pocket) indicates the purchase of any particular number of trees—be it only half a dozen—I would say without hesitation that you would probably get more landscape value and pleasure from your new treasures by grouping them together as a feature than by dotting them about here and there all over the garden where they can only be viewed one at a time.

Such a feature could well be made on a lawn. On a large lawn it could look well a little to one side of the main area so as not to appear lost, yet have mown grass all round it. The bed should be raised up very slightly towards the middle, near which one conifer larger than the rest and of a sturdy upright habit will look well dominating the lower varieties around it. In a large planting, other dominant specimens will need to be used to form fresh centres of interest at other spots and it is not at all a bad plan in planting to start with these dominant plants, adding the lower planting around them.

On a smaller scale the same principles can be followed in grouping your dwarf conifers to form a definite garden picture. If a good composition is achieved it is at all times pleasing to the eye and since many of the dwarf conifers change colour two or even three times a year the tone values of the group are constantly altering. Some of our plants put on their richest colouring during the winter and what could be expected to give more pleasure than such a group planted where it can be seen from a principal livingroom window from whence its winter beauty could be enjoyed in comfort whatever the weather happened to be outside.

Since, in addition to the scenic effect they create, your dwarf conifers will demand close examination and admiration as individual specimens there should always be sufficient paths (or even stepping stones) so that no tree is further from a path or other convenient viewpoint than, say, two metres.

In every case the background is important and needs careful consideration. In the large plantings referred to (a very good example is the Nisbet collection at the Royal Horticultural Society's garden at Wisley) the group will be large enough to hold one's attention from whatever direction one approaches it and isolation itself may be all the background that is necessary, but in smaller plantings it will generally be the case that our garden picture will mainly or always be viewed from one direction and here the background must be chosen (as a picture frame is chosen) to set off the picture and isolate it from its surroundings. A background of tall trees—at a respectful distance—is excellent and where space is limited an evergreen hedge may be the answer; or the group may be placed so that a fence or even a building will serve the purpose.

The use of dwarf conifers in rockeries and alpine gardens is, of course, well established and many would say that this is the best use for them. As well as suggesting an alpine atmosphere their evergreen sturdiness of itself sets off the usually low-growing flora around them and any who have attempted alpine gardening without the use of dwarf conifers will be surprised at the improvement brought about by the introduction of a few well chosen specimens.

For this class of work the selection of the suitable form of tree is especially important. It should always be remembered that one is seeking to reproduce a scene from nature in one of her wilder moods, so anything savouring of smugness is to be avoided and plants should be selected for each situation of a form which would be expected in just that situation in the wild. For this reason the globose forms and others of a neat and formal outline are in a general way the least useful. Wholly prostrate forms of the *Juniperus horizontalis* type should be used sparingly, for they almost all spread eventually over a large area that could be more usefully used for other alpines, but in this class both *Juniperus conferta* and *Juniperus procumbens* 'Nana' are useful plants because of their willingness to grow downhill. They are consequently valuable for covering banks or old tree roots, and the former will even hang down and cover vertical rock faces like an aubrieta.

The dwarf Picea are a very useful group. They range from low-growing forms which never reach much over 30–40 cm high but spread slowly outwards (examples are *Picea abies* 'Nidiformis', 'Repens' and 'Tabuliformis') through less

15. A corner of the Layne Ziegenfuss collection at Hillside Gardens,
Lehighton, Pennsylvania, U.S.A.

prostrate cushion and bun forms ('Pumila', 'Pumila Nigra' and 'Gregoryana' and
its various forms) to globose plants ('Clanbrassiliana') and pyramidal forms
('Remontii'). In this latter class comes the popular *Picea glauca* 'Albertiana
Conica'. This plant grows into a neat green cone which with a little attention
may, if you wish, be made to look as though it had been turned on a lathe. A
single specimen of this variety always catches the eye, and a group (for
preference of varying heights) can be most effective, but always—because of its
formal symmetry—it should be planted somewhere on the low ground and well
out in the open.

Low-growing varieties of irregular outline of the *Juniperus* × *media* 'Pfitzerana' type are very useful and this variety itself can be utilised in most alpine
gardens. It will in time become a large plant but it stands being kept to size by
heavy pruning better than most of us do.

Many of the real pygmies will be quite at home in suitable nooks and
crannies amongst the rocks and there are several of the slow-growing and bush-
like forms of Juniper which if planted young and deliberately left unpruned will
grow into a gawky, one-sided plant which will look most attractive at the foot
of a rock cliff, where it will appear as though the plant had so grown in an
attempt to reach up and outwards to the light. There is quite a colour range of
these, giving us scope for selections either toning or contrasting with the colour
of the rock cliff behind. *Juniperus* × *media* 'Blaauw' is a most attractive blue-grey.
'Kaizuka' is a rich mid-green. 'Plumosa' (green) and 'Plumosa Aurea' (a rich
golden-yellow for most of the year) and the two variegated forms, if left to
themselves, form lower-growing and more compact plants and may need some

training to give us the ruggedness of outline we want just here, but the rich colour of 'Plumosa Aurea' is worth the effort.

It is, however, on the higher parts of the rock garden, at the top of the rocky outcrops, where the greatest care in the choice of suitable varieties is so important. At a first glance these more prominent positions would seem just fine for showing off the beauty and symmetry of some dwarf tree of upright or pyramidal habit and so the tendency is to plant such a tree where in nature it would have been either blown out of the ground in a gale many years ago or at best have been so knocked about by the wind over the years as to have lost all pretension to symmetry of outline. We may not be able to analyse our failure but the eye is instinctively disturbed by such incongruity, whereas a dwarf pine in the same spot (planted with its stem well out of the upright and with its lower branches and all the foliage below the branchlets removed so as to expose the bare bones of the poor windswept veteran) will look just inevitably right and so be aesthetically satisfying. Several of the unsymmetrical cultivars of the Scots pine, *P. sylvestris* ('Beuvronensis', 'Nana', 'Westonbirt') and the many other dwarf pines now becoming available will do excellently.

For the larger spot the Mountain pine, *Pinus mugo* will be suitable, a very good example of its use being on the rock garden at Kew. Several very close-growing selections have been named, but as this pine varies considerably from seed it is often possible to pick out desirable plants in the nursery row.

For any situation more than three or four feet above the level of the path from which it is to be seen I personally feel that the spreading forms should be limited to those with definitely pendulous branch tips, as those with stiff, up-turned growing points give to my eye an unpleasant shock-headed effect. Plants of the form I prefer are *Juniperus × media* 'Pfitzerana', *Chamaecyparis lawsoniana* 'Tamariscifolia' and, of course, the dwarf weeping Cedar of Lebanon, *Cedrus libani* 'Sargentii'.

Juniperus recurva var. *coxii* is quite entitled to a paragraph to itself because of its unique charm as a young plant, especially when planted near water. A specimen in the Wansdyke Nursery about 1.5 m high is without question my best salesman. It has had the lower branches removed and the upper main branches trained out horizontally so that the hanging foliage is well spread out, sufficient of this having been removed to expose the trunk and main framework, and few indeed are the visitors who do not fall for its charm, although warned that (inasmuch as the tree is called the Coffin Juniper because of the demand for its timber in Burma for this purpose) they must expect it to get too big in time.

A few dwarf conifers are essential in the heather garden. Here, contrary to the general rule they should be isolated plants relatively few and far between, only enough of them being used to emphasize the open, windswept terrain. The prostrate forms are quite out of place but the choice may fall on any of those varieties which grow with a rugged, irregular outline such as the varieties of juniper already mentioned in this chapter, and here out in the open safer use can be made of the upright to conical forms. The dark blue-green mass of *Chamaecyparis lawsoniana* 'Ellwoodii' or the slender grace of *Juniperus communis* 'Suecica' or 'Hibernica' can make a delightful contrast with the low masses of the surround-

16. A group of well matured dwarf conifers in Joel W. Spingarn's garden at Baldwin, Long Island, New York, U.S.A.

ing heathers and I know of no better combination than the winter-flowering *Erica carnea* and the loosely conical shape of *Thuja occidentalis* 'Ellwangerana Aurea' with its golden foliage. This is at its best when the Erica are in flower and it seems to revel in the hardest winter weather that comes. A good example of the skilful use of dwarf conifers in this type of garden can be seen in the Valley Garden in Windsor Great Park.

In the United States, where large numbers of houses are of the prefabricated type erected on low walls of concrete, the development of what is there called foundation planting has been necessary. This consists of evergreens planted close to the house to hide the concrete foundations, and for this conifers are widely used. In this country where it is more usual to carry the facing brickwork down to ground level such planting is unnecessary but it is still quite usual for a path to follow the outline of the house at up to a metre or more away. A border so formed is always a problem. Its nearness to the house makes it architecturally important but it is always dry and frequently very draughty, both being conditions in which few plants are happy. Hence the sound advice given in books on garden layout to make it as wide as possible.

Provided that there is sufficient width (one metre being perhaps a fair minimum) several of the dwarf conifers can be used in such a border with good effect. Care should be taken to avoid overplanting. This tendency is inevitable because the need to cover unsightly foundations as soon as possible can easily lead to the use of varieties much too vigorous for such a restricted spot, but in this country we have no such excuse.

As a group the junipers are probably best able to deal with the dry conditions, and the semi-prostrate forms of *Juniperus × media* and *Juniperus sabina* are particularly useful. Where there is ample room for it to develop, a plant of *Juniperus × media* 'Pfitzerana' planted right at the main corner of the house can be very impressive, but in most gardens today it would be well to choose the

17. Part of Fred Bergman's collection at Raraflora, Feasterville, Pennsylvania, U.S.A. Note how the dwarf forms are kept away from tall trees.

compact form 'Pfitzerana Compacta'. Low-growing, conical and upright forms can be used to give a point of emphasis where needed, but these should not (for both practical and architectural reasons) be planted in front of windows. In this sort of situation, where the wall of the house forms the background, regard must always be had to its colour and tone in order to secure a good contrast, and in the choice of planting the amount of sunshine the plants will get should be borne in mind.

The entrance door to the house needs special attention. In a very simple small forecourt garden a pair of Irish yews (the golden form where the house walls are grey stone or dark red brickwork and the dark green form where the walls are of any light colour) may be all that is necessary to give simple emphasis to the doorway. Where there is greater room more elaborate planting can be attempted and where there is plenty of space a grouping of conifers to flank the entrance can be made quite a feature, especially if the ground rises towards the house, necessitating a low flight of steps. These large groups should be planned not only for the effect architecturally as one approaches the building but so as to give a picture from the doorway itself, from whence it will most frequently be viewed both by our visitors and ourselves. In all but the simplest schemes it is usually better to secure balance than to attempt symmetry.

In all these suggestions I do not want to give the impression that dwarf conifers should be used alone. Although, as I have said, they are usually most effective used in groups they readily and happily associate with other plants, provided these are not too exuberant. The evergreen azaleas and the smaller daphnes, for example, even when not in flower, make a good combination with dwarf conifers by virtue of their contrasting foliage texture, and doubtless the same can be said of most of the slow-growing broadleafed shrubs. Carpeting plants can be allowed to grow right to the trunks of the trees and thereby save much weeding, providing that care be taken to avoid the more rampant and invasive species and varieties. Many dwarf bulbs look beautiful when in flower (if planted in fairly bold groups rather than individually dotted about under the dwarf conifers) but the garden varieties usually look out of scale.

I am frequently asked whether any of the dwarf conifers are suitable as indoor plants and my invariable reply is to suggest that two or preferably three little trees should be established in pots so that they can be brought indoors in turn. By this system of horticultural shift work they should all continue in excellent health and a small tree or two can give a lot of pleasure to an invalid or to one whose own green-finger days are over, and they would need far less constant attention than do Bonsai specimens. The trees should be changed around every month or two. During their indoor shift they should have the coolest and lightest position available and they should be plunged to the rims in the garden during their off duty shifts.

In any garden a few selected dwarf conifers established in pots can be very useful in many ways. They can be used as ornaments in their own right in a cold greenhouse or on the terrace and they may be plunged here and there in the alpine garden or border wherever and whenever a note of evergreen is needed to emphasize the floral picture of the moment. It should be borne in mind that all conifers in pots will need care in the matter of regular watering and they will enjoy frequent heavy syringeings on summer evenings (all conifers like this), especially in the dusty atmosphere of large cities.

Amongst the miscellaneous uses to which dwarf conifers can be effectively put is the planting of graves. Provided that care be taken to select varieties that can be relied upon to remain dwarf and that full advantage is taken of the range of available colours and habits of growth, a simple group of dwarf conifers can be quite as effective as any attempt to grow flowers in such a restricted area, and of course will be far less trouble to maintain. It is a particularly useful solution to the problem set by those graves that are cared about but which are impossible to visit frequently.

CHAPTER THREE
CULTIVATION REQUIREMENTS

As a broad generalization covering the present chapter I can state that dwarf conifers are hardy and tough, do well in any ordinary soil and are of easy cultivation.

As regards their being hardy and tough: Whilst this is a fair enough general statement, they do in fact range on the hardiness scale from near indestructibility downwards to a few which need to be given a sheltered spot, and even in these cases winter hardiness appears to be more a dislike of strong wind than inability to withstand low temperatures.

In more detail again: Abies, Cedrus, Juniperus, Picea, Pinus, Thuja and Thujopsis seem to stand up to any winter weather, this being especially true as one would expect of the mountain forms such as *Abies balsamea* var. *hudsonia* and the low-growing forms of the tree junipers. The dwarf forms of Chamaecyparis, Cupressus, Podocarpus and the other genera with which we are concerned follow their full size relatives with respect to hardiness. That means to say that they will stand a great deal of exposure but may suffer in an extreme winter. Usually the golden and white-tipped forms are more susceptible to winter damage than the green forms and in all genera (except perhaps Juniper) the fixed juvenile forms seem to be the least reliable. These forms should therefore be given as much shelter as possible from cold winds or (what is worse) draughts. A few of the Podocarps are reliably hardy only in the milder parts of the British Isles.

Turning now to the matter of soil: My statement about dwarf conifers doing well in any ordinary soil can be amplified by stating that any garden soil we are likely to meet comes within that description. On soil overlying chalk or with a very high lime content choice should be limited to Juniperus and Taxus and, fortunately for those who have to garden under those conditions, these genera include a very wide range of colour, habit and texture forms, but other than this no worry need be felt about planting dwarf conifers in any soil in which gardening at all is possible. If conifers do well in your district you can be assured of success. If they are conspicuously absent from the local landscape it is much more likely to be an unsuitable climate than any peculiarity of the soil. In such conditions you may have to provide an immediate environment for your dwarfs that is more to their liking if they are to succeed.

An idea sometimes met with is that the dwarf conifers need peat. This may have arisen from a general practice with trade exhibitors at flower shows of using a thin covering of this material to complete their exhibits, but it has no substance; it may in fact lead to losses because of the difficulty of really firm planting in peaty mixtures. I know of one case where a collection of dwarf conifers given to a well known garden was planted in stations prepared by heavy additions of peat and losses occurred which might have been avoided had the trees been planted out straight into the soil and been trodden firmly.

Another notion that one meets is the idea that because dwarf conifers are choice and sought-after plants they need to be planted in exceptionally good soil. In a general way the truth is just the opposite to this, for both slowness of growth and ultimate dwarfness are functions of the rate of growth, and given a rich diet even the slowest of growers must be excused for responding with unusual and unwelcome vigour. Conversely, the strongest grower will be slow-growing if kept on near starvation diet. Considerable control can therefore be exercised over the future growth of any dwarf conifer as of any plant. So if you have only been able to obtain a very small specimen of some choice rarity, one that would be quite ineffective in the place you have in mind, the thing to do is to plant it temporarily in a good spot, encouraging it with a handful of bonemeal mixed thoroughly into the soil at the time of planting. If on the other hand you have large specimens that you do not want to increase greatly in size, plant them in the poorest soil you can find or (more effective still) use a container of some sort to restrict the root spread. This can be anything from a large flower pot to a derelict dust-bin with a few holes knocked in its bottom for drainage.

The check to growth resulting from being lifted and replanted is itself a useful deterrent to any plant and a specimen that is just right in a particular situation can be kept from increasing in size almost indefinitely by being lifted and replanted occasionally, the opportunity being taken to do a little discreet root pruning each time.

Arising out of this last suggestion I might point out what a great deal of fun can be had with dwarf conifers by getting right away from the idea that we are planting them in permanent homes. With large-growing trees of all kinds (and even down to such things as roses) this from the nature of the case has to be our outlook and the utmost we can do is to interplant our permanent trees with something quick-growing that can later be grubbed when it has served its purpose, but with the dwarf forms there is no need whatever to regard anything we do as finality. Each tree as it increases in size can be used in the situation for which it is ideally suited at the time and be moved into a large home when it needs one and is large enough to fill it adequately.

Once this idea has taken root in any real gardener's mind he will enjoy many happy hours during each summer, planning the autumn's moves. Special meetings of the Garden Planning Committee will be called to discuss this proposal and that amendment during the summer evenings when backs are beginning to ache too much for any more bending tonight, and as soon as there has been some real soaking rain to soften the ground the re-arrangements decided upon can be carried out in plenty of time for the little trees to settle down and make fresh roots in their new homes while the soil is still warm; in time too for the matter to be put right before the winter really sets in if, in spite of all the planning, it is felt that a mistake has been made. This paragraph will probably make me very

18. A well laid out exhibit of dwarf conifers. Another part of J. W. Spingarn's collection in Baldwin, Long Island, New York, U.S.A.

unpopular in the nursery trade because re-arranging one's trees can be nearly as much fun (fortunately not *quite* as much) as buying new specimens, but there is always the possibility of the gardener forgetting that a tree—especially a large one—is very liable to suffer from dryness at the roots during the first summer after a move of this kind and finding that he has to visit the nursery in search of a replacement for the tree he has unfortunately lost through his forgetfulness.

Dwarf conifers can either be purchased in pots or from the open ground according to the tradition in the nursery to which you go, some inclining towards growing all their stock in pots and others preferring to grow them in the more natural conditions of open ground cultivation. Still other firms keep their young stock in pots and grow the larger sizes under field conditions.

As a general rule plants from the open ground are stronger and more in character than their counterparts in pots and they will usually have a better root system. This is especially true of larger specimens that have been kept in a pot for too long (see Illus. 23). (Remember that the present vogue for containerising is for the benefit of the seller—not that of the plant or the buyer). On the other hand you can buy (and plant) dwarf conifers from pots at any part of the year, whereas nurseries carrying the whole of their stock in the open ground will probably be willing to take an order for autumn delivery but will refuse to serve you during the summer.

However your plant comes to you, never pop it into the ground just as it stands. If your plant has been growing in a pot the chances are that it will have its roots in a dense tangle with one or more long roots going round and round at the bottom of the pot. These long roots are of no more use to the plant than clock springs which they resemble and they should be cut hard back. Carefully unravel the tangled mass of smaller roots with as little damage to them as possible. Even if you have to wash most of the soil off in a bucket of water it is better to free the root system so that it can be spread out as the planting proceeds, with all the main roots radiating from the plants in their natural manner (this especially goes for what you have left behind of the clock-spring roots) than to plant the pot ball as it is. If plants from the open ground are delivered with the roots in a ball tied round with hessian or some similar material this must be removed. The root system in this case must be broken into sufficiently to enable sizeable roots to be spread out as the soil is back-filled. The aim always is to have the MAIN ROOTS SPREADING DOWNWARDS AND OUTWARDS, SEPARATED BY SOIL, IN THE SAME WAY THAT THE BRANCHES SPREAD UPWARDS AND OUTWARDS, SEPARATED BY AIR. In the case of very large specimens with a heavy ball it may be better to lower this into a hole dug to the exact depth before cutting the hessian away. In this case a small piece must be left in the ground where it will rot and do no harm, but the roots all round can be teased out of the ball and spread in the soil as previously described.

The essential thing in the case of either a pot ball or a hessian ball is to break up at least the surface of the ball and to ensure that some main roots radiate from it into the surrounding soil. Omission of this precaution is probably the greatest single cause of failure to establish balled plants, for if the ball (consisting almost certainly of soil with very different physical properties to the surrounding earth) is just dumped into a hole in the ground it is quite possible for capillary connection never to be established between it and its surroundings. In this case the plant, having drawn every trace of moisture out of the ball when growth commences in the spring, can perish from drought when the rest of the garden may still be too wet to do anything with. If, in addition, the ball is approximately spherical a wonderful ball-and-socket effect is produced and the poor plant rocks to and fro in every wind with no possibility of ever anchoring itself, for any new roots which do succeed in crossing from the ball into the socket are sheered off during the next breezy spell before they ever attain any mechanical strength.

Dwarf conifers can be successfully transplanted at any time from early autumn to late spring, but due to the danger of desiccation before a plant can re-establish itself, planting should not be done when cold weather is due. This means that the months of December, January and sometimes February are best avoided, especially in the case of very small plants. If the vulnerability of spring planted trees to dryness at the roots during the following summer is remembered, spring is probably the best time as the roots are then active and soon get hold in their new quarters, but human frailty being what it is autumn is probably the safest time. If sufficient trouble is taken, however, it is quite practicable to move conifers at any time of the year. During the hot summer of 1960 I moved a number of quite large specimens. The ground at the time was as dry as a brick and they were each lifted with a great block of soil of the consistency of concrete and brought home in the back of the car. They were stood for several days in a mist-propagation house, during which time the ball was frequently watered. When it was nice and soft all through and the foliage was fresh and

19. A part of the collection of dwarf *Picea abies* forms in the Pygmy Pinetum at Devizes, Wiltshire, England. (Note: These plants will require more space as they grow in size).

green from the effect of the mist the trees were planted out in a shaded corner to which no sunlight penetrated and I did not lose a single plant. They are now some of the best specimens in the Pygmy Pinetum.

For amateurs without mist houses the same effect could have been secured by very frequent spraying or syringeing and where natural shade is not available artificial shade can be provided by the erection of a rough timber tripod over the plant with two of its sides covered with hessian, canvas or any available opaque material. This wigwam should have one side left open towards the north and it should be large enough relative to the size of its occupant to allow air to circulate freely around the plant and yet shelter it from the sun throughout the whole day.

Trees purchased in pots during summer should not be planted in the way described above until the autumn. If you are impatient to see them in place they should be stood in a bucket of water for several hours and then be dropped into position (with or without the pot) and watered regularly until they can be dealt with thoroughly later on. Shading will always help a newly planted tree.

No one should attempt to grow plants of any kind indoors or under glass who is not prepared to shoulder conscientiously the full responsibility usually carried by Nature herself in the matter of water supply. All I therefore need to do here is to remind such that a dwarf conifer is probably more prone to suffer from its owner's lapses of memory than other plants because it is often left for years in a more or less pot-bound state and because conifers do not advertise their sufferings like most other plants do by wilting in time for the application of a quick refresher. When conifers show distress they are usually in a very bad way indeed and are probably beyond the point of recovery. Treatment in such circumstances is to stand the pot in a bucket of water for several hours until the whole ball is soaked through, and then to put the plant where it will be in complete shade, syringeing the leaves as frequently as possible until it recovers its usual bright, healthy appearance. It may ease its own burden of recovery by shedding some of its foliage (the gaunt, unfurnished appearance of many pot-grown plants is due to a succession of such crises in their lives) but it will soon show which way things are going, and the abandoned foliage can be rubbed off as soon as it is completely shrivelled and dry.

I have already remarked that newly planted conifers in the open need regular attention during their first summer, especially if May, June or July are dry months, and they should never be allowed to become dry at the roots. Their second year they are, of course, less vulnerable and after that most conifers can safely be left to themselves unless drought conditions develop. Note should be taken of the clause 'in the open' which qualifies the last but one sentence, for conifers planted in hollow stone walls, near buildings and in crazy paving and other inherently dry places will always need watering during the summer.

Almost all conifers thrive best in areas of high rainfall and in consequence of that they all enjoy being sprayed or syringed with water whenever the weather is warm and dry. This is especially so in the grimy atmosphere of cities where the foliage gets not only dry but coated with dust, and always the syringeing seems most effective when done during the evening, so that the leaves remain wet during the night.

Pruning is no mysterious art to be understood only by the initiated few; it is just the simple knowledge of how plants react to damage (in this case our pruning) applied with common sense and a clear idea of what we are trying to do in each case.

Pruning serves two purposes. In the early, formative years of the tree it usually accompanies staking of the central stem to form a trunk, and other practices which would come under the wider term, Training. This type of pruning may consist of either the removal of rival leaders and the lower or overcrowded branches where, as in the case of *Juniperus recurva* var. *coxii,* the beauty of the tree lies in an open habit, or the shortening of growing tips to encourage buds to break lower down in order to produce denser growth, where this is the effect required. In either case no amateur is likely to overdo matters and frequently he needs reminding of the importance of trunk training and formative pruning. I well might paraphrase the words of the wise king of old and say 'Train up a tree in the way it should go and when it is old it will not depart from it'.

Some judicious shortening of the growth after transplanting will always help a plant to re-establish itself after its move, by reducing the burden on the root system until it has had time to make new root hairs. In many cases, such as the prostrate forms of juniper, cutting back of the leading growths each spring for several years is necessary to encourage the plant to form a dense mat. This is exactly the same as the cutting back advocated in the gardening textbooks for newly planted hedges and is done for the same reasons.

The second object of pruning is to keep the tree within bounds. This can be done—and less successfully with some species than others—to a limited extent only, for the reason that hard pruning encourages strong growth. So if you try to restrict a tree to a size *greatly* below its natural inclination you are starting up a vicious circle and would be well advised to move the tree to a spot where it will have more room to develop and plant a dwarfer form in its place.

When I am asked about the pruning of dwarf conifers and the best tool to

20. Dwarf conifers at the United States National Arboretum, Washington, D.C., U.S.A.

use I always advise the use of nail scissors. I do this not only because a pair of nail scissors is in fact a very convenient tool but because by recommending its use I hope I am impressing the enquirer with the desirability of 'little and often' over against the leaving of pruning until stronger and larger tools are needed. A nurseryman uses a knife and for the heavier cuts this is the best tool *provided it is kept sharp.* Nail scissor pruning can be done at any time of the year (what an invitation to the gardener to while away the hours pottering about and fiddling with his trees!) but any heavy cutting is best done in late spring when life is active and new growth will soon cover the scars of battle.

Although this book does not deal with the art of Bonsai yet there are some things we can learn from the Bonsai technique and profit by if used with restraint. I have already suggested the use that can be made of root pruning in keeping our trees from putting on size and the necessity of staking certain varieties in their early years, and if in any particular case a curved trunk would be more pleasing to the eye than a straight one or a branch be required to grow in a particular shape or direction, no objection could be raised to our getting the effect we want by the use of a curved stake or a length of wire loosely twined corkscrew-fashion around the trunk or branch we wish to train until it takes the shape we have chosen. It is important to remember that the season's growth hardens or lignifies during the late summer and autumn, so any training devices should be in position by early August at the latest and will be found to have served their purpose by the winter, whereas once growth has hardened into wood it has become inert and will never change its shape. Force will be needed

21. Dwarf conifers trained to give special effects. *Chamaecyparis pisifera* var. *leptoclada*.

22. *Juniperus procumbens* 'Nana'.

to bend it where we want it to go and we shall have to hold it there by force in a state of internal stress until the following season's growth has hardened around it during the following autumn. Even then when we release the ties the mechanical strength of the old wood that has merely been held in a state of stress all the time will assert itself against the strength of the new wood and the plant will give a bit and take up a shape intermediate between its original and the one we want. Of course, if we have allowed two years' growth before taking the training in hand, not only shall we need to use greater force and stronger ties— we shall need to leave them in place for two autumns at least. Hence the importance of training young growth during that first summer.

Certain forms, particularly those with juvenile foliage, are prone to the browning of their leaves by scorching sun or keen wind. In the case of plants suffering in this way in more or less normal weather the answer is to move them to a more sheltered spot, but even the more robust forms may be affected during an exceptional winter or even a prolonged spell of cold wind.

In every case the nursing of a badly burnt plant back into health and symmetry is a difficult task and requires much patient care, sometimes extending over several years, but it is in some obscure way a rewarding one. If only the foliage tips are burnt all that is necessary is to wait until they are completely shrivelled and brown and then at some time when the foliage is quite dry vigorously beat, brush, shake or otherwise coax all the dead leaves to fall off. The wind will do it for you in time but the sooner the dead bits are gone the sooner the tree will recover its good looks. If large areas of foliage die it will indicate that some part of the branch system is also dead. Whether or not such a plant will ever recover a pleasing shape will depend firstly upon the distribution and extent of the die-back and secondly upon the ability of the species in question to break from old wood. In any event the dead patches must be cut away, for they are most unsightly. Dead tissue never comes to life again and the presence of dense areas of dead foliage will prevent the tree from ever regaining its shapeliness. Cutting these away will let light in, encouraging buds to break from the old wood, and a healthy plant will soon colonize the blank spaces. But here a word of caution is necessary: Do not be too eager to cut anything out until you are sure it is dead, for the plant may take some time making up its mind just how much of its branch system it is going to abandon and premature knife action may result in the loss of wood with life in it, where it perhaps can ill be spared from the tree. The safest course is to go over the plant several times at intervals during the spring, each time cutting out only what is indisputably dead, beginning with the browned foliage and only cutting into old wood when little pinheads of new growth indicate the points at which the plant intends to start refurnishing itself.

A very common misapprehension is that conifers, because they are ever-green, do not drop their leaves; but the only difference between an evergreen and deciduous plants is that the latter discard their leaves after a few months, leaving the branches bare during the winter and until the new growth commences in the spring, whereas evergreens hold on to theirs much longer—at least until the next year's leaves develop. The different species vary in their ideas of how long to keep their old leaves but they all let them ripen and fall off in the end. This can have two effects worth mentioning here. One is that certain conifers can look very bedraggled for a few weeks during the summer just when the old leaves are ripening and preparing to drop. This can easily be taken for a sign of ill health (or even impending death) but a close look at the foliage will soon disclose what is taking place and the tree will soon recover its good looks.

The other result of the dropping of the dead leaves is the tendency with many of the more bush-like and densely branched conifers for the dead leaves to collect and build themselves into a dense solid mass in the interior of the plant, especially amongst the lower branches. This is a common cause of the fastigiate forms of *Chamaecyparis lawsoniana* and *Thuja orientalis* becoming bare at the base, for the dense peat-like mass excludes light and completely inhibits growth buds. Gardeners should realize that this is a form of neglect, and they will often find a considerable improvement in the general appearance of a tree results from thorough spring cleaning of its interior. It is not at all unusual to be able to get a wheelbarrow full of debris out of a single large plant. A convenient tool for this work can be easily made out of a piece of stout wire bent into a hook, but the way I have found best is to use the garden hose with a narrow bore nozzle or with one's finger held against the open end so as to produce a high velocity jet, and to work this to and fro right in among the branches. There will probably be considerable doubt as to which has got wetter, you or the tree, but if you have persevered, at close enough range, all the dead rubbish will have been cleared away and you may very possibly be rewarded next spring by the appearance of new foliage much lower down the tree than you had ever again expected to see it.

Older plants of the dense and bushy forms, especially the juvenile forms of *Thuja orientalis* such as 'Rosedalis', consist of a dense surface covering of foliage but the interior will be found to contain much dead wood—the remains of branches that have failed to meet the competition for light and air. If as much of this dead wood as possible be cut away occasionally it will contribute to the health and longevity of the tree. Some of these forms tend to become untidy and irregular in outline as they age and the more open the interior of the plant can be kept the more encouragement there will be for buds to start into growth from the old wood and these will thicken the growth, colonize any bare patches and keep the tree vigorous and shapely in its old age.

Damage from heavy snow can be avoided (or at worst greatly minimized) if the trouble be taken to shake the plant free of the snow as soon as possible after it has fallen and before the subsequent effect of wind, rain, frost or a combination of them increases the burden of snow being carried by the plant to the point of damaging the main branches. Branches of fastigiate forms may need tying up (few gardeners would respond to advice to tie them up before the storm, I am afraid) but surprisingly little damage will have been done if action is taken immediately following the falling of the snow.

Since, as already pointed out, dwarf conifers cannot be raised from seed, they have to be increased vegetatively. The striking of cuttings on a commercial scale is carried out nowadays with quite elaborate equipment, in propagating

23. The Three Corpses—The sad but inevitable result of planting a pot bound specimen without proper care of the root system.

houses provided with controlled bottom heat and mist apparatus, but there is nothing to prevent the home gardener striking a few cuttings of his treasures with the simplest of apparatus. A cold frame on the north side of a hedge or low building where it is fully open to the light but receives no direct sunlight is ideal, but much can be done on a small scale with a few bell-jars or even a bottomless wooden box covered with a sheet of glass. The light (in the case of the cold frame) or the sheet of glass (in the case of the box) should be a close fit and unless the frame is a very substantial affair of brick or concrete it would be all the better for being sunk into the ground until the glass is at or a little above ground level. This sinking will greatly further our aim of sheltering the cuttings from fluctuating and extreme temperatures, which is the reason for the use of the cold frame at all. The wooden box can be similarly sunk, or two boxes can be used, one much larger than the inner one where the cuttings are to go and with the space between them filled up with soil. Sinking must not, of course, be done where there is the slightest danger of flooding.

Eight to ten centimetres of rooting medium should be provided. This could consist of 50 per cent sharp, coarse sand or grit, 25 per cent finely sieved soil and 25 per cent peat. The exact mixture is not important, provided it is what the gardener calls 'open'. This means that it cannot readily become sodden. So, provided the sand predominates and is coarse enough, the soil adds a little nutriment to feed the new roots we hope for and the peat buffers fluctuations in the moisture level, but the proportions are not critical.

In the taking and preparation of the cuttings standard gardening practice should be followed. There is nothing special about cuttings of dwarf conifers except that the cuttings will vary (according to the subject) from the usual 8–10 cm long down to about 2.5 cm in the case of some of the very slow-growing forms. They should be of well ripened one-year-old wood with or without a heel or small portion of second-year wood. One of the most important points with cuttings of all kinds (and dwarf conifers are no exception) is to make quite sure that the soil is well firmed around the base of the cuttings. It is useless to ram the soil at the surface if the base of a cutting is dangling in a pocket of air or loose soil. This is a very frequent source of failure.

Conifers do not seem to be very fussy regarding the time of year at which the cuttings are taken. It can be done either during the autumn or in early spring, but bearing in mind that the cuttings will have to remain in the frame for twelve months or longer and that they are more likely to suffer from excessive heat during the summer than extreme cold during the winter, autumn cuttings will have the advantage during the first and most critical six months.

I intend to be quite non-committal regarding the use of plant hormones as an aid to rooting, for although I usually use a powder dip myself I know several very experienced dwarf conifer 'fans' who maintain that conifers dislike the treatment and root better without it. A dip into a powder fungicide such as Orthocide (Captan) in any case is a wise precaution against the ingress of stem-rot before the cutting has had time to close its defences by forming callus tissues over the wound.

Even with such simple apparatus as described, reasonably good results can be expected from most varieties of Chamaecyparis, Cryptomeria, Juniperus, Picea, Taxus and Thuja, but Cedrus, Cupressus, Pinus, Pseudotsuga and some Abies and Picea range between 'Very Difficult' and 'Impossible', at least on any worthwhile scale, and in consequence the dwarf forms of these genera have to be propagated commercially by grafting, a process which calls for equipment and skills rather outside the range of this book. It might not be amiss, however, to remark that propagation by grafting is necessarily much more costly than the production of plants from cuttings and this is why these genera must always be offered by nurserymen at higher prices.

Most, probably all, conifers can be increased by layering. In some cases all that needs to be done is to lower a plant bodily into the ground (or earth it up) so that only the young growths at the tips of the branches are to be seen and leave it so for one or perhaps two growing seasons until a little exploratory digging at the side of the plant indicates that rooting has taken place freely up the buried branches. The plant can then be taken up and cut with sharp secateurs into two or more rooted pieces, each of which can be treated as a new plant. Where a whole plant cannot be sacrificed in this way the layering of a single branch in the normal textbook manner can always be relied upon to produce roots in time.

I have no experience of air-layering conifers but see no reason to suppose it would not be successful where no branch near enough to the ground is available for layering in the normal manner. But it is at best a cumbersome method—a propagator's last ditch.

CHAPTER FOUR
CLASSIFICATION AND NOMENCLATURE

In my earlier book I included a chapter on nomenclature which, since it attempted a simple account of this far-from-simple subject and provided an introduction to the Codes governing the naming of plants, was of much wider application than the dwarf conifers which were the subject of the book. Although it may have served some useful purpose, I now feel that such a treatment is out of place in a book of this kind, particularly since the same ground is covered much more adequately in other publications[1], and I here assume that my readers have taken the trouble to acquire a basic understanding of plant classification from the book recommended or some similar source, and I limit myself to the particular problems which arise from the application of the Codes of Nomenclature to ornamental conifers (amongst which the dwarf forms represent no separate problem) with only sufficient general references to the subject to enable the less fortunate reader to make at least some sense of it all.

These problems largely spring from the need for compliance with not one but two Codes, the first being the *International Code of Botanical Nomenclature* (often cited as ICBN and popularly referred to as the *Botanical Code*) and the second the *International Code of Nomenclature for Cultivated Plants* (often cited as ICNCP and popularly referred to as the *Cultivated Code*).

In addition to this dual obligation we face all the difficulties arising from the necessity of applying the codes retroactively to the work of writers who gave names to garden conifers before any codes were in being. Our task is the harder for the very brief and inadequate descriptions given by most of these early writers and the virtual non-existence of herbarium specimens to serve as types in the botanical sense.

One difficulty I find many gardeners have is to distinguish between identification, classification and nomenclature. Although today often combined in a single thought-flash they are distinct processes and botanical writers always distinguish between them and use the terms with precision. In human history (as it does today for scientific pioneers) identification came first, and the early need for distinguishing between a floating log and a crocodile must have had its moments. Classification into objects 'safe-' or 'dangerous to jump on' when crossing a river followed identification closely, together with an urgent need for the names (i.e., nomenclature) 'log' and 'crocodile' to warn the surviving members of the tribe. Today, when we send a plant specimen to the Botanical

[1]A book which I have found very helpful is *An Introduction to Plant Taxonomy* by Jeffrey, C. (J. and C. Churchill Ltd., London), 1968.

Garden for 'identification' we are in fact merely asking the botanist there to recognise our plant and fit it into its rightful place in an existing scheme of botanical classification and then to tell us its correct name under the Codes.

The development of any such scheme of classification would have been quite impossible had not botanists long ago noticed that on the one hand Nature herself had grouped her children into assemblages of individuals which were interfertile and recognizably distinct from all other assemblages and separated therefrom by genetically or otherwise controlled barriers preventing or at least restricting interbreeding, and that on the other hand despite these distinguishing differences, different such assemblages often showed similarities that more or less suggested larger and more comprehensive groups. These larger groups are of course now familiar to us as GENERA and the smaller assemblages as SPECIES. Nature having provided us, as is her wont, with anomalies and exceptions of all kinds, no cast-iron definition of either term of universal application has ever been or ever will be contrived. Moreover, since every attempt at classification (of any kind) depends, as it must do, to some extent on judgment and opinion and be based, as it must be, on the best knowledge available *at the time,* finality in botanical nomenclature can never be hoped for. But by laying down that the name of each species shall consist of a 'two-tier' binomial in Latin form consisting of a generic name (a noun) plus a specific epithet (an adjective, or a noun used in a similar way) the problem has been reduced to more or less manageable proportions, and by elaborating rules as to priority, valid publication, the avoidance of the repetition of a name within the forbidden degrees and so on, the Codes have at least secured a basis for stability.[2] Thereon, botanically speaking, hang all the law and the prophets.

With the higher categories in the botanical hierarchy—Families, Orders, Classes and Divisions—we do not here concern ourselves. We are spared anxiety above the rank of genus and even at that level we are much more fortunate in the conifer world than are many of our gardener friends whose interests lie in some other groups. D. R. Hunt of the Royal Botanic Garden, Kew, in an introduction to an up-dated *Reference List of Conifers*[3] drawn up at the time of the Royal Horticultural Society's Conifer Conference held in 1970, in referring to a similar list[4] prepared by the late W. Dallimore for the previous conference held in 1932, was able to write 'Since Dallimore's List was published both conifer taxonomy and conifer nomenclature have remained relatively stable'. In other words he is telling us that for the past 40 years or so there have been very few changes in either generic or specific names amongst the conifers.

[2]It is interesting in this connection to note that the *Botanical Code* on its very first page states 'The only proper reasons for changing a name are either a more profound knowledge of the facts resulting from adequate taxonomic study or the necessity of giving up a name that is contrary to the rules'.

[3]'Reference list of conifers and conifer allies grown out of doors in the British Isles'. D. R. Hunt. Article in *Conifers in the British Isles* (Proceedings of the Third Conifer Conference arranged by The Royal Horticulture Society, 1970) 1972.

[4]'Reference list of conifers grown out of doors in the British Isles'. W. Dallimore. Article in *Conifers in Cultivation* (Report of Conifer Conference held by Royal Horticultural Society in 1931) 1932.

And since this augurs well for similar stability in the future 'For what we have received may we be truly thankful!'.

But just as Nature refuses too much regimentation in the higher categories into which her large family can (anomalies and doubtful cases apart) be classified, so she claims room for manoeuvre within the most basic group of all—the species. So, even where the limits of species are not in dispute, differences between individual plants sometimes occur of sufficient importance for a botanist to take interest in, and for classifying these he can use the ranks below that of species available to him in the *Botanical Code;* i.e., the infra-specific categories—*sub-species* (not much used in the conifer world), *varietas* (plural *varietates*), and *forma* (plural *formae*). They are to him but minor matters but, of course, these are the very differences upon which the whole world of cultivated plants is built.

The *Botanical Code* was the first to be developed. But whilst the botanists were busy about their task of CLASSIFYING plants (this means all plants— past, present and future) and were using their Code to regulate botanical nomenclature, horticulturists were also working on the very same plants in quite a different manner. They, passing over all the others that failed to interest them, were SELECTING particular plants that would make 'good garden forms' or be for some reason or other of interest or value *seen through horticultural eyes,* and the *Cultivated Code* was introduced only when it became realised that these two matters—botanical classification and horticultural selection—were so different, so separate and distinct that the balance of advantage lay in having a second Code. The time lag between the appearance of the two Codes had a most unfortunate effect, one which has left us a legacy of trouble and confusion. Of this, more below.

The *Cultivated Code* accepts the species (and, of course, their names[5]) established under the *Botanical Code* as a basis or starting point and sets out only to regulate matters within each species that are of importance in horticulture. Terms it introduces are Clone, Cultivar and Group.

Most gardeners are familiar with the term Clone. It is defined as 'A genetically uniform assemblage of individuals . . . derived originally from a single individual by asexual propagation, for example, by cuttings, divisions, grafts or obligate apomixis'. The *Code* also defines the term Cultivar as 'An assemblage of cultivated plants which is clearly distinguished by any characters . . . and which when reproduced (sexually or asexually), retains its distinguishing character'. Article 11 of the *Code* sets out four classes of cultivar, but since three of these relate to sexually reproduced plants, a thing almost unheard of amongst ornamental conifers, in OUR PARTICULAR CASE a simplified definition of cultivar will therefore for practical purposes be 'One clone or several closely similar clones'. I would, however, warn my readers that this is a fortunate simplification applicable only to the ornamental conifers we are dealing with in this book (and not entirely without exception, even so) and it must never be thought of as a general principle.

Before any Codes were available it was traditional to name garden conifers,

---

[5] And also, any CHANGES of name—a fruitful source of horticultural discomfiture and irritation.

not by the use of a fancy name such as was usual even then amongst many other garden plants, but by adding one, two or even three Latin-form epithets to the specific name. Although this is no longer permitted, any such Latin-form name in use before 1st January 1959 is to be retained as a cultivar name. These names can, however, sometimes cause misunderstanding and confusion to the unwary in the following ways.

Firstly, gardeners who know that all botanical names are in Latin form and that cultivar names nowadays must be 'fancy' ones may not recognise that many of these older garden forms with their Latin-form names are cultivars and that the names are correctly so used, provided that the new typographical rules are followed. (Thus, in the case of Lord Clanbrassil's spruce, *Picea abies* 'Clanbrassiliana' and *Picea abies* cv. Clanbrassiliana are both correct, *Picea abies clanbrassiliana* and *Picea abies* var. *clanbrassiliana* are not).

Secondly, some early horticultural authors with tidy minds used the English words 'variety' or 'form' (often abbreviated to 'var.' or 'f'.) to distinguish the garden plants they were writing about from the plants normal to the species in question, and this can now give rise to the erroneous idea that those writers were using the botanical categories *varietas* or *forma* (these, unfortunately, having the same abbreviations) with the meanings in use today. The horticultural rather than botanical intention of the writer is paramount in any such case.

Thirdly, with only a *Botanical Code* available at the time, well meaning attempts were made to regulate these Latin-form cultivar names within this now-seen-to-be-inappropriate Code, and this has given to them a spurious botanical status. One writer to do this was the late Professor Alfred Rehder of the Arnold Arboretum of Harvard University, Jamaica Plain, Massachusetts, U.S.A. Rehder's *Manual of Cultivated Trees* is well known to all serious gardeners. It was followed by his *Bibliography of Cultivated Trees* published in 1949, a monumental work commenced in his 76th year (an object lesson to gardeners never to give up), which in 800 or more closely printed pages gives references to the sources of botanical and cultivar names, the valid names and synonyms of all the woody plants found in the second edition of the *Manual,* with some additions. Making the obvious choice from amongst the botanical categories available to him, the Professor sought to reduce the confusion in the nomenclature of what he called the 'clonal garden forms'[6] by listing them all, uniformly, as botanical *formae.*[7] With hindsight—now that there is a *Cultivated Code*—this is very generally regarded as having been unfortunate.

The *Cultivated Code* (Article 10, Note 2) states that the concept of cultivar is

---

[6]Although the term 'cultivar' had by that time come into limited use, Rehder uses the words 'clonal garden forms' with a similar meaning.

[7]Out of respect for probably the greatest taxonomist of all time, I must point out that a study of Rehder's Introduction (to his *Bibliography of Cultivated Trees*) makes it abundantly clear that the Professor was well aware of the insuperable difficulty of handling clonal garden forms by botanical methods, and leads to the conclusion that, were he with us today, he would be the first to welcome the provisions of the *Cultivated Code*. Even his remark (p. xi) 'The purpose of botanical nomenclature . . . is classificatory, whilst the purpose of horticultural [nomenclature] is selective' stamps the Professor as more up-to-date in his outlook in 1949 than are some of the taxonomists one is privileged to bump into in 1976.

essentially different from the concept of *varietas*. It could well have added the words 'and also of any other botanical category', since any such must always be a class of plants (the result of botanical classification) whereas a cultivar, whether it consists of a single clone or a thousand, is always a single entity seen through horticultural eyes (the result of horticultural selection). So although within a species the rank *forma* may as a general rule be regarded as the one most nearly approaching the concept of cultivar, it is still essentially different therefrom. The circumscription of a cultivar, however closely in any particular case at any particular time it may appear so to be, can therefore (because of this essential difference) never be the circumscription of a *forma* (nor of any botanical taxon) because, on the one hand, the latter concept must include individuals either existing or which may be found in the future which do not or will not fall within the circumscription of the cultivar, and because, on the other hand, a fresh selection giving rise to a new cultivar may at any time be made from within the *forma* (or as the case may be). It follows that any attempt to deal with the nomenclature of cultivars within the Botanical system is an impossibility. We cannot create a botanical combination out of a botanical non-entity. Such attempts may have succeeded in regimenting confusion: with the best of intentions they could never reduce it. As cultivars these plants began, cultivars they are now seen to be and (we must now add) CULTIVARS THEY HAVE BEEN ALL THE TIME.

The general trend amongst horticultural writers nowadays is to treat these names as cultivar names[8] and proposals to amend the *Cultivated Code* have been submitted which will regularize this, but the pseudo-botanical combinations proposed by Professor Rehder (and others) are still widely regarded as valid, even if regrettable. But it now seems that any proposed botanical combination *based only on the description of a cultivar* does not satisfy the requirements of the *Botanical Code* regarding valid publication, the horticultural coiner of the name not having had the requisite formative intention. It is therefore probable that this pseudo-botanical status given to cultivars will eventually be pronounced illegitimate, so the plan followed in this book is to treat the original cultivar names as having had uninterrupted validity. Adoption of this plan has required a great deal of research to ascertain the intention of the writer who first used the name. But since, whatever their ultimate fate, these pseudo-botanical names are part of botanical history and will continue to be met with in reference books I have here included them in the synonymy of the names I treat as valid. Translation of these decisions into correct typography is simple. All I have to do with these pre-1st January 1959 Latin-form cultivar names is to see that my printer uses single quote marks and capital initials and all is in order.

Where a cultivar epithet so treated is derived from a personal or a place name such as 'Maxwellii' or 'Beuvronensis' no more need be said, but if it

---

[8]The *Kew Handlist of Coniferae* 5th Edition, 1961, says of the coniferae 'The general practice was to bestow Latin, rather than fancy names on the cultivars, so that under such species as *Chamaecyparis obtusa* and *Juniperus chinensis* quite considerable numbers of varieties are listed which prove on examination to be cultivars and not variations of botanical standing . . . cultivars should . . . no longer be allowed to masquerade as botanical entities'.

consists of a descriptive adjective such as *pendula, fastigiata,* or *nana,* I have to consider, case by case, whether the description (although the name was given to a cultivar) also fits a CLASS of variants from the normal that is of sufficient botanical interest to justify recognition as a *forma.* But this is not, in any event, a matter that can be left to the printer. The cultivar named *Abies alba pendula* by Carrière did not (as it now seems) acquire botanical status or become a *forma* because someone once printed it *Abies alba* f. *pendula* Carr., and should I (or anyone) now feel it to be justified by the botanical circumstances in this or any other such case I would have to 'validly publish' the name as a new combination in compliance with the procedure laid down in the *Botanical Code,* supplying the so-far-missing botanical description, which in this case would have to include Carrière's plant along with all other variants—past, present or future—characterised by pendulous terminal growth. Were this ever to be done there would be a botanical taxon, *Abies alba* f. *pendula*—a class of plants—and falling within it three cultivars, Carrière's plant (this, the original clone, alone is entitled to bear the cultivar name 'Pendula'), another selection named 'Pendula Gracilis' by Sénéclause and the new American clone 'Green Spiral' (See Chapter V). Others might yet turn up!

But I have a much simpler course open to me, as a horticultural writer.

In addition to the terms Clone and Cultivar already discussed, the *Cultivated Code* introduces another concept—the Group—a useful provision, since it introduces a valuable element of classification into this Code, in which groups are simply defined as 'Assemblies of similar cultivars'. Since the descriptive adjectives under discussion (*pendula, fastigiata, nana,* etc.,) often relate to groups of this kind, I can well afford to leave the unfortunate pseudo-botanical names to their fate and use these Latin epithets where I find it convenient as Group names under the *Cultivated Code.* Thus, '*Abies alba*—PENDULA GROUP' (containing the cvv. 'Pendula', 'Pendula Gracilis' and 'Green Spiral') is just as precise and useful (not to say, simpler) to horticultural readers than *Abies alba* f. *pendula* would be, so this simple solution of a very thorny problem is adopted here extensively.

The *Cultivated Code* does not require the use of any typography to distinguish a group name, merely suggesting that if used between the specific name and cultivar name it (the group name) be placed within brackets. This typography will doubtless serve very well for the complex cases it is provided for, but in the present and simpler case, I can as a grower and seller of conifers see practical objection to an arrangement that can give rise to an impression that two additional words have been introduced into the middle of the name. At best it would give my customers reasonable grounds for the complaint that we are 'Back again to the polynomials', at worst it would lead to unintelligible orders, extra work for nurserymen, disappointment for customers and frustration all round.

I therefore distinguish my group names throughout by the use of Capitals and Small Capitals, and where the group name is used in relation to the name of a particular cultivar I avoid using it between the specific name and the cultivar name.

In my earlier book I was able to announce that better days, nomenclaturally speaking, were on their way since the Royal Horticultural Society had been appointed International Registration Authority for Garden Conifers. To do this gave me the greater pleasure for having played a leading part in getting the idea put forward, but I now regret having to admit that my hopes of early progress were not realised. At that time we were given to understand that the Council were of the opinion that they should accept the task of becoming International Registration Authority for whatever group of plants might be offered to them— a sort of horticultural *noblesse oblige*—but in the case of ornamental conifers it may perhaps not have been fully realised what a long and tedious (and hence costly) task the sorting of all the old names would be before any useful register could be compiled. This has apparently proved a serious handicap to progress. The Conifer Conference of 1970 came and went without any reference to the subject of names registration and now, fourteen years since I first wrote (unless developments are reported whilst this book is going through the press), there is still no Conifer Register.

It might be thought that if the wheels of time grind exceedingly fine despite their slowness, we might venture to hope that the Register, when at last it did appear, would be the end of all our (nomenclatural) problems, but this seems unlikely, since the duty of any Registration Authority, as it is laid down in the Code, is merely the preparation of a list of names of cultivars past and present and does not extend to the resolving of the knotty questions of which name applies to which plant in our gardens today. Since this is where most of our difficulties will still lie a register of a somewhat different kind (perhaps 'Data pool' would be a better term) is being built up at the Pygmy Pinetum at Devizes. This covers conifers of all sizes (not only the dwarf forms) and it is deliberately and intentionally plant oriented. Information of this practical nature is accumulating from personal contacts and correspondence with botanic gardens, arboreta and growers, large and small, throughout the conifer-speaking world and I invite further correspondence of the kind. I shall be glad to receive even the smallest contribution and of course shall be pleased to reciprocate by making the information already in the pool available to any enquirer who is interested. I am particularly interested to receive Names-lists of pineta and collections of conifers (not limited to dwarf forms) and I aim to put on record information of the location of authentic specimens of the rarer forms.

I am sometimes asked questions on the subject of introducing and naming new forms of dwarf conifer, mainly by gardeners who have raised a plant from a cutting found 'in the wild' or taken from a witch's broom or an isolated branch which shews an interesting mutation. Or the enquiry may come from a keen gardener who has a very old plant in his garden which is clearly a dwarf form because of its slow rate of growth.

The first thing, especially in the last mentioned case, is to make sure the plant is not known in cultivation elsewhere already, with a legitimate clonal name of its own. Widespread inquiry is the only safeguard. Unfortunately, botanic gardens are seldom in a position to commit themselves on this kind of question and the opinion of one or two specialist growers of dwarf conifers is probably the best resource.

Next, it is necessary to have the plant propagated and at least to some extent distributed. Because the definition of a clone begins 'An assemblage of individuals . . . ' a solitary plant does not qualify for recognition as a cultivar. If anyone in this situation is unable to do this himself or get it done by a local nursery, I might be able to help. Thirdly—and this is perhaps most important of all—is the question whether the new candidate for recognition has sufficient garden value and distinctiveness from the clones already in cultivation to justify its introduction as a new cultivar. Because of the known propensity of seedling variation to decrease with age and of mutations to reduce or disappear entirely in time, this should only be decided upon with the advice of, preferably, several persons of authority in the conifer world, given only after seeing established specimens of the new plant. Unchecked growth in the open ground for ten years would be the absolute minimum; 25 years would be better. Many over enthusiastic raisers of exciting new forms have indulged in hasty action that has added one more name to our lists but no more beauty to our gardens. The name chosen will need to be registered with the Royal Horticultural Society acting as International Registration Authority for Ornamental Conifers, but before an approach to them is made a copy of the *Cultivated Code* should be carefully studied.

It is to be hoped that when arrangements for registration are eventually determined they will include provision for the testing of novelties of this kind under some form of provisional registration, only to be confirmed after prolonged trial and eventual acceptance by the International Registration Authority.

I finish this chapter with a short section on a question which frequently puzzles gardeners 'Can a plant have two correct names?' The answer to this question as of so many that arise in life, is 'Well, Yes—and No'.

If you are thinking of the accepted botanical name, the answer is a clear 'No'.[9] Your dwarf-form Christmas tree is as truly *Picea abies* as the tallest Norway spruce in the world. If, on the other hand, you are thinking of a named variety in the garden sense, the answer will depend upon the particular circumstances of the case.

Firstly, there is only a purely imaginary boundary between plants originating 'in the wild' and those arising in cultivation. The subjects in Nature's vegetable kingdom do not recognise national boundaries and garden fences any more than do mosquitoes and many other subjects in her animal kingdom. Whatever man may do, they are all the same plants. The horticulturist propagating a variant found in the wild is creating and maintaining a cultivar, however the material reaches him, and the botanist must never overlook the fact that the latest, gaudiest and to him most repulsive garden variety is still only an expression of the genetic potentiality of the one or more species to which it owes its life.

It therefore follows that both the botanists and the horticulturists have their rights. Botanical nomenclature is classificatory, horticultural nomenclature is

[9]Cases of unresolved disagreement between botanists are here disregarded.

selective. So if a botanist says 'This natural variation from the normal is interesting, it is worthy of such and such an infra-specific botanical classification', he may so classify it and publish a new name (in Latin, of course) under the *Botanical Code*. If a horticulturist says 'This particular plant has a distinctive garden value, it is worth naming', he may find and publish a new cultivar name under the *Cultivated Code*. Both are correct names and it matters not at all who gets in first. But they will never both be naming EXACTLY THE SAME THING. A cultivar can never be identical with the taxon within which it lies, since it would in that case no longer be a cultivar entitled to a cultivar name: its botanical name would be adequate for its identification. This truth may be pictorially set out in the following way. Many horticulturists will know that the relationship between the different categories in the botanical hierarchy can be likened to 'Boxes within boxes'. Boxes representing species (one or more as the case may be) nest neatly within boxes representing genera. These, in turn, fit into larger boxes representing Families, and so on. We may extend this imagery by regarding infra-specific classifications as being partitions within the smallest of the boxes and thinking of cultivars as solid objects such as pebbles, of such size and shape that they can never fill the appropriate compartment exactly, *without leaving air spaces*. In the case we are considering the correct cultivar name is represented by the pebble and the correct botanical name by the sub-division in the species box in which the pebble rightly belongs.

CHAPTER FIVE
VARIETIES CURRENTLY
AVAILABLE

This will probably be my best read chapter. It is more than just the usual list of personal recommendations, but it stops well short of an attempt to describe every known form of dwarf conifer. Rather it is an attempt to bring together a reasonably complete list of the different forms that are at the time of writing known to be obtainable in British, Continental and American nurseries. Some of these are easily obtained and are stocked by most nurseries that sell conifers; others are rare and may need searching for amongst nurseries that specialise in the dwarf forms.

The descriptions, whilst more than a mere appraisal of the garden value of each variety, stop short of complete botanical descriptions. All I have attempted to do is to give such general descriptions as will help towards recognition and enable the garden use of each variety to be appreciated, with information in more detail where it is necessary for distinguishing between two or more forms of close similarity. In this the free use that has been made of photographs should help considerably.

Whilst I hope the remainder of this book will be of interest (and, perhaps, of use) to any garden-minded person, in this chapter I have assumed that my readers have some general knowledge of conifers and their dwarf forms (or have friends who do) and have access to some good general textbooks on conifers, especially as regards descriptions of the genera and species—matters outside the scope of this book.

IDENTIFICATION PLATES

This might be a good opportunity for giving a few explanatory details regarding the Identification Plates to be found on pages 52 to 137. It is not claimed that these will ensure recognition of every form of dwarf conifer illustrated, but studied together with the descriptions and with reference also to other photographs in the book they should enable anyone with some general knowledge of dwarf conifers to put the correct name to unidentified dwarf forms in many cases, and they are certainly adequate to show up the incorrectness of many existing labels.

All the photographs are natural size and should be viewed from a distance of twelve inches. In many cases the spray has been simplified by pruning away growth that would have been outside the picture plane. In some cases, where this would have resulted in unduly denuding the spray, the leaves or branches that have been pruned off have been laid alongside in as near their original position as possible. In these cases the spray has therefore been somewhat flattened, as though it had been confined between sheets of glass, so an actual spray from a plant of the variety illustrated may when held in the hand appear to be more congested than it does in the photograph. No attempt has been made to illustrate every variety; only those forms are included in which some peculiarity of foliage enables a picture of a small spray to have some recognition value.

DEFINITIONS

Before commencing my descriptions I need to define a few of the words I shall use, where these are given a restricted or particular meaning. For this I have good precedent, for Acts of Parliament (those models of light reading) usually have an 'Interpretation Clause' containing definition of words to be used in the Act, and even Humpty Dumpty himself told Alice 'When I use a word it means just what I choose it to mean—neither more nor less'.

Very well then, when I use the following words they mean just what I say in the following definitions—neither more nor less!

Compact   Probable size when mature, one-fifth to one-half that of the trees normal in the species.

Dwarf   Probable size when mature, one-twentieth to one quarter of the normal.

Pygmy   Probable size when mature, less than one-twentieth of the normal.

In the foregoing definitions no attempt at precision is possible. The proportion cited relates to the main dimension; normally this is the height, but in the case of prostrate forms it will be the spread. We are, of course, saddled with the words *compacta*, *nana* and *pygmaea* in some of the older cultivar names and these may or may not conform to these definitions.

Cultivar   An abbreviation of 'cultivated variety'. The term is defined in the *International Code of Nomenclature of Cultivated Plants*.

Cultivariant   Plants of a cultivar growing in a particular manner (not as yet recognised in the *Cultivated Code*) but of distinctive garden use (and therefore commercially necessary to distinguish in some way) and produced by (1) special cultural practices, or (2) the special selection of propagating material. An example of (1) is a standard rose tree. Prostrate plants of conifers resulting from grafting side shoots which retain their habit are examples of (2).

It is only the name (which may well be improved upon) which is new, the concept is as old as horticulture itself.

Glaucous   Appearing to have a whitish coating similar to the bloom of a grape; not necessarily easily rubbed off. Not used by me to describe merely a blue or grey-green colour (although often so used in garden literature).

Juvenile Foliage   See above Chapter I.

Lateral pair (of leaves)   That pair of leaves which, if a leaf spray be laid flat on the table, come from the sides of the shoot; i.e., those parallel to the table top.

Facing pair That pair of leaves of which one leaf faces upwards and one downwards towards the table. When lateral and facing pairs alternate, the arrangement is termed decussate.

Normal   This word is used to indicate what is characteristic of the species in some way (usually in the matter of size, or otherwise as will be clear in the context). It is preferred to the commonly used word 'typical' in order to avoid confusion with the special use of the word 'type' by botanists. A botanical 'type' may or may not be normal.

Reversion   The unwelcome appearance of vigorous, normal and arborescent growth upon a plant that is a 'dwarf form' as the result of some internal disturbance in the plant's make-up which had reduced its vigour; e.g., a variegation or a witch's broom.

TYPOGRAPHY

Botanical Names   Except where bold type is used, these are printed in italics, the botanical categories *varietas* and *forma* being abbreviated to var. and f.; e.g., *Juniperus communis* var. *montana*.

Cultivar Names   These are normally printed in Roman type and always with single quotation marks and initial capitals; e.g., 'Little Gem'.

Bold Type   Bold type is used for both botanical and cultivar names in side headings and where they introduce a plant not appearing under a separate heading.

Wrong Names   Where obsolete or illegitimate names have to be quoted to clear up a point of confusion, they are printed in italics, within double quotation marks and without initial capitals, to make the illegitimacy as obvious as possible; e.g., *"forsteckiana glauca"*.

ABIES AMABILILIS, A. BALSAMEA, A. CEPHALONICA

A. *Abies cephalonica* 'Meyers Dwarf'. Always a dense, flat-topped plant, usually wider than high. Short, dark green, lustrous leaves, stiff and radially held, giving a spiky appearance to the plant.

B. *Abies balsamea* 'Nana'. There are several garden forms of the dwarf Balsam fir. All have dark green, glossy foliage with white stomatic bands beneath, and are indestructibly hardy. 'Nana' forms a rounded bush with short leaves held radially (**C**), or nearly so.

D. – – 'Prostrata'. This forms a low, almost prostrate shrub with pectinate (i.e., in two flat, comb-like layers) foliage. A third clone 'Hudsonia' with longer leaves is intermediate in both habit and foliage.

E. *Abies amabilis* 'Spreading Star'. A prostrate cultivariant of the handsome Red Silver fir. On good soil it will eventually become a flat-topped plant 1 m high by several metres across, but few plants in cultivation are very large as yet. Although not much in evidence, the white underside of the leaf (**F**) is most attractive. The crushed foliage smells of tangerines.

IDENTIFICATION PLATE 2

ABIES KOREANA, A. LASIOCARPA, A. PINSAPO, A. PROCERA

A. *Abies lasiocarpa* 'Arizonica Compacta'. One of the best dwarf conifers. Forms a conical bush with silvery-grey foliage and large shapeless buds. The swollen joints are characteristic.

B. – – 'Roger Watson'. This interesting new form is always seen as a low, conical bush with a horizontal branching system and dark, grey-green leaves. The American form 'Conica' may be identical.

C. *Abies pinsapo* 'Glauca'. This and the golden form, although not dwarf forms, grow as low bushes for some years, but eventually develop a leader and become arboreal.

D. *Abies procera.* This species finds it difficult to develop leader growth from a side graft, so (especially in the glaucous form) will form attractive plants of the 'Prostrate' (cultivariant) type.

E. *Abies koreana* 'Piccolo'. A seedling with typical, but very short leaves, which forms an attractive, small, spreading plant. It will probably become large in time.

IDENTIFICATION PLATE 3

CEDRUS AND CEPHALOTAXUS

A. *Cedrus brevifolia.* A species distinct on account of its short leaves. It is not a dwarf, but is frequently grown as such in a pot, where it will be quite happy for some years. Grafted plants will only develop a leader if staked when young.

B. *Cedrus libani* 'Nana'. A rather variable plant, since dwarf Cedars of Lebanon can turn up in seed beds at any time. The two types of foliage illustrated are found also in larch, but that genus is deciduous.

C. – – 'Sargentii'. The dwarf weeping Cedar of Lebanon. Usually seen as a pendulous bush, but unless stem-trained as a young plant it will merely sprawl on the ground.

D. *Cephalotaxus harringtonia* var. *fastigiata.* Usually seen as an upright bush like an over-size yew. The leaves are held radially.

E. – – var. *prostrata.* As its name indicates, this is a prostrate form with wide-spreading branches with its foliage pectinate (i.e., in two flat ranks, like a comb). (**F**) shews the two stomatic bands on the underside of the leaves.

IDENTIFICATION PLATE 4

CHAMAECYPARIS LAWSONIANA 1

The garden forms of the Lawson cypress are difficult to illustrate by photography (and correspondingly difficult to recognise from the plates) because the foliage and leaf spray shape varies considerably with the age of the tree. Even within a single tree differences are noticeable, according to the relative vigour of each shoot. Sprays from growth of medium vigour only should be chosen for comparison, ignoring both the coarse, open growth often to be found on strong, leading shoots and the weak lateral sprays near the base of the plant.

A. *Chamaecyparis lawsoniana* 'Minima'. The rounded outline of the spray, with no leader dominance, is reflected in the globose shape of the bush and its numerous rising main branches with no central leader.

B. – – 'Nana'. The conical shape of the spray and the dominant central leader determine the shape of the tree, which is usually squatly-conical, with a central trunk.

C. – – 'Gimbornii'. As always, the spray shape is reflected in the shape of the tree—in this case an upright-oval, round-topped bush. The foliage is finer and neater, and lies in flatter sprays than in 'Minima'.

D. – – 'Filiformis Compacta'. This is the smallest of several thread-leaf forms. It forms a rounded mop-like bush with growth tips mostly pendulous. Much more vigorous, but with similar foliage is 'Duncanii'. 'Filiformis Erecta' and 'Masonii' are forms (not dwarf) with filiform foliage held stiffly erect.

E. – – 'Forsteckensis'. At its best this is a dense little bush of tight, congested growth. To preserve this, the more vigorous shoots (Arrow) by which the plant increases in size should be cut out.

F. – – 'Gnome'. The growth is similar to but denser than in the case of 'Forsteckensis', but the warning given regarding coarse, loose shoots applies equally to both forms. Neglected bushes may have put on strong and uncharacteristic growth so as to be scarcely recognisable.

G. – – 'Pygmy'. Of all the small globose forms this is the most well behaved, always forming a neat, globose bush like a miniature 'Minima'. The similarity in shape to the neat, rounded leaf sprays of that variety is noticeable.

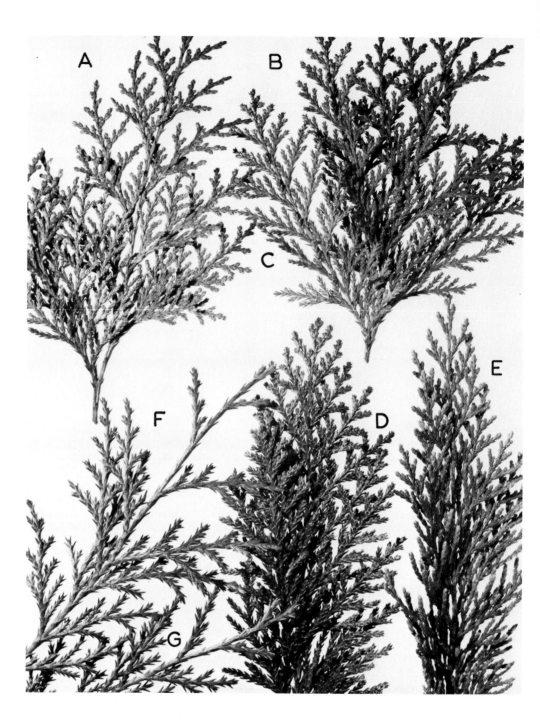

IDENTIFICATION PLATE 5

CHAMAECYPARIS LAWSONIANA 2, C. NOOTKATENSIS 1

The forms on this Plate are all wide-spreading bushes with no leader and all branch tips arching over. They are low-growing at first but eventually they can build up to 2 m or so high.

A. *Chamecyparis lawsoniana* 'Tamariscifolia'. Note the free-standing leaf tips and the triangular shape of the leaf spray. This form is slightly glaucous on the underside. There are, I believe, several clones in cultivation. The colour is light green.

B. – – 'Nidiformis'. Note the dense, overlapping foliage (both at front and back of spray) and the rounded leaf spray, usually curled. Slightly glaucous above, very glaucous beneath (**C**). The colour is greyish-green.

D. – – 'Dows Gem'. Note the coarse, open foliage, which lies in boldly curved sprays, imparting a good deal of character to the bush. The colour is a rich, dark green.

E. – – 'Knowefieldensis'. Note the long, parallel-sided sprays with the central stem always predominant. The resulting clearly defined, long, narrow, triangular outline is repeated in larger sprays on the plant. Colour: rich, mid-green; only very slightly glaucous below.

F. *Chamaecyparis nootkatensis* 'Nidifera'. From all prostrate forms of the Lawson cypress this can be distinguished by the absence of any glaucescence on the underside of the leaves. (**G**), and from *C. nootkatensis* 'Compacta' (see next Plate) it is distinct by the arching over habit of all terminal growths.

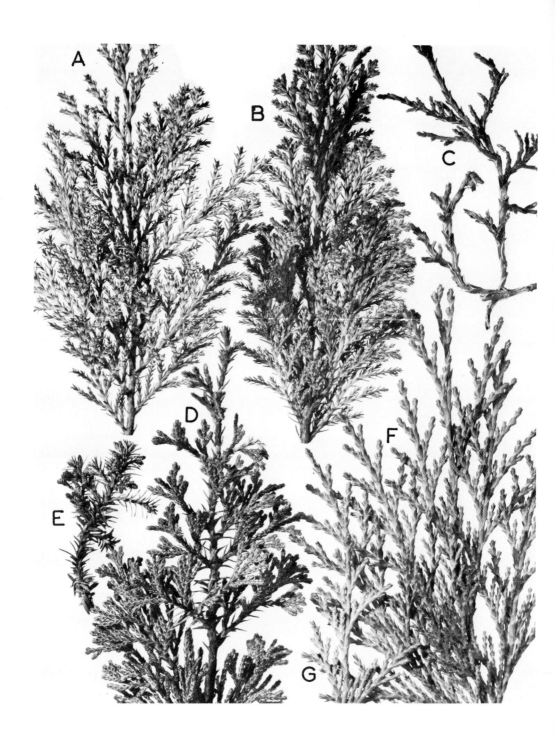

IDENTIFICATION PLATE 6

CHAMAECYPARIS LAWSONIANA 3, C. NOOTKATENSIS 2, C. THYOIDES 1

A. *Chamaecyparis lawsoniana* 'Fletcheri'. Not a dwarf form (although, alas, often sold as such). The juvenile foliage is attractive. The colour is grey-green. Habit: broadly fastigiate.

B. – – 'Ellwoodii'. Much slower in growth than 'Fletcheri', at least for a number of years, but old trees can be found which are quite tall. The foliage is dark green and is usually coarse and more or less adult at the top of an old specimen. Habit varies considerably, usually broadly fastigiate, or flat-topped with several leaders.

C. – – 'Lycopodioides'. Will become a large upright bush or small, rounded tree in time, but the pointed leaves and twisted shoots all over the plant are unmistakable.

D. *Chamaecyparis thyoides* 'Andelyensis'. Seen as a narrowly columnar tree, frequently carrying a heavy crop of seed-cones. (**E**) is a spray of juvenile foliage, which is almost always present in the lower part of the tree. Both the adult and the juvenile sprays shewn are carrying flowers.

F. *Chamaecyparis nootkatensis* 'Compacta'. Usually found as a large, upright bush, densely clothed to the ground with foliage which is of the same colour on both sides with no trace of glaucescence. All leading growths are held stiffly upright. (**G**) shews the underside of the leaf spray.

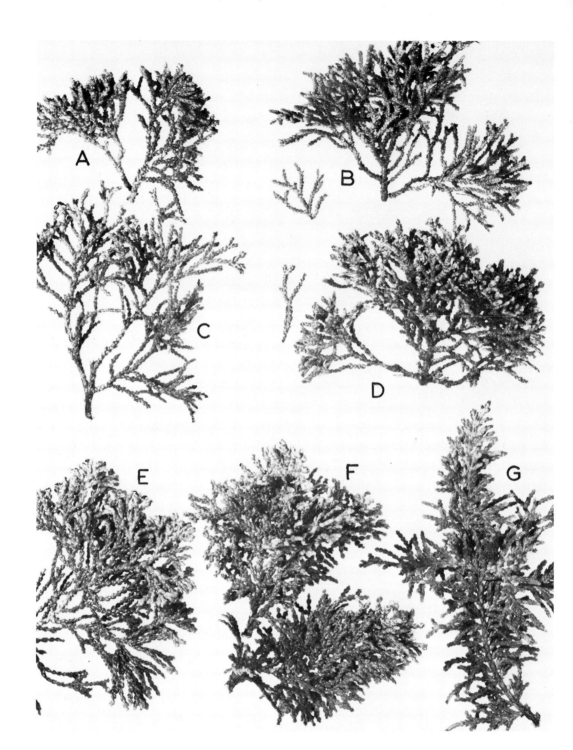

IDENTIFICATION PLATE 7

CHAMAECYPARIS OBTUSA 1

A. *Chamaecyparis obtusa* 'Caespitosa'. Always a tiny, bun-shaped plant with dark green, upcurved sprays, and tiny, tightly appressed leaves.

B. – – 'Minima'. A tiny, bun-shaped form similar to 'Caespitosa' but with light green foliage consisting of a dense mass of tetragonal branchlets, not the flat sprays of that variety.

C. – – 'Juniperoides'. Forms a small, bun-shaped or globose plant with foliage in open lace-like sprays with closely appressed leaves, more suggestive to me of the typical foliage of *C. thyoides* than of any juniper.

D. – – 'Juniperoides Compacta'. As its name indicates, a smaller and altogether denser version of 'Juniperoides'. Colour: yellow-green.

E. – – 'Chilworth'. Usually seen as an upright and miniature but tree-like plant. Leaf sprays noticeably down-cupped. Very uncommon.

F. – – 'Intermedia'. Intermediate between 'Nana' and the very diminutive forms shewn in **A to D**. Foliage is dense and a rich, dark green.

G. – – 'Compact Fernspray'. The spray is flat and fern-like. This variety is a diminutive version of the tree-like form 'Filicoides'. (See next Plate).

CHAMAECYPARIS OBTUSA 2

A. *Chamaecyparis obtusa* 'Kosteri'. A slow-growing upright or, more frequently, spreading bush with foliage in flat sprays in which each little group of leaves is twisted, one lateral turning upwards and the other downwards.

B. – – 'Nana'. Several slow-growing clones are in cultivation under this name. The true 'Nana' is very dense and slow-growing with very dark green foliage curved out of the plane of the spray.

C. – – 'Coralliformis'. The normal leaf spray is absent entirely, being replaced by a filiform type of growth which is always much twisted in all directions—so suggesting the name—but it lacks the small fasciated areas that characterise 'Torulosa'. 'Tsatsumi' is coarser and has its main shoots less contorted. The rounded leaf tips distinguish all these forms from *Chamaecyparis lawsoniana* 'Lycopodioides', which also is much coarser in every way, as is *C. obtusa* 'Lycopodioides'.

D. – – 'Nana Gracilis'. This is the popular variety that forms a bush of picturesque outline, seldom over 1.5 m (but grafted plants may grow larger). The foliage is a rich glossy mid-green in dense sprays which twist and turn in all directions, mainly upwards, so producing the characteristic irregular outline to the plant.

E. – – 'Filicoides'. Usually seen as a gaunt and open small tree, but a specimen that has been regularly trimmed can be quite dense and bushy. The foliage is in flat sprays.

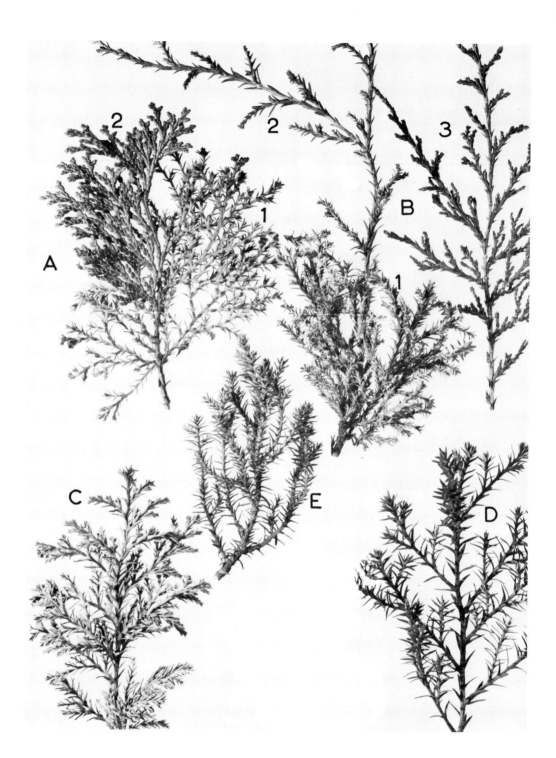

CHAMAECYPARIS OBTUSA 3, C. THYOIDES 2, C. PISIFERA 1

Seedlings of several species of Chamaecyparis and Thuja are very much alike because of the similarity in the seed-leaves (or juvenile foliage, as it is usually termed) and consequently are hard to tell apart until they grow up and develop the normal, adult foliage. So in those cases where freak retention of this juvenile foliage has given rise to a distinct garden variety, difficulties in recognition can arise. Leaf shape and the angle to the shoot, branching habit and colour (especially winter colour) are all factors that may be required to clear up the identity of any particular plant.

A. *Chamaecyparis obtusa* 'Chabo-Yadori' (often grown as 'Ericoides') has a mixture of juvenile leaves (at 1) and the normal adult *C. obtusa* foliage (at 2). The colour is the normal green of the species.

B. *Chamaecyparis pisifera* 'Squarrosa Intermedia' (See f. *leptoclada*). The specimen depicts: (1) The desirable wholly juvenile type of growth; (2) The loose type of growth by which the plant increases in size; and (3) the coarse, adult foliage which will take over if allowed to remain.

C. – – 'Squarrosa Dumosa'. The foliage of all juvenile (i.e., squarrose) forms of this species are very similar.

D. *Chamaecyparis thyoides* 'Ericoides'. This is the well known fixed juvenile form which makes a small, conical plant sometimes reaching to 1 m with upright branching habit and rather open, juvenile foliage. The colour of the leaves is dark green in summer, turning usually to a rich plum-purple in winter. This variety is not altogether hardy and often shews patches of dead foliage in spring.

E. – – 'Heather Bun' is the name suggested for a slow-growing selection long in cultivation, which forms a small, upright or ovoid bush with very diminutive foliage which distinguishes it from 'Ericoides' (with which variety it is nevertheless often confused). The colouring is the same.

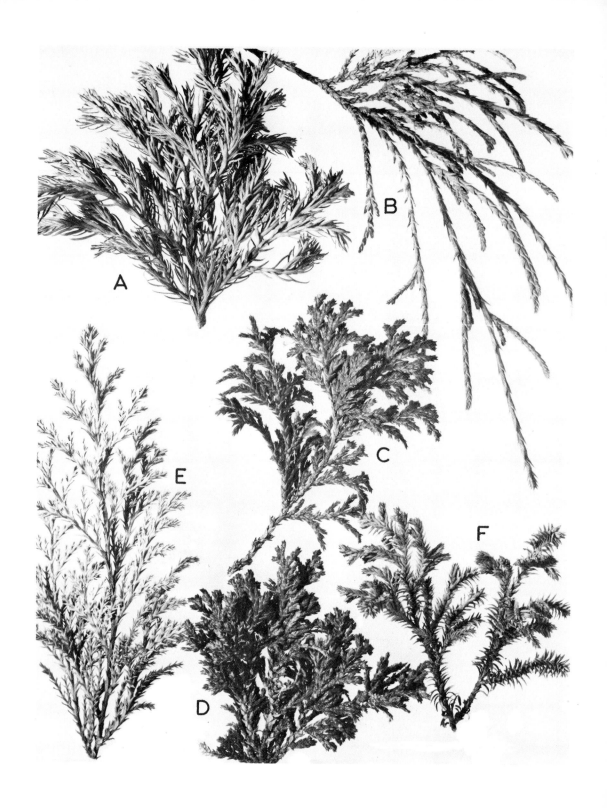

CHAMAECYPARIS PISIFERA 2

A. *Chamaecyparis pisifera* 'Boulevard'. This popular form can usually be readily recognised by its colour, which when the plant is doing well is a bright, silvery-blue (especially in shade). In hot, dry soils the colour can be disappointing, but the foliage is characteristic.

B. – – 'Filifera'. The word *filiformis* or *filifera* merely means 'in form like a thread', and there are several selections with this thread-like foliage in cultivation, in all of which the terminal growths are more or less pendulous. 'Golden Mop' is a popular garden form—a rich golden yellow if grown in an open spot. 'Filifera Compacta' is the commoner green form usually seen as a dense, rounded bush seldom over 1 m high by as much across.

C. – – 'Compacta' makes a wide-spreading, rounded bush (often irregularly broken up in an old plant) with adult but very densely set foliage in congested, more or less flat sprays of dark green, usually conspicuously glaucous beneath.

D. – – 'Nana' is a diminutive form of 'Compacta' with foliage that is similar to that variety but reduced in size in all respects. Several doubtfully stable variegated and colour mutations have been propagated and named. Several such variations can often be found on a single large plant. 'Compacta' and 'Nana' are quite distinct, but since growth of intermediate vigour occurs the identification of an isolated plant can be very puzzling.

E. – – 'Plumosa Aurea'. The semi-juvenile foliage of this form (of which there are several named selections in garden cultivation) should be compared with the adult foliage depicted in (**C**) on this plate and with the juvenile foliage in (**C**) on the previous plate.

F. – – 'Plumosa Compressa'. This attractive little bun-forming plant carries very variable foliage, as the plate shows, much of the foliage being much more 'squarrose' than 'plumose'. Because of this variability, selection of propagating material can give rise to apparently different forms, but these are not stable, and eventually the usual mixture of foliage types takes over.

CRYPTOMERIA JAPONICA 1

A. *Cryptomeria japonica* 'Compressa'. A dense, regularly globose plant not unlike the commoner 'Vilmoriniana' depicted at (**B**), but with rather denser growth, having more noticeably reflexed leaves. The foliage in the interior of the bush is blue-green. The winter colour is a deep purple-bronze.

B. – – 'Vilmoriniana'. A deservedly popular, globose variety, similar to 'Compressa' but marginally less dense in growth and less regular in outline. The leaves near the shoot tips are less spreading, the foliage is light-green in colour and this cultivar bronzes only slightly in winter.

C. – – 'Bandai-sugi'. Note the erratic growth pattern of the shoots. This produces a correspondingly irregular little bush. Growth in the more vigorous form 'Monstrosa Nana' and the still stronger-growing 'Monstrosa' shews the same irregularity in shoot vigour. Indeed only relative vigour seems to separate these forms.

D. – – 'Spiraliter Falcata'. This rather awkward name has priority for a 'screw-thread' variety usually seen as an upright bush or small tree with a fairly open habit quite unlike the following form.

E. – – 'Spiralis' (Granny's Ringlets). Note the difference between the foliage of this and the preceding form. 'Spiralis' is usually seen as a low, spreading bush but it will build up in time. The amount of twist on the leaves varies with the season.

F. – – 'Fasciata'. Usually seen as an irregular and rather unhappy-looking little bush. The tiny, mossy growth on the stems can be clearly seen.

G. – – 'Elegans Nana'. This is the form often grown as 'Lobbii Nana'. The juvenile foliage (unlike that of 'Elegans Compacta') is straight and stiff. An outstanding feature of this form is large dense clusters of male flowers during the winter.

CRYPTOMERIA JAPONICA 2

A. *Cryptomeria japonica* 'Globosa Nana'. This is usually a large bush, wider than high, with a dense thatch of foliage and all the terminal growths pendulous.

B. – – 'Jindai-sugi' makes a conical or upright bush or small tree with an upright and quite regular branching habit and growth and with densely held, mid-green foliage; retaining this colour during the winter.

C. – – 'Nana'. The rather more open habit and the widely varying thinness of the branchlets distinguishes this form from 'Jindai-sugi'. The colour is a light yellowish-green retained all the year, but 'Pygmaea', with very similar foliage, turns a deep crimson colour during the winter.

D. – – 'Globosa'. This makes a dense little bush, usually wider than high. The densely held juvenile foliage is not unlike that of 'Elegans Nana', but 'Globosa' never develops the clusters of flowers in winter characteristic of that cultivar; also it turns a striking brick-red colour during the winter.

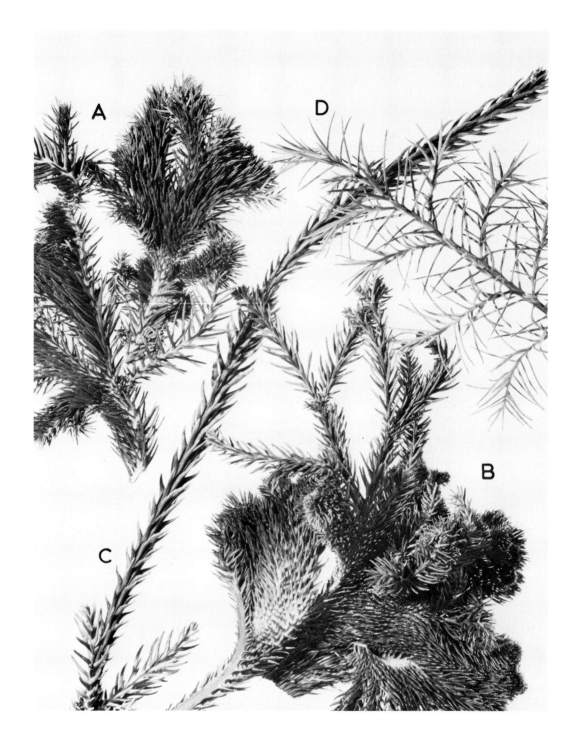

CRYPTOMERIA JAPONICA 3

A. *Cryptomeria japonica* 'Kilmacurragh'. The whole bush is covered with small fasciated areas. Foliage dark green.

B. – – 'Cristata'. Unlike 'Kilmacurragh', the monstrous cristate areas are very conspicuous, often the size of a man's hand, interspersed with quite normal foliage.

C. – – f. *araucarioides*. The specimen shown is typical of the long, thread-like (or snake-like) shoots of all this group, which are impossible to distinguish from the foliage alone.

D. – – 'Elegans Compacta'. This is merely a compact selection of the fixed juvenile form 'Elegans'. The long, frequently curved leaves are very soft to the touch and turn the usual rich plum-purple in winter.

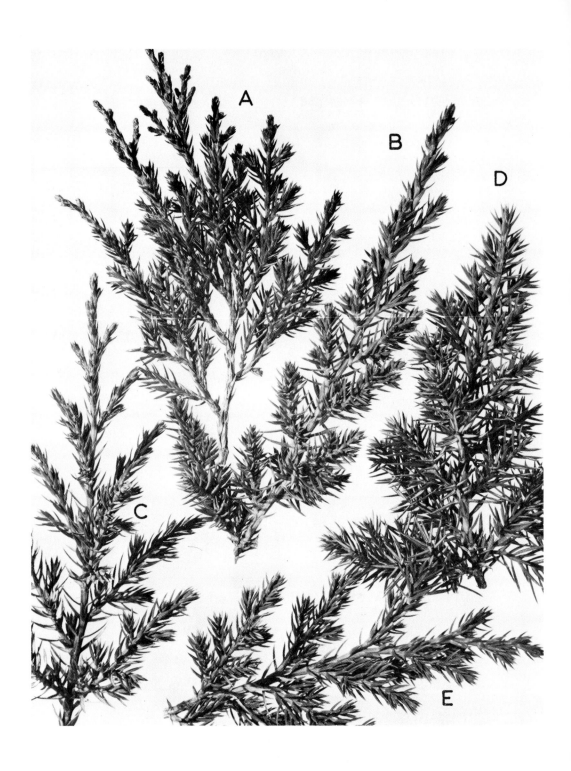

JUNIPERUS CHINENSIS 1

A. *Juniperus chinensis* 'Pyramidalis'. Usually an upright, more or less round-topped shrub with blue-grey foliage that is sharp and prickly. In young plants the leaves are wholly juvenile (acicular).

B. – – 'Stricta'. Usually a plant of distinctly conical outline. The foliage is similar to 'Pyramidalis' in colour, but it is soft to the touch. Older plants are often disfigured by the dead brown foliage which is retained on the plant for several years.

C. – – 'Monarch'. Seen as a columnar small tree with blue-grey foliage.

D. – – 'Obelisk'. An upright or conical small tree with the leader always sloping out of upright. Note the wide leaves with the broad band of stomata which gives the foliage a glaucous-grey colour.

E. – – 'San José'. A low-growing, flat-topped, spreading bush usually not over 50 cm high with exclusively juvenile foliage of a soft grey-green.

JUNIPERUS CHINENSIS 2, J. COMMUNIS 1

A. *Juniperus chinensis* 'Japonica'. As a young plant this is a spreading bush with mainly juvenile foliage, with very sharp closely spaced leaves. With age, it becomes a small columnar tree with mainly adult leaves.

B. – – 'Kaizuka'. Usually a tall bush or small tree of picturesque irregular outline and steeply sloping (never upright) stem and main branches. Adult foliage of a rich, deep mid-green predominates, but a few shoots with juvenile foliage may be present.

C. – – 'Echiniformis'. Usually seen as a very small bun or hemispherical plant with very congested growth and wholly juvenile foliage. For long it was listed under *J. communis* and can still be found thus labelled.

D. *Juniperus communis* var. *montana*. All forms are marked by the curved, boat-shaped leaf. This clone is 'Windsor Gem', a very slow-growing form, similar to but less than half as vigorous as 'Silver Lining' (See **F** on next Plate). **E, F, G,** and **H.** Two of the many so far un-named clones under test in the Pygmy Pinetum at Devizes, Wiltshire.

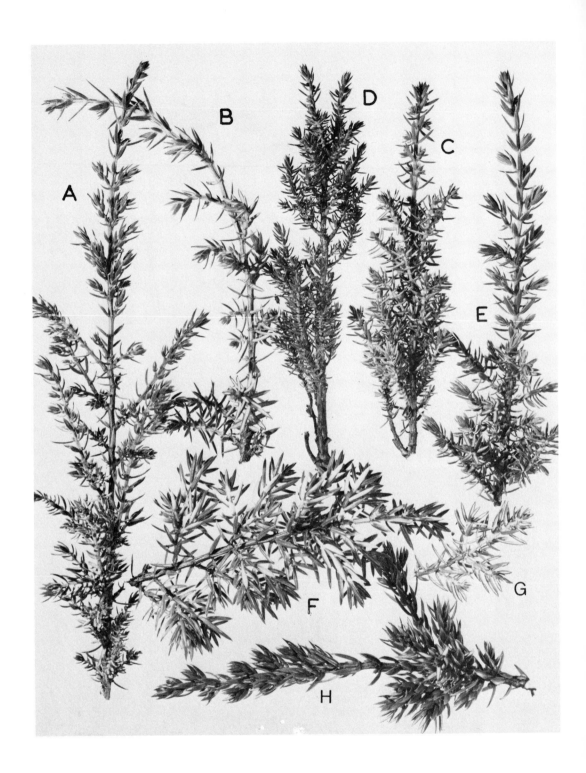

IDENTIFICATION PLATE 16

JUNIPERUS COMMUNIS 2

A. *Juniperus communis* 'Hibernica'. The well known Irish juniper. Always a strictly fastigiate plant.

B. – – 'Mayer'. A columnar, rather than fastigiate form, with short branches.

C. – – 'Compressa'. The popular diminutive fastigiate form. Always with a good leader, it tends to form a narrow and pointed plant.

D. – – 'Suecica Nana'. This clone although almost as slow-growing and equally fastigiate is distinctive in lacking leader dominance, so it forms a wider and blunt-topped plant.

E. – – 'Sentinel' ('Pencil Point'). A selection that is intermediate between 'Hibernica' and 'Compressa'.

F. – – 'Minima' ('Silver Lining'). A popular clone of var. *montana*. (**G**) shews the chalk-white underside of the leaves.

H. – – 'Gew Graze'. A very dense, slow-growing prostrate form, much more compact than 'Repanda'.

IDENTIFICATION PLATE 17

JUNIPERUS COMMUNIS 3

A. *Juniperus communis* var. *depressa.* A wide spreading ground-cover plant with its wide leaves facing downwards, so that the white upper sides (**B**) are not seen. Clones that are less prostrate, such as 'Dumosa' (**C**) have been selected and named. The foliage of all forms bronzes in winter.

D. – – var. *hemispherica.* Note the densely set, straight leaves. It forms a spreading but not prostrate bush.

E. – – var. *hornibrookii.* Note the very small leaves, characteristic of this botanical *varietas.* The clonal name 'Hornibrookii' should only be used for strictly prostrate forms. Other forms differing in habit should be kept distinct. One of these—

F. – – 'Edgbaston' tends to hold its branchlets in flat sprays, but the main branches are held up at + 30-45°.

G. – – 'Repanda'. In this popular group the (longer) leaves are incurved and lie forwards along the shoot. Several clones are in cultivation, all giving good, dense ground-cover.

JUNIPERUS CONFERTA, J. DAVURICA, J. PROCUMBENS, J. TAXIFOLIA

A group of useful prostrate or procumbent junipers.

A. *Juniperus conferta.* A wide spreading procumbent species in which the foliage is very prickly. The main branches spread along the ground with the branchlets rising so that the plant may rise to 80 cm, but several forms have been selected and named that are more prostrate.

B. *Juniperus taxifolia* var. *lutchuensis.* Very distinct from *J. conferta* in the much broader leaf, more prostrate habit, brighter mid-green colour and the entire absence of prickliness to the touch.

C. *Juniperus davurica* 'Expansa'. An easily recognised species because of its stout and rigidly horizontal, long main branches clothed with dense juvenile foliage over the greater part of the plant but with adult (squammiform) leaves on the strong main leader shoots. Dull grey-green.

The form 'Expansa Variegata' is similar, but blotched with a creamy-white variegation in irregular patches of varying size. Another form 'Expansa Aureospicata' is a less vigorous plant, carrying almost wholly juvenile foliage.

D. *Juniperus procumbens* 'Nana'. A popular mat-forming ground cover selection of which several clones are in cultivation, varying slightly in colour and relative vigour. Of these—

E. – – 'Bonin Isles' is a clone in cultivation in Britain, with somewhat larger leaves—a form intermediate between 'Nana' and the greater vigour that is normal to the species.

In all forms of *J. procumbens* the tips of the main shoots tend to turn upward and hold themselves just clear of the ground. The characteristic white smudges on the sides of the leaves can be seen in a few places in the plate.

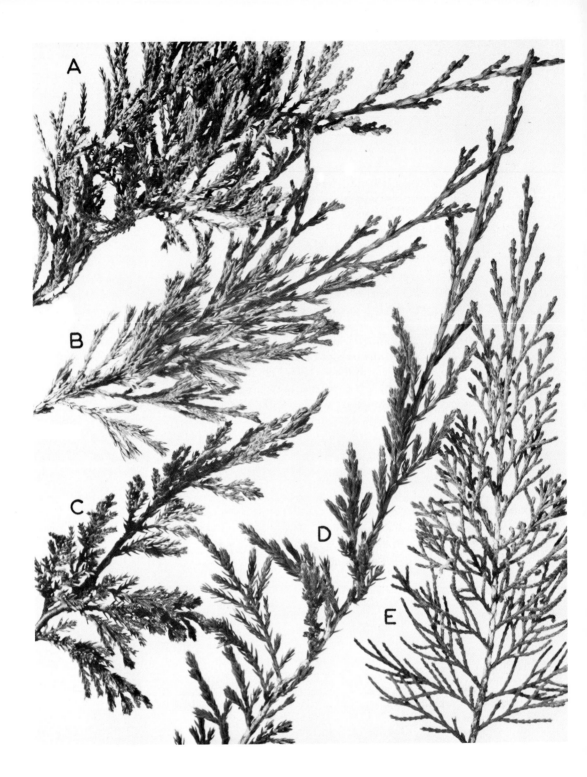

JUNIPERUS HORIZONTALIS

Of this species a very large number of selections have been made 'in the wild' and brought into cultivation. All are more or less prostrate plants, useful for ground cover.

A. *Juniperus horizontalis* 'Wiltoni'. A very prostrate form and a vigorous grower. The colour is a rich blue-green throughout the year.

B. – – 'Plumosa'. One of a group of forms making low, spreading (but not prostrate) bushes with main stems rising at angles varying from 30° to 45°. The colour is green, often turning to various shades of brown and mauve in winter.

C. – – 'Filicina Minima'. One of the slowest and neatest of the prostrate forms and one bearing predominantly juvenile foliage.

D. – – 'Prostrata'. A strong-growing, completely prostrate form with a much coarser look than 'Wiltoni' and quite different in colour. 'Prostrata' as grown in Britain is dark green, turning dull mauve in winter.

E. – – 'Douglasii'. The Waukegan Juniper. Green in summer with a glaucous grey bloom which turns a bright mauve in autumn.

JUNIPERUS RECURVA 1, J. SQUAMATA

A. *Juniperus squamata* 'Glassell'. A very slow-growing bush with numerous rising stems and tiny, grey-green leaves and a picturesque habit.

B. – – 'Loderi'. Always forms a closely columnar plant with a distinct leader which is erect, but the laterals nod slightly, as in all *J. squamata* forms.

C. – – 'Meyeri'. A vigorous bush or small tree. The foliage is blue-grey—the bluest form of any juniper—but the retention of the dead foliage on the lower branches detracts from the attractiveness of this cultivar. 'Blue Star' and 'Blue Carpet' are new selections of slower growth and less vigour.

D. – – 'Wilsonii'. Usually a rounded to spreading bush with all growing tips strongly recurved (turned downwards) and leaves often twisted to show much of the glaucous upper sides.

E. *Juniperus recurva* 'Coxii'. A tall-growing shrub or small tree with steeply pendulous, much over-crowded foliage, of a rich mid-green. The bark of the trunk is peeling. *J. recurva* itself has smaller leaves, and the form 'Castlewellan' has leaves so small as to give the foliage a thread-leaf appearance. All forms become large trees in time.

F. – – 'Densa'. A low bush, flat and wide-spreading at first, building up with age, but always with nodding tips at all growing points. Foliage is green.

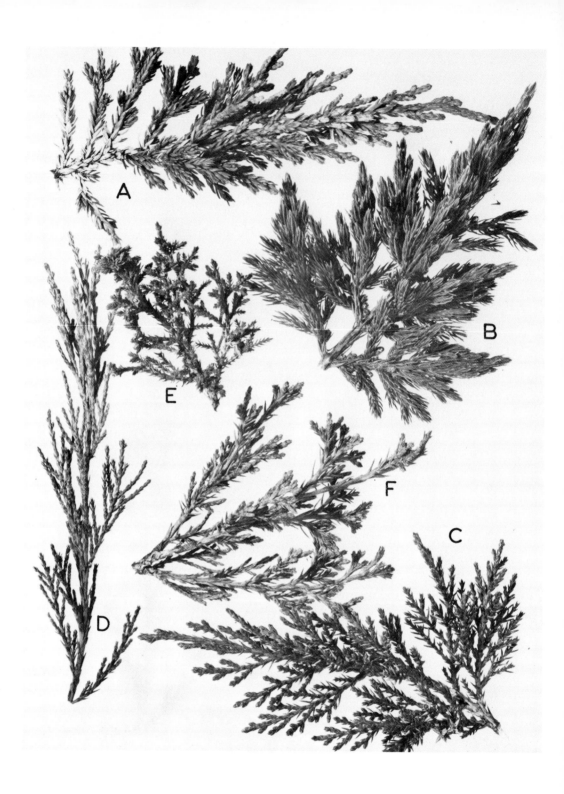

JUNIPERUS RECURVA 2, J. SARGENTII, J. SABINA, J. SCOPULORUM, J. VIRGINIANA

A. *Juniperus sargentii.* A wide-spreading ground cover plant.

B. *Juniperus recurva* 'Embley Park'. Distinct from other forms by its rich, mid-green colour.

C. *Juniperus sabina* 'Tamariscifolia'. Many forms of *J. sabina* carry only adult foliage, but all can be recognised by the pungent smell of the crushed and warmed foliage.

D. *Juniperus scopulorum* 'Skyrocket'. This is the most narrowly columnar of many selected garden forms of this species, all with similar foliage.

E. *Juniperus virginiana* 'Humilis'. Never seen as more than a low scrubby bush.

F. – – 'Globosa'. The most naturally globose dwarf conifer known.

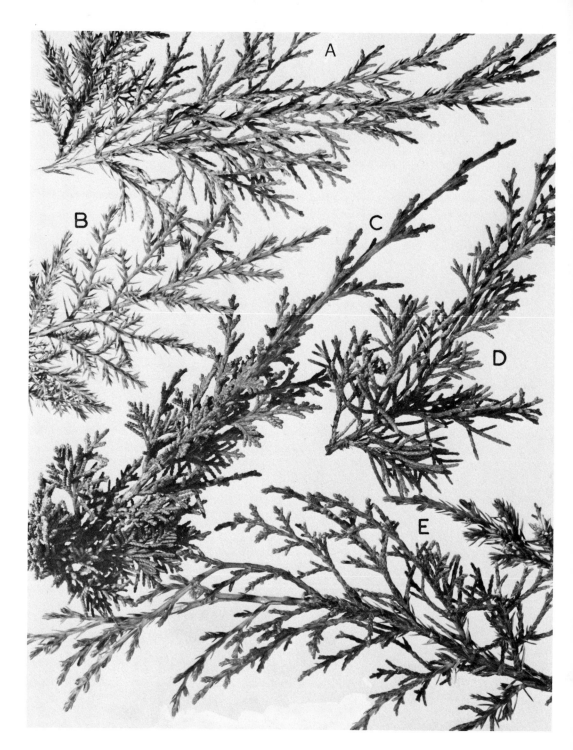

IDENTIFICATION PLATE 22

JUNIPERUS × MEDIA

The forms of this hybrid are frequently listed as *J. chinensis* but they constitute a well defined horticultural group, and the different cultivars all have at least a trace of the sour smell in the bruised and warmed foliage that is characteristic of *J. sabina*.

A. *Juniperus × media* 'Pfitzerana'. This is the prototype of quite a number of named selections that differ in colour and habit more than in foliage, so they cannot be distinguished by herbarium or photographic specimens—only by comparisons between living plants.

  'Pfitzerana' is a strong-growing, spreading plant, with its main branches rising at about 45°, fairly flexible and arching over so that all growing tips are distinctly pendulous.

B. – – 'Pfitzerana Compacta' [Hort. Eng.] Several compact forms of the 'Pfitzer' juniper are in cultivation. This, the 'Nicks Compact' of America, makes a much lower and slower-growing plant, and carries almost exclusively juvenile leaves and the additional area of stomata on the leaves imparts a greyish tinge to the foliage.

C. – – 'Blaauw'. An upright plant of irregular outline with steeply ascending branches and forward setting branchlets. The colour is a rich blue-green.

D. – – 'Shimpaku'. A very slow-growing little bush with almost wholly adult foliage of a soft grey-green. This form is much used in Japan for the manufacture of Bonsai plants. (Cf. 'Plumosa Cinerea').

E. – – 'Plumosa Aurea'. This is one of a group of forms differing from 'Pfitzerana' by their habit of growth. Although the final growing tips are still pendulous, the main branches are held at a steeper angle and the growth is distinctly stiffer, both in appearance and fact. This form has dull golden-yellow foliage; there are green and variegated forms appropriately named.

IDENTIFICATION PLATE 23

PICEA ABIES 1

The dwarf forms of the Norway spruce are difficult to recognize from foliage alone; so much depends upon habit of growth of the plant.

A. *Picea abies* 'Gregoryana'. Gregory's spruce is one of the easiest to recognise. It forms a dense little globose bush with narrow, needle-like leaves and very numerous, almost spherical, green, glossy buds, looking rather like glass beads, in every part of the bush. With age, this form gradually loses character and a very old bush can be unrecognisable.

B. – – 'Echiniformis' is very similar, but the leaves are much longer and less densely borne. Other forms with similar bead-like buds (but at the top of the bush only) are 'Parsonsii' and 'Veitchii'.

C. – – 'Pygmaea'. The Pygmy spruce is one of the oldest and best known forms and is well named. The congested habit and dense growth, the short, thick, rhombic leaves and large, coarse buds are well shown in the plate.

D. – – 'Humilis' is a congested version of 'Pygmaea' with a still denser habit and shorter leaves. Quite a different plant is often supplied under this name and some plants of continental origin may be found not to be true 'Humilis', despite their being so labelled.

E. – – 'Clanbrassiliana'. Lord Clanbrassil's spruce is another very old variety not always supplied true to name. The uneven vigour of growth shews up well in the plate, as does also its distinctiveness from the following form.

F. – – 'Elegans'. Knights Dwarf spruce is often mistaken for 'Clanbrassiliana', but its neat, globose shape, even as a very old plant, and the uniformly short leaves are quite distinct from the variability noticeable in the foliage of 'Clanbrassiliana'.

PICEA ABIES 2

The varieties on this plate are all low, spreading or procumbent forms.

A. *Picea abies* 'Nidiformis'. This forms a low, wide-spreading bush. The main branches radiating from the centre of a young plant rise and curve over at the growing tips so as to form a shallow nest-like depression, but this effect is lost as the plant ages. It has dark green, rather wiry looking foliage. A distinctive feature is the presence of minute, transparent hooks (visible only with a glass) on the lower edge of the leaf.

B. – – 'Pumila Nigra'. This forms quite a low plant wider than high, but since the main branches stand up at 45° and do not curve over, it always appears to be higher than a plant of 'Nidiformis' of similar size.

C. – – 'Decumbens' is very similar to 'Nidiformis' but the branch system is more horizontal so it forms a flatter plant. The foliage is yellow-green.

D. – – 'Tabuliformis' as the name implies, forms a flat-topped plant which spreads over a wide area with the foliage in quite regular, flat sprays, so that the plant can only gain height by fresh layers smothering the growth beneath.

E. – – 'Procumbens'. This is one of the strongest growers in this group. The vigorous, glossy foliage and the pronounced taper of the shoot outline can be clearly seen in the plate. The colour is a rich green.

PICEA GLAUCA, P. MARIANA, P. OMORIKA, P. ORIENTALIS

A. *Picea glauca* 'Albertiana Conica'. This distinctive form is popular for its neat, conical shape, the fine needle-like leaves and the delicate green colour when it flushes into new growth. It is frequently seen badly disfigured by attacks of red spider.

B. *Picea omorika* 'Nana'. Usually a conical bush, with glossy green foliage very glaucous on the upper side.

C. *Picea mariana* 'Nana'. A dainty little hemispherical plant with fine, silvery-grey leaves.

D. – – 'Pygmaea'. Smaller than 'Nana' in every way, and with much reduced leaf-size and rate of growth.

E. *Picea orientalis* 'Gracilis'. The short blunt-ended leaf is characteristic of all forms of this species.

PINUS BANKSIANA, P. DENSIFLORA, P. LEUCODERMIS, P. MUGO

A. *Pinus banksiana.* The form here is the pendulous cultivar 'Uncle Fogy' but the foliage is characteristic.

B. *Pinus mugo* 'Gnom'. Always seen as a more or less globose bush. The pale grey leaf sheaths are noticeable.

C. *Pinus densiflora* 'Umbraculifera'. Always seen as a dome-topped shrub or small tree. Leaves have been cut away to shew the mahogany-red buds.

D. *Pinus leucodermis* 'Compact Gem'. Always the deep green foliage is very dense. The bud has been exposed to view by cutting away of the needles.

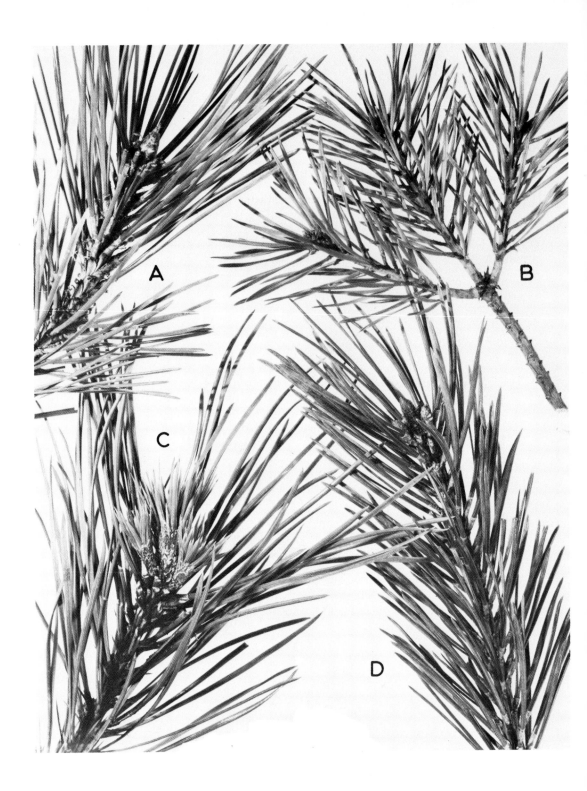

PINUS NIGRA, P. SYLVESTRIS

A. *Pinus nigra* 'Hornibrookiana'. One of a group of dwarf cultivars of this species in which the terminal bud and the leaves are very similar. Dull green.

B. *Pinus sylvestris* 'Beuvronensis'. This is the commonest of the dwarf Scots pines in cultivation. It forms a rather flat-topped bush. The length of needle will be much less on a plant in a container with a restricted root run. The foliage is greyish-green.

C. – – 'Globosa Viridis'. Another form frequently seen. It forms a globose to upright plant with dark green foliage. Note the long twisted leaves and the autumn flush of short, juvenile leaves covering the buds. A similar form that turns yellowish to yellow in winter—long grown as *P. nigra* 'Pygmaea'—is the cultivar 'Moseri'.

D. – – 'Watereri'. Eventually a rounded tree, this is usually seen as a distinctly conical bush with ascending branches and blue-green foliage.

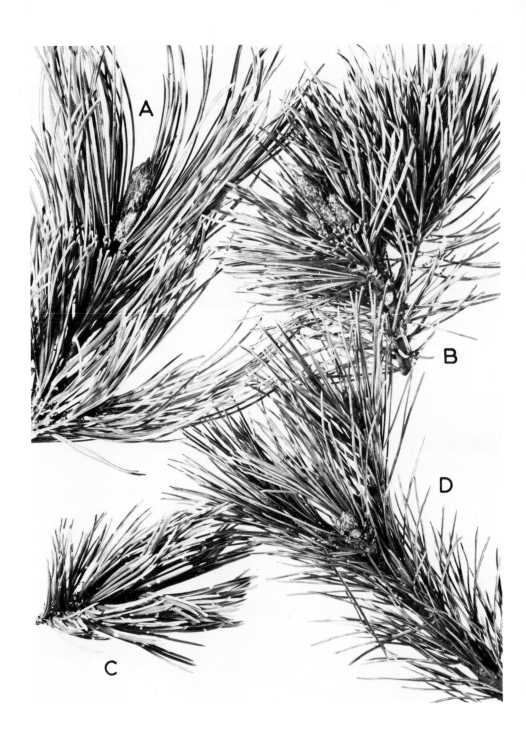

IDENTIFICATION PLATE 28

PINUS ARISTATA, P. CEMBRA, P. KORAIENSIS, P. PUMILA

A group of five-needle pines.

A. *Pinus koraiensis* 'Winton'. The feature at once distinguishing this species is the strongly toothed edge to the leaf, imparting to it a rough feel when drawn through the fingers.

B. *Pinus pumila*. Note the incurved leaves, the conspicuous white lines on the two inner faces and the tendency of the terminal bud to lengthen during the winter. The clone illustrated is 'Globe', but several selections differ only in habit.

C. *Pinus aristata*. The dark green leaves in close clusters and the numerous spots of white resin on the leaves are unmistakable.

D. *Pinus cembra*. Note the short, straight leaves in forward-pointing, closely held bundles, inconspicuous stomata and rather blunt tips.

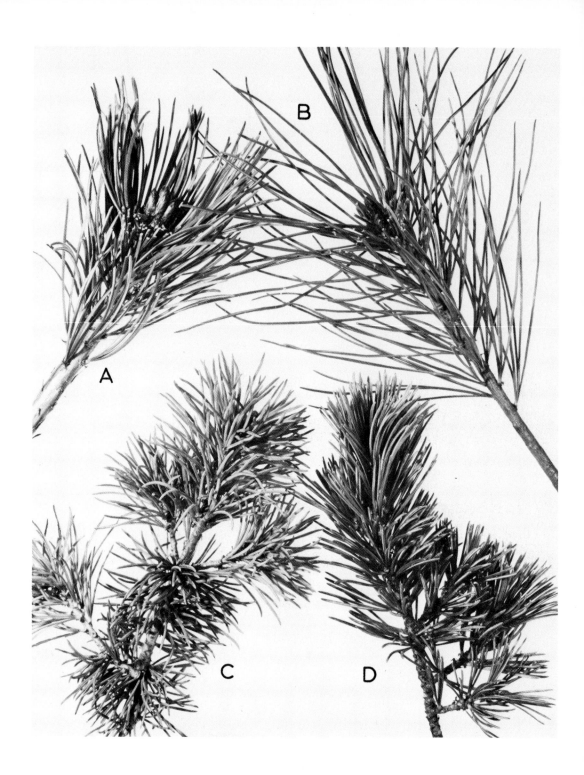

PINUS PARVIFLORA

A five-needle species that is very variable. In its native Japan it is a large tree, but only selected, slow-growing forms are usual in European cultivation. The short, twisted leaves in wide spreading bundles, dark blue-green, and (in most garden forms) conspicuous blue-white bands, give a characteristic look to the plant, which frequently bears cones, even when young. The young shoot is pale green.

A. *Pinus parviflora* 'Gimborns Pyramid'. One of several selections differing mainly or only in growth habit. Some leaves have been cut away to expose the terminal bud.

B. – – f. *aizu*. A geographical form of the species (not a dwarf) illustrating its wide variability. Some leaves have been cut away to expose the terminal bud.

C. – – 'Adcocks Dwarf'. Very distinct in its foliage, but will probably grow large in time.

D. – – 'Ha-tsumari-goyō' (= 'Brevifolia'). The distinction from 'Adcocks Dwarf' is very marked.

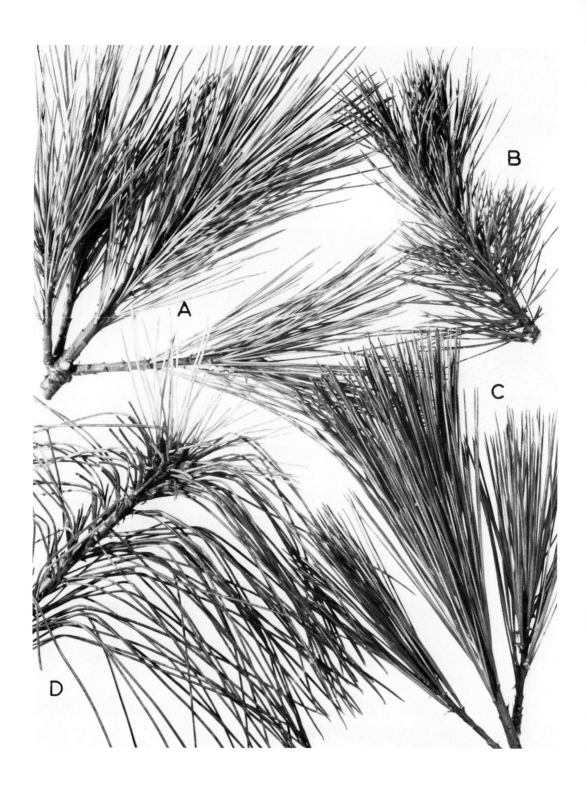

IDENTIFICATION PLATE 30

PINUS STROBUS, P. WALLICHIANA

This is another group of five-needle pines.

A. *Pinus strobus* 'Nana'. This is typical of the dwarf or slow-growing seedlings of this species that appear from time to time and of which there are several named clones in cultivation. They differ mainly in vigour and colour and intensity of the stomatic bands—this governing the apparent colour of the foliage.

B. – – 'Densa'. This represents one end of the range, and (**C**) 'Macopin' represents the other—this cultivar being perhaps better regarded as a compact, rather than dwarf form.

D. *Pinus wallichiana* 'Umbraculifera'. A rounded bush, reaching to 2 m high by as much across. The kink in the mature foliage is characteristic. It is often wrongly labelled *"P. strobus umbraculifera"*.

PODOCARPUS

A. *Podocarpus alpinus* seldom becomes more than a low, rambling bush with long straggling main branches and short laterals.

B. *Podocarpus nivalis*. This species remains a low bush in Britain. It varies considerably in size and shape of leaf. This specimen and (**C**) one with smaller leaves show the normal range. The colour is medium to dark green, but

D. – – 'Bronze' is a very slow-growing, small-leafed selection with foliage a rich coppery-brown.

E. *Podocarpus acutifolius*. Seldom more than a bush in Britain. The leaves are very sharp and the colour is a brownish-green.

F. *Podocarpus totara*. This will reach the dimensions of a small tree in Britain. The foliage is a dull yellow-green. In the allied species *P. cunninghamia* the leaves are much larger.

PSEUDOTSUGA MENZIESII

Botanists are not universally agreed as to the specific name here used and it may be found listed as *Pseudotsuga taxifolia*.

A. *Pseudotsuga menziesii* 'Fletcheri'. This is the commonest form in cultivation. It makes a broad, flat-topped plant, sometimes several metres across, with dull green leaves, lighter beneath.

B. – – 'Densa'. Of several cultivars with foliage and habit of the same kind this is probably the smallest in leaf size and rate of growth. The branch habit is noticeably horizontal.

C. – – 'Tempelhof Compact'. One of several dwarf forms selected in the seed beds, all marked by compact habit, reduced rate of growth and (usually) shorter leaves than normal.

D. – – 'Brevifolia'. A selection that eventually makes a small open tree but one that can be kept within bounds by pruning, with a fresh grass green colour.

E. – – 'Fretzii'. Another form usually seen as a bush or small tree, but with (**F**) dull, dark green foliage, very glaucous beneath.

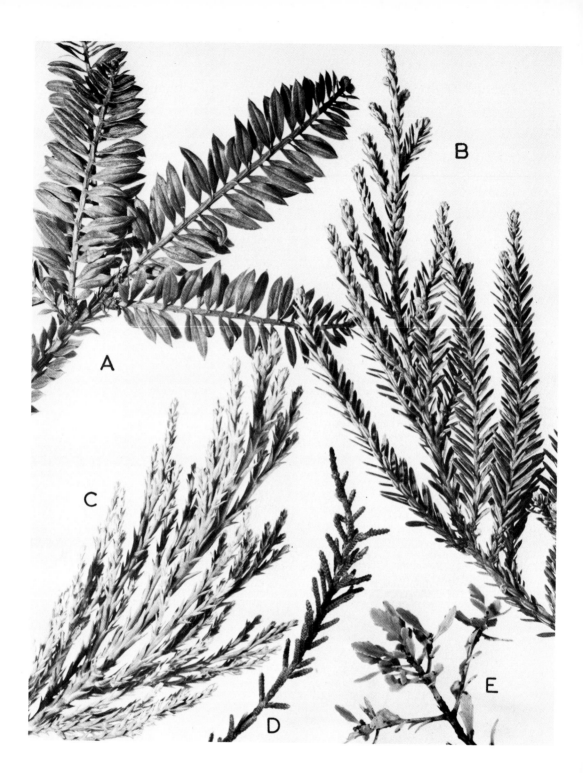

MICROCACHRYS, PHYLLOCLADUS, SEQUOIA, SEQUOIADEN-DRON

A. *Sequoia sempervirens* 'Prostrata'. The width and shape of the leaves distinguish this form. The colour is a soft grey-brown and the plant is very prostrate, unless strong leader growths have been allowed to take over.

B. – – 'Adpressa'. The creamy-white erect young shoots in early summer make this an outstanding plant, so long as it has been kept within bounds by the use of the knife.

C. *Sequoiadendron giganteum* 'Pygmaeum'. This contradiction in terms will become a very large bush in time, with foliage similar to that of the species but smaller in all its parts.

D. *Microcachrys tetragona.* A spreading, often rather straggling little bush with dark green foliage which is distinctly tetragonal (i.e., four-sided). It often sets tiny red cones.

E. *Phyllocladus alpinus.* A shrub or small tree from New Zealand, occasionally seen as a small shrub, unmistakable from its curious leaves (to be exact, cladodes), looking, as Mr. Hillier says, as though 'made by a small child out of plasticine'.

TAXUS BACCATA 1

A. *Taxus baccata* 'Amersfoort'. The broad, rounded leaf of this form is unmistakeable.

B. – – 'Paulina' is a rare form usually seen as a prosperous looking bush seldom over 1.5 m, with ascending branches and decurved leaves.

C. – – 'Compacta' is similar in habit to 'Paulina' but the leaves are much smaller.

D. – – 'Pygmaea'. The invariably short, thin leaves and neat regular growth of this very diminutive form produce a dainty little plant.

E. – – 'Nutans'. This is another diminutive form that makes a small, often squat bush with glossy dark green leaves, very irregular in size.

F. – – 'Epacrioides'. The longer, dull green leaves radially held at a wide angle to the stem distinguish this from—

G. – – 'Ericoides' in which the glossy leaves all lie distinctly forwards.

H. – – 'Nana' Knight. This very old form is the commonest of the miniature group. Growth is open and irregular and the leaves are a dark, glossy green and vary widely in size.

J. – – 'Fowle'. This is a clone of 'Adpressa' which slowly makes a dense bush, wider than high.

IDENTIFICATION PLATE 35

TAXUS BACCATA 2, T. CUSPIDATA

A. *Taxus baccata* 'Gracilis Pendula'. Always seen as a wide spreading bush with gracefully curved foliage.

B. – – 'Pendula'. This form is similar in habit to the foregoing, differing mainly in its less curved foliage.

C. – – 'Adpressa Variegata'. The foliage of all the 'Adpressa' group is similarly short, but this form carries a bright golden margin to every leaf.

D. *Taxus cuspidata* 'Nana'. Distinguishable from the English yew by the shape of the leaves and their yellowish tint beneath. 'Nana' forms a larger, taller bush than a similar form 'Densa'.

Note that some specimens in this plate show signs of damage by insect attack.

IDENTIFICATION PLATE 36

THUJA OCCIDENTALIS 1

A. *Thuja occidentalis* 'Hetz Midget'. A tiny globose plant with dark green foliage in circular, curved sprays.

B. – – 'Globosa Rheindiana'. Another miniature globose form with rather confused green foliage.

C. – – 'Caespitosa'. A low, hemispherical bun with dense, much flattened foliage, and an occasional spray of juvenile foliage.

D. – – 'Ohlendorffii'. Usually a low rounded bush with wholly or mainly juvenile foliage, but an old or neglected bush may have thrown up strong vertical thread-like shoots that are square in cross section. The variety 'Tetragona' also carries both forms of foliage, but it is a very much coarser and strong-growing plant, sometimes becoming a small tree. The upright shoots predominate and this section is almost exaggeratedly tetragonal, so there should be no confusion.

E. – – 'Pygmaea'. Usually an upright, irregular little bush with dark green glossy foliage very much flattened. Note the prominent resin glands.

F. – – 'Sphaerica'. Usually seen as a small globose or upright bush to which the open lacework appearance gives a dainty effect.

IDENTIFICATION PLATE 37

THUJA OCCIDENTALIS 2

A. *Thuja occidentalis* 'Globosa'. As its name indicates this form makes a regular globose bush, sometimes wider than high, with light green almost grey-green foliage.

B. – – 'Little Gem' forms a neat, rounded bush with much flattened, rich green foliage. The little growths all along the old wood which are characteristic of this form can be clearly seen in the photograph.

C. – – 'Woodwardii' forms a rounded bush, regularly globose even in age. The large, flat mid-green sprays are held vertically in a dense globose bush up to 1.5 m or more.

D. – – 'Filiformis'. A thread-leaf form with many of the branches thin and pendulous. The foliage is noticeably glandular, has the usual *Thuja occidentalis* smell when bruised and always one or two of the terminal shoots are flattened. See (**E**).

IDENTIFICATION PLATE 38

THUJA OCCIDENTALIS 3

A. *Thuja occidentalis* 'Ellwangerana Aurea' and (**B**) 'Rheingold' are golden forms which are frequently confused with each other. The former makes a conical plant up to 3 m high bearing (except when a young plant) wholly adult foliage. The latter is much more dwarf, it makes a rounded or squatly conical little bush always carrying a large proportion of juvenile foliage.

C. – – 'Ericoides'. This is the fixed juvenile form. Very soft foliage, dull green in summer and medium brown in winter.

D. – – 'Recurva Nana'. This form and 'Dumosa' (**E**) are frequently confused. They both form flattened globose plants and have flattened foliage in curved sprays, but whereas 'Recurva Nana' has only this type of growth, 'Dumosa' also carries some straight, thread-like upright shoots (**F**) on which the foliage is neither flattened nor recurved.

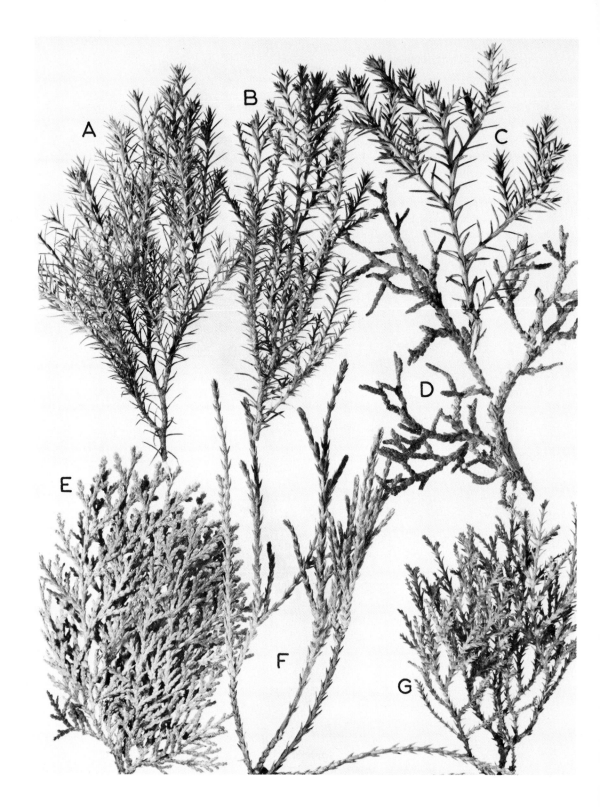

THUJA ORIENTALIS 1

A. *Thuja orientalis* 'Meldensis'. Forms an upright to globose bush with dark green juvenile foliage that is quite *rough to the touch*.

B. – – 'Rosedalis' (syn. *"rosedalis compacta"*). Makes a similar plant but the foliage is very *soft and supple*. Colour: in spring it is a butter-yellow, in summer a soft, pale green and in autumn it turns a dull purple-brown.

C. – – 'Juniperoides' (syn. *"decussata"*). Has the largest foliage of this group and is readily distinguishable by its winter colouring, which is a beautiful purple-mauve, heavily overlaid with a white glaucous coating, like a ripe grape.

D. – – 'Athrotaxoides'. A very rare, monstrous form.

E. – – 'Aurea Nana' is always seen as an ovoid or beeskip-shaped bush, reaching to 1 m only after many years. Colour: Golden-yellow in spring and summer, becoming green later.

F. – – 'Filiformis Erecta' is a thread-leaf form with branching in all the main parts of the bush strongly erect. The thread-leafed forms of this species can be distinguished from the *Chamaecyparis pisifera* 'Filifera' group by the freestanding leaf tips and from similar forms of *Thuja occidentalis* by the absence of glands or the pungent smell of the bruised foliage.

G. – – 'Minima' is the smallest form of any. It forms a low, rounded bush with semi-juvenile foliage that is stiff and quite harsh to the touch. It turns a dingy brown in winter.

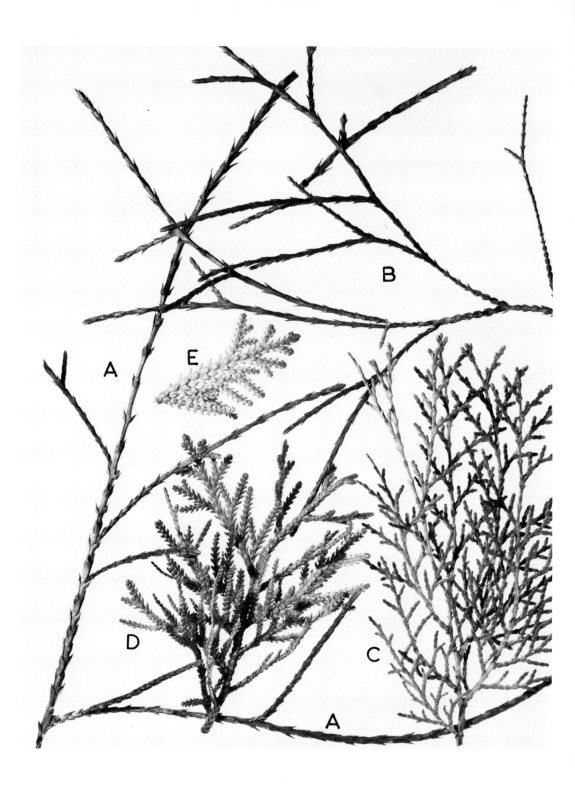

IDENTIFICATION PLATE 40

THUJA ORIENTALIS 2, THUJOPSIS

A. *Thuja orientalis* 'Flagelliformis' becomes a small tree with ascending main branches and pendulous branchlets. Strong leading shoots are much coarser than shown in the photograph. Colour: light, yellowish-green.

B. – – 'Filiformis Elegans'. The foliage is thinner than in 'Flagelliformis' and the colour is dark green.

C. – – 'Sieboldii'. Makes a globose or ovoid bush, eventually to 2 m. The dainty, lace-like foliage is golden-yellow at first, becoming light green later in the year.

D. *Thujopsis dolabrata* 'Nana' forms a low, spreading bush with very much flattened foliage. The photograph at (**E**) shows the glaucous underside of the spray.

IDENTIFICATION PLATE 41

THUJA PLICATA

A. *Thuja plicata* 'Rogersii' (syn. *"aurea rogersii"*). Usually seen as a dense little bush with all the growing tips a bright orange-brown, but it will become an upright bush to 1.5 m in time.

B. – – 'Collyers Gold'. A slow-growing form with flattened greenish-yellow foliage.

C. – – 'Stoneham Gold'. A slow-growing form similar to 'Collyers Gold', but with dark green foliage, bright orange-yellow at the growing tips.

D. – – 'Gracilis Aurea'. Differs from the type by its more slender foliage which, in a small plant, belies its ultimate size.

E. – – 'Hillieri'. Always a deep mid-green and with congested foliage. 'Pumila' is similar but very much more slow-growing.

TORREYA, TSUGA 1

A. *Torreya nucifera* 'Prostrata'. The long tapered and sharp-pointed leaves distinguish this species from Cephalotaxus. See Plate 2.

B. *Tsuga canadensis.* It is impossible to illustrate even a representative selection of the large number of dwarf garden forms that have been named.

C. 'Pendula'. This is the clone widely met with in Britain and in continental Europe. If not trained up when young, or top-worked it becomes merely a sprawling bush.

D. 'Cole'. This diminutive spreading form makes a completely prostrate little plant, with many of its main branches bare.

TSUGA 2

A. *Tsuga canadensis* 'Ruggs Washington Dwarf'. Usually seen as a globose to cushion-shaped plant, seldom over 45 cm.

B. – – 'Minima' makes a spreading or more or less pendulous plant reaching 3 m across, so it is not at all appropriately named.

C. – – 'Nearing' (syn. 'Jervis'). Similar in growth to 'Hussii' but still slower in growth and more compact.

D. – – 'Minuta'. A very dense flattened globe, only slightly faster growing than 'Abbotts Pigmy'.

E. – – 'Armistice'. The true plant makes a flat-topped (i.e., not pyramidal) plant.

F. – – 'Hussii' makes a dense, upright and picturesquely irregular small tree with short, dark green leaves.

G. – – 'Verkades Recurved'.

H. – – 'Jeddeloh'. A low, wide-spreading variety becoming popular in Europe.

AUTHORITIES AND SYNONYMIES

One major difference between my previous book on dwarf conifers and the present one is the inclusion here of authorities and synonyms. I hope the additional information will increase its value as a work of reference without detracting from the interest of the book for the general reader. To the horticulturist without botanical training it will be important to know that a person's name (often abbreviated) printed after any botanical name is that of the writer who is regarded as the 'authority' for that name, either on account of his having invented it or because he was the earliest writer to use it in compliance with the rules. Any different botanical names that follow (with their own authorities) are the 'synonyms'. These represent attempts by those other writers to find names for the same plant or group of plants which for some reason or another are now rejected—usually because the triumphant authority has 'priority' (this meaning that he got in first). Another troublesome situation is where a second author has used a name already in use for a different plant entirely, and this also is dealt with in the synonymy (usually by the use of the word 'NON').

To enable students to check up on the facts for themselves the author's name is often followed by a reference to the publication in which the name first appeared. To save space these are usually printed with so much abbreviation as to look almost meaningless to the uninitiated, but the rules for standardising these abbreviations, as well as rules to determine which name is to prevail when there are other claimants, are printed in the *Botanical Code*. They soon become familiar in use.

Many gardeners could accept the value of recording the 'authority' but would see no point in giving synonyms. 'If the name is wrong,' they would say, 'why not forget it?' The answer is that a great deal of information may have been recorded under these rejected names by these other writers which is none the less accurate or valuable on that account. For example *Pinus pinea, Pinus abies, Abies pectinata, Picea pectinata, Abies picea* and several other names have been used in the past for what we now call *Abies alba* Mill., so we should lose a lot by ignoring its synonymy, which leads us to all this hidden information.

Although full Botanical citation requires the inclusion of authorities as a means of securing accuracy, for some reason not clear to me the *Cultivated Code* does not seem to regard this as important. Why precision in nomenclature is regarded as being less important in horticulture (where commercial horticultural interests involving large sums of money may very well be involved) than it is in botany I cannot imagine. For my part I regard precision as being just as important in the nomenclature of cultivars as anywhere else. The *Cultivated Code* does not object, so I give authorities wherever they are known to me.

The system adopted throughout the chapter is as under:

Case	Information	Example
Species	Author's name No citations	*Abies alba* Mill.
Botanical 'var'. or 'f'.	Author's name No citations	– – var. *arizonica* Lemmon.
Pre 1st January 1959 Latin-form name now legitimately used as cv. name	No authority credited Citations within square brackets: (1) Basionym (i.e., earliest known use of name) (2) Pseudo-botanical name now reduced to synonymy (3) Any additional references considered of particular interest to readers	*Chamaecyparis obtusa* 'Filicoides' [*Retinospora filicoides* Veitch ex Gordon etc. . .] [*C. obtusa* f. *filicoides* (R. Smith) Beissn. in Rehd. etc. . . 1949 *.][1]
Previously published 'Fancy' cv. name to replace illegitimate name	Shortened author citation:[2] Krussm. 1960 Hillier 1964 Bergm. 1965 Den Ouden & Boom 1965 Welch 1966	– – 'Rigid Dwarf' Den Ouden & Boom 1965 [*C. obtusa rigida* etc. . .]
Legitimate cv. name published since 1st January 1959	Author's name Citation within square brackets	– – 'Gnome' Corley [Gar. Chron. etc. . .]
Suggested new cv. name to replace illegitimate or undesirable name.	The words—New name followed by normal citation of old names.	– – 'Skylands' New name [*Picea orientalis* 'Aurea Compacta' etc. . .]
New Cultivar	The words [New cv.] within square brackets	– – 'Green Velvet' [New cv.]

[1] Where a reference to the *Bibliography of Trees and Shrubs* (Rehder, 1949) includes the whole of his synonymy, this is indicated by an asterisk, thus . . . 1949 *.]

[2] These abbreviated references relate only to a small group of well known writers on conifers between 1960 and 1966.

The Abies or Silver firs, form a fairly large genus of forest-sized trees which have given rise to relatively few dwarf forms. They can be distinguished from their nearest relatives the Picea from the fact that the leaves when they fall leave disc-like leaf scars, whereas those of the latter genus leave small, prominent, peg-like projections.

The Abies, like certain other genera, mostly have two distinct forms of growth, the leader growth on which the leaves are radial and lateral growth on which the leaves are pectinate, or at most semi-radial. This lateral growth, as has been explained in Chapter I, in some species has little or no capacity for developing into true leader growth but will extend in a horizontal direction so, by propagation from lateral branches, prostrate forms of distinct garden use can be produced. As the entire plant in such a case consists really of a single branch the growth is always extremely one-sided, but as many of the firs have attractive foliage such plants can be of great garden value when used to clothe a bank or to accentuate a prominent position on a large rockery. Some of these had been named before the *Cultivated Code* put a ban on latinized names and these are with us under cultivar names such as 'Prostrata', 'Horizontalis' and 'Pendula', but in future any cultivars produced in this way (they are one form of 'cultivariant' see definitions at the beginning of this chapter) should be simply indicated by the specific name and cultivar epithet (if any) followed by the word (Prostrate) to indicate the cultivariant status.

Abies alba Mill. The Common Silver fir (for many years known as *Abies pectinata* D.C.) has long been in cultivation and several cultivars have been named, including dwarf forms. The foliage of this species is less attractive than some and this may be why these forms do not appear to have survived in cultivation. They may be conveniently grouped as follows:

NANA GROUP. *Forms that are compact or dwarf according to the definitions at the beginning of this chapter.*
      'Compacta'   'Tortuosa'
      'Nana'

PENDULA GROUP. *Forms that are tree-like but with pendulous growth tips.*
      'Green Spiral'   'Pendula Gracilis'
      'Pendula'
The prostrate forms referred to by Hornibrook [Dw. Con. Ed. 2, 20. 1938] were doubtless merely cultivariants.

– –'**Compacta**' [*Picea pectinate compacta* Parsons, Nurs. Cat. 65. 1887?; var. *compacta* Hornb. Dw. Con. Ed. 2, 19. 1938; *A. alba* f. *compacta* (Parsons) Rehd. Bibl. 11. 1949 *.] NANA GROUP. This is described as a seedling form making a dwarf roundish bush, broader than high, compact, branches crowded and with very shiny leaves. This clone originated with a plant at Rochester, New York,

U.S.A., that had been purchased from the one-time Parsons Nursery, Flushing, New York, and it probably is not now in cultivation. Any similar form arising in future will need to be registered under a new cultivar name.

– –'Green Spiral' [New cv.] PENDULA GROUP. This is the name given here to a pendulous form of which two trees planted in 1916 in the Secrest Arboretum at Wooster, Ohio, U.S.A., were long grown as 'Tortuosa', but the possibility that these represent the ultimate development in that reputedly dwarf variety is very remote. The trees, now about 10 m high, have a single, more or less erect but curiously twisted trunk and relatively few short and pendulous branches. These also tend to be twisted or incurved, in places bare, elsewhere covered with dense foliage. The trees have never formed cones.

This form has a certain attractiveness when màture, but it will doubtless be slow-growing and being so columnar may be used as a specimen where space is limited. It has recently been re-introduced to the American trade.

– –'Nana' [*Picea pectinata nana* Knight, Syn. Conif. 38. 1850 (Nom.); *Abies pectinata nana* (and *prostrata* pro syn.) Carr. Traité, 208. 1855.] NANA GROUP. This was described as a very dwarf variety of French origin, growing one or two feet high and smaller in all its parts. I cannot trace it in cultivation.

– –'Pendula' [*Picea pectinata pendula* (Nom.) Godefroy ex Knight, Syn. Conif. 38. 1850; *A. alba* f. *pendula* (Carr.) Rehd. Bibl. 11. 1949 *; *Pinus abies* var. *pendula* (Nom.) Lawson, Pl. Fir Tribe, 10. 1851; *Abies pectinata pendula* Hort. ex Carr. Traité, 207. 1855.] PENDULA GROUP. This clone was described by Carrière as having horizontal spreading branches, very pendulous at the tips. It originated about 1835 as a seedling on M. Godefroy's nursery at Ville d'Avray. Since this origin was known to an English nurseryman in 1851 it is a reasonable assumption that several old trees known in Great Britain answering to the description are of this clone, two examples being at Endsleigh Gardens, Milton Abbot, Tavistock, Devon. Only this clone is entitled to the cultivar name 'Pendula'.

– –'Pendula Gracilis' [*A. pectinata pendula gracilis* Sén. Conif. 14. 1867.] PENDULA GROUP. This clone was described as a vigorous and exceptionally beautiful variety obtained through a M. Massé (of whom nothing is known) and as having a straight trunk and slender side branches very long and hanging vertically down; bark a clear brown, covered with scarious pubescence. I obtained material from trees clearly answering to this description at Thorn House, Wembury, near Plymouth, the residence of N. Trahair.

– –'Tortuosa' [*Picea pectinate 2 tortuosa* (Booth) Loud. Arb. Frut. Brit. 2330. 1838; *Abies pectinate tortuosa* Carr. Traité, 206. 1855; Sén. Conif. 15. 1867.] NANA GROUP. This was described as a very bushy little tree of German origin with its branches and branchlets very much twisted and crooked, which gives it a very singular appearance. Slavin [Rep. Conif. Conf. 88. 1932] stated of the plant in Highland Park, Rochester, New York, 'A bushy dwarf with crowded, ascending branches and short, lustrous, bright-green leaves 11–19 mm long. Our plant is about 60 cm high × 1.25 m broad', but B. Harkness writes (26 March 1963) 'Lost from Highland Park collection'. Probably now lost to cultivation.

Abies amabilis Douglas ex Forbes. The Red fir has not produced any recorded dwarf forms, but plants propagated from side-branches remain stable and because of the rich foliage of this species these make attractive, spreading plants which eventually cover a considerable area. Such plants are cultivariants (see definitions above).

– –'Compacta' [*A. amabilis* var. *compacta* Hornb. Dw. Con. 17. 1923.] This was clearly a plant of the cultivariant type. It can now be regarded as lost to cultivation.

– –'Spreading Star' Den Ouden and Boom 1965 [*A. amabilis* 'Compacta' Meyer, Pl. Expl. **2**: 69. 1963; 'Procumbens' Hort.] At the opening of the section on Abies, I suggest that these cultivariants, whilst not justifying a new cultivar name, might be distinguished for practical purposes (pending official recognition in some future edition of the *Cultivated Code*) by the use of the suffix (Prostrate). But since this particular clone has been widely distributed under this name and appears stable the cultivar name is worth retention in this case. (Illustration 101).

Abies balsamea (L.) Mill. Whilst few truly dwarf forms of Abies have been reported (and fewer still brought into cultivation) this species has distinguished itself by giving us several forms which are among the best dwarf conifers we possess.

The Balsam fir is usually a tree 20–30 m high, but on the higher slopes of the White Mountains, New Hampshire, U.S.A., near the treeline, it is reduced to a low, variable but always more or less prostrate form having foliage of the same deep glossy green but with leaves shorter and wider than normal and with the habit and leaf arrangement variable, and of this form we have several clones in cultivation. Because of their origin, they are all indestructibly hardy.

– –'Andover' Wyman [Arnoldia **26**: 14. 1966.] This was a completely prostrate form with normal foliage found growing wild in the woods near Andover, New York, in 1957. Although obviously of slow growth the original plant had a spread of nearly 5 metres. It is probably an interesting example of a cultivariant arising in nature from accidental damage which had destroyed the trunk many years previously.

– – f. **hudsonia** (Bosc ex Jacques) Fernald & Weatherby [Rehd. Bibl. 12. 1949 *; f. *nana* (Nels.) Beissn. Conif. Ben. 70. 1887.] A glance through the synonymy given in Rehder's *Bibliography* shews the difficulty this useful group of dwarf firs has had to find nomenclatural peace. Amongst much uncertainty two things seem certain, these being that because of the different habitat of *A. fraseri*, early mentions of a prostrate form of that species must be taken to refer to an *A. balsamea* form and that early writers bandied the epithets *hudsonia, nana, globosa, prostrata* and others about (usually without descriptions and with little or no knowledge of the plants). I see no grounds for distinguishing a second botanical form, so the balance of advantage seems to lie with accepting f. *hudsonia* as covering all the dwarf and low-growing forms and continuing the use of the following as cultivar names.

– –'Hudsonia' Welch [Dw. Con. 107. 1966.] This is a clone (or more probably a group of similar clones), the most common form in European cultivation, with a flattened globose or cushion-forming habit and foliage that is semi-radial. The difference between 'Nana' and 'Hudsonia' can be clearly seen if a twig of last year's growth be snapped off and looked at from the broken end, and since the upper side of the twig of 'Prostrata' is quite clear of leaves, these garden forms are easily distinguishable. The rich glossy foliage and indestructible hardiness make all of these forms most desirable garden plants. (Illustration 102).

– –'Nana' [*Picea balsamea* var. *nana* Nels. Pin. 37. 1866; *A. balsamea* f. *nana* (Nels.) Beissn. in Rehd. Bibl. 12. 1949 *] is a clone which forms a globose or rounded bush seldom reaching 1 m which carries its (usually very short) leaves radially. (Illustration 103).

– –'Prostrata' [*Picea balsamea prostrata* Hort. ex Knight, Syn. Conif. 39. 1850] is an uncommon clone with a very prostrate habit and completely pectinate foliage.

Abies cephalonica Loud., the Grecian fir, has so far as I am aware only produced the following dwarf form.

– –'Meyers Dwarf' Den Ouden and Boom 1965 [*A. cephalonica* 'Nana' Meyer, Pl. Expl. **2**: 69. 1963; Hillier, Dw. Con. 10. 1964 and Man. 458. 1971] forms a slow-growing, flat-topped, spreading plant with rigid branchlets and leaves shorter than normal. It is a very attractive form which should be more freely planted. (Illustration 104).

Abies concolor (Gordon) Hild. The White or Colorado fir has given us several good dwarf conifers.

– –'Compacta' [*A. concolor violacea compacta* Beissn. Handb. 476. 1891; var. *glauca compacta* Hornb. Dw. Con. 20. 1923; var. *glauca* 'Compacta' Hillier, Dw. Con. 10. 1964.] This is usually seen as a dwarf, compact shrub of irregular growth, with stout, stiff, short (2.5 to 4 cm) and very glaucous leaves. It is certain that more than one clone is in cultivation, since this form turns up in the seed beds from time to time, but in a form doubtfully distinguished as **'Glauca Nana'** the blue colour depends much on soil and situation. (Illustration 105).

– –'Gables Weeping' Hebb [Arnoldia **30, 6**: 251. 1970] is a truly dwarf, spreading (and eventually pendulous) form that originated as a seedling in a nursery in Pennsylvania and was introduced by the Watnong Nursery, Morris Plains, New Jersey. At 18 years of age it is only 50 cm across. The foliage is a dark, greenish-grey, with the leaves straight, or nearly so and much shorter than normal. Since the branch habit is strongly pendulous, young plants must be stem-trained to form a leader. It is a very attractive plant. (Illustration 106). Another weeping dwarf form **'Elkins Weeper'** [New cv.] is still more strongly pendulous and needs careful training when young if it is not to become somewhat of a monstrosity, since the falling of the leaves the second year leave the branching pattern permanently exposed. The leaves are dark green, always curled up-wards. As with so many conifers the contrast between the old leaves and the fresh apple-green of the new leaves is most attractive in both of these weeping forms.

– –'Globosa'. [*A. concolor* f. *globosa* (Niemetz) Rehd. Bibl. 13. 1949 *.] A globose form raised in Hungary early in the century and no longer in cultivation.

– –'Green Globe' New name [*A. balsamea globosa* Hort. Amer.] A most attractive form, appropriately named, found growing in a local cemetery and introduced by Verkades Nursery of Wayne, New Jersey. One of the best dwarf conifers of recent years. With time it may develop a leader and become squatly conical. (Illustration 107).

– –'Pendula' [*A. concolor pendula* (Simon-Louis) ex Beissn. Mitt. d. d. d. G. **5:** 64. 1896; f. *pendula* (Beissn.) Rehd. Bibl. 13. 1949 *] was, according to the description given by Hornibrook [Dw. Con. 21. 1923] merely a cultivariant of the (Prostrate) type which could be produced anywhere at any time.

– –'Pigglemee' [New cv.] is a nice, very compact, globose form with annual growth only 3-4 cm, propagated from a witch's broom on an old plant of *A. concolor* var. *candicans* and introduced to the trade by Draijer B. V. of Heemstede, Holland. It has foliage of the same beautiful blue-grey and very much shorter leaves. It should be very popular when more freely available. (Illustration 108).

– –'Wattezii (Prostrate)' Welch [Dw. Con. 107. 1966.] The cultivar 'Wattezii' is a rather slow-growing form of the species with creamy-yellow foliage fading to white, and in this cultivariant form it is an attractive garden plant.

Abies delavayi Franchet is an attractive Chinese species of which I can find only one reference to a truly dwarf form. It is described [Hillier, Man. 459. 1971] as a dwarf, slow-growing form of the type. Winter buds orange-brown; leaves more or less radially arranged, 1-1.5 cm long, the margins recurved. It is listed as **'Nana'**, but under the rules a 'fancy' name will have to be found for it. Plants I have seen in America labelled *A. delavayi* 'Fargesii Prostrate' appeared to be merely cultivariants.

Abies fraseri (Pursh) Poiret. Fraser's Balsam fir is frequently confused with the very similar *A. balsamea*.

– – f. **prostrata** Rehd. [Bibl. 12. 1949 *; var. *prostrata* Hornb. Dw. Con. Ed. 2, 25. 1938.] The case for botanical recognition of the dwarf form of this fir is questionable since to the best of my knowledge only one clone is known, but by analogy with the similar variant in *Abies balsamea* (with which this form was always confused by early writers) it may for the present be retained. The clonal name should, however, be used for the only clone known in cultivation, which originated at the Kelsey Highlands Nursery, East Boxford, Massachusetts, U.S.A., in 1916. **'Prostrata'** Den Ouden and Boom 1965, then, is a low-growing but fairly wide-spreading shrub with horizontal branches and foliage which can be distinguished from *A. balsamea* by the paler colour of its shoots, covered with a reddish down, and by the leaves which at the base are set forward on the shoot. They are a pale yellow-green above and are more noticeably white beneath.

Abies homolepis Sieb. and Zucc. The Nikko fir is another species that is happy to grow as a prostrate cultivariant and such plants have been recorded from time to time. Unless propagated from a clone that is itself recognized as a named cultivar these do not themselves form a new cultivar and should be referred to merely as **Abies homolepis (Prostrate).** (Illustration 109). Because of their dense, glossy, dark green foliage these plants are most attractive, if given room to develop. I know of no truly dwarf form of this species in cultivation.

Abies koreana Wilson. Although eventually too big for most gardens, young plants of the Korean fir make excellent garden plants because of their neat habit and attractive foliage and because they bear their long, purple cones freely on quite young trees. Trees from seed grow naturally conical; grafted plants will eventually do the same but can be kept as 'dwarf conifers' for many years if never allowed to develop a leader.

– –'**Compact Dwarf**' Den Ouden and Boom 1965 [*A. koreana* 'Nana' Hort. NON Meyer, Pl. Expl. **2**: 70. 1963.] This is a slow-growing form without a leader, usually forming a squat or wide-spreading, flat-topped bush with much interlacing of branches. The short, stiff, bifid leaves (15 mm × 1.75 mm) standing out straight from the creamy-grey shoots give the plant a more open appearance than is actually the case. The buds are light brown, up to 3 mm in diameter. It is said never to cone. (Illustration 110).

Meyer described 'Nana' as 'An evergreen tree producing cones in abundance on trees no taller than a man'. Since most seedlings do this the description does not distinguish any particular clone, so the name 'Nana' should not be used in any clonal sense.

– –'**Piccolo**' [New cv.] is a new introduction from Holland. I do not know its ultimate size. It makes a plant similar to 'Compact Dwarf' but the leaves are even shorter (to 12 mm × 1.5 mm) relatively more broad and noticeably bifid at the tip, held pointing forward along the shoot. The buds are small (2 mm diam.) and a dark mahogany-brown.

– –'**Prostrate Beauty**' Den Ouden and Boom 1965 [*A. koreana prostrata* Hort.] I believe that the 'irregularly-growing, robust form with horizontal or a little up-curved branches, without a leader' described by Dr. Boom related to the plant distributed from the Arnold Arboretum and has no reference to the form described by Dr. Meyer (referred to under 'Compact Dwarf', above). It is a cultivariant that makes an attractive specimen, but it will only remain dwarf and spreading if any leading growth that develops is at once cut away. (Illustration 111).

– –'**Starkers Dwarf**' [New cv.] This attractive form makes a dense flat-topped rounded specimen about twice as wide as high, a plant 15 years old being 1.25 m by 50 cm high. The growth is very dense, with ascending main branches and an annual growth only about 7 cm. The foliage is a rich deep glossy green. This variety is reliably dwarf with no tendency to throw up leader growth. It is named for Carl Starker of Jennings Lodge, Oregon, U.S.A., who received the mother plant from an unrecorded source in Canada in 1960. (Illustration 112).

Abies lasiocarpa (Hook.) Nutt. The Alpine fir is usually represented in gardens by the following geographical variety which was formerly regarded as a separate species. Since at that time each species was credited with having a dwarf cultivar with the name 'Compacta', recognition of the name 'Arizonica Compacta' (below) avoids the duplication that would otherwise occur.

– – var. **arizonica** (Merriam) Lemmon. This variety owes its popularity in gardens to its greater vigour and the glaucous grey foliage resulting from a broad white band of stomata on each leaf above as well as the two bands below. Unlike many of the Silver firs it objects to growing as a prostrate cultivariant and grafted plants readily develop leader growth and soon form conical trees.

‒ ‒'**Arizonica Compacta**' New name [*A. arizonica* var. *compacta* Hornb. Dw. Con. Ed. 2, 22. 1938; *A. lasiocarpa* 'Compacta' Welch, Dw. Con. 108. 1966.] Although in my earlier book I suggested a shorter name, the use of this cultivar name is well established in the trade, and this should be recognised. It is one of our most attractive dwarf conifers. It originated as a seedling at the nursery of the late Jan Boer Gz of Boskoop, Holland. It forms a dense, regular, broadly conical plant, about half as broad as high, with extremely silvery-blue foliage. (Illustration 113).

‒ ‒'**Beissneri**' [*A. sub-alpina Beissneri* Hesse, in Mitt. d.d.d.G. **10:** 46. 1901; *A. lasiocarpa* var. *Beissneri* Hornb. Dw. Con. 22. 1923] was described as a curiously distorted form with sickle-shaped leaves curled and twisted around the distorted branches. It is now lost to cultivation.

‒ ‒'**Compacta**' [*A. sub-alpina compacta* Beissn. Mitt. d.d.d.G. **9:** 64. 1909; *A. lasiocarpa* f. *compacta* (Beissn.) Rehd. Bibl. 12. 1949 *; var. *compacta* Hornb. Dw. Con. 22. 1923.] This is described as a densely branched, fairly regular glaucous blue globular form originating in Germany. It seems no longer in cultivation.

‒ ‒'**Conica**' [*A. lasiocarpa* var. *conica* Hornb. Dw. Con. 21. 1923; f. *conica* (Hornb.) Rehd. Bibl. 12. 1949 *.] This is a compact form making a broadly conical bush with crowded and ascending branches; leaves very dense on the upper side of the shoot, very thin and fine (25 mm x barely 1 mm wide), grey-green in colour but with stomatic bands not nearly so noticeable as normal. Raised from seed in the Arnold Arboretum in 1873. It is not in cultivation in England, unless the following cultivar proves to be the same, in which case the new name is redundant.

‒ ‒'**Roger Watson**' [New cv.] I suggest this name in honour of the late Roger Watson of Taunton in Somerset, England, by profession an engine-driver, by nature a gentleman and by choice a keen gardener and connoisseur of alpines and dwarf conifers. The mother plant from Taunton is now only 1.5 m high, having increased on average but 75 mm annually since I first met its former owner. It has formed a broadly conical plant with an horizontal branch system densely clothed with foliage. The leaves (15 mm by 1.25 mm) are normal, the stomata being quite inconspicuous, resulting in a dark grey-green appearance. This form will strike from cuttings. Such plants are very slow to get away but once they form a leader they soon develop into a conical shape. It is a very attractive little tree.

Abies magnifica A. Murray. The Californian Red fir has not produced any true dwarf, unless the plant listed by Hillier is such, but the species can successfully be grown as a prostrate cultivariant, so this form can appear anywhere at any time.

‒ ‒ (**Prostrate**) New name [*A. magnifica prostrata* Beissn. Mitt. d.d.d.G. **13:** 141. 1904; 'Nana' Hillier, Man. 461. 1971.] Hillier describes this as a dwarf form with wide-spreading branches. It is probably a cultivariant which, if it lives up to its name, should make a magnificent lawn specimen.

Abies nordmanniana (Steven) Spach. The Caucasian fir is another species that will grow happily as a prostrate cultivariant and such have appeared under various names. [*A. nordmanniana horizontalis* Carr. Rev. Hort. 151. 1887; f. *procumbens* Browicz & Bugaia, Rosznik Arb. Korn. **3:** 73. 1958.]

– –'**Golden Spreader**' Den Ouden and Boom 1965 ['Aurea Nana' Hort.] When it becomes readily available this cultivar will certainly become popular in gardens because of its wonderful colour. This is a bright, clear, golden-yellow which is at its best in the depth of winter. It forms a flat-topped spreading plant, slow-growing (annual growth 4–5 cm), leaves slightly curved, 12–25 mm long by 1.75 mm broad, yellow above, paler beneath with two greyish-white stomatic bands. Since it reputedly arose as a seedling it is presumably a true prostrate form.

Abies pinsapo Boissier, the Spanish fir, is normally a large tree but grafts from a side branch develop at first into rather confused, bushy plants which, because of the interesting and unusual foliage, make useful dwarf conifers for several years, until they outgrow the description.

– –'**Aurea**' [*A. pinsapo aurea* Sén. Conif. 16. 1867] is a form with its young shoots and foliage richly diffused with yellow. It is a slow-grower.

– –'**Glauca**' [*A. pinsapo* f. *glauca* (Carr.) Beissn. in Rehd. Bibl. 9. 1949 *] has glaucous foliage and is a stronger grower than 'Aurea'. Other forms, '**Clarke**', '**Hamondii**' and '**Pygmaea**' mentioned in the literature, I have not been able to trace in cultivation.

Abies procera Rehd. The Noble fir (known for many years as *A. nobilis* Lindley) is another large tree willing to accept life as a humble cultivariant, and the attractive, densely set upcurved foliage, always more or less glaucous, results in excellent flat-topped, spreading plants which, despite such noble lineage, are surprisingly slow-growing. Any attempt by such a plant to send up a leader should at once be cut away, lest it takes over and the plant becomes arboreal.

– – (**Prostrate**) [*A. procera* f. *prostrata* (Hornb.) Rehd. in Rehd. Bibl. 14. 1949 *.] Plants thus labelled will be cultivariants propagated from a normal tree, and those distinguished as '**Glauca (Prostrate)**' [*A. procera* f. *glauca* (Ravenscr.) Rehd. in Rehd. Bibl. 14. 1949 *] will be similar plants resulting from side-grafts taken from a selected glaucous form of the species. These last are most attractive. (Illustration 114).

AUSTROCEDRUS

Austrocedrus is a small genus at one time included in Libocedrus, under which it is still sometimes listed. Only one species has a recorded dwarf form.

Austrocedrus chilensis Florin & Boutelje. The Chilean cedar has produced one dwarf form, **'Viridis Compacta'** [*Libocedrus chilensis viridis compacta* Sén. Conif. 107. 1868.] Described as a compact, pyramidal form of congested habit, it was raised from seed by Sénéclause, a French nurseryman. I have not been able to trace it.

CALOCEDRUS

In my earlier book I listed this as Libocedrus, but the transfer to Calocedrus is now recognised by most botanists so should be accepted by us poor horticulturists. Only one species interests us here.

Calocedrus decurrens (Torrey) Florin is a species which is usually seen as a tall, columnar tree of monumental proportions with dense, rich green foliage. Three dwarf forms have arisen in seed beds widely separated in space and time.

– –'Compacta' [*Libocedrus decurrens* f. *compacta* (Beissn.) Voss in Rehd. Bibl. 49. 1949 *] was described in 1891 as a compact, thick twigged form of rounded habit, similar to a conical form of *Thuja occidentalis*. Whether this conical form is now identifiable in European cultivation I cannot say.

– –'Depressa' [*Libocedrus decurrens depressa* (Scott) Gordon, Pin. Ed. 2, 426. 1875; *Libocedrus decurrens* var. *nana* Dall. & Jacks. Handb. 304. 1923.] This is a very dense, compact and globose form, growing as wide as high, which originated in the Scott Nursery at Merriott in Somerset, where the mother plant at 10 years was 1 m x 1 m. I now consider that the specimen at the Westonbirt Arboretum in Gloucestershire, near the Head Forester's office referred to in my earlier book [Welch, Dw. Con. 217. 1966] can be identified with this form, not only because of the relatively close association geographically of the two places but because a propagation of the Westonbirt tree, after 10 years growth in Devizes, corresponds exactly to Gordon's description of the mother plant of the same age at Merriott. The available description of 'Nana' is so inadequate that it does not merit independent recognition any longer.

– –'Intricata' [*Libocedrus decurrens intricata* Hillier, Dw. Con. 42. 1964.] This is a form raised from seed by James R. Noble of San Francisco, California, U.S.A., in 1938 and introduced to this country by the late Mr. A. H. Nisbet of Gosport. It forms a dense and very slow-growing but distinctly columnar plant. Unfortunately, this and the Somerset plant have become mixed in the trade. From foliar characteristics alone they are difficult to separate, 'Intricata' being only marginally smaller and denser in the spray, but in winter it bronzes much more than does 'Depressa' and the difference in habit as the plants develop is unmistakeable. (Illustration 115).

CEDRUS

The cedars are a small genus of four or five species all very much alike and distinguished by having branchlets of two kinds—long terminal shoots bearing scattered leaves, and short, spur-like shoots which bear tufts of leaves in false whorls. In this respect they are similar to the larches but being evergreen cannot be confused with that genus, which is all deciduous. The genus has given us several good dwarf forms.

Cedrus atlantica (Endl.) Carr. The Atlantic or Mount Atlas cedar is normally a tree to 40 m high, differing from *C. libani* mainly in branching habit and in the size of its cones. Since it is virtually indistinguishable from *C. libani* by foliage alone, any dwarf forms are listed under that species.

Cedrus brevifolia (Hook. fil.) Henry. The Cypress cedar is so popular a tree to grow in a container that many persons are under the impression that it is a dwarf species. This is not the case for in the open ground it becomes a tree upwards of 5 m high. Like all the cedars, this species varies in vigour and length of leaf both genetically and in its response to cultural treatment and method of propagation, so variations tend to be highly prized by their owners and receive names that are of doubtful validity and of still more questionable value. **'Compacta'** Hillier [Dw. Con. 12. 1964] is a cultivariant grafted from a scion taken from a glaucous tree, **'Epsteinianum'** [New cv.] is a seedling form with leaves marginally shorter than normal, and **'Horizontalis'** Hillier [Dw. Con. 12. 1964] is probably a cultivariant resulting from a graft taken from a side branch. In a pot or other container this cedar seems to remain dwarf indefinitely and because of its small leaves, which are nicely in scale, it makes a good subject for Bonsai.

Cedrus deodara (Roxb.) G. Don in Loud. The Deodar has the longest leaves and most graceful habit of all the true cedars. If not allowed to develop a leader, it can be grown as large wide-spreading bush. It has given the following dwarf forms, some of which are uncommon in cultivation.

– –**'Hesse'** Meyer [Pl. Expl. **2**. 87. 1963.] This was a very dwarf and dense form which originated in the nursery of H. A. Hesse at Weener, Ems, in Germany, but which is no longer listed by them. It is probably not now in cultivation.

– –**'Nana'** [*C. deodara* var. *nana* Hornb. Dw. Con. Ed. 2, 34. 1938.] It is a very slow growing form which makes a compact bush. There is a good specimen on the rock garden at Kew. In cultivation but very rare. (Illustration 116).

– –**'Pygmy'** [*C. deodara* 'Pygmaea' Amer. Hort. Mag. **39, 4**: 192. 1960; Hillier, Dw. Con. 12. 1964; Bergm. Pl. and Gar. **21, 1**: 25. 1965.] This is an extremely dwarf form with conspicuously glaucous foliage and an annual growth of only 6 mm. It was found by James Noble in a little nursery in California in or about 1943 in a row of normal seedlings. The original plant was in the Wm. T. Gotelli collection and is, I believe, now dead but several propagations are now established both in Britain and the U.S.A., so this unique little form is unlikely to be lost to cultivation. (Illustration 117).

Cedrus libani A. Rich. The Cedar of Lebanon has given us several dwarf forms which are very popular, partly because of their value as garden plants and partly perhaps on account of its Biblical associations.

– – f. **nana** (Loud.) Beissn. [Rehd. Bibl. 32. 1949 *] was described by Loudon merely as 'A very dwarf variety . . . dwarf and bushy'. This description would cover all the slow-growing plants in cultivation.

– –'**Nana**'. Consistency with the general plan of the book would require us to limit this cultivar name to the clone originally described by Loudon but dwarf forms of this cedar turn up in seed beds from time to time and the accepted horticultural use of 'Nana' to cover the whole group of such clones must be recognised. (Illustration 118). In these circumstances plants from the various forms in cultivation may show minor variations, but they do not justify separate recognition, even the clone 'Comte de Dijon' being more outstanding for its romantic name than in any other way. Opportunities here must surely have been missed. Loudon, writing in 1838, mentions an 'exceedingly beautiful' dwarf specimen with silvery foliage, but although he expressed surprise that it had not been propagated no one seems to have taken the hint, and amongst the many seedlings raised since then the genetic reshuffling in such a variable species must surely have combined foliage deviation with dwarfism by this time, but none has to my knowledge been recorded, unless 'Gold Tip' is such.

– –'**Comte de Dijon**' [*C. libani* 'Comte de Dijon' Barbier, Nurs. Cat. 1908] is a clone of 'Nana' originally distributed by the nursery firm Barbier of Orleans in France. This being the case it may be feared that many of the plants grown as 'Comte de Dijon' have no claim to the name at all.

Of the four authentic plants recorded by Hornibrook in 1938 only two remain. The tree in the National Botanic Garden at Glasnevin, Dublin, has now become a tree 5 m high by 4 m across, and the branching is distinctly horizontal and wide-spreading. The foliage is radial, the leaves are long, fine and needle-like, 20-25 mm long by about 0.5 mm diam., tapering gradually to a fine point, often curved slightly and occurring singly on the growing shoot; or shorter, 15-18 mm long, even thinner, and occurring in tufts on the spur-like growths which are characteristic of the species, and with somewhat shorter and often unsymmetrical points. Annual growth about 50 mm. This plant should now be regarded as the type plant, and the name 'Comte de Dijon' be withdrawn from all specimens not conforming to the Dublin plant, or to its co-survivor at Myddleton House, Enfield, Middlesex, England.

– –'**Gold Tip**' [New cv.] A seedling found by Fred Bergman of Raraflora, Feasterville, Pennsylvania, U. S. A., and at first distributed by him as "variegated form". It forms a large irregular bush with the foliage bright yellow in early summer, fading to a mixed yellow and green later.

– –'**Golden Dwarf**' [*C. libani* 'Prostrate' Krüssm. Nadel. Ed. 2, 81. 1960; *C. libani* 'Aurea Prostrata', Hillier, Dw. Con. 13. 1964.] It is a completely prostrate form with golden foliage. It is probably a cultivariant of the form 'Aurea'.

– –'**Nana Pyramidata**' [*C. libani nana pyramidata* Carr. Traité, 284. 1855] was a dwarf conical form, probably no longer in cultivation.

– –'**Sargentii**' [*C. libani* var. *pendula Sargentii* Hornb. Dw. Con. 26. 1923] is a very valuable dwarf and truly weeping form which should not be confused with *Cedrus libani* 'Pendula', which is a large tree. This form needs to be trained up as a young plant to the desired height and it will then form a graceful, dome-shaped bush with long curved sweeping branches. It is a most attractive plant in a prominent spot on a large rockery. It can also be grown successfully in a large pot or other container in which it can look most attractive with its long, pendulous branches sweeping down below the level of the top of the pot. Grown in this way it may look its best if kept rather open by pruning away some branches entirely. Unless trained up to a leader the plant, being unable to lift itself above the level of the ground, sprawls about in a most ungainly way. (Illustration 119).

CEPHALOTAXUS

This is a genus of small yew-like trees or shrubs comprising five species all from southern or eastern Asia. It shares with Abies and other species a reluctance to develop true leader growth from a side shoot and so lends itself to the production of prostrate cultivariant forms. In the foliage it is distinguishable from Torreya by the non-spiny pointed leaves with prominent mid-rib above but not furrowed beneath and by the more numerous bud scales, and from Taxus by its longer leaves with two broad, silvery bands beneath.

Cephalotaxus fortuni Hook., with its long, tapered green leaves, gives us in **'Prostrate Spreader'** Den Ouden and Boom 1965 [*C. fortunei* 'Prostrata' Hillier, Dw. Con. 15. 1964; 'Prostrate' Welch, Dw. Con. 114. 1966] an attractive widespreading conifer, suitable for ground cover in a shady position. It will cover a large area in time.

Cephalotaxus harringtonia (Forb.) K. Koch, has had a struggle to find for itself a settled name. The typical form reaches to tree size and the species is usually represented in gardens by the following variety and garden forms.
– – var. **drupacea** (S. and Z.) Koidzumi [Rehd. Bibl. 5. 1949 *] forms a dense, globose bush without a leader, which will become large in time. It has produced the following bud mutations. (Illustration 122).
– –**'Fastigiata'** [*C. pedunculata fastigiata,* Carr. Prod. et Fix. Var. 44, 1865; *C. harringtonia* f. *fastigiata* Rehd. Bibl. 5. 1949 *] is a distinct form with a very strongly fastigiate habit and very large dark green leaves. (Illustration 120). It becomes a small tree somewhat similar to the Irish yew in time but is very slow-growing. Golden and variegated forms have been recorded but seem to be no longer in cultivation. At the base of the plant almost always will be found a few branches having a pronounced horizontal habit. Propagation from such branches gives rise to the following garden form.
– –**'Prostrata'** [*C. pedunculata* var. *prostrata* Hornb. Dw. Con. 27. 1923 and Ed. 2, 36. 1938; *C. drupacea* var. *pedunculata* f. *prostrata,* Hornb. Rep. Conif. Conf. 80. 1932.] (Illustration 121). This is doubtless a cultivariant form of var. *drupacea,* which it resembles in every way except habit. It is suitable for a conspicuous spot on a large rockery or for filling in a blank space near trees.
– – var. **nana** (Nakai) Rehd. [Rehd. Bibl. 5. 1949 *] was described as 'a low,

spreading shrub to 2.5 metres high which develops several upright shoots and which spreads by suckers'. It was first reported from Japan and is perhaps doubtfully entitled to varietal rank, although it is said to come true from seed. The cultivar name '**Nana**' should be limited to the clone or clones raised at the Arnold Arboretum in 1922. '**Nana Compacta**' [*C. pedunculata* var. *nana compacta* Froebel ex Beissn. Handb. Ed. 2, 66. 1909] was doubtfully distinct from var. *nana* but is no longer in cultivation, and '**Gnome**' Hillier [Man. 467. 1971] is a dwarf form with short ascending stems and radially arranged leaves, forming a flat-topped dome, a selection made at the Hillier Nursery, Winchester, in 1970.

CHAMAECYPARIS

The Chamaecyparis or False cypresses, which at one time were included in the genus Cupressus, are a genus of six species, four of which give us most of our dwarf forms. These are *Chamaecyparis lawsoniana* (the Lawson cypress), *Chamaecyparis obtusa* (the Hinoki cypress), *Chamaecyparis pisifera* (the Sawara cypress) and *Chamaecyparis thyoides* (the White cypress of North America).

In each of these species we have forms with fixed juvenile foliage and colour forms and also variations in habit and vigour. For no apparent reason, in the case of *C. pisifera* custom has developed group names such as 'Filifera', 'Nana', 'Plumosa' and 'Squarrosa' and these appear in the cultivar names. The other species similarly occur in groups but because of the bar there now is on Latinized names it is not possible to introduce analogous terms into their cultivar names. I do, however, use group names in the tables at the head of each species which will enable readers to identify their plants more easily and help them choose a cultivar for a particular purpose.

Chamaecyparis lawsoniana (Murray) Parl. The Lawson false cypress has given rise to innumerable cultivars, amongst which are several good dwarf forms. These are mainly variations in colour and form, although there are one or two with peculiarities of foliage, and as all these cultivars are seedling mutants the variations are reasonably stable; i.e., they do not revert, although in most cases the peculiarity becomes less pronounced with age.

All forms have, however, one drawback which is that new growth will never break from the old wood. This means in gardener's language that they resent heavy pruning, so both formative and restrictive pruning must be done little and often, and always before it becomes necessary to cut into the old wood. It also means that the species characteristically has little capacity to recover from severe damage. Although most of the forms are hardy, should an exceptionally severe winter or strong gale kill off all the young growth on one side of a tree it will seldom be killed outright but it will never break again and recover its shape.

Of the colour forms, the white foliage and variegated varieties are usually the least tolerant of wind and these should always be given a sheltered spot. Next in sequence are the yellow or golden forms, some of which (notably

'Erecta Aurea') are intolerant of wind, others being more reliable in this respect. As a general rule the colour of all the yellow forms develops only in full sunlight, plants in the shade never achieving more than a pale yellowish-green. The green and blue forms are the most hardy and the most tolerant of shady conditions.

Many of the dwarf cultivars may be loosely grouped as follows:

ELLWOODII GROUP   *Forms that are mutations of the well known cultivar 'Ellwoodii'.*

'Bleu Nantais'	'Ellwoods Gold'
'Blue Gem'	'Ellwoods Pygmy'
'Blue Surprise'	'Ellwoods White'
'Chilworth Silver'	'Fleckelwood'
'Ellwoodii'	'Nyewood' (See 'Chilworth Silver')

FILIFORMIS GROUP   *Forms characterised by thread-leafed foliage.* This group includes several cultivars that are not dwarf forms.

'Duncanii'	'Filiformis Compacta'
'Erecta Filiformis'	'Lycopodioides'

MINIMA AUREA GROUP   *Very slow-growing golden forms.*

'Aurea Densa'	'Minima Aurea'
'Lutea Nana'	

NANA GROUP   *A large group forming plants that are globose or broadly conical and which are unlikely ever to exceed 2 m high—in many cases much less.* I prefer this name (although the word *minima* appears much earlier in the literature) since it is more truly descriptive of this group.

'Forsteckensis'	'Minima Glauca'
'Gimbornii'	'Nana'
'Globosa'	'Nana Albospica'
'Globosa Nana'	'Nana Argentea'
'Globus'	'Nana Glauca'
'Gnome'	'Pygmaea Argentea'
'Green Globe'	'Pygmy'
'Minima	

TAMARISCIFOLIA GROUP   *A group which form wide-spreading bushes without a leader.*

'Dows Gem'	'Nestoides'
'Grandi'	'Nidiformis'
'Knowefieldensis'	'Tamariscifolia'

‑ ‑'**Albovariegata**' [*C. lawsoniana albo-variegata* Veitch, Man. 232. 1881.] This be‑
comes a large ovoid or conical bush (not to be confused with 'Argenteovarie‑
gata' which is a very tall-growing form) with deep green leaves profusely
spotted and blotched with white. With age the plant will reach 2 m and tends to
become round-topped. Here and there about the plant there are small sprays
consisting wholly of pure white foliage, giving the bush quite a distinctive
appearance but these white growths are very prone to damage by frost. It is an
attractive variety which could well be more widely planted.

‑ ‑'**Aurea Densa**']*C. lawsoniana* var. *aurea densa* Hornb. Dw. Con. Ed. 2, 49. 1938.]
Minima Aurea Group. This is one of three very slow-growing golden forms
raised by W. H. Rogers of Red Lodge Nursery at Chandlers Ford, Hampshire,
England, which are very similar (Illustration 123), the others of the group being
'Lutea Nana' and 'Minima Aurea'. (Illustration 124).

'Aurea Densa' and 'Minima Aurea' both form very attractive conical golden
bushes, the colour being well maintained throughout the year. 'Aurea Densa'
tends to form a blunt-topped cone with the foliage quite stiff to the touch when
the bush is patted with the hand. 'Minima Aurea' forms a more ovoid (some‑
times conical) bush with the foliage softer to the touch and with a tendency to
hold its sprays edgewise in places, similar to the cultivar 'Minima Glauca'.

These two varieties are, however, so similar that I am sorry for any poor
nurseryman who gets his stock of young cuttings muddled, but if perchance later
you receive from him the wrong variety there is no need to be worried. For the
first five years you will discern no difference: for the next five years visiting
experts will argue with great enthusiasm as to which variety it is you have; for
the next five years the consensus of opinion will slowly verge in one direction or
the other. In the meantime in either case you will have had a treasure that after
fifteen years you would not part with whatever its name. You are unlikely to
live to see either variety exceed 1 m high by about half that amount across.

'Lutea Nana' is a stronger grower and is paler in colour than the previous
two. Although it is no longer propagated by its raisers, Jack Drake of Inshriach
Plant Nursery, Aviemore, Inverness-shire, tells me that it is the only one of the
three to be absolutely hardy in his part of Scotland. It has never been touched by
any kind of weather, whereas 'Aurea Densa' has been completely ruined,
although it just manages to survive, and 'Minima Aurea' nearly always gets
badly singed.

This only shows the impossibility of producing a 'Select List of Recom‑
mended Varieties' for any widely grown group of plants, even in so small an
area as the British Isles.

‑ ‑'**Chilworth Silver**' Hillier [List Conif. 4. 1970 (Nom.) and Man. 468. 1971;
'Nyewoods' Corley, Gar. Chron. **163, 2:** 29. 1968; Welch in Napier, Con. Brit.
Is. 49. 1972.] Ellwoodii Group. This is one of a number of grey or blue sports
from the popular 'Ellwoodii' that have appeared. It forms an attractive, slow‑
growing, upright bush with densely packed, silvery-blue foliage. It originated as
a sporting branch found on one of the original trees of 'Ellwoodii' in the village
of Chilworth near Southampton mentioned by Hornibrook, and young plants
were given by the late A. H. Nisbet of Gosport to H. G. Hillier, who introduced

it to the trade. Nisbet would not agree to the name 'Nisbets Silver', preferring it should commemorate the place of its origin. Although the name suggested by R. S. Corley may have priority the plant has been widely distributed as 'Chilworth Silver' and in view of its origin given here I suggest the retention of that name.

Similar blue-grey or silvery sports are turning up in various parts of the world. In France, **'Bleu Nantais'** a form with yellowish-green twigs and silvery, glaucous foliage has been introduced by the nursery firm Renault of Gorron. From New Zealand I have received **'Blue Gem'**, described as a very blue sport which occurred on the nursery of R. Barry, South Taranaki Nurseries, Hawera, about 1960, which is compact and pyramidal with foliage softer than that of 'Ellwoodii'. **'Blue Surprise'** also has semi-juvenile foliage, but it is of a much deeper blue colour.

– –**'Compacta'** [*C. lawsoniana compacta* R. Smith, Pl. Fir Tribe, 15. 1863; var. *compacta* (de Vos) Beissn. Zierg. Ed. 2, 452. 1884.] This is a slow-growing dense form with fan-shaped leaf sprays which when young could very well be taken for a strongly growing plant of 'Minima'. It forms a neat, broadly conical plant. The specimen at the foot of the rockery at Wisley described by Hornibrook as measuring 1.5 by 1.2 m in 1927 has now reached 4 by 3 m and has retained its shape and denseness well.

– –**'Dows Gem'** Welch [Nurs. Cat. 4. 1964; 'Dows Variety' Hort. Amer. and Dow's Nurs. Cat. ?; 'Noble's Variety' Hort. Eng.] TAMARISCIFOLIA GROUP. This variety makes a low bush with strong, coarse, very open foliage with a heavy white bloom on the underside of the leaf. It makes an attractive specimen for a large lawn. (Illustration 125).

– –**'Duncanii'** Duncan & Davies [Nurs. Cat. 108. 1953/4.] FILIFORMIS GROUP. This is an attractive form originating as a seedling in the Duncan & Davies nursery, New Plymouth, New Zealand. The picture shows the only mature specimen that I know in the British Isles and gives a good idea of the plant, which would form a fine specimen on a large lawn where it has room to develop into a plant 5 m across. The foliage is particularly graceful and attractive, especially so in such a large plant. (Illustration 126).

– –**'Ellwoodii'** [*C. lawsoniana* var. *Ellwoodii* Hornb. Gar. Chron. **1929, 1:** 50. 1929 and Dw. Con. Ed. 2, 38. 1938.] There is no need to describe this ubiquitous cultivar, which for all its popularity even with the Departmental Stores, is a most useful plant. It is a slow grower for several years after planting, although eventually outgrowing most situations, but with its blue-green juvenile foliage and upright oval outline, it has no real competitor in its class. (Illustration 127). Details of a number of colour sports and variegations that have appeared will be found below, and also under 'Chilworth Silver' (above).

If a young plant is carefully restricted to a single stem (in other words if grown as a 'cordon') 'Ellwoodii' will form a narrow, columnar plant as architecturally effective as the Irish juniper, a tree 3 m high by no more than 30 cm across being quite practicable.

– –**'Ellwoods Gold'** Corley [Gar. Chron. **163, 2:** 20. 1968; *Ellwoodii aurea* Hort.] ELLWOODII GROUP. This is a sport with habit and growth similar to 'Ellwoodii' but the foliage is bright yellow in early summer, becoming less marked by autumn.

– –'Ellwoods Pygmy' Welch [Nurs. Cat. 4. 1964; *Ellwoodii nana* Hort.] ELLWOODII GROUP. This is probably merely a cultivariant, the result of selection of weak side shoots as cuttings. I do not know the origin of this form, but the mother plant at the Pygmy Pinetum is obviously a very old plant only about 45 cm high and wider than it is high. Young propagations retain this bushy characteristic, especially if any tendency to form a leader in the young plant be checked at once. (Illustration 128).

– –'Ellwoods White' Den Ouden and Boom 1965. ELLWOODII GROUP. This is a slow-growing form with a clear creamy-white variegation. A similar mutation has occurred more than once and several forms are in cultivation. One such, 'Fleckelwood' Barry [Nurs. Cat. 1970—spelt Flecklewood] originated at the South Taranaki Nurseries, Hawera, New Zealand. It is grey-green with a small, evenly distributed white fleck throughout and has a rate of growth that is about two thirds that of 'Ellwoodii'. I have seen other variegated forms that are not worth distinguishing, even if they are distinguishable.

– –'Erecta Argenteovariegata' [*C. lawsoniana erecta argenteovariegata* (de Vos) Beissn. Mitt. d.d.d.G. **13**: 87. 1907.] This is a very old variety which seems to have been lost sight of. This is a pity as it is an attractive one. Its habit is very similar to the well known 'Erecta Viridis' from which it arose as a sport, but it is slower in growth and the whole plant is liberally splashed with large patches of a clear white variegation. Like all the 'Erecta' forms with fastigiate branching habit it tends to become bare near the ground in time, so should be planted in a spot where its feet will be hidden.

– –'Erecta Aurea' [*C. lawsoniana erecta aurea* de Vos, Fl. and Pom. **1**: 16. 1876; Den Ouden, Naaml. 14. 1937 (Nom.); var. *erecta aurea* Hornb. Dw. Con. Ed. 2, 50. 1938.] This is a descriptively named form that seems to have turned up more than once. As now known it is slow-growing and attractive when young on account of its habit and bright colour which is perhaps the brightest gold of any. It is not very hardy and with age becomes a large bush to 3 m, frequently seen much the worse for damage by snow or heavy winds.

– –'Ericoides' [*C. lawsoniana* var. *ericoides* Kent in Veitch, Man. Ed. 2, 206. 1900; Hornb. Dw. Con. Ed. 2, 38. 1938] and 'Squarrosa' Beissn. [Handb. Ed. 2, 543. 1909] were both recorded forms with persistent juvenile foliage. Both are lost to cultivation, probably because with age they (unlike the present author—or so I am told) outgrew their juvenility, but 'Erika' [New cv.], a completely juvenile form with grey-green foliage recently introduced by Don Hatch, Chantry Nursery, Honiton, Devon, doubtless represents a similar variation. At twelve years the mother plant is only 60 cm high by 40 cm across. It will be interesting to watch its behaviour in the future.

– –'Filiformis Compacta' [*C. lawsoniana filiformis compacta* Hort. ex Beissn. Handb. 77. 1891; Hornb. Dw. Con. Ed. 2, 42. 1938; *globosa filiformis* Hort.] FILIFORMIS GROUP. There are two cultivars one meets under this name, both being, as one would expect, plants with thread-like foliage. The correct name for an upright, tall-growing form with multiple stiff and erect branches is **'Erecta Filiformis'**

[*C. lawsoniana erecta filiformis* (Neumann) Beissn. Handb. Ed. 2, 544. 1909], whereas the true 'Filiformis Compacta' is a globose bush with very fine cord-like branches and tiny dark blue-green leaves, in which the branches seem barely strong enough to bear their weight and flop about in all directions, giving the bush the appearance of a wet mop. (Illustration 129).

This cultivar need never be confused with *Chamaecyparis pisifera* 'Filifera' since the foliage is very much thinner and is a blue-green, nor with any of the thread-leaf forms of *Thuya occidentalis* which are all much coarser and stiffer and have the characteristic rank odour if the foliage is bruised. The foliage is similar to but much finer than that of 'Duncanii'.

– –'Fletcheri' [*C. lawsoniana* var. *fletcheri* Hornb. Dw. Con. 31. 1923.] This well known columnar form has semi-juvenile foliage not dissimilar from 'Ellwoodii' but it is always a lighter and greyer-green in colour. When it was first introduced it was hailed as a wonderful subject for rock gardens, but since then it has shown its ability to romp away rapidly to a height of 5 m or more; so it is too big for inclusion in this book, were it not for the following circumstances.

– –'Fletcheri Nana' [*C. lawsoniana* var. *fletcheri nana* Hornb. Dw. Con. Ed. 2, 40. 1938.] In his second edition Hornibrook uses this name for low, bun-shaped plants produced by suitable selection of cutting wood from 'Fletcheri'. **'Fletchers Compact'** Den Ouden and Boom [Man. 80. 1965] is the name used by Den Ouden and Boom for another cultivariant—much slower in growth than the normal 'Fletcheri' but retaining its upright shape. Both these forms are merely cultivariants (see Definition above), so they are not entirely stable and plants of intermediate character can be found, but the names have a useful practical value. **'Kestonensis'** [*C. lawsoniana fletcheri* Keston variety Reuthe, Nurs. Cat. 1935.] This was discovered on the Reuthe Nursery at Keston in Kent in the 1920's in a bed of Lawson cypress seedlings. It is more squat and bushy than 'Fletcheri' and has a similar type of foliage, but is much more slow-growing.

– –'Fletchers White' Den Ouden and Boom [Man. 81. 1965] is a variegated form of 'Fletcheri'. It carries a nice, bold variegation of creamy-white. Plants grow rapidly and this form will probably turn out as big a plant as the 'Fletcheri' from which it was derived as a sport. It is not altogether hardy.

Other variegations have appeared. One—**'Gold Splash'** [New cv.] originating in New Zealand, carries patches of yellow variegation here and there all over the plant. It is an attractive plant.

– –'Forsteckensis' [*C. lawsoniana forstekiana* Beissn. Handb. 79. 1891; spelling corrected to *forsteckensis*, Mitt. d.d.d.G. **13**: 146. 1904.] NANA GROUP. This popular and well tried variety is indispensable in any collection. When well grown this cultivar produces a dense globose or broadly conical bush not over 60 cm high with main branches very densely set, main branches short, and all its growth very congested. It increases in size by sending out longer tips of normal foliage. These will eventually thicken up but the bush can be kept to any desired size and with foliage almost unbelievably congested and moss-like by the systematic removal of these longer growths. (Illustration 130).

There is, however, a much looser form in cultivation which forms a much larger plant. Hornibrook expresses the opinion that this is the result of propagation from the stronger branches referred to above, but I incline to the view that it is a separate clone. Of this variety there is a wonderful old specimen in Goatcher's Nursery at Washington in Sussex which is (I write from memory) over 2 m high and wider than it is high. This form is just as attractive as the slower-growing one but not, of course, suitable for use in the same position in the garden. A form occasionally met with, **'Tilgate'** Ingwersen, [Nurs. Cat. ?] is very similar.

From time to time variegated branches appear on plants of 'Forsteckensis', but I have never yet come across a case where the variegation has been stable, when used for propagation.

– –**'Gimbornii'** Den Ouden [Conif. 106. 1949; var. *Gimbornii* Groot. in Hornb. Dw. Con. Ed. 2, 50. 1938.] Nana Group. This forms a dense, compact, oval little bush seldom seen more than 1 m high. The main branches are thick, stiff and erect and the branchlets short. The foliage is a glaucous blue-green with the tips of the growing shoots purplish-blue during most of the year. It is similar to 'Nana Glauca' but it has finer foliage in narrower sprays. This cultivar originated as a seedling on the Von Gimborn Estate at Doorn, Holland. The mother plant reached a height of nearly 2 m but was killed outright by the very severe winter 1962–63. (Illustration 131).

– –**'Globosa'** [*C. lawsoniana globosa* de Vos, Fl. and Pom. **1**: 17. 1867; (Hort.) Den Ouden, Naaml. 15. 1937 (Nom.); 'Globosa' Meyer, Pl. Expl. **2**: 89. 1963.] Nana Group. Several globose forms are in cultivation besides the well known 'Minima Glauca' and, understandably, several of these have attracted a reference to their shape at their christening. This cultivar is apparently a very old variety introduced from continental cultivation into the United States in 1963 and apparently now more common there than in this country. Bergman [Pl. and Gar. **21,1**:30. 1965] described it as a 'Broadly globose shrub with ascending branches and rather thick, short branchlets, the tips of which recurve slightly. Leaves bright green. At 8 years, 6 inches high and 10 inches wide'. **'Globosa Nana'** I only know from several old plants in the Royal Botanic Garden at Edinburgh. Indistinguishable from 'Minima Glauca' when young it eventually develops into an ovoid bush intermediate in shape between that variety and the conical 'Nana.' **'Globus'** New name [*C. lawsoniana* var. *glauca* 'Globus'. Barabits, Magyar Fenyöújdonságok (New Hungarian Conifers) 55. 1965; Deutsche Baumsch. **5**: 139. 1966.] This is an attractive, slow-growing form raised by E. Barabits from seed collected from *C. lawsoniana* 'Glauca' in the Botanic Garden at Sopron in Hungary. It forms a globose plant with attractive silvery-grey foliage and thin stems. At 14 years of age plants reach 80 cm.

– –**'Gnome'** Corley [Gar. Chron. **167, 23**: 31. 1970.] Nana Group. This is a very diminutive bun-form raised from seed at Warnham Court, Horsham, Surrey, by the head gardener, W. Hart, and introduced to the trade by Heath End Nurseries, Farnham. It is similar to but much more slow-growing than the popular 'Forsteckensis' but is irregular in growth and apt to put out coarse growth and lose its attractiveness. If any such growth is cut away it will settle down as an attractive and congested little globose to broadly conical plant. (Illustration 132).

- -'**Green Globe**' Duncan & Davies [Nurs. Cat. 64. 1973.] NANA GROUP. This is a very attractive new form originating as a seedling on the Palmer & Sons Nursery, Glen Eden, Auckland, N. Z. It forms a tight little bun of congested rich, deep green foliage. I have only seen small plants in this country.

- -'**Juniperina**' [*C. lawsoniana* var. *juniperina* Kent in Veitch, Man. Ed. 2, 207. 1900; Hornb. Dw. Con. Ed. 2, 51. 1938] was described as 'A pyramidal dwarf form with minute leaves resembling those of a Savin juniper'. I cannot trace it in cultivation.

- -'**Knowefieldensis**' [*C. lawsoniana Knowefieldensis* Beissn. Mitt. d.d.d.G. **20**: 172. 1911; var. *knowefieldensis* Hornb. Dw. Con. 34. 1923 and Ed. 2, 53. 1938; *knowefieldensis glauca* Hort.] TAMARISCIFOLIA GROUP. As grown in the Pygmy Pinetum it is a wide-spreading, flat-topped, untidy looking plant. The foliage is very thin and fine—a deep, rich green above and only slightly glaucous beneath. The leaves are very small, densely set and appressed for most of their length, only the tips being free (and that not noticeably so as they are in 'Nidiformis' and 'Tamariscifolia'). They are borne in flat, parallel-sided sprays about 2.5 cm wide, on side shoots regularly set about 2 cm apart and all emerging at a constant angle of about 45° and regularly decreasing in length towards the dominant terminal shoot. The resulting triangular outline at once distinguishes this form from 'Nidiformis', and from 'Tamariscifolia' it is distinct by the mainly appressed leaf tips and the crowded, overlapping growth.

- -'**Krameri**' [*C. lawsoniana Krameri* Hort. ex Beissn. Handb. Ed. 2, 552. 1909.] This is a globose or shrubby variety of no great beauty, reaching to several metres high, with its main branches set horizontally, partly twisted and pendulous. The branch system is very irregular and contorted, the final growth cord-like.

- -'**Lutea Nana**' [W. H. Rogers Nurs. Cat. c. 1930.] See above under 'Aurea Densa'.

- -'**Lycopodioides**' [*C. lawsoniana lycopodioides* (Tottenham) Beissn. Handb. Ed. 2, 551. 1909.] FILIFORMIS GROUP. This is not a dwarf form, but its curiously twisted foliage makes it an interesting plant for several years. It might perhaps best be described as a thread-leafed form in which the threads are curled and twisted in all directions, somewhat in the manner of *C. obtusa* 'Coralliformis', from which it can at once be distinguished by the pointed leaves with their free standing tips. Beissner mentions a golden form which I cannot trace in cultivation. It was probably a mistaken reference to the *C. obtusa* form with this name. (Illustration 133).

- -'**Minima**' [*C. lawsoniana minima* R. Smith, Pl. Fir Tribe, 15. 1863; var. *minima* Hornb. Dw. Con. 29. 1923.] NANA GROUP. This is a yellow-green form and with '**Minima Glauca**' [*C. lawsoniana minima glauca* R. Smith, Pl. Fir Tribe, 15. 1863 and Rehd. Bibl. 53. 1949; var *minima* Hornb. loc. cit. (in part)] (Illustration 134), its glaucous equivalent, which is much better known, can be confused with '**Nana**' [*C. lawsoniana nana* Dauvesse, Gar. Chron. **1864**: 579. 1864; f. *nana* (Dauvesse) Beissn. Conif. Ben 34. 1887 and Rehd. Bibl. 53. 1949 *; var. *nana* Hornb. Dw. Con. Ed. 2, 43. 1938] (Illustration 135) and its glaucous form '**Nana Glauca**' [*C. lawsoniana nana glauca* Veitch, Man. 233. 1881; var. *nana glauca* Hornb. Dw. Con. Ed. 2, 45 1938.] Although these names had appeared before, the earliest descriptions of identifiable plants are those by Hornibrook, and the confusion may have been contributed to by his statement to the effect that the rather horizontal arrangement of the leaf sprays in 'Nana' always distinguish it from 'Minima' which, according to him, bears its branches turned rather edgeways. I have never met a large plant which would be 'Nana' by this criterion when approached from one point of the compass which would not equally be 'Minima' when seen from a different direction; and I think the fact of the matter is that this is not where the distinction lies. In 'Minima' the trunk is very short or is missing entirely and has its place taken by a series of upswept and more or less vertical main branches of approximately equal length, giving the bush a broadly globose outline, whereas 'Nana' will always be found to have a well defined central trunk and more horizontally held branches. This gives 'Nana' much more tendency to become a broad, squat pyramid as it ages. An old plant can have a surprisingly thick trunk nearly to its summit. So that, although there may be some truth in what Hornibrook says as to the arrangement of the leaf sprays, this is not a reliable criterion. On the other hand, the leaf sprays of 'Minima' have a neat rounded outline and give the whole bush a 'well-groomed' look, whereas in 'Nana' the leading shoots project beyond the laterals, making the leaf sprays much more broken in outline and this gives the bush a somewhat less neat and tidy appearance.

The use of the name 'Minima' illustrates the folly of using superlatives in cultivar names, for it is by no means the smallest form of the Lawson cypress. **'Pygmy'** New name [*C. lawsoniana minima Pygmy* Jackman Nurs. Cat. 76. 1968-69] would be more eligible for this distinction. It could be described as a diminutive form of 'Minima' with the same colour, globose habit and rounded leaf spray, but all on a reduced scale. It also shares the dependability of the larger plant in being free of the tendency of some of the small bun-forms to throw out coarse, out-of-character growth. It is certainly one of the best dwarf conifers we have.

– –**'Minima Aurea'** [*C. lawsoniana* var. *minima aurea* Hornb. Gar. Chron. **1929, 1:** 49. 1929 and Dw. Con. Ed. 2, 43. 1938; *minima aurea Rogersi* Hort.] See above under 'Aurea Densa'.

– –**'Nana Albospica'** [*C. lawsoniana nana alba* (R. Sm.) Nich. Dict. Gar. **1:** 304. 1884; *nana alba* Veitch, Man. 233. 1881; *albo-spica nana* Gord. Pin. Ed. 2, 424. 1875; *nana albo-spicata* Beissn. Handb. 78. 1891; *alba spica nana* Hornb. Dw. Con. Ed. 2, 41. 1938; *nana alba* Hornb. Dw. Con. Ed. 2, 44. 1938.] Nana Group. Seedlings (sometimes slow-growing and therefore dwarf) with milky white young growth turn up occasionally in the seed beds. At first they are attractive and numerous attempts have been made by early writers to find descriptive names for novelties of this kind, but with age they tend to have less appeal and I can only trace one form in cultivation today. Presumably all the other forms (if in fact, they were different) are now lost. The form we have is a slow-growing dwarf, conical plant, dense in growth. The main branches are short; the branchlets short and thin. The leaves are small, white at the growing points, elsewhere pale green. This variety pays for planting in rich soil as it is only when it is growing strongly that it has the 'white appearance to the whole plant' described by Hornibrook, and that only during the growing season. (Illustration 136).

The orthography of the present name is obscure but I have selected it as the one that best preserves established usage.

– –'**Nana Albovariegata**' [*C. lawsoniana nana alba variegata* Hornb. Dw. Con. Ed. 2, 44. 1938.] This form appears to be lost to cultivation, and to judge from the description given by Hornibrook this is no great loss.

– –'**Nana Argentea**' [*C. lawsoniana* f. *nana argentea* Beissn. Zierg. 452. 1884; var. *nana argentea* Hornb. Dw. Con. Ed. 2, 44. 1938 (pro syn.)] NANA GROUP. This form makes a dwarf, broadly ovoid shrublet with ascending branches tightly pressed together, and with its foliage in stiff, erect, grey-green sprays creamy-white at the growing tips. It is an uncommon form, not to be confused with 'Pygmaea Argentea', which makes a much smaller plant.

– –'**Nana Argenteovariegata**' [*C. lawsoniana* var. *nana argenteovariegata* Hornb. Dw. Con. Ed. 2, 45. 1938.] This is evidently a case of someone naming a plant too soon, for it is not a dwarf form. It is a densely growing pyramidal plant with pure white-tipped foliage appearing as though lightly covered with snow. Forms with white-variegated or white-tipped foliage turn up in the seed beds occasionally, and I fancy that more than one of these has strayed into cultivation.

– –'**Nidiformis**' [*C. lawsoniana nidiformis* Beissn. in Mitt. d.d.d.G. **10**: 74. 1901 and Handb. Ed. 2, 552. 1909 (*plumosa nidifera nana* Hort. pro syn.); *Chamaecyparis* × *nidifera* Hornb. Rep Conif. Conf. 72. 1932.] TAMARISCIFOLIA GROUP. Most later writers, following Hornibrook, appear to have confused this form with *Chamaecyparis nootkatensis* 'Nidifera' (see below). It forms a low, spreading plant very similar to 'Tamariscifolia' (for which cultivar it is often mistaken) vaguely suggesting a large bird's nest (hence the name), with radially spreading and horizontal or arching main branches and decurving branchlets. The foliage looks at a glance to be coarser than that of 'Tamariscifolia' and bears blue or grey-green foliage a little glaucous above and very glaucous beneath, much flattened (1.5 mm wide); the leaves very crowded, the lateral pair standing off at the free tips at 45°, the facing pair smaller, appressed, in shape a 45° triangle (variable), seldom glandular. The growth is in wide sprays in which many of the side branches twist out of the plane of the spray and almost all the ultimate shoots curve, some up, some down, as though the spray had been gone over with a flat-iron when wet, and in drying each little shoot had curled as it felt inclined. (Illustration 137). It is not altogether hardy. '**Grandi**' Clarke and Co. [Nurs. Cat. 2. 1950] I cannot distinguish from 'Nidiformis', but if as I am informed it is hardier it should be more widely known.

– –'**Pygmaea Argentea**' [*C. lawsoniana pygmaea argentea* Beissn. Handb. 79. 1891; *pygmea* (sic) *argentea* Backhouse, Nurs. Cat. 37. 1907/8; 'Backhouse Silver' Hort.] NANA GROUP. This popular cultivar is a dwarf form of very slow growth, forming a small globose or squatly conical bush with its main branches upright. The foliage is green, pale creamy-white at the tips and very densely set. When the plant is growing strongly the foliage is almost white in early summer and the whole bush then has the appearance of having been turned upside down when wet into a barrel of flour. (Illustration 138).

J. Backhouse & Son Ltd. record that it originated as a sport in their nursery at York and that it is perfectly hardy at York. It does, however, burn in strong sunlight.

– –'Rogersii' [*C. lawsoniana nana Rogersii* Den Ouden, Naaml. 15. 1937 (Nom.); Rogers and Son. Nurs. Cat. c. 1930] is a glaucous blue, globose variety with thread-like foliage raised from seed by Rogers and Sons of Red Lodge Nursery, formerly at Southampton but now at Chandlers Ford, Hampshire. It will grow to 2 m in time. The colour is similar to the well known tall variety 'Alumii' but the blue is not quite so intense and it seems to become less marked as the plant ages. It is not one of the 'Nana' group, so the simpler name is preferable. [See Den Ouden and Boom, Man. 94. 1965.]

– –'Tamariscifolia' [*C. lawsoniana* var. *tamariscifolia* Hornb. Dw. Con. 31. 1923.] In this cultivar the trunk is always entirely absent, and its place is taken by a number of main branches which grow upwards and outwards in such a way that although the plant will reach to 2 m high in time the top is always more or less flat and the width is about twice the height. The branching is very irregular and the branches appear to tumble about in all directions. The foliage is a light mid-green, slightly glaucous above, noticeably so below, much flattened as in 'Nidiformis' but wider (2 mm). The leaves are longer and narrower, the lateral pair standing off at 30° and the facing pair in the shape of a 30° triangle, nearly always noticeably glandular. The foliage is in wide sprays in which the length of side branchlets reduces regularly towards the dominant leader, resulting in a triangular outline quite different to the bluntly rounded spray of 'Nidiformis', and although there is much overlapping the spray lies in a flat plane. (Illustration 139).

It seems probable that there are several forms of 'Tamariscifolia' about and that we have several clones in cultivation derived from different seedlings. One such, **'Nestoides'**, introduced by Jack Manten of Vancouver, British Columbia, Canada, is stated to be quite hardy. Otherwise, the differences are not worth recognition.

– –'Tharandtensis Caesia' [*C. lawsoniana tharandtensis caesia* Buettner in Mitt. d.d.d.G. **43:** 431. 1931 and Hornb. Dw. Con. Ed. 2, 48. 1938 (and *forsteckensis glauca* Hort. pro syn.)] This could broadly be likened to a coarse, upright-growing form of 'Forsteckensis' with grey-green to blue-green leaves. This cultivar is much the better for having its long shoots pruned well back occasionally. This keeps the bush dense and postpones the degeneration into more or less typical *C. lawsoniana* foliage which is usually the ultimate fate of all these seedling forms. I have found it unsatisfactory on soil that had been dressed with lime.

– –'Wansdyke Miniature' [*Picea abies* 'Wansdyke Miniature' Den Ouden and Boom, Man. 251. 1965.] This plant, although mistakenly reported as a *Picea abies* form by Dr. Boom, was well described by him as 'A compact and regular form, just a miniature of a normal (*Chamaecyparis lawsoniana*); stem thick and strong for the size of the plant; foliage bluish-green. Found by H. J. Welch, Wansdyke Nursery, Devizes, England'. It is unremarkable as a small plant but in time, because of its thick trunk and columnar shape it develops into a veritable scale model of a mature Lawson cypress and so would be an excellent plant for a scenic railway or model village.

– –'**Wisselii Nana**' [*C. lawsoniana* var. *Wisselii nana* Groot. in Hornb. Dw. Con. Ed. 2, 52. 1938] is a charming little extremely slow-growing cultivariant from the well known tall cultivar 'Wisselii'. Cuttings of 'Wisselii' taken low down on the tree from weak shoots should give rise to plants of 'Wisselii Nana'. Such are, however, unstable, and tend to shoot up in time. Seedlings from 'Wisselii' are equally disappointing, but **'Little Spire'** a reputed seedling of 'Fletcheri' with 'Wisselii' as the pollen parent has the general habit of 'Wisselii' but it is much more compact and slow-growing, reaching less than 2 m in 12 years. It was introduced by Don Hatch, Chantry Nursery, Honiton, Devon.

'Wisselii' itself, after having hung about for several years will run up to 5 m and worse in a very short time, so is no use on a rock garden, but where there is room for a large bush it can be used with great effect by taking a young and well branched plant and cutting the leader right out so as to encourage the branches to develop, repeating this treatment with any strong vertical shoots to encourage sub-laterals. Grown in this way 'Wisselii' forms a large plant as wide as it is high and consisting of a mass of spire-like shoots. I should like to see an old plant on a large lawn that had been so pruned over a period of years.

Chamaecyparis nootkatensis (D. Don.) Spach. This is a species of tall tree with dull green foliage without any white glaucous marking on the underside. The leaves on the main axis are equal in length, appressed with free tips. It has given us several dwarf forms, all of which have inherited the hardiness with which this species is credited.

– –'**Compacta**' [*C. nootkatensis* var. *compacta* K. Koch, Dendrol. **2,2**: 166. 1873; f. *compacta* Rehd. Bibl. 51. 1949 *; *C. nutkaensis compacta viridis* Schelle, Wint. Nadel. 306. 1909.] This forms a dense rounded bush to about 2 m high with typical foliage. It is very hardy, but not particularly outstanding as a garden plant. (Illustration 140).

– –'**Compacta Glauca**' [*C. nutkaensis compacta glauca* Schelle, Wint. Nadel. 306. 1909; 'Glauca Compacta' Bergm. Pl. and Gar. **21,1**: 31. 1965.] Similar to 'Compacta' except that the leaves are glaucous. Mrs. Bergman remarks that semi-juvenile foliage is frequently present on the inner growths.

– –'**Compressa**' [*C. nootkatensis* f. *compressa* Silva Tarouca Nadel. 166. 1913] and '**Gracilis**' [*C. nutkaensis gracilis* Schelle, Wint. Nadel. 306. 1909] were recorded dwarf forms now apparently lost to cultivation.

– – var. **nana** Schneid. in Silva Tarouca [Nadel 166. 1913.] The description merely lists the forms referred to here, so this name is meaningless and useless save as a group name, should one ever be required.

– –'**Nidifera**' [*Thujopsis nidifera* Nich. Gar. and For. **2**: 568. 1889; *Thuja borealis* var. *nidifera* Mast. Gar. Chron. **7**: 108. 1890; *Cup. nutkaensis nidiformis* Hort. in Beissn. Handb. 83. 1891; NON *Chamaecyparis lawsoniana nidiformis* Beissn. Handb. Ed 2, 552. 1909; NON *Cupressus nidifera* Hornb. Rep. Conif. Conf. 72. 1932]. (Illustration 141).

The story of how the correct identity of this plant has been established after nearly a century of confusion and of how it has again been brought into cultivation is as interesting as any detective story. The plant clearly originated in the Rovelli nursery at Pallanza, Italy, as a seedling from *C. nootkatensis* (we have the recorded testimony to this of the nursery foreman there). It was first distributed by them as *Thujopsis nidifera* and as such it was mentioned by George Nicholson, then Curator at Kew, in an account of a visit to Italy published in *Garden and Forest*. Presumably Messrs. Rovelli sent specimens to Nicholson and also to Dr. M. T. Masters (who added it to his own herbarium, labelling it 'Thuiopsis nidifera ex Hort. Rovelli., *Cupressus nutkaensis* Hartw'.) and *Gardeners' Chronicle* printed a note of it.

My knowledge of languages is insufficient to say in how many of them phrases designed for 'passing the buck' can be found. The French can avoid responsibility by 'On dit'. In German there is 'Man sagt'. So Nicholson's remark in *Garden and Forest* (above) 'It is said to be a hybrid between *Chamaecyparis nutkaensis* and the Oregon cedar (*C. lawsoniana*)' does not fix for us the origin of that theory, but it certainly relieves Murray Hornibrook of the responsibility, usually laid at his door, of inventing the hybrid name in *Conifers in Cultivation*. Unfortunately a mistake of this kind, once made, tends to be perpetuated and this particular one has appeared in book after book.

When the new herbarium and library wing at Kew was brought into use the old Arboretum herbarium which had been largely assembled by George Nicholson, Curator from 1886 to 1901 and editor of *Dictionary of Gardening,* was incorporated into the main herbarium. In the course of this work a specimen (presumably now the type of our plant), accompanied by a letter to Nicholson dated 26th January 1890 from the Rovelli Nursery, and also the Masters specimen already mentioned, was found by D. R. Hunt, to whom I am indebted for much of the information here given.

Beissner in the first edition of *Handbuch der Nadelhölzkunde* gives a brief description of *Cupressus nutkaensis nidifera* Hort., relating presumably to our plant. In his second edition he makes no reference to the Nootka form but he introduces a new plant *Chamaecyparis lawsoniana nidiformis* Hort. His use of the word 'Hort.' (Hortorum = of gardens) here and the absence of any suggestion that he was amending his own earlier work make it clear that he was writing of a different plant even though he warns that the earlier name had been misapplied. It would seem that between 1891 and 1909 the Nootka form had been lost sight of and a very similar Lawson form had taken its place. Of this, more anon.

Hornibrook, with the hybrid theory in his mind assumed that Beissner's 1909 plant and the Rovelli plant were the same, which it is now clear was not the case. So with, on the one hand, the assurance that the plant had been raised from seed gathered from a plant of *C. nootkatensis,* and on the other, a report on a specimen of the plant he knew as 'Nidifera' which he had sent to Prof. Borthwick of Aberdeen (who replied that on the basis of the microscopic anatomy it was 'near *C. lawsoniana*) he settled for the hybrid theory and wrote accordingly for the 1932 Conference. It is an example of our propensity to ignore discordant facts once we have accepted a theory.

A note in Dr. R. Melville's hand on the Nicholson specimen at Kew reads 'This has no flavour of *Chamaecyparis lawsoniana* and is probably not a hybrid as suggested by Hornibrook [Dw. Con. ed. 2, 54, 1938.] The specimen does not match Hornibrook's description and is quite different from the *C.* × *nidifera* offered by Messrs. Hilliers. Moreover, it is different from the *C. lawsoniana* 'Nidiformis' described by Welch [Dw. Con. 126. 1966] and offered by him, of which there is a herbarium specimen at Kew. Both Hillier's plant and Welch's are forms of *C. lawsoniana* closely resembling *C. lawsoniana* 'Tamariscifolia' by which, incidentally, Hornibrook said *C.* × *nidifera* was "nearly always" represented in British gardens'.

In 1968, during a visit to Czechoslovakia, I had come across a very old plant of a dwarf form of *C. nootkatensis* with a graceful habit (quite unlike the widely known 'Compacta') at the Arboretum Meynany, formerly the home of Dr. Stefan Ambrozy, and I had asked whether cuttings could be sent to me. These were a long time reaching me but in February 1970, within a fortnight of my receiving from Mr. Hunt the above account of the finding of the herbarium specimens, these cuttings turned up. A specimen sent to Kew agreed with the type sheet and I now have sufficient stock to restore this attractive variety to cultivation.

Finally, in 1972, when I was in Italy on a horticultural conference I visited the one-time famous nursery at Pallanza, now a hotel, in the hope of finding the mother plant. The nursery having been sold in 1914, very little evidence of its former glory remained save some enormous Camellia plants and a few large conifers. Amongst these was a very old plant which H. G. Hillier, who was also in our party, agreed was *C. lawsoniana* 'Nidiformis'. It is a pity to have cleared up a conundrum of 80 years standing and then have to finish on a note of conjecture, but my guess is that at some time between Beissner's first and second editions the mother plant of *C. nootkatensis* 'Nidifera' was 'lost' (or sold) and the somewhat similar Lawson form began to be propagated and distributed in its stead. I have been unable to find *Thujopsis nidifera* listed in any of the Rovelli catalogues I have seen.

C. nootkatensis 'Nidifera' is an attractive garden form, appropriately named. The difference in the foliage from the nest-like cultivars of *C. lawsoniana* is very clear from Identification Plate No. 5. Also it is a much hardier plant.

Chamaecyparis obtusa (Sieb. and Zucc.) Endl. This species comes from Japan, where it forms a fairly large tree. The foliage is distinguished by its obtuse (blunt ended, i.e., not pointed) leaves with white, waxy, X-shaped markings beneath. The leaves are in pairs, alternately lateral and facing, the lateral pair much larger than the facing, both pairs appressed to the stem with only the blunt tips free. The species has given rise to numerous dwarf garden forms. These are probably all seedling mutations so are not liable to reversion. Nature normally preserves her species by making her freaks sterile, but just occasionally she lets one by and it is to just such an occurrence that we owe a number of most interesting and extremely dwarf forms of *C. obtusa*. For several years before the First World War a large plant of 'Nana Gracilis' in the Red Lodge Nursery near Southampton set viable seeds, although this dwarf form is usually sterile. The nursery foreman, George Gardner, sowed these and from them raised a large number of seedlings. The value of these was not at first realised but when

Hornibrook was writing his second edition a number of these seedlings were selected and given such names as 'Minima', 'Caespitosa', 'Laxa', 'Intermedia', etc. A number of the plants that were not selected were grown on and sold over the years to collectors in this country and in America and some of these have since been given names such as 'Verdonii', 'Bassett', 'Chilworth' and so on. I give a description of all the forms I consider worth separating. My descriptions of all these attractive little forms have been taken from the mother plants at Red Lodge Nurseries, and have been kindly verified for me by Mr. Verdon, the present proprietor, or his able assistant, Mr. D. A. Bunce.

The dwarf forms may be roughly grouped, as follows:

NANA GROUP.   *Dwarf forms unlikely to exceed one metre in height, even after many years.*

'Bassett'	'Nana Compacta'
'Chilworth'	'Nana Densa'
'Chimaanihiba'	'Nana Lutea'
'Flabelliformis'	'Pygmaea'
'Hage'	'Pygmaea Aurescens'
'Laxa'	'Rigid Dwarf'
'Nana'	'Tonia'
'Nana Aurea'	

(Note that 'Nana Gracilis', 'Kosteri', 'Repens' and 'Tempelhof' are too large for inclusion in this group.)

PYGMY GROUP.   *Diminutive forms, buns and the so-called 'tennis ball' conifers.*

'Caespitosa'	'Juniperoides Compacta'
'Intermedia'	'Minima'
'Juniperoides'	

Some of these very tiny forms are frost tender and liable to sun scorch in summer, so are plants for the cold greenhouse or a frame, but Joel W. Spingarn of Baldwin, Long Island, New York, has obtained quite a number of seedlings that are reliably hardy in the climate of New York. He writes: In the year 1966 Henry Weissenberger, a nurseryman at Baldwin, Long Island, New York, made available to me seed that he had collected from Chamaecyparis cultivars which had set cones that year, a most unusual event. The seed of *Chamaecyparis obtusa* 'Nana Gracilis' and *Chamaecyparis obtusa* 'Gracilis Aurea' germinated. The resulting plants ran the gamut, as Mr. Welch describes in other cases, from arboreal down to the most extreme dwarf forms. Some of the seedlings proved to be quite handsome. I have selected nine of the smallest for propagation, and show their growth habit in the table below. The following selections are completely hardy here. (Illustrations 152, 153, 154). The first five were grown from seed of *Chamaecyparis obtusa* 'Nana Gracilis'; the last four are from seed of *Chamaecyparis obtusa* 'Gracilis Aurea'.

Approximate Annual Growth	Name	Width		Height		Outline
		1973	1976	1973	1976	
¼″	'Pixie'	2¾″	3½″	1½″	3″	Flat globe
¼″	'Gnome'	2½″	3½″	2″	3″	Ball
½″	'Leprechaun'	3¾″	5½″	3¾″	5½″	Ball
¾″	'Golden Fairy'	4¾″	7″	3¾″	11½″	Pyramid
¾″	'Elf'	3½″	5½″	3½″	7″	Round-pointed top
½″	'Golden Sprite'	4½″	6½″	3″	4¾″	Tight flat bun
1¼″	'Golden Filament'	6″	11″	4″	8″	Spreading-filiform
1″	'Dainty Doll'	5″	9″	5″	12″	Blunt tapered top—leader formed
1″	'Golden Nymph'	5″	8″	5″	8½″	Round tufted-leader formed

LYCOPODIOIDES GROUP.   *Thread-leaf and monstrous (contorted) forms and similar foliage abnormalities.*

'Compact Fernspray'	'Lycopodioides'
'Contorta'	'Lycopodioides Aurea'
'Coralliformis'	'Spiralis'
'Coralliformis Nana'	'Torulosa'
'Filicoides'	'Tsatsumi'

– –'**Albospica**' [*Retinospora obtusa alba spica* R. Smith, Pl. Fir. Tribe, 38. 1863; *C. obtusa* f. *albo-spica* Rehd. Bibl. 53. 1949 *] is a slow-growing, rather open, conical form reaching to 2 m high, densely branched, the young shoots at first creamy-white, changing later in the year to pale green. Not one of the most attractive forms.

– –'**Bassett**' Welch [Dw. Con. 131. 1966.] NANA GROUP. This is one of the Red Lodge seedlings, less well known than some. It is not unlike 'Juniperoides' but it forms a much taller plant with ascending branches and the foliage is a darker green.

– –'**Caespitosa**' [*C. obtusa* var. *caespitosa* Rogers ex Hornb. Dw. Con. 44. 1923.] PYGMY GROUP. This is another of the Red Lodge introductions, one of the smallest. It forms a tiny, dense bun of very blue-green, cup-like sprays with tiny, tightly appressed, scale-like leaves. It is one of the smallest conifers in existence. (Illustration 142). Not unlike it for size is '**Minima**' [*C. obtusa* var. *tetragona minima* Hornb. Dw. Con. 43. 1923, corrected to var. *minima* in Ed. 2, 69.

1938.] PYGMY GROUP. In this variety the foliage is of a very light green, the cup-like cupressoid sprays of 'Caespitosa' are absent and in their place there is a close mass of ascending branches and branchlets that are tetragonal (i.e., four-sided) in cross-section. It is, if anything, even slower growing and smaller than 'Caespitosa', and usually forms a more dense, hemispherical cushion, a twenty-year-old plant being still but a few inches high.

– –'**Chilworth**' Welch [Dw. Con. 131. 1966] NANA GROUP. This is another of the forms we owe to Mr. Gardner's green fingers. It has not become so well known as some of the other forms but is sufficiently distinctive to justify its becoming better known than it is. It forms an upright and quite a tree-like little plant with light green, tiny leaf sprays which are recurved. It is a form which should appeal to Bonsai addicts. It takes on a dull brownish tinge in winter.

– –'**Contorta**' [*C. obtusa contorta* Den Ouden. Conif. 120. 1949] LYCOPODIOIDES GROUP. This forms a slow-growing, conical plant, eventually to 1.5 m, with dense foliage which is twisted and contorted in what, to my eye, is not a particularly attractive manner. The colour is deep green, bronzing in winter. Any tendency to throw out coarse, uncharacteristic growth should at once be checked.

– –'**Coralliformis**' [*C. obtusa lycopodioides* f. *coralliformis* Beissn. Handb. Ed. 2, 562. 1909; var. *coralliformis* Hornb. Dw. Con. Ed. 2, 64. 1938; var. *Tsatsumi* Slavin, Rep. Conif. Conf. 98. 1932.] LYCOPODIOIDES GROUP. This is usually seen as a low, rounded bush in which the normal sprays are entirely absent and instead the foliage is thread-like. The branches and branchlets are curled and twisted in a way that is said to be suggestive of coral and this constitutes the main attraction of the plant. (Illustration 143). It should not be confused with 'Lycopodioides' as its foliage has no trace of the coarse, bloated appearance of that variety, nor with *C. lawsoniana* 'Lycopodioides', as it lacks the pointed, free standing leaf tips of that variety, although the twisted growth is very similar. From 'Torulosa' it differs in not developing the fasciations that characterise that variety. As a young plant it is rather weedy looking and insignificant but it fills out in time, especially if any lanky growth is shortened back regularly. It makes a better plant if tied up when young until it has formed a leader and it will in time reach 2 m or more in height.

In my previous book I stated that I was unable to distinguish between 'Coralliformis' and a somewhat similar form '**Tsatsumi**' [*C. obtusa* var. *Tsatsumi* Slavin, Rep. Conif. Conf. 98. 1932; Hornb. Dw. Con. Ed. 2, 63. 1938.] This was because I had not then seen the true 'Tsatsumi', which I do not think is grown in England. The two forms are quite distinct, a fact that has been very much obscured by the description given by Slavin (repeated by Hornibrook) taken from a small plant, 50 cm by 1 m, that had evidently been much cut into for propagation material. B. Harkness, formerly Director of Parks, Rochester, New York, writes that the plant is now 4 metres high. Propagations from it show growth that is, like 'Coralliformis', entirely filiform and without fasciation, but the growth is much stronger and the plant more open. The branch system is much less ramified and is almost completely without the twisted, wavy contortions of the commoner form. As a young plant it soon forms a leader. In some

American collections there is listed **'Coralliformis Nana'** Bergm. [Pl. and Gar. **21, 1**: 33. 1965.] The validity of the name is doubtful but no doubt it is descriptive of the plant, which I have not seen. It is said to make a more stunted growth but otherwise to be similar to 'Coralliformis'.

– –**'Ericoides'** [*Retinospora ericoides* van Geert, Conif. de Pleine Terre 59. 1862; NON *C. obtusa* var. *ericoides* Boehmer, Nurs. Cat. 1899–1900; NON Hornb. Dw. Con. Ed. 2, 58. 1938; NON 'Sanderi' (see below).] Van Geert's *"retinospora"* is now impossible to verify; Boehmer's plant is otherwise identified. The name presumably refers to a form with fixed juvenile foliage. The best claimant known to be in cultivation is a plant that reached me under the vernacular name **'Chabo-Yadori'**. It is a dense bush with light green, truly juvenile foliage but with the tips of the branchlets here and there all over the bush showing small amounts of characteristic and unmistakeable adult *C. obtusa* foliage. (Illustration 144).

– –**'Filicoides'** [*Retinospora filicoides* Veitch ex Gord. Pin. Ed. 2, 263. 1875; *C. obtusa* f. *filicoides* (R. Smith) Beissn. in Rehd. Bibl. 54. 1949 (excl. synonymy, in part); NON *Retinospora filiformis* R. Smith, Pl. Fir Tribe, 39. 1863 (= A weeping form).] LYCOPODIOIDES GROUP. This is a fairly strong-growing cultivar usually seen as a small and rather open tree, but it can (by systematic shortening of all strong shoots) be grown as an attractive bush. It is characterised by the development of side shoots from the axial buds of the lateral leaves only, so has flat, fernlike sprays. (Illustration 145). This peculiarity of foliage is quite distinctive, so 'Filicoides' is unlikely to be confused, except with very similar foliage on *Thuja occidentalis* 'Spiralis'. This latter can at once be distinguished by the acrid smell of the bruised foliage characteristic of that species. **'Compact Fernspray'** Corley [Gar. Chron. **156; 10; 247**. 1964; 'Filicoides Compacta' Hillier, Dw. Con. 20. 1964; 'Pygmy Fernspray' Welch, Dw. Con. 133. 1966; 'Filicoid Dwarf' Den Ouden and Boom, Man. 104. 1965; *compacta* Hort.] This is a diminutive form of the above. It is a very attractive form with foliage similar but smaller in all its parts. There is a large specimen of this cultivar near the top of the rockery at Wisley.

– –**'Flabelliformis'** [*C. obtusa* var. *flabelliformis* Hornb. Dw. Con. Ed. 2, 68. 1938.] NANA GROUP. This forms a globose, later upright, plant with short, fan-shaped sprays. The leaves are tiny, a light green with a glaucous bloom. 'Flabelliformis' resembles 'Nana' and is scarcely worth distinguishing therefrom. It is one of the Red Lodge seedlings.

– –**'Gracilis'** is a very strong-growing variety not to be confused with 'Nana Gracilis' (below). It is not a dwarf form.

– –**'Hage'** [*C. obtusa nana* 'Hage' Den Ouden, Conif. 123, 1949.] NANA GROUP. This is a dwarf form with dark green foliage very similar to 'Nana', but the tips of the leaves sometimes turn yellow-brown in winter, and it forms a denser and more globose bush. It originated as a seedling of 'Nana Gracilis' on the Wm. Hage and Co. Nursery at Boskoop, Holland.

– –**'Intermedia'** [*C. obtusa intermedia* Den Ouden, Naaml. 17. 1937.] PYGMY GROUP. This is one of the Red Lodge forms, which as its name indicates is a pygmy form intermediate between 'Nana' and the very minute 'tennis-ball' cypresses. It is, in my opinion, the smallest form that can be considered practicable for the open garden, except in sheltered districts. The foliage is a very dark green. (Illustration 146).

– –'**Juniperoides**' [*C. obtusa* var. *juniperoides* Hornb. Dw. Con. 44. 1923.] Pygmy Group. This is another very dwarf globose form from Red Lodge with dark green foliage in open and rather wiry looking, fan-shaped, decurving sprays. (Illustration 147). Not to be confused therewith is another form '**Juniperoides Compacta**' [*C. obtusa* var. *juniperoides compacta* Hornb. Dw. Con. Ed. 2, 68. 1938] which, as the name would suggest, is generally similar in appearance but of more compact growth. The foliage is a yellow-green and the tiny, confused leaf sprays are down-cupped, with the tips drooping. (Illustration 148).

– –'**Kosteri**' [*C. obtusa* var. *nana Kosteri* Hornb. Dw. Con. Ed. 2, 62. 1938] is one of the most attractive forms. In habit and foliage it might be regarded as intermediate between 'Nana Gracilis' and 'Pygmaea', but it is quite distinctive because every spray of the plant is twisted, one lateral turning down and the lateral opposite turning up. This gives the plant a most distinctive appearance and it is quite characteristic of this variety, which with its almost glossy, mid-green foliage is therefore one of the easiest to recognise. Left to itself it forms a rather sprawling bush not unlike 'Pygmaea' but I consider that it is best grown with a central stem trained up as a leader. If this be done the horizontal branches spread out in layers like a wedding cake and the attractiveness of the foliage is then seen at its best. The layer effect referred to can be accentuated by a little discreet thinning out of the foliage. (Illustration 149).

– –'**Laxa**' [*C. obtusa* var. *laxa* Hornb. Dw. Con. Ed. 2, 68. 1938.] Nana Group. This was one of the biggest of Mr. Gardner's batch of seedlings from 'Nana Gracilis', but Messrs. Rogers who raised it tell me they have lost the variety and do not know who has it. A plant in the alpine house at Wisley, about 50 cm high, with dark green, open sprays, could well be the original seedling, but propagations from this plant seem unlikely to develop the 'loose, open-growing plant . . . intermediate between vars. *nana* and *nana gracilis*' of Hornibrook's description. Time will doubtless tell.

– –'**Lycopodioides**' [*Retinospora lycopodioides* Standish ex Gord. Pin. Suppl. 92. 1862; *C. obtusa* f. *lycopodioides* (Gord.) Beissn. in Rehd. Bibl. 54. 1949 *.] This is an interesting dwarf which forms a globose shrub when young and eventually becomes a tall, open shrub to 2 m. The main branches ascend and are rather few and irregular. The branchlets are thick and often cockscomb-like at the tips; the leaves are irregular, dense and set all round the branches. The foliage is dark green and the monstrous growth gives the whole plant a curiously bloated appearance. The variety tends to form a rather open and gaunt tree but this can be checked by pruning back strong growth when young. It suffers from some form of die-back and is seldom seen at its best. A much better garden plant is '**Lycopodioides Aurea**' [*C. obtusa lycopodioides* f. *aurea* Beissn. Handb. Ed. 2, 562. 1909] which is similar but slower-growing and with butter-yellow growths. (Illustration 150).

Several forms originating in Japan and with more or less monstrous foliage were introduced into Western cultivation during the last century and their vernacular names were recorded. [Beissn. Handb. Ed. 2, 561-2. 1909.] Of these,

f. *rashahiba* is probably 'Lycopodioides' as we have it today, but the forms f. *aonokujahuhiba*, f. *kamakurahiba*, f. *kanaamihiba*, f. *patsunamihiba*, f. *shamohiba* and f. *troubetzkyana* I have been unable to trace. I have come across several more or less monstrous or contorted plants in different parts of Europe, but none had to my mind any garden value and so nothing is lost by regarding these forms as lost to (Western) cultivation. The form 'Torulosa' (below) in some American collections may in fact be one of these old forms, but unless its original identity is still known in Japan it is now impossible to identify it, so it must stand on its own feet as a new cultivar.

– –'**Mariesii**' [*C. obtusa* var. *Mariesii* Kent in Veitch, Man. Ed. 2, 222. 1900; *Mariesii* Hort. Angl. ex Beissn. Handb. Ed. 2, 561. 1909 and *nana albo-variegata* Beissn. Handb. 96. 1891; var. *nana argentea* Hornb. Dw. Con. Ed. 2, 61. 1938; 'Dwarf White-tip' Hort. Amer.] This is a very attractive, slow-growing dwarf form which makes a conical bush to about 1 m high, characterised by the leaves being yellowish-white to milk white in summer, rather more yellowish-green in winter. The foliage is very thin and the bush tends to be open and sparsely covered unless checked by shortening the strong growing tips. I do not think we have more than a single clone in cultivation. On its own roots it grows very slowly and makes a low, rounded bush, but it is frequently grafted and according to what understock is used its vigour, colouring and even habit can vary. Probably it is this that has given rise to the conflicting names and descriptions. (Illustration 151).

– –'**Minima**' See above under 'Caespitosa'. (Illustration 155).

– –'**Nana**' [*C. obtusa nana* Carr. Traité. Ed. 2, 131. 1867; f. *nana* (Carr.) Beissn. in Rehd. Bibl. 54. 1949 (and syn. in part); var. *nana* Hornb. Dw. Con. Ed. 2, 60. 1938.] This is a very old cultivar of extremely slow growth, as a result of which the stronger-growing forms, particularly 'Nana Compacta' or 'Nana Gracilis' are sometimes offered for sale in its place. 'Nana' forms a very dense, flat-topped bush with a mainly horizontal branch system and foliage in densely packed tiers in neat, rounded, often cupped sprays of dark almost black-green. A very old specimen will be less than 1 m high by as much or less across. (Illustration 156).

– –'**Nana Aurea**' [*C. obtusa nana aurea* Carr. Traité. Ed. 2, 131. 1867; Krüssm. Nadel. Ed. 2, 101. 1960.] This is a more vigorous plant than 'Nana', reaching to 2 m with age. The fan-shaped foliage sprays are golden-yellow on the outside of the bush and yellowish-green away from the light.

– –'**Nana Compacta**' [*Retinospora obtusa nana compacta* Barron Nurs. Cat. 7. 1875 (bound in Gord. Pin.); *C. obtusa* 'Nana Compacta' Krüssm. Nadel. Ed. 2, 101. 1960; Welch, Dw. Con. 138. 1966.] This is the form still being widely distributed in Britain as 'Nana', from which it is quite different. It is a bright green form with the leaves glaucous beneath and it forms a dense, rounder plant. (Illustration 157). Although in colouring it is similar to 'Nana Gracilis' it is much slower and more open in growth and is without the tendency to form an upright plant which characterises that cultivar.

– –'**Nana Densa**' [*C. obtusa* var. *nana densa* Hornb. Dw. Con. 40. 1923; 'Nana Densa' Hillier, Dw. Con. 21. 1964.] Although Hornibrook reduced this form to a synonym of 'Nana' in his second edition, H. G. Hillier still maintains and offers it [Man. 473. 1971] as a separate cultivar. He is undoubtedly right, but 'Nana Densa' is so close to 'Nana' that both cultivars would only be required in a very large collection.

– –'Nana Gracilis' [*Retinospora obtusa nana gracilis* R. Smith, Pl. Fir Tribe, 39. 1863; *C. obtusa* var. *nana gracilis* Hornb. Dw. Con. Ed. 2, 61. 1938.] Despite its misleading name this is a very attractive, dense growing form reaching 2 m high in time, making a pyramidal bush with rich lustrous green, healthy looking foliage and a somewhat rugged and picturesque outline. It is too well known to need much description and should be in every garden where there is room for it. It is worth a little trouble to get a plant on its own roots. (Illustration 158). 'Graciosa' Den Ouden and Boom [Man. 105. 1965] is a sport of 'Nana Gracilis' with stronger and looser, bright green foliage. Both are too vigorous for our Nana Group.

– –'Nana Lutea' Welch [Dw. Con. 138. 1966.] This is a very nice golden form which arose as a sport on a plant of 'Nana Gracilis' and was introduced by Jan Spek of Boskoop, Holland. It forms a neat, compact little bush with leaf sprays about equivalent in vigour to 'Nana' but of a clear golden-yellow colour, well maintained throughout the year. (Illustration 159).

– –'Pygmaea' [*Retinospora obtusa pygmaea* Gord. Pin. Suppl. 94. 1862; *C. obtusa pygmaea* H. & H. Syn. Nadel. 253. 1865; var. *pygmaea* Hornb. Dw. Con. Ed. 2, 63. 1938.] Nana Group. This is one of the most desirable forms and a well grown plant always draws attention to itself. It forms a low, spreading bush always much wider than high, with the flat, fan-shaped sprays lying closely one above the other. (Illustration 160). The difference between this cultivar and 'Pygmaea Aurescens' [*C. obtusa* var. *pygmaea aurescens* Hornb. Dw. Con. Ed. 2, 63. 1938] is mainly one of colour, but in the Pygmy Pinetum the latter is definitely the stronger grower of the two, and it occasionally throws out strong horizontal shoots quite unlike the fan-shaped sprays of 'Pygmaea'. During the greater part of the year 'Pygmaea' is quite green and 'Pygmaea Aurescens' is brownish-green; in the autumn and winter 'Pygmaea' takes on a slight bronze colour whereas 'Pygmaea Aurescens' turns a rich copper-bronze. There should be no difficulty in telling them apart, but 'Pygmaea Aurescens' is not infrequently labelled 'Pygmaea'.

This is a variety that seems to be particularly susceptible to the influence of rootstock vigour when grafted. In the Westonbirt Arboretum near Tetbury in Gloucestershire there is a plant labelled 'Pygmaea' which is of an upright, pyramidal shape about 2.5 m high, although cuttings taken and rooted from this plant form normal prostrate plants. There is a similar plant at Messrs. Waterer's nursery at Knap Hill, Surrey.

– –'Pygmaea Densa' Hillier [Man. 474. 1971.] Nana Group. This rather doubtful name is listed for a plant described as a 'smaller, compact form' of 'Pygmaea'. It is probably the same plant I have received under the vernacular name 'Chima-anihiba' (sometimes spelt 'Chimohiba').

– –'Reis Dwarf' [New cv.] This is a curious form. The foliage is similar to that of 'Kosteri' and for a time it forms a neat bun-shaped plant, but it will sometimes throw up long, straggling shoots. Unless these are cut away it loses its original habit and becomes an upright, rather open shrub. The congested type of foliage reappears on these longer shoots so the plant lends itself to being trained into quaint and curious shapes.

– –'Repens' [*C. obtusa nana repens* Den Ouden, Conif. 123. 1949.] This is another prostrate form much the same in habit as 'Pygmaea' but very much stronger and coarser in growth and always green in colour, with no trace of bronze. It originated as a sporting branch of 'Nana Gracilis', to which it is apt to revert. (Illustration 161).

– –'Rigid Dwarf' Den Ouden and Boom 1965 ['Nana Rigida' Hillier, Dw. Con. 23. 1964 and Man. 474. 1971.] NANA GROUP. This is a distinct form, of dense upright growth and of a stiff and rigid appearance. The main branches sweep up to a nearly vertical position, the foliage is dark green with glaucous markings beneath.

– –'Sanderi'. See *Thuja orientalis* 'Sanderi'.

– –'Spiralis' [*C. obtusa* var. *spiralis* Hornb. Dw. Con. Ed. 2, 69. 1938.] LYCOPODIOIDES GROUP. This is an upright-growing form with a stiff habit; the sprays are cup-shaped and curiously twisted around the smaller branchlets; a very distinct and outstanding form, but not a particularly attractive one, at least when young.

– –'Tempelhof' Den Ouden and Boom [Man. 110. 1965.] This makes a compact, broadly ovoid to pyramidal bush eventually reaching 2.5 m. The leaf sprays are fan-shaped, green to yellowish-green, often with a brownish tint (similar to 'Pygmaea Aurescens'), especially during the winter.

– –'Tetragona Aurea' [*Retinospora tetragona aurea* Wm. Barron Nurs. Cat. 12. 1875; *C. obtusa* f. *tetragons* Rehd. in Rehd. Bibl. 53. 1949 *; f. *Barronii* Rehd. in Rehd. Bibl. 53. 1949 *; var. *filicoides aurea* Kent in Veitch Man. Ed. 2, 221. 1900; var. *tetragona* and var. *tetragona aurea* Hornb. Dw. Con. Ed. 2, 66. 1938 and later writers; 'Kojolcohiba' Welch. Dw. Con. 142. 1966.] In my earlier book I discussed several possible explanations of the mysterious disappearance of the alleged green form of 'Tetragona Aurea'. I am now entirely satisfied that there was no such plant and that the propagations received in 1871, having been at first kept in cold frames or other shaded situations remained the green colour that is characteristic of 'Tetragona Aurea' in such conditions, and that by 1875 they had been planted out in full sunlight and had developed their true colour. This being the case the name "*tetragona*" and all attempts at substitutes for it are invalidated under Article 42 of the *Cultivated Code* which requires the rejection of a cultivar name if the cultivar which it purports to be 'neither does nor did exist'.

The golden form when well grown is one of the most beautiful dwarf conifers we have. (Illustration 162). It is usually seen in gardens as a small or medium-size bush, but it would seem to respond considerably to the selection of propagating material (or perhaps, choice of rootstock in the case of grafted plants) because whilst there is, for example in the late G. L. Pilkington's garden at Grayswood Hill, Haslemere, Surrey, a plant of this variety about 6 m high, I have seen minute and obviously old and slow-growing bushlets only a few centimetres high. It is probable that virus infection plays a part in this variability.

It is distinct from all other forms both in its habit and colouring. The growth in a good plant is very congested, the main branches being long and gracefully curved, densely set and closely packed with secondary branches from the axils of both facing and lateral leaves, giving the tetragonal cross section to the twig from which it gets its name.

The colour in full sunlight is a rich bronze-gold but it only needs a relatively small amount of overshading from nearby trees or buildings for this to be reduced to a poor yellowish-green. On the other hand, in *full* shade it develops a dark, rich, blue-green which is quite attractive. The plant is not a particularly easy one to grow; it tends to throw its strength into the main leading growths and become bare at the base and in the interior of the bush. This characteristic seems to be accentuated by the susceptibility of this variety to drought in the summer and to wind scorch in the winter, both conditions apparently encouraging it to shed some of its foliage. It can be kept dense by regular shortening of strong shoots.

Here must be mentioned two forms which came to me from Messrs. Duncan & Davies Ltd., of New Plymouth, New Zealand. Of these **'Kojolcohiba'** is very similar to 'Tetragona Aurea' in foliage, but it is a strong grower and forms a conical plant with steeply ascending branches. In the Pygmy Pinetum it is a much better doer than 'Tetragona Aurea', being less sensitive to sun and wind.

Duncan and Davies now write "'**Fernspray Gold'** is a plant that we grew for many years under the name 'Tetragona Aurea', but which in recent years we believe was incorrectly named, as a plant we were growing under the name of 'Kojolcohiba' was found to answer to the description of 'Tetragona Aurea'. As we were unable to get any correct identification of this plant anywhere throughout the world, our Company in association with the Nomenclature Committee of New Zealand's Nurserymen's Association named it 'Fernspray Gold' and applied the name 'Tetragona Aurea' to the plant originally called 'Kojolcohiba'."

This attractive plant cannot now be positively identified with the var. *filicoides aurea* of Kent, although it could well be described as a golden form of 'Filicoides', having the same fern-like leaf spray. So the new name is very apt. On the other hand, 'Kojolcohiba' maintains its vigorous upright habit—quite distinctive from the growth in England of 'Tetragona Aurea'—so the retention of the distinction seems justified—at any rate in this country, although it may merely be that the local stock is affected by virus.

– –'Tonia' Den Ouden [Conif. 123. 1949.] NANA GROUP. This is a variegated sport from a plant of 'Nana Gracilis' which originated in the nursery of William Hage & Co. of Boskoop, Holland, in about 1928. Plants I have seen are much weaker in growth and with a smaller leaf spray than 'Nana Gracilis'. The variegation is uncertain and spasmodic, and apparently young plants may make several years' growth before any white patches appear. These are a clear white contrasting well with the dark green normal foliage, but I consider the plant more a horticultural curiosity than a thing of beauty.

– –'Torulosa' Bergm. [Pl. and Gar. **21, 1**: 33. 1965.] LYCOPODIOIDES GROUP. An upright, tangled shrub with erect leading shoots and with branches contorted and twisted, with filiform foliage not unlike 'Coralliformis' but having small fasciated tips here and there. Doubtless Mrs. Bergman accepted a name already in general use, but since the word torulose has quite a different meaning I rather fancy the original coiner of the name meant to choose 'Tortuosa'. The Code permits the correction of spelling mistakes, but scarcely a howler of this kind. Plants sometimes listed as *"torulosa nana"* seem to be merely young plants of 'Torulosa'—probably propagations from weak side-cuttings. (Illustration 163).

Chamaecyparis pisifera (Sieb. and Zucc.) Endl. This is another Japanese species of tree-like proportions which has given us a number of garden forms. Within the species we find true dwarfs, thread-leaf forms and forms with fixed juvenile and semi-juvenile foliage, but whilst these last retain their juvenile foliage they do not all remain dwarf, some of them being prepared to grow to a height of 9 m or more in this country. As a tree of this size with juvenile foliage is quite attractive they have their garden value but they cannot be regarded as dwarf forms. They do, however, stand heavy pruning, so can be kept within bounds to some extent.

The invention of the supposed genus *"Retinospora"* [Sieb. and Zucc. F. Jap. **2:** 36. 1842] to embrace a number of forms of conifer in Japanese cultivation, coupled with the habit that seemed prevalent at the time of applying the epithet *ericoides* (i.e., heath-like) to everything in sight bearing persistent juvenile foliage resulted in nomenclatural problems from which we are still not altogether free. For when, in European cultivation, the different forms went their individual ways, some developing patches of adult foliage and some even setting infertile cones, it became evident that *"Retinospora"* had been a mistake and the subsequent allocation of each form to its proper species (and also genus, for Thuja was involved as well) has been a matter of considerable difficulty. This difficulty has been largely overcome with time and further knowledge of the plants, but the sorting out of the nomenclature along conventional lines is a virtual impossibility, owing to the undiscriminating use by the nineteenth century writers of the many names now to be found in the literature. If botanical writers are under a basic misunderstanding regarding both the generic and the specific allegiances of the plants they describe, plants which they only know of in the writings of others or at most as young plants, it is too much to expect that they will leave behind them much of any real value to posterity. The treatment, here, therefore, particularly as regards the synonymies is not beyond argument, but I think it carries with it at least an air of probability and (being based on a knowledge of the plants now in cultivation rather than upon a probing into the probable intentions of writers of long ago) it will, I hope, provide a nomenclatural basis for present day use.

Many of the garden forms can be conveniently grouped, as under:

FILIFERA GROUP   *Forms carrying wholly thread-like foliage instead of the normal leaf spray.* This group corresponds to the botanical category f. *filifera* (see below).

'Filifera Aurea'	'Filifera Nana'
'Filifera Aureovariegata'	'Golden Mop'
'Filifera Flava'	'Sungold'
'Filifera Gracilis'	

LEPTOCLADA GROUP   *A small group with more or less persistent glaucous juvenile foliage with very small leaves.* This group corresponds to the botanical category f. *leptoclada* (see below).

'Dwarf Blue'   'Squarrosa Intermedia'
'Leptoclada'   'Squarrosa Minima'
'Plumosa Cristata'   'Squarrosa Pygmaea'
'Rucks Globe'

NANA GROUP   *A group of very diminutive bun-like forms carrying adult foliage,* corresponding to the botanical category f. *nana* (see below).

'Aurea Nana', see 'Strathmore'   'Nana Aureovariegata'
'Compacta'   'Nana Variegata'
'Compacta Variegata'   'Parslori'
'Minima Variegata'   'Pygmy' (= 'Tsukumi'?)
'Nana'   'Strathmore'
'Nana Albovariegata'   'White Pygmy'

PLUMOSA GROUP   *Forms with persistent semi-juvenile foliage. The free standing part of the leaf is short and held close to the stem. Leaves are folded along the mid-rib and there may be some slight difference between the facing and lateral pairs. A definite branching system is more or less in evidence.* This group corresponds to the botanical category f. *plumosa* (see below), and is not limited to dwarf forms.

'Plumosa Albo-picta'   'Plumosa Flavescens'
'Plumosa Aurea Compacta'   'Plumosa Juniperoides'
'Plumosa Aurea Nana'   'Plumosa Nana'
'Plumosa Compacta'   'Plumosa Pygmaea'
'Plumosa Compressa'   'Plumosa Rogersii'
    (met with under a   'Snow'
     variety of names)

SQUARROSA GROUP   *Forms with persistent juvenile foliage. Leaves resemble the seed-leaves; long, free standing, decurved; no distinction between facing and lateral pairs of leaves.* This group corresponds to the botanical category f. *squarrosa* (see below). This group also is not limited to dwarf forms.

'Boulevard'   'Squarrosa Dumosa'
var. *ericoides*   'Squarrosa Elegans'
'Green Velvet'   'Squarrosa Lombarts'
'Pici'   'Squarrosa Lutea'
'Squarrosa Aurea'   'Squarrosa Sulphurea'
'Squarrosa Aurea Nana'

– –'**Aurea Nana**' [*C. pisifera* f. *aurea nana* Beissn. Handb. 91. 1891; var. *aurea nana*

Hornb. Dw. Con. Ed. 2, 76. 1938, *aurea nana Fretsii* (pro syn.); *aurea compacta* Hort.] NANA GROUP. This unfortunate plant has had its ups and downs. Hornibrook tells us that it was lost sight of for many years after Beissner described it in 1891 but that it had just returned into cultivation when he wrote in 1938. It seems to have gone under for the second time very soon afterwards, and I have been unable to trace it in cultivation with certainty. I am now, however, satisfied that the cultivar 'Strathmore' described and pictured by Harrison [*Ornamental Conifers*, 66. 1975] is the plant we grow in this country under Beissner's name. But since this identification cannot now be verified, I consider that the balance of advantage lies with regarding Beissner's plant (with its uninspiring and confusing name) as lost to cultivation and accepting the cultivar name 'Strathmore' for the plant we grow. A description will be found under that name.

– –'**Boulevard**' Boulevard [Nurs. Cat. 3. 1960; *Retinospora K and C.,* Kempenger and Christiansen, Nurs. Cat. 1934; *C. pisifera squarrosa cyano-viridis* Hort.] SQUARROSA GROUP. This is quite a newcomer, and seldom does a fresh introduction amongst garden conifers make such a rapid advance in popularity. It arose as a sport on *Chamaecyparis pisifera* 'Squarrosa' many years ago, and although it is not a dwarf form it is deservedly popular for its attractive foliage and wonderful colour which, when well grown, is a beautiful and outstanding silvery blue-grey, and as it seems to stand heavy pruning it should be possible to keep it within bounds in a given situation for a good many years. On one American nursery I visited, I noticed that all the stock plants had developed adult foliage. I have not seen this anywhere in Europe, but whenever it appears it should at once be cut away.

In dry soils and in soils containing lime the true colour fails to develop and instead the plant assumes an unattractive dirty brown, but whatever the soil the colour always seems to be better in shade and although it seems thoroughly hardy the plant will give of its best colour when grown in a cold house, especially during the winter months. Sad confirmation of the depravity of man comes in a report reaching me that plants grown 'soft' in this way are sold to the holiday makers in Cornwall as house plants, under the name 'Cornish Blue'.

– –'**Compacta**' [*C. pisifera* var. *compacta* Hartw. u. Ruempl. Baume u. Str. 661. 1875; 'Compacta' Den Ouden and Boom, Man. 113. 1965.] NANA GROUP. This distinct cultivar has been much neglected by authors and even Hornibrook does not mention it. It forms a fairly compact, low-growing, bun-shaped bush bearing wholly adult foliage, mostly in compact, tightly packed sprays which are somewhat recurved, but occasionally it sends out much stronger growth which does not develop the normal congested foliage until the next growing season, and by this means the plant increases in size. It should not be confused with the much smaller and tighter plant 'Nana'.

– –'**Compacta Variegata**' [*C. pisifera* var. *compacta variegata* Hornb. Dw. Con. Ed. 2, 75. 1938.] NANA GROUP. This name was published for a sport from 'Compacta' with a fairly bold variegation in yellow to pale yellow flecks or splashes. In habit the plant is looser than the green form and in time will form a bush 1.5 m high by 2 m or more across. There is no general golden sheen over the whole plant. (Illustration 164).

– –'**Dwarf Blue**' Hesse [Nurs. Cat. 29. 1938/39] is indistinguishable from 'Squarrosa Intermedia'.

– – var. **ericoides** Reg. [Russ. Dendrol. Ed. 2, 27. 1883; Hornb. Dw. Con. Ed. 2, 70. 1938; *Retinospora squarrosa dubia* Veitch, Man. 250. 1881.] SQUARROSA GROUP. This is described as a plant not unlike *C. thyoides* 'Ericoides'. The only specimen known to Hornibrook is no longer in existence and so this form has been long regarded as lost to cultivation. In 1972 in an old garden in Scotland I came across what I at first regarded as a pale, bright green form of 'Squarrosa'. It was a very old plant and the foliage answered to Hornibrook's description of var. *ericoides*, but since the plant I found can only possibly (or at most, probably) be that form, and in view of the confusion already surrounding that sadly overworked epithet I have felt it best to introduce this attractive form under a new name, '**Green Velvet**' [New cv.] The habit and growth is quite typical of 'Squarrosa' but the colour and appearance of the plant from a short distance answer exactly to the name now given to it.

– – f. **filifera** (Sén.) Voss. [Rehd. Bibl. 55. 1949 *.] This is a botanical class embracing all the *forms characterised by thread-leaf (filiform) foliage in place of the usual leaf spray*. The cultivar that gave its name to this *forma* (and to our present group) is not a dwarf.

– –'**Filifera Aurea**' [*C. pisifera filifera aurea* (Veitch) Beissn. Handb. 91. 1891.] This cultivar, like 'Filifera', is not a dwarf and will form an erect plant 4-5 m high in time, but distinguishable therefrom is the popular cultivar, '**Golden Mop**' Welch [Dw. Con. 146. 1966; *C. pisifera filifera aurea nana* Hort.] FILIFERA GROUP. I do not agree with Den Ouden and Boom, [Man. 113. 1965] that this is the same as 'Filifera Aurea', since the habit is lower and the foliage is very much finer. Although slow to establish, this form develops into a dense, globose bush never over 1 m high and of the most wonderful gold colour, but unfortunately it is prone to sunburn. Although considered by the purists to be out of place in an alpine garden it is very effective in a group of dwarf conifers or when grown as a specimen in a sunny spot. The new cultivar '**Sungold**' is somewhat less spectacular as regards colour but has the great advantage of hardiness, so is becoming popular on the continent. Mr. Grootendorst, who introduced it, tells me that in hot climates it develops a golden-bronze colour and does not burn even in full sunlight.

– –'**Filifera Aureovariegata**' [*C. pisifera filifera aureovariegata* Beissn. Handb. 91. 1891.] This is a form with a creamy-yellow variegation in bold splashes all over the plant which is fairly strong-growing, forming in time a large bush 1-1.5 m high. It is then an attractive form and should be more widely planted than it is, but like all the thread-leaf forms it is rather insignificant at first and calls for a little patience.

– –'**Filifera Gracilis**' [*C. pisifera filifera gracilis* (Gord.) Beissn. Handb. 91. 1891.] This is a very attractive and uncommon form with foliage an unusual and attractive yellowish-green. Its foliage is slightly more slender and noticeably more regular than in the other 'Filifera' forms and it remains a dense little bush that should be seen more frequently than it is. It is occasionally offered as '**Filifera Flava**' [*C. pisifera filifera flava* Schelle. Winterh. Nadel. 301. 1909] which was described as being of a sulphur yellow colour and appears to be lost to cultivation.

– –'**Filifera Nana**' [*C. pisifera filifera nana* Beissn. Mitt. d.d.d.G. **6**: 58. 1897.] This is only a slower-growing bush form of 'Filifera', from which it probably arose by bud mutation. These have evidently occurred more than once in different places, since plants in cultivation vary noticeably, but insufficiently to justify separation. I once found a witch's broom on a plant of 'Filifera' having extremely fastigiate growth. Propagations therefrom, although of no garden value, retain this characteristic, so these mutations are normally stable. Any out-of-character growth should be cut out if it occurs. (Illustration 165).

– – f. **leptoclada** Sieb. [*Retinospora leptoclada* Sieb. Cat. Prodr. 6. 1861; *C. pisifera* f. *leptoclada* (Endl.) in Rehd. Bibl. 56. 1949 (in part); *Retinospora squarrosa leptoclada* (Sieb.) Gord. Pin. 297. 1858 and *Retinospora leptoclada* (Zucc.) Gord. Pin. Suppl. 91. 1862; *Chamaecyparis pisifera* var. *squarrosa intermedia* Hornb. Dw. Con. 49. 1923 and var. *squarrosa minima* l. c.; NON *Retinospora ericoides leptoclada* Mast. Journ. Linn. Soc. 352. 1896.] This early and rather phoney category covers a group of *forms in cultivation characterised by the persistence of at least some glaucous juvenile foliage consisting of very small leaves, often only at the base of an old tree,* and provides a suitable name for the Group in which such are listed here.

The epithet *leptoclada* (Latin = with slender shoots) appears very early in the literature of these forms but so far as I am aware no real attempt has hitherto been made to determine its application to plants in current cultivation. It first turns up in a catalogue of 1862 which I have not seen and the plant was evidently an importation from Japan, said to be one of several there called 'Nazu' (= a dwarf). Gordon confused it with what we now know as *Chamaecyparis thyoides* 'Ericoides', thinking the latter was (his words) 'only the primordial form of *Retinospora leptoclada*' and Masters confused it with our *Chamaecyparis thyoides* 'Andelyensis'. Since Hornibrook (who also knew only small plants) did a very similar thing, Gordon's mistake was understandable; Masters's was not and the perpetuation by Kent in Veitch [Man. Ed. 2, 232. 1900] of the same mistake still bothers us. Hornibrook's mistake is capable of a very simple explanation, as we shall see.

I am unable to make up my mind whether or not recognition of the group as a botanical form is justifiable or whether we are in fact only dealing with a single clone and a number of cultivariants. I much incline to the latter conclusion, but because the *Cultivated Code* does not yet recognise cultivariants the former treatment must serve us for the time being. In either case we are dealing with a clone (or, as the case may be, a group of clones) which in maturity carries for the most part adult foliage of a most uninteresting kind which no one would want to propagate and which is (or are) only kept in cultivation at all by propagation by means of cuttings consistently selected from the attractive, glaucous, juvenile type of foliage. This type of foliage is usually so little in evidence in a predominately adult tree that the identity of the two types of growth is often overlooked. So although Gordon gives a good description of an older plant, Hornibrook, thinking only of young specimens, describes his newly named 'Squarrosa Intermedia' as 'A most curious form of unknown origin with mainly or entirely juvenile foliage'.

So there the matter rests. I have seen old plants in several countries with hardly any juvenile foliage to be seen. So now those Superintendents and

Curators whom I have doubtless outraged by saying that their plants were 'Squarrosa Intermedia' gone to the devil will be able to label them *Chamaecyparis pisifera* 'Leptoclada' (or if they prefer it, f. *leptoclada*) with my blessing and—no doubt—much amusement.

The ability of young plants propagated from juvenile growth to retain this horticulturally attractive quality is not at all complete, and all the cultivars (or cultivariants if that is what they are) in the group are apt to throw out adult or semi-adult growth and this must be rigorously cut out if the plant is to retain its early beauty. They are impossible to distinguish from a study of the foliage alone, although (perhaps) differing in later behaviour. This may be due to clonal differences or merely the result of several 'cutting generations' of carefully selected propagating material, possibly with cultural and climatic differences playing a part. However this may be, the name serves us usefully for a distinct group of garden forms, all of them the better for an annual light clipping in early summer.

– –'**Leptoclada**' [*Retinospora squarrosa leptoclada* (Sieb.) Gord. Pin. 297. 1858; *Retinospora leptoclada* (Zucc.) Gord. Pin. Suppl. 91; var. *leptoclada* Kent in Veitch Man. Ed. 2, 232. 1900.] The application of this name is discussed above.

– – f. **nana** Beissn. [Handb. 91. 1891.] A group, recognisable both botanically and horticulturally, of *very diminutive bun-like little plants, carrying adult foliage.*

– –'**Nana**' [*C. pisifera* f. *nana* Beissn. Handb. 91. 1891; var. *nana* Hornb. Dw. Con. Ed. 2, 75. 1938.] This is one of the choicest of dwarf conifers. It makes a low, bun-shaped bush with dark bluish-green foliage, very glaucous beneath, in little fan-shaped sprays. (Illustration 166). '**Parslori**' Hillier [Man. 475. 1971] is a form that came to me from an Australian source. So far in the Pygmy Pinetum it has made a very neat, flattened, bun-shaped plant lower than 'Nana' and with lighter green foliage. '**Pygmy**' and '**White Pygmy**' are names suggested by R. S. Corley of High Wycombe [Bull. Alp. Gar. Soc. **38, 2:** 156. 1970] for two very tiny bun-forms bearing respectively green and white-tipped foliage which he received from Japan. Regarding the species in this case as constituting the 'cultivar class' under Article 50, this seems a pity since we already have *pygmaea* as a cultivar epithet several times and 'Pygmy' (according to Article 32) is only the same name in another language. It is to be hoped that Mr. Corley will be inclined to change his mind and put forward names less certain to cause confusion. A form '**Tsukumi**' which I have received from Japan is very similar. If it turns out to be the same it will solve this problem for us, since the Japanese vernacular name would have priority.

– –'**Nana Albovariegata**' Welch [Dw. Con. 147. 1966] is a form not mentioned by Hornibrook with a small, white and not very effective variegation. It sometimes carries a wholly white spray of foliage in the interior of the bush. The name, despite its Latin form, might scrape acceptance under Recommendation 12A of the *Cultivated Code;* the relationship of this Recommendation to Article 27 is obscure, but to invent a new 'fancy' name for an unimportant mutation of the present kind would seem to me to be absurd, rules or no rules.

– –'**Nana Aureovariegata**' [*Retinospora pisifera nana aurea-variegata* R. Smith, Pl. Fir Tribe, 30. 1863; *C. pisifera nana aureo-variegata* Beissn. Handb. 92. 1891.] This, as quite correctly described and named by Hornibrook, is a form of 'Nana' making the same very dense bun-shaped cushion but with a wonderful golden sheen all over the plant. It looks its best in sunshine and is a most desirable variety, reliably dwarf and slow-growing, but is apt to revert to the green form in patches. These should be cut away at once.

– –'**Nana Variegata**' [*C. pisifera nana variegata* Sén. Conif. 57. 1867] is a variegated form of 'Nana' similar to 'Compacta Variegata' but smaller in every way. '**Minima Variegata**' [Hort. Eng.] is a still more diminutive form with a similar clear, yellow variegation. The name may be invalid and need replacement but it is accurately descriptive.

It is possible that all these forms (perhaps 'states' is a better word) have a common origin and that the forms of 'Compacta' were derived from the 'Nana' forms (or *vice versa.*) by the selection of cutting material. This theory is perhaps borne out by the fact that the variegated forms are variable and that intermediate forms can often be found in different parts of the same bush. For this reason, care should be taken by pruning and the selection of propagating material to preserve the types I have described. Even 'Nana', which Hillier [Dw. Con. 27. 1964] tells us is a 'very consistent variety', does not always behave itself as well as it might, so should be watched for growth out of character.

– –'**Pici**' Barabits [Deutsche Baumsch. **5**: 139. 1965] SQUARROSA GROUP. This is a form raised from seed in 1953 by Elemer Barabits of Sopron in Hungary. It is slower growing than 'Squarrosa Dumosa' but is very similar to that variety in summer. In winter it turns a warm bronze but is quite hardy. The mother plant is in the Botanic Garden at Sopron in Hungary.

– – f. **plumosa** (Carr.) Beissn. [Rehd. Bibl. 55. 1949 *.] This botanical epithet covers *all forms with persistent semi-juvenile foliage. The free standing part of the leaf is shorter and closer to the stem. Leaves are folded along the mid-rib and there may be some slight difference between the facing and lateral pairs. A definite branching system is more or less in evidence.*

– –'**Plumosa**'. With the cultivar that gave its name to this group and its golden form 'Plumosa Aurea' (Illustration 167) we have nothing to do in this book as they are both forms which will reach to 10 m. The word 'Plumosa' is used in this connection to indicate a semi-juvenile type of foliage that is intermediate between the juvenile 'Squarrosa' foliage with its long, free standing leaves and the small-leaved adult type, and it has no connection with the botanical term 'plumose' (which means 'feather-like') for which I prefer the word 'frondose' (i.e., like the frond of a fern).

In most of the 'Plumosa' forms the leaf is much shorter and is pressed close to or attached to the stem for part of its length with only the tip standing free, and the branching system shows a definite pattern, with the tendency for the laterals to lie in the same plane, giving just the suggestion of being frondose. Unfortunately, consistency has not always been achieved in the naming of these forms and there are several cases where the epithet used belies the group to which the cultivar belongs.

– –'**Plumosa Albopicta**' [*Retinospora plumosa albo-picta* Veitch Man. 248. 1881; *C. plumosa argentea* Sén. Conif. 57. 1867; *C. squarrosa variegata* Carr. Traité, 139. 1855.]

This is a slow-growing form which makes an upright bush eventually to about 2 m, with exceptionally small leaves. These are dark green with numerous small areas of white which give the whole plant a speckled appearance.

It is attractive, especially as a young plant, but as the variegation is quite ineffective seen at a distance it should be planted close to a path or in a spot in which it would be observed from close at hand. The variegation is retained throughout the year, but is brightest in the spring and summer. The forms described by Carrière and Sénéclause cannot be distinguished from the present form for which I retain Veitch's name as best preserving established usage.

- –'**Plumosa Argentea**'. See 'Plumosa Albopicta' above.

- –'**Plumosa Aurea Compacta**' [*C. pisifera plumosa aurea compacta* Hort. ex Beissn. Handb. Ed. 2, 570. 1909.] The early descriptions of this and the following form are too brief to be of much help. These golden forms come and go in the nurseries as fresh mutations occur (and sometimes disappear as the mother plant ages). Since the description in my earlier book at least related to plants in current production probably the best thing is to leave well alone. Nomenclature must be our servant, not our master.

This forms a slow-growing globose (later sometimes upright) bush to ultimately 1.5 - 2 m. The foliage is a golden-yellow and is much nearer to 'Squarrosa' than to 'Plumosa'. Each leaf has two strongly-marked bands of white on the underside. (Illustration 168).

It is extremely difficult to distinguish between young propagations of this cultivar and 'Plumosa Rogersii' described later, but the white marking on the underside of the leaves of the latter is slightly less prominent and also it will soon throw up a leader and begin to assume its characteristic conical shape, whereas 'Plumosa Aurea Compacta' soon develops into a rounded little bush.

- –'**Plumosa Aurea Nana**' [*C. pisifera plumosa aurea nana* Hort. ex Beissn. Handb. 88. 1891 (pro syn).] This is just a slow-growing form of the larger plant, presumably derived from it by selection of weak-growing cutting material. It bears rather small and typically 'Plumosa' foliage, which in the early summer is a beautiful golden-yellow. It is variable in the trade, and there are probably several clones in cultivation. Some forms later turn to a dull green but the best form retains its golden colour throughout the year.

- –'**Plumosa Compacta**' [*C. pisifera plumosa compacta* Den Ouden, Conif. 128. 1949.] This is a rather strong-growing form raised by Den Ouden which does not seem to be in cultivation. I have not seen it. The name should not be used for a dwarf form of any kind.

- –'**Plumosa Compressa**' [*C. pisifera* var. *plumosa compressa* Hornb. Dw. Con. Ed. 2, 74. 1938; *Thuja occidentalis* 'Silveriana Nana' (Spaan) Hort. Amer.] This is probably the smallest form of *C. pisifera*. It was raised from a sporting branch of 'Squarrosa' by Van Nes of Boskoop. It is a most popular and attractive slow-growing little plant, bearing both 'Squarrosa' and 'Plumosa' type foliage of diminutive size which seems to vary in colour in different situations and seasons. (Illustration 169).

In its young state it looks like a tight, glaucous green moss, and by a little systematic clipping in early summer with a pair of nail scissors it can be induced to form a small bun of an almost unbelievably solid appearance and tightness of foliage, but normally older plants show variation of foliage and colour; because of this variability, propagations have been made from time to time of likely branches, and to these have been given a wonderful variety of names. It would appear that as these names become more complex they became more difficult to memorize and more easy to quote differently next time, for one meets every possible combination of the words *nana, compacta, aurea, glauca* and others. I once received a nice little plant labelled *Chamaecyparis pisifera "plumosa flavescens aurea compacta nana"* which seemed to me to be carrying the joke a little too far. The variations certainly are not sufficiently stable to justify retention of all these names but I see Hillier does retain the name **'Plumosa Compressa Aurea'** [Man. 475. 1971] for a form distinguished by foliage gold tinged in summer.

This plant is susceptible to frost injury. In the spring as soon as new growth commences the dead growth should be cut out and usually a season's growth will close over the gap.

– –**'Plumosa Cristata'** [*C. pisifera plumosa cristata* (Onuma) Beissn. Mitt. d.d.d.G. **9**: 67. 1900; 'Plumosa Cristata' Bergm. Pl. and Gar. **21, 1**: 36. 1965.] LEPTOCLADA GROUP. This seems the most distinctive of any of the group, if the picture and description given by Mrs. Bergman are maintained in other soils and situations. I saw a form when in the United States in 1970 that I think was this. I was told that it maintained the tight growth of the plants I saw and never misbehaved by producing loose growth, but propagations now growing as young plants in the Pygmy Pinetum shew little or no improvement on 'Squarrosa Intermedia' in this respect.

– –**'Plumosa Flavescens'** [*Retinospora plumosa flavescens* de Vos, Sempervirens **3**: 228. 1874; *C. pisifera plumosa flavescens* Beissn. Handb. 90. 1891; *Retinospora plumosa sulphurea* Hort. ex Den Ouden, Conif. 128. 1949.] This is quite a distinct and attractive form which is seldom met with. It forms a conical or globose bush never over 1 m high and its cultivar name (which means 'yellowish' or 'turning yellow') is quite descriptive of the foliage. This is smaller in the leaf and neater than in any other of the 'Plumosa' varieties, and at first is sulphur yellow at the growing tips. It turns green by the autumn.

– –**'Plumosa Juniperoides'** Hort. Amer. [*C. pisifera 'Plumosa Aurea Compacta'* Bergm. Pl. and Gar. **21, 1**: 35. 1965.] This distinct form might, at a casual glance, be mistaken for 'Plumosa Compressa', having the same closely packed juvenile leaves and neat habit. It differs in being of much stronger growth and in holding its relatively broad leaves forwards and clasping the shoot (unlike the strongly decurved leaves of 'Plumosa Compressa'), especially on the young shoots, to which they impart a tetragonal effect that no doubt suggested the name. It is golden-yellow in early summer, turning green later. (Illustration 170).

– –**'Plumosa Nana'** [*C. pisifera* var. *plumosa nana* Hornb. Dw. Con. Ed. 2, 74. 1938.] This, according to Hornibrook, was a sub-globose form which has been lost to cultivation but **'Plumosa Nana Aurea'** [Hornb., l.c.] is quite a distinct and very uncommon variety which forms a low, compact, bun-shaped cushion. The leaves are much more of the 'Squarrosa' type than 'Plumosa' and are strongly recurved, a rich golden-yellow. A twig taken from the plant could be mistaken for 'Plumosa Aurea Compacta' or 'Plumosa Rogersii', but the low, slow growth and the bun-shaped habit of the plant make it distinct.

– –'**Plumosa Pygmaea**' Welch [Wansdyke Nurs. Cat. 4. 1961 and Dw. Con. 150. 1966; *C. pisifera* 'Pygmaea' Hillier, Man. 476. 1971.] On the rock garden in the National Botanic Garden at Glasnevin in Dublin there is a very old specimen about 2 m high bearing this name, and although I have not been able to trace it in the literature, I am assuming that because of its age it must have been published at some time or other and therefore be legitimate. The plant could be roughly described as a green form of 'Plumosa Rogersii'. Young plants form the same cone-shaped bush and it is an attractive plant which should be better known, having the great advantage that it seems to be thoroughly wind resistant.

– –'**Plumosa Rogersii**' [*C. pisifera plumosa aurea compacta Rogersii* Rogers, Nurs. Cat. 2. c. 1930; var. *plumosa Rogersii* Hornb. Dw. Con. Ed. 2, 75. 1938.] This is a very popular form which forms a conical plant with golden-yellow foliage which is much nearer 'Squarrosa' than 'Plumosa' and which retains its colour all the winter. It arose as a sport from 'Plumosa Aurea'. Unfortunately it is a little wind tender, especially in the spring, so should be given a sheltered spot.

– –'**Snow**' Hillier [Man. 476. 1971] PLUMOSA GROUP. This is a recent introduction from Japan the origin of which I do not know. Hillier describes it as a dwarf, bun-shaped bush with mossy, blue-grey foliage tipped with white, tending to burn in the sun or cold wind. (Illustration 171). It is, I think, a plant for the alpine house, like the similarly white-tipped *Cryptomeria japonica* 'Knaptonensis'.

– –'**Sopron**' New name [*C. pisifera* 'Repens' Barabits Deutsche Baumsch. **5**: 139. 1966.] This is an interesting low-growing, wide-spreading form raised from seed in 1955 by E. Barabits of Sopron in Hungary. It carries adult foliage of a light green. I suggest this name as I believe the Latin-form name first used is not acceptable under the Rules.

– – f. **squarrosa** (Zucc.) Beissn. & Hochst. [Rehd. Bibl. 55. 1949 *.] This is a botanical epithet covering *all forms with persistent juvenile foliage not included in f. leptoclada. Leaves resemble the seed-leaves; long free standing, decurved; no distinction between facing and lateral pairs of leaves.* It includes all the cultivars listed in the Group of the same name.

– –'**Squarrosa Argentea**' Hort. [*C. pisifera* 'Squarrosa Argentea Compacta' Welch, Dw. Con. 151. 1966.] This is probably a mutation or selection from f. *squarrosa* and is marginally slower-growing, at least for some years, so is popular as a cheaply produced 'dwarf conifer'. The silver-grey juvenile foliage is attractive. Like all the 'Squarrosa' forms, it stands up to heavy pruning.

– –'**Squarrosa Aurea**' [*Retinospora squarrosa* var. *aurea* Nels. Pin. 77. 1866; Welch, Wansdyke Nurs. Cat. 4. 1962.] This is an old variety, now seldom mentioned or planted. It has golden-yellow foliage and is a beautiful plant when happy, but as it dislikes sun, frost and wind it needs careful placing. There are trees several metres high in the Royal Botanic Garden, Edinburgh.

– –'**Squarrosa Dumosa**' [*C. pisifera squarrosa dumosa* Beissn. Handb. 87. 1891; *plumosa nana* Hort.] This is a most attractive and truly dwarf form which forms a dense, globose bush that is never seen over 1 m in height, with fairly large leafed foliage which in summer is a quiet grey-green but which in winter takes on a most attractive metallic bronze appearance, giving the whole bush the suggestion of the beauty of old pewter. (Illustration 172). It should be much more widely known than it is. **'Squarrosa Lombarts'** is similar, but a much more vigorous plant, attractively coloured in winter.

– –'**Squarrosa Intermedia**' [*C. pisifera* var. *squarrosa intermedia* Hornb. Dw. Con. 49. 1923; 'Dwarf Blue' Hort. Europe (in part).] LEPTOCLADA GROUP. This form is well known in England, where its easy rooting qualities endear it to nurserymen. When properly grown it is seen as a low, rounded bush with tightly packed, congested foliage of the 'Squarrosa' type but smaller in leaf than in any of those forms. (Illustration 173). But from time to time (it seems prone to do this more in some years than in others) it throws out longer shoots with more open foliage. If it is desired to keep the bush small and dense looking these should be cut away, but it is by means of these longer shoots that the plant increases in size and they normally develop the congested type of foliage the following year. But occasionally strong coarse growth bearing adult foliage appears and unless this is cut out at once the plant will go into a Dr. Jekyll and Mr. Hyde routine and end up as f. *leptoclada* gone to the devil, like many a good plant before it.

– –'**Squarrosa Lutea**' [*C. pisifera squarrosa lutea* Den Ouden, Naaml. 18 1937 and Conif. 129. 1949] is a sport from 'Squarrosa' with smaller habit and yellowish-white foliage which arose in the nursery of Koster Bros., in Holland, and is distinct in colour and habit from 'Squarrosa Aurea' already described. **'Squarrosa Aurea Nana'** listed by Hillier [Man. 476. 1971] may well be the same, from the description given. I do not know it.

– –'**Squarrosa Minima**' [*C. pisifera* var. *squarrosa minima* Hornb. Dw. Con. 49. 1923; f. *minima* (Hornb.) Rehd. Bibl. 56. 1949 *; 'Squarrosa Argentea Pygmaea' Hillier, Dw. Con. 28. 1964; 'Argentea Pygmaea' Bergm. Pl. and Gar. **21, 1:** 35. 1965; 'Squarrosa Pygmaea' Spingarn. Bull. Amer. Rock Gar. Soc. **24, 2:** 41. 1966; Hornb. (pro syn.) Dw. Con. 49. 1923.] LEPTOCLADA GROUP. I regard these as all the same as, or at the most as derivatives of 'Squarrosa Intermedia'. Since any desirable differences in tightness and slowness of growth may be the result of regular pruning, mutation or years of careful selection of propagating material by particular nurserymen, its value to collectors and connoiseurs may be real enough but it is impossible to reduce to writing. **'Rucks Globe'**, introduced by J. W. Spingarn of Baldwin, Long Island, New York, originated from an extremely slow-growing mutation found by Wm. Ruck, nurseryman of Merrick, also of Long Island, New York.

– –'**Squarrosa Sulphurea**' [*C. pisifera* '*Sulphurea*' Kent in Veitch, Man. Ed. 2, 225. 1900.] This, as its name indicates, is a variety with sulphur yellow foliage. It forms a dense, conical plant and in spring and early summer is outstanding because of its colour, but this turns to green later in the year and by winter the plant has only its neat outline and soft looking foliage to distinguish it. (Illustration 174). **'Squarrosa Elegans'** was, according to Hornibrook [Dw. Con. Ed. 2,

71. 1938] a compact form with light yellow foliage not burning in the sun. There are certainly more than the single clone in cultivation, but they are difficult to separate.

– –'**Strathmore**' Harrison [Orn. Con. 66. 1975.] NANA GROUP. Harrison does not tell us the origin of this name and does not know the exact origin of the plant he uses it for. Above under 'Aurea Nana', I make a shrewd guess of its identity but suggest that since this cannot be proved—if it ever could be done, would only perpetuate an undesirable name—that this name be accepted for this unfortunate but attractive cultivar, which slowly forms a wide-spreading or roundish bush having foliage of a rich, golden-yellow colour at its best in the depth of winter, but otherwise typical of *C. pisifera.*

Chamaecyparis thyoides (L) Britton et al. This is a tree-like species from North America which has given us several attractive dwarf forms. In the type, the twigs are slender and bear triangular, sharply pointed leaves. The side twigs alternate, forming short, erect, fan-shaped sprays which are held irregularly, i.e., not in flat sprays as in the other species in this genus. Most of the leaves are marked on the back with a resinous gland. In nature it frequently is found growing in marshy ground or swamps, so the dwarf forms will presumably feel at home in such conditions.

– –'**Andelyensis**' [*C. sphaeroidea andelyensis* Carr. Traité. Ed. 2, 123. 1867; f. *andelyensis* (Carr.) Rehd. Bibl. 51. 1949 (and syn. in part); *Retinospora leptoclada* Veitch, Man. 244. 1881 and *C. thyoides leptoclada* (Nom.) op. cit. 238 and (as var.) Kent in Veitch, Man. Ed. 2, 232. 1900; *Retinospora leptoclada* Mast. Journ. Linn. Soc. **31.** 352. 1896.] This well known variety is not, strictly speaking, a dwarf but it is so very slow-growing that it can be used without much immediate concern regarding its ultimate height, which can be several metres. (Illustration 175).

It slowly forms a tall, pointed column with upright branches bearing mainly adult foliage and coning freely. It was much planted years ago but now that we have other columnar forms available it is less in demand, which is rather a pity. Veitch in his first edition gives an account of this cultivar and its origin as a seedling in a Nursery at Andelys in France, its introduction at an exhibition in Paris and subsequent purchase by an English nurseryman. It is such an excellent account that it leaves Veitch with no excuse for adopting the purchaser's change to *leptoclada,* a name already in use for a form of *Chamaecyparis pisifera* (see above), and thereby introducing confusion into the nomenclature of both species.

– –'**Andelyensis Nana**' [*C. thyoides* var. *andelyensis nana* Hornb. Dw. Con. Ed. 2, 78. 1938.] This form is identical with 'Andelyensis' in all respects except habit. It forms at first an upright rounded bush which tends to increase laterally more than in height with age. It is doubtless a cultivariant, produced from deliberate selection of weak-growing lateral growth for cuttings. It is therefore apt to throw up the strong vertical growth characteristic of 'Andelyensis' and this should be at once cut out if the dwarf characteristic is to survive. (Illustration 176).

– –'**Conica**' [*C. thyoides* 'Conica' Den Ouden, Conif. 131. 1949] I do not know, but as it is described as a sport from 'Andelyensis' (and unstable at that) its right to recognition as a separate cultivar name must rest on minor characteristics such as foliage (juvenile), habit (conical) and slowness of growth.

– –'**Ericoides**' [*Retinospora ericoides* (Zucc) Gord. Pin. 294. 1858; *Chamaecyparis ericoides* Carr. Traité, 140. 1855; *C. thyoides ericoides* Sudw. U.S. Dept. Agric. For. Serv. Bull. **14**: 79. 1897.] This is another early introduction from Japan and recorded as grown there under the name of Nazu (= dwarf.) It is a fixed juvenile form, so its reputed appearance in a French seed bed in 1940 as recorded by Den Ouden and Boom [Man. 120. 1965] may be equally true, and this may account for the recognised variability of 'Ericoides' in the trade. It forms a regular, very close-growing, compact, pyramidal bush, eventually to about 1.5 m high. The colour is a dark grey-green in summer, turning to deep purplish or violet-brown in winter. (Illustration 177). It forms an attractive bush but is apt to be damaged by cold winds and dislikes dry conditions. One occasionally comes across this plant labelled *"chamaecyparis pisifera ericoides"* or even *"thuja orientalis ericoides"*, but this sort of mistake should not be necessary. '**Ericoides Glauca**' [*C. thyoides* var. *ericoides glauca* Fitsch. in Beissn. Handb. Ed. 3, 527. 1930] was doubtless descriptively named, but I have not been able to trace it.

– –'**Heatherbun**' [New cv.] I have received from several sources a very diminutive and slow-growing form with wholly juvenile foliage similar to that of 'Ericoides' but smaller in all its parts. The growth is consequently very tight and dense and it forms a round-topped little bush quite unlike the conical habit of 'Ericoides'. It changes colour like 'Ericoides', from which it may have originated as a bud sport, but it seems to be quite stable and reliable in cultivation. It is a most desirable form with the same rich, plum-purple winter colour.

– –'**Nana**' [*C. thyoides* var. *nana* Loud. Encyc. Trees 1075. 1842; var. *nana* Hornb. Dw. Con. Ed. 2, 80. 1938.] This name has long been in use, but for what plant is impossible to say. Hornibrook tells us it was a densely branched blue-green dwarf form making a small round almost spherical bush. In this, only the shape distinguishes 'Nana' from 'Andelyensis Nana' described above. Had the description made any reference to juvenile foliage it could reasonably have been identified with 'Heatherbun' (above), but since it does not we can perhaps best leave 'Nana' as Hornibrook left it—'Lost to cultivation'.

– –'**Pygmaea**' [*C. Sphaeroidea pygmaea* Carr. Traité. Ed. 2, 124. 1867; *C. thyoidea* var. *pygmaea* Hornb. in Rep. Conif. Conf. 80. 1932 and Dw. Con. Ed. 2, 80. 1938] is a very tiny form, probably from seed, since the foliage and growth suggests much more what is normal to the species (but on a much reduced scale) than it does a mutation from 'Andelyensis'. It forms a flat, cushion-shaped bush with numerous short, spreading branches and blue-green foliage. It is a most desirable little plant.

CRYPTOMERIA

Cryptomeria japonica (L. fil.) D. Don is the solitary occupant of this genus. In nature it is a very tall tree but it is extremely variable from seed and has given us some of our best dwarf conifers (although many forms grown as dwarfs are no such thing, as time will reveal). These vary considerably and an assorted group of Cryptomeria cultivars can be so diverse as to give rise to considerable surprise that they are all variants of a single species.

They are (with the exception of the white-tipped forms) quite hardy, but most forms turn colour in the winter, the colour varying from a slight bronzing to a rich, reddish-bronze or purple. In some cases the winter colouring provides a valuable means of distinguishing between varieties.

A number of forms in Japanese cultivation were sent to Europe during the nineteenth century. These were accorded the usual nomenclatural treatment of the times, being given (for the most part) Latin-form names and inadequate descriptions by European writers. They are presumably still with us today, presenting us with the usual problem of which name goes with which plant.

Although their popularity has fluctuated somewhat in that country, garden cultivation in Japan has also continued. Japanese nurserymen are as prone, it seems, to give names lightheartedly to their treasures as are nurserymen anywhere else, and Japanese writers as capable of writing about cultivars with insufficient acquaintance with the plants themselves as their counterparts the world over. So the nomenclatural legacy they have in Japan seems roughly the same as ours. There is also an additional question 'Which Japanese form is the same as which European one?' To this additional problem, time, distance, language and even alphabet all contribute. I have made contact with sources of information which I hoped would bridge the gap and have been corresponding both with Japanese nationals and Europeans resident in the country, but we have more or less reached the mutual conclusion that the interchange of growing material is the only ultimate solution. This is being arranged, but it is quite a long term project. In the meantime I have sorted out the European forms as well as I can. I also include such data as I have on the Japanese cultivars. This represents some progress; the two streams have been brought together into a single channel; but they are still two streams, so the treatment here must be regarded as tentative. It must be just as difficult in Japan to decide for instance, whether 'Enkō-sugi' is the same as our 'Araucarioides' as it is for us to decide whether 'Araucarioides' (when we have made up our minds which plant we mean) is their 'Enkō-sugi'. I hope this attempt will stimulate interest, both in the East and in the West, and I shall be pleased to hear from anyone able to correct or add to my information.

Japan it seems, has yet to produce her own Beissner or Hornibrook. The Floras available treat inadequately of *varietates* and do not deal with cultivars at all. Left thus without a guide, horticultural names in use have varied down the years. Old names have given way to new, names have been switched, usage today is frequently regional. So the vernacular equivalents quoted in some of the older European books are often worse than useless.

For these reasons the following table is only put forward as a basis for further study of this bilingual problem.

Japanese	European	Remarks
Birodō-sugi	Compressa	= Velvet Cloth
Chabo-sugi	f. *nana* Carr.	Chabo = Very dwarf
Eizan-sugi	f. *uncinata* S & Z	A mountain near Kyoto
Enkō-sugi	f. *araucarioides*	= Monkey throat
Ito-sugi	Dacrydioides	
Kusari-sugi	Spiraliter Falcata	
Mankichi-sugi	Monstrosa	
Mankitiana-sugi	Monstrosa	
Ōgon-sugi	Aurea	= Yellow
Okina-sugi	Nana Albo-spica	= Old man
Ōsaka-tama-sugi	Vilmoriniana	Tama = A ball
Sekka- or Sekkwa-sugi	Cristata	= Fasciated
Yawara-sugi	f. *elegans*	= Soft
Yore-sugi	Spiralis	= Spiral
Yatsubusa-sugi	Elegans Nana	

– – f. **araucarioides** (Henk u. Hochst.) Beissn. [Rehd. Bibl. 43. 1949 *.] *All those forms characterised by rope-like or snake-like foliage, the result of strong main shoots and a paucity or irregular incidence of lateral shoots.* Horticulturally, these constitute the

ARAUCARIOIDES GROUP

'Araucarioides'   'Ito-sugi'
'Athrotaxoides'   'Kewensis'
'Dacrydioides'   'Lycopodioides'
'Enkō-sugi'   'Selaginoides'
'Hōō-sugi'

In my previous book I have referred to the uncertainty in the nomenclature of the various forms with snake-like foliage. Since these variants turn up in the seed beds from time to time it is certain that we have more clones in cultivation than there are names in the literature. In this difficult group I have had the help of Professor Dr. H. Kruse of Jochi-daikoku (Sophia University), Tokyo, who has supplied me with descriptions of the Japanese cultivars. Although slow-growing at first they all become large shrubs or trees in time.

– –'**Araucarioides**' [*C. japonica araucarioides* Sieb. Nurs. Cat. 5. 1861; Sén. Conif. 61. 1868.] A cultivar introduced from Japan by Dr. von Siebold into the Netherlands in 1859. It was described by Sénéclause as 'An outstanding, ornamental tree, with bright or dark green leaves, the colour persisting throughout the winter'. This description would cover most of or all the tree-like forms now in cultivation in Britain having a well defined central leader. (Illustration 178).

– –'**Athrotaxoides**' [*C. japonica athrotaxoides* Sén. Conif. 62. 1868.] ARAUCARIOIDES GROUP. A form that was found in a seed bed in France, now probably lost to cultivation, unless the plant in the Botanical Garden at Copenhagen [Krüssm. Handb. taf. 44 (top right) 1972] is this cultivar.

– –'**Bandai-sugi**' [*C. japonica* var. *Bandai-sugi* Grootn. ex Hornb. Dw. Con. Ed. 2, 82. 1938; and Hort. Japan.] This is a popular garden variety. It is usually seen as a low globular bush, but with age it can reach to 2 m high. The foliage is very congested and irregular, all the branches being thick and the leaves thick, broad and tapered. The growth is most erratic, some of the branchlets being of fairly strong growth with stiff straight foliage pointing forward at an angle of 30°, very slightly incurved; other shoots being very short with short, closely set leaves, some not more than 3 mm long. The colour is green, turning a dull bronze in winter. (Illustration 179).

– –'**Compressa**' [*C. japonica compressa* Den Ouden, Conif. 134. 1949; probably 'Birodō-sugi' Hort. Japan.] This is one of two pygmy globular forms very popular in gardens, the other form being 'Vilmoriniana' (described below). They both have short, densely set, neat, juvenile foliage and both form dense, globular bushes. They are of about equal garden value and are often confused with each other, but they differ in that the leading shoots in 'Compressa' never project above the general surface of the bush as they do in the case of 'Vilmoriniana' (giving that variety a somewhat less neat and tidy appearance); in that the leaves in 'Compressa' are slightly more decurved than they are in 'Vilmoriniana' (giving the shoot a more rosette-like appearance looked at from the end), and in that 'Compressa' colours to a rich red-bronze in the winter compared to the much less pronounced colouring of 'Vilmoriniana'. Finally, the foliage on the interior of the bush is blue-green in the case of 'Compressa' and yellow-green in 'Vilmoriniana'.

– –'**Cristata**' [*C. japonica cristata* Beissn. Mitt. d.d.d.G. **10**: 79. 1901; 'Sekka-sugi' Hort. Japan.] There are several forms in cultivation characterised by abnormality in parts of the foliage. The form commonly grown under this name forms a fairly tall, upright bush or low tree to 3 m high with some of its foliage quite normal but developing monstrous foliage here and there. (Illustration 180). The cristations occasionally are as large as a man's hand on young plants, but become much smaller in maturity. The plant mentioned by Hornibrook as growing at Kilmacurragh, Rathdrum, County Wicklow, is of quite a different type and is now called '**Kilmacurragh**' Welch [Dw. Con. 157. 1966.] In this cultivar the foliage is juvenile and the whole bush is covered with fasciated shoots. The original plant is still at Kilmacurragh (having now reached the height of 6 m) to serve as our type plant and there are specimens in the National Botanic Garden at Glasnevin, Dublin, the Royal Botanic Garden, Edinburgh, and in the Pygmy Pinetum at Devizes. (Illustration 181).

– –'**Dacrydioides**' [*C. japonica dacrydioides* Carr. Traité. Ed. 2, 193. 1867.] ARAUCAR-

IOIDES GROUP. This form was rather briefly described as 'having long branches set well apart, very slender, rather pendulous'. A distinctive feature recorded was that the leaves, shorter and more slender than normal and irregular in size and spacing along the shoot were of a rusty brown as are some of the Dacrydiums from New Zealand. This description of distinctive colouration (although the time of the year it was recorded was not stated) is repeated by several later writers, but Krüssmann [Nadel. Ed. 2, 112. 1960] adds 'Never with a single trunk'. He also gives a good illustration of an old plant in a park at East Mosca in Biella, Piedmont, Italy—a spreading bush about 1 m high by about 2 m across.

– – f. **elegans** (Jakob-Makoy) Beissn. [Rehd. Bibl. 43. 1949 *] is merely a form in a fixed juvenile state which probably originated in China, although it could turn up in a seed bed anywhere. It is not dwarf, but **'Elegans Compacta'** Welch [Dw. Con. 157. 1966; *C. japonica elegans nana* Veitch, Man. 218. 1881; var. *elegans nana* Bean, Trees. 440. 1914; Dall. & Jacks. Handb. 183. 1923; Hornb. Dw. Con. Ed. 2, 87. 1938; 'Elegans Nana' Den Ouden and Boom, Man. 125. 1965] is probably a bud mutation, since it retains the soft, curved, tapered leaves and the mauve winter colour of 'Elegans' but does not become more than a large bush. It should not be confused with the following cultivar. (Illustration 182).

– –**'Elegans Nana'** Hort. [*C. japonica* 'Lobbii Nana' Welch, Dw. Con. Ed. 2, 159. 1966; *C. japonica* var. *pygmaea* Hornb. Dw. Con. Ed. 2, 84. 1938; NON var. *Lobbii Nana* Dall. & Jacks. Handb. 183. 1923; 'Yatsubusa-hiba' Hort. Japan.] This is the form for which in my earlier book I hesitantly accepted the name 'Lobbii Nana' under which I found it at Kew. It has juvenile foliage which is shorter than in 'Elegans Compacta' and the leaves are straight and stiff looking. The growth is dense and in winter every leading shoot carries a crowded cluster of male flowers. (Illustration 183).

The choice between this epithet and 'Elegans Compacta' is difficult. Both first appear with descriptions inconclusive as to what cultivar was in the writers' minds. The first appearance of both names together [Dall. & Jacks. Handb. Ed. 3, 255. 1948] tells us of var. *elegans compacta* 'Habit very dwarf and compact with the juvenile type of leaves' and of var. *elegans nana* 'A dwarf plant of dense habit with crowded leaves of the juvenile type.' Faced with this sort of thing the choice must to some extent be arbitrary. The choice of 'Elegans Compacta' for the form with soft, curly foliage, and 'Elegans Nana' for the form with stiff, straight leaves and abundant male flowers best preserves existing usage in Britain and in continental Europe.

– –**'Enkō-sugi'** [*C. japonica* 'Araucarioides' God. ex Krüssm. Handb. 104. 1972; 'Viminalis' Hillier, Man. 477. 1971.] ARAUCARIOIDES GROUP. This is a slow-growing, irregular shrub (2–4 m) without a distinct central leader, having long, stiff, coarse, whip-like main branches that at intervals along their length produce clusters of short, side branches. Needles differ in length according to the season of growth (forming branches of varying thickness) being usually long, thick, stiff, curved towards the branch and dark green. Old specimens may develop dense and constant tufts at the ends of the branches, with branchlets of nearly equal length; but young plants have few tufts and less branchlets.

– –**'Fasciata'** [*C. japonica* var. *fasciata* Dall. & Jacks. Handb. Ed. 3, 255. 1948.] This is a collector's piece, more a curiosity than a thing of beauty, usually a low stunted bush with some healthy looking foliage but with the old wood studded with a curious, moss-like, leafy excrescence (one can hardly call it growth) which gives the bush an unhealthy appearance.

– –'Globosa Nana' [*C. japonica* var. *globosa nana* Hornb. Dw. Con. 58. 1923; 'Lobbii Nana' Hillier, Man. 477. 1971] is an attractive dwarf form which bears normal foliage but the trunk is entirely missing and it consequently forms a globose bush. It is densely set with branches and the branchlets are pendulous. It is rather slow in getting going as a small plant, but eventually forms a bush 1-2 m high by as much or more across, and it would form an attractive lawn specimen. (Illustration 184). Hornibrook's choice of this name was rather unfortunate for it has left the way open for the name **'Globosa'** [*C. japonica globosa* Lombart Nurs. Cat. 19. 1942/43; Den Ouden, Conif. 135. 1949] to be since used for a different cultivar. I have not seen large plants of 'Globosa' but it would appear that it is going to form a smaller plant than 'Globosa Nana'. The plants I have seen are low-growing, much wider than they are high. The juvenile foliage has straight, stiff pointed leaves, shorter than in 'Yatsubusa-hiba' (which the plant somewhat resembles, except that it is without any trace of monstrosity), but the outstanding feature of 'Globosa' to my mind is the awful colour that it turns in the winter. This is a most unattractive bright red, the colour of a rusty tramp steamer.

– –'Hōō-sugi' [Hort. Japan.] Araucarioides Group. A slow-growing small (2-3 m) tree, similar to 'Ito-sugi' but differing in the following features: branches snake-like, swung elegantly in different directions, needles very short, sometimes of scale-form, of nearly equal length, giving the impression of a thin braided rope, dark green. The name means 'Phoenix-Cryptomeria'; it is used for various forms, this being the form cultivated around Tokyo.

– –'Ito-sugi' Krüssm. [Handb. 106. 1972.] Araucarioides Group. A form selected by Prof. G. Isa of Kyoto University, and therefore more exactly called 'Kyoto-ito-sugi', to distinguish it from other gardeners' forms: ('Ito' means 'thread'). It forms a small (2-3 m) tree of pyramid form, with a single trunk as central leader, branches regular but scarce and thin, more crowded near the top in older plants, with branchlets crowded at the tips of the branch, tips swung straight upwards, needles short, of nearly equal length (but of variable length on old plants), light (grass) green.

– –'Jindai-sugi' [*C. japonica* var. *Jindai-sugi* Hornb. Dw. Con. Ed. 2, 83. 1938.] This popular variety forms a compact, conical bush with erect and spreading branches. The foliage is very regular and dense, with short, stiff, straight leaves pointing forward at a narrow angle. The colour is a nice soft green which is retained all the year. What a pity a few more of these forms were not imported from Japan under their vernacular names! (Illustration 185).

– –'Kewensis' [*C. japonica* var. *kewensis* Hornb. Dw. Con. Ed. 2, 85. 1938.] Araucarioides Group. This was a name used by Hornibrook for a plant then at Kew that I cannot now trace. It does not appear to have been propagated so the name may be disregarded.

– –'Knaptonensis' [*C. japonica* var. *knaptonensis* Lyttel, My Garden **7**: 360. 1934;

Hornb. Dw. Con. Ed. 2, 83. 1938.] Hornibrook tells us that this originated as a witch's broom on a plant of 'Nana Albospica' (described below) and, as one would therefore expect, when true to type it consists of a congested mass of irregular shoots. These are a glistening white, but it shows a tendency to revert to the looser, dirty creamy-white of the mother variety. It is an extremely attractive plant when well grown, but as it dislikes wind and frost it is really a plant for the cold greenhouse. (Illustration 186).

– –'**Lobbii Nana**' [*C. japonica* var. *lobbii nana* Dall. & Jacks. Handb. 183. 1923 and Ed. 3, 255. 1948; NON var. pygmaea Hornb. Dw. Con. Ed. 2, 84. 1938; NEC var. *Lobbii Nana* Hort. Kew, l.c., (pro syn.); NON Welch, Dw. Con. 159. 1966; NON Hillier, Man. 477. 1971.] This plant is a mystery. Dallimore & Jackson first describe it as 'Of dwarf habit'. When preparing for their second edition, Dallimore (or it may have been Jackson, or they could have been egging each other on) let himself really go and came up with 'Of dwarf habit with green leaves'. Since then no one has seen or heard of any such plant and even Hornibrook seems to have funked the problem for he does not mention it. In my first edition I used the name with much hesitation for a form thus labelled growing in the alpine garden at Kew. I now identify this plant as 'Elegans Nana'. The cultivar listed as 'Lobbii Nana' in Hillier's Manual is 'Globosa Nana' and so I consider 'Lobbii Nana' should be treated as lost to cultivation.

– –'**Lycopodioides**' [*C. japonica* var. *lycopodioides* Carr. Rev. Hort. 226. 1885; Beissn. Handb. 147. 1891.] ARAUCARIOIDES GROUP. This form was described as a very irregular shrub with its main stems almost devoid of branches or very irregularly branched; branches sometimes upwards of a metre long and uniform in diameter like a length of rope. Here and there, the branches are thinner and bear shorter leaves, giving a peculiar appearance to the shoot. Carrière tells us it is a dwarf plant imported direct from Japan. Beissner says that *C. japonica lycopodiformis* Hort. (Changed to *lycopodioides* Ed. 2, 483, 1909) is 'a monstrous, dwarf form, in growth resembling Lycopodium', so his plant cannot be distinguished from Carrière's.

– –'**Monstrosa**' [*C. japonica monstrosa* Beissn. Handb. Ed. 2, 482. 1909; var. *monstrosa* Hornb. Rep. Conif. Conf. 73. 1932.] This is hardly a dwarf form since it forms an upright, columnar or rounded bush to 2 m or more high. (Illustration 187).

Although the plant Beissner took his description from was columnar there seems no doubt that he was describing the form widely grown under this name today, but it usually forms a round-topped tree. Beissner accurately describes the coarse, irregular growth with partly coarse branches with long stiff pointed leaves and partly short branchlets crowded with similarly short leaves. It could very well be described as an exceedingly coarse, outsize version of 'Bandai-sugi'.

– –'**Monstrosa Nana**' [*C. japonica* var. *monstrosa nana* Hornb. Dw. Con. Ed. 2, 83. 1938.] This unfortunate plant, if it exists, has had much difficulty to establish an identity. The specimen described by Hornibrook is no longer to be found and his brief description does not altogether exclude the form I now identify as 'Elegans Nana' so the name 'Monstrosa Nana', amongst others, has been widely used for that other unfortunate plant. Specimens of 'Monstrosa Nana' that I have come across have all had the peculiar growth habit that is characteristic of both 'Bandai-sugi' and 'Monstrosa' but have been of a scale and vigour intermediate between those two forms. This agrees with Hornibrook's description. Growth characteristics and vigour can vary so greatly with the age of a plant and rootstock vigour that the existence of three clones different in scale but so alike otherwise needs some further verification, but in the meantime I suggest the use of the cultivar name 'Monstrosa Nana' be limited accordingly.

– –'**Nana**' [*C. japonica nana* Hort. ex Knight, Syn. Conif. 22. 1850; f. *nana* (Carr.) Beissn. in Rehd. Bibl. 43. 1949 *.] The epithets *nana* and *pygmaea* appear within months of each other in the middle of the nineteenth century, either without descriptions or with descriptions so brief that all we can now say with any assurance at all was that the writers were giving names to cultivars the identity of which is now lost.

Since nomenclature is to be our servant, not our master, and as we have two cultivars in cultivation very similar but distinguishable, I have conveniently assumed that those early writers, the cunning old rascals, knew all the time that there were the two plants to need the two names, and in the absence of any indication in the descriptions as to which was meant by which, I use 'Nana' for the form that is much the commoner of the two today. 'Nana' therefore is a dwarf, congested, slow-growing form to about 2 m high. The main branches are very thin and erect, the branchlets are horizontal with the tips pendulous. The leaves vary in length. On main branches they are up to 15 mm long, at first appressed to the stem but the free part curving quickly out to an angle of 50°, but elsewhere they are short to very short, accentuating the thinness of the branches. (Illustration 188).

This variety remains green in winter, or at most turns a dull metallic green, but an otherwise barely distinguishable and uncommon variety, '**Pygmaea**' [*C. japonica pygmaea* Baxter in Loud. Hort. Suppl. 592. 1850; NON var. *pygmaea* Hornb. Dw. Con. Ed. 2, 84. 1938] turns a rich reddish-bronze.

– –'**Nana Albospica**' [*C. japonica nana albo-spicata* Beissn. Handb. Ed. 2, 483. 1901; *argenteo variegata* Sén. Conif. 62. 1868; *alba variegata* Young in Gord. Pin. Ed. 2, Nurs. Cat. 9. 1875.] The white-tipped group, if that is what they are, are difficult. What plants Sénéclause or Maurice Young wrote of cannot now be determined; it is a reasonable presumption they and Beissner's dwarf form and the plant at Isola Madre on Lake Pallanza were one and the same. Since Hornibrook's objection to regarding 'Nana albo-spica' as a variegated form of 'Nana' was based on a misconception of that form as we know it today, Den Ouden and Boom's acceptance [Man. 127. 1965] of this name as best preserving present usage is fully endorsed by me. 'Nana albo-spica', therefore, can fairly be described as a white variegated form of 'Nana' in which the whole of the young growth is a creamy-white which gets duller with age, eventually becoming a pale green.

This cultivar is somewhat hardier than 'Knaptonensis' derived from it and will normally stand outside during a winter, the older foliage turning a pink-bronze.

– –'**Selaginoides**' [*C. japonica* var. *selaginoides* Bailey, Cult. Conif. 143. 1933.]

ARAUCARIOIDES GROUP. Bailey gives a description which does not distinguish it from 'Viminalis', of which cultivar it may be a synonym.

- –'Spiralis' [*C. japonica* var. *spiralis* Sieb. and Zucc. Fl. Japan **2**: 52. 1870; 'Yoresugi' Hort. Japan; 'Granny's ringlets' Hort.] There are two quite different forms with the foliage twisted spirally round the branches. The present form is known in specimens of tree-like dimensions, but the garden variety (which may have been derived from the larger tree as a cultivariant) is normally seen as a low, congested little bush, unmistakable on account of the thick, incurved, and twisted foliage. This peculiarity varies with the season, being most noticeable in winter. (Illustration 189).

- –'Spiraliter Falcata' [*C. japonica spiraliter falcata* Carr. Rev. Hort. **1876**: 340. 1876; 'Kusari-sugi' Hort. Japan; *Spiralis elongata* Hort.] This variety forms a much taller, upright bush and carries longer and thinner branches than in 'Spiralis' and they all tend to twist and curve. It bears much thinner, narrower leaves, rather irregular in size. These two spiral forms are quite distinct, even as small plants. (Illustration 190).

- –'Vilmoriniana' [*C. japonica* var. *Vilmoriniana* Hornb. The Garden, **87**: 37. 1924 and Dw. Con. Ed. 2, 88. 1938.] This is one of the most popular dwarf conifers. It forms a compact, roughly globular bush never seen more than 1 m high by as much through with very neat foliage and closely recurved leaves. The differences between this cultivar and 'Compressa', the only one likely to be confused with it, are given under that variety. (Illustration 191).

- –'Viminalis' [*C. japonica* var. *viminalis* Hornb. Dw. Con. 56. 1923; var. *selaginoides* (Rovelli) Dall. & Jacks. Handb. Ed. 3, 255. 1948.] ARAUCARIOIDES GROUP. Hornibrook states that the name was in use in Italian horticulture at the end of the 19th century. I have been unable to establish that it was at that time validly published but the historical fact clearly adds authority to Hornibrook's description which tells us that 'it makes a low, rather loose shrub sending out long, slender, snake-like branches with few or no side branchlets. The branches grow on yearly from the terminal bud and retain their foliage. The occasional side branches are usually also single and short, but at times they are crowned with a whorl of smaller branchlets'. Apart from a curious reference to 'tufting' in Carrière's second description of 'Lycopodioides' which is so at conflict with the rest of his two descriptions that we must, I feel, regard it as a mistake, this is the only reference to the formation of 'whorls' on secondary branches, but this is so characteristic of many plants in European cultivation that it must serve to distinguish this form from all others. It cannot be regarded as a dwarf form, since plants of tree-size are to be found shewing this feature. (Illustration 192).

CUNNINGHAMIA

Cunninghamia lanceolata 'Compacta' Barabits [Deutsche Baumsch. **5**: 139. 1966.] This interesting dwarf form is, so far as I know, the only recorded dwarf form of a genus which itself is uncommon in our gardens. It was selected in 1955 as a seedling by Istvan Bano, the manager of the Forestry Experimental Station at

Kamon, in Hungary. It has the normal juvenile foliage of the species except that it is smaller in all its parts and has a reduced rate of growth. It is an exceptionally healthy, winter hardy form, easy to propagate vegetatively and it is of a neat, globose shape. It has made a notable addition to the range of dwarf conifers available to our gardens. (Illustration 193).

CUPRESSUS

The true cypresses form a genus of a dozen species, only two or three of which can be regarded as hardy in the British Isles. At one time the genus included all the species now known as Chamaecyparis, and many nurserymen still use the name Cupressus in the wider sense. In this they are perhaps less influenced by conservatism and reluctance to change than by a conviction that the old name is better known by the public and so is a better commercial proposition than the new name, which so many customers regard as an irritating tongue-twister.

Cupressus glabra Sudw. is now distinguished from *C. arizonica* Greene, under which name it had been grown for many years. It is normally a tall, pyramidal tree with glaucous grey foliage, but it has given us one good dwarf form.

– –'**Compacta**' [*C. arizonica* f. *compacta* (Schneid.) Rehd. Bibl. 50. 1949 *.] This cultivar forms a dense, conical or ovoid bush, very slow-growing, with typical foliage of an attractive grey-green. (Illustration 194). In the true plant the foliage is very congested, but in **'Crowborough'** [New cv.] it is somewhat less dense, so this makes a larger plant, to 2 m.

Cupressus goveniana var. *pygmaea*. See *C. pygmaea*.

Cupressus lambertiana Hort. Austral. See *C. macrocarpa*.

Cupressus macrocarpa Hartweg., well known as the fast-growing 'Cypress' (at one time so popular for hedges and shelter planting but now being rapidly ousted by the bi-generic hybrid *Cupressocyparis leylandii*) has given rise to a number of seedling variants, particularly golden forms, which only need brief mention here as they all grow too large in time to be classed as dwarf. Many of these have originated in Australia or New Zealand where they are very popular. Mr. Davies of the nursery firm of Duncan & Davies once told me that in that country they never grow 'Macrocarpa' in pots, a practice he thinks may largely contribute to their reputation for unreliability in this country.

There is also a small group of very diminutive forms. These are not garden plants at all. In some cases they are not hardy out of doors in a hard winter, but they are sought after by collectors and are usually a point of interest to visitors, partly I think because most of them know the species well in its usual, arboreal form and are so surprised to see such a tiny representative thereof a few centimetres high growing in a pot, in such striking contrast to all the other *Cupressus macrocarpa* trees they know.

R. S. Corley of High Wycombe, who has studied these forms very closely, has kindly allowed me to give extracts from his article in *Gardeners' Chronicle* of 5 May 1962 (see below).

– –'**Coneybearii Aurea**' Hazlewood [Hazlewood Bros., Epping, N. S. W. Nurs. Cat. 1933.] This is an Australian form of unrecorded origin which eventually forms a flat-topped tree with rich, golden-yellow foliage in thin pendulous branches. It is too big to classify as a dwarf, but young plants are very dense and bushy for some years and attractive on account of their colour. See 'Saligna Aurea' below.

– –'**Globe**' Den Ouden and Boom 1965 [*C. macrocarpa* 'Globosa' Hillier, Dw. Con. 32. 1964; var. *compacta* Hornb. Dw. Con. 59. 1923 (Nom. illegit.)] is a dwarf, globose bush with a dense habit and scale-like leaves. Its normal growth is compact, but if any loose shoots appear they should be cut out. At the time Hornibrook suggested a name it had not been propagated so was not, technically, a cultivar.

– –'**Golden Pillar**' [New cv.] Of all the recently introduced seedlings this has probably the best claim for inclusion here. It is an extremely fastigiate small tree with bright golden-yellow foliage and at first it forms a columnar plant which is a valuable combination. It originated as a seedling in a Dutch nursery and was introduced by Geo. Jackman & Sons Nursery, Woking in Surrey, in 1955. (Illustration 195).

– –'**Gold Spread**' [New cv.] I have received this plant from R. Barry of South Taranaki Nurseries, Hawera, in New Zealand. He described it as a wide-spreading but truly horizontal golden form, very slow-growing and dense. The original plant is 75 cm high by nearly 5 m across at 15 years of age. The origin of this form is obscure. Barry received it from Australia as 'Horizontalis Aurea' but both 'Horizontalis' [Harrison, Trees for South Hemisph. 117. 1959; *C. lambertiana horizontalis* Hort. Austral.; *C. macrocarpa lambertiana* Hort. Austral.] and the golden form 'Horizontalis Aurea' [*C. lambertiana horizontalis aurea* Hort. Austral.; *C. macrocarpa* 'Lambertiana Aurea' Lord, Trees for Austral. Gar. 1948] are trees of upright habit and noticeably horizontal main branches. It may have arisen, like 'Greenstead Magnificent' (see below) as a mutation, or perhaps it is the result of propagations that have retained the horizontal habit; i.e., it is a cultivariant. It seems a very promising plant.

– –'**Greenstead Magnificent**' New name [*C. macrocarpa* 'Greenstead Magnifica' Hall, Seed and Nursery Trader, Jan. 1970.] This interesting variant occurred as a bud mutation 8 metres up on a 40 year old specimen of 'Horizontalis' growing near a vineyard at Hope Valley, South Australia. After 8 years, propagations have formed plants 1 m wide by 30 cm high, so it would seem to be reliably dwarf. It forms a dense, low-growing plant, almost prostrate in habit, with blue-grey foliage pendulous at the tips, the blue colour being more intense when growing in shade. It was introduced to the trade by Mr. Roger Hall of C. F. Newman & Sons, Tea Tree Gully, South Australia, who first described it in an Australian trade journal and in *Australian Home Gardener* May 1970.

– –'**Minima**' [*C. macrocarpa minima* Corley, Gar. Chron. **151, 18**: 326. 1962; 'Minimax' Den Ouden and Boom, Man. 141. 1965; 'Nisbets Gem' Welch. Dw. Con.

165. 1966.] We now come to the group of seedlings that have given us extremely dwarf forms, the others being 'Pygmaea' and 'Woking'. 'Minima' is the hardiest of the group. (Illustration 196). It was raised many years ago by R. Menzies at the Golden Gate Park, San Francisco, California, U.S.A., and was sent by the late James Noble to A. H. Nisbet who had made a notable collection at Gosport in England. It forms at first a low, rounded bush with neat, congested and mainly juvenile foliage and as it is much easier to propagate than the other forms it will always be in easier supply. Following Mr. Nisbet's death in 1967 I purchased his collection and many of his plants including this one are now in the Pygmy Pinetum at Devizes, where it is being propagated. It makes a picturesque little tree, but any coarse growth must at once be removed. In view of the date of its introduction I now consider the name under which it has circulated for so long must be acceptable, so the fancy names suggested by Dr. Boom and myself must be regarded as superfluous.

– –'Pygmaea' [*C. macrocarpa* f. *pygmaea* A. B. Jackson, Gar. Chron. **151, 15**: 267. 1938; var. *pygmaea* Hornb. Dw. Con. Ed. 2, 90. 1938.] This is the only form referred to by Hornibrook in his second edition. He tells us that the mother plant was raised from seed in 1929 by a Mr. Marcham of Carshalton Nursery and passed into the possession of W. Bentley, of Quarry Wood, Burghclere, Hampshire. It subsequently became part of the collection of the late G. L. Pilkington of Grayswood Hill, Haslemere, Surrey. Mr. Pilkington grew it in the open ground for several years, but disaster overtook it during the drought of 1960. It was then a spreading little tree about 45 cm high and about the same in width, although over thirty years of age. Fortunately it had been propagated and is available in the trade, but is still very rare in cultivation.

It was originally described as having foliage of two kinds, the lower leaves decussate and broadly awl-shaped about 1 mm long and the upper leaves towards the growing tips of the shoots scale-like, appressed, glandular below. Mr. Corley describes the plant at thirty years as having rich green foliage, almost entirely adult, with only a vestige of the juvenile foliage remaining on some lower branchlets. The habit of Mr. Pilkington's plant was decidedly irregular and most remarkable for its extreme density of foliage, with tightly packed cockscomb-like formations in bosses. Mr. Corley's plant, at twenty-four years of age, is showing signs of developing the same cockscomb-like growths. (Illustration 197).

– –'Saligna Aurea' [*C. macrocarpa aurea saligna* Hodgins, Victoria, South Austral. Nurs. Cat. 1948; Lord. Trees for Austral Gar. 1948; 'Saligna Aurea' Hort. Austral. (in part).] I have received a plant under this name from R. Barry of South Taranaki Nurseries, Hawera, N. Z. He tells me it never develops a trunk unless a leader is trained and strongly staked. A 3–4 m specimen with a dense thatch of nearly vertical weeping cords is very impressive.

I prefer the epithets to follow in the normal order, but D. F. Francis of the Botanic Gardens, Adelaide, South Australia, writes that this form appears from descriptions to be identical with the earlier-named 'Coneybearii Aurea', and if this proves correct this name will be superfluous—but it is hardly a dwarf!

– –'Sulphur Tip'. This descriptively named, slow-growing cultivar was found as a seedling and introduced to the trade by Don Hatch of Chantry Nursery, Honiton, Devonshire.

– –'Woking' Corley [Gar. Chron. **151, 18:** 326. 1962.] Mr. Corley gives also the history of this form, the mother plant of which, at Jackman's nursery at Woking, was an irregular dense column about 60 cm high by 1 m across. This plant unfortunately died in 1958 at the approximate age of twenty years. Mr. Corley's specimen is pyramidal and its leaves are entirely juvenile, broadly awl-shaped, bright green, about 1 mm in length, arranged in four ranks, and densely set on the numerous short branchlets, the annual growth of these being about 2 cm. The form seems quite stable in pot cultivation, for which it is suitable, being only marginally hardy in the open ground. (Illustration 198).

Cupressus pygmaea (Lemm.) Sarg. Although for long regarded as a variety of *C. goveniana*, Wolf and Wagener [El Aliso. **1:** 195. 1948] regard this as a distinct species. They say that it forms cone-bearing dwarf trees a meter or so high when growing in sterile soils but that trees in richer soils are not at all dwarfed. Since they add, as a footnote, that similar sized dwarf cone-bearing individuals can be found in stands of most of the other American Cupressus species in extremely sterile soils it would seem that this species has acquired its name under false pretences. Grafted plants in the Pygmy Pinetum show little or no dwarfing tendency; propagation from cuttings and subsequent culture at 'subsistence level' may be more successful. It would be interesting to learn whether seed collected from the dwarf trees transmits the dwarf character.

Cupressus sempervirens L. The Mediterranean Cypress has two recorded dwarf forms, **'Fortuselli'** [*C. fastigiata fortusellii* Carr. Traité. Ed. 2, 149. 1867] and **'Monstrosa'** [*C. fastigiata monstrosa* Carr. l.c.] Although Hornibrook gave a description of each of these they were probably already lost to cultivation when he wrote. I can find no trace of either. The following, although by no means dwarf, is so outstanding that it is worth mentioning here.

– –'Swanes Golden' [Swane Bros. Nurs. Cat. 1961.] This is a bright golden-yellow small tree of compact and very slender growth, worth planting for its outstanding colour and its columnar habit even although it grows too large in time for many garden situations. It arose as a seedling on the nursery of Swane Bros. Pty. Ltd., of Sydney, N. S. W., from seed of *C. sempervirens* 'Stricta' collected in Canberra. Plants in New Zealand are 3 m high and 1 m across, at 15 years.

Cupressus torulosa D. Don. The Himalayan cypress has given rise to but a single recorded dwarf form. **'Nana'** [Gord. Pin. Ed. 2, 100. 1875] was described as 'a very compact form' and seems to have been lost sight of. If it was a starveling such as seems to be the case with all the American cypresses (see above), no doubt one day it found times had changed for the better and began to grow normally.

– –'Gold Spangle' [*C. torulosa Aurea* Hort. Austral.; *C. funebris aurea* Hort. N. Z.] This is another plant I have received from R. Barry of the South Taranaki Nursery, Hawera, N. Z. He describes it as a hardy and very attractive tree, reaching 2 to 3 m, golden-yellow in summer, paling to greenish-yellow in winter, but the foliage is attractive at all seasons, never scorching in summer sun.

DACRYDIUM

Although this genus includes about sixteen species, all from the Southern Hemisphere, relatively few are widely known in Britain and of these only one comes within our range for size.

Dacrydium laxifolium Hook. fil. is a prostrate or sub-erect shrub in nature with slender trailing branches, but in cultivation in this country it is usually seen as a specimen in a pot, although it is quite hardy.

It is interesting as being the smallest known conifer, fruiting specimens no higher than 7–8 cm occurring in the wild, but it has no particular beauty. Even a prize specimen most uninitiated folk would be apt to pass by, thinking it to be some form of heather not in flower. It is a collector's plant in this country. (Illustration 199).

– –'**Blue Gem**' [New cv.] This is a very good blue form that was collected in the wild, and introduced by the Otari Native Plant Museum in Wellington, New Zealand. I understand that it is in some collections under the uneuphonious name 'Homers Tunnel' after the spot near where it was found. I have altered the name ('Blue') under which I received it in compliance with the Code, to identify it unless an acceptable cultivar name has already come into use in its native land.

FITZROYA

The genus Fitzroya contains only a single species, but as this was at one time called *F. patagonica,* confusion sometimes occurs.

Fitzroya cupressoides (Mol.) Johnst. comes from southern Chile, where it forms a large tree, but in this country it seldom grows beyond a large bush or small tree, except in very sheltered situations.

It is interesting on account of its unusual foliage, which consists of small shiny leaves which, cupressus-like, are attached to the shoots save for a pointed triangular tip which is free standing and ending in a sharp, tiny, incurved point. It is, however, unmistakeable for that genus because the leaves are in whorls of three. The branches are usually thickly furnished with short branchlets and in older plants are pendulous. It stands pruning, so can be kept down to size and those in search of the unusual could try it as a hedge plant.

JUNIPERUS

This large genus, comprising upwards of 40 species, is a very useful one. Most of the Junipers are extremely hardy and tough, they stand hot, dry conditions well and varieties can be safely planted on limy soil or where there is a chalk subsoil. They are, however, prone to damage by aphis, scale and certain rusts.

The Junipers are evergreen trees and shrubs, often with thin flaking bark, with finely divided branchlets and two types of leaves, the juvenile or acicular (i.e., needle-like) leaves and the adult, scale-like leaves (sometimes the word 'squammiform' is used to describe these) which in the different species sometimes occur separately or both together on the same tree. Several scales unite to form a berry-like fruit containing one or more seeds. As befits the genus with the largest distribution throughout the Northern Hemisphere it has given us many useful garden forms. These come in every conceivable size, colour and texture, and in shape they range from the completely prostrate form of *Juniperus horizontalis,* through spreading, globose and pyramidal forms to perhaps the most spectacularly needle-like plant known, *Juniperus scopulorum* 'Sky Rocket'. As well as green forms of every hue there are golden, glaucous, blue-grey forms and variegated forms and some of the plants take on rich purple hues in the winter.

It is a genus that must have sadly tried the patience of botanists because, particularly on account of the habit that many of the forms have of clothing themselves wholly or mainly with juvenile foliage when young and changing over gradually and leisurely (sometimes incompletely, and in some cases not at all) to adult foliage in the mature plant, and its other habit—in species that are characteristically dioecious—of not running invariably true to type, it does not lend itself to being studied by the normal methods of orthodox botany, which rely mainly upon herbarium specimens and little if at all upon the knowledge and study of living plants.

There are several species of Juniper which never become large trees and these can therefore be used in gardens equally as well as the dwarf forms of taller-growing species. The persistent juvenile habit of others is an invitation to make use of them at this stage of their life, since many of these are most attractive both in foliage and in habit, which in the early years is often regularly conical.

Since the Junipers, along with Yews, tolerate calcareous soils (quite a different thing to needing such conditions) better than any other genera, those whose lot it is to garden on limestone or chalk may regard themselves fortunate that the Junipers cover such a wide range in colour, habit and texture.

I have had a great deal of help with the Junipers from Herman J. Grootendorst of Boskoop, Holland, who has had a lifetime of experience in growing and studying this important genus.

Juniperus africana Hort. N. Z. See *J. chinensis.*

Juniperus chinensis. L. The Chinese juniper. This is a very difficult and perplexing species with many nomenclatural problems.

In 1946 an American nurseryman named P. J. Van Melle of Poughkeepsie, New York, who was interested in the Chinese juniper and its cultivated forms, published his findings in the American publication *Phytologia* and the following year these were collected and republished in book form entitled *Review of Juniperus Chinensis*. This was published by the New York Botanical Garden from whom copies can be obtained by writing to Publications Department, The New York Botanical Garden, Bronx Park, New York, New York 10058, U. S. A. Briefly, Van Melle complains that the original species *J. chinensis* L. was inadequately defined by Linnaeus when he named it, that *J. sphaerica* Lindl. was subsequently quite unjustifiably reduced to a variety of *J. chinensis* and that *J. chinensis* var. *sheppardii* should have been recognised as a distinct species and that in result (what with all the garden forms that have appeared and a whole group of natural and garden hybrids with the prostrate species *J. sabina*) the name *J. chinensis* has come to include, as he puts it, 'everything but the kitchen stove—a loose aggregate, incapable of definition in terms of a species'.

To overcome this he proposed to limit the use of *J. chinensis,* to resuscitate *J. sphaerica* and to raise *J. sheppardii* to specific status. He also proposed a new hybrid species *J.* × *media* to contain all the more or less bush-like forms in which *J. sabina* blood—or should it be sap?—was discernible by the characteristic savin odour of the crushed foliage. He also separated certain garden forms being grown as cultivars of *J. chinensis* and identified them with another species *J. davurica* and he regarded *J. chinensis* 'Sargentii' as a separate species.

In support of all these suggestions he clearly did an immense amount of work both amongst the literature and herbarium specimens of all these Junipers and amongst the living plants, but like persons always tend to do once they have found a tenable theory, he disregarded every contribution from earlier botanical work that did not support his proposals. That many of these early writers were often mere copyists or at best were writing with but limited knowledge of the Junipers of which they wrote is only too clear (e.g., many of them as young plants bearing predominantly juvenile foliage are quite unlike the same trees as adults) so he had good grounds for exasperation over much of the literature he was trying to sort out, but Van Melle's work has not been fully accepted in the botanical world. Rehder says [Bibl. 649. 1949] 'An evaluation of the classification of these Junipers as proposed by Van Melle is not possible without further study and must be left to a future monographer of this group' and when I asked one of the leading English taxonomists about it his reply was 'Van Melle is probably right, but a lot more work will have to be done on these junipers before we can accept all he says—it will mean scrapping so much in all the books'. And that seems to sum up the general attitude.

In these circumstances each subsequent writer has had to make up his own mind how far he will follow Van Melle's recommendations. I notice for instance that Hillier accepts the new hybrid *J.* × *media* but does not agree with the transfer of the cultivars 'Expansa' and 'Expansa Variegata' to *J. davurica,* although this latter is now the practice in the nursery trade in Holland, where on the other hand *J.* × *media* has only recently come into general use.

To avoid confusing the reader I will not set out Van Melle's proposals in full (anyone interested can study his work for themselves) but I should give a word of warning that the nomenclature of this species, or group of species if that is what it ultimately becomes, is subject to review. To make the position of the present book clear, come what may, I here treat Van Melle's proposals as follows:

1. Van Melle's main proposals are not accepted.
2. The transfers to his new hybrid species *J.* × *media* are accepted (but see my notes on his use of 'pseudo-botanical' names for cultivars below).
3. The transfers to *J. davurica* are accepted.
4. Recognition of *J. sargentii* as of specific rank is accepted.
5. Van Melle's differentiation between *J. procumbens* 'Nana' and *J. squamata* 'Prostrata' is completely rejected. I am of the opinion that Van Melle could only have had *J. procumbens* 'Nana' to examine and that both the photographs on his plate XII are of that cultivar.

J. chinensis normally comes as an upright or conical tree upwards of 20 m high so that most of its geographical varieties and cultivated clones are outside the scope of this book, but the alleged hybrids with *J. sabina* are usually classed as dwarf forms and so are included under *J.* × *media*. *J. chinensis* usually bears both adult and juvenile leaves on the same plant, the former small, usually in pairs, closely flattened to the branches, broadly triangular and blunt at the apex; the latter being usually ternate (only occasionally in opposite pairs), 5-10 mm long, awl-shaped and sharply pointed; very densely set on the plant. The species is dioecious (that is to say, the male and the female flowers are borne on separate plants), so only female clones carry the berries. The difference between this and the two most nearly related species, *J. scopulorum* and *J. virginiana,* are noticed under those species (below). When berries are present, since they are much larger than the fruit of either *J. scopulorum* or *J. virginiana* the distinction from either of those species is conclusive.

– –'**Ames**' Haber and Lantz [Iowa Farm Sc. **2, 11:** 10. 1948.] The late Prof. T. J. Maney, sometime of Iowa State College, introduced four interesting new Junipers (the others are 'Maney', 'Iowa' and 'Story'), selections from a large number of seedlings raised by Dr. Vernon Stoutemeyer from Japanese seed (reputedly of an upright form of *J. sargentii* but evidently from a glaucous plant of *J. chinensis*) sown about 1934. 'Ames' makes a small, compact upright tree well clothed with foliage, giving a very dense appearance. The colour is blue-green and it makes an attractive specimen. It is very hardy.

– –'**Aurea**' [*J. chinensis aurea* R. Smith, Pl. Fir Tribe, 18. 1863; Young, Nurs. Cat. 3. 1875; f. *aurea* (Young) Beissn. in Rehd. 60. 1949 *.] This, as Hornibrook points out, in time grows too large to be regarded as a dwarf conifer, but being of slow growth it should be retained as long as possible on account of its wonderful colour, this being a brilliant golden-yellow during the spring and summer if the plant is grown in full sunlight, but it becomes less outstanding by winter. It is a male clone originating as a branch sport on a normal tree in M. Young's Nursery at Milford, Godalming, in Surrey, and introduced by him to the trade. It bears juvenile and adult foliage in approximately equal amounts.

– –'**Blue Point**' [New cv.] is a recent introduction in America where it is described as making a symmetrical, conical tree with dense, blue-grey foliage.

– –'**Carrière**' It is not now possible to be certain, but I believe Carrière's *J. japonica aurea* [Traité. Ed. 2, 32. 1867] renamed *J. chinensis* var. *Carrière* by Hornibrook [Dw. Con. Ed. 2, 105. 1938] was our *J.* × *media* 'Plumosa Aureovariegata'. I consider that his reference to the foliage being *grêles* (pock-marked) with yellow indicates this plant.

– –'**Columnaris**' and '**Columnaris Glauca**' are too tall-growing for inclusion here.

– –'**Echiniformis**' [*J. oxycedrus echiniformis* Knight, Syn Conif. 11. 1850; *J. hemisphaerica* Gord. (NON Presl) Pin. 96. 1858 and *J. echinoformis* Rinz; *J. oxycedrus echinoformis* Van Houtte (pro syn.); *J. communis echinoformis* Beissn. Conif. Ben. 41. 1887 and Handb. 137. 1891.] This curious little plant has suffered much from the coiners of names. Certainly it has no affinity with either *J. communis* or *J. oxycedrus* so has now found a more likely resting place here. It forms a tiny little flattened or rounded bush with short, irregular, crowded branches and very tiny leaves. Its slow rate of growth and apparent weakness of constitution in Britain may be due to a virus, for whilst it seems hardy, quite established plants suddenly may die back. It is a great favourite with owners of alpine houses, under which conditions very fine specimens can be grown, given enough patience. Gordon and some others confused it with *J. communis hemisphaerica* Presl and so the description of the plant and its origin by these writers are a useless hotch-potch. It seems reasonably certain that 'Echiniformis' was first sent out by a nurseryman Rinz of Frankfort. Whence he received it is not known, but it would hardly have been a wildling found on Mt. Etna. It seems to be a much better 'doer' in the United States than in Britain. (Illustration 200, 201).

– –'**Dropmore**' [New cv.], a form collected by Frank L. Skinner at Dropmore, Manitoba, Canada, is a similarly extremely slow-growing bun-forming plant with a very dense habit and highly ramified branching habit and a dense, neat thatch of very decussate adult or semi-adult foliage, in which the very small (to 3 mm long) leaves are held closely forward so that the plant entirely lacks the starry-eyed look of 'Echiniformis'. (Illustration 202).

– –'**Iowa**'. This is another of Professor Maney's introductions the history of which is given under 'Ames' above. 'Iowa' forms an elegant, informal pyramid densely covered with blue-green foliage. It is more spreading and less compact than 'Ames' and more green in colour. Juvenile and adult foliage are equally proportioned.

– –'**Japonica**' [*J. japonica* Carr. Traite, 33. 1855 (excl. synonymy); *J. chinensis* f. *japonica* (Carr.) Lipa in Rehd. Bibl. 61. 1949 *; var. *nana* Hochst. Conif. 90. 1882; *J. japonica* Carr. Traité. Ed. 2, 32. 1867, (incl. var. pyramidalis); *J. chinensis* 'Nana'

Welch, Dw. Con. 172. 1966; f. *oblonga* Slavin, Rep. Conif. Conf. 102. 1932; var. *Veitchii* Hornb. Dw. Con. Ed. 2, 101. 1938; NON var. *japonica* Vilm. Hort. Vilm. 58. 1906; NON *japonica* (Vilm.) Elwes & Henry, Trees **6**: 1432. 1912.] Hornibrook seems to have made a valiant attempt to unravel what is usually referred to as 'The Japonica Tangle', this being the confusion amongst several *J. chinensis* forms that resulted from the free and light-hearted use made of the word *"japonica"* both as a specific and as a varietal name by nineteenth century writers on conifers. But in spite of all his trouble I, personally, remain uncertain as to just how many forms he was trying to leave with us. Van Melle, on the other hand, convinced himself that the title could be dropped entirely. I find it impossible to make head or tail of his synonymy. In his zeal to eliminate the epithet *"japonica"* entirely he found no place for the plant here listed as *J. chinensis* 'Japonica', so he had to put undoubted references to our plant where best he could.

Van Melle was such a stickler for taking into account the differences in habit and foliar characteristics of these junipers at varying ages and the importance of studying trees at all stages of growth that it is strange that he did not also appreciate the importance of following the changes as they took place in particular plants over a period of years. Had he done so he would have been saved a curious mistake. Referring to Veitch's description 'It is a dwarf bush, sometimes with only one stem but oftener with a divided one; in the latter case the branches or divisions of the stem assume a procumbent habit', Van Melle says 'There is no juniper . . . which behaves in so variable a manner'. But in this he was wrong.

I originally obtained propagating material of 'Japonica' from two sources, one a spreading form bearing mostly juvenile foliage, the other form an upright plant with a good proportion of adult foliage. Apart from this the two samples were indistinguishable. As often happens on a busy nursery there was difficulty in keeping the two forms separate—the prostrate form and the upright form would persistently get mixed—or so I thought until I noticed that one by one the spreading plants were changing sides. They did this not by throwing up a leader but by pulling up their main branches, at first to a steep angle, eventually to the vertical. Eliminating double leaders being second nature to a nurseryman when on his rounds I never secured plants with Veitch's 'divided leader' but have no doubt some of the plants would have so developed, left to themselves, and of course a couple of snips with secateurs would have kept any young plant in procumbent shape indefinitely.

With this growth characteristic known there is no difficulty in accepting apparently divergent accounts that neither Hornibrook nor Van Melle could reconcile. I have no doubt that Carrière, Gordon, Veitch, Slavin and Nicholson were all writing about the same plant but at different stages of growth. When preparing his second edition Carrière was fooled by the behaviour of some of his plants into treating them as var. *pyramidalis* and also there seems to have been widespread uncertainty about the relationship to *J. procumbens*. Otherwise the name serves us well as a cultivar name for a plant which usually starts life as a fairly low bush with two or three ascending main branches bearing adult foliage at their tips but densely covered throughout the rest of their length with juvenile foliage which is very densely set and extremely prickly. This prickliness is one of the main characteristics and is so pronounced that it is advisable to wear gloves when handling the plant. It is an attractive garden form and capable because of its prickliness of holding its own against animals, red Indians, commandos and (nowadays of course) spacemen.

Eventually, however, left to itself, it becomes a small, more or less upright little tree, the proportion of adult to juvenile foliage increasing as time goes on, and often varying considerably on different sides of the same tree. The colour (especially in the adult foliage) is an attractive, rich green. (Illustration 203).

– –'**Japonica Variegata**' [*J. japonica variegata* Carr. Traité. Ed. 2, 31. 1867; *J. chinensis japonica aureo-variegata* Veitch. Conif. 288. 1881; 'Kaizuka Variegated' Hort. Amer.] I have no doubt that we should thus identify the plant widely grown in America as 'Kaizuka Variegated' (an invalid name in any case). The plant tallies with Carrière's description, and it is quite clearly a variegated form of 'Japonica' with no affinity whatever with 'Kaizuka'.

– –'**Kaizuka**' [*J. chinensis Kaizuka* Yokohama Nurs. Cat. 1920; *J. sheppardi* var. *torulosa* (Eastwood) Van Melle, Review, 28. 1947; 'Hollywood Variety' Hort. Amer. (in part); 'Torulosa' Hort. Amer. (in part).] This attractive form will grow eventually to tree-size but it is slow-growing and for many years in its early stages is a most desirable plant, having a picturesque, rugged outline with a tendency for its trunk or main branches to be slightly out of upright and this character should not be modified by pruning or staking.

Part of the attraction of this plant is the picturesque effect given by the irregular crowding of the branchlets into dense mop-like clusters which often form cylindrical effects (hence the word 'Torulose'—not to be confused with the word 'tortuosa' which means twisted) along the branches. In the best form the foliage is a bright, rich green which will hold its own with the green of *Chamaecyparis obtusa* 'Nana Gracilis' but there are clones in cultivation in which the colour is a much duller bluish-green. If Van Melle ultimately gets his way he will have elevated this form into a botanical variety of his proposed species *J. sheppardii*. In that event his proposed *J. sheppardii* var. *torulosa* would cover all these colour forms, leaving the cultivar name 'Kaizuka' still available for the bright green form which is the one we want in our gardens. (Illustration 204).

– –'**Maney**' is the third of Professor Maney's introductions the history of which is given under 'Ames' above. 'Maney' forms a semi-erect but spreading bushy plant with a blue cast to the foliage. It thus fills a useful place between the upright form normal to *J. chinensis* and the *J. × media* spreading forms. It looks well either massed or grown as a specimen in a small garden. (Illustration 205).

– –'**Obelisk**' Den Ouden [Conif. 154. 1949.] This is a very attractive form introduced by F. J. Grootendorst & Sons of Boskoop, Holland, which becomes a narrow, pyramidal plant to about 3 m high. The main branches and branchlets are spreading and short and stout, the leaves are very densely set, juvenile, directed forward, slightly decurved with apices very sharply pointed, 10–15 mm long with the underside glaucous. The whitish upper side of the leaves being turned outwards give the plant a distinctive glaucous grey appearance. A slight slope to the leader seems to be characteristic of this variety and for formal situations would be a defect.

This variety, together with the two stronger-growing cultivars '**Monarch**' and '**Olympia**' (not classed as dwarfs), is of similar origin to Professor Maney's four American introductions (see under 'Ames' above), having been raised from seed received from Japan as 'an upright form of *J. sargentii*' but which must have come from a glaucous form of *J. chinensis*. (Illustration 206, 207).

– –'**Pyramidalis**' [*J. japonica* SENSU (Carr.) Sargent Gar. and For. **10**: 421. 1897 (NON Carr.); *J. chinensis* f. *pyramidalis* Beissn. Handb. 120. 1891; NON *J. japonica* var. *pyramidalis* Carr. Traité. Ed. 2, 32. 1867; *J. squamata* 'Campbellii' Krüssm. Nadel. Ed. 2, 160. 1960.] Having shewn (see under 'Japonica' above) that the plant given this name by Carriere neither does nor did exist, we are free under Article 42 of *ICNCP* to accept it as the correct (even if misleading) name of a plant Sargent described as 'of distinct compact habit with many erect branches with bluish-green juvenile foliage . . . it retains its peculiar compact juvenile habit'. Beissner tells us that it forms a dense, slim blue-green column bearing at first acicular leaves and squammiform leaves later, and is a male clone. Den Ouden adds that the leaves are sharp, and that it was introduced from Japan into Belgium by Dr. von Siebold in 1845. It is significant that neither the word 'pyramidal' nor 'conical' appears in any of these descriptions. Nor is there any mention of a strong central leader. Instead we read of a compact column of a distinct or a peculiar shape and of many erect branches, and one account notices the sharpness of the leaves. These clearly distinguish this form from 'Stricta' below, with which this cultivar is frequently confused. The picture (Illustration 208, 209) clearly shows the 'peculiar' round-topped column that is distinctive of 'Pyramidalis' in contrast to the very stiff conical outline of 'Stricta'. Furthermore, the foliage of 'Pyramidalis' is relatively soft to the touch when stroked upwards.

– –'*Rockery Gem*'. See *Juniperus sabina*.

– –'**San José**' [*J. japonica* 'San José' Clarke, Nurs. Cat. 1935; *J. chinensis* 'San José' Clarke, Amer. Nurs. **88, 7**: 40. 1948.] This attractive dwarf form was found by W. B. Clarke, a nurseryman of San José, California, in 1935, mixed in with a planting of *J. chinensis*. It lies low on the ground and displays a mixture of adult and juvenile foliage and has I understand become extremely popular in California. The foliage is sage green. It was at first regarded as a low-growing form of 'Japonica', but it can always be distinguished from it by its lower habit of growth and its softer foliage, which has none of the prickliness characteristic of 'Japonica'. Young plants carry wholly juvenile foliage. (Illustration 210).

– –'*Shimpaku*'. See *Juniperus × media*.

– –'**Shoosmith**' Den Ouden and Boom 1965 [*J. chinensis nana Shoosmith* Southside Nurs. Cat. 1930] is a dwarf compact, globose or pyramidal form.

– –'**Spartan**' Den Ouden and Boom 1965 [*J. chinensis densaerecta* 'Spartan' Monrovia Nurs. Cat. 6. 1961-62] is a fast-growing, dense plant with a narrowly growing pyramidal or columnar outline and a rich, mid-green colour. A very useful plant for a focal point, but hardly a dwarf.

– –'Story' This is the last of the four introductions by Professor Maney referred to under 'Ames' above. 'Story' forms an upright and slender symmetrical small tree with horizontal branching and dark green foliage. It needs careful staking and training when young.

– –'Stricta' [*J. excelsa stricta* (Rollisson) Gord. Pin. Ed. 2, 144. 1875 (and f. *glauca* pro syn.); Nich. Dict. Gar. **2:** 212. 1885; f. *stricta* (R. Smith) Rehd. Bibl. 60. 1949 * (and Hort. Amer.); *J. chinensis pyramidalis* f. *glauca* Slavin Rep. Conif. Conf. 103. 1932; *stricta* Den Ouden, Conif. 156. 1949; *J. procera* var. *africana* Hort. N. Z. (in part).] Gordon tells us 'This beautiful variety forms a tall, dense, narrow, conical head, tapering gradually from the ground to a sharp terminal point and is of a fine silvery glaucous colour. It originated in the nursery of Messrs. Rollisson at Tooting'. Since the description of this plant and the first description of 'Pyramidalis' (see above) are so different, each clearly relating to a plant well known in cultivation today it is surprising that there has been so much confusion between these two names. This may largely be due to the comedy of errors that saddled a more or less columnar plant with the epithet 'Pyramidalis' and so has left a noticeably pyramidal plant to face life as 'Stricta', but the fact is that there is hardly a writer on either side of the Atlantic who has not helped this confusion along.

'Stricta' becomes too large in time but it serves us well as a garden plant, for in its young stages it forms a regularly conical bushlet with ascending branches and wholly juvenile foliage of a very beautiful, light blue-grey. Brushed with the hand, the foliage feels distinctly prickly. It remains an attractive plant for some years but eventually its habit of holding on to its dead foliage for several years gives the plant an unhealthy appearance, by which time it is usually best to replace it.

The true *J. excelsa,* a species native to Greece, is not hardy in Britain.

– –'Titlis' [Draijer. Nurs. Cat. M. 1972/73] is a new form introduced by the nursery firm Draijer B. V. of Heemstede, Holland, and described as a somewhat irregular and very compact fastigiate form with silvery-blue foliage, very sharp to the touch. I have not seen it.

– –'Variegata'. [*J. chinensis femina variegata* R. Smith, Pl. Fir Tribe, 18. 1863; *albovariegata* Veitch. Man. 288. 1881.] This variety which received its present name some years before Veitch suggested the name "*albovariegata*" quoted by Hornibrook, forms a slow-growing but eventually large, conical bush which is worthy of a better position than the rough corner assigned to it by Hornibrook, as its blue-green foliage (very similar in colour to 'Stricta') with its combination of juvenile and adult foliage, both types being irregularly but often liberally splashed with a creamy-white variegation, can be very effective when seen from close at hand. The plant is especially attractive when its neighbours are green or of some other, contrasting, colour.

Juniperus communis L. is a dioecious species easily distinguishable by its leaves from most of the other Junipers which give us dwarf forms. They are invariably awl-shaped and grow straight out at a wide angle from the stem, never clasping it as in *J. sabina* and many other species. The branchlets are triangular with projecting ridges and the leaves are in whorls of three. The leaves are stalkless and taper from a swollen base to a sharp point, their upper surface having a single broad band of stomata (in a few forms partly divided by a faint mid-rib), their lower surface being convex and bluntly keeled. (Illustration 211).

J. communis is truly circumpolar, being widely distributed throughout Europe, Asia and North America and although usually found as a small upright tree it also occurs widely as low-growing or prostrate shrubs. These come in almost infinite variation and in no clear distribution pattern, thus making any logical taxonomic treatment almost impossible. They often make excellent garden plants and numerous selections have been made in the wild and brought into cultivation. These have thereby become cultivars, one by one, despite their wildling origin.

These low-growing forms have long been recognised by botanical writers and numerous attempts have been made to deal with their taxomony. In 'the literature', *alpina, cambricus, canadensis, communis, davurica, densa, hemispherica, intermedia, nana, pygmaea, rebunensis,* and *sibirica* appear as specific epithets, and in various intra-specific ranks can be found *alpina, β, γ, canadensis, communis, dealbata, depressa, hemisphaerica, hornibrookii, intermedia, minor, montana, nana, nana compacta, prostrata, saxatilis* and *sibirica.*

The nomenclatural pendulum has over the years swung through all the available categories, (species, sub-species, *varietas* and *forma*) but the general consensus of opinion has been to treat these interesting Junipers as varieties of *J. communis*. I have elsewhere [Gar. Chron. **166, 5:** 14. 1969] argued the case for continuing this practice. The theory that the selection of appropriate rank for any taxon is a matter of botanical judgment and that each worker has unfettered choice is stoutly maintained by botanists, but it is not always so, since sometimes quite different considerations override. So my lack of deference to so recent and so eminent authority as *Flora Europaea* is probably more apparent than real since, as a matter of editorial policy, the only infra-specific rank recognised in that monumental work is sub-species. These low-growing forms therefore had to be recognised at that rank or NOT AT ALL. Editorial limitations, like Railway Regulations, can put an author in a similar predicament to the ticket collector who told the old lady 'Cats is dawgs and parrots is dawgs, but your canary is a hinsect'.

I therefore here set myself two tasks; firstly, to simplify and rationalise the botanical confusion that has resulted from past attempts to cope with the innumerable variations and intermediate forms and their sporadic appearance in the wild, and, secondly, to suggest a way out of the horticultural confusion that has resulted from an objectionable practice of using valid botanical epithets for cultivars (clones). I deal with the first of these problems by retaining only vars. *communis, depressa* Pursh., *hemisphaerica* (Presl) Parl., *hornibrookii* Hornb. and *montana* Aiton (see below). Whether or not these suggestions are accepted, by shewing that many of the names to be found in the literature were invalid or merely superfluous I hope I have reduced the botanical tangle considerably. In the bad old days the term variety was used rather inconsistently by writers, and the drastic reduction of the number of varieties here recognised puts several of these into an anomalous position, since one cannot have a *varietas* within a *varietas*. Where such a name has been validly published for a minor variation with a discernible local distribution the category *forma* seems appropriate and several reductions in status are proposed.

There remains, however, the separate problem of horticultural nomenclature. Since, as I have already mentioned, the selected forms grown in cultivation are cultivars, I believe the first step is for horticulturists to recognise the difference and stop using botanical names and cultivar names indiscriminately.

Every seedling or wildling brought into cultivation must fall into one or other 'var.', so no objection can be raised to labels such as *J. communis* var. *montana* Ait. Of the many dozens of the selected wildlings only a handful have been named (or are worth naming) as cultivars and if the clonal name is unknown (or is non-existent) that is as far as the identification needs to go—or, indeed, can go. A plant so labelled would quite properly have to share its identity with other plants botanically within the same *varietas,* even although to a gardener's eye they may look different. It so happens, however, that the botanical categories here retained also represent well defined horticultural divisions, so their epithets suggest themselves for use as names for the Groups into which the numerous cultivars fall. But as I have elsewhere explained, the botanical *varietas* will always, in theory, be a larger concept than the Group that bears its name. The net must always be larger than the fish it catches.

In my previous book [Dw. Con. 180. 1966] I wrote 'There seems to be a need for a study of the various clones in cultivation and scope for a little restrained naming of worthwhile garden forms'. I have since attempted to collect together all the clones of garden merit that I have been able to find. As a result I now have a collection of about 70 forms being grown for comparison and study. Some of these are of known clones, others not, these having come to me under one or other of the pseudo-botanical names which I now suggest should be discarded. Some may turn out to be identical. In my earlier book I made a rather unfortunate start with the cultivar name 'Silver Lining' which has turned out to be superfluous. In this book will be found several additional cultivar names. As the forms in my collection grow and their garden value becomes apparent, I hope to proceed with a little more 'restrained naming of worthwhile garden forms'. In the meantime I invite correspondence from anyone interested in the taxonomy of this group and, in particular, would be grateful to receive young plants or propagating material of unknown but potentially good garden forms. I intend in due course to distribute authentic material of all the newly named clones to botanic gardens and nurseries, but for the present, the classification of the variations of *J. communis* L. will be as follows.

– – var. **communis.** When you partition off one part of a room it is undeniable that you are at the same time partitioning off the remainder of the room and this *varietas* owes its existence to a useful botanical rule that says, roughly speaking, that when a varietal name is established, automatically what remains within the species becomes a *varietas* having as epithet the specific epithet repeated. Since var. *communis* has this rump-like character it serves us well as a Group name for a number of good garden forms which otherwise might attract the title 'Miscellaneous'. So, since it sounds better, we may horticulturally speak of the

COMMUNIS GROUP

f. *aurea*	'Kiyonoi'
'Bakony'	'Mayer'
'Bruns'	'Pencil Point'—
'Columnaris'	Syn. 'Sentinel'
f. *compressa*	'Sentinel'
'Compressa'	f. *suecica*
f. *cracovia*	'Suecica Nana'
'Hibernica'	

There are numerous other forms, selections from the wild, that vary only slightly. Sometimes they have been selected only for their hardiness in a particular climate, so are difficult to distinguish in growth habit and foliage.

– – var. **depressa** Pursh. Fl. Am. Sept. **2**: 646. 1814. [Rehd. Bibl. 57. 1949 *; var. *canadensis* Loud. **4**: 2490. 1838.] *The low-growing forms of J. communis L. found in eastern North America. A prostrate low shrub with branches ascending at tips; leaves upturned, rarely almost spreading, linear, acuminate-sublate, to 15 × 1.6 mm, with a narrow (as broad as, or less than each green margin) glaucous (stomatal rows distinct) band above.*

This is the common wild juniper of eastern North America. It is a low-spreading, shrub never more than 1 m high and occurs sometimes in large groups, there being a very good illustration in *Cultivated Conifers in North America* by L. H. Bailey, 1933, Plate XXXIX. It thrives in dry, sandy, stony or gravelly soil, is extremely hardy and is a rapid, vigorous grower. It is very useful for massing in front of trees or in the wild or moorland garden. The leaves are 8–10 mm by 1.5 mm, oval to lanceolate, with a long and finely drawn out transparent tip. These make the plant prickly to the touch. The lower side of the leaf is prominently keeled, yellowish to brownish-green in summer, sometimes touched with darker brown near the tips, and turns brown in winter, unless grown in full shade. The leaves are in whorls of three and each leaf is sharply curved near its base and twisted so as to face the ground, consequently the white stomatic band ½ to ⅔ the total width of leaf (not quite reaching to its base) on the upper side of the leaf is not seen. The leaves at the strong growing tips are strongly appressed to the stem and the growth is in irregular, flat sprays.

The name serves us as a title for the

DEPRESSA GROUP

'Depressa Aurea'	'Effusa'
'Depressed Star'—See Montana Group	'Gimborn'
'Dumosa'	'Vase'

– – var. **hemisphaerica** (Presl) Parl. Fl. Ital. **4**: 83. 1867; [*J. communis* var. *saxatilis* (Attrib. to Pall. Fl. Ross. **1, 2**: 12. and t. 54. 1788 by) Willd. Sp. Pl. **4, 4**: Ed. 2, 854. 1806 (pro syn.); Suring. Mitt. d.d.d.G. **38**: 330. 1927, nom. illegit.; *J. hemisphaerica* Presl, Del. Prag; 142. 1822; Endl. Syn. Conif. 12. 1847; *J. communis* ssp. *hemisphaerica* (Presl) Nym. Consp. Fl. Europ. 676. 1881; *J. nana A. montana* Endl. Syn. Conif. 14. 1847; *J. communis* var. *montana* Hornb. Dw. Con. Ed. 2, 110. 1938; NON *J. hemisphaerica* (Presl) Gord. Pin. 96. 1858.] *The low-growing forms of J. communis L. found in the high mountainous regions of Europe, Asia and northern Africa and distinguished by their bushy habit and densely set, broad, thick, usually tapered leaves, sharply up-curved at the base and thence straight, ending in a long prickly tip.* (Illustration 211).

This has the reputation of not being hardy in Britain and only one selection, to my knowledge, is in cultivation. There seems no objection to using the cultivar name in this case. The name was at one time mistakenly used for the diminutive plant here regarded as *J. chinensis* 'Echiniformis'.

– – var. **hornibrookii** Grootn. ex Hornb. Dw. Con. Ed. 2, 111. 1938 [*J. communis* var. *prostrata* Hornb. Dw. Con. 68. 1923; NON Beissn. Mitt. d.d.d.G. **5**: 55. 1896.] *The low-growing forms of J. communis L. distinguished by their bushy, prostrate or mat-forming habit and by their very small, straight, widely spreading and loosely set leaves with long, sharp tips, with stomata above in distinct rows not embedded in a waxy coat.*

Although it is arguable that var. *hornibrookii* is botanically not distinguishable from vars. *communis* and *montana* because of the infinitude of intermediate forms, they constitute a well understood horticultural division which we can call the

Hornibrookii Group

'Edgbaston'	'Inverleith'
'Hornibrookii'	'Prostrata' Hornb., NON Beissn.

– – var. **montana** Aiton, Hort. Kew. **3**: 414. 1789. [*J. minor montana* Bauh. Pinax 489. 1596; *J. communis* γ L. Sp. Pl. 1040. 1753; *J. communis* Lamarck, Encyc. Meth. Bot. **2**: 625. 1788; *J. nana* Willd. Sp. Pl. **4, 2**: 854. 1806 (in part); *J. communis alpina* Gaud. Fl. Helv. **6**: 301. 1830; *J. communis* 3 *nana* Loud. Arb. Frut. Brit. **4**: 2489 and Fig. 2344. 1838; *J. nana alpina* Endl. Syn. Conif. 14. 1847; *J. communis* var. *nana prostrata* Hornb. Dw. Con. Ed. 2, 110. 1938; *J. communis* ssp. *nana* Syme in Sowerby, Engl. Bot. Ed. 3, **8**: 275. 1868; Franco in Bot. Soc. Brot. **36**: 112. 1962; Flora Europaea **1**: 38. 1964; *J. sibirica* Loddiges ex Burgsd., Anleit. Sich. Erzieh. Holzart **2**: 127. 1805; *J. communis* var. *jackii* Rehd. Mitt. d.d.d.G. **1907, 16**: 70, 1908; *J. communis* var. *minima* Grootn. Mitt. d.d.d.G. **53**: 200. 1940.] *The low-growing forms of J. communis L. found in Greenland, the British Isles, and through Europe, the Himalayas, India and to Japan and in western North America and distinguished by the prostrate, often mat-forming habit and thick, broad and relatively short, boat-shaped, upcurved leaves which because they are densely set (especially so on the young growing shoots) are frequently subimbricate. The leaves carry a broad white (in the American forms often conspicuously so) stomatal band more than twice the width of each green margin, are bluntly* *keeled below and terminate in a point which varies in shape considerably (often in different parts of the same plant) but is always obtuse relative to the long fine point normal to the species, and is sometimes drawn out at the tip to a short point.* (Illustration 212).

Horticulturally these are easy of recognition and readily fall into the

MONTANA GROUP

'Berkshire'	var. *prostrata* Beissn.
'Depressed Star'	'Repanda'
'Derrynane'	'Silver Lining'—See 'Minima'
'Gew Graze'	'Soapstone'
f. *jackii*	'Windsor Gem'
'Minima'	'Zeal'
'Nana Aurea'	

Most of the plants in gardens at present labelled *alpina, nana, sibirica, saxatilis* and all the other old names here reduced to synonyms belong to var. *montana* Ait. and, if so, should be so labelled unless their cultivar name (if any) is used.

– – f. **aurea** (Carr.) Rehd. [Bibl. 57. 1949 *; *J. communis aureovariegata* Beissn. Handb. 138. 1891; var. *aureo-variegata* Kent in Veitch, Man. Ed. 2, 171. 1900.] COMMUNIS GROUP. In a species so variable in habit it is not surprising that 'sports' with golden foliage have turned up in the various different groups, and that the names built up around the word *"aurea"* have multiplied. Beissner describes **'Aureovariegata'** *as of normal habit but with golden foliage.* Although a mutation of this kind may have occurred more than once, none has established itself in cultivation, so this name will serve to cover all the upright golden forms there may be, unless and until a form turns up of sufficient garden value to justify a new cultivar name.

– – *'Aureospica'.* See 'Depressa Aurea'.

– – **'Berkshire'** [New cv.] MONTANA GROUP. This is a very attractive and extremely slow-growing, bun-forming selection named from the area where it was found. The mother plant was growing in the Arnold Arboretum under the accession number 814/166 and the provisional label *'J. communis* (Special)'. It is a most desirable form, even in small gardens unable to accommodate the stronger-growing members of the species. (Illustration 213).

– – f. **compressa** (Carr.) Rehd. [Bibl. 57. 1949 *; *J. communis compressa* Carr. Traité, 22. 1855; *J. hibernica compressa* Hort. (pro syn.); *J. communis* var. *columnaris* Hornb. Gar. Chron. **1929, 1:** 50 and Dw. Con. Ed. 2, 113. 1938.] COMMUNIS GROUP. Although I do not for one moment believe Veitch's statement [Man. 275. 1881] repeated by Nicholson [Dict. Gar. **2:** 212. 1884] that this dainty and rather delicate little treasure is found on the Pyrenees at 5000 feet of elevation yet it lends an air of respectability to its claim for recognition as a botanical *forma* and this suits us very well horticulturally, for there is evidently more than one clone in cultivation under this name, although they are virtually impossible to tell apart. The name used collectively should in any case be restricted to narrowly columnar dwarf forms and, ideally, the cultivar name **'Compressa'** should be limited to the well known, minute, columnar plant so universally popular, with its steeply ascending branches, pointed apex and tiny leaves, about 5 mm by 1 mm, and an average annual growth of 5 cm or less—a tiny replica of the Irish juniper. Unfortunately it is not an easy plant, being very prone to damage by wind, frost and red spider. (Illustration 214). **'Columnaris'** Hornb. [Gar. Chron. **1929, 1:** 50. 1929.] What plant Hornibrook had in mind when he coined the name is now impossible to ascertain, so it is probably best to regard 'Columnaris' as lost to cultivation. See 'Sentinel' and 'Suecica Nana'.

– – f. **cracovia** (Carr.) grad. nov. [*J. communis* var. *Cracovia* Carr. Traité, 21. 1855; *cracovica* Loud. Arb. Frut. Brit. **4:** 2490. 1838.] Communis Group. Polish Common juniper, found in the neighbourhood of Krakow in Poland. It makes a very robust, upright tree with long leaves. The single clone in European cultivation could properly be referred to as **'Cracovia'**.

– –**'Depressa Aurea'** [*J. nana canadensis aurea* Beissn. Handb. 133. 1891; *J. communis* var. *depressa aurea* Hornb. Dw. Con. Ed. 2, 109. 1938; *J. communis* 'Golden Vase-shape' Bergm. Pl. and Gar. **21, 1:** 47. 1965 (?); var. *aureo-spica* Rehd. in Bailey, Cult. Everg. 199. 1923; f. *aureo-spica* (Rehd.) Lipa in Rehd. Bibl. 58. 1949.] This is a most attractive plant which has had a struggle to establish its correct name. The change from *"canadensis aurea"* is easily understood; it follows from the publication of the varietal name *depressa*. (Illustration 215). The varietal name *"aureospica"* was coined by Rehder (as it now turns out, superfluously) since the botanical machine into which he was hopefully pushing everything, under the ideas prevalent at the time, would not accept quadrinomials.

'Depressa Aurea' is at its best in late May, when its golden-yellow colour is at its peak. Later it becomes a dull bronze and by winter, almost green. It makes a sturdy bush, with its branches much more ascending than (as Hornibrook doubtless intended to say) those of 'Nana Aurea'. (Illustration 216).

– –**'Depressed Star'** Den Ouden and Boom [Man. 164. 1965; *J. communis* var. *prostrata* Beissn. Handb. 133. 1891; NON Hornb. Dw. Con. 68. 1923; *J. communis* 'Prostrata' Den Ouden and Boom, Man. 169. 1965.] Montana Group. Unless, in coining this name Den Ouden and Boom [Man. 163. 1965] were describing a cultivar of var. *depressa* Pursh that has since been lost sight of (a possibility contra-indicated by their description of 'Depressed Star'), it would seem that they have left us with a small problem. Since, following the use of the name 'Depressed Star' for a specimen of *J. communis* var. *prostrata* Beissn. at the Proefstation at Boskoop in Holland the name has come into general use for that cultivar, common sense suggests leaving well alone, particularly since there is a clone of var. *hornibrookii* in English cultivation under the cultivar name 'Prostrata'. 'Depressed Star', then, is a broad, wide-spreading shrub with a mainly horizontal branching system and leaves broad and decurved, with a silvery band above but held so that only the green undersides are seen, changing to brown in late autumn. (Illustration 217).

Clones of the true var. *depressa* that have been selected and named, vary mainly in habit. **'Dumosa'** [*J. communis depressa dumosa* Den Ouden, Conif. 160. 1949], **'Effusa'** [*J. communis effusa,* Den Ouden, Conif. 160. 1949], **'Gimborn'** [*J. communis depressa* 'Gimborn' Den Ouden, Conif. 160. 1949] and **'Vase'** [*J. communis* 'Vase Shaped' Kuml. Friendly Evergreens, 173. 1946] are shrubby forms, increasingly upright in the order given, the first three having been seedlings selected on the Gimborn estate, Doorn, Holland, and the third being an American selection introduced by D. Hill Nursery Co., Dundee, Illinois, U.S.A. 'Vase' colours to a rich chocolate brown in winter and, especially as a young plant, is an attractive form. These shrubby forms all become more wide-spreading as they age. (Illustration 218).

Of these, I understand that the European selections are no longer in production, plants labelled 'Effusa' usually being 'Repanda' or a clone difficult to distinguish therefrom.

– –'Gew Graze' [New cv.] MONTANA GROUP is an interesting and attractive new introduction not unlike 'Repanda' but with much larger (10 mm × 2 mm) leaves but slower growth and less prostrate habit. The foliage remains green during the winter. It was selected by Dr. D. E. Coombe of Cambridge University 'in the wild' near the Lizard, in Cornwall, where a once quite extensive local population is in danger of extinction by heath fires. It does not seem sufficiently distinctive for recognition botanically, but it makes an attractive and quite 'different' garden plant and could become popular when better known. 'Gew Graze' is a female clone. **'Soapstone'** [New cv.] is the male clone from the same collection by Dr. Coombe. As a young plant in the Pygmy Pinetum it is distinct only by fractionally shorter leaves, but it turns red-bronze during the winter, at which time the two forms are easily distinguished, even in non-flowering plants.

– –**'Hemisphaerica'** (see p. 212.) This name can be used for the only clone that, so far as I am aware, is in cultivation. I received it some years ago from the National Botanic Garden, Glasnevin, Dublin, under the name *montana* (see also *J. chinensis* 'Echiniformis' above). (Illustration 219).

– –**'Hibernica'** [*J. hibernica* Lodd. Nurs. Cat. 1836; *J. communis* f. *stricta* (Carr.) Rehd. Bibl. 57. 1949 *; var. *fastigiata* Bean, Trees. 671. 1914.] COMMUNIS GROUP. *J. communis* is one of several conifer species that come either as more or less columnar trees or as low-growing or spreading shrubs. The latter on the whole are more useful in our gardens, but the upright kind (probably more typical of the species) have also given us several good garden forms. These all occur within var. *communis* as defined above and constitute no real botanical entity, so I consider the advantage lies in treating them as cultivars. The rules for deciding the priority of varietal epithets when botanical names are changed sometimes bring to the surface a long forgotten and almost unused name but the rule for cultivars is more simple—basically, we retain the first name used for that cultivar. And fortunately, as in this case, it is usually the name in general use.

'Hibernica', therefore, is the well-known Irish juniper forming a tall, narrow columnar tree with tightly packed vertical branches. Several other selections of upright or fastigiate forms have been given cultivar names. **'Bakony'**, a Hungarian selection is claimed to be hardier in winter and **'Kiyonoi'**, an American selection is said to be a dark green form which withstands the summer heat better than does 'Hibernica', but all are rather large-growing for inclusion in this book.

– –**'Hornibrookii'** [*J. communis* var. *Hornibrookii* Grootn. ex Hornb. Dw. Con. Ed. 2, 111. 1938; *J. communis* var. *prostrata* Hornb. Dw. Con. 68. 1923; NON Beissn. Handb. 133. 1891.] This is the original clone found by Murray Hornibrook in

County Galway in Ireland. It was there a perfectly prostrate mat, flowing down over rocks and absolutely following their contours. (Illustration 220). It is very popular for rockeries because of its neat habit and dainty leaves, but in cultivation so many forms with similar foliage but dissimilar growth habit have been introduced that the time has come to distinguish a few by new cultivar names. It will be difficult to maintain these distinctions in commercial cultivation because of the existence of intermediate clones, but the following are readily separable in the Pygmy Pinetum and I shall be pleased to supply material to establish these clonal forms. I suggest that the name 'Hornibrookii' should be limited to the very prostrate and *slow-growing* male form with leaves 5 by 1 mm (rarely to 8 mm by 1.25 mm) and an annual growth of 50 to 80 mm. In this form the older leaves are often twisted, so that the wide (always more than half the total leaf width) stomatic band shews and this gives a somewhat grey look to the plant as a whole. The clone I have as **'Prostrata'** Hort. Eng. [*J. communis* var. prostrata Hornb. Dw. Con. Ed. 2, 113. 1938; NON Beissn. Handb. 133. 1891] has the same horizontal habit as 'Hornibrookii' but is very much more vigorous and strong-growing. For this reason, since it shares the small leaf and dainty look it tends to be distributed in place of the dwarfer plant, which is a pity.

In both the previous forms the habit is quite prostrate, all the main branchlets lying quite horizontal, but **'Edgbaston'** [New cv.] differs both in foliage and habit. The stomatic band is narrower (less than half the total width of leaf) and the underside is a dull, dark green. The habit is much more erect. It forms a wide-spreading plant but the main branches rise at + 30–40°. This makes the brown branches and the regular, flat spray of the numerous branchlets much more noticeable. Finally, in **'Inverleith'** [New cv.] we have a plant that retains the dainty leaf size of the flatter-growing forms, but it forms a dense bush nearly as wide as high. The mother plant is in the Royal Botanic Garden at Edinburgh, built on the gardens of the former Inverleith House—hence the name. (Illustration 221).

– – f. **jackii** (Rehd.) nov. grad. [*J. communis* var. *Jackii* Rehd. Mitt. d.d.d.G. **1907, 16:** 70. 1908 and Man. 10. 1927.] MONTANA GROUP. This is a local variant occasionally met with in Oregon and northern California with long, whip-like main branches, often reaching over 1 m in length unbranched, save for occasional clusters of short branchlets. The plant has no garden value. It bears leaves characteristic of var. *montana* and, consistently with the general treatment in this book, has no claim to varietal status.

– –'**Minima**' Grootn. [Mitt. d.d.d.G. **53:** 200. 1940; var. *nana prostrata* Hornb. Dw. Con. Ed. 2, 110. 1938; 'Silver Lining' Welch. Dw. Con. 182. 1966.] MONTANA GROUP. I am now satisfied that the clone named by Herman J. Grootendorst in 1940 and my plant are one and the same, so—used as a cultivar name—his name has priority and my own rather more euphonious effort is redundant. It forms a very prostrate plant which is hard and rough to the touch but not prickly, with strong leading growths which nod at the growing tips. Young twigs are distinctly triangular, pink above, green below; older branches brownish-purple. Entre-noeud up to 10 mm, less towards tips of shoot. Leaves 5-8 mm by 1.5-2 mm, upcurved, but narrow at the base and bluntly pointed; each leaf viewed from above or the side being boat-shaped, rather like a Venetian gondola. The leaves are shiny green below but the whole leaf is covered with a heavy glaucous bloom (easily rubbed off) giving the plant a grey-green appearance which is maintained throughout the year. Above, the leaves carry a very wide band of minute stomata covered with a chalky white bloom and as many of the leaves are twisted so that this whiteness is seen especially near the centre of the plant, the general effect is most attractive. It is a fairly strong grower, but is a poor transplanter and is slow to establish itself. (Illustration 222).

- –'**Nana Aurea**' [*J. communis nana aurea* Beissn. Zierg. Ed. 2, 461. 1884; *aurea* (Hort. Holl.) Beissn. Handb. Ed. 2, 625. 1909; NON *aureus* Nich. Dict. Gar. Suppl. 455. 1900.] MONTANA GROUP. This is a low, flat-spreading form with main branches nodding at the tips. The leaves are silvery-white, striped with green edges above, but golden-yellow to brown-yellow below, this colour being more or less retained throughout the year. It is very easily distinguished from all other forms, but it is not a very good doer, so is seldom planted. (Illustration 223).

- – var. *prostrata* Beissn. See var. *montana,* above.

- –'**Repanda**' [*J. communis* var. *repanda* Grootn. Mitt. d. d. d. G. **53**: 200. 1940.] HORNIBROOKII GROUP. 'Repanda' is a very dense, prostrate clone (or group of clones) always forming a neat, circular plant, very useful as a ground cover. The whole plant is very soft to the touch with no trace of prickliness. The twigs are very supple. Leading shoots send out their laterals in regular flat sprays but the branching towards the centre of the plant is irregular and twigs stand up at all angles. The twigs are light brown with entre-noeud up to 10 mm, usually much less. The leaves vary in size, up to 10 mm by 1.5 mm, and are *upcurved so that they lie close to the shoot,* the underside is dark, dull green, prominently keeled but with a sunk mid-rib, the upper side with an ill defined, broad stomatic band, light grey in colour but largely hidden from view because of the way the leaves are held. (Illustration 224).

It is certain that more than one clone is in circulation under this name, the difference between them being mainly the habit. The new cultivars 'Gew Graze' and 'Soapstone' might come in here. A clone that is much less prostrate wrongly circulates in Britain as 'Effusa' (See under 'Depressa', above) and '**Derrynane**' [New cv.] is a very prostrate female clone found growing as a flat carpet, following the contours of the rock beneath, on a headland at Derrynane in Kerry in Eire. In cultivation it makes an attractive ground cover plant that berries freely. The group from which it came is evidently a local population similar to that found by Dr. Coombe in Cornwall, since it also contains male plants.

- – var. **saxatilis.** I have elsewhere shewn [Taxon **17,** 5: 545. 1968] that this much used name was never validly published until it had become redundant, so it should no longer be used in any combination. Plants labelled *J. communis saxatilis* in gardens are usually var. *montana* Ait., or one of its named clones.

- – f. **suecica** (Mill.) Beissn. [Rehd. Bibl. 57. 1949 *] the Swedish juniper, is mostly found as a more or less columnar tree with fastigiate branching and the tips nodding. Leaves bluish-green. There are probably several clones in cultivation.

- –'**Suecica Nana**' [*J. communis* var. *suecica nana* Bailey Cult. Conif. Ed. 2, 189. 1933.]

It being described by Bailey as 'a dwarf columnar form of var. *suecica,* usually not exceeding 1 metre' is unlikely to mean that it originated in Sweden, and in Britain this name is used for a looser and freer-growing edition of 'Compressa'. Although the branching of both are equally fastigiate, each little shoot of 'Suecica Nana', if closely examined, will be seen to have much less leader dominance, so even as a young plant it is usually blunt-topped by comparison with 'Compressa', which usually terminates in a single shoot, this resulting in a pointed little tree. It will make a plant 1.5 m high by not more than 30 cm across, but without some assistance from the knife such old plants usually become a bit irregular in outline towards the top. It seems much more wind resistant and hardy than 'Compressa' and is, of course, quicker growing, but 'Suecica Nana' is apt to throw out loose, strong growth. This should be cut out as soon as it appears. (Illustration 225).

I do not feel able to be definite on the point, but in my experience the true 'Compressa' does not make this coarse growth. If this be correct, the presence of such growth on any plant would indicate that it is 'Suecica Nana' rather than 'Compressa'. The coarse growth, if propagated, gives plants of the normal 'Hibernica' type. (Illustration 226).

– –'**Windsor Gem**' [New cv.] MONTANA GROUP. This name I suggest for a distinctive, diminutive and attractive form of which there are several well established plants in the Saville Gardens, Windsor Great Park, the origin not being on record. It has foliage and habit similar to 'Minima' but with the leaf size and rate of growth very much reduced. The picture gives a good impression of the plant. (Illustration 227).

– –'**Zeal**' [New cv.] MONTANA GROUP. This is another selection with quite a different habit, as will be seen by the picture which was taken in a garden in Devonshire of a very old plant whose origin is not on record. It is very slow-growing, and the upright habit shews up both the dark green undersides and the white stomatic band on the upper-sides of the foliage, giving a dark blue-green overall appearance. (Illustration 228).

Many cultivars of the MONTANA GROUP can only be rooted with difficulty and stocks have to be built up by grafting. In case such treatment adversely affects the vigour such plants should be planted deeply to encourage scion rooting.

Juniperus conferta Parl. This is a procumbent, dense, mat-forming species from Japan which makes a useful garden plant. In its native habitat it grows on the seashore, so presumably would be a valuable plant for coastal gardens. It forms a wide-spreading shrub with brownish bark, thick main branches, and dense, erect branchlets. The leaves are crowded, overlapping, about 12 mm long, awl-shaped and green, each tapering to a sharp point. (Illustration 229). These points give a distinctly prickly feel to the plant when brushed with the hand and this at once distinguishes it from another prostrate juniper which has long been grown in England as *J. conferta* var. *maritima* but which the Japanese botanist Satake has now identified as *Juniperus taxifolia* var. *lutchuensis.*

– –'**Blue Pacific**' is a selection listed by Monrovia Nursery, Azusa, California, U.S.A. It has a low, trailing habit and a blue-green colour that suggested the name chosen for it.

– –'**Boulevard**' [New cv.] is a very prostrate selection with all its main branches growing horizontally, so that the shoots are readily seen. The colouring is normal.

– –'**Emerald Sea**' is a clone introduced by the United States Department of Agriculture in 1972. It was discovered on low sands near the shore of Ashiara, Ibaraki Prefecture, Honsho, Japan. It is very salt tolerant and forms a dense, low mat, remaining quite prostrate. It is recommended for ground stabilisation on sand dunes and for ornamental ground cover. The foliage is emerald green during summer and autumn, becoming more yellowish in tone in the winter.

Juniperus davurica Pallas. According to Van Melle, *Juniperus davurica* is a very common and widely distributed species in eastern Asia, but as far as I am aware it is only found in cultivation in the following form and its variegated counter-parts.

– –'**Expansa**' [*J. chinensis* var. *parsonsii* Hornb. Dw. Con. Ed. 2, 96. 1938; var. *expansa* Grootn. Mitt. d.d.d.G. **53**: 207. 1940; *J. davurica* var. *parsonsii* (Hornb.) Van Melle, Review, 30. 1947 (and synonymy).] It has always apparently been assumed (with what justification I cannot say) that our green form is not the typical *J. davurica,* so the plant in cultivation has always been saddled with a varietal name. The plant forms at first a low, flat, spreading bush which for some years may not exceed 30-50 cm in height, but ultimately it builds itself up into a dome-shaped mound 3 m across and up to about 1 m high at the centre. Although not claiming priority, the epithet 'Expansa' best preserves existing usage. (Illustration 230).

It is not a prostrate juniper. Individual plants in open, uncrowded situations develop stout and very rigid, horizontally-spreading primary branches which do not rest upon the ground but extend themselves horizontally just clear of it. Because of this characteristic, it is important not to plant this juniper too deep and I have noticed that when set so that the main branches are touching the ground, the plant does not prosper and the growth becomes uncharacteristic, lacking the sturdy, horizontal-branching habit that it normally has. It carries a mixture of adult and juvenile foliage, one attractive feature being the prominent development of long, slender, filiform, adult, ultimate branches arranged in more or less dense, rich looking foliage sprays. The whole plant has a strong and robust appearance looking as though it would be none the worse for being slept on by a cow.

– –'**Expansa Aureospicata**' [*J. chinensis* var. *expansa* f. *aureo-spicata* Grootn. Mitt. d.d.d.G. **53**: 207. 1940] is a form with butter-yellow variegation. It is less vigorous than 'Expansa Variegata' and carries mainly juvenile foliage.

– –'**Expansa Variegata**' [*J. chinensis* var. *expansa variegata* Hornb. Dw. Con. Ed. 2, 94. 1938; *J. davurica* f. *variegata* Van Melle, Review, 31. 1947] is similar to 'Expansa' but with bold splashes of creamy-white variegation here and there over the plant on both adult and juvenile foliage. This variegation is apt to suffer during the winter frosts, but it appears again with the new season's growth.

Juniperus horizontalis Moench is a species from North America in which numerous forms have been selected and named. They are all more or less prostrate plants and nearly all are good growers and capable of covering a large area. Having been regarded at one time as a prostrate variety of *J. sabina,* at another as a variety of *J. virginiana* and even, by one authority, simply as *J. prostrata,* plants can still be found incorrectly labelled.

The main branches are long, the branchlets very numerous, short and dense. The leaves on the cultivated forms are mainly needle-shaped, often in whorls of three, green or blue-green, frequently colouring to blue or mauve tones in the winter, 2-6 mm long and standing free at the tips, with very sharp points; convex on the underside, with a gland. On mature foliage the leaves are scale-like and loosely imbricate.

Like all junipers, this species and its cultivars withstand hot, dry situations, growing under town conditions and tolerating moderately alkaline soils. They grow slowly at first and can therefore be disappointing for a couple of years, but eventually produce excellent ground cover, especially useful in covering steep, rough banks. They are usually much improved by pinching back the leader growths during the summer for two or three seasons after planting to induce a dense branch system, and thereafter by an occasional hard pruning. Although long known in cultivation it is only now being widely planted for ground cover. A large number of clones have been selected and named, especially in the United States of recent years, and the number now available in the trade is, surely, many more than is necessary. Several are difficult to distinguish, once they have left the nursery of their origin and I believe there is some confusion in some collections in that country.

- – 'Admirabilis' [Plumfield Nurs. Cat. 1936] is similar to 'Emerson' but is a male clone. It has prostrate main branches, with branches and branchlets held at a steep angle. The foliage is dense. The leaves are all juvenile, a yellowish-green with a heavy grey bloom, especially on the upper sides of the leaves. It is a vigorous plant reaching to 30 cm high, but spreading to several metres.

- – 'Adpressa' (Since the noun Juniperus is feminine, the Latin-form epithets [adjectives] should follow suit. Hence *adpressa,* not *adpressus*). This is one of a number of the earlier selections introduced by the Plumfield Nursery, Fremont, Nebraska. It makes a very dense and prostrate plant never over 25 cm high but spreading widely. Foliage green with whitish-green pointed tips. It is not always found true to name.

- – f. **alpina** (Loud) Rehd. [Journ. Arn. Arb. **6**: 203. 1925.] Although Rehder's description was based on a single clone, this is a botanical form found in the Manitoba province of Canada, although possibly only a single male clone is in cultivation. It is a rather atypical form which carries its one-year branches nearly erect, becoming horizontal by the second year. By this means it spreads over a large area, never reaching over 50-60 cm high. The leaves are exclusively awl-shaped, 3-4 mm long, more or less bluish or greyish changing to a dull purple in autumn. It is a rather rank grower and is therefore not a good ground cover plant. (Illustration 231). It seems to need yearly snow-cover.

- – '*Aunt Jemima*'. See below, under '*Plumosa Compacta*'.

- – '**Bar Harbor**' Teuscher [New Flora and Silva **8**: 194. 1936; *J. horizontalis* var. *Bar Harbor* Hornb. Dw. Con. Ed. 2, 120. 1938.] This form comes from Mt. Desert Island, Maine, where it grows in crevices on the rocky coast and may frequently be found well within reach of the salt spray. It is a ground hugging form with its matted growth covering large areas and rooting from the long branches. In colour it is a pleasant grey-green resulting from a white glaucous bloom over its true green colour. In autumn and winter it turns a delicate mauve-purple. Being a population in the wild several clones may have found their way into cultivation. These differ slightly but some plants labelled 'Bar Harbor' are certainly no such thing. Bar Harbor being a place name the spelling should not be altered. (Illustration 232).

– –'**Blue Acres**' is a new Canadian selection by Professor C. E. McNinch of Guelph. A prostrate spreading form with blue-green foliage, blue when it first appears.

– –'**Blue Chip**' [*J. horizontalis* 'Blue Moon' Thomsen—name withdrawn] is a low-growing selection with bright blue foliage well maintained throughout the year. Raised from seed about 1940 in the Asagar M. Jensen Nursery in Denmark. The colour is outstanding. I understand that the name was changed to avoid confusion with *J. scopulorum* 'Blue Moon'.

– –'**Blue Horizon**' [New cv.] is a recent selection which makes a very low-growing, creeping plant which remains low and open, never mounding up in the centre as 'Wiltonii' does, to which cultivar it is otherwise similar.

– –'*Blue Moon*'. See 'Blue Chip'.

– –'*Blue Rug*'. See 'Wiltonii'.

– –'*Blue Wilton*'. See 'Wiltonii'.

– –'**Coast of Maine**' is a form I have not found listed in America, although presumably that is whence it came. It is a low-growing form making flattened mounds. Foliage grey-green, purplish in winter. From the descriptions, it could turn out to be identical with 'Grey Carpet'.

– –'**Douglasii**' [*J. horizontalis* f. *douglasii* Rehd. Mitt. d.d.d.G. **1915, 24:** 214. 1916.] This is one of the earliest selections (1855) from the one-time Douglas Nurseries, Waukegan, Illinois (hence it is sometimes listed as the Waukegan juniper.) It is a close-growing form with very small leaves tightly appressed. Main branches horizontal or nearly so, all branchlets ascending at a steep angle. Side branches turning upwards so as to produce a V-shaped spray (i.e., not flat.) The foliage is grass green but covered all over with a glaucous bloom giving a rich grey-green appearance which changes to a soft greyish mauve in winter. Shoots are orange-brown at the growing tips. Teuscher [New Flora and Silva **8**: 195. 1936] tells us 'To see this Juniper as it grows naturally is a revelation. Its main branches are entirely buried in the sand, only the branchlets coming above the surface, where they form a dense, soft carpet which follows in every detail the outline of the dune . . . the natural habitat suggests the proper treatment of this juniper in cultivation . . . not very well suited for use in the rock garden, but for sandy gardens, especially for dune gardens it offers one of the finest lawn substitutes'. (Illustration 233).

– –'**Dunvegan Blue**' [New cv.] is a form that was collected on the banks of the Peace River near Dunvegan and introduced by the Beaver Lodge Nursery, Alberta, Canada. It is described as creeping close to the ground and as being of silvery-blue colour. I have not seen it.

– –'**Emerald Spreader**' Monrovia [Nurs. Cat. 6. 1973] is a new form, patented in U. S. A., described as ground hugging and bearing numerous laterals clothed with green foliage, giving the plant a dense, feathery appearance. The colour should be a welcome change from the far too numerous blue selections.

– –'**Emerson**' Marshall ex Wyman [Amer. Nurs. **117, 1**: 121. 1963; 'Marshall' Marshall Nurs. Cat. 1929; More, Green Thumb **13, 3**: 32. 1956; 'Black Hills Creeper' Hort. Amer.] This form was found in the Black Hills of South Dakota by Geo. A. Marshall, Arlington, Nebraska, and Professor Emerson of the University of Nebraska. At first it was distributed as Black Hills Creeper but was given its present name in honour of one of its finders. The plant is very prostrate, seldom exceeding 30 cm, blue in colour, this colour being well maintained throughout the winter. It is slow-growing and drought resistant, and is a female clone.

– –'**Eximia**'. As seen at Phytotektor Nursery, Winchester, Tennessee, U.S.A., in 1970, this appeared somewhat more upright than 'Emerson' and was a lighter green.

– –'**Filicina**' [*J. horizontalis filicinus* Plumfield Nurs. Cat. 1936; More, Green Thumb **13, 3**: 36. 1956 and **15, 3**: 93. 1958; *filicinus minimus* Hort. Amer.] This is a very prostrate, slow-growing and dense form with delicate green foliage in fern-shaped sprays. A female clone—and a very dainty, lady-like looking plant.

– –'**Glauca**' [*J. horizontalis* var. *glauca* Hornb. Dw. Con. Ed. 2, 120. 1938.] This is an unsatisfactory name, since it has been loosely used for several blue selections. The clone described by Hornibrook—a very flat and coarse spreading form with steel blue, whipcord-like foliage selected by Professor Sargent, then of the Arnold Arboretum—is not now in cultivation and the epithet 'Glauca' is widely used (especially in European nurseries) for the clone described below as 'Wiltonii'.

– –'**Glenmore**' More [Green Thumb. **13, 3**: 32. 1956] is a dwarf form, one of the lowest and slowest of the species, main branches horizontal, held just clear of the ground, branchlets thin, a dull light brown; leaf sprays nearly upright; leaves all juvenile, very closely set, medium green, tips brownish in winter. A female form, selected by Robert E. More, in Wyoming. A neat little plant, but because of the way the leaf sprays are held, of less value for ground cover than the more rampant forms. (Illustration 234).

– – f. **glomerata** Rehd. [Journ. Arn. Arb. **6**: 202. 1925.] Although Rehder records that this form had been found more than once in the wild it is probable that only a single clone is in cultivation and for this the cultivar name '**Glomerata**' is in order. It is a most distinctive variety carrying long, often twisted, pinkish-brown main branches, mostly rising at a steep angle and bearing juvenile leaves nearly appressed. The branchlets are short, mainly vertical or nearly so, and they carry very dense, rich green foliage and tiny leaves in flat sprays almost suggestive of one of the tiny forms of *Chamaecyparis obtusa*. If the strong-growing leader growths are regularly pinched out this type of foliage will slowly develop into a dense mat a few cm only in height. The colour turns rather dull in winter.

– –'**Green Acres**' is similar to 'Blue Acres' (above) in origin and description, saving for the colour, which is a dark green.

– –'**Grey Carpet**' Kammerer [Bull. Morton Arb. **6**: 40. 1931] is a creeping form with long, trailing branches forming low cushions. It differs from 'Bar Harbor' by its somewhat more green foliage.

– –'**Grey Pearl**' is a small, compact-growing plant, grey in colour, selected and introduced by Thomsens Planteskole, Skalborg, Denmark.

– –'**Hermit**' [New cv.] This form was found growing on Hermit Island, Maine, by Dr. R. B. Livingston, University of Massachusetts, Amherst, Massachusetts, and propagations have been growing for several years at the University of Vermont and the Arnold Arboretum as 'Livingston No. 11'. *Juniperus* 'Hermit' is described as 'a vigorous, dense, spreading plant (similar to Pfitzer juniper in habit). It was registered [Arnoldia **33**: 205. 1973] as a possible hybrid between *J. virginiana* and *J. horizontalis,* but Dr. Livingston writes (30 May 1974) that it is a *J. horizontalis* form, found many miles outside the range of *J. virginiana.*

– –'**Hughes**' is a strong-growing new form selected by the Cedar Rapids Nursery of Iowa, U. S. A. It has a wide-spreading but ascending branch system and as a young plant has very much the habit of *J. virginiana* 'Grey Owl', but the foliage is grey-green. Useful for ground cover in a rough spot, or under trees. (Illustration 235).

– –'**Humilis**' [*J. horizontalis* var. *humilis* Hornb. Dw. Con. Ed. 2, 121. 1938.] This is another name supported by inadequate description. Unless anyone can shew that he has the original clone referred to by Hornibrook it should not be used. All we know of it is that it was very slow-growing and had prostrate branches and very short erect branchlets with recurving tips.

– –'**Livida**' [*J. horizontalis lividus* Plumfield Nurs. Cat. 1941] forms a dense mat of yellow-brown main branches and many side branches pointing forwards, all completely prostrate to the tips. Branches are numerous and very short, seldom rising to 45° even at the centre of the plant (at least when young—I have not seen an old specimen). Foliage is all juvenile, the leaves are very small except on strong-growing main shoots, much resembling *J. sabina* 'Tamariscifolia'. Colour is actually a deep grass green, but a heavy grey bloom all over the plant gives it a greyish appearance.

– –'**Livingston**' Hebb. [Arnoldia **33**: 205. 1973] is another of Dr. R. B. Livingston's finds on Hermit Island, Maine; introduced by the University of Vermont. It is described as 'a procumbent plant generally 15-20 cm high; foliage steel-blue in summer, bluish-green in winter, mostly scale-like, minute; occasional fruit, light blue, with bloom. The plant is much branched and growth is dense'.

– –'**Marcella**' As seen in the U. S. National Arboretum, Washington, D. C., and the Arnold Arboretum, Jamaica Plain, Massachusetts, this was a ground hugging variety never over 13 cm high with short main shoots and many laterals, and dense juvenile foliage with small leaves. The plant is lower and better for ground cover than 'Petraea' and is of a lighter green. I do not think it is always found true to name. A female clone.

– –'**Petraea**' This is another early selection which should give way to later cultivars. It forms a spreading plant about 20 cm high with main branches arising at a steep angle and tending to become bare near the ground, so it is not so good for ground cover as the more prostrate forms. The foliage is juvenile, dark bluish-green, turning dull mauve in winter. It is a female clone.

– –'**Planifolia**' [*J. horizontalis planifolius* Plumfield Nurs. Cat. 1941.] This is a rapid grower, with long, palmy, silver-blue branches. Grows 20–25 cm high. Solid cover. Should be useful where quick cover is desired.

– – f. **plumosa** Rehd. [Journ. Arn. Arb. **6**: 204. 1925.] The botanical status may be open to question, but it gives us a convenient name for a distinct group of cultivars—the

PLUMOSA GROUP

– –'**Plumosa**' [*J. horizontalis* var. *plumosa* Hornb. Dw. Con. Ed. 2, 121. 1938; *J. communis depressa plumosa* Andorra Nurs. Cat. 8. 1919 (Spring).] This, the Andorra juniper, forms a flat-topped, open spreading shrub, never over 50 cm high but spreading laterally by means of main branches radiating from the centre of the plant. The branches rise at an angle of about 45° (reminiscent of the Pfitzer juniper) and bear dense, awl-like foliage loosely appressed and arranged in plumes. The foliage is a light grey-green, becoming purplish-plum colour in the winter. (Illustration 236). It was discovered in 1907 and introduced by the Andorra Nurseries of Philadelphia, Pennsylvania. The name is, however, sometimes loosely used to cover a number of sports or selections that have been named in the United States. Of these, the best known in Europe is '**Plumosa Compacta**', a selection similar to 'Plumosa', but making a much denser plant and one which stays 'full' at the centre. The grey-green foliage turns bronzy-purple in winter. (Illustration 237). '**Youngstown**' is very similar except that it remains greener throughout the winter, except in colder areas. '**Aunt Jemima**' ['Plumosa A. J.' Hort. Amer.] is a selection made in 1957 and introduced by the D. Hill Nursery Co., Dundee, Illinois, U. S. A. Its growth is very low and spreading with a blue-green colour retained throughout the growing season. It will make a densely clothed bush 1.5 m across by only 20 cm high, reminiscent of the pancakes of Aunt Jemima fame. '**Fountain**' is another D. Hill selection, which makes a flat-topped but higher bush than 'Aunt Jemima'—to 40 cm, and is a more rapid grower.

– –'**Prince of Wales**' Wyman [Arnoldia. **29, 1:** 3 1969.] A form collected in the wild near High River, Alberta, in 1931. This was first propagated by the Canada Dept. of Agriculture Research Station, Morden, Manitoba, in 1931 with commercial introduction in 1967. In the words of Dr. W. A. Cumming, Director of the Morden Station, it is 'very procumbent, forming a dense mat 10–15 cm in height, foliage both acicular and scale-like, bright green in colour, younger foliage with a bluish tinge caused by a waxy bloom. Exposed foliage tinged purplish-brown in the winter months'.

– –'**Procumbens**' [*J. horizontalis* f. *procumbens* Slavin, Rep. Conif. Conf. 106. 1932.] This identification was, I think, a mistake. Plants I have seen always turn out to be a form of *J. procumbens* 'Nana'. The description given by Slavin would support this suggestion. The name should be dropped.

– –'**Prostrata**' [*J. horizontalis* var. *prostrata* Fulling, Bull. New York Bot. Gar. **14**, 118. 1929; Grootn. Mitt. d.d.d.G. **53**: 212. 1940.] As I know it, this is a prostrate, dense and mat-forming variety, making a plant up to 30 cm high by 3–4 m across. Main branches are long, stout and prostrate but with tips slightly turned up, the branchlets are numerous and densely set, covering the ground; the sprays are blue-grey with the tips purplish; the leaves are mostly awl-shaped and thin but towards the growing tips are scale-like, a glaucous green. It is one of the best prostrate forms and one that has been in cultivation a long time, but often found wrongly named. Plants supplied in Britain as *J. horizontalis* are usually of this cultivar. (Illustration 238).

– –'Pulchella' [*J. horizontalis pulchella* More, Green Thumb, **16**: 32. 1959] is a very slow-growing and dense, compact variety, forming a symmetrical mat-like plant seldom over 10–15 cm high but more than 1 m across, with trailing branches and greenish-grey, acicular leaves borne on numerous, almost vertical branchlets in fern-like sprays. Claimed by the late Mr. Robert E. More to be an exceptionally hardy form, withstanding sun, shade and drought.

– –'Repens' Grootn. [Mitt. d.d.d.G. **53**: 212. 1940] is a similar form, but looser and of less garden value.

– –'Turquoise Spreader' Monrovia [Nurs. Cat. 6. 1973] is a new selection patented in America, which remains quite flat and low but makes a vigorous, wide-spreading plant with neat, juvenile foliage with very small leaves. The colour is a beautiful jade green.

– –'Variegata' [*J. horizontalis* f. *variegata* Slavin, Rep. Conif. Conf. 106. 1932.] The Variegated Creeping juniper is an attractive and vigorous prostrate form with a creamy-white variegation. It is all the better for an occasional hard cutting back, as the variegation is much more effective in the denser growth thereby secured.

– –'Venusta' Raraflora [Nurs. Cat. 1966] is a ground hugging, dense form of a much darker shade of bluish-grey, but otherwise similar to 'Glauca'. A female clone.

– –'Viridis' [*J. horizontalis* var. *viridis* Grootn. Mitt. d.d.d.G. **53**. 213. 1940] is a prostrate, densely branched, broad shrub, 50–60 cm high; branches horizontal, branchlets spreading, covering the branches; leaves for the greater part awl-shaped with pointed apex, light green above, sometimes slightly blue bloomy beneath. It is a female form and distinctive by its green colour in summer, but is otherwise not outstanding.

– –'Wapiti' Buckley [Amer. Nurs. **161, 2**: 14. 1967] is a recent introduction from Beaver Lodge, Alberta, Canada, and extremely hardy. Young plants are upright and soon form a solid, dense mass of a fine textured, dark lustrous green. Found by John Wallace near the Wapiti River south of Beaver Lodge in 1952 and released by the Experimental Farm in 1959. Mature plants are 30–40 cm high and with a spread of 3 metres.

– –'Webberi' Sherwood [Nurs. Cat. 1971–72] is a new form which makes an extremely low, mat-like spreading plant. The foliage is green with a glaucous blue sheen.

– –'Wiltonii' Vermeulen [Nurs. Cat. 4. 1953; listed also as Wilton Creeping Juniper, 4. 1955; as Wilton Carpet Juniper, 15. 1957 and as 'Blue Rug', 11. 1964; *J. horizontalis* 'Blue Wilton' More, Green Thumb. **13, 3**: 32. 1956 and **15, 3**: 93. 1958; *J. horizontalis* 'Glauca' Hort. Europe.] The colour is bright blue, well maintained throughout the year. It was found on Vinalhaven, an island off the coast of Maine, by Jacob C. van Heiningen of the South Wilton Nurseries,

Wilton, Connecticut, and was grown by him as "*J. horizontalis* var. *glauca*". Under this incorrect name the F. J. Grootendorst & Sons Nurseries imported it into Holland around 1933 and introduced it just before the war. Being one of the finest blue carpeting Junipers at the time it caught on and is now grown by tens of thousands in Continental Europe. As the name 'Glauca' was (in the U. S. A.) being loosely used for several other collected blue leaved forms John Vermeulen listed it as 'Wiltonii' after the town where Jacob van Heiningen lived. (Illustration 239).

– –'**Winter Blue**' is a new form in habit similar to 'Plumosa' but which is of a pleasing light green in summer, becoming quite a bright blue in winter.

Juniperus × media Van Melle. This is the name of the hybrid suggested by the late P. J. Van Melle (see above) as a convenient way of dealing with a large group of junipers which as he pointed out 'constitute a reasonably homogeneous group of considerable practical importance'. They are all more or less evidently hybrids between *J. chinensis* and *J. sabina,* the evidence of the sabina influence being the characteristic 'savin' odour of the foliage when bruised. As would be expected this is stronger in some forms than in others.

The foliage of a number of useful junipers regarded as forms of *J. virginiana* are also marked by the same smell, but I do not think this warrants their transference to the present species. If *J. sabina* has been loose enough to flirt with an American cousin as well as a neighbour, it seems to me that another hybrid species will have arisen. In cultivation, junipers with quite mixed ancestry may well exist, but for the present I leave them as cultivars of *J. virginiana.*

As most of the spreading forms formerly treated as cultivars of *J. chinensis* (and in many books still so regarded) are transferred to *J. × media* this is now an important group in the dwarf conifer firmament, but I would warn my readers that they will probably find them listed under *J. chinensis* in some textbooks on conifers for some time to come. Van Melle gave pseudo-botanical rank to all the forms he knew in cultivation, on the assumption that they had originated in the wild and could once again there be found. The many new forms since his day are clearly cultivars and common sense lies, I feel, in treating all these forms, both old and new, as cultivars.

They group themselves simply as follows:

PFITZERANA GROUP.   *Spreading bushes with main branches ascending at an angle and arching over so that the tips are pendulous (more so in some forms than others), carrying some juvenile and some adult foliage but mainly a form of semi-juvenile foliage in which the lower half of the leaf clasps the stem closely, the upper half standing off stiffly at an angle.*

'Arctic'	'Kallays Compact'
'Armstrongii'	'Kohankies Compact'
'Fruitland	'Kosterana'—See *J. virginiana*
'Gold Coast'	'Mathot'
'Hetzii'	'Mint Julep'
'Hills Blue'	'Nicks Compact'— See 'Pfitzerana Compacta'

'Old Gold'	'Pfitzerana Glauca'
'Pfitzerana'	'Sea Spray'
'Pfitzerana Aurea'	'Silver Tip'
'Pfitzerana Compacta'	'Sulphur Spray'

PLUMOSA GROUP. *Bushes carrying almost exclusively adult foliage, with prominent, vigorous, nodding leading shoots with short laterals pointing forward and very short sub-laterals carrying the foliage in dense tufts. As all the growing tips curl over the effect is vaguely suggestive of ostrich plumes.*

'Blaauw'	'Plumosa Aurea'
'Globosa'	'Plumosa Aureovariegata'
'Globosa Aurea'	'Shimpaku'—See 'Globosa Cinerea'
'Globosa Cinerea'	'Shimpaku Gold'—See 'Globosa Aurea'
'Plumosa'	'Tremonia'
'Plumosa Albovariegata'	

– –'**Arctic**' Hill [Nurs. Cat. 5. 1972.] PFITZERANA GROUP. This is a selection which makes a wide-spreading plant 2 m across by no more than 50 cm high. It grows rapidly and is reputedly very much hardier than most of the PFITZERANA GROUP. The colour is bluish-green.

– –'**Armstrongii**' [*J. chinensis Armstrongii* Armstrong Nurs. Cat. 42. 1932; "var." Bailey, Hortus Suppl. 1935; *J. × media* var. *Pfitzeriana* f. *Armstrongii* (Bailey) Van Melle, Review, 29. 1947; *J. pfitzeriana nana* Hort. Amer.] is a low-growing shrub of the 'Pfitzerana' type but of more compact and lower growth, seldom reaching much beyond 1 m high. The leaves are mainly scale-like except at the base of the bush. Foliage is soft to the touch, of a bright yellowish-green colour. A sport of 'Pfitzer' introduced by the Armstrong Nurseries, Ontario, California, U. S. A., in 1932. (Illustration 240).

– –'**Blaauw**' [*J. chinensis* 'Blaauw' Den Ouden and Boom, Man. 149. 1965; Blaauw's Varietät Grootn. Mitt. d.d.d.G. **53**: 206. 1940.] PLUMOSA GROUP. This is a dense growing and upright cultivar in which the differentiation in vigour between the leading shoots and the sub-laterals is very pronounced so that the relatively few, strongly growing main branches striking up at a steep angle give a characteristically rugged outline to the plant which is most attractive. The colour of the foliage, a rich blue-grey, is an additional attraction. It is quite distinct from 'Globosa Cinerea' in habit although somewhat similar in colour. (Illustration 241).

– –'**Fruitland**' [New cv.] PFITZERANA GROUP. A recent introduction described as a vigorous wide-spreading plant, but retaining the dense foliage of 'Pfitzerana Compacta'. The colour is bright green. I have not seen it.

– –'**Globosa**' [*J. chinensis* var. *globosa* Hornb. Dw. Con. 62. 1923; *J. × media* var. *globosa* Van Melle, Review, 29. 1947 (excl. synonymy); *J. virginalis globosa* Yokohama Nurs. Cat. 33. 1921/22 (and earlier?); *J. virginiana globosa* (Hort. Eng.); *J. japonica Bandai-sugi* Hort. Amer. (in part.)] PLUMOSA GROUP. 'Globosa' and its

colour forms have had an interesting and amusing history. They first came on to
the western scene as importations into this country and the United States from a
Japanese nursery of plants labelled *"Juniperus virginalis globosa"*. These were
certainly nice, globose plants and came in three colours green, gold and grey,
and they apparently sold well. After a while the fact that there was no *"J.
virginalis"* known to botanists was noticed and it was thereupon assumed that the
correct name should have been *"J. virginiana globosa"*, so the next few customers
received plants under this name and thus labelled they can still be found. Later it
was seen that they were not a *J. virginiana* form at all but were cultivars of *J.
chinensis,* so Hornibrook in his second edition described them as *"J.c. globosa"*,
"J.c. globosa aurea" and *"J.c. globosa cinerea"*, respectively.

Finally, it was found that they had not even any moral right to the
designation *"globosa"*, for the plants remaining unsold, deprived of the careful
attention from the knife to which they had been accustomed in their native
Yokohama were beginning to develop a habit that was by no means globose.

The present position, therefore, is that 'Globosa' differs from 'Plumosa' only
in minor respects. It forms a more symmetrical plant, the branches are much
shorter and stand at wide angles all over the plant and the foliage is a lighter
shade of green. The true 'Globosa' is rare in cultivation, but the difference
between the forms is slight and both are only needed in a very complete
collection. 'Globosa' is a female form.

– –'*Globosa Aurea*'. Lost to cultivation. See 'Plumosa Aurea' below.

– –'**Globosa Cinerea**' Hillier, 1964 [and Man. 488. 1971; *J. chinensis* var. *globosa
cinerea* Hornb. Dw. Con. Ed. 2, 95. 1938.] PLUMOSA GROUP. This is very close to
the cultivar 'Blaauw', so much so that, especially in young plants, they are
difficult to tell apart. 'Globosa Cinerea' does not, however, throw up quite such
strong leader growth and the angle of divergence of side shoots is greater, so it
forms a much broader plant of less rugged outline; also the foliage, especially in
wintertime, is more a grey-green than the blue-grey of 'Blaauw'. As in the case
of the green forms, these two grey varieties are too close together for both to be
needed in the average garden, and my choice would always rest with 'Blaauw'
(see also 'Shimpaku' below).

– –'**Gold Coast**' [*J. chinensis aurea* 'Gold Coast' Monrovia Advert., Amer. Nurs. **184,
2**: 1971.] PFITZERANA GROUP. A new form patented in America and introduced by
Monrovia Nursery Co., Azusa, California, U. S. A. It has a fairly low, broad-
spreading habit, more dense than in the typical 'Pfitzer' and with each growing
tip a rich, golden-yellow, which is described as deepening in cold weather. As
might be supposed, it is difficult to distinguish from the older form 'Old Gold'.

– –'**Hetzii**' [*J. glauca hetzii* Hetz. Fairview Nurs. Cat. 4. 1937; *J. chinensis* 'Glauca
Hetz' Wyman, Amer. Nurs. **117, 1**: 115. 1963.] PFITZERANA GROUP. This is hardly
a dwarf form since it grows to 5 m high, but where there is room for it to
develop fully it is an attractive plant. The main branch system is spreading, the
branchlets are numerous, well clothed with foliage, the leaves being mainly
small, adult, but always with some juvenile leaves, all conspicuously glaucous.
(Illustration 242). It is widely used as an understock for grafting.

– –'**Hills Blue**' [*J. chinensis* 'Pfitzerana Blue' D. Hill, Nurs. Cat. 5. 1939.] PFITZER-

ANA GROUP. This is close to 'Pfitzerana Glauca'—perhaps in colour lying between that and *J. virginiana* 'Grey Owl', turning less purple in the winter, and making a lower and flatter plant.

- –'**Kallays Compact**'. PFITZERANA GROUP. This is one of a number of compact forms of the Pfitzerana juniper, all arising no doubt from bud mutations. This one, which originated in the Kallay Nursery, Painesville, Ohio, U. S. A., is one of the most popular. It is of a deep green colour and carries a preponderance of juvenile foliage. It makes a flat-topped plant which seldom exceeds 80 cm but which will spread to nearly 2 metres. It is sometimes sold as 'Pfitzerana Compacta'—a name belonging to the 'Nicks Compact' of American nurseries. (Illustration 243).

- –'**Kohankies Compact**' [*J. chinensis* 'Kohankies Compact' Wyman, Amer. Nurs. **117, 2**: 64. 1963.] PFITZERANA GROUP. According to Wyman, this is a compact-growing sport from 'Pfitzerana' originating at the former Kohankie Nursery, also at Painesville, Ohio, but it is quite unlike its foster parent. It is very dense and almost globose. It is not recommended by Wyman because of not being hardy at the Arnold Arboretum, but possibly in a milder climate it might be of value.

- –'*Kosterana*'. See *J. virginiana* 'Kosteri.'

- –'**Mathot**' [*J. chinensis* 'Mathot' Den Ouden, Conif. 154. 1949; Meyer, Pl. Expl. **2**: 121. 1963.] PFITZERANA GROUP. This is very similar to 'Kallays Compact' in growth, but is denser; the leaves are all juvenile, in pairs, to 7.5 mm long, with bluish-green bands above, green below. As the upper side of the leaves are turned outwards the plant has a generally glaucous appearance. It originated on the Mathot Nursery, Boskoop, Holland, in 1940.

- –'**Mint Julep**' Monrovia [Advert. Amer. Nurs. **124, 2**: 1971.] PFITZERANA GROUP. A recent introduction, patented in U. S. A. It makes a rather flat, spreading bush, fairly compact but with long, arching main growths. The colour is a deep, rich, mid-green. It is a valuable introduction because of its colour.

- –'**Old Gold**' [*J. chinensis pfitzeriana* 'Old Gold' Grootn. Nurs. Cat. 11. 1958/59.] PFITZERANA GROUP. This is a very attractive form, descriptively named. It forms a much more compact plant than the typical 'Pfitzerana' and the lovely bronzy-golden colour goes right through the plant. This clearly distinguishes it from 'Pfitzerana Aurea', in which the golden colour at its best is limited to the young growth. The colour is retained throughout the winter. It arose as a sporting branch in the F. J. Grootendorst & Sons Nursery in Boskoop, Holland. (Illustration 244).

- –'**Pfitzerana**' [*J. chinensis pendula* Späth, Mitt. d.d.d.G. **5**: 28. 1896; Franchet. 1884 (?); *J. chinensis Pfitzeriana* Späth, Nurs. Cat. 104. 1899–1900; *J. media* var. *Pfitzeriana* Van Melle, Review, 19. 1947.] This is a good example of the growth in popularity of a good plant. When Hornibrook wrote his second edition in 1938 he evidently (from the paucity of his description) had not seen a plant, but now it is one of the most widely planted conifers and is so well known as not to need a description here. It is planted by the thousand each year, mainly I expect because of its picturesque outline as a young plant. One excellent use for it is to mask the presence of a manhole-cover on a lawn. This, its vigour and characteristic habit of growth enables it to do effectively in a short while and yet permit free access to the drains beneath on lawful occasions, but I wonder how many planters of this excellent juniper bear in mind its ultimate size. In the Arboretum Trompenburg in Rotterdam, for instance, there is a specimen large enough to afford complete shelter for quite a number of persons during a shower. (Illustration 245).

Its picturesque habit of growth is due largely to the preponderance of a semi-juvenile type of foliage and its habit of throwing up its strong main branches at an angle of 45°, from which angle the tips of the leader and the principal laterals arch over so that all the growing tips are pendulous. The foliage is a light yellowish-green but owing to the fact that the juvenile foliage (of which the centre of the bush mainly consists) shows the white uppersides, the general effect is that of a grey-green colour.

An engraving of the mother plant in the Späth nursery shows a broad, pyramidal tree with gracefully arching branches and this is probably whence Hornibrook took his description. Sceptics who find it hard to believe that 'Pfitzer' will submit to such treatment will be amused by a photograph in *Die Gartenwelt* [403. 1900–01] which clearly shows the leader of this same tree, although several metres high, still trained up to a bamboo cane!

Van Melle [Review, 81. 1947] traces the history and probable introduction of this juniper, which was known in France and Belgium before Späth renamed it for his nurseryman friend W. Pfitzer of Stuttgart. (Hence, from a rule of Latin, the correct spelling is 'Pfitzerana', not 'Pfitzeriana'). Späth's plant is a male form, so if it is the origin of the ever increasing number of variants they must all have arisen as bud sports. As Van Melle points out, this means that the mutations are themselves mutable (i.e. subject to further change, or to reversion) so careful selection of propagating material is important.

– –'Pfitzerana Aurea' [*J. chinensis pfitzeriana aurea* D. Hill. Nurs. Cat. 4, 1937; var. *pfitzeriana aurea* Grootn. Mitt. d.d.d.G. **53**: 207. 1940] has the typical Pfitzerana growth but with a tendency to a flatter habit, the branches being held at an angle of 30°. The branchlets and leaves are a bright golden-yellow in summer but become yellowish-green by the winter.

– –'Pfitzerana Compacta' [*J. chinensis* 'Nicks Compact' Wyman, Amer. Nurs. **117,1**: 116. 1963.] This is another sport from the Pfitzer juniper which Wyman considers one of the best of the compact junipers. It forms a flat-topped plant to nearly 2 metres across but only 30 cm high, of excellent compact form with stiff, thick branches and very prickly foliage. It was introduced by Bobbink and Atkins Nursery, Rutherford, New Jersey, U. S. A., in 1930 as *J. chinensis pfitzeriana compacta*. It carries mainly juvenile leaves, the white upper sides giving quite a greyish cast to the green colour. (Illustration 246).

– –'Pfitzerana Glauca' [*J. chinensis pfitzeriana glauca* Sherman, Texas Nurs. Cat. 1940; *J. × media* var. *pfitzeriana* f. *glauca* Van Melle, Review, 29. 1947.] This is another sport with its foliage varying between silvery-blue and a dull greyish-blue. The foliage of 'Pfitzerana Glauca' is very prickly, which distinguishes it at once from 'Hetzii', which is quite soft to the touch. 'Pfitzerana Glauca' forms a taller plant than 'Hills Blue' and colours more noticeably in winter. Several variegated sports have also appeared. Of these, one named **'Silver Tip'** is attractively speckled with creamy-white similarly to *J. × media* 'Plumosa Albo-variegata', but it is not a good doer.

- –'**Plumosa**' [*J. chinensis* var. *plumosa* Hornb. Dw. Con. 66. 1923 and Ed. 2, 102. 1938; *J. × media* var. *plumosa* Van Melle, Review, 30. 1947] is a broad, spreading shrub, seldom over 1.5 m high with long main branches and numerous short side branches all pointing strongly forwards, the sprays being crowded and plume-like, with all growing tips curved gracefully over. There is usually a small amount of juvenile foliage near the base of the plant. Unless otherwise trained in its early days it limits itself to relatively few main branches and when one of these predominates the plant has a lop-sided development which may or may not be an advantage according to the situation. The colour is deep green. It is a male clone. (Illustration 247).

- –'**Plumosa Albovariegata**' [*J. chinensis* var. *plumosa albo-variegata* Hornb. Dw. Con. Ed. 2, 106. 1938; *J. × media* var. *plumosa* f. *albovariegata* Van Melle, Review, 30. 1947] is similar to 'Plumosa' with a somewhat lower and more spreading habit and with its foliage liberally peppered with a small creamy-white variegation.

- –'**Plumosa Aurea**' [*J. chinensis* 'Plumosa Aurea' Den Ouden and Boom, Man. 157. 1965; *J. chinensis* var. *globosa aurea* Hornb. Dw. Con. 63. 1923 and Ed. 2, 95. 1938; *J. chinensis* f. *aureo-globosa* Van Melle, Review, 29. 1947; *J. virginalis globosa* (Yellow), Yokohama Nurs. Cat. 1910?; *J. japonica globosa aurea* Bobbink and Atkins Nurs. Cat. c. 1916; NON *J. chinensis* var. *plumosa aurea* Hornb. Dw. Con. 66. 1923 and Ed. 2, 103. 1938; NON *J. × media* var. *plumosa* f. *aurata* Van Melle, Review, 30. 1947.] PLUMOSA GROUP. This is the most decorative colour form of this group. It forms an attractive flat-topped, spreading bush wider than high with mainly adult foliage in gracefully arching sprays, the foliage and branchlets yellow-green in spring, the colour becoming more pronounced through the year until by winter it is a rich golden-bronze. (Illustration 248). In my previous book I stated that there is no golden form of 'Globosa' since fresh importations from Japan always turn out to be the cultivar 'Plumosa Aurea' of the trade. I have since seen a form with the same colouring but having the erect habit mentioned by Hornibrook as characteristic of 'Plumosa Aurea' as he used the name in 1938. Illustrations 248 and 250 distinguish the two forms unmistakably. There has clearly been a name switch here since 1938 and as the more spreading form has become so widely known as 'Plumosa Aurea', common sense suggests retaining this usage (as permitted by Article 27c of the Cultivated Code—despite its posing a problem with the synonymy) and accepting the name '**Tremonia**' (see below) for the form distinguished by the more upright habit.

- –'**Plumosa Aureovariegata**' [*J. chinensis* var. *plumosa* f. *aureovariegata* Van Melle, Review, 30. 1947] is a slower-growing form with its deep green foliage carrying a deep yellow variegation, usually somewhat irregularly. (Illustration 249).

Where there is room for such a group to be seen from a little distance away, a remarkable colour and texture effect could doubtless be obtained by planting a large group of these 'Plumosa' forms, including 'Blaauw' and 'Globosa Cinerea' for their contribution in colour, the rich green of the taller-growing *J. chinensis* 'Kaizuka' at the back or centre of the group.

- –'**Sea Spray**' [New cv.] PFITZERANA GROUP. This is a new form, patented in the

United States by Hines Wholesale Nurseries, Santa Ana, California, in 1972. It is a rapid grower reaching 2 metres across, very low-growing (never over 20 cm) with blue-green foliage very dense all over the plant. It is said to be very hardy and resistant to root rot. It was found as a sport of *J.* × *media* 'Pfitzerana Glauca' by Frank J. Serpa of Freemont, California, in 1963.

– –'**Shimpaku**' Welch [Dw. Con. 198. 1966.] PLUMOSA GROUP. This is a very slow-growing and delightful dwarf form of the Plumosa group, with dull, greyish-green foliage. It is a form much used by the 'manufacturers' of Bonsai trees, by whom it is frequently misnamed Sargent's juniper (see below), but when it becomes freely available it should become very popular as a garden plant or for use in troughs.

Herman J. Grootendorst of Boskoop, Holland, considers it to be identical with 'Globosa Cinerea', 'Shimpaku' being merely that variety growing 'on its own roots'. A golden form which I have received as 'Shimpaku Gold' appears to be a diminutive 'Plumosa Aurea'. Since the latter form is another that is usually supplied as a grafted plant, this could well confirm Mr. Grootendorst's statement, but the special requirements of the Bonsai cult justify retention of the separate name for commercial reasons. See also under *J. sargentii.*

– –'**Sulphur Spray**' Grootn. [Dendroflora **6**: 78. 1969.] PFITZERANA GROUP. This is a colour sport from 'Hetz' with pale sulphur yellow foliage found about 1962 and introduced by L. Konijn and Co., Arboretum Tempelhof, Ederveen, Holland.

– –'**Tremonia**' New name [*J. chinensis* var. *plumosa aurea* Hornb. Dw. Con. 66. 1923 and Ed. 2, 103. 1938.] PLUMOSA GROUP. Under 'Plumosa Aurea' above I state a case for retaining that name for the wide spreading plant for which it is in general use. The more erect form which Hornibrook doubtless had in mind was first brought to my notice in the Dortmund-Brunninghausen Botanic Garden by G. Krüssman who has suggested the name. 'Tremonia' is identical with 'Plumosa Aurea' in colour but its habit is that of 'Blaauw'. (Illustration 250).

Juniperus procera var. *africana,* Hort. N.Z. See *J. chinensis* 'Stricta'.

Juniperus procumbens (Endl.) Miq. This is a procumbent species not always seen in good health. In time it will cover a large area, for plants 1 m high by 7 m across are known. The main branches are stiff, stout and rampant, all growing tips tending to turn upwards. The leaves are in threes, linear-lanceolate, sharp-pointed, 6-8 mm long; concave above, with two glaucous bands; convex beneath. (Illustration 251). An invariable characteristic of this species is a pair of prominent white smudges on the underside of each leaf, one on each side near its base.

– –'**Nana**' [*J. procumbens* var. *nana* Grootn. ex Hornb. Dw. Con. Ed. 2, 122. 1938; *J. japonica nana* D. Hill, Nurs. Cat. 1904 to 1942; *J. chinensis* var. *japonica* SENSU Vilm. Hort. Vilm. 58. 1906 (most probably); *J. squamata* f. *prostrata* SENSU Van Melle, Review, 99 (and particularly Plate XII—bottom) 1947; *J. japonica* 'Green Mount' Hort. Amer. (in part)] is a slower-growing decumbent form with proportionately thicker stems and shorter and wider leaves. It forms a dense mat and is a much more desirable garden plant than the typical form, being

TABLE OF COMPARISON OF JUNIPERUS PROCUMBENS AND CERTAIN RELATED SPECIES

Species	Habit	Branchlets	Length	Point	Leaves Habit of Growth	Upper side	Lower Side	Fruit
J. procumbens	Low, spreading shrub with stiff, ascending branchlets, shoots turning up at ends.	Stiff with *glaucous ridges*.	$1/4$–$1/3$ in	Spiny pointed.	Adherent except upper part.	Concave. Broad white stomatic band. Green mid-rib *not* extending to apex.	Bluish-green, with two white spots or smudges‡ from which two glaucous lines run down the edges of the pulvini.	Sub-globose. About in across. 2-3 seeded.
J. recurva	Graceful shrub or small tree. Thin light-brown bark peeling off in strips.	Not glaucous.	$1/8$–$1/4$ in	Hard; sharp.	Densely overlapping. Curved.	Concave. Whitened. Persisting several years after death.	Convex. Channelled only near base.	Ovoid to ½ in long. 1 seeded. Seed pitted, dark purplish-brown.
J. squamata	Decumbent shrub,* branchlets thick, always tending to nod at tips.† Foliage much more closely packed than *J. procumbens*.	Green, grooved.	$1/64$–$1/4$ in	Finely pointed.	Crowded, overlapping, loosely appressed. Straight or slightly curved. Persisting as dry brown scale.	Two greyish white bands.	Convex. *Grooved from base to near apex.*	Ellipsoid. ¼–½ in long. Reddish-brown to purplish-black. 1 seeded.
J. morrisonicola	Shrub or small tree of open habit with ascending, terete branches and all growing tips bending over.	Green, 3-angled.	$1/8$–$1/64$ in	Lanceolate, sharp-tipped.	Spreading; densely set and persistent to second year.	Concave; glaucescent.	Grey glaucous. Slightly keeled.	Globose. ¼ in diam. Dry, black, glabrous.

* Not true of some varieties.   † Only very slightly so in the fastigiate form *J. squamata* 'Loderi'.   ‡ Not always clearly present in *J. procumbens* 'Nana'.

particularly useful for ground cover or planting so as to trail downhill over rocks or a tree root. (Illustration 252, 253).

The epithet *procumbens* having been at one time or another applied to several species of juniper, and *J. procumbens* as we know it today being (like so many other species) variable and capable of producing attractive dwarf, ground-hugging forms (more than one of which has been brought into cultivation), we have here a problem not capable of resolution by poring over the old descriptions. We can only sort out the plants as we grow them today.

First claim to the name 'Nana' must surely go to the plant brought home from Japan by Arthur Hill about the turn of the century and listed by the D. Hill Nursery Company as *J. japonica nana* from 1904 onwards until 1942, since when it has been listed as *J. procumbens* 'Nana'. It makes a very dense plant and is of a distinctly blue-green colour. How the other form in American cultivation reached that country I cannot say. This is mid-green in colour and is, I think, the form generally known in Europe, and in the Pygmy Pinetum there is a form— **'Bonin Isles'**, which Will Ingwersen tells me was given to his father by a friend who collected it (presumably in the Bonin Isles south of Japan) many years ago, exact records not being available. It has the same dense, mat-forming habit as 'Nana' but is a much stronger grower—vigour is intermediate between that form and the normal *J. procumbens*.

In these garden forms the characteristic white smudges are not always discernible to the naked eye on every leaf and the plant may have to be searched over until a leaf is found on which they can be seen, and always the marks are much smaller than in the type species. 'Nana' is often confused with *J. squamata* 'Prostrata'. Apart from the presence of the smudges which will always identify *J. procumbens,* the growing tips of all forms of this species tend to turn upwards, whereas all forms of *J. squamata* nod, more or less, according to the variety (see table above).

Every plant I have seen in the United States labelled *J. squamata* 'Prostrata' was a form of *J. procumbens,* a situation for which Van Melle's wrong picture is probably largely to blame. Variegated plants seen labelled as forms of *J. procumbens* were *J. davurica.*

Juniperus recurva. Buch.-Hamilton. This species has no claim to be regarded as a dwarf, but var. **coxii** (Jacks) Melville. makes such an attractive plant for some years if well grown that it is well worth planting, even although one knows at the time that it will have to come out after ten years or so. After all, gardeners are willing to go to a lot of trouble over annuals and bedding plants knowing that their usefulness will be limited to less than that number of months, so I can see no possible objection to planting a tree on these terms. The cultivar name **'Coxii'** is equally correct, if the cultivar name is preferred. (Illustration 254).

As its name, Coffin Juniper, indicates it forms a large timber tree in its native land, but when small it is an outstandingly graceful little tree with rich green foliage and very pendulous branches. It is especially effective when planted to overhang a garden pool with its trunk leaning over at an angle, towards the water.

The leader needs tying up for several years and the lower branches must be cut away and the foliage thinned drastically as the tree grows, to bare the trunk and display the graceful habit.

- – 'Densa' [*J. recurva* var. *densa* Carr. Traité, 27. 1855; Gord. Pin. 106. 1858; *J. densa* Gord. Pin. Suppl. 32. 1862, with *J. recurva nana* pro syn.; *J. recurva* var. *squamata* Veitch Man. Ed. 2, 185. 1900; *J. recurva* 'Nana' Welch, Dw. Con. 202. 1966.] 'Densa' is a form which, like the arboreal *J. squamata* var. *fargesii,* indicates a connection between the two species by showing intermediate characteristics, and I place it here because it is generally found under this species, rather than as myself having much conviction on the point. It is a picturesque, low, spreading plant with all its growing points strongly recurved; the leaves are much shorter than in *J. recurva* 'Coxii' but are of similar colouring. It builds up slowly in the centre of the bush, but is always much wider than high. The foliage is not unlike that of *Juniperus squamata* 'Wilsonii', but the plant has a more spreading habit. Also the general colour of the foliage is green, not grey as it is in that variety and in the diminutive form 'Glassell', for which *J. recurva* 'Densa' is sometimes mistaken, they being very similar in habit as small plants. The foliage has a strong smell suggestive of turpentine. (Illustration 255).

- – 'Embley Park' Welch [Wansdyke Nurs. Cat. 6. 1961; *J. recurva* var. *viridis* Hillier, Dw. Con. 39. 1964.] This plant is an attractive garden variety making a wide-spreading bush with densely packed, rich, deep green foliage. It was first noticed in a derelict rock garden at Embley Park, near Romsey, Hampshire (at one time the home of Florence Nightingale and now a boy's school), and it was named by Mr. Hillier var. *viridis* on the assumption that it had been sent home by the plant collector George Forrest and so was established in the wild, but following the plan of this book, I prefer to use the cultivar name. (Illustration 256).

It is a very attractive plant which should be much better known. Save for three plants at Embley Park, the only mature specimen I have seen is in a cottage garden at Headfort, County Kells, in Ireland. It does better in semi-shade.

Juniperus rigida. Sieb. and Zucc. This is a somewhat variable species which grows too big in time but it forms an interesting plant or small tree for some years. Its popular name, the Needle juniper, is well earned and it is not a plant to be handled carelessly or without gloves. On the other hand its specific name is misleading as it is of a graceful, pendulous habit. It would make an interesting specimen for a large lawn.

- – var. **nipponica** [*J. rigida* ssp. *nipponica* (Maxim.) Franco in Bol. Soc. Brot. **36**: 119. 1962; *J. communis* var. *nipponica* (Maxim.) Wils. Conif. & Tax. Japan, 81. 1916.] A procumbent shrub with yellow-brown branchlets and lustrous leaves, deeply concave and whitish on the upper side, which is found wild in the mountain zone of Japan and which has been grown as *J. communis* var. *nipponica* is now understood to be a mountain variety of this present species.

Juniperus sabina L. is a very variable, spreading or procumbent shrub widely distributed on the high mountains of Europe and Asia, and one in which the numerous named selections are much better garden plants than is the type. All forms have a characteristic, disagreeable, pungent odour to the foliage when bruised, and a bitter taste. Both juvenile (awl-shaped) and adult (scale-like) leaves are usually to be found on any plant, both kinds appearing in opposite pairs.

– –'**Arcadia**' Grootn. ex Den Ouden. [Conif. 175. 1949; 'Russian Savin No. 3' (Hort Amer.)] is one of four hardy selections (the others being 'Broadmoor', 'Buffalo' and 'Skandia') made from many thousands of seedlings imported by the D. Hill Nursery Co., Dundee, Illinois, U.S.A., from a government forestry station in Russia in 1934. All are proving resistant to the juniper blight which is seriously troubling most plants of *J. sabina* in the mid-west and so they are proving popular in the United States. 'Arcadia' is a grass green colour and its habit resembles a diminutive plant of 'Tamariscifolia', but the leaves are predominantly scale-like and small. It will make a dainty looking plant 1.25 m across and 50 cm high. (Illustration 257).

– –'**Blue Danube**' Blaauw [Nurs. Cat. 1956; 'Blaue Donau' Hesse Nurs. Cat. 41. 1961/62] forms a low shrub with wide-spreading branches having their tops curved upwards. The branchlets are crowded, the leaves mainly scale-like but the awl-shaped leaves inside the plant are a light greyish-blue. It is not in my opinion a particularly outstanding form, but being very hardy, is widely planted on the continent.

– –'**Broadmoor**' More [Green Thumb. **13, 3**: 33. 1956; Russian Savin No. 4 (Hort. Amer.)] This is a dwarf, low, staminate form, wider spreading and stronger than 'Arcadia'. It looks when young like a neat version of 'Tamariscifolia' but the plant tends to build up at the centre with age. The main branches are strong and spreading horizontally; the branchlets short and reaching upwards; the sprays very short and occurring mainly on the upper side of the branchlets. The foliage is bright green.

– –'**Buffalo**' More [Green Thumb **13, 3**: 33. 1956.] This is another of the Russian seedlings. (see 'Arcadia' above.) It is a wide-spreading form which stays lower than 'Tamariscifolia'. Bright, deep green, bearing berries when quite young and very hardy.

– – f. **cupressifolia** (Aiton) Lipa [Rehd. Bibl. 63. 1949 *.] This is another early varietal name of uncertain application. It is generally described as a low-growing, berry bearing shrub with bluish-green, wholly adult foliage. '**Femina**' [Hesse], '**Holmbury Hill**' and '**Musgrave**' (below) are selected clones that have received names.

– –'**Erecta**' [*J. sabina* Hort. Holl.; *J. sabina cupressifolia* Hort. NON Ait.] Dutch Savin juniper. This form approaches the normal form of the species. It is a tall, loose-growing shrub, with a predominance of adult foliage but with branches all ascending at a steep angle. It is not a particularly good garden plant and is hardly worth distinguishing from *J. sabina* in its typical form.

– –'**Fastigiata**' [*J. sabina* f. *fastigiata* (Beissn.) Vos in Rehd. Bibl. 63. 1949 *] is a narrowly columnar plant most unlike the normal *J. sabina* and by no means a dwarf form. I feel its claim on this species is very doubtful. (Illustration 258).

– –'**Hicksii**' [*J. sabina* var. *hicksii* Grootn. Mitt. d.d.d.G. **53**: 210. 1940] is a rather strong-growing shrub with branches at first ascending, becoming procumbent as the plant ages. Its foliage is dark bluish-green with a dull mauve tint in the winter and as it is mainly juvenile with the white upper sides of the leaves showing, the plant has an attractive, greyish-blue cast.

– –'**Knap Hill**', distributed by the nursery of that name near Woking, Surrey, I am unable to distinguish from *J.* × *media* 'Pfitzerana'.

– –'**Musgrave**' [*J. sabina* 'Musgrave's Variety' Ingwersen, Nurs. Cat.] is a low, spreading form which closely covers the ground, carrying mostly tightly appressed adult foliage, but awl-shaped leaves occur here and there over the bush and in the centre of the plant. The foliage is glaucous. It was found in a garden in Surrey and was introduced by the Ingwersen Nursery, East Grinstead, Sussex.

– –'**Rockery Gem**' [*J. chinensis* 'Rockery Gem' Grootn. Dendroflora **4**: 68. 1967.] This variety arose as a seedling selected on the nursery of Le Feber and Co., Boskoop, Holland. In 1969 the mother plant there was 1.25 m across on a short stem, plants in the nursery rows being much lower. The main branches are horizontal with numerous branchlets densely set at the sides and top; foliage is all acicular leaves 5 mm long, green below and with a wide glaucous band above. The leaves on weak shoots in the centre of the plant stand off at 45° shewing the glaucescence clearly; leaves on strong-growing shoots lie closer and give a green appearance, although the general effect, seen from a little distance, is grey-green. Although introduced as *J. chinensis,* the appearance of the plant and the characteristic *sabina* pungence of the foliage indicate its affinity with the latter species. (Illustration 259).

– –'**Skandia**' [*J. sabina* 'Skandia' Grootn. Nurs. Cat. 9. 1953/54; 'Scandens' Hillier, Dw. Con. 40. 1964.] This is the last of the four Russian seedlings (see 'Arcadia' above). It is a very low-growing form of dense habit. The foliage is predominantly juvenile, dark green but with glaucous bloom which gives the plant a greyish overall appearance. (Illustration 260).

– – f. **tamariscifolia** (Ait.) Koehne [Rehd. Bibl. 63. 1949 *.] This is found growing wild on the mountains of southern Europe so it is clearly entitled to botanical recognition, but since the cultivated plants are a single clone (or a group of clones so similar as to be indistinguishable) the use of the name cultivarwise is justifiable—as well as being almost universal.

– –'**Tamariscifolia**', then, is a low, spreading shrub carrying mostly juvenile, pointed leaves in opposite pairs, small and loosely appressed. It has been widely planted in the past, having a happy knack of fitting into the garden planting scheme at several points, but unfortunately it is very prone to juniper blight, caused by a fungus known as *Phomopsis juniperovora* which causes die-back of branches and even the death of the tree. The blight is almost impossible to control even under nursery conditions so the continued planting of this popular plant can, alas, no longer be recommended. (Illustration 261).

– –'**Thomsen**' Den Ouden and Boom [Man. 190. 1965.] A form selected in 1957 and introduced in 1960 by Thomsens Planteskole, Denmark. It is a compact, bushy shrub with fine, dark green adult foliage.

– –'**Variegata**' [*J. sabina* var. *variegata* Carr. Traité, 36. 1855; f. *variegata* (West)

Beissn. in Rehd. Bibl. 63. 1949 *.] This varietal name appears very early, but Carrière's description is the earliest to afford any real conviction that he was writing about the clone well known in cultivation today. It is an upright to spreading shrub with closely set branches and dark green adult foliage irregularly sprinkled with white variegation. It is quite an attractive form which could well be more widely planted.

– –'**Von Ehren**' [*J. sabina vonehron* Kuml. Friendly Evergreens, 178. 1946; 'Von Ehron' Hort. Amer.] is an upright, spreading form with light green foliage, with very small, adult leaves. Left to itself it forms a rather loose, open plant with no particular attraction (at least when young), but in America I understand it is in much demand sheared into a dense, globose shrub.

Juniperus sargentii Takeda ex Koidzumi 1919 [*J. chinensis* var. *Sargentii* (Henry) Rehd. Bibl. 61. 1949 *; NON *J. chinensis sargentii* SENSU Newsum, Dwarfed Tree Manual 74. 1960; NEC Yashiroda, Plants & Gardens, **22, 2:** *Front cover illus.* and 45. 1966; NON *J. sargentiae* SENSU Yashiroda, Bonsai Plants. 1, 22 and 48, 1960 (and other writers on Bonsai trees).] Sargent's juniper is a prostrate shrub discovered by Dr. Sargent on the coast of northern Japan, very useful for ground cover as it is hardy, very accommodating as to soil and situation and remarkably disease free. (The plant so much used by Bonsai addicts is *J.* × *media* 'Shimpaku'.)

It has been at one time or another described as *J. procumbens* and as *J. chinensis* var. *sargentii,* and as always in such circumstances can still be found growing under any name it has once carried. The last mentioned is still recognised by some writers on the coniferae but I follow Van Melle in treating it as a distinct species. It forms a low mat-like, spreading shrub with stout, prostrate main branches and short ascending branchlets. The leaves are in whorls of three; keeled below, concave with a raised mid-rib above, up to 8 mm long by 2 mm broad and quite free-standing on the main branches, but very much smaller, very closely set and loosely appressed on the branchlets and growing tips, giving them a cord-like appearance. The foliage has a very unpleasant smell of camphor when bruised, quite unlike any other juniper I know. Colour and habit variations have been selected as follows:

– –'**Compacta**' [*J. chinensis sargentii compacta* Noble, Journ. Calif. Hort. Soc. 1950.] Much more compact in growth with juvenile leaves dark green, very glaucous above, adult leaves light green with a dark green margin.

– –'**Glauca**' [*J. chinensis* var. *sargentii* f. *glauca* Grootn. Mitt. d.d.d.G. **53:** 207. 1940.] In this more vigorous form the main branches are ascending at a steep angle and the foliage is blue-green. (Illustration 262).

– –'**Viridis**' [*J. chinensis* var. *sargentii* f. *viridis* Grootn. Mitt. d.d.d.G. **53:** 207. 1940.] A form lacking the glaucous bloom and hence appearing greener than the type.

Juniperus scopulorum Sarg. The Western Red cedar (Brit.) or Rocky Mountain juniper is normally a pyramidal tree to 12 metres. Many selections of dense growth and attractive colour have been named and brought into cultivation, but most of these are too large for mention here. The foliage is in a general way similar to *J. virginiana,* a closely related species, but its branchlets are shorter and the foliage is more densely set, more or less tetragonal, 1 mm across; leaves adult, tightly appressed, tips pointed, juvenile leaves spreading.

– –'Admiral', introduced by the Mount Arbor Nurseries, Shenandoah, Iowa, U. S. A., is a broad, pyramidal shrub with grey-green foliage.

– –'Gareei' [*J. scopulorum* var. *gareei* Grootn. Mitt. d.d.d.G. **53**: 209. 1940] is a dwarf, rounded, compact bush reaching to 1.5 m; branches spreading; foliage whitish-blue. Originally selected by a Mr. Garee of Noble, Oklahoma. Wyman records that a 20 year old specimen measured over 3 m across by 1.25 m high.

– –'Globe' [*J. scopulorum globosa* Wyman, Amer. Nurs. **117**, 2: 13. 1963] as its name indicates, is a variety of globose habit; to 2 m high in time, with silvery-grey, juvenile foliage.

– –'Hillborns Silver Globe' New name [*J. scopulorum* 'Hillburn's Silver Globe' Hillier, Man. 491. 1971.] A selection that makes a medium sized more or less globose bush with very attractive silvery-grey foliage.

– –'Repens' [*J. scopulorum* var. *repens* Hornb. Dw. Con. Ed. 2, 126. 1938; var. *palmeri* Grootn. Mitt. d.d.d.G. **53**: 209. 1940; 'Palmeri' Den Ouden and Boom, Man. 194. 1965.] This is a strong-growing but completely prostrate form found on the hills near Lake Windemere, Kootenay District, British Colombia, Canada. It is a dwarf form with prostrate branches similar to *J. horizontalis* 'Prostrata', branches spreading; branchlets directed forward, prostrate but with tips slightly turned up, leaves awl-shaped, 5 mm long, bluish-green.

– –'Silver King' is a dwarf and spreading form, reaching to 50 cm high by 2 m diam. Densely branched and spreading with more or less filiform foliage of silvery-blue. An American patented variety which originated from seed in the nurseries of C. White, Walla Walla, Washington, U. S. A.

– –'Silver Star'. Bergm. [Pl. and Gar. **21, 1**: 49. 1965.] This cultivar is described as a wide, low-growing shrub of spreading habit, with young growths at first a vivid, light green, soon becoming silvery. It slowly reaches 30 to 40 cm high and 1.25 m across.

– –'Skyrocket' Den Ouden and Boom [Man. 205. 1965; *J. virginiana* 'Skyrocket' Grootn. Nurs. Cat. 1964/65; *J. chinensis* 'Skyrocket' Grootn. Nurs. Cat. 11. 1957; *J. scopulorum pillaris* Wyman, Amer. Nurs. **117, 2**: 13. 1963.] This is not a dwarf form, but as it must be one of the most narrowly columnar trees in existence it can be used with great effect for a number of years in a situation where a strong vertical line is needed in the garden picture. It is widely known and needs no description from me. (Illustration 263).

– –'Tabletop' More [Green Thumb, **13, 3**: 33. 1956 (and picture); 'Table Top Blue' Hort. Amer.] The name is misleading, for 'Table Top' will form a flat-topped shrub to 2 m by 5 m across with wide-spreading main branches, branchlets thin, pale yellow-brown; leaves very small, closely appressed, conspicuously blue. Female plants bear berries which add considerably to the attractiveness of the plant.

– –'Welchii'. With a name like this it should be good, but unfortunately it is not a dwarf form, so I cannot bring it in here. It is described as silvery-grey with 'less silver in old age', so it would appear that extreme poverty stares me in the face eventually.

Juniperus squamata Buch.-Ham. ex Lamb. [Elwes and Henry, Trees **6**: 1420. 1912] is a very variable species from Central Asia, usually a low, procumbent shrub with thick, prostrate main branches and numerous short erect branchlets, but sometimes a small tree. The leaves are crowded, in whorls of three, the upper part 4-5 mm long by 1 mm, standing free, often rather boat-shaped, with two bands of stomata above, green beneath, pointed; dead leaves very persistent. All growing tips incline to nod. I do not think the typical form is in British cultivation, but several *formae* and cultivars are recognised, certain of which fall into the following natural groups.

MEYERI GROUP   Leaves long and blue in colour

'Blue Carpet'	'Holger'
'Blue Star'	'Meyeri'

WILSONII GROUP   Leaves short and green in colour

'Forrestii'	'Prostrata'
'Glassell'	'Pygmaea'
'Loderi'	'Wilsonii'

– –'**Blue Carpet**' Van de Laar [Dendr. **9**: 47. 1972] MEYERI GROUP. This is a slow-growing sport from 'Meyeri' that originated on the nursery of Jac. Shoemaker, Boskoop, Holland. In ten years it has made a spreading plant about 25 cm high by 1.5 m across.

– –'**Blue Star**' P. de Vogel [Dendr. **2**: 46. 1965.] MEYERI GROUP. This cultivar is one of the most promising new dwarf conifers to be introduced of recent years. This form originated in the nursery of Gebr. Hoogeveen of Reeuwijk in Holland, where in a block of stock plants of *Juniperus squamata* 'Meyeri' one plant began to grow more compactly and later produced two very compact shoots. Used as cuttings, about 1950, these gave rise to the new form. 'Blue Star' forms a very slow-growing, low, rounded or squat plant about as broad as high with very dense foliage in which the leaf shape is similar in colouring to the juvenile foliage usually found in the lower part of a plant of 'Meyeri', but the foliage is more crowded on the branchlets and the plant never throws out the strong leader growth characteristic of 'Meyeri', so it stays dense and squat, and so far it has remained stable in cultivation. (Illustration 264).

– –"*campbellii*". See *J. chinensis* 'Pyramidalis'.

– – var. **fargesii** Rehd. and Wils. in Sarg. [Pl. Wils. **2**: 59. 1914; Rehd. Bibl. 58. 1949 *.] This is an upright form of tree size with green foliage and pendulous habit very similar to *J. recurva* 'Coxii'. It is rare in cultivation but there is a good specimen at Embley Park, near Romsey, Hampshire.

– –'**Forrestii**'. There is a distinct form falling within the WILSONII GROUP in cultivation in Britain with foliage similar to the cultivar 'Wilsonii' but having a more upright habit—intermediate between that form and the fastigiate 'Loderi'. It is probably one of the '985' seedlings, and this name may need to be replaced by a fancy name under the Code. In America I have seen this or a similar plant being grown as 'Campbellii', a name to which the same remarks probably apply. Confusion has been added to by the use of the latter name quite wrongly for *J. chinensis* 'Pyramidalis' by some growers.

– –'Glassell' Ashberry [Min. Trees and Shrubs, 82. 1958.] WILSONII GROUP. This is a dwarf and extremely slow-growing form with branches ascending at steep, picturesque angles and short, curved branchlets. Foliage is as 'Wilsonii', but much shorter and denser. It is an ideal plant for a trough garden, as its branching habit gives a 'Ye olde gnarled apple tree' appearance to the tiniest plant, especially if all its foliage is nipped off except at the growing tips. It should appeal to Bonsai addicts.

– –'Holger' [New cv.] This is a reputed hybrid between *Juniperus squamata* 'Meyeri' and *Juniperus × media* 'Pfitzerana', one of several raised by the late Holger Jensen of the Ramlosa Plantskola, Helsingborg, Sweden, in 1946, but I treat it here under this species since its growth and habit, although intermediate between the parents, lies closer to *J. squamata*. It forms a wide-spreading plant (the mother plant now measures 2 m by 2 m) and in spring the young growth is yellow, giving a beautiful two-tone effect against the glaucous blue older foliage. (Illustration 265).

– –'Loderi' [*J. squamata* var. *Loderi* Hornb. Rep. Conif. Conf. 74. 1932; *J. wallichiana* var. *loderi* Hornb. Gar. Chron. **85**: 50. 1929.] WILSONII GROUP. Although not one of the Wilson seedlings this also seems to have come from a stray seed in a mixed packet and it certainly is one of our present group, differing from the other cultivars only in habit. 'Loderi' forms a dense, columnar bush of the habit of *J. communis* 'Compressa', for a giant specimen of which it can be mistaken at a distance. Even in this fastigiate form the characteristic nodding at the growing tips is just discernible. (Illustration 266).

– –'Meyeri' [*J. squamata* var. *Meyeri* Rehd. Journ. Arn. Arb. **3**: 207. 1922.] Although Professor Rehder may have correctly identified this now deservedly popular plant as *J. squamata* (he having the advantage of fruiting material) an attempt to confer botanical status on a plant found, not 'in the wild' but in a Chinese flower pot, is clearly not for us to follow today. 'Meyeri', then, forms a large handsome bush (or if stem-trained as a young plant—a small tree) with strong-growing luxuriant main shoots and short branchlets, gracefully curling over at every growing tip, quite one of the most beautiful of conifers, or indeed of all plants, when well grown. The foliage is dense and of a beautiful blue-grey. Leaves are long, straight and sharp-pointed, 6-10 mm long by 1.5 mm broad. (Illustration 267).

As this cultivar has the annoying habit found in this species and holds on to its dead leaves for several years it tends to develop a half-dead appearance in time. This can be overcome by regular hard pruning (as is advocated for black currants) to encourage strong young main branches and plenty of new wood. The foliage and habit is so unlike all forms of *J. squamata* in cultivation that I wonder whether it may turn out to be of hybrid origin. I understand that it fruits readily in the United States and I should be interested to hear from anyone who has raised seedlings.

– –'Prostrata' Den Ouden and Boom [Man. 197. 1965; NON f. *prostrata* (Hornb.)

Rehd. Bibl. 58. 1949 *; NON Van Melle, Review, 99. 1947; NON Teuscher, New Flora & Silva **8**: 193. (fig. 66) 1966; and other writers.] WILSONII GROUP. Although it is virtually impossible to distinguish between *J. procumbens* and *J. squamata* from examination of the foliar parts alone, the difference in habit even in young plants is noticeable. Typical *J. procumbens* always shows the unmistakeable white smudges at the base of the leaf. The mat-forming dwarf forms in cultivation also have these marks, but much less noticeably so and sometimes they are visible on a few leaves only, here and there. But the long, sturdy main shoots, densely clothed with very short laterals, held stiffly along the ground except just at the tip are very different to the tendency of the growing tips of all forms of *J. squamata* to nod in a rather apologetic manner. Whether or not seeds of *J. procumbens* could have found their way into the distribution of Wilson's collection 985 I cannot say, but Hornibrook's description [Dw. Con. Ed. 2, 126. 1938] of the plant he raised from that source (now no longer traceable in cultivation) and Slavin's account [Rep. Conif. Conf. 108. 1932] of his own plant of similar origin both suggest that other species to me much more than any form of *J. squamata* that I know, and I rather think this could be the origin of the mat-forming clone of *J. procumbens* (NON 'Nana' SENSU D. Hill) which I found widely grown in the eastern United States as *J. squamata prostrata*. Whether or not this be the case, all subsequent mention of *J. squamata prostrata* based on Hornibrook needs to be examined critically.

'Prostrata' as we have it in Britain has thick, woody, horizontal main branches carrying more or less erect branchlets bearing leaves longer and less wide than in the 'Wilson' group, but otherwise similar. All growing tips arch over noticeably. Another clone in circulation, **'Pygmaea'**, so named because of its smaller leaves and neat habit when small, has the same vertical branching system but develops in time into a rounded, spreading bush. It is possible that these two cultivars are more representative of the typical *J. squamata* than any others in cultivation. (Illustration 268).

– – f. **wilsonii** Rehd. [Journ. Arn. Arb. **1**: 191. 1920] E. H. Wilson sent home from China several consignments of *J. squamata* seeds. These were distributed widely both in America and Europe under his collection No. 985 and it turned out a veritable 'surprise packet'. The seeds produced an assortment of undoubtedly *J. squamata* forms which developed in cultivation into more or less conical bushes usually with several stems close together and with their short, crowded branchlets usually recurved at their tips. Leaves are shorter and (relatively) broader than in the normal *J. squamata* (which is doubtfully in cultivation) and more imbricate. These Professor Rehder lumped together so it is not surprising that Van Melle regarded f. *wilsonii* as 'something of a loose number'. It serves us correspondingly well as a group name for a number of clones in cultivation well separated from each other in garden use by their habit.

– –'**Wilsonii'**. The clone in cultivation under this name (presumably that from which Professor Rehder took his description) forms a rounded bush about as broad as high. It has the short, broad, boat-shaped leaf that characterises the whole group, but these stand off at 80-90°, exposing the white stomatic bands, and in this clone all the growing tips arch over noticeably. (Illustration 269).

Juniperus taxifolia Hooker and Arn., a Japanese species seldom met with in cultivation has given rise to a procumbent form which is a valuable garden plant.

– – var. **lutchuensis** (Koidz.) Satake, Bull. Nat. Sci. Mus. Tokyo **6**: 192. 1962 [*J. conferta* var. *maritima* Wils. ex Nakai, Bot. Mag. Tokyo. **36**: 105. 1922; *J. lutchuensis* Koidz. Bot. Mag. Tokyo. **32**: 138. 1918] is a prostrate plant not unlike *J. conferta* but differing from that species by its flatter leaves (less deeply grooved above, and with the mid-rib sometimes evident) its much more prostrate habit and the lack of prickliness to the foliage when brushed, or of pungency when crushed. It is one of the few conifers that will fall down the face of a rock wall like an Aubrieta and with its dense growth and fresh, grass green foliage is a useful ground cover plant and deserves to be much more widely known. (Illustration 270).

Juniperus virginiana L. This species is mostly a tall, upright tree, but it is variable from seed and has given us a few shrubby and several spreading forms. The leaves are usually adult, but frequently juvenile leaves are present in small tufts even on old trees. The juvenile leaves are in pairs, 3-6 mm long with a sharp point, concave and glaucous above except at margins, green and convex below, pointing forwards. The adult leaves are very small and are in four ranks (giving a somewhat tetragonal cross-section to the twigs, which are very thin), overlapping, closely appressed (except, occasionally, at apex) with a glandular depression on the back.

J. *virginiana* is closely related to *J. scopulorum*, being the equivalent in eastern North America of that species in the west of the continent. It is clearly distinguishable from *J. scopulorum* in its flowering parts and in its habit of ripening its seeds the first year, but in the dwarf forms where we are usually restricted to foliar characteristics, the two species are often difficult to separate. From *J. sabina* forms it is readily distinguishable by the absence of the true savin odour and taste to the foliage. *J. chinensis* is distinct by its much larger (5-7 mm) fruit (when present), the coarser (i.e., thicker) growth, the awl-like leaves usually in threes (seldom in pairs) and more widely occurring over the tree, and by the sour, resinous scent of the warmed, crushed foliage.

Some American nurserymen affirm that a cedar-apple gall prevalent on the local *J. virginiana* never attacks *J. scopulorum* or *J. chinensis* forms. Anything, I suppose, can aid diagnosis. Alan Mitchell considers that the crushed foliage of *J. virginiana* smells of paint or soap.

– –'**Blue Cloud**' [*J.* × *media* 'Blue Cloud' Hillier, Dw. Con. 36. 1964.] This is an alleged hybrid raised from seed from *Juniperus virginiana* 'Glauca' with *J.* × *media* 'Pfitzerana' as the pollen parent. It forms an interesting large bush of similar parentage to 'Grey Owl' (below) in which the glaucous grey foliage is very dense in the interior of the bush, but long, twisted, whiskery young shoots thrown outwards at all angles give an untidy but picturesque look to the plant. (Illustration 271).

– –'**Chamberlaynii**' [*J. virginiana Chamberlainii* Knight, Syn. Conif. 12. 1850; *Chamberlaynii* (Carr.) Rehd. Bibl. 62. 1949 *; NON Hillier, Dw. Con. 41. 1964.] I regret having added to the confusion over this cultivar by writing of it in my earlier book as a prostrate form. I have been unable to trace whose name was thus honoured nor how he himself spelled it, but 'Chamberlaynii' was early described as a tall, pendulous tree. I have seen several such specimens in collections in France.

– –'Globosa' [*J. virginiana* var. *globosa* Beissn. Mitt. d.d.d.G. **15**: 134. 1904.] This makes a truly globular plant, being probably one of the most naturally globose conifers we have, even large plants having the appearance of having had some artificial help in keeping their neat shape. (Illustration 272).

A specimen fifty years old in the Arnold Arboretum, Jamaica Plain, Massachusetts, U. S. A., is only 4.5 m high and is an excellent rounded and densely branched specimen. Except in small plants the foliage is mainly adult with small leaves and fine twigs densely set, the leaves being green. It is one of the most attractive dwarf conifers we have and has been in cultivation many years. Close to it is '**Dumosa**' [*J. virginiana* var. *dumosa* Carr. Traité, 45. 1855] a form which was described as a bushy variety with a rounded, spreading head and with leaves either very acutely pointed, spreading and straight, or squammiform, closely imbricated in four rows. It seems no longer in cultivation and since Carrière knew plants 4 m high it must have been a compact form, rather than a dwarf. '**Microphylla**' [Sén. Conif. 101. 1867] was another early introduction no longer to be found. It formed a slender, pyramidal bush with short, twisted branches and very small, acicular leaves.

– –'Grey Owl' Grootn. [Nurs. Cat. 14. 1949/50.] This is another useful plant with the same supposed parentage as 'Blue Cloud'. 'Grey Owl' makes a much lower-growing and more wide-spreading plant and needs plenty of room in which to develop. The branches are thin, the leaves are small, appressed, a soft silvery-grey with the growing tips sometimes tinged with purple in winter. (Illustration 273).

– –'Horizontalis' [*J. virginiana* var. *horizontalis* Hornb. Dw. Con. Ed. 2, 12. 1938; NON *horizontalis glauca* Kumlien, Friendly Evergreens, 183. 1948 and colour plate.] This is an unsatisfactory name: any plants I have seen (see Hillier, Dw. Con. 41. 1964) or received under this name turning out always to be a strong-growing form of *J. horizontalis*. One thing is certain: Hornibrook's description was not of the cultivar *'Horizontalis Glauca'* [Kumlien l.c.], a form found many years ago by Professor Sargent on an exposed cliff site along the coast of Maine and introduced by D. Hill Nursery Co., which has very stiff branches, thick, rugged foliage and a bright bluish colour. The name 'Horizontalis' should be dropped as a case of mistaken identification by Hornibrook. (See also 'Reptans' below).

– –'Humilis' [*J. virginica humilis* Loddiges, Nurs. Cat. 42. 1826; *J. virginiana humilis*. Sén. Conif. 100. 1867; 'Repens' Nisbet ex Hillier, Dw. Con. 41. 1964 (?); 'Monstrosa' Welch, Dw. Con. 213. 1966. and Hort. Eng. (in part).] This is an extremely diminutive plant which forms a low, spreading bush with very small, acicular leaves borne in quite dense tufts, from which very thin growing shoots stand out horizontally in every direction. It is dark green in colour, the young growth turning dull mauve-pink in the winter.

- -'**Kobold**' Den Ouden and Boom [Man. 202. 1965] was described as a dense, globose form raised from seed on a nursery in Boskoop, Holland. Possibly no longer in cultivation.

- -'**Kosteri**' [*J. virginiana* var. *Kosteri* M. Koster & Co. Nurs. Cat. **14**: 23. 1877; Jäger u. Beissn. Ziergeh. 466. 1884; *J. chinensis kosterana* Boom, Ned. Dendrol. 99. 1942.] This forms a low but wide-spreading and eventually large bush, probably of mixed parentage. It is often confused with *J.* × *media* 'Pfitzerana' but it makes a much lower and wider spreading plant.

- -'**Monstrosa**' [*J. virginiana monstrosa* Carr. Traité. Ed. 2, 46. 1867; NON Welch, Dw. Con. 213. 1966.] Carrière's description 'A variety very remarkable for the quantity of "witches' brooms" which issue from all parts of the bush' is hardly adequate to identify any form ever seen by me in cultivation. It is probably lost to cultivation (See 'Humilis' above).

- -'**Nana Compacta**' [*J. virginiana nana compacta* de Vos, Handb. 242. 1887; Beissn. Handb. Ed. 2, 594. 1909; 'Tripartita Nana' Nisbet ex Hillier, Dw. Con. 42. 1964] is a bush up to about 1 m, more or less globose but much less regular in outline than 'Globosa' and bearing mainly juvenile foliage on its crowded branchlets. The leaves are greenish-grey above, green below, turning dull purplish-green in winter. (Illustration 274).

- -'**Pendula Nana**' [*J. virginiana pendula nana* Hillier, Nurs. Cat. 194. 1935 (and earlier?); 'Chamberlaynii' Hillier, Dw. Con. 41. 1964 and Man. 493. 1971] is a very small, slow-growing form with a strongly pendulous habit so that, as described by Mr. Hillier under the cultivar name 'Chamberlaynii', it makes an almost prostrate grey-green mat unless trained up in its early days. In the Pygmy Pinetum I have a small plant that was so trained to a height of 30 cm or so and is now planted where it is flowing down over the face of the rockery where in time I think it will make a most attractive specimen.

- -'**Pumila**' [*J. virginiana pumila* Den Ouden, Conif. 183. 1949; NON *humilis* Hort. ex Gord. Pin. Ed. 2, 156. 1875 (pro syn.); NON 'Monstrosa' Hillier, Dw. Con. 41. 1964 (?).] As I have it this is a form not unlike 'Globosa' but forming a flattened (not globose) bush and with the foliage a rich mid-green, maintained throughout the winter. I have not been able to verify the statement made by Den Ouden that it was raised at Silverdale in Lancashire.

- -'**Reptans**' [*J. virginiana* f. *reptans* (Beissn.) Rehd. in Bibl. 62. 1949 *.] The early use of names such as *J. virginiana horizontalis* cited by Rehder almost certainly relate to *J. horizontalis* forms of some kind, and since Beissner's description of the plant in the Botanic Garden at Jena (which has long since been lost) points the same way, the cultivar 'Reptans' should be regarded as being 'lost to cultivation', or at least 'not now identifiable'. Plants I have received from Germany under this name were unmistakeably a strong-growing *J. horizontalis* form, and I have already suggested (above) that Hornibrook's 'Horizontalis' was also a case of mistaken identity.

    This leaves us without any recognised prostrate clone of *J. virginiana*, unless (a possibility I have not investigated) 'Chamberlaynii', normally seen as a tall pendulous tree will make a prostrate plant if not trained up to a stem in the nursery.

- -'**Silver Spreader**'. A wide-spreading, low-growing American form with silvery-grey foliage, raised from seed and introduced by the Monrovia Nursery Co., Azusa, California, U.S.A., about 1955. It is similar to the European 'Grey Owl', but the foliage is a bright silvery-green.

– – 'Sky Rocket'. See *J. scopulorum*.

– – '**Tripartita**' [*J. virginiana tripartita* R. Smith, Pl. Fir Tribe, 22. 1864; f. *tripartita* (Sén.) Beissn. in Rehd. Bibl. 62. 1949 *] is a strong-growing form which makes a large spreading bush 2–2.5 m across by nearly as much high. It usually throws several stiff main branches from near the ground level and bears a mixture of adult and juvenile foliage which is green, turning to dull purple in winter. It is not in my opinion a particularly attractive form, but is useful where a fairly large and wide-spreading plant is required, being roughly the equivalent of *J.* × *media* 'Pfitzerana', but it is more upright and of a stiffer habit of growth, lacking the graceful, nodding tips of that variety. (Illustration 275).

LARIX

This is a small genus of forest trees much in demand for timber production. The leaf arrangement is similar to that of Cedrus, for which genus plants can be mistaken when in young foliage in early summer. The important distinction is that Larix is deciduous, whereas Cedrus is evergreen. Several pendulous forms have appeared but they are not dwarfs, and of the compact or truly dwarf forms recorded as having arisen from seed none is still in cultivation. This is probably because in time their rate of growth became normal, and the plants became arborescent. The genus is prone to witches' brooms but a number of attempts to propagate these by grafting have not succeeded in fixing the dwarfism induced by the brooming. The following are the only dwarf forms known to me to be in current cultivation. These seem reasonably stable, but no doubt individual plants may revert in the end.

These dwarf forms have the beautiful, soft-green spring foliage characteristic of the genus and their dense, picturesque branch pattern is an added attraction during the winter.

Larix decidua Mill. The European or Common larch with grey, glabrous shoots, has given us in '**Corley**' Hillier [Man. 494. 1971] a slow-growing, small, leaderless bush of rounded habit. It was found as a witch's broom by R. F. Corley of High Wycombe, Buckinghamshire, and introduced to the trade by Hillier's Nursery, Winchester.

Larix kaempferi (Lamb) Carr. [*L. leptolepis* (Sieb. & Zucc.) Gord.] The Japanese larch, with its red twigs, has given rise to several bush-like forms, presumably from seed, and two attractive garden forms from witches' brooms.

– – f. **minor** [*L. leptolepis* f. *minor* Rehd. Bibl. 29. 1949 *; *dumosa* Beissn. Mitt. d.d.d.G. **11**: 73. 1902.] Since these bush-forming seedling variants have appeared more than once, this name will cover them unless and until a form appears that is worthy of a cultivar name. I do not know of any such plants in current cultivation.

– –'Nana' [*L. decidua* 'Nana' Hillier, List Conif. 8. 1970. Nom.] The mother plant at the Pygmy Pinetum came from Hillier's Nursery labelled *L. leptolepis* 'Nana', although I do not think it has ever appeared in any of that firm's catalogues, and whether it is the same plant mentioned, without description, in the check list issued at the time of the 1970 Conifer Conference I cannot say. The plant is a very dainty little bush, very close jointed and slow-growing, and since most of the lateral buds develop into shoots the growth is very congested and compact. The leaves are in dense clusters 8–10 mm long.

– –'Varley' [New cv.] This is an attractive variety. It was found by M. J. Varley on a plant of Japanese larch near Ormskirk, Lancashire, in 1968. The tree was about 8 m high and the broom about 2 m from the ground and very near the trunk. It was introduced to the trade by the Wansdyke Nursery, Devizes, Wiltshire.

The annual growth is about half that of 'Nana' (above) and as the leaves are longer (10–15 mm long—occasionally more) the result is a very dense little bush indeed.

MICROBIOTA

Microbiota decussata Komarov is the sole representative of this genus of which little is yet known with certainty, since it has affinities with Juniperus and Thuja. It was discovered in 1921 on a mountain in southeastern Siberia, near Vladivostock, but has hardly yet found its way into cultivation. It forms a wide-spreading, flat-topped plant looking not unlike a low-growing specimen of *Chamaecyparis lawsoniana* 'Tamariscifolia'. Although it turns a rather dull brown in winter it is quite hardy (as its origin would indicate) and it seems to tolerate shade. A full account of this interesting species is given by J. R. P. Van Hoey Smith [Int. Dendro. Soc. Year Book. 50. 1972.] (Illustration 276).

MICROCACHRYS

Microcachrys tetragona, the sole occupant of this genus, in its native Tasmania is a low, straggling evergreen bush with long, slender, whipcord-like branches. It is hardy in Britain but is usually grown in an alpine house, where it soon gets out of hand unless the branches are regularly shortened to encourage a bushy habit which is not natural to the plant.

The tiny leaves are in four regular ranks, giving a tetragonal effect to the shoot and they persist for several years. It will often set its tiny red cones in captivity and is an interesting little plant when well grown. (Illustration 277).

MICROSTROBOS

As is often the case with a small, rare and unimportant genus, Microstrobos has had a struggle to establish its identity, having been included by some botanists with Dacrydium and by other writers called Pherosphaera. One only of the two known species is in English cultivation at all, so far as I know.

Microstrobos fitzgeraldii (F. Mueller) Garden & Johnson. A small, densely branched, low-growing shrub, occurring under shelving rocks at the base of waterfalls on the Blue Mountains west of Sydney, Australia. It is now extremely rare, since it can only survive in the constant spray and under the protection against fire of the overhanging rocks, so it is probably now one of the rarest conifers in the world.

A rooted cutting from a nurseryman friend, David S. Thomson of Summertown, South Australia, struggled to keep alive on a rather dry pocket on the rock garden in the Pygmy Pinetum until the donor himself paid me a visit and explained the plant's peculiar requirements. Potted up and stood in a corner of the mist house it has since grown rapidly and seems thoroughly at home. Readers fortunate enough to secure a plant and who have no mist house could probably give it the regular splashing it likes by arranging a small water tank with a strip of cloth hanging over its side, serving as a wick to release an occasional drop of water and arranging for this to fall onto some hard surface just over the plant so as to make a tiny splash.

PHYLLOCLADUS

Of this genus of evergreen trees and shrubs, natives of Tasmania, only one species is of interest to us here.

Phyllocladus alpinus Hooker Fil. is in cultivation a small shrub, remarkable mainly for its curious, thick phylloclades. These are leaf-like branches which look and act like leaves but carry the female flowers on their margins. **'Silver Blades'** Hillier [*P. alpinus* var. *minor* Hillier, Dw. Con. 42. 1964] introduced by Hillier & Son Nurseries, Winchester, in 1968, is a slow-growing shrub with small, neat, diamond-shaped cladodes of silvery blue. Hillier [Man. 498. 1971] says the colour is best seen on plants grown under glass, and I understand that he no longer regards it as distinguishable.

PICEA

This important genus of forest trees has given us a large number of dwarf forms, many of which have originated by propagation from witches' brooms, a phenomenon which is common in the genus. The leaves of Picea always spring from a peg-like stalk which remains on the shoot at leaf fall. This at once distinguishes any spruce from the round leaf scar of Abies or the oval scar of Pseudotsuga.

The dwarf spruces are among the aristocrats of the dwarf conifer world, but unfortunately this is a group in which great difficulty exists as regards identification and nomenclature.

Picea abies (L.) Karsten [*P. excelsa* Lam.] The Norway spruce is normally a conical tree up to 50 m high but the dwarf forms are of all sizes down to small bun-like plants never over 50 cm high. Those forms which originated by propagation from a witch's broom tend to revert (i.e., to throw out strong, healthy, normal growth), and seedling variants tend to grow coarse and out of character in time. In both cases the garden value of the plant can be preserved indefinitely by regular and systematic cutting away of all strong growth as it appears.

The Norway spruce alone has given rise to eighty dwarf forms (perhaps I should be more correct in saying eighty names) and several of the other species add their quota, and many of them are difficult to distinguish. In 1938 Hornibrook wrote 'One could fill a good-sized garden with the dwarf forms of the Norway spruce' and he could with equal truth today add the words ' . . . as to the correct names of many of which one's visitor-experts will all disagree'.

The absurdity of trying to create pseudo-botanical combinations out of what are basically cultivars is particularly in evidence in this group. Professor Rehder's *Bibliography*, for example, would leave us with no less than thirty-four *formae*, a situation I am sure no botanist, past, present or future would advocate.

Hornibrook made a valiant attempt to collect together all the then known cultivars and to provide better descriptions and additional names where necessary, but even so it is difficult and often impossible to identify a plant from his descriptions and there are many new cultivars now in cultivation, so in my earlier book I attempted to record the characteristics of these cultivars much more thoroughly and systematically than had ever previously been done.

One major obstacle to authoritative identification is that botanical writers have seldom taken much real interest in these dwarf forms, so some of the earlier descriptions are quite inadequate to identify the plant intended. Another difficulty is that many of these forms are very variable and liable to reversion (especially is this the case where a dwarf form has originated from a witch's broom) so that plants are liable to be mistaken for closely related forms. Also, there were (and still are) many unnamed clones in cultivation which add to the confusion by being circulated under the name of a close relation.

By far the most difficult aspect of this work was the locating of plants of unimpeachable identity to serve as my types, for even in the best collections there are plants which are clearly different from plants similarly labelled elsewhere and so I had to restrict myself to a description of those varieties in which the diagnostic position was reasonably clear. Murray Hornibrook's work was taken as the basis. Some of his descriptions clearly related to the plants I described in more detail in my book, but in some cases I had to fall back upon the balance of probability or a consensus of opinion from several reliable sources.

Since then, several other forms have been 'sorted out' and are added here, but (alas!) further study has shewn that several of the cultivars described in my earlier book were wrongly identified and these mistakes I must now, with apologies, correct. Even now it is impossible to claim that finality has been reached, so readers who can help by bringing to my notice the whereabouts of mature specimens whose age or recorded history gives authority to the names under which they are being grown, especially of the cultivars here omitted, are invited to communicate with me through the publishers or by writing to me direct at The Pygmy Pinetum, Devizes, Wiltshire. Information limited to even a single form will be appreciated.

In the use of my descriptions several points need to be borne in mind. One is that it is quite impossible to distinguish the various forms during the summer months, from the time the young buds swell and burst until the new dormant buds are well formed in the autumn.

Of the characteristics recorded, some are more variable than others. Habit, for instance, varies considerably with the age of a plant, annual growth with its vigour, the colour of shoots and foliage is affected by soil and climate, pubescence and other characters vary with the season—so these characteristics must be used with caution. On the other hand, leaf shape, the angle at which the leaf is held to the twig and the side twig to the main shoot, the angle of the main side branches to the horizontal; the size and arrangement of the buds, especially in the terminal cluster, and the disposition of the leaves at this part of the shoot are usually stable throughout the life of the plant and so have greater diagnostic value.

The prostrate and procumbent forms have been a particularly difficult group. As always, the older descriptions are too sketchy to carry any certainty and Hornibrook in some cases gave names to plants he had not seen. I have allocated the published names amongst all the different cultivars I have been able to find, according to the best available evidence, but I must admit to having been finally reduced to rather arbitrary action in one or two cases, so I am far from claiming to have had the last word on this subject. I think my descriptions, however, should be adequate to identify each clone I deal with and if further research requires any changes in the names I have used it should cause no great difficulty. The basis of my choice of name is given in the course of each description. But at best all these forms are variable and, to repeat, many unnamed forms are in cultivation.

– –'**Acrocona**' [*P. abies* f. *acrocona* (Fries) Fries in Bot. Centr. 138. 1893; *P. excelsa acrocona* Fries in Bot. Notiser. 256. 1890.] Although occasionally seen as a normal tree, 'Acrocona', being slow-growing, makes a useful 'dwarf form', interesting because of the curious and very large cones carried on the tips of the main branches. (Illustration 278).

– –'**Beissneri**' [*P. abies* var. *Beissneri* Hornb. Dw. Con. Ed. 2, 138. 1938; *P. excelsa* f. *Maxwellii* Beissn. Handb. 366. 1891.] This old cultivar illustrates well the problem of correctly identifying plants in cultivation today from which to verify or amplify early descriptions. My description in *Dwarf Conifers* [222, 1964] was taken from a plant in a well authenticated collection, despite its partial disagreement with the description given by Hornibrook. Plants reaching Devizes from other sources also have lacked the "flat, compact growth, comparable with 'Procumbens' in vigour and arrangement, the globular or broadly ornate buds and the dark mahogany-brown shoots" described by Hornibrook and have, with age, turned out to be the cultivar 'Nana'. I must therefore, with apologies, withdraw my own description and continue the search for a plant answering to that recorded by Hornibrook. **'Barryi'** [*P. excelsa* f. *Barryi* Beissn. Handb. 365. 1891; *P. abies* f. *Barryi* (Beissn.) Rehd. Bibl. 22. 1949 *] is another cultivar I have been unable to trace. Hornibrook considered it to be "related to 'Beissneri'", so my suggestion that the name might represent a coarse form to which that cultivar might revert may stand. A good picture in Silva Tarouca [Nadel, Ed. 2, 47. 1923] illustrates just the sort of plant one would expect and shoots of a dark mahogany brown colour would be confirmatory. (Illustration 279).

– –**'Brevifolia'** is a descriptive name that has been loosely employed by several writers at various times for plants with short leaves, such as may turn up in a seed bed at any time. These are not necessarily dwarf forms and the name cannot now be identified with any clone in cultivation, so it can no longer be used with any precise meaning. **'Crippsii'** [Hornb. Dw. Con. Ed. 2, 156. 1938; *Abies excelsa brevifolia* Cripps ex Gord. Pin. Ed. 2, 8. 1875.] Although I have not been able to trace this form in cultivation it should be mentioned here as one clone for which the name *"brevifolia"* had been used. It was characterised by very small, yellow-green leaves very densely borne, arranged radially. From Hornibrook's description 'Crippsii' must have been remarkably close to 'Ohlendorffii', if it was not, in fact, the same clone.

– –**'Capitata'** [*P. excelsa capitata* Croux ex Bailly, Rev. Hort. 395. 1889; *P. abies* var. *capitata* (Carr.) Bailey, Cult. Conif. 104. 1933; Hornb. Dw. Con. Ed. 2, 139. 1938.] This distinctive form is seldom, if ever, to be found true to name. Hornibrook was clearly mistaken in identifying a plant at Kew ('Nana' or a related form?) with Croux's plant which Bailly described as forming a more or less spherical bush having a curious biennial habit of growth, one year putting out straight shoots each terminating in a capitate cluster of buds which during the following year develop into globular clusters of shoots (*têtes-de-loups*). The bush being built up of these tight clusters has a distinctive and bizarre appearance not met with, he tells us, in any other cultivated form. In this he was undoubtedly correct, but this biennial habit makes any casual recognition of 'Capitata' very difficult. Some years ago I received a small plant of an unrecognised form which has now developed this kind of growth pattern but it is still too soon to identify it with certainty. (Illustration 280).

– –**'Clanbrassiliana'** [*Pinus clanbrassiliana* Loddiges, Nurs. Cat. 12; 31. 1820; *P. abies* f. *Clanbrassiliana* (Laws.) Rehd. Bibl. 22. 1949 (and synonymy, in part); var. *Clanbrassiliana* Hornb. Dw. Con. Ed. 2, 152. 1938; NON Annesley, Beaut. and Rare Trees, 33. 1903 (and photo).] Although several misspellings of Lord Clanbrassil's name are to be found, the double 's' used here is now accepted. This was the earliest dwarf form of the Norway Spruce to be discovered, having been first described in 1836, and since the original tree is still alive in Tollymore Park, near Newcastle, County Down, Northern Ireland, in a spot open to the public for all to see, the confusion over its identity is surprising and quite unnecessary. It may be partly due to a tendency years ago to regard 'Clanbras-siliana' as a collective name covering any dwarf form of *P. abies* that might turn up. (Illustrations 281, 282).

Lord Clanbrassil's spruce, together with Knight's Dwarf spruce (*P. abies* 'Elegans') and the Pygmy spruce (*P. abies* 'Pygmaea'), was the first named clone of witch's broom origin on record. Lord Clanbrassil planted his now famous tree in 1798 and the cultivar was offered in a trade catalogue of 1820. The date of introduction of Knight's Dwarf spruce is not known, but the specimens nearly 5 feet high referred to by Richard Smith must have been of a great age by 1863 and the dates recorded by Hornibrook put the plants of 'Pygmaea' at Leonards-lee at about the same age. But very soon, alas, confusion set in. A Knight's Dwarf spruce planted at Castlewellan was believed to be a propagand of the Clanbrassil plant—many years later to mystify Hornibrook by the colour of its twigs. Forbes [Pinet. Woburn 90. 1839.] writes of a variety "*elegans*" described for him by one Smith, a nurseryman of Ayr, as 'an elegant-growing tree, more slender than (the arboreal) *P. abies* var. *carpatica*'—clearly not at all the same form. Loudon [Arb. Frut. Brit. 2295. 1838.] speaks of three varieties (probably our present three) all in one breath, applying a remark true enough of the true 'Elegans' (i.e., 'it is said to be a dwarfer plant than 'Clanbrassiliana') to Smith of Ayr's plant. Gordon. [Pin. 6. 1858.] gets the description right, but quotes the authority and synonymy wrong. Finally, we have Henry [Trees Gt. Brit. 1343. 1912.] remarking (of 'Clanbrassiliana') 'this form has been found growing wild in . . . Sweden', a statement that, read carefully in its context, cannot have any meaning other than that witch's brooms turn up also in that country! This, of course, they do.

'Clanbrassiliana' forms a broad and spreading, a globose or sometimes a squatly upright bush (eventually a small, round-topped, multi-stemmed tree); very slow-growing and with a crowded branch system, with large, conical, red-brown buds and rather wiry looking foliage in which each leaf appears curved, is held edgeways, is widest about midway along its length and tapers thence gradually to a fine point with a drawn out sharp tip. One feature always met with in the true plant is the noticeable difference in vigour (i.e., annual growth and leaf length) at different parts of the plant, and sometimes between adjacent shoots. The branching system is spreading with the main side branches ascending at 10-20°, more at the crown of the plant. The leaf spray is flat, slightly up-cupped, so that the bush is more or less regular in growth but without any noticeable appearance of growth in layers.

BUDS: Medium red-brown, long-conical with sharp points, 4-5 mm (termi-nal), 2-3 mm (other), glossy, very resinous in winter so as to make the buds then appear light grey in colour. Number in terminal cluster 1-3, rarely 4; frequently there are two additional horizontal buds near terminal cluster and again at the base of the current year's growth and (rarely) one additional bud half-way. Buds are prominent because of their size and bright colour.

BUD SCALES: Large, pointed, fringed with resin, closely appressed.

LEAVES: Medium, bright to dull mid-green. Leaves emerge at a narrow angle to shoot, those on top of shoot are straight, elsewhere they curve away sharply near their base and are thence straight or (most frequently) curved outwards. *They are widest at the centre*, are thick and flat in cross section with a raised mid-rib and are *held edgeways to the shoot*. The upper half of the leaf tapers gradually to a long fine point, ending in a fine long drawn out tip pointing forwards, sharp to the touch. Two to three broken rows of stomatic lines above and below, not extending to tip. *Size*: 5-10 mm (or more) by 0.5-0.75 mm wide, with slight sheen, arranged radially to semi-radially, held at 60-80° horizontally and 30° above and 70-80° below (angles measured at the tips of the leaves). Aberrant leaf[1] at 90-100°, not always present. Leaves on top of shoot point forward, nearly hiding shoot. Leaves form oval to tapered outline. There is no concentration of leaves around terminal bud, but normal leaves point forward at 30° and end in line with each other, giving a squared off appearance. Leaves are set close together, and are flexible to the touch.

SHOOTS: Light grey-brown above, creamy or greenish-white below, glossy, glabrous. Pulvini are not prominent.[2] Shoots are thin and flexible; annual growth 20-50 mm, very noticeably variable between strong shoots carrying long leaves and weak shoots bearing short to very short leaves.

Any tendency to coarseness of growth should be checked by cutting away growth that is out of character before it gains control.

– –'Clanbrassiliana Elegans' [*Pinus picea* var. *clanbrassiliana elegans* Lawson, Pl. Fir Tribe 17. 1851; NON *Picea excelsa* var. *clanbrassiliana elegans* Hornb. Dw. Con. 93. 1923; NON Sén. Conif. 25. 1868; NON Welch, Dw. Con. 225. 1966.] After such a negative synonymy it seems a pity to have to leave on the statute book a name that has been so misapplied and which properly only belongs to a form no longer in cultivation. Lawson tells us it "differed from 'Clanbrassiliana' in the colour of the leaves which is pallid green", and this is all we know about this cultivar. Because of the then prevalent loose use of the name 'Clanbrassiliana' to cover any dwarf form of the Norway spruce, all subsequent writers confused Lawson's plant with either Knight's Dwarf spruce (i.e. 'Elegans') or the non-dwarf 'elegant tree' for which Smith of Ayr incorrectly also used the epithet 'Elegans'. Hornibrook, for instance, gives us a good description of the true 'Elegans', but to be on the safe side adds 'It is much faster in growth (than Clanbrassiliana) and is more irregular and looser in habit'. Loudon clearly had the true 'Elegans' in mind as he wrote, but wrongly cited Smith of Ayr as the authority. Sénéclause described 'Clanbraziliana Elegans' as a broadly conical bush to 70 cm, with short, stout branches and pointed leaves 4-6 cm in length, so he already could not have had the right plant in mind.

– –'Clanbrassiliana Plumosa' [*P. excelsa* var. *clanbrassiliana plumosa* Hornb. Dw. Con. 94. 1923; Beissn. Handb. Ed. 2, 234. 1909.] This name, according to Hornibrook, arose out of a misidentification by Beissner. It is no longer in cultivation, if it ever was.

– –'Clanbrassiliana Stricta' [*Abies excelsa* var. *clanbrassiliana stricta* Loud. Arb. Frut. Brit. 4. 2295. 1838; Hornb. Dw. Con. 92. 1923.] Although in my previous book,

[1]For fuller description of aberrant leaf see below under *P. abies* 'Merkii'.

[2]Pulvini are the cushion-like swellings on the twigs below each leaf stem.

on the strength of a large specimen grown under this name in the National Botanic Garden, Glasnevin, Dublin, I suggested that this form might not be worth separating, I have since seen in the United States a small plant with so unmistakeably a fastigiate branch system that I think I may have been wrong. So mature specimens of more or less columnar shape may yet come to our notice. (Illustration 283).

– – f. **compacta** (Kirchn.) Rehder. [Rehd. Bibl. 22. 1949 *; *P. abies.* var. *compacta pyramidalis* Hornb. Dw. Con. Ed. 2, 158. 1938.] *Forms differing from the type by a reduced rate of growth and little or no leader dominance so that they form compact, rounded shrubs, seldom or never reaching the size of small trees.*

Such form a distinct horticultural group within which several clonal names have appeared, but they are all too strong-growing for inclusion here and none can now, to my knowledge, be identified in cultivation. Any desirable clones in this group should be registered and distributed under new clonal names.

– – f. **conica** (Endl.) Rehder [Rehd. Bibl. 21, 1949.] *Forms differing from the type by a reduced rate of growth but retaining more or less normal leader dominance so that they form compact and noticeably conical plants, seldom or never reaching the size of small trees.*

Within this group may be placed several selections too strong-growing for inclusion here and to these also my remarks under f. *compacta* apply. But here should be mentioned **'Conica Elegans'** [*P. excelsa* var. *elegans* (var. *conica elegans*, pro syn.) Hornb. Dw. Con. 103. 1923; *P. abies* f. *elegans* (Forbes) Rehd. Bibl. 21. 1949 *.] This is the *Abies excelsa pygmaea* of Smith of Ayr, described by him for Forbes [Pinet. Woburn. 90. 1839] as 'an elegant tree, more slender-growing plant than the (arboreal) *Abies excelsa* var. *carpatica*, with solitary leaves about 12 mm long, slightly curved, somewhat four angled and marked with narrow, silvery lines'. Beissner [Handb. Ed. 2, 233. 1909.] says that plants 4 m high retain their conical shape. It is clearly a very different plant from Knight's Dwarf spruce, the sole rightful claimant to the name *Picea abies* 'Elegans'.

– –**'Decumbens'** [Hornb. Dw. Con. 160. 1923; NON Welch, Dw. Con. 226. 1966.] Procumbens Group. Hornibrook has left us a somewhat sparse description of this cultivar with no mention of the source of his material, which was probably a single plant. In my earlier book I gave a fuller description from the only specimen I had been able to find claiming the name. Not only does this not entirely agree with Hornibrook's description (e.g., in the colour of the leaf), with age it has proved inferior to the reliable cultivar 'Nidiformis' in every respect. I therefore consider it not worth perpetuating, so I do not repeat the description here. The outstanding characteristics of Hornibrook's plant seem to have been the resemblance to a rhubarb leaf suggested by the arching over and spreading out of the branches and branchlets, together with the very dark green colour of the foliage. This should facilitate recognition, should this cultivar ever turn up, but it is probably now lost to cultivation.

– –**'Diffusa'** [*P. excelsa* var. *diffusa* Hornb. Dw. Con. 120. 1923.] From the bad record of survival of these dwarf spruces in the climate at Kew I expected to have to put this name on the 'Lost to Cultivation' list, especially as it had never apparently strayed into commercial production, but several years ago I came across several old plants in a cottage garden in Gloucestershire which appear to be of this variety, and two of these are now in the Pygmy Pinetum at Devizes.

They answer very well to Hornibrook's description except that instead of making a wide-spreading bush like the plant at Kew mentioned by Hornibrook in his first edition (but apparently no longer there in 1938) my plants have formed very attractive beeskip-shape bushes about 1.5 m tall and the same across and are maintaining this shape and a dense uniform outline by sending up several nearly vertical shoots carrying radial foliage at the crown of the plant in addition to the normal side shoots carrying the thin, flattish, semi-radial foliage described by Hornibrook.

Apart from the different habit and the yellower green of the foliage, 'Diffusa' differs from 'Pumila' only in minor respects, as follows: Terminal bud cluster contains 1-5 buds making buds more noticeable; mid-rib of leaves is slightly raised; the (usually transparent) leaf tips always point forwards; leaves are narrower (0.75-1 mm) but closer together so as to hide upper side of shoot and finish with usually a broken circle of short, stiff (not drooping), needle-like leaves pointing forward at 20° around the terminal cluster; the shoots are thinner and the annual growth is greater (50-60 mm). The 1-2 year leaf spray is flat but by the third year it is twisted out of the plane of the spray, resulting in a very dense and solid looking plant.

'Diffusa' is a reliable and attractive garden form of great decorative value and should be better known than it is. (Illustration 284).

– –'**Dumosa'** [*P. excelsa* var. *dumosa* Carr. Traité, 249. 1855; *P. abies* var. *dumosa* (Carr.) Bailey, Cult. Conif. 104. 1933.] This cultivar was, I regret to say, misidentified in my earlier book, so the description there should be disregarded. I have not been able to find an authenticated specimen. It has long borne a reputation for putting out coarse growth and so losing its dwarfness, so it probably is no longer in cultivation. It must have been close to 'Microphylla'.

– –'**Echiniformis'** [*Abies excelsa echiniformis* Laws. Nurs. Cat. 8. 1875; *P. abies* var. *echiniformis* (Gord.) Bailey, Cult. Conif. 104. 1933.] The Hedgehog spruce forms a very slow-growing, neat, globose or cushion-shaped plant of dense, irregular and congested growth. It is often confused with 'Gregoryana' and occasionally with 'Veitchii' (and also, with no justification whatever, with *Picea glauca* 'Echiniformis').

Buds: Light brown with slight sheen and light yellow-green centres where not covered with scales; large buds cylindrical with rounded tips, 1-3 mm diameter, very irregular in size. Growth is very congested and irregular and may occur in either of two ways, viz., strong shoots 15-20 mm long with normal leaves and a small terminal cluster (3-5 buds of assorted sizes), or a congested type of growth in which a cluster of buds has developed into a mass of short shoots 3-5 mm long with tiny leaves, each carrying its own terminal cluster, the effect being a congested mass of buds and leaves up to 15 mm across. These two types of growth often alternate. There is an occasional lateral bud on the long shoots, near the base. These large bud clusters are a very prominent feature on some plants, but are not always present.

Bud Scales: Usually small and very closely appressed, but occasionally they are pointed, loosely appressed and with tips free.

Leaves: Medium, dull, yellow to grey-green, sharply turned out at base, thence straight or slightly curved forward, parallel, with the top half tapered to a sharp, more or less symmetrical point, sometimes drawn out to a short tip, *very sharp to the touch*, very narrow but thick and of rhombic cross section, but held *flat*; the mid-rib not being prominent. Three to four very broken rows of stomatic lines above and below, extending to tip. *Size*: 12-15 mm or occasionally longer by 1-1.25 mm wide with slight sheen, arranged radially and held at all angles to the shoot. Occasional shoots bear much wider and thicker leaves. No aberrant leaf. The uppermost leaves on the strong shoots stand off at 70-90° (or even more) in a roughly star-like ring, *below* the terminal cluster. The large bud clusters are a confused mass of buds and small to very small leaves pointing more or less forward. *Leaves on strong shoots are few and spaced well apart*, and are stiff and prickly to the touch—hence the popular name.

SHOOTS: Light brown with slight sheen, glabrous. Pulvini are flattened, giving shoot a crocodile leather appearance. Relative to their length the shoots are thick and very stiff. The erratic development of the buds gives a congested and completely patternless growth.

– –'**Elegans**' [*Abies excelsa elegans* Knight, Syn. Con. 36. 1850; (Knight) Carr. Traité, 249. 1855; R. Smith, Pl. Fir Tribe, 4. 1863 (Knight's dwarf spruce); *P. excelsa* var. *Clanbrassiliana* Annesley, Beaut. and Rare Trees. 33. 1903 (and illus.) and of some English nurseries; 'Clanbrassiliana Elegans' Welch, Dw. Con. 225. 1966; NON *Abies excelsa elegans* Smith of Ayr ex Loud. Arb. Frut. Brit. 4: 2295. 1838 (and elsewhere); NON *P. abies* f. *elegans* (Forbes) Rehd. Bibl. 21. 1949 *.] Although Knight's Dwarf spruce was one of the three earliest garden forms of the Norway spruce to have received a clonal name it has long struggled against the confusion that arose between it and the variety 'Clanbrassiliana' on the one hand and the very different plant misnamed 'Elegans' by Smith, a nurseryman of Ayr, on the other (See 'Conica Elegans' above). It forms a globose or very squatly conical plant with a branching system of no clear pattern and with very dense uniform growth. The main branches rise at 10 to 45°; the leaf spray is basically flat but each little shoot arches over downwards so that the whole spray droops. The photograph by the late Earl Annesley is undoubtedly of this form, and there are many old specimens, including several fine plants at Wakehurst Place in Sussex. (Illustration 285). It is still one of the best and most reliable forms, and should be more widely planted.

BUDS: Medium, red-brown, ovoid, with blunt (occasionally long) point, 2-3 mm (terminal), 1.5-2 mm (other), with slight sheen. Solitary terminal bud, with usually a pair of sub-terminal buds; other lateral buds few; buds noticeable.

BUD SCALES: Medium, rounded, not fringed, appressed.

LEAVES: Medium, bright mid-green, straight or curved backwards, widest at the centre, rhombic, held edgeways, narrowing gradually to a long, symmetrical point drawn out to a long, fine, translucent tip, sharp to the touch. One (occasionally two) rows of very small stomata above and below, extending to tip. *Size*: 6-8 mm long by 0.5-0.75 mm wide, glossy, arranged imperfectly radially, held at 50-60° horizontally, 20-30° above and 50° below. Aberrant leaf at 90°. Leaves on top of shoot point forward, partially hiding shoot. Leaves form an oval outline. Leaves are set close together and are stiff to the touch.

SHOOTS: Light yellow above, very pale yellow below, glossy, glabrous.

Pulvini are prominent. Shoots are thin and very flexible. Annual growth 20-30 mm, side shoots at 60-70° to branch. Bud sheaths persistent three years, dark brown to black.

Although in their buds and leaf shape this form and 'Clanbrassiliana' are much alike, the habit is quite different and 'Elegans' never has the noticeable difference in leaf size and vigour that is characteristic of that other form.

– –'**Ellwangerana**' [*P. excelsa ellwangeriana* Beissn. Handb. 366. 1891; *P. abies* f. *Ellwangeriana* (Beissn.) Rehd. Bibl. 22. 1949 *.] This forms a dense, robust and spreading plant with ascending branches but no central leader. Growth from lateral buds lies in a flat spray, but where terminal buds are numerous these develop clusters of almost radial shoots, giving a somewhat tufty look to the plant. Makes a good sized bush in time, but is useful on the larger rockery, especially as the bush can be kept in character indefinitely by cutting out all very coarse growth as it appears. (Illustration 286).

BUDS: Medium orange-brown, conical, with sharp point, 3-5 mm, uniform all over the plant, resinous in winter. Number in terminal cluster up to ten, lateral buds very numerous, sometimes in clusters. Buds noticeable because of their number, but intermingled with leaves.

BUD SCALES: Medium, pointed, fringed with resin, very closely appressed.

LEAVES: Dark, bright, mid-green, mostly straight, occasionally curved upwards, parallel, thick and stout, mid-rib prominent above and below, with a symmetrical, medium point slightly drawn out at the tip, sharp to the touch. Two to three rows of glistening white stomatic lines above and below. *Size*: 12-15 mm long by 1 mm wide (width very uniform all over the plant), with slight sheen, arranged almost radially on strong shoots, elsewhere semi-radially, held at 60° horizontally (up to 90° on some shoots, less than 60° near the tips), 20° above and 40° below. There is an occasional aberrant leaf, at 90°. Leaves on top of shoot point forward, not hiding shoot. Leaves form tapered outline, with a few short leaves, pointing forward, amongst the terminal buds. Leaves are set close together, and are very stiff to the touch.

SHOOTS: Medium orange-brown above and below with slight sheen, hairy. Pulvini are very prominent. Shoots are very thick and stiff; annual growth 40-60 mm, side shoots at 45° to branch.

– –'**Formanek**' Svoboda [Zpravy Bot. C.S.S.R. 130. 1966.] PENDULA GROUP. In November 1968 I saw this form which was raised from seed of unrecorded origin and planted out on the rockery at Pruhŏnice in 1932. It had made a pendulous plant 1.5 m diameter × 1.0 m high, closely following the face of the rocks amongst which it grows. It was named for V. Formanek who found it. It is not yet in general circulation in Britain, but its slowness of growth and pendulous habit should make it a valuable acquisition.

– –'**Globosa Nana**' [*P. abies* var. *globosa nana* Hornb. Dw. Con. Ed. 2, 144. 1938.] For my earlier book I selected as my 'type' a plant in the National Botanic Garden at Glasnevin in Dublin, a source that, from its close association with Murray Hornibrook I regarded as unimpeachable. But with age, propagations therefrom have at Devizes outgrown any claim to this name and can only now be regarded as falling within the cultivar 'Globosa' [Hornb. Dw. Con. Ed. 2, 172. 1938] a collective epithet he regarded as covering all similar and rather vigorous clones.

One aspect of these dwarf cultivars of *P. abies* is that the more one studies them, the less one feels one knows with any degree of certainty. This is due to a combination of reasons. Apart from the well-known inadequacy of many of the early descriptions, which often reduces the identification of the old names with the plants now in circulation to the level of intelligent guesswork, later writers (including, alas, the present one) who have attempted to supply fuller descriptions have sometimes examined only a single, unrecorded plant. Since seasonal changes, mutations, the nutritional status of the plant, its age and any pruning it has undergone can drastically affect its claim to be truly representative of the clone to which it belongs, so even where the new 'type' has not been actually misidentified (as has happened on this occasion) the amplified description may be suspect. Hornibrook describes 'Globosa Nana' as a sub-form of 'Pygmaea'— more vigorous, coarser, more frequently monstrous and carrying projecting branches similar to 'Nana'. Since the growth of 'Pygmaea' is notoriously variable, sufficiently so as to give rise at one end of the 'vigour scale' to a separate cultivar (i.e., 'Humilis') it must be allowed similar latitude at the other end. But so far, defining the line of demarkation between 'Globosa Nana' and the equally variable 'Nana' (and, come to that, 'Beissneri' and 'Capitata') has so far beaten me. Most of these forms tend to throw up a leader, thereby becoming conical; one good snip with secateurs converts any such plant into a 'rounded spreading bush', so such entries in descriptions are unreliable. Most of the plants I have cherished over the years under these different names have turned out to be 'Nana'. None has exhibited the dark-brown shoots distinguishing 'Beissneri', nor the tufts of upright shoots characteristic of 'Capitata'.

– –'Gregoryana' [*Abies excelsa Gregoryana* Paul ex Gord. Pin. Suppl. 4. 1862; *Picea abies* f. *Gregoryana* (Gord.) Rehd. Bibl. 22. 1949 *.] This is one of the slowest-growing and most attractive forms. When young it forms a dense, bun-shaped to globose plant which could be roughly described as a closer-growing form of 'Echiniformis', but the *leaves are shorter and closer set and held edgeways,* and 'Gregoryana' lacks the strong shoots often thrown out here and there by that variety, so forms a smaller, denser looking plant. With age both 'Gregoryana' and 'Echiniformis' are apt to lose the simple globose form which is their main attraction, the plants opening up into a cluster of globose masses somewhat suggesting a small, inverted bunch of grapes, but this tendency can be checked indefinitely by careful 'stitch-in-time' pruning. (Illustration 287).

BUDS: Very pale yellow-green, invariably globose, tips not covered with scales, 1-1.5 mm in diameter (terminal buds) with slight sheen, not resinous in winter. Number and size of buds in terminal cluster very variable (up to ten or more), with one or two lateral buds at base of strongest shoots only. Buds very noticeable because of their number.

BUD SCALES: Small, pointed, not fringed with hairs, very closely appressed.

LEAVES: Medium, dull grey-green, apparently round like a needle but actually rhombic in section, held edgeways, straight, parallel, with the top quarter tapering gradually to a sharp, symmetrical point slightly drawn out to a fine tip, a little sharp to the touch but much less so than in 'Echiniformis'. One to two (rarely three) rows of stomatic lines above and below extending to tip. *Size*: 8-12 mm long by 0.5-0.75 mm wide, glossy, arranged radially, held irregularly at all angles, but mainly at 70-90°. The uppermost leaves on the shoot stand out in a star-like circle at the base of the terminal cluster, *exposing all its buds*. Because of its congested growth these interlock with leaves from adjoining shoots, forming an impenetrable mass. An occasional short leaf points forwards. Leaves are set close together, and are stiff to the touch.

Shoots: Light brown with slight sheen, slightly hairy. Pulvini are prominent, brown. Shoots are thick but flexible. Annual growth is very variable from 5 to 20 mm. The erratic development of the buds gives a congested, patternless growth which is so dense as to smother all foliage in the interior of the plant.

Gordon tells us that it was raised at the Cirencester Nursery. This probably means that a witch's broom was found by a customer and brought to Richard Gregory (at that time owner of the nursery) for propagation. John Jefferies joined the firm as a young man and his great grandson Robert writes that the earliest reference he can find is in a catalogue of October 1856 with the title *Ornamental Trees & Shrubs cultivated by John Jeffries (successor to Mr. Gregory)* in which *Abies gregori* is offered as 'the best of all dwarf varieties' at 2/6 to 5/-. By 1873 they were priced at '2/6 to 21/-'. At the higher figure you probably received a beautiful plant in those days. There must be very few nurseries with such an enviable family record—or so fine a collection of their own catalogues!

– –'**Gymnoclada**' [*P. abies* var. *Gymnoclada* Hornb. Dw. Con. Ed. 2, 172. 1938.] Hornibrook gives a good description of this curious form whose chief distinction lies in the fact that most of the current year's growth, and also the older branchlets, are almost entirely defoliated except at their extreme tips, and it is astonishing that a plant defoliated for practically the whole of the year should not only live but continue to grow. It arose as a seedling in a Dutch nursery and was introduced in 1938 by the firm Den Ouden and Son of Boskoop, Holland, but is no longer propagated. Such curious forms appear from time to time. I received material from J. W. Archer, of the following form, which is somewhat similar to, but perhaps less grotesque than 'Gymnoclada'. In '**Tufty**' [New cv.] the branchlets do not defoliate—the leaves along the shoot merely shrink in length during the summer except at the tip, where the full length leaves remain around the terminal bud in a sort of tuft. It is quite distinctive, but rather more curious than beautiful.

– –'**Highlandia**' [*P. abies highlandia* Slavin, Rep. Conif. Conf. 116. 1932; var. *highlandia* Hornb. Dw. Con. Ed. 2, 162. 1938.] is a form grown at Highlands Park, Rochester, New York, U. S. A., for many years and named after its place of origin. Hornibrook describes it as similar to 'Pumila' but with a stiffer habit and more compact growth. I have not found it in cultivation in this country.

– –'**Horizontalis**' [*P. Abies excelsa horizontalis* R. Smith, Pl. Fir Tribe, 7. 1864.] Richard Smith describes this form as 'An extraordinary plant'. He adds 'admirably suited for rock work or wild scenery', but the customers were unconvinced, it would seem, for nothing further has been seen or heard of this form.

– –'**Hornibrookii**' [*Picea excelsa Hornibrookii* Den Ouden, Naaml. 29. 1937 and Conif. 210. 1949.] This is a form sent by Murray Hornibrook to the Den Ouden

Nursery in Boskoop and introduced thence to the trade. Originating, presumably, as a witch's broom, it is an attractive and well behaved form that deserves to be better known than it is. It forms a squat flat-topped bush to 1 m high by as much again across with a congested habit. The main branches are mostly more or less horizontal but otherwise in no clear pattern. (Illustration 288).

BUDS: Bright medium brown, conical or ovoid with sharp point (terminal) or rounded tip (other), 3-4 mm (terminal), 2 mm (other), glossy, not resinous in winter. Number in terminal cluster three to four, lateral buds numerous. Terminal bud inconspicuous, laterals more noticeable.

BUD SCALES: Small, indistinctly seen, closely appressed.

LEAVES: Dark, bright, mid-green, straight, parallel-sided, thick but flat, with tiny hooks on lower edge, similar to the cultivar 'Nidiformis'; mid-rib prominent on underside of leaf, with sharp point drawn out to a minute tip, sharp to the touch, 2-3 rows of stomatic lines above and below, extending to tip. *Size:* 8 mm to 10 mm long by 1 mm wide, with slight sheen, arranged pectinately, held at 50° horizontally and 30° above and 60° below. Aberrant leaf at 90° or more. Leaves on top of shoot point forward, hiding shoot. Leaves form tapered outline. Terminal and sub-terminal buds almost hidden by cluster of leaves pointing forwards. Leaves are set close together and are stiff to the touch.

SHOOTS: Light brown above, yellowish-white below, glossy, glabrous. Pulvini not prominent. Shoots are thin and flexible, with annual growth 30-60 mm; side shoots at noticeably irregular angle to branch.

– –'Humilis' [*P. excelsa humilis* Beissn. Handb. 364. 1891.] This horticultural curiosity forms a small, dense, globose plant of very congested growth with no clear growth pattern. Parts of the plant may consist of a congested mass of close growth in which the buds and leaves are more or less normal and healthy in appearance and size, and other parts which are a still denser mass of tiny buds and leaves. It is almost certain that this form arose by selection of propagating material from the dense growth occasionally seen on plants of 'Pygmaea' ('Humilis' could well be described as a diminutive form of that cultivar) for plants that are intermediate in character are to be found.

As a pot plant or on a small rockery it can be quite attractive, since the growth in a good specimen is almost unbelievably congested, but to many people it is more curious than beautiful.

BUDS: Light bright orange (lighter in centre), 2-3 mm (terminal buds) down to less than 1 mm (other), with slight sheen, resinous in winter. Number in terminal cluster varies considerably from one to eight or more, so that congested parts of the plant are little more than a dense mass of buds. As a result, buds are very prominent. (Illustration 289).

BUD SCALES: On large buds are medium, pointed and very closely appressed.

LEAVES: Dark, bright, mid-green, straight or (occasionally) curved backwards, parallel-sided and very thick, with prominent mid-rib, narrowing abruptly to a sharp point slightly drawn out (on large leaves) to a fine tip. Two to three very broken rows of stomatic lines above and below, extending to tip. *Size*: 2-10 mm long by 1 mm or less wide, glossy, arranged radially. Irregularly held at all angles from 10° to 75° to shoot, and on some strong shoots arranged spirally at the tip, where a dense cluster of short leaves pointing forward surround the terminal cluster without hiding it. Where the growth consists of a confused mass of buds the leaves are very small indeed. All leaves are set close together, and are stiff to the touch.

SHOOTS: Light grey above, very light grey below, glossy, glabrous. Pulvini are prominent. Shoots are thick and stiff; annual growth anything from 5 to 30 mm, side shoots at all angles to branch.

– –'Hystrix' [*Picea excelsa* var. *hystrix* Hornb. Dw. Con. 108. 1923.] This form is seldom met with. Small plants from material sent to me from the Arnold Arboretum in 1967 correspond with Hornibrook's description save for the buds, which are conical and certainly not minute. The foliage bears a superficial resemblance to 'Elegans' but the growth is open and irregular and the plants are much less attractive.

– –'Inversa' [*Abies excelsa inverta* Smith ex Gord. Pin. Suppl. 4. 1862; R. Smith, Pl. Fir Tribe, 7. 1867 (and Nurs. Cat. earlier?); *P. excelsa inverta* Beissn. Conif. Ben. 60. 1887, spelling altered to *inversa* in Handb. 361. 1891; *P. abies* f. *inversa* (Gord.) Rehd. Bibl. 21. 1949 *.] PENDULA GROUP. Whether the *Abies excelsa inverta* described by Gordon in 1862 was different to the *Abies excelsa pendula* he had mentioned four years earlier [Pin. 5. 1858] or whether the change was the result of an early bit of horticultural one-upmanship on the part of Richard Smith of Worcester (which I very much expect it to have been) it is now impossible to say, but it seems difficult to reconcile the latter's description—'The most elegant weeping form of the Norway spruce . . . of free growth and under ordinarily favourable circumstances calculated to attain a height of from 50 to 80 feet' with the clone so widely grown under this cultivar name today. It is even uncertain to what extent Beissner had a particular clone in mind, so we had better accept his spelling and continue using the name for a truly pendulous form that needs to be stem-trained when young, otherwise it becomes merely a prostrate or trailing plant. The regular development of the three terminal buds give a flat two-year spray, in which the growing tips are held up at 10° (i.e., 10° above the plane of the spray), but on pendulous branches these, of course, hang down almost vertically. (Illustration 290).

'Inversa' is quite easily distinguishable from 'Reflexa' by its thin flexible branches and by the colour and type of its foliage.

BUDS: Medium dull brown, long ovoid with blunt point, 5-6 mm (terminal buds), 3-4 mm (other), dull, resinous in winter. Number in terminal cluster one, but always two sub-terminal buds and on strong shoots one pair of lateral buds midway along the shoot. Buds inconspicuous.

BUD SCALES: Large, pointed, fringed with resin, loosely appressed, with tips free and sometimes recurved.

LEAVES: Light, bright, mid-green, straight, or occasionally very slightly curved up or forwards, parallel-sided, thick, rhombic in section, held edgeways, mid-rib prominent, especially on lower side of leaf, the top quarter tapering to a medium, symmetrical point usually with a blunt tip, not at all sharp to the touch. Two or three (or more below) rows of rather small stomata extending to tip. *Size*: 8-12 mm long (longest at centre of shoot) by 0.75-1.25 mm wide, glossy, arranged semi-radially, held at 60-65° horizontally (noticeably uniform), 30° above and 40-50° below. The aberrant leaf at 90°, borne also by the sub-terminal buds, is long and very noticeable. Leaves on top of shoot point forward, not hiding shoot. Leaves form an oval outline finishing with an open circle of shorter leaves pointing forward around terminal bud (not obscuring it) often noticeably twisted. Leaves are set close together, and are stiff to the touch.

SHOOTS: Medium brown above and below, glossy, pubescent. Pulvini are prominent, orange-red. Shoots are thinnish and flexible. Annual growth 30-50 mm, side shoots uniformly held at 50-60° to branch.

– –'Kalmthout' R. de Belder [Journ. Roy. Hort. Soc. **94**: 90. 1969.] This name has been given to a form of which the mother plant at the Arboretum Kalmthout in Belgium is over 5 m high by nearly 10 m across. In foliage and branch structure it agrees with 'Nidiformis', but it is difficult to believe that the effect of rootstock vigour can be so pronounced, and unless propagations 'on their own roots' prove otherwise, it must be regarded as a very different clone—compact, perhaps, but certainly not dwarf.

– –'Kamon' [*P. abies* 'Kamon' (Bano) Barabits, Deutsche Baumsch. **5**: 140. 1966.] This attractive variety arose in the Kamoni Arboretum in Hungary as a witch's broom on a tall tree of *Picea abies* 'Cranstoni', which is a very tall, sparsely-branched, open variety. With its dense habit and thick lustrous foliage, it is one of the best new dwarf conifers I know. It is very slow-growing, trees 10 years old reaching only 60 cm. (Illustration 291).

BUDS: Dark orange-brown, long-conical, with sharp point, 5 to 7 mm (terminal), 4 to 5 mm (other), dull, not resinous in winter. Terminal bud solitary, 2 to 6 sub-terminal buds but other lateral buds rare. Buds inconspicuous.

BUD SCALES: Medium, rounded, not fringed with resin, on most buds closely appressed.

LEAVES: Dark, dull, blue-green, straight (curved below), sides parallel, square in cross section, mid-rib not prominent, with sharp point slightly drawn out to a hooked tip, sharp to the touch. Many rows of minute stomatic lines above and below, extending to tip. *Size:* 15 mm to 18 mm by 1.25 mm, with slight sheen, arranged radially, held at 45° horizontally (variable) and 20° above and curving to 90° below. No aberrant leaf. Leaves on top of shoot point forward, completely hiding shoot. Leaves form a parallel outline with a cluster of very small leaves around, but not hiding terminal bud. Leaves are overlapping, flexible and are stiff to the touch.

SHOOTS: Medium, brown-red above and below, dull, minutely pubescent. Pulvini are very prominent. Shoots are very thick and stiff; annual growth 30 mm to 70 mm, side shoots at 45° to branch, variable.

Due to the irregular development of the lateral buds there is no clear branching pattern, and it forms a very dense irregular but picturesque plant wider than high.

– –'Knaptonensis' [*P. excelsa* var. *Knaptonensis* Hornb. Dw. Con. 95. 1923.] I do not think this form is any longer in cultivation.

– –'Little Gem' Den Ouden and Boom [Man. 240. 1965.] This well named, delightful little plant appeared as a witch's broom on a stock plant of 'Nidiformis' in the Grootendorst nursery at Boskoop in Holland about 1958. Growth on the mother plant was gradually cut away to encourage development of the broom which finally was cut up for propagation and the mother plant destroyed. It forms a more bun-shaped plant than 'Nidiformis' but otherwise could be described as similar to that variety but smaller in all its parts. So far it has shown no sign of reversion. Being so very slow-growing, it can never become in easy supply. (Illustration 292).

– –'**Mariae Orffi**' Den Ouden [Conif. 211. 1949; *P. excelsa* 'Mariae Orffi' Hesse, Nurs. Cat. 28. 1936.] A dwarf, flat-globose, very compact, slow-growing form, branchlets very short, yellowish-brown; winter-buds conical, small, yellowish-brown, surrounded by leaves; leaves radial, on older branchlets pectinate, 6-8 mm long, four angled, slightly sickle-shaped, light yellowish-green, apex blunt and yellowish coloured.

– –'**Maxwellii**' [*Abies excelsa Maxwellii* Maxwell (Geneva, N.Y.) Nurs. Cat. 23. 1873; *P. abies* f. *Maxwelli* (R. Smith) Rehd. Bibl. 23. 1949 and syn. (in part); *P. excelsa* var. *Maxwellii* Hornb. Dw. Con. 103. 1923; NON *P. excelsa* Maxwellii Hort. ex Beissn. Handb. 366. 1891; NON Slavin, Rep. Conif. Conf. 117. 1932.] This originated from a witch's broom on the Maxwell Nurseries at Geneva, New York, which continued to grow until destroyed by an ice storm in 1967. (Illustration 293). It carried two distinct types of growth. Cuttings taken from the 'tight' growth result in flat-topped plants (the 'true Maxwellii' of the trade) whereas propagations from the 'loose' growth give rise to the stronger-growing, rounded type of plant that mystified Hornibrook and for which he raised the name 'Pseudo-Maxwellii' (see below). Since both types of material are in fact equally authentic this situation is bound to give rise to confusion. Bernard Slavin, for example, was evidently taking his description from a plant of the loose form (i.e., Hornibrook's 'Pseudo-Maxwellii').

Although the development of growth intermediate in character may cause further difficulty, the two distinct forms seem to be in cultivation, so the nomenclature is best left as Hornibrook left it. His descriptions distinguish the two forms reasonably well.

– –'**Merkii**' [*P. excelsa* var. *merkii* Beissn. Zierg. Ed. 2, 440. 1884; Hornb. Dw. Con. 109. 1923; *P. abies* f. *Merkii* (Beissn.) Rehd. Bibl. 22. 1949 *; *P. abies* var. *Merkii* Hornb. Dw. Con. Ed. 2, 163. 1938.] In my earlier book I had to leave certain forms over for further study where I was not satisfied that I had been able to run to earth an authentic specimen.

One cultivar thus left over was 'Merkii'. This form has long presented difficulty. Its origin seems unrecorded. Beissner [Handb. Ed. 2, 235. 1909] describes it as 'A dense, short-leaved, roundish, low-growing dwarf form at first wider than high, but developing into a broadly conical plant'. Hornibrook in his second edition gives a fuller description but as he expresses doubt as to whether the cultivar was still in cultivation it is difficult to see how he came by the added information. He also confuses identification by drawing attention to what I have called the 'aberrant leaf'; i.e., a leaf sticking out at an angle to its neighbours at the base of each lateral bud. By not mentioning this elsewhere he has given a widespread impression that this aberrant leaf is peculiar to 'Merkii', and since it is in fact not at all uncommon a number of forms have from time to time been wrongly 'identified' (and distributed) as this cultivar.

In 1968, however, I found in the interesting and extensive collection of dwarf conifers at the Stadt Dortmund-Brunninghausen Botanical Garden a mature plant the origin of which was not on record which answers well to Hornibrook's description and which the Directeur, Herr Krüssman (author of *Handbuch der Nadelgehölze* [1972] and numerous other horticultural books) agreed should be identified as the true plant. The following description was taken from this plant in November 1968. The name should not be used for any other form.

A very dense, broad, squat plant 70 cm high × 1.0 m diameter with a central leader. The irregular branching system and irregular leaf angle give a tousled appearance to the plant which is quite attractive. The long aberrant leaf commented on by Hornibrook is quite noticeable. (Illustration 294).

Growth is very dense and irregular; the branching system has no clear pattern, the main branches rising at varying angles; the angle of emergence of lateral branches varies also, between 30° and 45°.

BUDS: Light crimson-brown, conical with blunt or sometimes rounded tip, 3–4 mm (terminal), 2–3 mm (other), glossy, not resinous in winter. Usually a solitary, large, rounded, terminal bud; lateral buds numerous. Buds are noticeable, two or three buds being frequently fused together into a single mass.

BUD SCALES: Small, rounded, not fringed with resin, very closely appressed.

LEAVES: Light, bright, mid-green, curved at base, thence straight, parallel-sided, thick but flat, held edgeways, mid-rib occasionally prominent; tapering gradually to a long acute point drawn out to a long fine tip, sharp to the touch. 2 to 3 rows of small and inconspicuous stomatic lines above and below, extending to tip. *Size:* 10 mm to 14 mm by 0.75 mm to never over 1.0 mm; glossy, arranged radially to semi-radially, held at widely irregular angles, usually about 45–50° horizontally and 30° above and 50° below. Long aberrant leaf at 80–100° is conspicuous. Leaves on top of shoot point forward, not hiding shoot. Leaves form a parallel outline terminating in a thick cluster of (usually short) leaves pointing forward and nearly covering the terminal bud, are spaced apart and are flexible to the touch.

SHOOTS: Light yellow above, very light grey-green below, with a slight sheen, glabrous. Pulvini are prominent. Shoots are fairly thin and very flexible; annual growth 3–8 cm, side shoots at 30–45° to branch, the angle very variable all over the plant.

– –'Microphylla' [*P. excelsa microphylla* Carr. Traité, 251. 1855.] The name was doubtless used by Carrière for one particular clone which bore very small leaves. Similar seedlings occasionally arise. They are not dwarf forms.

– –'Minutifolia' Grootn. ex Hornb. [Dw. Con. Ed. 2, 157. 1938], on the other hand, to judge by Hornibrook's description, originated as a witch's broom many years ago. It seems to have been a rather curious little plant with tiny leaves and very prominent light brown-red buds, but I have been unable to trace it. Specimens doubtless still exist in collections.

– –'Microsperma' [*P. excelsa microsperma* Mast. Kew Hand List 67. 1896; Hornb.

Dw. Con. 116. 1923; *P. abies* f. *microsperma* (Hornb.) Rehd. Bibl. 22. 1949 *; (see also under 'Nana Compacta' below).] This old cultivar forms a broadly conical plant with a spreading, symmetrical branch system, the branches standing up at all angles from horizontal (to 60° in the case of the strongest branches). The shoots which develop from the terminal and the 'half-way' clusters referred to below are too crowded to lie in a flat spray. The upper ones commence at an angle of 20° and arch gracefully over. This slight arching effect, repeated all over the plant, gives a characteristic appearance to this variety.

This is an attractive form which looks as though it would become large eventually. Its foliage, held edgeways is not unlike a form of *P. orientalis*. The arching twigs and the flattened terminal bud cluster, repeated about mid-way along the year's growth on strong shoots, is quite characteristic. It should be better known than it is. (Illustration 295).

BUDS: Bright, dark red-brown conical (leading buds ovoid) with sharp points, 4-6 mm (terminal), 2-4 mm (other), with slight sheen. Number in terminal cluster 5-8 (more on main leader growths), always (on lateral shoots) in two definite groups on each side of the terminal bud. A second and similar cluster is found half-way along strong shoots; otherwise there are few lateral buds. Buds are conspicuous.

BUD SCALES: Small, pointed and blunt, fringed with hairs, loosely appressed.

LEAVES: Dark bright mid-green, curved abruptly away from shoot at base and thence slightly forward forming an elongated 'S' shape, with parallel sides, rhombic in section, held edgeways, mid-rib not prominent, with a sharp, oblique point and a sharp tip not drawn out but often ending in a slight suggestion of a hook, not sharp to the touch. One to three long straight rows of stomata above and below extending to tip. *Size:* 6-8 mm long by 0.5-0.75 mm wide, longest at the centre of the shoot, glossy, arranged imperfectly radially, held at 70° horizontally, 20-30° above and 40-50° below. Aberrant leaf at 90°. Leaves on top of shoot point forward, not hiding shoot. Leaves form a parallel outline and finish in a double circle of very short, straight leaves held at 30° around the terminal bud but not hiding it from view. The buds in the terminal cluster carry the aberrant leaf. Leaves are set very close together, and are stiff to the touch.

SHOOTS: Medium brown above, medium grey-brown below, glossy with slight sheen, dull, very slightly pubescent. Pulvini are prominent, orange-brown. Leading shoots are very thick, but laterals are thin and flexible. Annual growth 30-50 mm, side shoots held at 40-90° to branch, the previous year's bud scales persistent and noticeable—very dark brown.

– –'Mucronata' [*Abies excelsa* var. *mucronata* Loud. Encycl. 1027. 1842; *P. abies* f. *mucronata* (Loud.) Rehd. Bibl. 22. 1949 *.] This is a very old cultivar originating in France which forms a broadly conical plant with growth uniform and regular and very dense. The main branches sweep up to 60° (or occasionally to 90°) these branches bearing their leaves radially. It is a robust and strong-growing variety which gets large in time: easily recognizable by the curved main branches and the numerous large buds.

BUDS: Bright, medium orange-brown, ovoid, with blunt point, 7-8 mm (terminal), 4-6 mm (other), dull. Solitary terminal bud, but lateral buds numerous, especially so near terminal bud, and buds are a prominent feature of the plant because of this.

BUD SCALES: Large, pointed, fringed with resin and closely appressed, except the uppermost scales on the main terminal buds, which look rather like a tiny hyacinth bulb.

LEAVES: Dark, bright blue-green, thick but flat; mid-rib not prominent; straight except that top third is curved upwards slightly; parallel, top quarter tapering very gradually, ending abruptly in a fine tip only slightly drawn out; sharp to the touch. One to three broken rows of stomatic lines above and below, not extending to tip. *Size:* 10-17 mm long by 1 mm wide, glossy, arranged almost radially, held somewhat irregularly at 40-50° horizontally and 30-40° above and (occasionally) below. Aberrant leaf at 90° or more. Leaves on top of shoot point forward, not hiding the shoot. Leaves form a more or less parallel outline, with a cluster of short, round leaves, pointing forward, around but not hiding the terminal bud. Leaves are spaced well apart and are stiff to the touch.

SHOOTS: Light orange-brown above and below, glossy, very slightly hairy. Pulvini are prominent. Shoots are very thick and very stiff, annual growth 20-50 mm, side shoots are held at 30-45°, usually in a flat spray.

– –'Nana' [*P. excelsa* var. *nana* Carr. Traité, 249. 1855; *P. abies* f. *nana* (Carr.) Rehd. Bibl. 22. 1949 *; *P. excelsa nana* Beissn. Handb. Ed. 2, 235. 1909; NON *Abies nana* Loud. Arb. Frut. Brit. 2295. 1838.] The true 'Nana' forms a broadly conical plant to 1.5 m high with most erratic growth. Main shoots at 45° above horizontal, this angle varying considerably. Parts of the bush are of close and relatively uniform growth, but at the top and here and there at the sides strong, coarse vertical shoots will arise. These will often follow up with the normal growth the following year. (Illustration 296).

It is not, at a quick glance, unlike a very coarse edition of 'Pygmaea' but these occasional coarse, vertical shoots with their distinctively different, sparse, divergent, noticeably square and often curved leaves are quite unlike that variety.

BUDS: Light orange-brown round-ovoid with rounded tip. Size very variable, from 2 to 6 mm (terminal) 1 to 2 mm (other), dull. Sometimes one large terminal bud, sometimes many smaller buds of different sizes in an irregular cluster, lateral buds very uncommon. Buds inconspicuous.

BUD SCALES: Large, thick and pointed, fringed with hairs, loosely appressed.

LEAVES: Medium bright mid-green, usually straight, but noticeably curved outwards on a few coarse shoots. Small leaves rhombic, large leaves square, with blunt, noticeably oblique point, slightly drawn out to a very fine tip, very sharp to the touch. Two to four broken rows of stomatic lines above and below not extending to tip. *Size:* very variable, from 2 to 16 mm long (sometimes even less on congested shoots) by 0.5-1.5 mm wide; glossy, symmetrically radial, normal leaves held at 10-20° but this angle is increased up to 70° on the coarse shoots, and the outline of the shoot is similarly variable. A cluster of much shorter leaves, pointing forwards, completely covers the terminal bud, where solitary. Leaves are overlapping on weak, and are spaced widely apart on coarse, shoots and are very stiff to the touch.

SHOOTS: Light orange above and below, glossy, glabrous. Pulvini are very prominent. Shoots are very thick and very stiff; annual growth variable, from 5 to 50 mm (on the strong, coarse shoots to 100 mm), side shoots at 45° to branch, this angle varying considerably.

– –'**Nana Compacta**' Den Ouden and Boom [Man. 243. 1965; Welch, Dw. Con. 238. 1966; *P. excelsa nana compacta* Hesse, Nurs. Cat. 29. 1950/51.] In my earlier book I included a full description of this form, based on the only plants then available—these being quite small. With time they have turned out to be identical with or indistinguishable from 'Microsperma', so there would be no point in retaining the name.

– –'**Nidiformis**' [*P. excelsa nidiformis* Beissn. Handb. Ed. 2, 630. 1909; var. *nidiformis* Hornb. Dw. Con. 101. 1923] PROCUMBENS GROUP. A variety originating in Germany which is one of the commonest and most reliable dwarf forms of the Norway spruce, and is usually found true to name. It forms a spreading to prostrate plant of dense and fairly regular growth. The main branches at first rise at 50–70° and arch over to 10° at the growing tips. This habit tends to leave a cone-shaped depression in the centre of young plants to which the variety owes its name, but this characteristic is usually lost as the plant ages. (Illustration 297).

It can be distinguished by the presence of a row of tiny, vicious, glassy hooks (too small to be seen by the naked eye) on the lower edge of every leaf. So far as I know this characteristic is shared only with 'Decumbens', in which variety the hooks are fewer and present only on a few of the leaves. In 'Decumbens', also, the leaves are wider and of a lighter green and they form a parallel (not tapered) outline and lack the wiry look that is a characteristic feature of 'Nidiformis'. As with all these low-growing forms 'Nidiformis' will cover a large area in time, building up height slowly at the centre.

BUDS: Dark brown, ovoid, with blunt point, 1–2 mm (terminal), 1–1.5 mm (other). Terminal bud solitary with usually two sub-terminals, and occasionally one other lateral. Buds are inconspicuous.

BUD SCALES: Medium, rounded, not fringed with hairs, very closely appressed.

LEAVES: Dark, dull, mid-green, curved out sharply at base, thence straight or slightly curved forward, with parallel sides, rhombic, with a series of sharp transparent hooks on the bottom edge of the leaf which ends in a sharp, very oblique point, rather drawn out to an up-turned tip, slightly sharp to the touch. One to two rows of stomatic lines above and below extending to tip. *Size:* 5–7 mm long by 0.5–0.75 mm wide; with slight sheen, arranged imperfectly radially, held at 80–90° horizontally, 30° above and with an occasional leaf at 80° below. Aberrant leaf at 90°. Leaves on top of shoot point forward, not hiding shoot. Leaves form a tapered outline, with circular ends, where a few shortish leaves point forwards, not hiding the bud. Leaves are set close together and are very wiry both in appearance and to the touch.

SHOOTS: Light yellow-grey above, almost white below, glossy, glabrous.

Pulvini are prominent. Shoots are thin and very flexible; annual growth 30–40 mm; side shoots at 30–70° to branch (noticeably variable).

– –'**Ohlendorffii**' [*P. excelsa* var. *Ohlendorffii* Späth, Nurs. Cat. 37. 1904/5; Hornb. Dw. Con. 118. 1923; *P. abies* var. *Ohlendorffii* (Späth) Bailey, Cult. Conif. 106. 1933; Hornb. Dw. Con. Ed. 2, 174. 1938; *P. orientalis pygmaea* Ohlend. ex Beissn. Handb. 376. 1891.] A very old German form, said to have been raised from seed about 1850. It forms a globose plant (later becoming broadly conical) with an ascending-spreading branch system and branchlets growing at all angles, not in flat sprays. Many of the growing shoots arch over slightly. In a young plant growth is dense and regular, but with age the outline becomes irregular because of strong branches which sweep up to form sub-leaders. (Illustration 298).

This is the plant commonly met with in the trade under this name. It corresponds only reasonably well with the description given by Hornibrook, as the leaves at their tips in the cultivar I am describing always curve away from the shoots and the branches are not in fan-like sprays as he suggests. It was at first thought to be a form of *P. orientalis*, the foliage being not unlike that of that species, but is now accepted as belonging to *P. abies.*

BUDS: Bright medium to dark orange-brown, long ovoid with pointed tip, 2–3 mm occasionally more (terminal), 1.5–2 mm (other), glossy. Number in terminal cluster irregular, usually 3–5, occasionally up to ten on very strong shoots, with usually one or two lateral buds on strong shoots. Buds very noticeable, especially in young plants.

BUD SCALES: Small, rounded, often fringed with white resin, very closely appressed.

LEAVES: Light, bright yellow-green at first, darkening to dull green by the autumn. All leaves begin at a narrow angle to the stem and curve outwards and backwards, especially so in case of leaves on lower side of shoot, and are square or round like a needle, parallel for most of their length but tapering at each end and ending with an oblique, sharp point, much drawn out to a fine tip pointing forwards along the shoot, not sharp to the touch. One to four irregular rows of very small stomatic lines above and below, not extending to tip. *Size:* 4–8 mm long by 0.5–0.75 mm wide, glossy; arranged radially on leading shoots and on small plants, semi-radially on side growth of older plants, held (at their tips) at 40–50° horizontally, and 10–30° above and 60° below. Aberrant leaf at 90°. Leaves on top of shoot point forward, almost hiding shoot. Leaves form parallel or tapered outline ending in a double circle of short leaves pointing forwards (10–30°), covering but not hiding the terminal bud. Leaves are set very close together, and are stiff to the touch.

SHOOTS: Light brown above, very light brown below, glossy, glabrous. Pulvini are prominent. Shoots are thin and flexible. Annual growth 30–60 mm, side shoots held irregularly at 40–50° to branch.

– –'**Pachyphylla**' [*P. excelsa* var. *pachyphylla* Hornb. Dw. Con. 102. 1923 and (*P. abies*) Ed. 2, 175. 1938.] This is one of the most distinctive forms, although by no means the most beautiful. It forms a squat (later an upright) plant of extremely slow growth, and bears thick, fleshy leaves quite unlike those typical of the species. It seldom makes sufficient growth to provide material for propagation, so will always be rare. The 'small plant at Glasnevin' of which Hornibrook wrote in 1938 is still less than 1 m high by half as much across, so that 'Pachyphylla' could claim to be reliably dwarf, but it is merely a curiosity. It is much sought after by collectors. The cultivar 'Kamon', with somewhat similar foliage, makes a more attractive plant. (Illustration 299).

BUDS: Medium brown, globose, 2-3 mm (terminal), 1-2 mm (other), with slight sheen, solitary terminal bud, lateral buds rare, occasionally one or two at base of current year's growth. Occasionally no terminal bud develops and this leads to the ultimate death of the shoot. Buds inconspicuous.

BUD SCALES: Medium, rounded, so closely appressed as to be indistinguishable as separate scales.

LEAVES: Medium, dull mid-green, curved forwards, tapered to each end, the upper side convexed, the lower side keeled, giving a boat-shaped cross-section; very thick and fleshy in appearance, ending in a very blunt, oblique point, not drawn out, but occasionally ending in a short nipple-like tip, not sharp to the touch. Five to six rows of stomatic lines above and three to four below, sometimes extending to tip. *Size:* 10-15 mm long by 1.25-1.5 mm wide, glossy, arranged radially, held at all angles 20-90°, standing out more in the centre of the shoot than at either end and noticeably spirally arranged, ending at the tip with a circle of small leaves not covering the bud. Leaves are spaced widely apart, and are very stiff to the touch.

SHOOTS: Very light grey above, medium grey below, glossy, glabrous. Pulvini are prominent. Shoots are thick and stiff. Annual growth 5-20 mm.

‒ ‒'Parsonsii' [*P. excelsa Gregoriana* f. *Parsonsii* Hornb. Dw. Con. 98. 1923; *P. abies* f. *Parsonsii* (Hornb.) Rehd. Bibl. 22. 1949.] Although Hornibrook first described this and the cultivar 'Veitchii' as forms of 'Gregoryana', they can each well stand as separate cultivars and the inclusion of the word 'Gregoryana' merely tends to give an impression (especially in view of Recommendation 12A of the *Cultivated Code*) that they have arisen as a mutation from that cultivar, which I do not think is the case. 'Parsonsii' is similar to 'Gregoryana' in its tiny, pale, globose buds but it makes a looser and more open bush, usually wider than high; the annual growth is greater, the branching more horizontal, even drooping at the sides of the bush, and the leaves are long and flat (quite unlike the needle-like leaves of 'Gregoryana') and never truly radial on the shoot, even at the top of the plant. Near the ground the leaf arrangement becomes pectinate and the buds are ovoid.

‒ ‒'Parviformis' [*Abies excelsa parviformis* R. Smith, Pl. Fir Tribe, 7. 1864; *P. abies* f. *parviformis* (Maxw.) Rehd. Bibl. 22. 1949 *.] This name, in rather loose use today amongst some collectors for any unrecognised diminutive form, should be restricted to the clone described by Richard Smith as . . . 'A peculiarly interesting and very dwarf variety, horizontal in its branches and exceedingly slow in growth'. Although far from complete, this description is quite specific and I have never met a plant which it fits.

‒ ‒ f. **pendula** Laws. [*Abies communis pendula* Laws. Agric. Man. 366. 1836; *P. abies* f. *pendula* Rehd. Bibl. 21. 1949 *; f. *inversa* (Gord.) Rehd. l.c.; *P. abies* var. *reflexa* (Carr.) Hornb. Dw. Con. Ed. 2, 168. 1938.] *Forms differing from the habit normal to* *the species in having all their terminal shoots noticeably pendulous.* This suggests a name for the

PENDULA GROUP

'Formanek'	'Pendula Major'
'Inversa'	'Pendula Monstrosa'
'Pendula'	'Reflexa'

– –'**Pendula**'. Unless and until the clone referred to by Lawson can be identified, this should not be used as a cultivar name and any pendulous clone worth introducing should be registered as a new cultivar. 'Pendula Major' Sén. [Conif. 29. 1867] and 'Pendula Monstrosa' Beissn. [Handb. Ed. 2, 229. 1909] are recorded names of such forms.

– –'**Phylicoides**' [*P. excelsa phylicoides* Carr. Traité, 251. 1855; "var." Hornb. Dw. Con. Ed. 2, 176. 1938] can hardly claim to be a dwarf form as it grows into a large open bush or a gaunt small tree. The foliage is quite distinct—the leaves are yellow-green the first year, becoming blue-green the second season. *Size:* 6-7 mm long, parallel-sided, rhombic in cross-section, held edgeways, often curved away from shoot. The side branches are few and frequently quite pendulous. It is quite unlike any other cultivar of *P. Abies,* but is more of a curiosity than a plant of beauty or garden value.

– – f. **procumbens** (Carr.) Rehd. [Bibl. 22. 1949 * (incl. *Picea excelsa* var. *prostrata* Schn. in Silva Tarouca, Nadel. 30. 1913; *Picea abies* f. *tabulaeformis* (Carr.) Rehd. Bibl., l.c.] *Forms differing from the habit normal to the species in not developing a leader and having a pronouncedly horizontal main branching system, resulting in a procumbent or prostrate plant much wider than high.* This gives us a name for the

PROCUMBENS GROUP

'Decumbens'	'Pumila Nigra'
'Nidiformis'	'Repens'
'Procumbens'	'Tabuliformis'
'Pseudo-prostrata'	

– –'**Procumbens**' [*P. excelsa procumbens* Carr. Traité, 241. 1855; *P. abies* f. *procumbens* Rehd. Bibl. 22. 1949.] Although lending its name to the horticultural group (and also to the botanical *forma* for anyone wishing to take notice botanically of these curious variants) this is also the legitimate name of a cultivar still very much with us.

'Procumbens' forms a very strong-growing and healthy looking, flat-topped, procumbent plant with foliage in stiff, widespread, flat (slightly up-cupped) sprays held at 20-30°. The leaves are longer than in any other low-growing variety I have seen and reduce regularly in length from the base of the year's growth to the terminal bud. The invariable development downwards of the supernumerary sub-terminal bud (where it occurs) is characteristic. (Illustration 300).

There is a good plant of this form at Red Lodge Nursery, Chandler's Ford, Hampshire, and a fine specimen on the bank near the front door at Jermyns, Ampfield, near Romsey, Hampshire, the residence of Mr. H. G. Hillier.

BUDS: Light orange-brown, conical with sharp point, 4-5 mm (terminal), 3-4 mm (other), dull, not resinous in winter. Number in terminal cluster usually three. Where a fourth bud is present *it always points downwards;* lateral buds are numerous and occur all round the shoot. Buds are inconspicuous.

BUD SCALES: Small, rounded, fringed with hairs, very closely appressed.

LEAVES: Light, bright, mid-green straight, parallel-sided, thick but flat, mid-rib sunk, with top half of leaf tapering to a sharp symmetrical point, slightly drawn out to a transparent tip, sharp to the touch. Three rows of stomatic lines above and below extending to tip. *Size:* 10-17 mm long (shortest above and towards the tip of the shoot) by 1-1.5 mm wide, glossy, arranged semi-radially, held at 60-80° horizontally, 20-30° above and an occasional leaf at 40° below. Leaves on top of shoot point forward. Shoot has a very noticeably tapered outline ending in an irregular and variable cluster of small leaves pointing forward or nearly so around the terminal bud, but not hiding it. Leaves are set close together, and are very stiff to the touch.

SHOOTS: Medium orange-brown, glossy, glabrous. Pulvini are prominent. Shoots are very thick and stiff. Annual growth 50-100 mm, side shoots at 70° to branch.

'Procumbens' starts into growth two weeks before 'Tabuliformis'.

– –'Prostrata' [*P. Excelsa* var. *prostrata* Schn. in Silva Tarouca, Nadel, 230. 1913.] See f. *procumbens* above.

– –'Pseudo-Maxwellii' [*P. abies Maxwellii* Slavin, Rep. Conif. Conf. 117. 1932; *P. excelsa* var. *pseudo-Maxwellii* Hornb. Dw. Con. 105. 1923.] I have explained the origin of this form under 'Maxwellii' (see above). Slavin's description was probably responsible for the widespread distribution of the form of looser and more open growth with different leaf arrangement, buds, etc., of which Hornibrook complained, especially as regards European nurseries, and which he distinguished by the name 'Pseudo-Maxwellii'. I have myself observed noticeable differences in habit and vigour between my own plants in Devizes and propagations therefrom which I saw growing in the United States. Always the vigour was greater in America, so I do not accept Dr. Boom's statement [Man. 241. 1965] despite its endorsement by some continental nurserymen, that there is only a climatic variation giving a spurious appearance of there being two distinct varieties. I cannot possibly believe that an American form could be so disloyal to the land of its birth as to maintain its true character only in Europe and not at home. The difference being essentially one of relative vigour I think the truth must be that the European material is the 'Pseudo-Maxwellii' of America willing to grow normally at home, but that because of the usual reduction of vigour in European cultivation it answers more closely to the description of 'Maxwellii' whilst on this side of the Atlantic.

– –'**Pseudo-prostrata**' [*P. abies* var. *pseudo-prostrata* Hornb. Dw. Con. Ed. 2, 168. 1938.] PROCUMBENS GROUP. The second form referred to by Hornibrook is distinguishable (with difficulty) from 'Procumbens', but is rare in cultivation. Since it is inferior in every respect from the more usual form described above, this is no misfortune and this form merits no perpetuation, either on paper or in our gardens. It is, as Hornibrook tells us, a somewhat stronger grower with annual growth up to 14 cm. The main shoots stand up starkly at a steeper angle, giving a much coarser look to the plant and the foliage is dull, so that the rather sleek, well-groomed look of the better form is quite lost. (Illustration 301).

– –'**Pumila**' [*Abies excelsa pumila* R. Smith, Pl. Fir Tribe, 5. 1867; *P. abies* f. *pumila* (R. Smith) Voss in Rehd. Bibl. 23. 1949 *.] 'Pumila' and its associated colour forms present a difficult group, for the descriptions we have inherited would suggest that they are identical in all respects save colour of foliage. It would, however, be nearer the truth to say that all they have in common is a leaf which is widest at about one-third of its length from the base (tapering thence gradually to the tip), and the habit of carrying their leaves semi-radially and lying in distinct ranks or rows, the leaves in each rank being shorter and pointing more nearly forward than those in the rank below it. In a single twig this arrangement is quite neat but it gives a rather jumbled appearance to the plant viewed as a whole. (Illustration 302).

'Pumila' is very much less common than 'Pumila Nigra' (described below) which has quite a different habit of growth, but as Hornibrook merely describes the latter as 'similar to the type, but with much darker green foliage' confusion has perhaps been inevitable, and as the leaf shape is shared also with 'Clanbrassiliana' a mix-up with that already sadly distracted plant is also apt to occur. There are several plants of 'Pumila' as I now describe it, in a bold and very effective group about midway along the entrance drive at Grayswood Hill, Haslemere, Surrey.

'Pumila' forms a low, spreading bush with a more or less irregular outline and with the lower branches wide-spreading and procumbent, but the upper ones more erect. The foliage is a rich, bright mid-green. The sprays are slightly up-cupped but because of the small angle of divergence of the side branches there is much overlapping of shoots, so the flat 'plate-like layers' described by Hornibrook are often much obscured. The whole bush has a very soft and cushiony feel, and the foliage is everywhere uniform and regular, lacking the irregular leaf size between one shoot and another which is an invariable feature of 'Clanbrassiliana'.

BUDS: Light orange, conical-ovoid with blunt point, 2-2.5 mm (terminal), 1.5-2 mm (other), dull. One horizontal pair of lateral buds close to the solitary terminal bud, rarely one additional bud ⅔ along shoot. Buds inconspicuous.

BUD SCALES: Medium, rounded, not fringed with hairs or resin, appressed.

LEAVES: Light, bright mid-green, turned out at base, thence straight, thin and flat, mid-rib prominent, widest at ⅓, upper ⅔ with a long taper to a sharp, oblique point drawn out to a very fine, transparent tip, not at all sharp to the touch. One or two rows of stomatic lines above and below, extending to tip. *Size:* 6-10 mm long by 0.5-0.75 mm wide, glossy, arranged semi-radially in

ranks, the lowest held at 60° (upper ranks at a lesser angle) horizontally, 20°
above and with leaves in the lowest rank hanging irregularly to 70° below.
Aberrant leaf at 80-90°, borne by sub-terminal buds. Leaves on top of shoot
point forward, not hiding shoot. Leaves form a parallel outline with leaves of
normal length continuing to the very tip of the shoot and are held forwards and
downwards so as to give a drooping appearance to the shoot. Leaves are spaced
well apart and are flexible and soft to the touch.

SHOOTS: Medium yellow-brown above, medium yellow below, glabrous.
Pulvini are prominent. Shoots are thin and very flexible. Annual growth 20-30
mm, side shoots held at 40-50° to branch.

- -'**Pumila Argentea**'. Murray Hornibrook's original plant, presented to the
National Botanic Garden, Glasnevin, Dublin, is now a large tree of no distinctive character or peculiarity in colour of foliage. It may have been, at the time
he described it, a case of chlorosis due to some mineral deficiency in the soil in
which it had been potted, but in any case the name can now be dropped.

- -'**Pumila Glauca**' [*Abies excelsa pumila glauca* Veitch, Man. 71. 1881; *P. abies* var.
pumila glauca Bailey, Cult. Conif. 106. 1933.] As occasionally met with in Britain,
this is very similar to the following cultivar 'Pumila Nigra'. In some plants the
branches rise perhaps a little more steeply, but other than that the only
difference I can detect is that the stomata are more numerous and show up a
glistening white under a ×25 magnification, instead of the dull white of 'Pumila
Nigra'. This is sufficient to give a barely discernibly glaucous look to the leaf
examined closely with the naked eye, but the plants as a whole are indistinguishable. I do not think the difference is worth maintaining, except in very
comprehensive collections—if that.

- -'**Pumila Nigra**' [*P. excelsa pumila nigra* Beissn. Handb. 365. 1891; *P. abies pumila
nigra* (Beissn.) Slavin, Rep. Conif. Conf. 118. 1932.] 'Pumila Nigra' is the
commonest of the group which carries the name and is an excellent and reliable
variety. It forms a wide-spreading plant, seldom reaching to 1 m high but
covering a large area in time.

The regular development of the horizontal pair of lateral buds produces a
spray which basically is flat, but as all the shoots twist upwards, and as the
narrow angle of divergence results in considerable overlapping the effect of
flatness is lost after the second year and the general effect is that of a dense,
irregular plant with *all the main growing shoots rising stiffly at an angle of 30–45° all
over the plant.* Of all the forms which form low, wide-spreading plants 'Pumila
Nigra' carries its main branches at the steepest angle and can thus be readily distinguished from the truly procumbent forms even at a distance. (Illustration 303).

There are large specimens in the rockery at the Botanic Garden, Bath, and
at Stourhead in Wiltshire, near the main entrance.

BUDS: Light orange-brown, conical with blunt point, 2.5-3 mm (terminal),
2-2.5 mm (other), dull, resinous in winter. Solitary terminal bud with a
horizontal pair of laterals very close and frequently also one or two midway
(also horizontal), seldom any others. Buds are inconspicuous.

BUD SCALES: Small, rounded, fringed with resin, very closely appressed.

LEAVES: Dark, dull, blue-green turned out at base, thence straight, thin and flat, tapered to each end, widest at one-third from base, tapering gradually but narrowing abruptly to a blunt, oblique point drawn out to a minute, transparent tip pointing forward, a little sharp to the touch. The mid-rib is raised, giving the leaf an appearance of being grooved. Two to four broken rows of small, creamy-white stomata above and below extending to tip. *Size*: 8-12 mm long (less on top of shoot and towards the tip) by 1.0 mm wide, glossy, arranged semi-radially in distinct ranks, each rank at a different angle, giving a dense and untidy look to the shoot; held at 40-60° horizontally, 20° above (and 30-70° below wherever the long leaves in the lowest rank hang forwards and downwards). Aberrant leaf at 80-100°. Leaves on top of shoot point more or less forward, almost hiding shoot. Leaves form a tapered outline squared off abruptly at the tip, where a circle of very small leaves pointing forward at 0-30° and often twisted cover but do not hide the terminal bud. Aberrant leaves borne by the sub-lateral buds project and so are very noticeable. Leaves are set very close together, and are stiff to the touch.

SHOOTS: Medium brown above, medium orange-brown below, glossy, glabrous. Pulvini are prominent. Shoots are thin and very flexible. Annual growth 30-50 mm; side shoots at 50° to branch, this angle being noticeably uniform all over the plant.

– –'**Pumilio**' [*P. excelsa pumilio* Sén. Conif. 29. 1867.] Sénéclause described this as 'a very dwarf variety with relatively thick branches on which the pulvini are very prominent. The branchlets are short, erect and numerous and the slender leaves are triagonal, grooved on all three faces, 6-12 mm long, dark green, glaucous, ending in a sharp point. A beautiful little bush barely reaching 40 cm high'. I include this forgotten variety because the description, as those by Séneclause usually were, was of a plant he knew and consequently specimens sent out from his nursery (should any survive) could be recognised from it today—even although they will by now have greatly exceeded his 40 cm. It is certainly not 'Pumila' as we know it today, nor any of its forms.

– –'**Pygmaea**' [*P. excelsa pygmaea* Carr, Traité, 250. 1855 (excl. synonymy); *P. abies* f. *pygmaea* (Loud.) Rehd. Bibl. 22. 1949 *; *P. excelsa* var. *pygmaea* Hornb. Dw. Con. 99. 1923 and (*P. abies*) Ed. 2, 143. 1938.] 'Pygmaea' is, next to 'Clanbrassiliana', the oldest recorded dwarf form of *P. abies* and they both remain equally popular, but unlike the latter variety, 'Pygmaea' seems to have been able to maintain its identity and so is usually found truly named. There are some very old plants in existence, including those at Leonardslee, Horsham, Sussex. The history of these plants was recorded by Hornibrook and they have now added more than a quarter of a century to their age without much increase in size, so the variety can be regarded as reliably dwarf, provided that (as a former head gardener at Leonardslee once privately admitted to me to having always done) any strong, coarse growth be cut out of the bush as soon as it develops. (Illustration 304).

If, as I believe, 'Humilis' is a cultivariant resulting from selection of cutting wood from the particularly tight, congested growth that occasionally develops in a plant of 'Pygmaea', the distinction between these two cultivars (as I suggest also in the case of the 'Gregoryana' group) is somewhat arbitrary, and intermediate forms occur.

'Pygmaea' forms a very slow-growing, globose to broadly conical bush usually seen less than 1 m high, although capable of reaching twice that height after a century or so of steady growth. The growth is very dense and congested, and in its own irregular way uniform all over the bush, except that an abnormally strong shoot will sometimes appear here or there as a result of which the plant develops a rugged and picturesque outline, and occasionally (due perhaps to a local concentration of the virus—or whatever agent it is that caused the dwarfing in the first place) a branch will develop an extremely dense habit with the shorter leaves, reduced shoot growth and the abnormal bud-formation associated with 'Humilis'. There is an interesting example in the Pygmy Pinetum at Devizes in which the two types of growth are in such contrast that it is difficult to realize they are on the same plant.

BUDS: Medium orange-brown, globose (large buds cylindrical with rounded tip), 2 mm (terminal), 1 mm (other), glossy or with slight sheen, not resinous in winter. Up to three buds in terminal cluster, but most shoots carry a solitary terminal bud. Lateral buds are frequent at base of current year's growth, otherwise rare.

BUD SCALES: Variable—sometimes large and pointed, more often small, rounded and tightly appressed.

LEAVES: Dark, bright, mid-green, straight, rhombic to nearly square, parallel-sided, narrowing abruptly to a symmetrical point with a very fine drawn out tip, sharp to the touch. Two to three broken rows of stomatic lines above and below, usually extending to tip. *Size:* 5-8 mm long by 1 mm wide, with slight sheen, arranged radially on strong shoots, discernibly set spirally on shoot and often twisted, occasionally noticeably so; held at 30-45°, the leaves on lower side of shoot longer and at a wider angle than those above and finishing with a circle (frequently of smaller) leaves pointing forward around but not hiding the terminal bud, often twisted. Leaves are set very close together, especially on the weaker shoots, on which they are also much smaller than on strong shoots.

SHOOTS: Light to very pale yellow or grey, glossy and glabrous. Pulvini are prominent. Shoots are thick but relatively flexible. Annual growth 10-30 mm, very variable, the different shoots, even adjoining ones, differing noticeably in vigour and size of leaf. Side shoots are at 30-45° to branch, the angle being very variable.

The habit is congested, the branching system irregular and following no particular pattern, and the foliage is usually sufficiently dense to smother all growth in the interior of the plant.

– –'**Reflexa**' [*P. excelsa reflexa* Carr. Rev. Hort. 259. 1890; *P. abies* var. *reflexa* Hornb. Dw. Con. Ed. 2, 168. 1938.] PENDULA GROUP. This is a truly pendulous form which requires to be stem-trained to the required height unless it is to be grown as a prostrate plant. In this form it can be very effective if planted at the top of a large rockery down over which its branches will cascade, the growth in the centre of the plant building up into a dense mat of lusty, stiff branches richly clothed with foliage. As with so many of the forms with dark foliage it is particularly attractive during early summer, when the soft green of the new foliage makes a vivid contrast with the old. It is the strongest-growing and most outstanding of any of the pendulous forms of *P. abies*. (Illustration 305).

BUDS: Bright, light orange-brown, long ovoid, with blunt point, 6-8 mm (terminal), 5-7 mm (other), dull, resinous in winter. Number in terminal cluster 3-6, lateral buds numerous, especially on strong leading shoots. Buds are very prominent, especially in winter.

BUD SCALES: Large, pointed, fringed with resin, loosely appressed with upper part recurved, sometimes curled right back.

LEAVES: Dark, dull grey to blue-green, usually straight or nearly so, the mid-rib prominent, with parallel sides with the top quarter of its length tapering gradually to a symmetrical, medium point with a blunt, transparent tip, not sharp to the touch. One to four broken and irregular rows of stomata above and below, extending to tip. *Size*: 10-12 mm long by 1-1.25 mm wide, with slight sheen, arranged radially, the upper leaves short, lying along the shoot, the lower leaves long and hanging forwards and outwards, held uniformly at 30-35° horizontally, 10-15° above and 50-60° below. The aberrant leaf, being long and held at 90°, is very noticeable. Leaves on top of shoot point forward, partly hiding shoot. Leaves form a parallel outline, finishing with a thin circle of short, needle-like leaves pointing forwards and usually closely appressed to the terminal bud; often twisted. Leaves are set close together, and are stiff to the touch, appearing stiffer than they are.

SHOOTS: Light grey above and below, dull, pubescent. Pulvini are prominent, orange-red. Shoots are very thick and stiff, annual growth 50-120 mm; side shoots held at 60° to branch, each growing branch forming a saucer-shaped spray with slightly recurved shoots (hence the name) which only become pendulous the second year.

– –'Remontii' [*Abies excelsa Remontii* R. Smith, Pl. Fir Tribe, 5. 1872; *P. abies* f. *Remontii* (R. Smith) Rehd. Bibl. 21. 1949 *.] 'Remontii' is an attractive and popular form, but not one of the most dwarf. It eventually makes a conical bush of about the shape of the well known *P. glauca* 'Albertiana Conica' and it reaches to about 3 m high. The foliage is a bright mid-green and the growth is neat and regular, in flat sprays with a regular ramification (due to the development of the two sub-terminal buds) distinctly traceable back into the older growth. The growing tips are at ±5° but the growth is too dense to have any appearance of being in layers.

Where a larger specimen is required this is one to be recommended. There is a fine specimen in the National Pinetum at Bedgebury, Kent. (Illustration 306).

BUDS: Light orange, conical or ovoid with blunt point, 2-3 mm (terminal), 1-2 mm (other), glossy. Solitary terminal bud with one or two laterals very close to terminal bud, other lateral buds very rare. Buds noticeable.

BUD SCALES: Medium, pointed not fringed, closely appressed.

LEAVES: Light to medium, bright mid-green, curved out near base, thence straight; widest at centre, held edgeways, mid-rib prominent, with the top half tapering abruptly to a slightly drawn out tip, not sharp to the touch. One to three broken rows of stomatic lines above and below extending to tip. *Size*: 5-7 mm long (always the longest leaves are below, hanging down) by 0.5-0.75 mm broad, with slight sheen, arranged imperfectly radially, held at 60-80° horizontally and 30° above and 70-90° below. No aberrant leaf. Leaves on top of shoot are short, and point forward, not hiding shoot. Leaves form a tapered outline (sometimes noticeably so) and finish at the tip with a close circle of very short leaves pointing forwards, with their tips reaching to the tip of the terminal bud. Leaves are set close together, and are flexible to the touch.

SHOOTS: Medium brown above, light brown below, with slight sheen, glabrous. Pulvini are prominent. Shoots are fairly thick, but flexible; annual growth 20-30 mm; side shoots at 50-60° to branch.

– –'Repens' [*P. excelsa repens* Simon-Louis, Mitt. d.d.d.G. **7**: 85. 1898; Hornb. Dw. Con. 111. 1923; *P. abies* var. *repens* (Simon-Louis) Bailey, Cult. Conif. 106. 1933.] PROCUMBENS GROUP. 'Repens' forms a prostrate to spreading plant which gradually builds up in the centre by superimposition of later growth. The growth is regular, dense and uniform. The regular development of the two sub-terminal buds year by year results in a regular, flat leaf spray and as the angle to the horizontal at the growing tips is ±5°, the growth appears noticeably in layers.

The following description was made from the two old plants in the National Botanic Garden at Glasnevin, Dublin, part of the original Murray Hornibrook collection received in 1921-2. (Illustration 307).

BUDS: Bright medium orange-brown, conical to ovoid with sharp point, 3-4 mm (terminal), 2-3 mm (other), with sheen. Number in terminal cluster three, with usually one lateral bud additionally on each side. Buds inconspicuous.

BUD SCALES: Medium, pointed, fringed with hairs, very closely appressed.

LEAVES: Light, bright mid- to yellow-green (the colour being variable), twisted out at base, thence straight, widest at the centre, flat, wiry looking and narrow but relatively thick, with the mid-rib prominent, tapering to a sharp, symmetrical point, slightly drawn out to a fine tip sharp to the touch. One or two broken rows of stomatic lines above and below extending to tip. *Size*: 8-10 mm long by never over 1 mm wide; glossy, arranged semi-radially but much flattened, the leaves twisted to bare the stem beneath, held at 70° horizontally, 30° above and 60° below. Aberrant leaf at 80-90° or more. Leaves on top of shoot point forward, not hiding shoot. Leaves form tapered outline, ending in a cluster of shorter leaves radiating at all angles, not hiding the bud. Leaves are set closer together than their narrowness suggests and are flexible to the touch.

SHOOTS: Medium orange-brown above, light brown below, with slight sheen, glabrous. Pulvini are not prominent. Shoots are thin and very flexible. Annual growth 30-50 mm, side shoots held at 45-50° to branch, uniform all over the plant.

– –'Sargentii' [*Picea excelsa* var. *Sargentii* Hornb. Dw. Con. 120. 1923 and (*P. abies*) Ed. 2, 166. 1938.] This was one variety omitted in my earlier book because of lack of verification. But in view of Hornibrook's inclusion of 'Sargentii' in the 'Pumila' group in his second edition and his reference to the plants in the Grootendorst nursery I have identified it, not without some hesitation, with the plant in the Grootendorst Nursery at Boskoop, Holland. It is curious that although it was sent to Hornibrook by Professor C. S. Sargent from the Arnold Arboretum it is not (so far as I am aware) mentioned in any American listing. (Illustration 308).

As thus identified, it is very close to 'Pumila Nigra', differing only in its lighter green, shorter leaves more densely borne (so as completely to hide the shoot from above and also all the buds) and by its denser, tidier and (as a small plant) more procumbent habit. One difficulty with this identification is the shape of the leaf cross-section, which is not round as recorded by Hornibrook.

– –'Sherwoodii' Sherwood [Nurs. Cat. 1945.] A semi-dwarf of fairly rapid growth, requiring plenty of space, forming (if prevented from developing a leader) a wide-spreading plant of rugged, picturesque outline.

– –'Tabuliformis' [*P. excelsa tabulaeformis* Carr. Prod. et Fix. des Var. 52. 1865; Beissn. Handb. 365. 1891; *P. abies* f. *tabulaeformis* (Carr.) Rehd. Bibl. 23. 1949 *; *P. abies* var. *tabuliformis* Hornb. Dw. Con. Ed. 2, 169. 1938.] PROCUMBENS GROUP. This forms a spreading plant, usually seen as a low, prostrate mat with horizontal branching system and foliage in flat regularly tri-pinnate sprays with the growing tips tending to droop, held at 0 to -5°. The foliage itself is not particularly dense but as there is much overlapping of shoots, the plant builds up a dense thatch at the surface of the plant and gains height with age by the smothering of the growth beneath. Growth in older plants is consequently in distinct layers, but always the top of the plant is flat, hence the name. (Illustration 309). There is a very old plant in the National Botanic Garden at Glasnevin, Dublin, from which this description is given, and another in which the layer effect is very evident at Jermyn's House, Ampfield, Hampshire, the residence of Mr. H. G. Hillier, which I think is the same cultivar.

BUDS: Medium orange-brown, ovoid (occasionally almost globose), with sharp point, 2-3 mm (terminal), 1-2 mm (other), dull, not resinous in winter. Solitary terminal bud with one or two subterminals (alternate), occasionally one or two lateral buds, on strong shoots only. Buds almost invisible.

BUD SCALES: Large, rounded, not fringed, loosely appressed.

LEAVES: Medium bright yellow-green, straight but twisted at base, sides parallel, rhombic in cross-section, held edgeways, the mid-rib prominent, with the top quarter tapering to a long, sharp point sometimes a little drawn out to a sharp tip, not sharp to the touch. One to four rows of stomatic lines above and below extending to tip. *Size*: 7-10 mm long (longest in the centre of the shoot) by 0.5-0.75 mm wide; with slight sheen, arranged semi-radially, held at 60-70° horizontally, 20° above and occasional leaves to 40° below. Aberrant leaf at 90°. Leaves on top of shoot point forward, not hiding shoot. Leaves form an oval outline ending in a thin circle of leaves around the bud. Leaves are set rather wide apart and are flexible to the touch.

SHOOTS: Light brown above, medium grey below, glossy, glabrous. Pulvini are prominent. Shoots are very thin and flexible. Annual growth 20-30 mm, side shoots held at 50-60° to branch, the angle noticeably uniform all over the plant.

– –'Veitchii' [*P. excelsa gregoriana* f. *Veitchii* Hornb. Dw. Con. 97. 1923; *P. abies* f. *Veitchii* (Hornb.) Rehd. Bibl. 22. 1949 *.] This uncommon form, although I think it is a distinct clone, shares certain characteristics of 'Gregoryana' and 'Parsonsii', forms already described. It forms a globose or flat-topped plant in which, at the crown of the bush, the foliage is indistinguishable from 'Gregoryana'— having the same shiny, beadlike, globose buds and the radial, needle-like leaves of that form—but at the sides the foliage has the long, flat, semi-radial leaves and ovoid buds of 'Parsonsii'.

– –'Wagner' [New cv.] This very diminutive and attractive form arose on the

Wagner Nursery at Blakesley, Pennsylvania, U.S.A., and was introduced to the trade by Hillside Gardens, Lehighton, Pennsylvania. It forms a bun-shaped little plant with very thin, dark green needles 10 mm × 0.75 mm and annual growth of only 30 mm.

– –'**Waugh**' Hillier [Dw. Con. 48. 1964 and Man. 500. 1971.] When young this variety, which evidently originated as a witch's broom, forms a rather open little bush with thick shoots and widely spaced leaves as in 'Nana', but after a few years it tends to grow rank and coarse. It is a disappointing form.

– –'**Wansdyke Miniature**' Den Ouden and Boom [Man. 251. 1965.] This name arose through a misunderstanding. The plant I found and showed to Dr. Boom is *Chamaecyparis lawsoniana* 'Wansdyke Miniature'. His description fits the plant exactly but *Picea abies* 'Wansdyke Miniature' neither does nor did exist.

– –'**Wills Zwerg**' is a German form which, despite the name, makes a conical tree upwards of 2 m high, so it is hardly to be regarded as a dwarf form. It would fall within the group defined as f. *conica* (see above).

Picea bicolor (Maxim) Mayr. Alcock's spruce is a Japanese species, normally a tree to 40 m, but it has given us two excellent garden forms.

– –'**Howells Dwarf**' [New cv.] The only specimen I have seen, at the Vermeulen Nursery, Neshanic Station, New Jersey, U.S.A., was a flat-topped bush about 1.5 m high with attractive arching branches, but it will, I fancy, grow rather large in time. For a while it was distributed in the United States as Howells Dwarf Tiger-tail spruce, but it has no connection with the true Tigertail spruce, *P. polita*. (Illustration 310).

– –'**Prostrata**'. This came to me from Pruhŏnice in Czechoslovakia. It has formed a very attractive, prostrate plant. Whether this is anything other than a cultivar-iant I cannot yet say, but so far the young plants remain low and spreading. It will probably need a new name under the *Code* before it goes into commercial circulation.

Picea glauca (Moench) Voss. The White spruce is usually a tree up to 25 m, the species being widely distributed in Canada and the eastern United States, and it has given us several good dwarf forms. It can always be distinguished by its glabrous shoots from the pubescent shoots of *P. mariana*. *P. glauca* now includes (in var. *albertiana*) a geographical variant from Alberta, Canada, that was at one time treated as a separate species. The change gives rise to a nomenclatural conundrum in the case of the following cultivar.

– –'**Albertiana Conica**' [*Picea albertiana conica* Bean. Gar. Chron. **69**: 255. 1921; *P. glauca* f. *conica* Rehd. Bibl. 26. 1949 *; *P. alba* Link var. *Albertiana* f. *conica* Hornb. Dw. Con. 82. 1923.] It is always of interest to know how plants have reached our gardens and Dr. Donald Wyman of the Arnold Arboretum, writing in *The American Nurseryman* for 1st November 1961, gives the following account of the origin of *P. glauca* 'Albertiana Conica'. (Illustration 311).

'In 1904, when Professor J. G. Jack and Alfred Rehder of the Arnold Arboretum were doing a little botanizing work together in southwest Canada, they found themselves at Lake Laggan, Alberta, in the Canadian Rockies, waiting for a train. When they found the train was several hours late, they wandered off into the woods nearby and found four dwarf evergreen seedlings, all of uniform size, which were different from anything they had seen before. These they dug and shipped back to the Arnold Arboretum at once. They later turned out to be dwarf varieties of the white spruce, *Picea glauca*, and were named by Rehder *P. glauca conica*. It was found that these trees could be propagated by cuttings and in due course they were distributed throughout the botanic gardens and nurseries of the northern temperate regions of the world'.

Dr. Wyman goes on to relate of his having many years later found reversion on a large plant of this cultivar and of having saved seeds from that plant from which all the seedlings came as normal *P. glauca*. This fact, and the recent appearance of several mutations resulting in tiny, almost ridiculously miniature sports, point unmistakably to the probability that the four seedlings were the progeny of viable seeds set in one particular year on a witch's broom in the vicinity (which itself may well have disappeared before 1904). This all poses a series of problems for those people who would let Codes rule instead of serve them. Do botanists really wish to regard such pranks of Nature as botanically recognisable? If so, in the case of a plant once listed as a *forma* of a species that has since itself been reduced in rank, is our plant a *forma* within the new *varietas* or a *forma* of the nowadays all-embracing species?

By using the name in a cultivar sense we avoid these problems since the *Cultivated Code* lays down (Article 7) that cultivated plants are named at three main levels: genus, species and cultivar. As horticulturists we may discreetly also avoid prying into the question of whether or not cuttings rooted from more than one of the wildlings brought into cultivation were distributed from the Arnold Arboretum (i.e., whether we have more than one clone in cultivation) and continue to use the cultivar name that we are so well accustomed to. 'Albertiana Conica', then, is now one of our most prized dwarf conifers. It naturally forms a dense, conical bush (with a little trouble taken in cutting out any unwanted growth such as a duplicate leader, it can be retained to a height of 2 m or more, looking as though it had been turned out on a lathe) with attractive fine, dense, soft grass green foliage especially attractive in early summer. It is unfortunately a little intolerant of wind and liable to damage by red-spider and mites.

Buds: Medium red-brown, cylindrical with rounded tip, 2 mm (terminal), 1.5 mm (other), not resinous in winter. Number of terminal cluster usually three, lateral buds numerous (on strong shoots only). Buds inconspicuous.

Bud Scales: Small, rounded, very closely appressed, persisting for several years.

Leaves: Light, bright, grass green, aromatic when crushed, reflexed at base thence straight or curved forward or downwards; very thin, fine and round in section like a needle, grooved, parallel, tapering gradually to a sharp point with a long, fine tip, not sharp to the touch. One row of stomata above and below, not extending to tip. *Size*: 8-12 mm long by not more than 0.5 mm wide, dull, arranged radially, held at widely varying angles, the longest leaves below the shoot hanging forwards and downwards. No aberrant leaf. Leaves form an irregularly parallel outline and finish with a dense clump of short leaves pointing forwards covering but not hiding the bud; along the rest of the shoot the leaves are set spaced well apart. Leaves are flexible and are soft to the touch.

SHOOTS: Light yellow, glossy, slightly hairy. Pulvini are prominent, orange in colour. Shoots are thin and flexible; annual growth 30-60 mm, side shoots at 30-70° to branch.

As has already been mentioned, several bud sports on 'Albertiana Conica' have been noted of recent years and when propagated these have given rise to attractive little plants. They all have the typical foliage but with much smaller leaves and a greatly reduced annual growth. **'Alberta Globe'** De Vogel [Dendroflora **5:** 69. 1968] originated on the nursery of C. Streng. Jr., Boskoop, in Holland. It forms a globose plant with leaves 6 to 9 mm long. (Illustration 312). **'Lilliput'** [New cv.], another Dutch form, was introduced by the firm Le Feber & Co., also of Boskoop, who tell me it was raised from seed. It forms a miniature 'Albertiana Conica' with leaves 3 to 4 mm long by 0.5 mm broad and an annual growth of 15 mm. The mother plant at 10 years is barely 50 cm high. **'Little Globe'** Wyman [Arnoldia **29:** 6. 1969] originated as a witch's broom at the Waterford works of Wayne, New Jersey, in the United States in 1959 and was introduced by Verkades Nursery, Wayne, New Jersey. It is a tight-growing globose form with an average growth of about 38 mm annually. It has large rounded buds and is very attractive with light green growth darkening to a bluish-grey later in the year. (Illustration 313). The original witch's broom was destroyed by fire some years ago. **'Laurin'** Arnold in Kordes [Nurs. Cat. 49. 1973] is another pyramidal form introduced by the German nursery firm Heinrich Kordes of 2202 Bilsen/Holstein. It originated as a three-bud mutation on the nursery of Reinhold Arnold, at Alveshohe, near Bilsen, in 1950. It has very thin needles 5-10 mm long, a fastigiate branching habit and an annual growth of 2 cm. Finally, **'Tiny'** [New cv.], a British contribution, appeared as a witch's broom at the Red Lodge Nursery, Chandlers Ford, Hampshire, about 1961. The broom is extremely tight, with needles 5-7 mm long, square in cross-section and very densely borne. The glossy, ovoid buds are very small, in scale with the rest of the plant and are noticeable because of their deep mahogany-red colour. All these forms are inevitably much alike.

– – 'Aureospicata'. See P. Mariana.

– – **'Cecilia'** New name [P. glauca 'Witch's Broom', Spingarn, Nurs. Cat. 1973.] An attractive form originating with a witch's broom found by Greg Williams near the Skippack Highway, northeast of Philadelphia, Pennsylvania, U.S.A. It forms a neat, slow-growing upright plant with dense, congested foliage and with thick and very densely held silvery-grey leaves rather suggestive of a Blue spruce, but with blunt tips.

– – **'Echiniformis'** [P. alba var. echiniformis Carr. Traité, 239. 1855; P. glauca var. echiniformis (Carr.) Hornb. Rep. Conif. Conf. 81. 1932; "P. echiniformis glauca" of some nurseries] forms a low, dense, cushion-shaped plant with closely set branches and thick, greyish-green foliage curved forward along the shoot, which is completely covered from view by the leaves, as are also the terminal buds. (Illustration 314).

The whole plant has a curious limp appearance quite unsuggestive of a hedgehog and it bears no resemblance whatever to the shining globose buds and long, straight, stiff, needle-like leaves of *P. abies* 'Echiniformis'.

BUDS: Medium brown, variably cylindrical to globose, yellow-green at centres with rounded tip, 2–3 mm (terminal), 1–2 mm (other), dull or with slight sheen. Number in terminal cluster (ill-defined) 3, buds noticeable.

BUD SCALES: Medium, rounded or sometimes pointed, closely appressed or with pointed tips free.

LEAVES: Light, dull, yellow-green, with a heavy bloom which gives a grey or blue-green effect, curved, parallel-sided and round like a needle, with an obtuse, oblique point with short tip. *Size*: 5–7 mm long, very narrow, very glaucous, arranged radially, held at 40–45° horizontally and 20° above. Leaves are set close together, and are flexible.

SHOOTS: Medium brown above and below, glabrous and very flexible. Annual growth 15–30 mm, occasionally more, side shoots at 45° to branch.

– –'**Nana**' [*Abies alba nana* Jacques, Ann. Fl. Pom. **5**: 326. 1836; *P. glauca* f. *nana* (Jacques) Rehd. Bibl. 25. 1949 *.] 'Nana' forms a conical or globose plant with upright-spreading main branches which carry large and prominent buds, and with more or less flat sprays with straight and (to all appearances) stiff branchlets which are held at all angles from horizontal towards the sides of the bush but ascending steeply at its centre. It is quite rare in cultivation and is at once distinguishable from the commoner 'Echiniformis' by its habit of growth and large brown buds.

BUDS: Bright medium brown. Strong terminal buds, globose, 4–5 mm; other buds, conical with sharp points, 1–4 mm, dull. Number in terminal cluster one, with 4–5 side buds, arranged spirally, very close to terminal bud on leading shoots, more distant on laterals, with the horizontal pair dominant. Seldom more than one other lateral bud. Buds are very prominent and noticeable, especially at the top of the plant.

BUD SCALES: Thin, papery, pointed, not fringed with resin, loosely appressed.

LEAVES: Very light, bright grey-green, straight, with parallel sides, thick and needle-like, ending in a blunt, oblique point sometimes slightly drawn out to a transparent tip, not sharp to the touch. Three to four rows of stomatic lines above and 2–3 below, not extending to tip. *Size*: 5–7 mm long (according to the vigour of each shoot, but uniform in length on each shoot) by less than 1 mm wide, dull, arranged radially on upright shoots, imperfectly radially on side branches, held at 40° horizontally, 20° above and 40° below. No aberrant leaf. Leaves on top of shoot point forward, partially hiding shoot. Leaves form a parallel outline ending with double circle of short leaves around the terminal bud like the petals of a half-closed daisy. Leaves are set close together and are stiff to the touch.

SHOOTS: Medium grey above and below, dull, glabrous. Pulvini are prominent. Shoots are of medium thickness and very flexible although (because of their straightness) they appear to be stiff. Annual growth 25–45 mm; side shoots held at 50° to the branch.

This form is in cultivation in Britain and there is a good specimen in the

National Pinetum at Bedgebury in Kent. But the cultivars **'Compacta Gracilis'**, **'Compressa'**, **'Nana Glauca'** and **'Tabuliformis'** listed by Hornibrook, I have been unable to trace. They are probably lost to cultivation.

Picea jezoensis (Sieb. and Zucc.) Carr. The Jezo spruce has not, so far as I am aware, produced for us any truly dwarf forms, unless the named clones used in the Bonsai trade in Japan are such, but the golden variety **'Aurea'** [*Picea ajanensis aurea* (P. Smith) Beissn. Handb. 389. 1891] when grown as a prostrate cultivar, makes a low, widespreading bush, very attractive with its ochre-yellow foliage, at its best in mid-winter. It will doubtless get large in time.

Picea mariana (Mill.) Britton, Sterns and Poggenberg [*Picea nigra* Link.] The Black spruce is another American species of large tree dimensions in nature that has given us one or two delightful dwarf forms. At the northernmost limit of its range it is dwarfed by the climate to a shrub a few feet high and several of these have long been in garden cultivation. The young twigs of *P. mariana* forms are minutely pubescent and this distinguishes them from *P. glauca* forms, which are glabrous (devoid of hairs).

– –'**Aureovariegata'** [*P. nigra aureovariegata* Hesse ex Beissn. Handb. Ed. 2, 264. 1909 and (as *P. mariana*) Fitsch in Beissn. Handb. Ed. 3, 251. 1930; *P. glauca* 'Aurea' Hillier, List Con. 10. 1970 (and earlier Nurs. Cat. ?) altered to *P. mariana* 'Aurea' Man. 502. 1971.] Several coloured and variegated forms of both *P. glauca* and *P. mariana* have turned up and have been given descriptive Latin-form names, but perhaps because either the poor colouration or its rather fleeting seasonal nature has not resulted in particularly attractive trees they all seem to have disappeared, with the exception of this form. It was grown and distributed for many years as *P. glauca* 'Aurea', but it seems certainly a form of *P. mariana* and I see Hillier now lists it as *P. mariana* 'Aurea'. It is, however, closer to the description of 'Aureo-variegata' given by Beissner—'A form in which a lovely golden-yellow hue shews through the blue-green ground colour' than to his description of 'Aurea'—'A wholly shining golden form'.

– –'**Beissneri'** [*P. mariana* var. *Beissneri* Rehd. Mitt. d.d.d.G. **14**: 213. 1915.] Although slow-growing, this is hardly a dwarf form as it is a conical tree that will reach 5 m or more, but the German nursery firm H. A. Hesse, Weener-on-Ems, Germany, list a dwarf form **'Beissneri Compacta'** which they describe as a globose to pyramid dwarf form to 2 m high by as much broad, with leaf shape and colour as in the species. (Illustration 315).

– –'**Doumetii'** [*P. nigra doumetii* Carr. Traité, 242. 1855] is another pyramidal form densely furnished with fine, thin silvery green leaves, but as it reaches 5 m or more, it is too large for consideration here.

– –'**Ericoides'** [*Picea nigra ericoides* Bean, Trees and Shrubs 2: 160. 1914; *P. mariana* f. *ericoides* (Bean) Rehd. Bibl. 25. 1949 *.] As already mentioned, several shrubby mountain forms have been brought into garden cultivation. These are difficult to distinguish, partly because they are not entirely stable and so plants will occasionally respond to lowland cultivation by throwing out coarse and quite uncharacteristic growth, and partly because of the propensity of early writers on conifers to bandy names about without any personal knowledge of the plants they represented. For instance, Carrière [Traité, 242. 1855] introduced a dainty, fastigiate form with short, needle-like leaves as 'Fastigiata', but quotes the name 'Pumila' as a horticultural equivalent, although 'Pumila' had been previously used by Knight [Syn. Conif. 36. 1850] without a description but presumably relating to the form already being grown by Wm. Barron at the Elvaston Nurseries, near Derby, where in 1875 the mother plant measured nearly 4 m through by less than 2 m high. Although clearly these were quite different plants the two names were repeatedly treated as synonyms by later writers. Other cases of the same kind occur and I have come to the conclusion that it is not always possible to reconcile the old descriptions with each other, or with the plants we have today.

The first description of 'Ericoides' [Bean] was 'a rounded bush with very slender leaves, never more than 8-9 mm long, almost heath-like, young shoots thin, much branched, downy the first two or three years. It has been grown in gardens for 50 years . . . grows very slowly'. This delightful little plant has grey-brown shoots, and its tiny leaves (7-9 mm × less than 0.5 mm) are so narrow as to give a wiry look to the foliage, and they are held out stiffly at a wide angle to the shoot. The (inconspicuous) stomata impart a grey tone to the green foliage. These features make it very distinct from 'Nana' and from the following cultivar with its incurved leaves and red-brown shoots. (Illustration 316).

Hornibrook [Dw. Con. Ed. 2, 186. 1938] gives the following description of what was clearly a different plant:

'BUDS: Minute, ovoid; crimson-brown; terminal bud girt with a ring of almost imperceptible scales from which spring subulate points of varying lengths.

'BRANCHLETS: Very thin and flexible; pale crimson-brown covered with not very dense minute pubescence; annual growth 2.5 cm to 3.5 cm.

'LEAVES: Arranged as in *P. excelsa*; very thin and heath-like; dark blue-green; 5 to 8 mm; incurved; slightly twisted, with one stomatic line on two sides and three on the other two.' On the same page he adds that a plant at Arnold Arboretum was conical and of irregular growth with foliage presenting a 'furry' appearance—whatever that might mean. There is a form in cultivation which (apart from the references to the Arnold Arboretum plant, which may well have been a reverting specimen) answers well to this description and is worthy of recognition. I suggest for it the name **'Ruddigore'**. [New cv.]

- -'**Fastigiata**' [*Picea nigra fastigiata* Carr. Traité. 242, 1855; *P. mariana* f. *fastigiata* (Carr.) Rehd. Bibl. 25. 1949 *.] I have given the record of this form in the previous account of 'Ericoides'. It might be difficult to shew that the identical clone originating with M. Briot had been found, should one ever turn up, but Carrière's description is quite clear, and I at any rate know of no such fastigiate plant.

- -'**Nana**' [*P. alba nana* Carr. Traité, 239. 1855; *P. mariana* f. *nana* (Beissn.) Rehd. 25. 1949 *; *P. glauca* 'Echiniformis' Hort. Holl. (in part.)] This is the form most frequently met with in Britain. It is somewhat variable and it may be that there are several clones in cultivation. This might be considered to justify the use of the botanical category f. *nana*, but the clonal differences (if that is what they are) are slight and difficult to define and so I prefer to retain the name as a cultivar epithet. 'Nana', then, is quite one of the best conifers we have, reliably dwarf (seldom seen over 50 cm) forming a neat, round little bush with fine, short, bluish-grey foliage held radially on shoots which all more or less radiate from the centre of the plant, giving it a very well mannered and *petite* appearance, a delightful little plant if the coarse shoots that develop occasionally are cut out immediately. (Illustration 317).

BUDS: Medium brown, globose, 2 mm (terminal), 1 mm (other); dull, not resinous in winter. Terminal bud usually solitary or with one very small bud adjoining, but with several lateral buds not far distant. Buds are noticeable.

BUD SCALES: Small, pointed, not fringed with hairs or resin; tips free standing.

LEAVES: Actually a dark, dull blue-green, but the numerous large white stomata give the plant an almost blue-grey appearance; straight, round in section, parallel, tapering gradually to a long sharp point (frequently noticeably oblique, giving a curved appearance to the leaf) sometimes much drawn out to a long fine tip, not sharp to the touch. Two to four rows of very prominent stomatic lines above and below, extending to tip. *Size*: 7-12 mm long (shortest on upper side of shoot) by less than 0.5 mm wide, with slight sheen, arranged radially, held at 40-70° horizontally and 20-30° above and with the lower leaves curved to 80° below. Aberrant leaf at 70-80°, not very noticeable. Leaves form a parallel outline rather squared off at the tip, where leaves shorter than usual form a single circle around the terminal bud. Leaves are set fairly close together, and are very flexible.

SHOOTS: Medium brown above and below, dull, very hairy. Pulvini are not prominent. Shoots are thin and very flexible. Annual growth 30-50 mm. The growth of shoots from three or four lateral buds (often more vigorous than from the terminal bud itself) gives a dense and congested pattern of growth with no trace of the usual flat leaf spray. The branches are at all angles, mostly pointing outwards.

From 'Echiniformis' it differs in its longer and wider leaves, pointing forwards and bearing the prominent white stomata which give to the plant the much more 'blue-green' general look noted by Hornibrook [Dw. Con. Ed. 2, 187. 1938.]

– –'**Pumila**' [*P. nigra pumila* Hort. ex Knight, Syn. Conif. 36. 1850; *Abies nigra pumila* Barron, Nurs. Cat. 3. 1875.] This is another problem plant. I have already noticed the long-standing confusion between this form and Carrière's variety 'Fastigiata'. Apart from Barron's statement that the mother plant was nearly 4 metres across we have no description whatsoever of 'Pumila'; I cannot bring myself to believe that the twelve very dwarf plants found by the late H. den Ouden [Den Ouden and Boom, Man. 270. 1965] were of this form and so I feel we must regard 'Pumila' as lost to cultivation. Much more probably those plants were of the following form which has so long been distinguished by collectors that the validity of the name may safely be presumed.

– –'**Pygmaea**' Welch [Dw. Con. 257. 1966; *P. mariana* 'Pumila' Den Ouden and

Boom, Man. 269. 1965; *P. nigra pygmaea* Hort.] This delightful little plant differs from 'Nana' only in size. The leaves are from 5-7 mm in length, and the annual growth seldom exceeds 30 mm (often it is much less). It is exactly 'Nana' in miniature and should not be confused with 'Echiniformis'.

Picea × mariorika Boom. This interesting hybrid arose spontaneously on the nursery of G. D. Boehle at Westerstede, Germany, where the two parent species (*P. mariana* and *P. omorika*) were growing in close proximity. Of the many seedlings raised most were arboreal forms intermediate between the two species, but the following selections have resulted in attractive dwarf conifers, although their ultimate size is not yet known.

– –'**Gnom**' (Jeddeloh) Krüssm. [*P. omorika* 'Gnom' Handb. 216. 1972; Jeddeloh Nurs. Cat. 19. 1972/73] forms a broadly conical plant of very dense habit. (Illustration 318).

LEAVES: Very broad (up to 20 mm by 2 mm), dark green below and with two bands of stomata and a broad central green band above; cylindrical with very long sharp and prickly points.

BUDS: Light brown in colour and of two kinds—small rounded buds 2 mm diameter (not showing separate scales) appear on weak shoots and larger (up to 6 mm) dark brown oval buds (on which separate scales can be distinctly seen) appear on leaders and main shoots. The foliage is much darker in general tone than in *P. omorika* 'Nana'. It was introduced by the Jeddeloh Nursery at Oldenburg, Germany.

– –'**Kobold**' [New cv.] This forms a wide-spreading, hemispherical and very dense plant reaching to 1 m high by about twice as much through. (Illustration 319).

BUDS: Blunt-ovoid, 2-3 mm (terminal). Terminal bud solitary, bud scales often projecting.

LEAVES: Dark green below, straight or slightly curved, with 3-4 rows of stomata above. *Size:* 8-12 mm long by 0.5 mm wide, held radially, the terminal bud surrounded by leaves.

SHOOTS: Red-brown with minute, scattered pubescence, pulvini prominent, thick and stiff to the touch. Annual growth 5 mm. This form was selected about 1951 and introduced by the Jeddeloh Nurseries, Oldenburg, Germany.

– –'**Machala**' Grootn. [Dendroflora **8**: 74. 1971; *P. omorika* 'Nana' Jeddeloh, Nurs. Cat. 19. 1972/73.] This variety was raised by Herr Machala, Director of Conifer Nurseries in Czechoslovakia, and exhibited jointly by Boot and Co. N. V. and Th. Streng Nurseries of Boskoop at the Flora Nova Exhibition in Holland, 1970. The plant shewn was compact, broadly globose, with thin, soft, grey-blue leaves, silvery on the underside. A plant in the Rombergpark at Dortmund-Brunninghausen received from the raiser in 1965 which I saw there in 1968 then measured 70 cm across by only 30 cm high, but G. Krüssmann, the Director, writes that it is now 1 m across and 80 cm high. The foliage is a dense, bluish-green colour, young shoots greenish-white beneath.

– –'**Tremonia**' [New cv.] This name is suggested for a more or less globose form, the mother plant of which is in the Westfalen Park at Dortmund-Brunninghausen. G. Krüssmann, Director of Parks in that city, tells me it was purchased in 1958 and is now a globose bush 2 m across and 1.10 m high, somewhat loose in growth with the young growth a bit nodding; needles very fine, green with no glaucous tinge. I am not entirely satisfied as to its distinction from 'Kobold'. (Illustration 320).

Picea × moseri Masters. This hybrid between *P. jezoensis* and *P. mariana* var. *Doumetii*, raised about 1900 in the Moser Nursery, Versailles, although ultimately a small tree, serves for many years as an attractive dwarf conifer because of its slow growth, dense habit and closely set leaves, green above, and with wide, silvery stomatic bands below, which gives an attractive two tone look to the plant.

Picea omorika (Pančić) Purkyne. The Serbian spruce, although a pyramidal tree to 30 m, has given us several dwarf forms.
– –'**Berliners Weeper**' [New cv.] is a truly upright form marked by an extremely pendulous habit, with even its main branches hanging down stiffly so that it forms a narrow plant that makes a fine specimen for even a small garden, although even there it may grow too large in time.
– –'**Expansa**' Den Ouden [Conif. 237. 1949.] This unusual cultivar forms a wide-spreading, almost prostrate shrub, not more than 1 m high but covering a large area, with ascending branches and typical foliage. It is, I think, merely a cultivariant, since propagations are very apt to throw up a leader and become arborescent. The same is, I believe, true of prostrate plants sometimes grown under 'Pendula' and similar names.
– –'**Nana**' [*Picea omorika* var. *nana* Grootn. ex Hornb. Dw. Con. Ed. 2, 188. 1938] forms a globose to conical plant of a pleasant informal outline and attractive foliage. The leaves are slightly convex above, a medium yellow-green without stomata; below they have up to seven rows of closely packed white stomata in each of two noticeable, broad, glaucous bands. As the leaves are twisted to show both sides the foliage has a bi-coloured appearance which gives an attractive look to the plant, especially if it is planted on raised ground where it is seen from below. The effect of a few strong-growing side branches is to give an uneven outline to the plant. (Illustration 321).

BUDS: Light medium brown, long ovoid, with blunt point, 3–4 mm (terminal), 2–3 mm (other), dull, not resinous in winter. Number in terminal cluster 3–5, lateral buds unusual. Buds inconspicuous.

BUD SCALES: Large, narrowly pointed, not fringed with hairs or resin, very loosely appressed.

LEAVES: Dark, bright, yellow-green above; convex, with a prominent mid-rib below; straight, parallel and with rounded or very obtuse point with a tiny pointed tip, not sharp to the touch. No stomata on upper side, two broad bands of up to seven rows of white stomata below, not extending to tip. *Size*: 7–8 mm long by 1.5 mm wide, dull, arranged semi-radially on lateral shoots, held at 80–90° horizontally and 20° above (often curving to 0°) and irregularly below. No aberrant leaf. Leaves on top of shoot point forward, almost hiding shoot. Leaves form a parallel or slightly tapered outline with a semi-circular end where leaves a little shorter than normal project beyond the terminal bud, partly hiding it from view. Leaves appear (because of their width) to be very close together, and are stiff to the touch.

SHOOTS: Light brown above and below, dull and very hairy. Pulvini are prominent. Shoots are thick but not very stiff. Annual growth 20-40 mm, side shoots held at 60° to branch. The growth is irregular and informal and very dense; the branching system is ascending, strong branches rising at 30-50°, others at 0° to 20°, never below. Foliage is in flat sprays, with each shoot slightly arched.

Picea orientalis (L.) Link. The Oriental spruce is normally a tall, densely branched pyramidal tree, but it has given us several dwarf forms. The leaves are arranged semi-radially and are much shorter than in *P. abies*; a dark, shining green; rhomboidal to square in cross section with a blunt, oblique or rounded point. The leaf cushions (pulvini) are usually much swollen.

‒ ‒ f. **aurea** (Otto) Beissn. [Rehd. Bibl. 24. 1949 (but for 1897 read 1887, twice); *Picea orientalis* f. *aureo-spicata* Beissn. in Rehd., l.c.]

Forms differing from normal in having the young foliage a bright yellow or golden hue, sometimes turning to the dark green characteristic of the species later in the year. It suggests a name for the

AUREA GROUP

‘Aurea	‘Early Gold’
‘Aureospica’	‘Skylands’

The correct treatment of this group is virtually impossible to determine, because from the scattered descriptions in the early literature it is now not possible to say what plants were in the writers' minds. Since the earliest epithet used is fortunately the most descriptive it serves us well as the name for this well defined horticultural group, and also for the following very old cultivar.

‒ ‒‘**Aurea**’ [*P. orientalis aurea* Beissn. Handb. Ed. 2, 255. 1909; Hesse Nurs. Cat. 1892.] This and the name ‘Aureo-spicata’ [l.c.] pose for us the question—‘Does one accord priority to the earliest appearance of a name or to the earliest valid publication of an identifiable description?’ Although conflicting early references are available, the first simultaneous use of both names I can trace is in the second edition of Beissner's *Handbuch der Nadelhölzkunde*. Here, contrary to what he wrote in the first edition of 1891, Beissner uses ‘**Aureo-spicata**’ for a variant in which ‘the young growth is a rich creamy-yellow turning to dark green by late summer, the contrast with the old foliage (while it lasts) being very attractive’, and transfers the name ‘Aurea’ to another form ‘with golden-bronze colouring which is persistent; this having been brought into cultivation in the Hesse Nursery at Weener (Ems) in West Germany’. Since this both embodies common sense and follows current usage in the trade I accept it here. (See also ‘Skylands’ below.) ‘**Early Gold**’ is a clone differing from ‘Aureo-spicata’ only in its date of bud-break.

Neither plant is dwarf but they make attractive plants for pot culture until they become too large.

– –'**Gowdy**' Wyman [Amer. Nurs. **114, 9**: 108. 1961.] This is not a dwarf. It is a slow-growing, upright form which makes an attractive small tree, but it will get large in time.

– –'**Gracilis**' [*Picea orientalis gracilis* A. Kort, Conif. Arb. Kalmthout Nurs. Cat. 1903; *P. orientalis* var. *nana* Hornb. Dw. Con. 126. 1923; NON Carr. Rev. Hort, 120. 1891; var. *gracilis* (Beissn.) Hornb. Dw. Con. Ed. 2, 189. 1938.] Although ultimately a small tree, this form is very slow-growing and is interesting when young or kept as a pot plant. It forms a round-topped (eventually pyramidal) bush, very densely set with branches carrying short, radially set leaves of a very bright grass green. The development of all the buds in the terminal cluster and the lateral buds results in little trace of a flat spray, especially as several main branches are apt to rise at a steep angle and become sub-leaders, so there is much interlacing of branchlets, some of which grow inwards towards the centre of the plant. There seem to be several very similar clones in cultivation, so the following details may vary somewhat between one plant and another. (Illustration 322).

Buds: Medium red-brown, with sharp point, 2-3 mm (terminal buds no larger than the others and quite hidden) with slight sheen. Number in terminal cluster 1-6, lateral buds numerous on strong shoots. Buds are inconspicuous.

Bud Scales: Medium, rounded, not fringed with hairs or resin and closely appressed.

Leaves: Medium, very bright mid-green, straight or slightly curved forward, with sides parallel, round like a needle with upper quarter of their length tapering to an oblique, medium point not drawn out at the tip or sharp to the touch. One to four very broken rows of stomata above and below, not extending to tip, especially on lower side, where they are sometimes only near the base of the leaf. *Size:* 5-7 mm long by 0.5-0.75 mm wide, noticeably glossy, arranged radially everywhere, held at 50° horizontally, and 40° above and 50° below. Aberrant leaf at 60-70°. Leaves form a tapered outline ending at the tip in a bunch of leaves pointing forward in a close cluster, completely hiding the terminal bud, especially on the leading shoots. Leaves are set close together on weak shoots but on leaders are wider apart and are stiff to the touch.

Shoots: Medium brown above, light brown below, glossy, hairy. Pulvini are prominent. Shoots are thin and very flexible (except for the strong leader growths). Annual growth 30-70 mm. Main side shoots held at 40-60° to the branch.

– –'**Nana**' [*P. orientalis nana* Carr. Rev. Hort. 120. 1891.] I regret having to withdraw the description of this cultivar given in my previous book, which turned out to be a clone of 'Gracilis'. The true 'Nana' is a very rare form, quite distinct on account of the dark green colour of the foliage. It forms a very slow-growing globose or ovoid bush of often congested growth. (Illustration 323).

Buds: Conical, 3 to 4 mm, terminal bud often projecting beyond a cluster of congested sub-terminal buds.

Leaves: Dark green, curved, lying forwards towards shoot, rhombic in cross-section with blunt point, tip not drawn out. *Size:* 6 to 7 mm long, held semi-radially, a few irregular, inconspicuous lines of stomata, fairly widely spaced.

SHOOTS: Brown, very short, crowded and held at varying angles.

– –'Pygmaea' [*Abies orientalis pygmaea glauca* R. Smith, Pl. Fir Tribe. 6. 1874 (Nom.); NON *Picea orientalis* f. *pygmaea* Beissn. Conif. Ben. 63. 1887 (NEC Ohlend.) Handb. 376. 1891.] The subsequent identification of the Th. Ohlendorffii plant as a form of *P. abies* does not invalidate the prior use of the name by Richard Smith of Worcester. Although unaccompanied by a description, the name itself is descriptive and so may reasonably be used for an extremely diminutive form at the Pygmy Pinetum which has the same colouring as 'Gracilis', but a somewhat more open habit, leaves only 3–5 mm long and an annual growth of 20 mm. It is not noticeably glaucous.

– –'Skylands' New name [*P. orientalis* 'Compacta Aurea' Hort. Amer.] AUREA GROUP. This name is suggested because of the questionable validity of the Latin-form name under which this plant has been circulated and the confusion that already exists over the use of the epithet 'Aurea'. It is a fairly slow-growing form with rich golden-yellow foliage which retains the colour well throughout the year. Young plants need to be stem-trained until a leader develops, or else may remain quite prostrate plants. It is a most desirable acquisition. Unfortunately it tends to burn in strong sunlight.

Skylands Farm was the unpretentious name of an estate of 1400 acres bought in 1922 by Clarence MacKenzie Lewis, a banker and financier. He started collecting plant material from several American and European sources, and by the time of his death the collection was well known horticulturally. The property was bought in 1953 to house a religious community and became known as Shelton College. Unfortunately the new owners cared little for the ideals of their predecessor and by the time the State of New Jersey acquired Skylands in 1966 no gardens or farm lands were recognisable. It is now known as the Ringwood State Park, and better days have dawned for the collection.

Several of the plants lost during the dark days were propagated by one or two American nurseries, doubtless under the influence of Lewis's head gardener, Stuart Longmuir, who (I am pleased to add) is still there, no doubt feeling much happier than he used to be. This attractive plant being one of these, 'Skylands' seems an appropriate name.

– –'Weeping Dwarf' Den Ouden and Boom. Man. 278. 1965 [*P. orientalis* 'Pendula' Hillier, Dw. Con. 49. 1964.] A dwarf and compact form with pendulous branchlets, the foliage being otherwise normal.

Picea pungens Engelm., the Colorado spruce, is one of the most beautiful of trees, especially in its glaucous blue forms, several of which have been selected in the seed beds and are distributed under cultivar names. These are all tall-growing conical trees, but any one of the forms can give rise to the procumbent cultivariant form (see below) by the use of graft scions taken from a side branch. It should always be borne in mind that such a plant consists essentially of the lowest branch of quite a large tree (and one freed, moreover, from the usual competition for sustenance and light) so it must be expected to cover quite a large area. Given the room to develop, however, these procumbent forms can be most spectacular, because of their wonderful colour.

The species has also produced several seedlings of compact habit. They usually have a shortened leaf length to match the reduced annual growth and these, when propagated, tend to form globose or flat-topped shrubby plants which because of their size are more suitable for small gardens. I believe, however, that each of these forms left alone and given sufficient time will eventually form a leader and attempt to develop the conical habit of the species, even if in any particular case a tree takes so long to do this that all it can in the end achieve is a rather misshapen monstrosity. This knowledge is, however, doubly useful. In the case of the cultivariant forms, it warns us to cut out any aspiring branches if we wish to preserve the procumbent habit we so desire, and in the case of the compact, shrubby forms it warns us to view with caution the descriptions of habit and shape given in the textbooks, since a little early pruning can have great effect on the later growth of a particular plant.

– –'**Blue Trinket**' Konijn ex Grootn. [Dendroflora **6**: 78. 1969.] A compact, conical form, like a compact form of the cultivar 'Endtz'. Raised from seed and introduced by the L. Konijn & Co. Nursery, Pinetum Tempelhof, then at Reeuwijk, Holland.

– –'**Compacta**' [*P. pungens* f. *compacta* Rehd. Bibl. 27. 1949 * and Pl. and Gar. **5, 3**: 165. 1949 (and synonymy); Hornb. Dw. Con. 127. 1923 (and illus.)] This is the oldest form to have been recorded, and I reproduce below part of an article by the late Alfred Rehder which is understood to have been the last article written by him before his death at the age of eighty-five.

It appeared in *Plants and Gardens,* Autumn 1949 (the Brooklyn Botanic Garden Record), a copy of which was kindly sent me by Henry Teuscher, of the Botanic Garden at Montreal, who was the guest editor for that issue.

'*Picea pungens* f. *compacta.* From typical *Picea pungens* Engelm. (*P. parryana* Sarg.) this form is chiefly distinguished by its habit, forming a dense, compact flat-topped bush broader than high, with horizontally spreading branches closely set with short shiny yellow branchlets; leaves crowded; rigid; spiny-pointed, slightly incurved, ¼ to ¾ inch long, dark green, with 4 or sometimes 3 stomatic lines on each side.

'The original plant was, according to Sargent, 3 feet high in 1897. According to Hornibrook, the plant at the Arnold Arboretum was 7 feet high and 12 feet in diameter in 1923 and now it is about 8 feet tall and 14 feet in diameter.

'*Picea pungens* f. *compacta* was raised from seed sent by Dr. C. C. Parry from Pike's Peak, Colorado, in 1863, to the Harvard Botanic Garden, as stated by C. S. Sargent in Gard. and For. **10**: 481. 1897, where under *Picea parryana* the following note appears: "Among the seedlings raised from Dr. Parry's first seeds is a dwarf form which is still less than 3 feet in height and a handsome, broad, round-topped bush". Grafts of this plant were received at the Arnold Arboretum in February 1890. This clearly shows that the statement made by several authors, that this form originated at the Arnold Arboretum, is not correct'.

– –'*Compacta Thume*'. See 'Thume'.

– – f. **glauca** (reg.) Beissn. [Syst. Eintheil. Conif. 35. 1887; Rehd. Bibl. 26. 1949 *; *P. pungens* f. *coerulea* (Beissn.) Voss in Rehd., l.c.; *P. pungens* f. *argentea* (Rosenthal)

Beissn. in Rehd., l.c.] *Plants differing noticeably from the normal by conspicuous glaucous bands of stomata on the leaves, giving the whole tree a distinctive whitish, grey or blue appearance.* Here would come 'Endtz', 'Fürst Bismarck', 'Hoopsii', 'Koster', 'Lombarts', 'Moerheim', 'Spek', 'Thomsen', 'Vuyk' and other arboreal, conical clones. Although far from being satisfactory as a botanical designation because of the infinitude of intermediate colour forms, *Glauca* serves as a useful collective term covering all these clones, but neither it, *Argentea* nor *Coerulea* should be used in any clonal sense, save as follows.

– –**'Glauca (Prostrate)'** Welch [Dw. Con. 262. 1966; *P. pungens tabuliformis* Ordn. ex Beissn. Mitt. d.d.d.G. **18**: 286. 1919: 'Glauca Procumbens', 'Glauca Prostrata' (and similar names) Hort.] This is how I suggest that all procumbent plants (cultivariants) propagated from an unidentified glaucous mother plant be distinguished. Such plants from known clones could be **'Koster (Prostrate)'**, **'Moerheim (Prostrate)'**, or as the case may be. Since these are plants being grown in a particular way that is not yet recognised in the *Cultivated Code,* (and one which, moreover, is not entirely stable) they are not entitled to recognition as distinct cultivars. (Illustrations 324, 325).

– –*'Glauca Compacta Thume'*. See 'Thume'.

– –*'Glauca Globosa'*. A synonym of, or a form indistinguishable from 'Montgomery'.

– –**'Glauca Nana'** [*P. pungens glauca nana* H. A. Hesse Nurs. Cat. 49. 1962-63 (and earlier?); 'Compacta Glauca' Hort. Amer. (in part)] is a slow-growing form said to have originated in America. It is grey, rather than blue, and normally forms a rather flat-topped, spreading plant. The leaves are long (to 25 mm) almost symmetrically radial, straight and with an extremely fine point, giving the foliage a very harsh and prickly feel. (Illustration 326).

– –**'Gotellis Broom'** [New cv.] This originated in a witch's broom that appeared on a plant of *P. pungens* 'Glauca' in the Gotelli collection, now in the United States National Arboretum in Washington, D.C. It forms an attractive little flat-topped plant usually wider than high with an annual growth of 25 mm and very short laterals but with disproportionally large (15 to 20 mm × 1.5 mm wide) leaves which have the minute rows of stomata and the (easily rubbed off) white bloom all over the leaf, giving the usual glaucous grey-white colouring to the foliage.

– –**'Hunnewelliana'** [*P. pungens* f. *Hunnewelliana* (Hornb.) Rehd. Bibl. 27. 1949 *; *P. pungens* var. *Hunnewelliana* Hornb. Dw. Con. 128. 1923.] Murray Hornibrook gives us the history and description of this form, writing of it in 1923 as a dwarf form. Both at the Wellesley Pinetum and at the Arnold Arboretum, plants have, after some years, thrown up a leader and become tall trees, so this form hardly merits attention here.

– –**'Moll'** [*Picea pungens glauca* 'Moll' Krüssm. Nadel. Ed. 2, 215. 1960] is a compact seedling form found by Peter Moll, Baumschule, Heisterbacherott, Germany. It forms a neat, dense, conical plant of irregular growth with short leaves. It makes a much larger plant than 'Montgomery'. (Illustration 327).

BUDS: Large, orange-brown, scales on terminal bud reflexed.

LEAVES: Greyish-green, straight, tips prickly, held radially, very closely set and short.

SHOOTS: Noticeably thick.

– –'**Montgomery**' [*P. pungens glauca* 'Montgomery' Teuscher, Journ. New York
Bot. Gar. **50**: 113. May 1949; *P. pungens globosa* Den Ouden, Conif. 244. 1949; *P.
pungens* 'Glauca Globosa' Hillier, Dw. Con. 50. 1964.] The history of the clone
'Montgomery' is well recorded and the mother plant is still available in the New
York Botanical Garden as our type. The leaves are straight or nearly so and set
forwards at 75°, not over 20 mm long and with very sharp tips, giving a feeling
of prickliness when grasped. Den Ouden and Boom give as the origin of
'Globosa' that it was raised from seed in 1937 in Boskoop, Netherlands, but I
now understand that this cannot be verified. Herman J. Grootendorst (verbal
communication September 1969) expressed to me the opinion that 'Globosa' was
synonymous with 'Montgomery', it having reached Holland from America and
having been propagated as 'Globosa' before its true identity was known.
(Illustration 328).

– –'**Thume**' New name [*P. pungens glauca compacta* (Thume) Hort. Amer.] From time
to time compact forms with glaucous blue foliage or blue forms of compact
habit turn up in the seed beds and eventually find their way into cultivation with
names in which the words *"compacta"* and *"glauca"* usually appear, sometimes in
different order, sometimes in combination with another name in an attempt to
achieve distinctiveness. The result is a confused situation in which it is virtually
impossible to say how many clones we have or which name belongs to which.
Fortunately they are all good garden forms, but a study of this group is
desirable, using mature plants not used for propagating from, since this alters
the growth characteristic of a plant considerably. 'Thume' is a form which is in
cultivation in the United States. It seems very close to 'Montgomery' in colour,
but is much more vigorous and soon forms a definitely conical plant. The foliage
is set forwards at 60° but the leaves (to 20 mm) are curved forward and so feel
soft to the touch when the hand is drawn forwards through the plant.

Picea schrenkiana Fisch. and Mey. An Asian species named after the Dr. Schrenk
who found it. It has supplied us with one dwarf form.

– –'**Globosa**' [*P. schrenkiana globosa* Schelle, Winterh. Nadel. 86. 1909; (Schelle)
Beissn. Handb. Ed. 2, 243. 1909.] I have recently received this rare form from
Pruhŏnicĕ in Czechoslovakia, so it should soon be available in this country. It is
described as forming a large, globose bush.

Picea rubens Sarg. The Red spruce of North America is normally a slender conical
tree. The following dwarf forms have appeared.

– –'**Nana**' Den Ouden and Boom [Man. 286. 1965.] A seedling form originating on
the Van Gimborn Estate at Doorn in Holland in 1908. It formed a compact
conical plant 1.2 m high in 44 years. I cannot find it in cultivation.

– –'**Pocono**' [New cv.] This was found in 1966 as a seedling in the wild on the
Pocono Mountains in the United States by Layne Ziegenfuss, Hillside Gardens,
Lehighton, Pennsylvania, U.S.A., and when I saw the mother plant in June 1974
it was a congested little plant 20 cm high and the same across, with a neat, tufted
habit.

Picea sitchensis (Bong.) Carr. The Sitka spruce, normally a tall tree, has not, to my knowledge, given us any reliably dwarf forms from seed, but the following cultivar has been recently introduced.

– –'**Strypemonde**' [New cv.] This form originated as a witch's broom on a 50 year old tree on the Strypemonde Estate in Holland. At an estimated age of 40 years the broom had a diameter of 40 cm. Propagations retain the very compact habit and a plant 8 years old measures 20 cm high by 30 cm wide. (Illustration 329).

BUDS: Light brown.

LEAVES: Very short, 0.6 to 1 cm; green below, very glaucous blue above, giving the whole plant quite a different appearance to normal *P. sitchensis*.

PINUS

The pines seem, for some reason not apparent to me, to be the most glamorous of all the conifers, with a particular appeal to poets, and the dwarf forms share in this attraction for some people to an accentuated degree. Several species either are mere shrubs or are so slow-growing that they can be made use of for some years, especially if grown in a pot. Other species have produced slow-growing seedlings or have given us dwarfs by the propagation of witches' brooms.

The pines sort themselves (with the usual tantalizing exceptions) into two groups: those bearing their needles in bundles of two and those bearing their needles in bundles of five. In attempting to identify any pine, the number of needles in the bundle is the first fact to establish; but since non-conforming bundles occur, it is well to examine the whole tree before deciding the point. The shape of the leaf is determined by the fact that the leaves, however many they may be, must together form a circular bundle.

The TWO-NEEDLE GROUP includes *banksiana, contorta, densiflora, echinata, leucodermis, mugo, nigra, pinaster, resinosa, sylvestris* and *virginiana*.

The FIVE-NEEDLE GROUP includes *albicaulis, aristata, cembra, flexilis, koraiensis, monticola, parviflora, peuce, pumila, strobus* and *wallichiana*.

In addition, several species have varieties in which the needles grow together (var. *monophylla*) and the species *cembroides, radiata* and *rigida* have three needles in each bundle.

The species with two needles are relatively easily distinguishable by reference to a good textbook on the coniferae, and all I can attempt here is a description of the dwarf forms. Botanists have frequently studied the cross-section of pine needles and most textbooks hopefully include simple diagrams of these to help in recognising the different species. But, alas, the species most alike in other respects shew the least differences in leaf cross-section and the wide range of variation within each species reduces the value of this study considerably.

Although the five-needle pines provide us with a goodly number of our finest dwarf conifers, their identification provides us with an almost equal number of problems. For not only have botanists changed their minds in the past as to what should or should not be regarded as a separate species,—even today opinions differ in different parts of the world as to how many species we are dealing with. An additional complication arises from the fact that the textbook descriptions are related to the typical form in each species, so much of the information given (such as the size and habit of the tree and details of the cones) is of no value in the identification of a garden cultivar, in which (apart from the possibility of hybridisation) the divergence of a cultivar from what is normal to the species can well be greater than the difference between that species and another. Even such apparently factual data as the length of leaf must be treated with caution, for we may be trying to identify the cultivar 'Brevifolia' of a species that normally runs to a longer leaf.

In these circumstances the inclusion here of a complete key is impossible and the descriptions of the different species must therefore only be considered as pointers and should not be relied on except as supplementary to the full descriptions and keys to the species to be found in any good modern textbook on the coniferae, of which there are several available. In this group the number and position of the resin glands provide us with a useful means of identifying the species to which cultivars belong. These may be clearly seen if a leaf be cut through cleanly with a razor blade and examined through a good magnifying glass.

Pinus albicaulis Engelm. FIVE-NEEDLE GROUP. A small tree-like species from the Rocky Mountains which in **'Nobles Dwarf'** den Ouden and Boom, 1965; [*P. albicaulis* 'Nana' Hillier, Dw. Con. 50. 1964] has given us a dwarf, shrubby form of compact habit, first heard of in the James Noble collection of dwarf conifers in California many years ago, presumably being a selected seedling. It is still a very rare form.

Pinus aristata Engelm. Bristle-cone pine. FIVE-NEEDLE GROUP. This species has received much publicity because gnarled old specimens on the White Mountains of California have been shown to be over 5000 years old, making them the oldest living things in the world. An attractive slow-growing little tree, with dark green, closely bunched foliage liberally sputtered with white resin spots. (Illustration 330). I believe this mountain form is now thought, at least by some botanists, to constitute a distinct species, in which case it will be known as **Pinus longaeva** Bailey, D. F. [Ann. Mo. Bot. Gar. **57**: 210. 1971] but it has received so much publicity as *P. aristata* that I daresay it will be a long time before the horticultural public accept the change.
– –'**Cecilia**' [New cv.] is a very tight, congested seedling found by J. W. Spingarn of Baldwin, Long Island, New York, U.S.A., in a local nursery. It forms a globose plant without a leader. Annual growth is about 2.5 cm. It was originally named 'Baldwin Dwarf' by Mr. Spingarn.

Pinus banksiana Lamb. Jack pine. TWO-NEEDLE GROUP. This very hardy North

American species is usually seen as a small sinuous tree, sometimes no more than a gnarled shrub. Although itself of little garden value the species has distinguished itself by producing one very interesting weeping form and in setting viable seeds on witches' brooms. An account of how this has been turned to good account by several experimental workers in the U.S.A. will be found above in Chapter I. The following clones have been selected and named.

- – 'Chippewa' [New cv.] This is one of four selections made by Alfred J. Fordham and myself in June 1974 from amongst a large number of such seedlings raised at the Arnold Arboretum, Jamaica Plain, Massachusetts, U.S.A. At that time the mother plant was an irregular little bun about 45 cm across by 20 cm high. The stiff main branches are spreading outwards and upwards, the branchlets are numerous, with no regular pattern, mostly curved upwards and outwards. The leaves are small and of varying length, 10 to 12 mm on strong shoots, less (often much less) on weak shoots, and this gives an open look to the little plant viewed from above. It should make an excellent plant for the smaller alpine garden. (Illustration 331).

- – 'Manomet' [New cv.] Another of the Arnold Arboretum seedlings. In June 1974 it had made a squat or globose plant about 50 cm each way. The plant had no main leader but divided at ground level into several stout ascending branches with an irregular pattern of side branches in whorls of two or more held at 60° to the main shoot but mostly curved forwards and upwards, so that most of the growing shoots are more or less upright. The leaves have a slight sheen and have numerous very inconspicuous bands of stomata. They are uniform in length (15 to 17 mm × 1 mm) and are in very closely spaced, wide-spreading bundles held at a wide (80 to 90°) angle, straight or nearly so. It forms a sturdy looking little plant of somewhat irregular outline. (Illustration 332).

- – 'Neponset' [New cv.] This is the third of the four selections referred to under 'Chippewa', above. Making a stronger plant, in June 1974 'Neponset' had made a low-growing, flat-topped plant 1 m across by only 25 cm high. The main branches are horizontal and very stiff and the laterals are short and held more or less upright. The leaves are straight and glossy, with several lines of inconspicuous stomata on both sides, in widely spreading clusters held edgeways at a wide angle to the shoot, about 15 mm × 1.25 mm, often with a cluster of longer leaves at the end of the previous year's growth. Leaves persist for three or four years, giving a very dense look to the plant. (Illustration 333).

- – 'Schoodic' [New cv.] This is a clone selected by Alfred Fordham at the Arnold Arboretum in June 1974 from a number of seedlings raised by him from seed collected from a stunted plant found on the coast of Maine. The seedlings varied from a compact form with a normal trunk to completely prostrate plants and included many grotesque, irregularly branched forms whose only value would be to clothe sand dunes or occupy a similarly wild situation. The selected form is a completely prostrate, mat-forming plant with irregular, twisted, horizontal branches and fairly open foliage with leaves 25 mm × 2 mm, not very dense. At this size it was still a somewhat straggly plant, but will probably fill out in time. (Illustration 334).

- – 'Uncle Fogy' A. G. Johnson ex Hebb [Arnoldia 30, 6: 259. 1970.] This interesting form originated as a naturally pendulous Jack pine found in a garden of a house in Richfield, Minnesota, owned by Mrs. Cora Wylder. The mother tree is 3 m high with drooping branches reaching to the ground, but unless top-worked, propagations form prostrate plants, suggesting that the pendulous habit of the mother tree originated from a mutating branch that 'took over'. Mr. Johnson writes (December 3rd 1973) correcting the spelling from Uncle Fogey to Uncle Fogy. (Illustration 336).

– –'**Wisconsin**' [New cv.] This is the last of the Arnold Arboretum seedlings. In June 1974 the mother plant was a dense, low, rounded bush 60 cm across by 35 cm high and of a somewhat irregular outline. The plant soon divides into several ascending main branches and a dense, irregular mass of laterals and sub-laterals all pointing outwards and upwards, these last being thin (2 mm) and flexible. The leaves are straight, very densely set and very small, the length increasing along the season's growth from 7 mm or less to 12 mm by 1 mm, rarely more. The clusters are open, occasionally near the top of the shoot spreading widely and twisted. It forms a very neat and attractive plant which should be reliably dwarf. (Illustration 335).

Pinus caribbaea Morelet. The Caribbean pine. I have heard of the occurrence of a witch's broom on this uncommon species. This has been grafted and so will presumably give rise to a dwarf form, but as this is a tropical species it will not help us much in Britain or other temperate areas.

The increased interest in dwarf conifers nowadays has stimulated a keen look-out for witches' brooms. Since, as in the case of the Norway spruce *Picea abies,* different brooms can give rise to indistinguishable forms, in the commoner pines such as *P. sylvestris* we already have a surfeit of very similar forms. But amongst the rarer pines dwarf forms arising from witches' brooms might still be worth introducing. If the finders are unable to make arrangements locally, I shall be willing to graft a few scions for them, sharing results on the 'odds and evens' rule, (i.e., I grade and number the resulting plants, keep the odd numbers and return the even numbers). It would, however, be wise to make contact with me by letter at the Wansdyke Nursery, Devjzes, Wiltshire, England, before attempting to send propagating material.

Pinus cembra L. The Arolla or Stone pine. FIVE-NEEDLE GROUP. This species makes a small tree with foliage usually rich and dense, covering the shoot. In the wild it is found from the Central European Alps to the Carpathians at high altitudes and in a second area from northeastern Russia through Siberia. It becomes more dwarf as the eastern edge of the distribution is approached so that in Japan this plant becomes *P. pumila.* There is therefore reasonable ground for regarding that species as a variety of *P. cembra* and it is therefore not surprising that uncertainty exists as to the correct classification of some of the dwarf forms.

BUDS: Long-ovoid with long pointed tip, *seldom elongating much during the winter.*

BUD SCALES: Long, pointed, often free at the tips.

SHOOTS: Heavily coated with felt-like pubescence, orange at first, darkening to brown or dark grey.

LEAF SHEATHS: Falling the first year.

LEAVES: Short (7-9 cm), stiff and straight, persisting for three to five years, pointing forward in closely held bundles, margins bearing widely spaced teeth, not continued to the (blunt-pointed) tip. Rich green colour on outside face, stomatic bands on inner faces inconspicuous. Two resin canals, deep within the leaf.

– –'Aureovariegata' [*P. cembra aureovariegata* Sén. Conif. 111. 1867; var. *aurea* Fitsch in Beissn. Handb. Ed. 3, 337. 1930.] Not a dwarf form, but very slow-growing for many years and a nice golden-yellow, at its best during the winter.

– –'Chalet' Vermeulen [Nurs. Cat. 2. 1972.] A new, compact selection which slowly forms a dense, rounded column of soft bluish-green. Introduced by Vermeulen Nursery, Neshanic Station, New Jersey, U.S.A., in 1972.

– – var. chlorocarpa Beissn. [Mitt. d.d.d.G. **8**: 113. 1899; Kew Handlist 48. 1925] is not a dwarf, and var. *chlorocarpa* SENSU Hillier [Dw. Con. 51. 1964 and Nurs. Cat. 193. 1964 (and earlier?)] is now listed under *P. pumila*.

– –'Globe'. See *P. pumila*.

– –'Jermyns' Hillier [Man. 507. 1971; *P. pumila* 'Jermyns' Hillier, Dw. Con. 53. 1964.] An exceedingly slow-growing, compact bush of dwarf, conical habit, raised in the Hillier and Sons Nursery, Winchester, England.

– – 'Nana' Hort. See *P. pumila* 'Compacta'.

– – var. pumila [*P. cembra pygmaea* Loud. Arb. Frut. Brit. 2276. 1838; Carr. Traité, 297. 1855; *P. cembra* var. *pumila* (Pall) Kew Hand-List 99. 1896.] This is an obsolete name for what is now accepted as a distinct species, *Pinus pumila* Regel. See below.

– – 'Pygmaea' [Hort. Europe, in part.] See *P. pumila* 'Pygmaea'.

Pinus cembroides Zucc. The Pinyon pine is a very rare three-needled Mexican species which, in its var. **monophylla** (Torrey & Fremont) Voss, provides us with the curious 'one-leaf pine' which is sufficiently slow-growing to add interest to even a small garden for a number of years. The single leaf is actually two leaves growing as one and occasional separated pairs can be found here and there.

Pinus contorta Douglas. Beach pine. TWO-NEEDLE GROUP. Normally a medium-size tree; two dwarf or slow-growing forms are on record.

– –'Goldchen' [New cv.] is a form originating from a mutation on a tree in the Jeddeloh Nursery, Oldenburg, Germany. When it becomes available it should become popular because of its colour, which is a bright golden-yellow.

– –'Spaans Dwarf' New name [*P. contorta minima* Hort.] This is named in honour of the late J. Spaan of Rosburgh, Washington, U.S.A., who first distributed it. It forms a sturdy, rather open little tree about 75 cm high and as much through with a very stout, sloping trunk and thick, rising main branches. (Illustration 337).

BUDS: Cylindrical, with obtuse, rounded tip, brown; terminal bud in cluster of 3 to 4 is 12 mm long by 4 mm diam., the side buds being much smaller.

BUD SCALES: Very closely appressed and heavily covered with blobs of resin. The shoot is grey-brown and rough in texture almost hidden by the closely set leaves.

LEAF SCALES: Scaly, dark brown, persisting (as scars) on third year bare branches.

LEAVES: Thin, mid-green (15 mm long by 1 mm in diameter, longest near the tip of the shoot), very closely set, held forward and with bundles spreading; straight or slightly curved outwards. Stomatic lines on both sides and the toothed margin are clearly seen with a glass.

It is a most desirable little plant, which should become very popular.

Pinus densiflora Sieb. and Zucc. (= *Akamatsu* Hort. Japan.) Japanese Red pine. TWO-NEEDLE GROUP. This pine is allied to our native *P. sylvestris* but is distinct therefrom in its longer and more slender, bright-green leaves bearing only a few scattered stomata and with the basal sheath soon dropping. Mayr [Mon. Abiet. Jap. Reich. 91. 1890] listed twenty-three garden forms which he knew or had heard of in Japan, but of these I only know of six in western cultivation. These all grow slowly but in time become small trees, so they should perhaps be classed as compact forms rather than dwarfs. Since Mayr (following the custom of the time) gave all these cultivars Latin-form varietal names, thus claiming for them a pseudo-botanical status that we no longer recognise, the 'one correct name, the single name by which it is internationally known' (See Art. 35 of the *Cultivated Code*) of each of these forms must be the vernacular Japanese cultivar name recorded by Mayr, but since the Latin-form epithets have long been established in western use as cultivar names and are unlikely to change, I give these as commercial synonyms, as allowed by the *Code*. The same treatment would be appropriate for any other of Mayr's varieties that may reappear in western cultivation. Acknowledgment of help I have received over these Japanese cultivars will be found under *P. parviflora*.

– –'**Aka-bandaishō**' = '**Globosa**' [*Pinus densiflora* var. *globosa* Mayr, Mon. Abiet. Jap. Reich. 91. 1890; f. *globosa* (Mayr) Beissn. Handb. Ed. 2, 438. 1909.] A slow-growing variant which forms a low, hemispherical plant with branchlets and leaves short and congested. It turns up in the seed beds from time to time. The name is often abbreviated to 'Bandaisho'.

– –'**Aka-hitoha-no-matsu**' = '**Monophylla**' [Mayr and Beissn., l.c.] A form with many of its needles joined together. Hitotsuba-akamatsu is a synonym. In the sub-form 'Kataha-hitoha-akamatsu' one only of each pair of needles is stunted.

– –'**Aka-senmo matsu**' = '**Tortuosa**' [Mayr and Beissn., l.c.] Several selections have been brought into cultivation with abnormal foliage. 'Aka-senmo matsu' has some of its leaves more or less spirally twisted.

– –'**Alice Verkade**' New name [*P. densiflora* 'Tanyosho Seedling No. 4', Verkade, Nurs. Cat. 1972.] This is a very attractive dwarf pine which makes a wide-spreading, bun-shaped plant with very dense, mid-green foliage. It was selected from amongst a batch of mutant seedlings that appeared in a single sowing of seed from a tree of *P. densiflora* 'Tanyosho' regularly used as a source of understocks for grafting in the Verkade Nursery, Wayne, New Jersey, U.S.A. Its ultimate size is not known. (Illustration 338).

– –'**Enkō-shō**' = '**Longiramea**' [Mayr and Beissn., l.c.] A somewhat pendulous form with leaves one third the normal length (Cf. *Cryptomeria japonica* 'Enkō-sugi').

– –'Hai-iro-matsu' = 'Argentea'. A variant with the leaves turning from the normal green to greyish yellow.

– –'Hase-matsu' = 'Mollis' has leaves soft and grey-blue, as in *P. parviflora*.

– –'Heavy Bud' New name ['Large bud' Vermeulen Nurs. Cat. 15. 1972.] This, another selection from the same batch of seedlings, forms a much quicker-growing and larger plant than 'Alice Verkade' (above). It is outstanding during the winter because of the very large brown buds which suggested the name. The foliage is the same rich mid-green.

– –'Hebe-matsu' = 'Anguina' Kobayashi [*Matsu-zukan* 59. 1975.] Snake pine. A form with twisted, snake-like branches.

– –'Jano-me' = 'Oculis Draconis' [Mayr and Beissn., l.c.] This is a slow-growing form with the terminal leaves carrying two yellow bands so that the shoot when looked at from the tip shows alternate whitish-yellow and green rings, suggesting a dragon's eye. But never having seen a dragon I cannot vouch for this. It forms an attractive small tree for those who like variegated plants. The variegation is at its brightest during the autumn. The cones are a bright blue and make a good colour contrast with the foliage. **'Shidare-janome-matsu'** = **'Oculis-draconis Pendula'** [Mayr and Beissn., l.c.] is a pendulous form with long, hanging branches and a regular pattern of yellowish circles on the top leaves of each shoot. 'Sagari-janome-matsu' is a synonym. (Illustration 339).

– –'Kakuyō-shō' = 'Hospitalis' [Mayr and Beissn., l.c.] has both short and long leaves, the latter at the growing tips.

– –'Kōkin-sho' = 'Rubro-aurea' has leaves that turn reddish in late autumn, forming stripes of green-red to red-yellow. 'Beni-nishiki-matsu' is a synonym.

– –'Mitsuba-akamatsu' [*P. densiflora* f. *subtrifoliata* Hurasawa.] This form has a proportion of its leaves in bundles of three. This is not uncommon as a phase in small plants of this species.

– –'Nishiki-akamatsu' = 'Aspera' [Mayr and Beissn., l.c.] A dwarfish form with very thick bark, deeply cracked. Rare in cultivation.

– –'Ōgon-akamatsu' = 'Aurea' [Mayr and Beissn., l.c.] There are several selections in cultivation with yellow colouring. In this form the leaves become light yellow during the autumn and winter. In the cultivar **'Akebono'** Kobayashi [*Matsu-zukan* 59. 1975] the leaves are at first yellow, becoming green by late summer.

– –'Ōgon-shibore' = 'Aurescens' [Mayr and Beissn., l.c.] has yellow leaves, green at the base.

– –'Ori-tsuru' = 'Recurva' [Mayr and Beissn., l.c.] There is a large, spreading and rather picturesque tree of this cultivar in the Royal Botanic Garden, Edinburgh. The leaves are very peculiar. They are thin, and some are buckled and twisted at the tip as though touched by a hot flame; but the interesting habit of the Edinburgh tree, if characteristic of this form, would of itself make it worth planting where there is room for it to develop. (Illustration 340).

– –'Pumila' [*P. densiflora pumila* Hesse Nurs. Cat. 19. 1930/31.] A variety of unknown origin, probably a seedling raised in a European nursery. It forms a dense, rounded shrub or small tree with long, blue-green leaves, held forward close to the shoot (especially at certain times of the year) giving the foliage a tufted appearance. Otherwise it is similar to 'Tagyō-shō' (below).

– –'**Sekka-akamatsu**' = '**Cristata**' Kobayashi [*Matsu-zukan*. 59. 1975.] A form with some of the branches fasciated like a cockscomb.

– –'**Shidare-akamatsu**' = '**Pendula**' [Mayr and Beissn., l.c.] A form with a strongly pendulous habit which needs to be top-worked or stem-trained if it is not to become merely a prostrate plant. Planted at the top of a wall down which its branches have plenty of room to fall it makes a most effective large specimen, since the leading growths recurve in an attractive manner. (Illustration 341). Another cultivar '**Shidare-ōgon-akamatsu**' = '**Aurea Pendula**' [Mayr and Beissn., l.c.] has long, hanging branches with yellow leaves. 'Sagari-ōgon-shō' is a synonym.

– –'**Shiraga-matsu**' = '**Variegata**' [Mayr and Beissn., l.c.] As might be expected several variegated forms have received cultivar names. 'Shiraga-matsu' has some of its leaves the normal green, some with yellow stripes and some almost wholly yellowish-white. A variant '**Chuya-matsu**' has white leaves at the base of the shoot and green higher up. The name means 'Day and Night'. In '**Tatejima-akamatsu**' = '**Vittata**' the variegation consists of stripes along the length of the leaf and in '**Tsuma-jiro akamatsu**' = '**Albo-terminata**' [Mayr and Beissn., l.c.], as one would expect, the white variegation occurs at the leaf tips only. Lastly, in '**Tora-fu akamatsu**' = '**Tigrina**' [Mayr and Beissn., l.c.] the variegation occurs in an irregular pattern suggesting the stripes on a tiger.

– –'**Tagyō-shō**' (often incorrectly spelt 'Tanyō-shō) = '**Umbraculifera**' [Mayr and Beissn., l. c.] forms a dense, round-topped bush, eventually a tree to 3 m high with the trunk dividing into several stems at a broad angle and with rich green, typical foliage. It bears cones very much smaller than the type, often freely borne on quite young plants. It is a very attractive tree which could be well made more use of on larger rockeries. (Illustration 342). A variant with yellow leaves amongst the green is '**Ōgon-tagyo-sho**'.

– –'**Tanyo-akamatsu**' [*P. densiflora* f. *parviphylla* Uyeki] is a selection with very short leaves.

– –'**Tengu-su**' (='Goblins Nest') The Japanese work *Matsu-zukan* gives an illustration, without description, of an obviously diminutive globose form. Tadahito Aritaki, owner of a private arboretum at Koshigaya-Shi, Saitama-Ken, Japan, writes that this is "the results of the radio-activity" and that the name is provisionally suggested as a collective name to cover a group of such plants. The illustration is certainly of a delightful little plant, but the unexplored possibilities if this sort of thing becomes general are staggering.

– –'**Utsukushi-akamatsu**'. In the Japanese book *Matsu-zukan* it is recorded that this natural form is found in the Koga district of Shiga Prefecture and also in the Okayama, Mijagi and Iwate Prefectures. These are small trees reaching only to 2–3 m but ranging in their branching habit from single-stemmed trees of normal habit, to multiple-stemmed trees which form broad, rounded (occasionally strikingly flat-topped) trees. It would seem that this would justify recognition as a botanical *forma* within which doubtless would come the cultivars 'Globosa' and 'Umbraculifera', as well as recent selections such as 'Alice Verkade'.

– –'**Yatsubusa-akamatsu**' = '**Octopartita**'. [Mayr. and Beissn., l.c.] This is an unsatisfactory name, since the word *Yatsubusa* is frequently applied to any congested or diminutive plant, but it is used in this context for a cultivar with congested habit, short branches and short, dense leaves. The book *Matsu-zukan* [p. 24] gives an illustration of an obviously very dwarf form named **'Tengu-su'**, a translation of which, I understand, would be 'Goblins Nest', but whether this is the same I cannot say.

Pinus echinata Mill. Short-leaved pine. Two-Needle Group. A widely distributed North American species which has given us one dwarf form—**'Clines Dwarf'** [New cv.] discovered by Eugene Clines, a nurseryman of Canton, Georgia, (presumably as a witch's broom) and introduced to cultivation by Joel Spingarn of Baldwin, Long Island, New York. It is a prostrate form with annual growth to 7.5 cm.

Pinus flexilis James. Limber pine. Five-Needle Group. A small, western North American species allied to *P. albicaulis*. The leaf bundles are nearly closed but separated from each other and they lie forwards along the shoot, giving a somewhat bedraggled look to the foliage. Several slow-growing selections have been introduced.

– –**'Glenmore Dwarf'** Scott Wilmore [Nurs. Cat. 7. 1949; Den Ouden and Boom, Man. 309. 1965.] Very slow-growing, forming a small, grey-blue, upright plant becoming pyramidal with age, with the main branches ascending or upswinging so that all growing tips are vertical or nearly so. The foliage is very dense, the leaves 40 mm x 1.25 mm in closely held bundles becoming shorter and tighter near the tips of the leader and branches, accentuating the dense look of the plant. Colour is yellowish-green but the numerous bands of white stomata on all faces give a greyish cast.

– –**'Nana'** [*P. flexilis nana* Noble, Journ. Calif. Hort. Soc. 78. 1951.] A dwarf bushy form with very short (about 3 cm long) leaves and flexible branches. Found by James Noble of California at Echo Lake in the Sierra Nevada Mountains in 1947.

– –**'Pendula'** [New cv.] This is not by any means a dwarf form. It makes a wide-spreading tree several metres across. There is a fine specimen at the U.S. National Arboretum, Washington, D.C. (Illustration 343).

P. griffithii. See *P. wallichiana*.

Pinus koraiensis Sieb. and Zucc. (= *Chosen-matsu* Hort. Japan.) Korean pine. Five-Needle Group. This species resembles *P. cembra* but the leaves are larger and with a blunter apex.

BUDS: Reddish-brown, cylindric-ovoid, 10 to 18 mm long, apex abruptly pointed, resinous.

BUD SCALES: Appressed, sometimes with tips free.

SHOOTS: Heavily coated with long, dense pubescence, yellow-brown or orange during the early part of the year, becoming darker by autumn.

LEAVES: 10 to 12 cm long by over 1 mm broad; blue-green with very conspicuous white stomatic bands on the inner faces and sometimes also stomata on the outer face; the bundles are loosely held, being widely spreading by the second year. *The margins are strongly toothed throughout their whole length, giving a rough feel to the edge of the leaf.* Resin canals three, one at each corner.

– –'Tortuosa' [*P. koraiensis* var. *tortuosa* Mayr, Mon. Abiet. Jap. Reich. 94. 1890] and 'Variegata' [Mayr, l. c.] are descriptively named forms described by Mayr, but neither was a dwarf.

– –'Winton' Hillier [Dw. Con. 52. 1964 and Man. 509. 1971.] An extremely beautiful, wide-spreading garden form, eventually reaching 2 m high by over twice as much through. It possesses characters intermediate between *P. koraiensis* and *P. cembra*—the leaves are not toothed to the apex and the number of resin canals is variable. I cannot distinguish between this plant and *P. pumila* 'Pygmaea' (see below).

Pinus leucodermis Ant. Bosnian pine. Two-Needle Group. This species can also be found listed as *Pinus heldreichii* var. *leucodermis,* or as a variety of *P. nigra,* a species with which it is closely allied. A medium sized tree with very dense, rigid and erect dark-green foliage. It is variable from seed and slow-growing forms can be found in seed beds. Of these are the following:-

– –'Aureospicata' [*P. leucodermis aureo-spicata* Hesse, Nurs. Cat. 31. 1952/3; *P. heldreichii* 'Aureospicata' Den Ouden and Boom, Man. 312. 1965.] A slow-growing form, eventually reaching to 3 m, with needles remaining yellow at their tips. Found in the seed bed at the H. A. Hesse Nursery at Weener, Ems, Germany, and introduced by them into cultivation. (Illustration 344).

– –'Compact Gem' [*P. heldreichii* 'Compact Gem' Den Ouden and Boom, Man. 312. 1965; *P. leucodermis* 'Compacta' Hillier, Dw. Con. 52. 1964; *"dwarf form"* Hort. Eng.] A compact, slow-growing bush, which at 10 years reaches no more than 3 m. (Illustration 345).

LEAVES: Dark-green, up to 10 cm by 1.25 mm and all distinctly curved.

BUDS: To 14 by 6 mm, dark brown with pale grey tips. Leaf sheath 10 mm long, pale grey, forming an eye around the bud 15 mm in diameter. It is clearly a selected seedling.

– –'Pygmy' Den Ouden and Boom [Man. 313. 1965; *P. leucodermis* 'Pygmaea' Krüssm. Deutsche Baumsch. **14:** 48. 1962; NON 'Pygmy' Hillier, Man. 510. 1971.] This is a still slower-growing form the history of which has, I believe, been tangled up with that of 'Schmidtii'. It is certainly a seedling, but whether it originated at Průhonice in 1952, as stated by Den Ouden and Boom, is doubtful. As I saw it in the Jeddeloh nursery at Oldenburg, Germany, in September 1972 it was a rounded bush 20 cm high with deep, mid-green, straight stiff leaves uniformly 40 – 50 mm long.

BUDS: Plump (10 × 5 mm) much drawn out to a long point, scales tightly appressed but discernible separately because of the colour, which gives a striped effect. Leaf sheaths 7 mm long, white, forming an eye around the bud 12 – 14 mm in diameter. (Illustration 346).

– –'Schmidtii' Welch [Rep. Conif. Conf. 50. 1972; *P. heldreichii* Christ var. *leucodermis* (Ant.) Markgraf f. *Schmidtii* Pilat, Jehličnaté 276. 1964; *P. leucodermis* 'Pygmy' Hillier, Man. 510. 1971.] However the battle for establishing the correct name may go, I shall always prefer the name that honours the finder, a great dendrologist and a very gallant gentleman.

In the autumn of 1926 the late Eugen Schmidt, then Secretary of the Czechoslovakian Dendrological Society, found a remarkable and very slow-growing conifer in the mountains of Bosnia, near Sarajevo. This tree, which was certainly over 100 years old, was about 3 m high, a compact, round-topped conical shape. A grafted plant at Průhonicě on *P. sylvestris* as understock is still only 0.5 m high after 41 years, so the form is reliably dwarf. It forms a dense globose to broadly conical plant with short, congested branches densely covered with sharp, bright green needles.

It was described in 1964 by Dr. Pilat of Prague as a botanical form of *P. leucodermis* but the leaves are lighter than is typical of this species and as *P. mugo* is growing close to the original tree, Herr Schmidt always maintained that the plant he had found was a hybrid, *P. leucodermis* × *P. mugo*. Since this sets a problem for the botanists I prefer to use the epithet as a cultivar name. Neither the original tree nor propagations from it have ever set cones. Being so slow-growing it will always be a rarity. (Illustration 347).

Pinus monticola Dougl. ex D. Don. Western White pine. FIVE-NEEDLE GROUP. Normally a tall tree, this species is the western equivalent of *P. strobus* from eastern North America, and it differs therefrom by its stouter and stiffer leaves and its brown, finely downy shoots.

– –'**Minima**' [*P. monticola* var. *minima* Lemmon, Bienn. Rep. Calif. State Board Form. **2**: 70-80. 1888.] Although Lemmon described this as a botanical form, expressing the opinion that it might warrant recognition as a separate species, the only clone I know in cultivation is a plant which I received from the Arnold Arboretum some years ago as *"pygmaea"* which in seven years has made a neat conical plant 30 cm high densely clothed with dark-green foliage. It is an attractive garden plant which deserves to be better known.

Pinus mugo Turra. [*P. montana* Mill.] Dwarf Mountain pine. TWO-NEEDLE GROUP. A very variable species with a distribution in nature throughout Europe from the Pyrenees to the Balkans. As well as the type (sometimes referred to as var. *mughus* or var. *mugo*) botanists recognise three geographical variations: vars. *pumilio* (Haenke) Zenari, *rostrata* (Ant.) Hoopes and *rotundata* (Link) Hoopes. The only constant distinction lies in the shape and size of the cones but the latter two varieties are more usually of arboreal size and so are outside the scope of this book. They are often listed as *P. uncinata* Mill. (Illustration 348).

All the varieties vary considerably from seed and even of var. *pumilio* the expectation from seedlings would be plants too large for most rockeries, but excellent for use on a rough embankment or where space permits. But selected, close-growing forms have been named and are propagated by grafting and these are excellent garden plants. As it is difficult to say under which botanical *varietas* these cultivars should be listed I make no such attempt. They are difficult to distinguish by description alone.

– –'**Compacta**' [*P. mugo compacta* D. Hill, Book of Everg. 30. 1924; var. *compacta* Bailey, Cult. Everg. 316. 1923; 'Compacta' Den Ouden and Boom, Man. 320. 1965.] This American selection forms a large, dense, almost globose plant with slender dark green leaves. There is a coloured illustration of it in Kumlien [The Friendly Evergreens, 196. 1946.]

– –'**Corleys Mat**' [New cv.] This is a very low-growing form selected from a nursery seed bed by R. S. Corley of High Wycombe. It forms a flat-topped plant never over 20 cm high but spreading out over the ground. The shoots are thick; the foliage is dense, with leaves long (to 10 cm) in open bundles, usually curved outwards and twisted, a bright mid-green. A very similar selection has been made on the Jeddeloh nursery at Oldenburg, Germany.

– –'Gnom' [*P. montana mughus* 'Gnom' den Ouden, Naaml. 35. 1937.] A form selected and introduced by the Den Ouden Nursery, Boskoop, Holland. It forms a dense and at first squat—eventually more or less globose—shrub with stout, twisted branches and numerous branchlets. Winter buds oblong-conical, resinous, in clusters of 3–5; leaves crowded, 3.5 to 4.5 cm long, parallel-sided, dark green with long, grey, papery scales and fairly obtuse tips. (Illustration 349).

– –'Hesse' Hesse [Nurs. Cat. 139. 1954.] This is an attractive selection forming a large, squat or upright, rounded bush of very dense growth.

BUDS: Orange-brown, cylindrical, with a long tip coated with resin, the terminal bud measures 15 × 8 mm in a cluster of (up to 3) smaller buds.

LEAVES: A rich mid-green, long (up to 70 mm), noticeably twisted, held at a very wide angle, making the winter buds conspicuous.

It was introduced by the H. A. Hesse Nursery, Weener, Ems, Germany, about 1940. (Illustration 350).

– –'Humpy' [New cv.] A seedling of var. *pumilio* selected in the Draijer B. V. Nursery in Heemstede, Holland, in 1970. It forms a squat, very attractive, compact little plant, extremely slow-growing. The dark green leaves are not over 15 mm long and have an annual growth of only 30–40 mm. The winter buds, although small (8 × 3 mm), stand out conspicuously because of their red-brown colour. (Illustration 351). **'Pincushion'** [New cv.] a selection which I saw at Raraflora, Feasterville, Pennsylvania, U.S.A., as a very flat-topped plant 30 cm high and 0.9 m across, is very similar.

– –'Kissen' New name. A seedling form of var. *pumilio* selected in the seed bed at the Jeddeloh Nursery, Oldenburg, Germany, where I saw it in September 1973 being grown under the illegitimate name *"brevifolia"*—a dense, flat, bun-shaped plant 75 cm across by only 30 cm high, with very short (10 mm long) dark green leaves and annual growth never over 50 mm. Terminal cluster of 3 to 5 very prominent buds, cylindrical (10 × 5 mm) with blunt points, all heavily encrusted with white resin. It is a very attractive little plant, especially when viewed from above. (Illustration 352).

– –'Knapenburg' Draijer, [Nurs. Cat. 24. 1972; *P. mugo* 'MG' Grootn. Dendroflora **4:** 69. 1967.] A seedling selected and introduced to the trade in 1970 by the Draijer B. V. Nursery, Heemstede, Holland. H. J. Draijer tells me it forms a squat, spreading bush of irregular outline and dense growth. (Illustration 353). Dark green needles 30 cm long and uniform in length throughout the bush. Winter buds 15 × 5 mm, cylindrical, red-brown, coated thinly with resin.

– –'Kobold' Den Ouden and Boom [Man. 321. 1965; *P. montana mughus* 'Kobold' Hooftman, Nurs. Cat. 1951.] This is another selection that makes a fairly dense, rounded bush. It was introduced to the trade in 1951 by the H. F. Hooftman Nursery, Boskoop, Holland.

BUDS: Conspicuously brown, in terminal cluster of 3 to 5, widely set, varying from 5 to 12 mm long, with blunt apex.

SHOOTS: Thick.

LEAF SHEATHS: Rather long, membraneous.

LEAVES: Crowded, straight, 2 to 3.5 cm long by 1 mm broad, bright green.

– –'Kokarde' Den Ouden and Boom [Man. 322. 1965; *P. montana mughus* 'Kokarde' Reinold ex Krüssm. Nadel. 222. 1955.] A rather curious form which was found in the Reinold Nursery at Dortmund, Germany, in 1952, in which each leaf, as it grows, alternates in colour between dark green and yellow, giving an appearance of rings of golden variegation which is not unattractive. The effect is more pronounced some years than others. '**Variegata**' [*P. mugo* var. *variegata* Nels. Pin. 121. 1866], now lost to cultivation, may have been a similar form.

– –'Mops' Den Ouden and Boom [Man. 322. 1965; *P. montana mughus* 'Mops' Hooftman Nurs. Cat. 1951.] This is a selection introduced by the Hooftman Nursery, Boskoop, Holland, in 1951 which has become popular in Britain. It makes a neat and more naturally globose plant than does 'Gnom' to which it is otherwise very similar both in foliage and bud. The leaves are shorter, 2 to 4.5 cm long by 1.5 to 1.8 mm wide, tapering to a long fine tip and with the bundles more open than those on 'Gnom'. (Illustration 354).

– –'Slavinii' Den Ouden and Boom [Man. 324. 1965; *P. montana* var. *mughus* f. *slavinii* Hornb. Gar. Chron. **1927, 1:** 147. 1927.] A dwarf, dense, spreading form raised by the late B. H. Slavin at Rochester, New York, U.S.A., which he states [Rep. Conif. Conf. 132. 1932] had made a plant nearly 2 m across by less than 60 cm high. The branchlets are held erect, the leaves somewhat crowded, lustrous dark green.

– –'Spaan' [New cv.] I received this unusual little form from the Morton Arboretum, Lisle, Illinois, U.S.A., where I saw it as a low, spreading plant. The leaves are extremely short, so the plant has a curious appearance—perhaps it is more curious than beautiful. It was found by the late J. Spaan, who distributed it as the 'Pygmy Mugo Pine'.

BUDS: Reddish-brown in clusters, usually with a few short leaves around the bud arising from its base.

LEAVES: Dark green, 1-2 cm long, often much curved and in open clusters.

– –'Trompenburg' [New cv.] A seedling form that was found in the Arboretum Trompenburg at Rotterdam. J. R. P. Van Hoey Smith writes that the mother plant, now forty years old, measures only 50 cm high by 1.20 m across, and grows 5 cm annually, so it is a reliably dwarf plant.

– –'Winter Gold' [New cv.] As seen by me in 1969 in the Draijer B. V. Nursery, Heemstede, Holland, where it originated, it was a somewhat open bush with light green needles 3-4 cm long, usually twisted. These turn a bright yellow during the winter, but in a mild winter in Britain the colouring is less pronounced. (Illustration 355).

BUDS: Small, 10 x 4 mm, very heavily coated with resin.

LEAVES: Long, twisted in spreading clusters, held at wide angle to shoot (up to 90° on older wood) 7-8 cm long × 1.5 mm wide, gradually tapering to a rather obtuse point.

Pinus nigra Arnold. Black pine. TWO-NEEDLE GROUP. This is another normally arboreal species consisting of several geographical varieties to which it is difficult and unnecessary to allocate the dwarf forms. These are mostly selected seedling forms with a reduced rate of growth but in most cases they are sufficiently strong-growing to be more accurately described as compact, rather than dwarf.

– – var. **balcanica** (Beissn.) Fitsch. in Beissn. [Handb. Ed. 3, 400. 1930.] A dwarf, cushion-form of dense growth and short, fine, dark green leaves. A local form from the Balkans, not known in cultivation. Another form I have not been able to trace is '**Prostrata**' [*P. laricio* var. *prostrata* Beissn. Mitt. d.d.d.G. **12**: 26. 1903.]

– –'**Globosa**' [New cv.] The mother plant of this form is a dense globose plant 2.5 m high and as much through in the United States National Arboretum at Washington D.C., U.S.A. I do not know the history of this plant, but presumably it was a selected seedling. (Illustration 356).

– –'**Hornibrookiana**' Slavin [*P. nigra Hornibrookiana* Slavin, Rep. Conif. Conf. 132. 1932.] This is an interesting old form raised from a witch's broom found on an Austrian pine in Seneca Park, Rochester, New York, by B. H. Slavin. He described it in 1932 as 'a low, somewhat shrubby plant with many stout, ramified, ascending branches covered with stiff, straight sharp-pointed lustrous, dark green leaves 5 cm long. It has a very compact, stubby appearance'. (Illustration 357).

– –'**Monstrosa**' [*P. laricio monstrosa* Carr. Traité. Ed. 2, 494. 1867.] Although originally described as a dwarf, the form now in cultivation under this name is no such thing.

– –'**Moseri**'. See *P. sylvestris* 'Moseri'.

– –'**Nana**' [*Pinus laricio nana* Carr. Traité, 385. 1855; *P. nigra* f. *pygmaea* (Carr.) Rehd. Bibl. 38. 1949; NON *P. nigra* var. *nana* Grootn. ex Hornb. Dw. Con. Ed. 2, 201. 1938 (Nom illegit); *P. nigra* 'Nana' (Draijer) Grootn. Dendroflora **6**: 78. 1969.] In his first edition Carrière describes this as 'A form, only reaching a few metres, which by the arrangement of its branches and its numerous short branchlets forms a broadly conical bush', but he inaugurated a long period of confusion by quoting *P. laricio pygmaea* Hort. as a synonym. Three years after Carrière's publication of 'Nana', Gordon [Pin. 169. 1858] published the name *pygmaea* (see below) for a prostrate form found in the wild on Mount Amaro in Italy. Unfortunately, in his index, Carrière reversed the usual typographical practice and used italics for the varietal epithets that he recognised and normal type for his synonyms. Although he made this clear in his *Avis* (p. 634) it fooled the late Professor Rehder who consequently listed *"f. pygmaea"* instead of the *"f. nana"* which Carrière had clearly intended. All very involved and difficult!

Hornibrook's later use of the name 'Nana' for a broadly pyramidal form with one distinct leader, described to him by H. J. Grootendorst was consequently illegitimate. Mr. Grootendorst told me in 1963 that this form was never propagated and that the original plant at Wageningen had disappeared, so at least one problem seems to have sorted itself out, but what I consider can be accepted as the true 'Nana' was recently found in Switzerland and has been reintroduced to cultivation by Draijer B. V. It forms a dense bush as wide as high. (Illustration 358, 359).

BUDS: 15 × 8 mm, sharply pointed, brown but heavily coated with creamy-white resin during the winter.

LEAVES: Dark green, 60–70 mm long by 1.5 mm wide, slightly twisted. The contrast between the bright, dark green foliage and the large, coated buds is most attractive in the autumn.

– – f. **pygmaea** Rauch ex Gord. Nov. Grad. [*Pinus laricio pygmaea* Rauch ex Gord. Pin. 169. 1858; NON *P. nigra* var. *pygmaea* Rehd. Bibl. 38. 1949; NON Hornb. Dw. Con. Ed. 2, 202. 1938 and Hort. Eng.] A very dwarf geographical form from the highest region of Mount Amaro in Italy. It has its branches lying flat on the ground with stiff, slightly curved leaves. The cones are spherical and smaller than those of *Pinus pumilio*. I have been unable to trace the reference to Rauch. I have a plant that answers to this description and presumably it can still be found on Mount Amaro. Holiday makers please note!

Unfortunately the confusion between the terms *nana* and *pygmaea* opened the way for Rehder to use the latter name for a now unidentifiable dwarf globose form and for Hornibrook to elaborate a description of two such globose forms known to him, distinguishable from each other by the foliage of one form turning a sickly yellow in winter. In so doing he seems to have overlooked the clear description given by Gordon (to which neither of his plants fitted by any stretch of the imagination) and he does not appear to have even checked the species. His green form has long been recognised as a *P. sylvestris* form ('Globosa Viridis,' which Hornibrook does not mention,) but for no apparent reason his 'sickly yellow' form has only recently come under the same suspicion. A very old specimen of this form is growing in the University Botanic Garden at Cambridge, and as a result of microscopic examination of the leaf structure it has now been established that this also is a *P. sylvestris* form. The colour varies from year to year. In the winter of 1970–71 it was a very bright yellow so this form can, I feel, with reasonable certainty be identified as *P. sylvestris* 'Moseri', itself until recently also regarded as a *P. nigra* form.

– – **'Strypemonde'** [New cv.] This form arose as a witch's broom on a 40 year old specimen of *P. nigra* on the Strypemonde Estate, Holland. (Illustration 360). It forms a rather coarse, open, heavy looking plant having a certain charm, but it is not particularly dwarf since a plant in the Arboretum Trompenburg, Rotterdam, at 18 years measured 1.70 m high by 2 m across.

BUDS: Large, broad (to 25 × 12 mm) creamy-white or pale grey, with the basal scales decurved.

LEAVES: Dull, dark or grey-green, 5–10 cm long (very variable) straight or nearly so and held up very stiffly in dense clusters around the large buds. A similar form **'Schovenhorst'**, named for the estate in Putten, in Holland, whence it came, differs in that many of its older leaves are twisted and carried at varying angles all over the plant, giving it a much more untidy appearance. In this form the buds are smaller and much narrower (20 × 10 mm), greyish-brown and with peeling bud-scales, giving the bud a striped appearance.

Pinus parviflora Sieb. and Zucc. (= *Goyō-matsu* Hort. Japan.) Japanese White pine. FIVE NEEDLE GROUP. This is regarded by some Japanese botanists as consisting of two species, *P. pentaphylla* Mayr, found wild in the northern part of Japan (having affinity with *P. strobus*) and *P. himekomatsu* Miyabe and Kudo, native to the southern end of that country, having rough bark and seeds with short wings (and a general affinity with *P. cembra*). Other authorities regard the two forms as varieties of a single species, and since they are said to interbreed freely in the area common to the two forms they are here so treated. Although a large tree in the wild, *P. parviflora* is usually represented in Great Britain by a rounded or flat-topped tree with cones erect and held above the very glaucous foliage, but the probable existence of more than one clone makes generalisation difficult. (See 'Glauca' below.)

BUDS; Ovoid, 5 mm long, brownish-yellow, slightly resinous.

SHOOTS: Pale green, sparsely covered with minute pubescence which does not cover the shoot.

LEAVES: Persisting for 3 to 4 years, widely spreading, twisted; 5 to 8 cm long (the shortest of any in this group) dark blue-green on outer face and with conspicuous blue-white stomatic bands on the inner faces, giving a glaucous appearance to the whole tree; margins are finely toothed, apex blunt. Two resin canals, close together near surface of leaf.

Mayr [Mon. Abiet. Jap. Reich. 1890.] described a number of cultivars in 1890, most of which are rare in cultivation (in Europe at any rate). One or two forms have long been in European cultivation and of recent years several seedling forms have been selected and given cultivar names. Because of their slow growth as young plants these make good garden conifers, although it is probable that several of those described below will shew themselves with age to be much more vigorous than their behaviour as small plants suggests.

A difficulty in the way of recording the forms in Japanese cultivation is that the vernacular names do not differentiate between the following: (1) Local provenances varying mainly in foliage or habit and in their suitability for cultivation as Bonsai, (2) garden cultivars in the Western sense of the word, and (3) selected clones used for Bonsai. With the help of Professor H. Kruse of Jochi-daigaku (Sophia University) in Tokyo I offer a tentative horticultural classification. The first group, the principal local variations, are provisionally treated as *formae* (as permitted under Article 34 (2) of the *Botanical Code*), the second group appear as cultivars. Professor Kruse has sent me a book *Matsuzukan* (= *Pines - Illustrated*) published in 1975. So far as I know this is the first book to describe the cultivars found in Japanese horticulture and it is very well illustrated in colour. Unfortunately for many readers the text is wholly in Japanese, but Professor Kruse has kindly supplied me with translations. A very extensive list of my third group, (i.e., selected clones used for Bonsai—many of them not dwarfs and hardly meriting recognition as cultivars in Western usage) is given by Wm. N. Valavanis in Volume Two of *Encyclopedia of Classical Bonsai Art* published by Symmes Systems, P. O. Box 8101, Atlanta, Georgia 30306, U.S.A., in 1976. Qualities highly prized in this group are the readiness to put out roots and/or new growth-buds from old wood, the tendency to develop a thick trunk quickly, pliable branches, rugged bark, short, straight needles and bi-annual bud-break.

The word *Goyō* means five-needle pine. *Yatsubusa* is a general term often used to describe any plant with congested foliage and in this context refers to selections with short leaves (and therefore popular for Bonsai) that are natural dwarfs. *Hime* means Princess and is used for any diminutive plant. *Shidare* = Pendulous. *Ōgon* = Yellow or golden. *Negishi* = Short-leaved. *Nishiki* = Having rough bark.

– –'**Adcocks Dwarf**' C. R. Lancaster [Gar. Chron. **159**: 109, 1966.] Selected in the seed bed at Hilliers Nursery, Winchester, and named for its finder, Graham Adcock, the foreman propagator. Very slow-growing and congested.

LEAVES: Short, 15 to 25 mm long, slender and spreading, exposing the stomata and thus giving a greyish appearance to the plant. The habit of producing a numerous, crowded cluster of buds at the tips of all the leading shoots results in dense growth. (Illustration 361).

– – f. **aizu** (Provisional name.) Possibly a form of *P. pumila* originating from the Aizu district in the northern part of Fukushima prefecture. Valavanis states that the needles are thick with a white stomatic line, and that the branches are thick and brittle.

– –'**Aoi**' is a clone with deep green needles, popular for Bonsai because of its good trunk formation.

– –'**Bergman**' Bergm. [Pl. and Gar. **21, 1:** 53. 1965.] This is a form selected as a seedling by F. W. Bergman of Raraflora, Feasterville, Pennsylvania, U.S.A. It forms a wide-spreading, rounded shrub with many main shoots. Leaves 70 mm long, bluish, twisted. The erect winter buds are up to 30 mm long. This seedling shows characteristics of both the Japanese and the Korean white pines. At 15 years, 40 cm high by 90 cm wide. (Illustration 362).

– –'**Brevifolia**'. See '*Ha-tsumari-goyo*'.

– – f. **fukushima** (Provisional name.) A geographical form from the Fukushima prefecture north of Tokyo. It is a strong-growing plant with annual growth up to 20–25 cm and short leaves (about 25 mm long) in fairly closely held bundles standing out at 80–90° from the stem. The stomata are inconspicuous, so the general colour of the foliage is green. I am unable to distinguish this form from f. *shiobara*, below.

– –'**Fuku-zu-mi**' [New cv.] This is an attractive form with very short (30 mm) and fine (less than 1 mm in breadth) twisted leaves in widely spreading bundles. Several rows of proportionately small glaucous white stomata on the two inner faces, give a glaucous blue. I have seen it only as a dense, neat, bun-shaped plant 40 cm across by only half as high. It is slow-growing but I do not know its ultimate size.

– –'**Gimborns Ideal**' Den Ouden and Boom [Man. 333. 1965.] This is one of a number of forms selected on the van Gimborn Estate at Doorn, Holland, there raised from seed. Den Ouden and Boom describe it as forming a large shrub with upright branches to 8 m, leaves rather fine, glaucous green. Even if the height given is a misprint for 3 m, the plant will need plenty of garden space, but like all forms of this pine it is attractive when small. It was introduced to the trade by L. Konijn & Son, now of Tempelhof, Bruin-horsterpad 6-8, Ederveen, Holland.

– –'**Gimborns Pyramid**' Den Ouden and Boom [l. c.] This is another introduction with the same history as the previous cultivar, branches densely borne, branchlets erect; leaves very glaucous, especially in spring, but the illustration they give [p. 332] is certainly not a pyramidal plant. Other selections from the van Gimborn Arboretum are 'Tempelhof' and 'Venus'. Both are too strong-growing to be considered dwarf forms, but the former is said to tolerate industrial conditions.

– – *Ginshō goyō*. This is a loose term used for any form with glaucous leaves.

– –'Glauca' [*P. parviflora* f. *glauca* Beissn. Handb. Ed. 2, 358. 1909] is described as a tree to 20 m, so is by no means a dwarf form. A clone which forms a low, spreading tree with glaucous foliage is the form in general cultivation in Britain as *P. parviflora*.

– –'Gyokkasen'. Unfortunately the book *Matsu-zukan* gives no textual description of this nor of several other cultivars illustrated therein. The illustration shews a plant with short and very thick, wide-spreading blue-green leaves and small, rounded buds.

– –'Gyoku-sho-hime' (= Jewel-decorated princess). The illustration (in *Matsu-zukan*) shews a plant with short (about 1 cm) but not crowded leaves amongst which the numerous bluntly-rounded buds are clearly visible. 'Hagoromo' is a synonym.

– –'Hakko' (= Eight ropes) The illustration (in *Matsu-zukan*) is of an obviously very slow-growing form with numerous very short, congested, slightly twisted leaves, 2 cm long. 'Kaneko' is a synonym.

– –'Hakkodo goyō'. A name sometimes used for *P.* × *hakkodensis,* a hybrid (or intermediate) form between the northern and southern provenances.

– –'Ha-tsumari goyō' = 'Brevifolia' Mayr. [*P. parviflora* var. *brevifolia* Mayr. Mon. Abiet Jap. Reich. 94. 1890.] An ascending, narrow tree with few branches and branchlets with short, very thick and stiff, blue-green leaves in tightly held bundles. This variation has turned up more than once in the seed-beds (See 'Negishi', below) and there are probably more than a single clone in cultivation. My description is of the clone 'Brevifolia' of English gardens.

– –'Hime-goyō-matsu' = 'Nana' [*P. parviflora nana* Carr. Traité. Ed. 2, 385. 1867.] A plant of apparently enfeebled constitution, lost to European cultivation, but since it was reported in 1961 in the United States [Nordine, Rep. Plant Prop. Soc. Conf. **11**: 24. 1961] it is probably still known there. It may have been used for more than one clone.

– –'Ibokan goyō'. (= Warty bark) with thick, long leaves, so named on account of its peculiar bark, which is very rough and coarse.

– –'Ichi-no-se'. A selection similar to 'Kokonoe' with similar leaves and longer buds.

– –'Ja-no-me goyō' = 'Oculus draconis' [*P. parviflora* var. *oculus draconis* Mayr, l.c.] A form with foliage variegated in stripes, supposed to look like an eye when viewed from the bud-end. Rare in European cultivation.

– –'Kamuro goyō' = 'Tortuosa' *P. parviflora* var. *tortuosa* Mayr, l.c. A form with leaves curled spirally round the stem, like a corkscrew.

– –'Koba goyō'. A cultivar with short leaves mentioned by Mayr.

– –'Kokonoe' (= Nine folds). This is one of the most popular clones. The illustration (in *Matsu-zukan*) shows a congested form with rather short, yellowish-green and frequently twisted leaves, partly covering the very numerous buds.

– –'**Koku-hō**' (= State treasure.) The illustration (in *Matsu-zukan*) shows a form with short and rather yellowish-green foliage, often twisted, and long pointed buds.

– –'**Koraku goyō**'. A very compact and congested form with yellow-green needles. Similar to 'Kokonoe'.

– – f. **laevis** Hayashi. An uncommon variant found in Hokkaido and central Honshu, having very smooth bark. 'Tado-hada-goyō' is a synonym.

– –'**Miyajima**'. A long cultivated form mentioned by Mayr, with very short needles, shorter even than in 'Negishi-goyō'. 'Miyajima' is a place name. Mayr also mentions a similar form, 'Eigoro-goyō', which I have been unable to trace in cultivation.

f. **nasu** (See f. **shiobara**.) After the war, likely plants from the volcanic Mt. Azume in Fukushima Prefecture and from the volcanic Nasu district in the adjoining To-chigi Prefecture were collected and trained as Bonsai. Such by now are highly prized specimens of the art, and many of them have been propagated and are the mother plants of the many clones distinguished by names used in the Bonsai trade but having no separate existence gardenwise. Of these 'Aoi', 'Bandai', 'Bun-ka', 'Chitose-gawa', 'Hatsu-shimo', 'Ju-man-goku', 'Ki-kusui', 'Momo-yama', 'Musashi-no-hikari', 'Nywaku', 'Nasu-musume', 'Otori', 'Rai-u', 'Ro-ku-ho, 'Sa-daijin', 'Shiki-shima', 'Shi-sho', 'Shun-mei-kan', 'U-daijin', 'Yama-biko' and 'Zuisho' are listed clones. The often fanciful names are doubtless descriptions of the mother plant which doubtless her daughters are expected to emulate in due course. But since propagation is sometimes from seed, even this may be questionable.

– –'**Negishi goyō**' [*P. pentaphylla* var. *brevifolia* Mayr, l. c. *P. parviflora* var. *brevifolia* Beissn. Mitt. d.d.d.G. **9**: 95. 1900 - SENSU Hornb. Dw. Con. Ed. 2, 203. 1938.] Mayr's classification of *P. pentaphylla* as a species distinct from *P. parviflora* permitted him two ff. *brevifolia*. Subsequent rejection of this distinction has resulted in much confusion and probably the only remaining use for the name is as a collective or group name to cover all the selected clones with unusually short leaves—now very numerous and all very much alike. Hornibrook's description 'making as a rule a low, broad pyramid, but occasionally making a rounded bush' distinguishes it from the erect form described under 'Ha-tsumari-goyō'.

– –'**Nishiki**' (= Rough bark or brocade.) A selection with blue-green straight ñeedles. This cultivar is named for the cork-like bark, which bears deep longitudinal fissures. The term is also loosely used for any form with rough bark, as well as for selections of *P. thunbergii* var. *corticosa* Makino.

– –'**Oritsuru goyo**' = '**Recurva**' [*P. parviflora* var. *recurva* Mayr, l. c.] A form having the tips of some of its leaves suddenly curved back, as though broken. 'Ikari-matsu' is a synonym.

– –'**Ryuju**' (= Dragon's longevity.) The illustration (in *Matsu-zukan*) shews a form with very thick leaves bearing prominent blue stomatic bands, straight or curved forwards towards the small, dark coloured, pointed buds. Eventually it will make a large tree.

– –'**Sa-daijin**' (= Minister of the left - An old title.) The illustration (in *Matsu-zukan*) shews a form with short, wide-spreading but irregularly held leaves partly covering the buds, which develop freely. The bark is more rough than in the cultivar 'U-daijin'.

– – f. **shikoku** (Provisional name.) A local form from Shikoku Island, west of Japan, described by Valavanis as characterised by short needles and rough bark. Clones listed in this group are 'Aki-goten', 'Beni-kagami', 'Bun-raku', 'Dai-mon-ji', 'Fuji-musume', 'Getu-ko', 'Go-ko-haku', 'Hara-koro', 'Kanzan', 'Kin-dai-shi', 'Sei-yu', 'Seto', Tai-koh' and 'Tama-hime'.

– –'**Shimofuri goyō**' = '**Variegata**' [*P. parviflora* var. *variegata* Mayr, l.c.] Some of the leaves are yellowish-white all over, some are variegated yellowish-white and green, and some are wholly green.

– – f. **shiobara** (Provisional name.) A local form named for the town Shiobara in the Nasu district, prefecture of To-chigi, north of Tokyo. Valavanis describes the needles as short, thin and light green. I do not suppose that the selections referred to above (see f. *nasu*) justify separate botanical recognition.

– –'**Todo-hada goyō**'. See f. *laevis*.

– –'**Tsuma-jiro goyō**' = '**Albo-terminata**' [*P. parviflora* var. *albo-terminata* Mayr, l. c.] A form with short glaucous leaves with yellow-white growing tips. (*Tsuma* = Tip. *Jiro* = White.)

– –'**U-daijin**' (= Minister of the Right - An old title.) The illustration (in *Matsu-zukan*) shows a form with short, thick, dark blue, glaucous leaves and small but long-pointed buds. It is popular for Bonsai because of its attractive bark and the flexibility of its branches which facilitates wiring and training.

– –'**Yatsubusa**' is apparently a name rather loosely used to cover any dwarf forms with short leaves, numerous buds and a congested, dense habit.

– –'**Zuiko**' (= Happy light.) The illustration (in *Matsu-zukan*) is of a form with dark green, short, thick, twisted leaves and small green buds.

– –'**Zuisho**' (= Happy luck.) The illustration (in *Matsu-zukan*) shows a single shoot, with short yellow-green leaves and long extended, bluntly pointed, brown buds.

Pinus peuce Grisebach. Macedonian pine. FIVE-NEEDLE GROUP. This mountain species from the Balkans has given us one most attractive slow-growing form, presumably from seed.

– –'**Arnold Dwarf**' [New cv.] I suggest this name for a form which came to me from Arnold Arboretum as 'Nana', a name now unacceptable under the *Cultivated Code*. It has made an upright little bush with very dense foliage. It is a very promising dwarf conifer. (Illustration 363).

Pinus pinaster Sol. Maritime pine. TWO-NEEDLE GROUP. This normally arboreal species seems prone to variation and the name '**Nana**' [*P. pinaster* var. *nana* Nelson, Pin. 124, 1866; Hornb. Dw. Con. Ed. 2, 204. 1938] has on two occasions been used for dwarf specimens, but none such is to my knowledge at present in cultivation.

Pinus ponderosa Douglas. Western Yellow pine. TWO-NEEDLE GROUP. A coarse-growing species with long leaves—a most unpromising source of dwarf forms, but one tree has sported a witch's broom that has been propagated. How dwarf the resulting plants will turn out to be I cannot say.

– –'Canyon Ferry' New name [*P. ponderosa* 'Canyon Ferry Dwarf' Berg ex Hebb, Arnoldia **32, 6.** 281. 1972.] In 1966 Clayton Berg of Valley Nursery, Helena, Montana, U.S.A., discovered a broom on an old specimen of *P. ponderosa* growing along the east shore of the Canyon Ferry Reservoir, Lewis and Clark County, Montana. Scion material was sent to the Morton Arboretum in 1969. The name commemorates the place of origin and the adjective 'dwarf' is unnecessary and indeed disfavoured under the *Cultivated Code*.

Pinus pumila (Pall.) Regel. (= *Hai Matsu* Hort. Japan.) Japanese Stone pine. FIVE-NEEDLE GROUP. This shrubby species was at one time regarded as a geographical form of the European species *P. cembra,* with which it has much in common. It is usually seen as a large, wide-spreading shrub. (Illustration 364).

BUDS: Cylindrical-conical (10 mm × 4 mm), apex blunt, reddish-brown, resinous, *often elongating during the winter.*

BUD SCALES: Apex filiform and partly free.

SHOOTS: Stout, green at first, becoming reddish to grey-brown by the second year.

LEAF SHEATH: Falling away the second year.

LEAVES: Short (35 - 50 mm long), densely bundled, *slightly incurved,* margins widely toothed or sometimes not toothed at all, green on the outer face, bearing 5 to 6 *conspicuous stomatic lines* on the two inner faces.

– –'Chlorocarpa' [*P. cembra* var. *chlorocarpa* (*nana* pro syn.) Hillier, Dw. Con. 51 1964, NON Beissn. Mitt. d.d.d.G. **8:** 113. 1899; *P. pumila* 'Compacta' Hillier, Man. 513. 1971.] Seedlings of compact habit turn up from time to time but they are very much alike. The clone at one time distributed under the unsatisfactory name "var. *chlorocarpa*" is no longer distinguished in the Hillier Nursery, Winchester, whence plants are now distributed under the name 'Compacta'. This is described as 'a small shrub up to 2 m of dense, erect, bushy habit; the branches crowded with large bunches of glaucous leaves. Very effective on a large rock garden or border edge'.

– –'Compacta'. See 'Chlorocarpa' (above).

– –'Draijers Dwarf' Draijer [Nurs. Cat. (Trade) 24. 1972/73; 'Kg. 1.' Draijer ex Grootn. Dendroflora **4:** 68. 1967.] A compact, spreading, slow-growing form found in a seed bed on the Draijer B. V. Nursery at Heemstede, Holland.

BUDS: Dark or grey-brown.

LEAVES: 3-4 cm long, thin.

Annual growth 5 to 6 cm. It received a Gold Medal when exhibited at the Flora Nova in Holland in 1970. (Illustration 365).

– –'Dwarf Blue' Den Ouden [De Broomkw. **10.** 52. 1954; Den Ouden and Boom. Man. 342. 1965 (in part).] With, it seems, three names to allocate between two cultivars, Den Ouden and Boom identified this plant, which they tell us was selected and distributed by the Den Ouden Nursery, Boskoop, Holland, with a seedling originating many years previously in the German nursery of H. A. Hesse at Weener-on-Ems, and distinguished therefrom a plant distributed as

'Glauca' by another Boskoop nurseryman, Hugo F. Hooftman. The descriptions given are scanty but there is a good photograph of 'Dwarf Blue' (Illustration 366) which forms a most attractive flat-topped spreading plant much wider than high with leaves 30-40 mm long in wide-spreading bundles exposing the stomatic bands which are much whiter than is usual in *P. pumila*.

Unless the Hooftman plant is a different clone, the description given of it ties it rather more convincingly with plants at the Pygmy Pinetum received as 'Nana'. (See below.)

– –'**Globe**' Draijer ex Grootn. [Dendroflora **6**: 79. 1969; *P. strobus pygmaea* Den Ouden, Conif. 299. 1949; P. cembra 'Globe' (and *P. cembra globosa* Hort. Holl., pro syn.) Den Ouden and Boom, Man. 301. 1965.] This is a most attractive form found in the Gimborn Pinetum at Doorn, Holland. It forms a perfectly globose plant reaching 2 m across after many years. (Illustration 367).

LEAVES: Variable in length (40 to 60 mm long by 1 mm wide) straight or slightly curved, held forward in open clusters giving a very dense look to the plant. Stomatic lines very conspicuous giving a blue colour to the foliage.

It cones when quite small, the red male flowers in spring being very attractive. It is one of the best dwarf conifers we have.

– –*'Jermyns'*. See *P. cembra*.

– –'**Nana**' Hesse ex Den Ouden and Boom [Man. 342, 1965; Hesse Nurs. Cat.(?); *P. pumila* 'Glauca' Hooftman, Nurs. Cat. 52. 1943.(?)] The specimens at Devizes are slow-growing and in 15 years have formed rather open-centered, low shrubs with strong main branches and leaves in bundles that are less spreading than in 'Dwarf Blue', so that the stomatic bands are less prominent and the overall effect is greyish rather than blue.

– –'**Pygmaea**' [*P. cembra pygmaea* Carr. Traité, 297. 1855; NON Loud. Arb. Frut. Brit. 2276. 1838; 'Pygmaea' Den Ouden and Boom, Man. 301. 1965; *P. pumila* var. *yezo-alpina* Isii et Kusaka in Iwata et Kusaka, Conif. Jap. Illus. Ed. 2, 214. 1954; Yezo-haimatsu Isii, Journ. Jap. Forestry Soc. **22**: 581. 1940.] This very interesting cultivar, although untypical of either species has rather greater affinity with *P. pumila*, so—despite its having been widely distributed as a *P. cembra* form—I prefer to list it here. This gives the additional advantage of avoiding confusion arising from old references to this name dating from before *P. pumila* became recognised as a separate species. Although long known in European cultivation, I think (from the description) it must be identified with a local variation found in the islands of Hokkaido, Chishima and Sachalin, which differs sufficiently from the plants found in Honshu to have been given recognition by some Japanese botanists. If this be the case then the priority of Carrière's epithet will need consideration. Meanwhile I use it 'cultivarwise' in safety! (Illustration 368). Unless identical with 'Pygmaea', Mr. Hillier's *P. koraiensis* 'Winton' is probably a different clone of this island variety.

'Pygmaea' forms an irregular, picturesque, more or less flat-topped bush to 1.5 m.

BUDS: Cylindrical, with an obtuse point drawn out to a fine tip. Terminal bud 5 mm diam., long (often lengthening during the winter), two to three smaller buds in clusters, mid-brown.

BUD SCALES: Pointed, rough texture, fringed with resin, loosely appressed.

SHOOTS: Very stout, covered with woolly pubescence.

LEAVES: Variable in size. At the base of the shoot they are 40-50 mm long by 0.75 mm broad and curved, usually forwards. Nearer the tip of the shoot the leaves are noticeably larger (to 90 mm by 1 mm) standing off at 60° but the separate bundles twisted and frequently curved downwards towards the end of the leaf. Six rows of stomata on inner faces, conspicuous. Edges sometimes finely and irregularly serrulate. Tip blunt. Although the branch system is open, the long twisted leaves and foliage retained for 3 years give a dense and somewhat tousled look to the plant. Iwata et Kusaka state that the leaves often carry three resin ducts,—the upper one being sometimes internal, the other sub-epidermic, two being nearer to the corner than is usual in *P. pumila*. There are minor differences also in the cones.

– –'Saphir' Draijer ex Grootn. [Dendroflora **8**: 74. 1971.] This arose as a seedling in the Draijer B. V. Nursery, Heemstede, Holland. It forms a spreading plant of irregular outline without a leader but with two or more main branches rising at picturesque angles. Leaves short, to 15 mm and thin, widely spaced on the stem but in dense clusters at the base of the usually twisted bundles. Dark brown buds 10 x 3 mm in multiple clusters sometimes much elongated. **'Säntis'** [New cv.] is another selection in the seed beds on the same nursery. (Illustration 369). H. J. Draijer tells me it forms a more or less upright plant with several erect branches and an annual growth of 6 to 8 cm.

LEAVES: Straight (6 – 7 cm long) blue-grey.

A feature of many of these slow-growing forms of seedling origin is that they are apt, in certain years, to put out coarse and quite uncharacteristic growth. This should be cut right out if the attractive, slow-growing, congested quality is to be retained.

Pinus radiata D. Don. Monterey pine. THREE-NEEDLE GROUP. This species is attractive in mild areas because of its bright, shining mid-green foliage. Elsewhere, although it is quite hardy the foliage burns badly in cold winds. I have received a very interesting account of the finding of several witches' brooms on this species in New Zealand where I understand it is widely planted, but so far I only have small propagations so cannot yet say how hardy they will be in this country.

– –'El Dorado' Johnson ex Hebb [Arnoldia **33**: 206. 1973] is a dwarf seedling registered by Dr. Leroy C. Johnson, manager of the U.S.D.A. Forest Service. It was grown from seed sown in 1960 and is described as being of slow growth and compact form and with extremely compact foliage. A description with photographs is to be found in the *Journal of Heredity* [**63, 5**: 293. 1972]. It is stated to be very hardy.

– –'Isca' [New cv.] The mother plant of this interesting form is a rounded tree over 4 m across, so this new cultivar is a compact rather than a dwarf form. Mr. J. R. P. van Hoey-Smith first drew my attention to this plant in a garden in Exeter, Devon. In foliage it is quite typical and it would be well worth planting for its colour and shape in a sheltered area. 'Isca' is the Roman name for Exeter.

Pinus resinosa Ait. Red pine. Two-Needle Group. This important timber tree has on more than one occasion produced dwarf forms from seed (see above Chapter I).

– – f. **globosa** Rehd. [*P. resinosa* f. *globosa* Rehd. Bibl. 35. 1949 *.] *Forms differing from normal by a much reduced rate of growth and leader dominance so that they form broadly globose plants never more than a few metres high.*

– –'Globosa' Den Ouden and Boom, 1965 [*P. resinosa* var. *globosa* Rehd. Journ. Arn. Arb. **3:** 41, 1922.] Prior claim to this cultivar name must go to a plant found by George Carpenter at Wolfeboro, New Hampshire, and sent to the Arnold Arboretum in 1920. It is described as globose, densely branched, strong-growing; branchlets very crowded, pale yellow; winter buds conical; leaves very densely crowded forming tufts; unequal in length. It is hardly a dwarf since this plant is now 5 m or so high.

– –'Quinobequin' [New cv.] This is a selection made by Alfred J. Fordham and myself in June 1974 from amongst the seedlings he had raised at the Arnold Arboretum. (Illustration 370). Most of the forms that did not shew reversion to the normal tree-like habit of the species shewed signs of coming within the description of f. *globosa* (above) but this and the following clone were very diminutive plants of potential value in small gardens. 'Quinobequin' was a small bun-shaped plant 20 cm across by 15 cm high lacking a central leader but with a spreading branch system. Annual growth 9 cm; leaves 50 × 1 mm in open bundles (sometimes widely so) so that the foliage becomes a mass of indistinct origin. The other clone '**Nobska**' was a very diminutive plant 15 cm × 10 cm, similar to 'Quinobequin' but even smaller in every respect. Annual growth 6 cm and leaves 50 mm long. (Illustration 371). Both are attractive little plants that will become popular when they are freely available in the trade.

– –'Watnong' [New cv.] This very diminutive form was found as a witch's broom on a tree in Far Hills, New Jersey, by Don Smith of the Watnong Nursery and introduced by him. It forms a tiny, globose plant with very small and narrow needles 40 mm by 1 mm, of a rather dull, pale green colour.

Pinus rhaetica Bruegger. A hybrid between *P. mugo* and *P. sylvestris* that has occurred spontaneously more than once. The following interesting pine— clearly a hybrid—is only placed here provisionally. It is possibly a hybrid between *P. nigra* and *P. sylvestris* var. *engadensis* Heer.

– –'Karel Stivin' [New cv.] In November 1968 I was taken by Dr. A. Pilát of Prague to the Alpine Nursery at Cernoliče (now a Department of the Academy in Průhoniče) where we met the former owner and saw the mother plant. This had been raised from seed sown in 1956. A difference in the cotyledons on this one plant was noticed in the seed bed and it is now a squat bush 90 cm by 80 cm across, of dense but irregular habit, with two main stems. The main branches are at 90° sweeping up to a congested branchlet system consisting mostly of vertical shoots, very much ramified. The buds are long, parallel-sided with obtuse points, very variable in size—where solitary to 15 × 5 mm, where in clusters (up to 5) much smaller. The scales are indiscernible to the naked eye and the buds are sometimes encrusted with resin. The leaves vary in size from 30 ×

1.25 mm to 70 × 1.5 mm on shoots of equal vigour, the short leaves being straight, or nearly so, the longer leaves curved and twisted. The leaves are green, with extreme tips yellow, the leaf scales being persistent. The leaves are persistent for three years or more and this gives a very dense appearance to the plant. It is a very attractive dwarf pine.

Pinus rigida Mill. Pitch pine. THREE-NEEDLE GROUP. This important timber tree is one of the species on which witches' brooms have been found bearing cones containing viable seeds. Above in Chapter I will be found an account of experiences in several research centres in the United States in the raising of seedlings, a proportion of which retain the dwarfism inherited from their mothers. No doubt in the fullness of time selections of good garden forms will be made and introduced into cultivation.

– –'**Sherman Eddy**' [New cv.] This was found by Sherman Eddy, a landscape architect at Boston, Massachusetts, in the Pocono Mountains and given to Weston Nurseries at Hopkinton, Massachusetts, who introduced it. It makes a compact, pyramidal plant, with very long light green needles in tufts. It is particularly attractive when the new leaves develop, at which times it can be imaginatively likened to a Koala bear.

Pinus strobus L. Weymouth pine. FIVE-NEEDLE GROUP. This species is an important timber tree in eastern North America, long known in European cultivation. It seems prone to produce dwarf forms. Of these several must have been in cultivation in the nineteenth century and they were given clonal names by early writers accompanied by such inadequate descriptions that it is not possible to use them nowadays with any precise meaning. Such are *brevifolia, compacta, compressa, nana, pendula, pumila* and *tabuliformis*. (*Umbraculifera* is now listed under *P. wallichiana*.) I therefore disregard them here in any clonal sense. It is better to introduce and register desirable new forms under new cultivar names than to perpetuate uncertainty.

An interesting account is given by A. J. Fordham [Arnoldia, **27, 4-5**: 29–50. 1967] of experiments at the Arnold Arboretum in the sowing of viable seeds collected from witches' brooms on several species of pine and several selections of his seedlings have been given names and will be found in this book. A résumé of this and other experimental work is given in Chapter I.

So far as *P. strobus* is concerned, the degree of variation is almost unbelievable. The seedlings at Arnold Arboretum range between plants of quite normal growth through every imaginable degree of dwarfness down to tiny plants which look more like a tuft of coarse grass than anything—horticultural curiosities and nothing more.

When such a genetical outbreak occurs it raises a nomenclatural problem that would baffle any system of classification. That it does occur outside the research station, is I think, borne out by the description of *P. strobus* var. *minima* recorded by Hornibrook in 1923. Nature has her own way of regaining her dignity. By the use of sterility and the naturally low survival rate in the wild of such oddities she ensures a return to normality in the end, but when man interferes by selecting plants that interest him horticulturally and by propagating clones vegetatively this process of recovery is halted and so we must name our treasures and group them as best we can, both botanists and horticulturists being in similar plight.

– –'**Bloomers Dark Globe**' Vermeulen [Nurs. Cat. 2. 1973] is a slow-growing seedling form of fairly open habit with a thick short trunk and stout, steeply ascending main branches with almost every growing shoot standing up at 70 - 90°. The leaves (70 - 80 mm long) are in fairly closely held clusters, pointing forwards, the colour being dark green with 3-4 conspicuous stomatic lines on the inner faces, giving a very deep, greyish-blue appearance which is most attractive. (Illustration 372).

– – f. **brevifolia** (Carr.) Rehd. [Bibl. 34. 1949 *.] A botanical category (if one is required) to cover all plants differing from normal by a markedly reduced length of leaf. It should not now be used in any clonal sense.

– –'**Densa**' [*P. strobus* var. *densa* Masters, Kew Handl. 101. 1896; Nordine, Proc. Int. Plant Prop. Soc. **11**: 24. 1961.] NANA GROUP. A clone grown under this name in America makes a compact and very dense plant, with very short (40 mm) and extremely fine needles. I only have a small plant, but it looks an extremely interesting form, especially if it remains as dwarf as the size of the needles suggests.

– –'**Hershey**' [New cv.] This is an American selection which originated in a large witch's broom on the Hershey Estate, Pennsylvania, of which I have only seen small plants. They were more open and irregular in outline than other forms and so 'Hershey' probably ranks as a compact, rather than dwarf form.

– –'**Hillside Gem**' [New cv.] MINIMA GROUP. This is a very dwarf form found by Layne Ziegenfuss at Whitehaven, Pennsylvania, about 1964. At 10 years the mother plant in Hillside Gardens, Lehighton, Pennsylvania, is a stunted little plant 75 cm high by 50 cm across, with an open, ascending branch system and very small (30 mm × 0.75 mm) leaves. The winter buds are in capitate clusters.

– –'**Hillside Weeper**' [New cv.] NANA GROUP. This was found as a mutant seedling by Layne Ziegenfuss at New Ringold, Pennsylvania, about 1966. The mother plant at Hillside Gardens, Lehighton, Pennsylvania, is now 1.75 m high by 1.25 m across, an irregular growing plant with a rather twisted trunk and an irregular branching system with the terminal growths spreading or sometimes pendulous. The foliage is normal.

– –'**Horsford**' [New cv.] NANA GROUP. Found as a seedling by Wm. Horsford in Vermont and introduced to the trade by Greg Williams of Hardwick, Vermont. It forms a neat, bun-shaped plant with diminutive foliage, very thin needles and annual growth 20-25 mm.

– –'**Jericho**' [New cv.] NANA GROUP. This is another form from America. It originated with a witch's broom on Long Island, New York, U.S.A., and was introduced by Joe Cesarini, then of Sayville, Long Island, New York. It forms a more or less upright bush with thin stems and thin straight leaves (60 - 70 mm), pale yellow green with inconspicuous stomata, held closely forwards in bundles not spreading widely. (Illustration 373).

– –'**Macopin**' [New cv.] NANA GROUP. This cultivar originated with a witch's broom found by Wm. Gotelli and George Erhle at Macopin, New Jersey. It forms a rounded bush of fairly open habit, with thick stems and long (70 - 80 mm) dark green leaves with conspicuous white stomatic bands (giving a blue overall cast) held forward at varying angles in (often) widely open bundles. (Illustration 374).

– –'Merrimack' [New cv.] Minima Group. This is a selection made by Alfred J. Fordham and myself in June 1974 from amongst the large number of seedlings raised by him from viable seeds collected from witches' brooms, an account of which is given above. At that time it had made a low, hemispherical bush about 45 cm across by half as much high, with a dense branching system and short, closely packed leaves. (Illustration 375). 'Uncatena' is another selected seedling. It had made a still more diminutive plant only about half the size of 'Merrimack' and correspondingly reduced in all its parts. (Illustration 376).

– – f. minima Nov. Comb. [*P. strobus* var. *minima* Hornb. Dw. Con. 143. 1923.] *Forms differing from the normal by a very much reduced rate of growth, resulting in diminutive plants or shrubs seldom if ever exceeding 1 metre.*

The name was used by Hornibrook for a clone no longer indentifiable in cultivation, but it serves us for a group name to cover the very diminutive forms now becoming popular, the

Minima Group

'Hillside Gem'	'Northway Broom'
'Merrimack'	'Uncatena'
'Minima'	

– –'Minima' (see above). Probably no longer in cultivation.

– – f. nana (Knight) Nov. comb. [*P. strobus nana* Hort. ex Knight, Syn. Conif. 34. 1850; Gord. Pin. 240. 1858.] *Forms differing from normal by a much reduced rate of growth, resulting in plants of shrub-like proportions, seldom if ever reaching to 3 metres.*

This name was used in a very loose way by several early writers in relation to clones then in cultivation which cannot now be identified, but it serves us well as a name for the

Nana Group

'Densa'	'Macopin'
'Hillside Weeper'	'Ontario'
'Jericho'	'Radiata'

– –'Nana'. An old name used by several writers for now unidentifiable clones. Although useful still as a loose, collective name, it should no longer be used in any clonal sense.

– –'Northway Broom' [New cv.] Minima Group. Found as a witch's broom on the Northway Highway, New York, by Greg Williams of Hardwick, Vermont, this forms a very attractive flat-topped plant with short (30 mm) and very narrow leaves held in open clusters showing up the conspicuous white stomatic bands. Annual growth 30 mm.

- –'**Ontario**' Nordine [Proc. Plant Prop. Soc. **11**: 24. 1961.] NANA GROUP. This forms a rounded plant with short (32 mm) needles. It was found in a block of seedling White pine in Durand Eastman Park on Lake Ontario, Rochester, New York. It seems to have a tendency to put out coarse growth and so lose its dwarfness.

- –'**Prostrata**' [*P. strobus* f. *prostrata* (Beissn.) Fern & Weath. ex Rehd. Bibl. 34. 1949 *.] A form with normal foliage and growth but with a completely prostrate habit. It makes a large plant in time but does not attempt to form a leader. It is a plant that needs to be used in the right spot. (Illustration 377).

- –'**Radiata**' [*P. strobus* var. *radiata* (*P. strobus nana* Hort. pro. syn.); Hornb. Dw. Con. 141. 1923.] NANA GROUP. This is one clone of the 'Nana' group that can be identified with certainty. It forms a low-spreading plant, wider than high. (Illustration 378).

> BUDS: Small, cylindrical (to 8 mm × 3 mm) light brown.
>
> BUD SCALES: Long, tapered, loosely appressed.
>
> SHOOTS: Thin, greenish-brown, glabrous.
>
> LEAF SHEATHS: Inconspicuous, soon falling away.
>
> LEAVES: Long, thin (to 8 cm × 0.75 mm), margins toothed, tapering towards the tip, medium green outside, inner faces with fairly noticeable grey stomatic bands. Leaves held stiffly forward at 10° except near the tip of the shoot (where a slight widening of the angle produces a discernible tuft) and around the terminal bud (where a cluster of short—3 cm—leaves helps to hide the buds almost completely.)

- –'**Tabuliformis**' [R. Smith, Pl. Fir Tribe, 42. 1864.] This, described as 'a very dwarf variety with small, glaucous foliage and forming a dense, spreading head from 36–60 cm', and '**Umbraculifera**' [*P. strobus umbraculifera* Knight, Syn. Conif. 34. 1850; Carr. Traité, 304. 1855; NON *P. Strobus* var. *umbraculifera* Hornb. Dw. Con. Ed. 2, 209. 1938 (for which see *P. wallichiana* 'Umbraculifera')] are forms that, if they ever separately existed, are now lost to cultivation.

Pinus sylvestris L. Scots pine. TWO-NEEDLE GROUP. This, our only native pine in Britain, is also widely distributed throughout northern Europe and Asia. As is to be expected in such a case, several (arboreal) geographical forms have been distinguished and given names, but these may be ignored in dealing with the nomenclature of the dwarf garden forms, most of which have originated from witches' brooms (less frequently from seedlings) and so must be regarded as clones.

There are now quite a number of these (far more than our garden needs require) since this widely grown species is prone to these curious growths. Although each broom will, in theory, give rise to a different dwarf form, mostly they are so much alike that only those shewing some clearly marked distinctiveness should be taken notice of. Every witch's broom is no more likely to be a winner than is every seedling.

A paper entitled "A Guide to the Named Variants of Scots Pine" by A. Carlisle,

Department of Forestry, University of Aberdeen [Forestry **31, 2**: 203-224. 1958] traces the origins of no less than 144 infra-specific epithets to be found 'in the literature'. Being written from the forestry point of view the garden forms we are interested in here are but lightly dealt with, but it is a most valuable piece of painstaking research, a must for anyone who would study this species and its variants.

– –'**Albyns**' Nordine [Proc. Int. Plant Prop. Soc. **18**: 263. 1968.] This originated as a seedling at the H. A. Albyn Nursery at Newark, Ohio, which at a time when all the remainder of the batch were trees of 4-5 m high, had formed a prostrate specimen 2.5 m across by only 40 cm high. It seems reliably dwarf since old specimens at the Dawes Arboretum at Newark, and in the Morton Arboretum, Lisle, Illinois, have retained this prostrate characteristic form. It was originally distributed as 'Albyns Prostrata' but there seems no need for the longer name.

– –'**Argentea Compacta**' [*P. sylvestris argentea compacta* Ordnung, Mitt. d.d.d.G. **8**: 133. 1899; Beissn. Handb. Ed. 2, 434. 1909.] This descriptive epithet has been applied to more than one dwarf form with silvery-grey foliage, but prior right to the name must, I think, lie with the form widely distributed for many years under this name by the Hesse Nursery, Weener, Ems, Germany, where the two mother plants were (1973) rounded, dome-topped trees 5 m high and across. (Illustration 379). The origin is not on record, but Herr Kache, then dendrologist at the Späth nursery accepted the name [Gartenwelt, 59. 1918] and wrote of 'the silvery-white glaucescence which covers the needles, the colour very bright by late summer'. Young plants seen at the Jeddeloh Nursery had formed an upright, oval bush, open in growth, with some interior foliage. Leaves to 60 mm × 1.75 mm, held very close to shoot, usually incurved, always twisted in an irregular manner; numerous very well defined rows of stomata on both sides of leaf, giving a bluish-white appearance to the plant. Both branching and leaf angle narrow but not so as to hide the terminal cluster of buds.

SHOOT: Greenish-brown, much grooved, giving a shrivelled appearance. Terminal buds stout (up to 15 mm × 5 mm), cylindrical, narrowing abruptly to an obtuse point; uniform orange-brown all over, with scales outlined with resin.

– – f. **aurea** (Veitch) Beissn. [Rehd. Bibl. 36. 1949 *; as "var." Veitch, Man. 157. 1881.] *Forms differing from the type by a change in colour of the leaves to a conspicuous golden-yellow during the winter months.*

There are several clones in cultivation, so this name serves us for the

AUREA GROUP

'Aurea'	'Gold Medal'
'Gold Coin'	'Moseri'

– –'**Aurea**' [*P. sylvestris aurea* Otto. Sieboldia **2**: 208. 1876; and later writers.] This form is not dwarf. It grows slowly but eventually forms a medium-size tree.

BUDS: Cylindrical, tapering to a blunt tip (to 15 mm long by 5 mm diam.)
BUD SCALES: Narrow, pointed, free—often decurved.
LEAVES: Long, stout (to 70 mm × 2 mm), held forward, the angle widening near terminal buds where leaves are curved forwards; the bundles are twisted

and open. Stomatic lines clearly visible by the naked eye. It turns a good golden colour in winter and is very effective if viewed from the south against a dark background of evergreens or buildings. During the rest of the year the foliage is the normal green and the plant is quite unremarkable. **'Beissnerana'** [Schwer. Mitt. d.d.d.G. **5:** 77. 1896] was either identical or is lost to cultivation, so the name need not be retained.

– –'Aureopicta' [*P. sylvestris aureopicta* Sén. Conif. 142. 1867.] This was described as 'A beautiful variety, remarkable because its leaves are predominantly a lovely golden-yellow, the variegation being constant'. I have not met with any tree answering to this glowing picture.

– –'Bakony' Barabits [Magyar Fenyőújdonságok 65. 1965; and Deutsche Baumsch. **5:** 140. 1966.] This is a rather strong-growing cultivar, becoming an upright-branching conical tree nearly 2 metres high in 16 years, although very slow-growing and squat as a young plant. It originated with a large witch's broom on a Scots pine with silver foliage noticed by Elemer Barabits of Sopron University, Hungary, in the Fenyofo district.

BUDS: 10 to 15 mm long by 4.5 mm diam., cylindrical, abruptly pointed; medium brown, much coated with resin, especially so the sub-terminal buds which are sometimes coated up solid, but the tips of the buds are free of resin.

LEAVES: Slightly falcate and twisted, 30 - 40 mm long, covered on both sides with very noticeable white bands of stomata. These give a very silvery-grey look to the foliage.

– –'Bergman' [New cv.] This is a very diminutive form which I have received from F. W. Bergman of Raraflora, Feasterville, Pennsylvania, U.S.A., where in 1970 the mother plant was a very flat-topped plant 0.9 m diam. and only 50 cm high. The foliage was not unlike that of 'Beuvronensis' but very much more dense and with shorter needles, giving a very dense and solid look to the little plant.

– –'Beuvronensis' Den Ouden and Boom [Man. 354. 1965; *P. sylvestris beveronensis* Transon ex Beissn. Handb. 233. 1891 (spelling corrected to *beuvronensis* in Ed. 2, 434. 1919); *P. sylvestris* var. *beauvronensis* Hornb. Dw. Con. Ed. 2, 211. 1938.] This cultivar originated as a witch's broom and was introduced to cultivation by the Transon Frères nursery at Beuvron, near Orleans (so this spelling must be accepted) but the name has been loosely used for several witch's brooms that have crept into cultivation and it is now difficult to claim that the original clone is still with us. It is impossible to make much sense of Hornibrook's description of the leaves—I have never seen a specimen with leaves 'about ½″ . . . mostly pressed tightly face to face by disproportionately long (about ¼ inch) leaf-sheaths', unless on a freshly transplanted tree or a half-starved specimen in a pot. The clone in general acceptance in Britain today is a flat-topped shrub, seldom reaching 1 m high but often wider-spreading, with a more or less horizontal main branch system and with the side branches held at 80°, usually curving forwards towards the light. Annual growth 60-70 mm.

BUDS: Long ovoid, mahogany-red (up to 8 mm by 3 mm), 2 to 3 in cluster; buds noticeable, considering their small size.

BUD SCALES: Thin, papery, narrow and pointed; edges encrusted with resin, loosely appressed to bud, often turned back.

SHOOT: Light brown, furrowed.

LEAF SHEATHS: Silvery-grey, 4 mm long, thin and papery, persistent one year.

LEAVES: To 40 mm by 1.5 mm, tapering gradually to a long sharp point, pointing forwards at 45°, often slightly curved, always twisted, the cluster well open; edges finely serrulate. Stomata on both sides (distinct lines barely perceptible with the naked eye) giving a glaucous grey tone to the foliage.

This makes a very picturesque tree, especially seen against the sky and if it has been planted with the main trunk well over at an angle and has had the lower branches and foliage removed from time to time to 'expose its bones'. (Illustration 380).

– –'**Bugattii**' and '**Bujotii**' are old names we can discard. The latter was a mistake by Sénéclause for a *Pinus nigra* form and my guess is that the name 'Bugattii' owes its origin to an illegible label! Neither is known in cultivation today.

– –'**Compressa**' [*P. sylvestris compressa* Carr. Traité, Ed. 2, 483. 1867; Den Ouden and Boom, Man. 354. 1965.] I have not found this form in cultivation. Carrière tells us it is to var. *fastigiata* what *Juniperus communis* 'Compressa' is to *J. c.* 'Hibernica', so it should be easy to recognise and Hornibrook [Dw. Con. Ed. 2, 211. 1938] gives us a good description to check it by should it turn up. A 'narrow, fastigiate form with its branches compressed against the main stem . . . annual growth 35 mm to 50 mm' should be unmistakable.

– –'**Doone Valley**' Hillier, [Man. 514. 1971.] This form originated as a witch's broom mutation on a tree near the Great Pond, Frensham in Surrey. J. W. Archer writes that it was one of several found by him and R. S. Corley of High Wycombe on the same visit in August 1958. Three grafts were raised at 'Doone Valley' (the name of Archer's residence at the time). Material from one of these was taken in 1961 by G. Adcock, head propagator at the Hillier Nursery, Winchester, who introduced it to the trade. (Illustration 381).

It forms an upright bush of pleasing irregular outline.

BUDS: Cylindrical with an obtuse point in clusters of 4-5, leader bud 10 mm × 4 mm, the others much smaller, bright orange-brown.

BUD SCALES: Inconspicuous and closely appressed, coated with white resin except at the tip.

SHOOTS: Dull brownish-green, deeply grooved, glabrous.

LEAF SHEATHS: Small and tightly clasping the leaves, brown with white edges.

LEAVES: 40-50 mm × 1.5 mm, straight or nearly so, slightly twisted; held at 60° in spreading bundles. Numerous lines of fine stomata on both sides of leaf. Leaf is grooved on outer face and ends in a long, narrow tip.

Material from another of the brooms found at Frensham has been sent to me by R. S. Corley and the resulting young plants look promising, being of dense growth and quite distinctive in colour.

– –'**Genevensis**' [Hornb. Dw. Con. Ed. 2, 212. 1938], '**Pygmaea Microphylla**' [Sén. Conif. 144. 1867] and '**Umbraculifera**' [Hornb. l.c.] are all names of prostrate cultivars (presumably originating from witches' brooms) which we can discard since none of them is in cultivation. Should a very old plant of any of these forms come to light, the descriptions in the literature should be quite adequate to establish its identity.

– –'**Globosa**' [*P. sylvestris* var. *globosa* Hort. ex Laws, Pl. Fir Tribe, 43. 1851; *P.*

sylvestris pygmaea Hort. Beissn. Nadel. 233. 1891; var. *pygmaea* Hornb. Dw. Con.
145. 1923 and Ed. 2, 213. 1938.] Although the 'Globular Scots Fir' has been little
noticed by authors, it (or an acceptable replacement) is with us today indisputably a 'small tree, compact in form, with stout branches and short stiff leaves'.
There is a good specimen in the Royal Horticultural Society's garden at Wisley,
in Surrey, from which the following description was taken. (Illustration 382).

DORMANT BUDS: Cylindrical with long point, leader buds with a cluster of
3-4 smaller buds, red-brown.

BUD SCALES: Appressed but distinguishable, pointed, fringed with resin.

SHOOTS: Greyish-brown, rough and grooved.

LEAF SHEATHS: Small, closely clasping the leaves, blackish-brown.

LEAVES: Fairly short and narrow (30-40 mm by 1.25 mm), stiff, straight,
twisted, held closely forward at 40° in bundles not widely spreading; numerous
minute stomata in distinct lines giving a grooved appearance. Leaves taper to an
obtuse point.

I have no doubt this is the plant described by Beissner (followed by
Hornibrook) as 'Pygmaea', with "*globosa nana* Hort." cited as a synonym.

– –'Globosa Viridis' [*P. sylvestris globosa viridis* Beissn. Mitt. d.d.d.G. **9**: 240. 1900; *P.
sylvestris* var. *pygmaea* Rehd. ex Hornb. Dw. Con. Ed. 2, 202. 1938 (the green
form).] I have already (see above under *P. nigra* f. *pygmaea*) explained the
misidentification of this plant by Hornibrook, but on the whole his description
fits our plant very well. It forms a globose, ultimately ovoid bush densely
clothed to the ground with long, shaggy foliage which is of a deep mid-green,
and it has peculiarities that should make it easy to recognise. (Illustration 383).

WINTER BUDS: These are completely hidden by a dense cluster of short,
bright green juvenile leaves that develop in late summer, often referred to as
'Lammas growth'.

SHOOTS: As the shoots develop in spring these leaves also lengthen. They
appear singly (i.e., not in pairs) and clasp the lower part of the shoot like juniper
leaves. (This is probably the origin of Hornibrook's statement that the annual
growth is 'inappreciable'—actually it can reach 15 cm.) Normal adult leaves
develop later.

LEAF SHEATHS: Small, papery, black.

LEAVES: The normal leaves are large (80-90 mm long by 2.0 mm wide)
tapering gradually to a long sharp point, held closely forward along the shoot,
irregularly curved and often twisted, giving the plant a dense but shaggy
appearance. The green colour persists throughout the winter.

This annual reversion to juvenility is quite distinctive, being found otherwise, so far as I am aware, only in the cultivar 'Moseri', which differs from
'Globosa Viridis' in its winter colouring.

– –'Gold Coin' [New name.] AUREA GROUP. I suggest this name for a reliably dwarf
form in cultivation in Britain which seldom exceeds 2 m high.

BUDS: (10 × 3 cm),

LEAVES 40 mm × 1.5 mm, usually straighter and stiffer and the colour a
more intense golden-yellow than in 'Aurea', from which this form is mainly
distinguishable by the reduced size of all its parts.

– –'Gold Medal' [New name.] AUREA GROUP. This name I suggest for a truly diminutive form, with buds only 5 mm long by 2.5 mm diam., and leaves not more than 25 to 30 mm by 1.0 mm. Apart from its diminutive size this form has the brightest winter colouring and retains it the longest in the spring. Two seventy year old plants of unrecorded origin at Pyrford Court, Ripley, Surrey, are about 1.5 m high.

– –'**Grand Rapids**' Nordine [Proc. Int. Plant Prop. Soc. **11**: 25. 1961.] Roy M. Nordine reports that this was found by C. E. Morris in a planting of Scots pine on park land at Grand Rapids, Michigan. The original plant is about 1.25 m wide by 40 cm high, a dwarf form with good green colour.

– –'**Hibernia**' New name [*P. sylvestris nana hibernica* Jeddeloh, Nurs. Cat. 33. 1972/3.] This new form originated as a large witch's broom found by the German nurseryman J. zu Jeddeloh at Glendalough in the Wicklow Mountains in Ireland in 1960, and was at first distributed under a name that has had to be replaced under the *Code*.

The mother plant which I saw in the Jeddeloh Nursery in September 1973 had formed a rounded bush 1.25 m high by as much across fairly open in habit but with foliage persisting in the interior of the plant, giving it a dense appearance. Leaves up to 15 mm × 1.5 mm usually curved at the base and twisted so as to show the numerous rows of stomatic bands which are clearly discernible on both sides of the leaf, giving a blue-grey look to the foliage. Angle of branching is very wide (as in 'Beuvronensis', with which this form might be confused). Leaves are held at a wide angle shewing up prominently the rather small red-brown buds which are encrusted with resin during the winter. (Illustration 384).

– –'**Hillside Creeper**' [New cv.] makes a strong-growing, completely prostrate plant useful for ground cover in an open spot. It is never over 30 cm high but will spread to several metres. It was a seedling selection by Layne Ziegenfuss of Hillside Gardens, Lehighton, Pennsylvania, and forms a congested mass of interlacing branchlets with deep, rich, mid-green foliage which turns yellowish-green during the winter.

– –'**Iceni**' [*Pinus sylvestris* var. *iceni* Mercer and Hay, Gardens & Gardening **4**: 9. 1953.] This semi-dwarf form was found as a seedling near Icknield Way, the Roman road that crossed the territory of the ancient British tribe the Iceni. It forms a rather loose bush with quite normal foliage and, is to my mind, of no particular interest.

– –'**Moseri**' Nov. comb. [*P. laricio Moseri* Moser, Journ. Soc. Hort. France, Ser. 4, **1**: 53. 1900; *P. nigra* f. *Moseri* (Moser) Rehd. Bibl. 38. 1949 *; var. *Moseri* Hornb. Dw. Con. Ed. 2, 201. 1938; *P. nigra* var. *pygmaea* Rehd. ex Hornb. Dw. Con. Ed. 2, 202. 1938 (the yellow form).] Aurea Group. This is a very old globose form raised by a nurseryman at Versailles, making a plant about 2 m through, with foliage turning yellow or yellowish in the winter. The colour varies, being a much brighter yellow in some winters than others. For many years this was supposed to be a variety of *P. nigra* but recently by means of microscopic examination of the leaf structure it has been found to be a *P. sylvestris* form. A very old tree in the University Botanic Garden at Cambridge, England, probably the origin of most of the plants in cultivation in this country, is indistinguishable from authentic plants of *P. sylvestris* 'Moseri' received from France, where it is once more in production by the Renault Nurseries, Gorron, Mayenne.

It shares the same general description and some of the peculiarities (i.e., the short leaves around the terminal bud and along the shoot) of 'Globosa Viridis' but the leaves, although much twisted, are usually straighter and they are held at a wider angle (45°) to the shoot. The difference in winter colouring is, of course, conclusive.

– –'**Nana**' [*P. sylvestris nana* Knight, Syn. Conif. 26. 1851; Carr. Traité, 373. 1855; Sén. Conif. 144. 1867; Slavin, Rep. Conif. Conf. 136. 1932; NON Gordon, Pin. 186. 1858; NON R. Smith, Pl. Fir Tribe, 36. 1864; *P. sylvestris* f. *nana* (Carr.) Lipa in Rehd. Bibl. 36. 1949 (excl. synonymy); *P. sylvestris* var. *nana* Hornb. Dw. Con. Ed. 2, 212. 1938 but NON Ed. 1, 146. 1923; 'Glauca Compacta' Hort.] This name (together with *pygmaea,* a name which some early authors used interchangeably with *nana*) has long presented us with a problem. Carrière's description reads: "This variety is very distinct by its habit and especially its size; it never becomes more than a very small bush, upright and compact, and of stunted growth. It is to *P. sylvestris* what the cultivar 'Clanbrassiliana' is to *Picea excelsa.*"

The early descriptions are inadequate and sometimes conflicting. Hornibrook adds to the confusion by giving a good description in his first edition [Dw. Con. 146. 1923] of a plant that later turned out to have been 'Watereri' and by writing of the latter as 'Pumila' as though that were a different form, and by switching his description of 'Nana' in his second edition [Dw. Con. Ed. 2, 212. 1938] to quite a different form without offering any explanation and by hedging on his (mistaken) separation of 'Pumila' from 'Watereri'. The first description of an identifiable plant was given by Slavin, and fortunately an original, labelled tree in the Durand Eastman Park, Rochester, New York, described in 1961 as 'A dense, slow-growing plant about 2 m high by 1.25 m across with a central leader, and pyramidal in outline, the needles are steel blue' is still available there, so there need be no uncertainty as to the true claimant to this name. A plant of this cultivar at the former Skylands Farm, now Ringwood State Park, New Jersey, was propagated and mistakenly put into cultivation under the name 'Glauca Compacta', so this name should no longer be used.

'Nana' forms a fairly regular conical tree with thick branches and rather stiff-looking leaves.

Buds: Cylindrical, 10 by 5 mm, abruptly tapering to an obtuse point, glossy red-brown.

Bud Scales: Pointed, loosely appressed, heavily coated with white resin.

Shoots: Light brown, rough.

Leaf Sheaths: Short (4-5 mm), dark brown or black, usually with white, papery tips.

Leaves: Held at a very uniform angle 30-35° all over the plant; *Sizes* 35 to 45 mm by 1.5 mm, usually straight or nearly so but often twisted. The colour is yellow-green, but 7-8 well defined and discernible rows of rather dull stomata on the outer face and a similar number of less well-defined bands on the inner face impart a somewhat glaucous tinge, the overall effect (in winter) being grey rather than blue. (Illustration 385).

– –'**Nisbets Gem**' New name [*P. sylvestris* 'Beuvronensis—Nisbet's form' Hort.] This is a form of unrecorded origin in the late A. H. Nisbet's collection at Gosport, Hampshire. It differs from 'Beuvronensis' in its shorter (25 to 30 mm), narrower (1.0 to 1.25 mm), straighter and often less twisted leaves, very much more closely set and held at a wider angle. The shoots, also, are stouter and stiffer, and it forms an upright, or conical little tree.

– –'*Pumila*'. See 'Watereri'.

– –'**Pygmaea**' [*P. sylvestris pygmaea* Knight, Syn. Conif. 26. 1850; NON Beissn. Nadel. 233. 1891 and Ed. 2, 434. 1909; *P. sylvestris nana* Gord. Pin. 186. 1858; R. Smith, Pl. Fir Tribe, 34. 1864; NON *P. sylvestris* var. *pygmaea* Hornb. Dw. Con. 145. 1923 and Ed. 2, 213. 1938.] It was fortunate that Knight differentiated between the 'Dwarf Wild Pine' and the 'Pygmy Wild Pine' when introducing the epithets *nana* and *pygmaea* for it gives us ground for talking our way out of the confusion resulting from the happy-go-lucky use by later writers of the two names interchangeably, confusion helped along nicely by Beissner (followed by Hornibrook) using *pygmaea* for another plant altogether, i.e., our 'Globosa'.

The earliest descriptions of 'Nana' at least agree that it was a conical form. The earliest description of the Pygmy Scots fir [Gord. Pin. 186. 1858] despite his calling it 'Nana' was—'A very dwarf variety, not growing more than one or two feet high but spreading widely in a horizontal direction and having very stunted branches and leaves'. Richard Smith's description of the Pygmy Scots fir follows Gordon suspiciously closely but he does add 'As it becomes old the numerous branches form a wide-spreading bush'. Beissner, alas (followed by Hornibrook), wrote of a quite compact globose form with stiff blue-green leaves and tells us he had seen beautiful globose plants up to 4 m, similar to the green form 'Globosa Viridis'—clearly not our present plant (see above).

In the Pygmy Pinetum there is an old specimen from an unrecorded source which answers to Gordon's description exactly, so far as it goes, and it is even characterised by the 'numerous branches' mentioned by Richard Smith. The plant is about 30 cm high but already is spreading out widely. Three or often four sub-terminal buds develop on each shoot and grow almost as vigorously as the leading shoot (annual growth 8-12 cm) but as all the shoots curl and twist so as to lie more or less horizontally the result is a dense thatch over the top of the plant, little or no gain in height but a steady increase in the lateral spread of the plant. (Illustration 386).

BUDS: Cylindrical with an obtuse point (8 mm × 3 mm) in a terminal cluster of 3 or 4 buds, often of nearly equal size; a rich, mahogany-red, very noticeable because of the colour contrast with the foliage.

BUD SCALES: Closely appressed and with an 'oily' look but without resin.

SHOOTS: Pale yellowish-green, thin, furrowed, glabrous; set at 70–80°, always twisted or sinuous.

LEAF SHEATHS: Small, mid-brown, persistent, leaving scars the third year.

LEAVES: Long (30–50 mm × 1.0 to 1.25 mm), straight or nearly so, twisted, tapered to a long fine point; held stiffly at 45° in open bundles; minutely and irregularly serrulate, both sides bearing numerous rows of minute stomata.

– –'**Pyramidalis Compacta**' [*P. sylvestris* var. *pyramidalis compacta* Hornb. Dw. Con.

147. 1923.] This form was distributed for some years as 'Nana' by some nurseries, but specimens in the Pygmy Pinetum correspond well with Hornibrook's description, so we may revive the use of this name. It well describes the plant, which is a narrow pyramid with a very thick trunk and ascending branches, on which the leaves persist for several years. From 'Nana' and 'Watereri' it is distinct by its more fastigiate habit, the smaller buds and the narrower angle of the closely packed and shorter leaves.

BUDS: Long-oval, 8-10 mm long by 3-4 mm diam. Often 1 or 2 much smaller buds in cluster; mid-brown, not prominently seen.

BUD SCALES: Pointed, of irregular outline; thin, papery, thickly encrusted with resin, recurved on terminal bud.

SHOOTS: Mid-brown, furrowed, with light sheen, glabrous. Branchlets all at narrow angle (40 to 50°), thick, but flexible.

LEAF SHEATHS: Persistent for two years, silvery-brown, darkening to black the second year.

LEAVES: Persistent for several years, 25 to 40 mm by 1.0 to 1.50 mm, the top third tapering gradually to a blunt tip. Leaves are held stiffly forward at 20-30°, are usually straight or nearly so, often slightly twisted, with many (noticeable) strong lines of stomata on both sides, margins irregularly finely serrulate.

– –'**Repens**' [New cv.] This is an attractive and very slow-growing form sent to me from the United States. It forms a low, almost mat-like plant, spreading over the surface of the ground but never exceeding about 20 cm in height. The growth is very irregular, the shoots varying considerably in vigour. (Illustration 387).

BUDS: Globose to ovoid, 5 mm long, dark red-brown, coated with resin.

LEAVES: Variable in length, 30 to 50 mm, and noticeably wide in proportion (2 mm); stiff, usually straight, or nearly so, slightly twisted; several strong lines of stomata on outside of leaf and numerous crowded lines of minute stomata on the inside face.

I have been unable to trace the origin of this name. If it was not in use before 1st January 1959 it will need replacement with a fancy name to comply with the *Code*. The mother plant was at the one time Skylands Farm (now the Ringwood State Park) so that would be a good name to perpetuate in such event. I understand that the plant (no longer there) was 1.25 m across by only 20 cm high.

– –'**Riverside Gem**'. Krüssm. [Handb. 262. 1972.] This was found by Bernard Harkness as a witch's broom in Riverside Cemetery, Rochester, New York, and introduced to the trade by Vermeulen Nursery, Neshanic Station, New Jersey. It forms a sturdy, squat or conical bush, probably not over 3 m high, with a stout trunk and thick, ascending branches. The shoots are glabrous, dark grey-brown, noticeably streaked, held at right angles but curving forwards and upwards. The leaves are variable with shoot vigour, but never over 50 mm by 1.5 mm; broad, tapered and held at a wide angle (85-90°) in widely open bundles in which the leaves twist away from each other; minutely serrulate and with numerous rows of inconspicuous but discernible stomata on both sides. Annual growth 10 cm.

– –'**Saxatilis**' [*P. sylvestris saxatilis* Carr. Traité. Ed. 2, 483. 1867; Den Ouden and

Boom, Man. 357. 1965; Bergm. Pl. and Gar. **21.1**, 53. 1965.] This is one of two low-growing forms which I saw at Raraflora, Feasterville, Pennsylvania, and which were said to have been received from a local resident by the name of Levy, now deceased, who claimed to have received them many years previously from Murray Hornibrook. This one fits his description well—low, prostrate and flat-topped, with a dense, mat-like growth; branchlets slender and crowded. Leaves 25 mm long, fine and twisted, dark bluish-green. At 16 years the mother plant was 15 cm high by 50 cm across. The other plant reputed to have come originally from Hornibrook is a low-growing and spreading, dense form which always makes a remarkably flat-topped plant. Fred Bergman has grown and distributed this as 'Nana Compacta', but I have not been able to trace this name and since it is not a very distinctive one (and probably not acceptable under the *Code*) Bergman and I feel it right to revive an old name—**'Tabuliformis'** [*P. sylvestris tabulaeformis* Barron Nurs. Cat. 7. 1875; 'Nana Compacta' Hort. Amer. (in part)]—that was used many years ago for a form that has never hitherto been identified. Of this form we only have the description implicit in the name itself, but so far as it goes it exactly fits our plant—which is quite remarkably 'table-forming' in its flat-topped habit.

– –**'Variegata'**. [*P. sylvestris variegata* Carr. Traité, 373. 1855.] The clone given this name was described by Carrière as 'of tender growth; leaves partly variegated with yellowish white'. Variegated forms turn up from time to time. They are mostly rather unattractive in the variegation and often, like Carrière's plant, lacking in vigour, but **'Inverleith'** [New cv.] is a very attractive form originating in the Royal Botanic Garden, Edinburgh, which has a clear, bright creamy-white variegation. Although not a dwarf, it grows slowly and makes an excellent subject for pot culture for some years. (Illustration 388).

– –**'Viridis Compacta'** [*P. sylvestris* var. *viridis compacta* Hornb. Dw. Con. 148. 1923.] This can only be regarded as a semi-dwarf since it makes a small, open tree, distinctive on account of the colour of its foliage, which Hornibrook records as a vivid grass green. Specimens I have seen have had this open, tree-like habit and noticeably green foliage, but the leaves were otherwise normal and were certainly not a vivid grass green. Part of Hornibrook's description was perhaps mistakenly taken from a plant of 'Globosa Viridis', a form which he only mentions, incorrectly, as his *P. nigra* var. *pygmaea* (Green form).

– –**'Watereri'** [*P. sylvestris* f. *watereri* (Beissn.) Rehd. Bibl. 36. 1949 *; *P. sylvestris* f. *pumila* Beissn. Handb. 233. 1891; *P. sylvestris nana* den Ouden, Naaml. 37. 1937; (Name sometimes spelled *wateriana* or *watereriana*).] This is a form about which confusion is quite unnecessary because the original tree is still growing on the Knap Hill nursery near Woking in Surrey. It was found on Horsell Common about 1865 by the late Anthony Waterer Senior, and the original tree, now about 8 m high is in excellent health. It is an upright form which becomes too large for classification with the truly dwarf forms; it is probably a seedling. Unless (as is probable) it appears in an earlier catalogue of the Anthony Waterer Nursery, the name 'Pumila' might claim priority, but because of the confusion arising with *P. pumila* and *P. mugo* var. *pumilio* I fully agree with Dr. Boom and the Kew Handlist in preferring to use the name 'Watereri'. (Illustration 389, 390). Den Ouden and Boom [Man. 358. 1965] record the origin of this confusion, which apparently arose out of the old, sad, familiar story of a lost label. A Dutch nurseryman raised some young trees from scions taken from a nice plant which he had admired in a German garden. The owner had forgotten the name but he could remember that the plant had come from the nursery firm of Waterers (of Bagshot, Surrey), so the young plants were distributed under the name *P. watereriana.* The name was reduced to its present form by Beissner in 1902, he not at the time recognizing it as the same cultivar he had written of as 'Pumila' in 1891.

'Watereri' forms an upright, pyramidal bush (eventually a small tree) with the main branches curving outwards and upwards so that all the growing tips are ascending. From 'Nana' it differs in its greater vigour, longer (60–70 mm by 1.75 mm), more widely spaced, usually curved and always noticeably twisted leaves and by the colour. Although the leaf is deep green, the several, well-defined and noticeable bands of glistening white stomata on both sides of the leaf result in a distinctly blue overall effect.

– –'**Windsor**' Hillier [Man. 515. 1971.] This form originated as a witch's broom on a tree in the Great Park, Windsor. Hillier's *Manual* describes it as a 'dwarf, bun-shaped form of slow growth. Leaves very small, greyish-green'. Propagations from this broom have, however, not proved reliably dwarf, so this name is not worth retention.

Pinus thunbergii Parl. (= *Kuromatsu* Hort. Japan). Japanese Black pine. Two-Needle Group. This tough, hardy, large tree is easily recognisable by its large mosque-shaped, silky-white buds. Mayr [Mon. Abiet. Jap. Reich. 89–90. 1890] lists ten variants, but of these only the following seem to be in European cultivation. None appear to have been dwarf forms. (On the use of the Japanese vernacular names see under *Pinus densiflora* above).

– –'Janome-matsu' = '**Oculis-draconis**' [*P. thunbergi* var. *oculus-draconis* Mayr Mon. Abiet. Jap. Reich. 90. 1890.] A form in which the leaves are variegated in bands, rather fancifully supposed to look like a dragon's eye. This peculiar colouring is most marked in the autumn and is not apparent in young plants. A variation called '**Benijanome-Kuromatsu**' changes its whitish 'eye' into a beautiful pink in winter.

– –'**Kashima-matsu**' and '**Mikawa-matsu**'. These I understand to be names used in the Bonsai industry rather than in horticulture, the former having short leaves, a short trunk and a short and congested branch system, a variation that comes readily from seed and has been known for two centuries or more for its suitability for bonsai culture, and the latter a general term for specimens collected from the Mikawa district (Aichi Prefecture) selected for outstanding leaf and/or bark qualities, and also, loosely, for similarly desirable forms.

– –'**Kuro-bandaisho**' = '**Globosa**' [*P. thunbergii* var. *globosa,* Mayr l.c.; 'Compacta' Hillier, Man. 515. 1971.] A dense, hemispherical large bush or low tree, with numerous branchlets reaching the ground.

– –'Nishiki' = 'Corticosa' is a collective or group name for a variation frequently found in the wild on the many small islands lying between Honshu and Shikoku (and in great demand for Bonsai) in which the bark is very thick and fissured, with winged excrescences similar to *Euonymus alatus*. Selected clones are '**Arakawa Sho**' (= Rough-bark pine) with thick bark, deeply and densely cracked; '**Ganseki-matsu**' (= Rock-stone pine) with hard and thick longitudinal ridges and '**Kikko-sho**' (= Tortoise-shell pine), with the bark thick and fissured in a tortoise-shell pattern.

– –'Ōgon-kuromatsu' = 'Aurea' [Mayr l.c.] A variant in which some of the needles are yellow, some green. In '**Shirago-kuromatsu**' = '**Variegata**' [Mayr l.c.] some needles are whitish-yellow all over, some green with a whitish-yellow sprinkling.

– –'Shidarematsu' = 'Pendula' [Mayr l.c.] I do not know this form, but suspect that the 'Prostrata' and 'Tabuliformis' of some American listings are plants of this cultivar that were not stem-trained as young plants. 'Sagarimatsu' is a synonym.

– –'Tora-fu Kuromatsu' = 'Tigrina' [Mayr l.c.] A variegated form with irregular whitish transverse striping of the leaves, suggesting the pattern on a tiger.

Pinus virginiana Mill. Scrub pine, Virginia pine. TWO-NEEDLE GROUP. This is the last of the native pines from which dwarf forms have been raised at the Arnold Arboretum from seed collected from witches' brooms. The following selections were made by Alfred Fordham and myself in June 1974.

– –'Nashawena' [New cv.] This selection had in 10 years formed a spreading plant 1.25 m across by less than half as much high, with foliage not very dense so that the congested branching system is exposed. (Illustration 391).

– –'Pocono' [New cv.] This had made a plant of similar size, densely clothed with green foliage. (Illustration 392).

Pinus wallichiana Jackson. [*P. excelsa* Wallich; *P. griffithii* McClell.] Bhutan pine. FIVE-NEEDLE GROUP. This Asian species having had so much trouble to acquire a stable name, it is not surprising to find its garden forms have had difficulties of the same kind.

– –'Nana' Den Ouden and Boom [Man. 310. 1965; *P. excelsa nana* Knight, Syn. Conif. 34. 1850; R. Smith, Pl. Fir Tribe, 35. 1872; Hornb. Dw. Con. 134. 1923.] Although the early references are *nomina nuda* (i. e., they give the name but no description), R. Smith tells us it was 'a dense, dwarf bush with leaves much shorter and more silvery than the species'. This distinguishes it from the following cultivar.

– –'Umbraculifera' [*P. strobus* var. *umbraculifera* Hornb. Dw. Con. Ed. 2, 209. 1938 and Hort. Eng.; NON Carr. Traité, 304. 1855; *P. wallichiana* 'Nana' Hillier, Man. 516. 1971.] This form, of which Hornibrook gives a picture, was for long regarded as a dwarf form of *P. strobus* but its transfer to this species is fully justified. It does not, however, fit the description given by R. Smith of 'Nana' which seems to be no longer in cultivation (it may well have been nothing but a dwarf form of *P. strobus*). 'Umbraculifera' is quite an attractive form, making a dome-shaped bush or small tree, easily distinguishable from any form of *P. strobus* by its drooping leaves, often kinked near their bases. (Illustration 393).

PODOCARPUS

Although a large genus of evergreen trees or shrubs, mostly from Australia or New Zealand, only a few species are hardy enough for use outside in Great Britain. As a broad generalization, the Podocarps are of the same ornamental value as the Yews, for which at first sight they can be mistaken. Many species are important trees in their native countries, but when raised from cuttings in Britain they remain shrub-like, and so qualify for inclusion here. All the forms listed have so far proved hardy in Wiltshire.

Podocarpus acutifolius Kirk. Although a tree up to 10 m high in New Zealand, this is usually seen in Britain as a small bush with stiff and long main branches and short branchlets usually in whorls of three. The foliage is radial on shoots and standing out at 80-90°, the leaves narrow and flat (15-25 mm long by 1-3 mm broad) on a short flattened stem, tapering very gradually to a fine, prickly point, grooved above and with two narrow stomatic bands below. The colour is a brown to orange-green according to the season. (Illustration 394).

Podocarpus alpinus R. Brown ex Mirbel. This species forms a low straggly bush with small leaves (12 mm by 2 mm) crowded, indistinctly two-ranked, blunt or sharp pointed; the upper sides dull, dark green; bands of stomata with prominent mid-rib beneath. It is very slow-growing and of no particular attraction as a small plant. In its early years long, straggly growths should be shortened to encourage a dense habit. Not very ornamental, but useful for a rough bank.

Podocarpus cunninghamii Col. [*P. hallii* T. Kirk.] This species forms a large bush with brownish-green, linear-lanceolate, stiff sharp-pointed leaves. These are larger than in the related species *P. totara* and on young, vigorously growing plants they may measure from 2.5 to 5.0 cm long. The trunk has thin, papery, peeling bark. (Illustration 395).

Podocarpus hallii. See *P. cunninghamii*.

Podocarpus nivalis Hook. (fil.) forms a dense shrub up to 1 m high, usually wider than high, with leaves closely and irregularly arranged all round the shoot, 7-20 mm long by 1.5 mm wide, shortly and stoutly stalked, thick and leathery, pointed or blunt at the apex, margins thickened; dull green above, keeled and with two ill defined white stomatic bands below. The fruit is a bright red. (Illustration 396).

It is hardy and suitable for a fairly bold spot on a rockery. In the Pygmy

Pinetum there are three forms, varying in size and shape of leaf, and I am informed by Dr. Trevor Davies of New Zealand that the species is variable on a regional basis.

– –'**Bronze**' Welch [Dw. Con. 278. 1966; 'Aureus' Hillier, Man. 517. 1971.] A slow-growing form with leaves not over 10 mm long, a dull coinage bronze in colour. An attractive little plant.

– –'**Jacks Pass**' [New cv.] A form collected in the wild and brought into cultivation by Campana Nurseries of Christchurch, New Zealand. Named for the area in the South Island where it originated. It is a compact, upright form which retains its attractive light green colour throughout the winter.

Podocarpus totara D. Don ex Lamb. At home this species is an evergreen tree 15–25 m or more high but in cultivation in Great Britain it is usually seen as an upright to spreading bush, densely clothed with long, flat and fairly broad (15–25 mm by 3–4 mm) leaves, ending in a sharp and slightly prickly point; leaves borne more or less radially, light yellow-green with a sunk mid-rib above and two broad white bands of stomata below. (Illustration 397).

– –'**Aureus**' [*P. totara* 'Aurea' Hort. N. Z.] A colour form somewhat euphemistically named—the colour is more Tuscan yellow than gold.

The Podocarps, being gentlemen, must have masculine epithets.

PSEUDOTSUGA

Only two of the five species in this genus (which is neither spruce, fir nor hemlock) have given us recorded dwarf forms, but they have suffered several changes of name. *Ps. menziesii* was for a long time regarded as *Ps. douglasii* (its vernacular name is Douglas fir, or, sometimes—to help on with the confusion a little—Oregon pine), then for a time it was *Ps. taxifolia*. This was before it received its present name, which let us hope it will be allowed to retain. *Ps. glauca* was at one time regarded as a geographical variety of *Ps. menziesii* and there seems even now some residual doubt as to its right specific status, and as is usual when such changes are made the old names linger on in labels and catalogues and cause much confusion.

The Pseudotsugas are most closely allied to Abies but they vary in that their cone scales are persistent, and they are distinguishable by their narrower leaves, soft to the touch, with coloured bases, and the beech-like buds.

Pseudotsuga menziesii (Mirb.) Franco [*Ps. taxifolia* (Poiret) Britten ex Sudworth.] The botanical pointer having now, let us hope, settled at the use of this specific name, together with several *varietates* thereof for the geographical forms at one time regarded as species, perhaps I should attempt an allocation of the cultivars. But the differences are so small that, in the absence of the fruiting parts, the botanical position of some of the dwarf forms is indeterminate. I therefore list them all as cultivars of *Ps. menziesii*.

A large number of dwarf forms have been named from time to time. Of those listed by Hornibrook, 'Astley', 'Cheesemanii', 'Compacta', 'Compacta Glauca', 'Compacta Viridis', 'Dumosa', 'Globosa', 'Leptophylla', 'Nana', 'Nidiformis' and 'Pygmaea' are apparently not now in circulation in England, although several of them are listed in some American collections. A number of new forms have recently been reported, some of which are seedlings of slow growth and (usually) neat foliage. These make attractive young specimens but they will probably aspire in time to dimensions beyond those expected of dwarf forms.

– –'Brevifolia' [*Ps. douglasii brevifolia* Mast. Journ. Linn. Soc. 244. 1891.] This is a very slow-growing, picturesque, eventually tree-like form with short, pale green leaves, straight or but slightly curved, arranged radially and standing out stiffly in all directions, with a pleasant fragrance when crushed. The buds are broadly ovoid with rounded tips. It differs from 'Fretzii' (below) in its narrower, apple-green leaves, and Mr. Hillier states [Dw. Con. 57. 1964] that it is less tolerant of lime than that variety.

– –'Compacta' [*Ps. taxifolia* f. *compacta* (Beissn.) Schn. in Rehd. Bibl. 16. 1949 *.] A garden form inadequately described in 1891 and impossible to identify today—certainly no botanical *forma*. Compact clones introduced into cultivation should be registered under cultivar names.

– –'Densa' [*Ps. taxifolia* f. *densa* Slavin, Rep. Conif. Conf. 137. 1932; *Ps. menziesii mucronata compacta* Hort. Amer. (in part)] is a dwarf, spreading, flat-topped bush with irregular, horizontal branches, much ramified to form matted branchlets clothed with leaves shorter than those of the species (12-20 mm). Bailey [Cult. Conif. Plate xxi 1933] gives a good illustration of this cultivar. (Illustration 398).

– –'Fletcheri' [*Ps. douglasii* var. *Fletcheri* Fletcher, Nurs. Cat. 1915; *Ps. glauca* var. *Fletcheri* Hornb. Dw. Con. Ed. 2, 225. 1938.] This cultivar is by far the commonest form in England and it is one of the most attractive of all dwarf conifers. Hornibrook gives a full account of its origin in his second edition. (Illustration 399). It forms a rounded or flat-topped, picturesque, spreading bush with (sometimes glaucous) leaves, radially set, or nearly so, 2-3 cm long (occasionally, on weak growth, much less) by 1.5-2 mm wide, twisted at the stem, thence usually straight but often gracefully curved and twisted, parallel, ending abruptly in a fine tip; green above with a sunk mid-rib, keeled below with two glaucous bands; winter buds long (7-10 mm), conical, finely pointed, red-brown, with bud scales tightly appressed except at the base of the bud. The plant is soft to the touch. 'Fletcheri', 'Cheesemanii' and 'Nana' were all found in the same batch of seedlings.

– –'Fretzii' [*Ps. douglasii* f. *fretsii* Beissn. Mitt. d.d.d.G. **14**: 74. 1905] is a slow-growing, curious form which makes a broad, conical bush (eventually becoming a small tree) with twisted ascending branches, very short branchlets and conical red buds coated with resin during the winter. The leaves are broader and shorter than in the typical form, 8-12 mm by 2 mm wide, a dark, dull green above, arranged radially and usually much recurved. It is a form of interest to collectors but of no great beauty. As it is usually seen as a rather straggly, open bush it would probably pay for a little pruning in its early years.

– –'Glauca Nana' New name [*Ps. glauca* var. *nana* Hornb. Dw. Con. 155. 1923; *Ps.*

m. 'Nana' Den Ouden and Boom, Man. 375. 1965; Hillier, Man. 519, 1971.] Since I am, for the purposes of this book, listing the cultivars without regard to their varietal standing in a botanical sense, the inclusion of the word 'glauca' in the cultivar name is justified by common sense if possibly not by strict adherence to the rules. The full history is recorded by Hornibrook [Dw. Con. Ed. 2, 225. 1938.] It is similar to the better known cultivar 'Fletcheri' but differs in being of more upright habit and stronger growth. The leaves are more radially arranged, longer (to 25 mm long), stiffer and the foliage is of a more glaucous blue colour, due to the bluish-white stomatic bands on the underside.

- –'Globosa' [*Ps. taxifolia* f. *globosa* (Beissn.) Schwerin in Rehd. Bibl. 16. 1949 *.] This is another old clone, long since lost to cultivation, to which my remarks under 'Compacta' apply.

- –'Hillside Pride' [New cv.] This is a diminutive form which was found by Layne Ziegenfuss in 1951 in a plantation of Douglas firs being grown for Christmas trees. At 23 years the mother plant is a neat conical plant 80 cm high by 50 cm across. The branch system is ascending, the foliage is very dense, the colour dull, dark-green; the leaves are small (15 mm × 1.5 mm) held at 80°. At first sight the plant could be mistaken for a form of *Abies balsamea*. (Illustration 400).

- –'Holmstrup' Krüssm. [Handb. 293. 1972.] A seedling form from the Jensen Nursery, Holmstrup, Denmark. It forms a dense, conical little bush with ascending branches and dark green leaves. It will probably reach tree-like dimensions in time.

- –'Little Jon' Wyman [Arnoldia **29,1**: 7. 1969.] A very slow-growing seedling form found by Albert Ziegler near Wrightsville, Pennsylvania, U.S.A., in 1967. It forms a small, dense pyramidal plant with thin dainty branches and with very dainty (to 15 mm by 1 mm), light green leaves with two bands of stomata beneath. At 10 years the mother plant was 45 cm high.

- –'Oudemansii' [*Ps. douglasii* var. *Oudemansii* Grootn. ex Hornb. Dw. Con Ed. 2, 223. 1938] is another collector's item which also grows very slowly but eventually reaches tree stature. Its habit is pyramidal with ascending branches, the leaves are 10-16 mm long by 2 - 3 mm wide, parallel-sided and rounded at the tip, dark shining green above with two light green stomatic bands below.

- –'Pumila' [*Ps. glauca* var. *pumila* Hornb. Dw. Con. 155. 1923.] A very old form, raised in the Anthony Waterer Nursery, Knap Hill, Woking, Surrey, during the last century and given a First Class Certificate when exhibited at a Royal Horticultural Society Show as long ago as 1899, but still quite rare. It forms an upright or less wide-spreading bush, but is otherwise similar to 'Fletcheri'.

BUDS: Small (7 mm by 3 mm), dark red-brown.

LEAVES: Very densely set and regular, 25 mm by 1.5 mm, light yellow-green, very pale beneath, usually tapering to a much finer point than in 'Fletcheri'.

- –'Slavinii' [*Ps. taxifolia pyramidata* f. *Slavinii* Slavin, Rep. Conif. Conf. 137. 1932] was described as being semi-dwarf and of conical habit, broad at the base, narrowing towards the top, leaves crowded, short, 15-18 mm long, a bright green.

- –'Tempelhof Compact' Den Ouden and Boom [Man. 377. 1965.] An introduction from the L. J. Konijn & Co. Nursery, Arboretum Tempelhof, Bruinhorsterpad 6-8, Ederveen, Holland. A plant in the Pygmy Pinetum is a round-topped little tree 30 cm high by 40 cm across with a very compact, irregular habit and with dense foliage of small (20 mm by 1.25 mm) dark green leaves with a broad band of stomata and a thin green mid-rib below, very closely set on the shoot, held semi-radially. The brown buds are very small (6 mm by 2 mm at the most) but they are very numerous and show up well against the blue-green foliage. It is an attractive form, and reliably dwarf, we suppose, since Dr. Boom tells us that the original findling was only 60 cm high at 20 years of age. (Illustration 401).

SEQUOIA

Sequoia sempervirens (D. Don) Endl., the Giant redwood, now stands alone in this genus, the Wellingtonia or Mammoth Tree of California (formerly *S. gigantea*) having had the generic name Sequoiadendron specially invented for it, although many people treat this as a joke and continue to use the old name.

Although one of the tallest trees in the world *S. sempervirens* has given us three excellent dwarf forms (or forms that, at least, we can use as such, by regular resort to the knife).

– –'**Adpressa**' [*S. sempervirens adpressa* Carr. Traité. Ed. 2, 211. 1867; NON Veitch, Man. 212. 1881; *S. sempervirens albospica* Veitch l.c.] This dwarf form is probably only a cultivariant of a tall variety of the species known as 'Albo-spica', as it will occasionally throw up strong vertical growth with small, appressed leaves radially set. These must be cut right out at once if the dwarf characteristic is to be preserved, but if this be done 'Adpressa' will remain indefinitely a low, densely branched bush. In the summer when all the crowded, upright shoots are tipped with creamy-white it is probably the most beautiful dwarf conifer in existence. It breaks into bud freely from old wood and is improved by an occasional hard cutting back. (Illustration 402).

– –'**Nana Pendula**' [*S. sempervirens* var. *nana pendula* Hornb. Dw. Con. 156. 1923; NON *S. sempervirens nana pendula* Hilling, Proc. Roy. Soc. **76**: 105. 1951.] It is quite possible that this too is a cultivariant, but this time of the weeping form known as 'Pendula', which is described as having branches arched over and (in old trees) spreading over the ground. Cuttings of weak shoots taken from such a tree could be expected to produce plants of 'Nana Pendula' if stem-trained when young. (Illustration 403).

It is quite distinct from 'Adpressa' by its sprawling, open habit of growth and from 'Prostrata' (below) by its narrow leaves.

– –'**Prostrata**' [*S. sempervirens prostrata* Gilmour, Journ. Roy. Hort. Soc. **78**: 6. 1953; *nana pendula* **76**: 1951, NON Hornb. Dw. Con. 156. 1923; 'Cantab' Hort.] is one of the most remarkable of dwarf conifers. It originated in a bud mutation on a tree in the Cambridge University Botanic Garden (hence the name 'Cantab' sometimes met with) which gave rise to a branch with flat leaves almost twice the usual width. Plants raised from cuttings taken from this branch had a completely prostrate habit, at least for some years.

Allowed to grow in this way the plant merely forms a wide-spread, dense, sprawling mat of no particular beauty, but if in its formative years one branch be trained up into a vertical leader the branches will spread out stiffly in horizontal layers and eventually it will become a large spreading plant, which with its wide leaves of an attractive and unusual shade of grey-green will seldom fail to attract attention.

I consider that it is most effective when planted against a wall or in front of a large rock so that it can only develop in a half circle. It will never increase in height without further stem-training (the process is basically the same as the production of an espalier fruit tree) but it will spread out horizontally to cover a large area in time. Any strong branches *carrying radially set foliage* that sweep up from the horizontal must, however, be cut away at once if the character of the plant is not to be lost. Such growths are true leaders and will take over the plant if allowed to remain. The leaves are sometimes killed in a hard winter. The plant is unharmed, but because the leaves persist for several years the dead, brown remains spoil its beauty for a long time, so it should be given a sheltered position if possible. (Illustration 404).

SEQUOIADENDRON

Sequoiadendron giganteum (Lindl.) Buchholz [syn. *Wellingtonia gigantea* and *Sequoia gigantea*] the Mammoth tree, itself growing to 100 metres or more, has given us one dwarf form in **'Pygmaeum'** [*S. gigantea* f. *pygmaea* Beissn. Handb. 463. 1891] but as would perhaps be expected of a pygmy giant it makes quite a large bush, 3-4 m high. The growth is relatively crowded and dense, but any strong leader growth that appears must be cut out in good time if the plant is not to become arboreal. (Illustration 405).

TAXUS

Taxus is a genus of six or seven species which are all very hardy and accommodating as to soil and situation, thriving equally in acid or alkaline soil, standing pruning and clipping well and succeeding even in dense shade. This makes the Yews a useful group even in the island climate of Britain, and in the more extreme climate of North America they are grown by the million and there many named forms are on the market which are very difficult to distinguish. The Yews are normally dioecious; that is to say, the male and female flowers are on separate plants and of course only female clones bear the 'berries'. An occasional branch may change its sex for no apparent reason.

The truly dwarf forms are few, but a number of named forms are sufficiently slow-growing to be mentioned here. These, like the varieties of *Juniperus communis*, seem to run either to a narrow fastigiate form or to a low and spreading habit. This is due to the fact that Yews propagated in the customary manner from side cuttings seldom if ever succeed in developing a true leader.[1] The plants are therefore all cultivariants. In the case of the fastigiate forms the absence of a leader escapes notice since one or more fastigiate branches serve the purpose, but vegetative propagations of other forms will result in anything from an upright-spreading to a completely prostrate bush, according to the branching habit of the seedling mother plant. This peculiarity has resulted in much confusion in the nomenclature, since every seedling is a potential mother of a new spreading clone, so any attempt to treat them as botanical *formae* is farcical. A living Herbarium of Taxus was established at the Secrest Arboretum at the Ohio Agricultural Research Centre, Wooster, Ohio, U.S.A., in 1942, and an account of nearly one hundred cultivars, with good descriptions and (in many cases a photograph) will be found in the publication L. C. Chadwick, and R. A. Kenn, *A Study of the Genus Taxus,* Ohio Agric. Res. and Dev. Centre (Bulletin 1086, May 1976). Only a small proportion of these, however, come within the scope of this book.

Taxus baccata L. is the Common or (in America) English yew. The leaves are spirally arranged, but on side branches are twisted into a pseudo-pectinate arrangement; linear, 12–13 mm long by 1.5–2 mm wide, gradually tapering to a fine point; dark (sometimes almost black) green above and pale green, grey or yellowish with faint stomatic lines below. There are several striking golden and variegated forms, but generally the foliage is a dark green, which in a mass can become somber, so the Yews should be planted with restraint.

The forms we are concerned with here can be grouped as follows:

ADPRESSA GROUP

f. *adpressa*
'Adpressa Aurea'
'Adpressa Erecta'
'Adpressa Pyramidalis'
'Adpressa Variegata'
'Amersfoort'
'Fowle'

FASTIGIATA GROUP

'Columnaris'
'Fastigiata'
'Fastigiata Aurea'
'Fastigiata Aureomarginata'
'Fastigiata Aureovariegata'
'Standishii'

NANA GROUP

'Compacta'
'Epacrioides'
'Ericoides'
'Knirps'

PROCUMBENS GROUP

'Cavendishii'
'Dovastoniana'
'Dovastonii Aurea'
'Expansa'   ....*continued*

1. The *Taxus cuspidata* 'Capitata' of the American nursery trade appears to be an exception (i.e., to the customary failure of yew cuttings to develop a true leader) but *T. cuspidata* often makes a multi-stemmed tree, so 'Capitata' may be no real exception to the rule after all.

NANA GROUP

'Minuta'
'Monstrosa'
'Nana'
'Nutans'
'Page'
'Parvula'
'Paulina'
'Pygmaea'

PROCUMBENS GROUP

'Gracilis Pendula'
'Horizontalis'
'Jacksonii'
'Pendula'
'Procumbens'
'Prostrata'
'Pseudo-procumbens'
'Recurvata'
'Repandens'

– – f. **adpressa** (Carr.) Beissn. [Rehd. Bibl. 3. 1949 *.] *Forms differing from the type in bearing short (6 - 10 mm) and broad (2 - 4 mm) leaves with obtuse points.* It serves us as a name for the ADPRESSA GROUP.

– –'Adpressa' [*T. baccata adpressa* Carr. Traité, 520. 1855; The Garden, **29:** 149, 221 and 268. 1896.] Although this form is said to turn up in seed beds, the clone in cultivation is stated to have originated in the Dickson Nurseries at Chester in 1828. It forms a large spreading shrub (eventually a small tree), with densely crowded branches and leaves that are much shorter and relatively broader than the common form, only 6 to 12 mm long by 2 to 4 mm broad, with a round apex ending in a sharp point. It is a fruiting form, the red aril being shorter than the seed so that the latter projects, and it comes mainly true from seed.

– –'Adpressa Aurea' [*T. baccata adpressa aurea* Beissn. Mitt. d.d.d. G. **6:** 56. 1892] is a much more attractive form with growth similar to 'Adpressa' but forming a very much less vigorous plant, not exceeding 1.5 m high. The leaves on young growth are golden-yellow, elsewhere yellowish; female flowers only. Much more frequently seen is another variegated form **'Adpressa Variegata'** [*T. adpressa variegata* Nels. Pin. 171. 1866] with leaves persistently pale golden-yellow with a central green stripe. It forms a dense bush and grows much larger than 'Adpressa Aurea'. There is a fine specimen at the Westonbirt Arboretum in Gloucestershire, on the north side of Mitchell Drive near Down Gate. (Illustration 406).

Several habit variants are recorded, having presumably arisen as seedlings— **'Adpressa Erecta'** [Nels., l.c.; *T. baccata adpressa stricta* Carr. Traité. Ed. 2, 732. 1867] described as a large, broadly conical shrub with main branches erect, a female clone, and **'Adpressa Pyramidalis'** [Den Ouden, Conif. 331. 1949] a Dutch seedling that is similar, but with fastigiate main branches.

– –'Amersfoort' Meyer [Baileya **9, 4:** 133. 1961.] ADPRESSA GROUP. A curious, slow-growing form with stiff open habit resulting from ascending main branches and few short branchlets. The leaves are numerous, oval, set radially, 5 - 8 mm long by 3 - 4 mm wide, rounded at the apex and abruptly pointed, dark glossy green above, lighter beneath. The leaves are slightly convex and this, with the raised mid-rib above, gives a curious thick appearance to the leaves and the whole plant is not at a glance unlike *Olearia nummularifolia.* It is more of a curiosity than a thing of beauty. (Illustration 407).

It can be readily distinguished from 'Adpressa' by its stiff habit, and by its *thick* leaves being twice as long as wide and radially set on the branches, whereas 'Adpressa' has a lax habit, the leaves are pectinate and are three times as long as they are wide.

– –'*Argentea Minor*' Hort. See 'Dwarf White'.

– –'**Cavendishii**' [*T. baccata* var. *Cavendishii* Hornb. Rep. Conif. Conf. 76. 1932; NON SENSU Welch, Dw. Con. 286. 1966.] PROCUMBENS GROUP. All the description Hornibrook gives us is "a low-growing, almost prostrate variety, somewhat similar to 'Repandens', but differing from it by its wider spread and its curved, more pendulous branchlet-tips". In *Dwarf Conifers* [286. 1966] I regret having given a description of a strong-growing form which further study has convinced me cannot be identified as 'Cavendishii'. Den Ouden and Boom [Man. 394. 1965] add details that doubtfully distinguish it from 'Repandens'.

Many of these prostrate, spreading forms are very difficult to distinguish. I have been unable to trace the origin of the name 'Cavendishii' nor any specimen of sufficient age and recorded history to claim authenticity, so I feel it must be regarded as 'lost to cultivation'.

– –'**Columnaris**' [*T. baccata columnaris* Carr. Traité. Ed. 2, 738. 1867; var. *columnaris* Hornb. Dw. Con. Ed. 2, 238. 1938.] FASTIGIATA GROUP. I have not been able to find this as a distinct form. The descriptions were taken, I think, from young plants of 'Fastigiata Aureomarginata' which, with age, would have developed the greater vigour and longer leaves characteristic of that cultivar.

– –'**Corona**' [*T. baccata* 'Nissen's Corona' Nissen, Nurs. Cat. 19. 1957; 'Corona' Den Ouden and Boom Man. 394. 1965.] This is one of four selections made by J. Nissen, a nurseryman of Aprath near Wuppertal in Germany, about 1934. 'Corona' makes a symmetrical, round but flat-topped plant with a habit suggestive of a crown, often with age several times as wide as high. Leaves are bright green.

– –'**Compacta**' [*T. baccata compacta* Beissn. Mitt. d.d.d.G. **19**: 120. 1910.] NANA GROUP. This is one of the most attractive forms in this group. It forms a compact, oval, or conical bush of ascending branches, 1.3 m across; branches regularly spreading, compact branchlets crowded, 4-6 cm long, brown; leaves radial, 10-12 mm long, 1.5 mm broad, curved slightly, sickle-shaped, shining dark green above, paler and with a dark mid-rib beneath.

The different forms in this group are difficult to distinguish in print although quite distinct 'in the flesh'. The growth on newly transplanted bushes is usually quite uncharacteristic, so only established plants should be identified from book descriptions.

'Compacta' is nearest to 'Paulina' in appearance but is much smaller in all its parts.

– –'**Decora**' [*T. baccata* var. *decora* Hornb. Dw. Con. Ed. 2, 240. 1938; 'Decora' Hillier, Dw. Con. 60. 1964.] There is some mystery here. The plant grown in England under this name is a very distinct form; a very slow-growing and most attractive garden variety, forming an upright flat-topped bush with arching branches and lustrous foliage. The leaves are unusually large, up to 30 mm long by 3-4 mm broad, and are all curved upwards. (Illustration 408).

This agrees closely with Mr. Hillier's description but not with Horni-brook's, who says of 'Decora' that it is 'one of the tiniest of all yews and the only real pygmy among the flat-growing forms'. Which variety he was actually writing of cannot now be ascertained, but it was certainly not our present plant.

- –'**Dwarf White**' Den Ouden and Boom [Man. 396. 1965; 'Argentea Minor' Krüssm. Handb. 305. 1972, and Hort. (in part).] Although I see that Krüssman recognises the Latin-form name I prefer to retain the name suggested by Boom, on the ground that it is now in general use for this form which is a very slow-growing low bush with its young leaves variegated with narrow silver margins. It is not particularly effective seen from a distance, but is interesting as a pot plant or on a rockery. It gets large in time. (Illustration 409).

- –'**Epacrioides**' [*T. baccata epacrioides* R. Smith, Pl. Fir Tribe, 41. 1867; var. *epacroides* Hornb. Dw. Con. Ed. 2, 234. 1938.] Nana Group. This is a very old dwarf form, considered by some writers as synonymous with 'Ericoides'. Hornibrook, however, rightly distinguishes them, since in the Pygmy Pinetum there are specimens clearly marked by the distinctions he describes.

'Epacrioides' forms a twiggy little, upright or spreading bush with a rather irregular branch system and branchlets of varying length. Leaves about 15 mm by 1.5 to 2 mm wide, dull green, arranged radially and with the older leaves standing off quite stiffly at 80° from the stem.

- –'**Ericoides**' [*T. baccata ericoides* Standish and Noble, Ornam. Trees. 102. 1852; f. *ericoides* (Carr.) Pilger in Rehd. Bibl. 3. 1949 *; var *ericoides* Hornb. Dw. Con. Ed. 2, 233. 1938.] Nana Group. This is another very old form of very slow growth which makes a small bush (seldom reaching 1 m) with no leader and with numerous slender, erect branchlets. The growth is somewhat more regular than in 'Epacrioides' and the leaves are similar in size and arrangement, but they are distinctly glossy. The young leaves are almost appressed to the shoot (giving to the bush a very fanciful heath-like appearance) and even the older leaves are held pointing forwards, so that they look shorter than the corresponding leaves of 'Epacrioides'.

- –'**Expansa**' [*T. baccata expansa* Carr. Traité. Ed. 2, 738. 1867; NON Dallm. Holly Yew & Box 198. 1908; var. *expansa* Hornb. Dw. Con. Ed. 2, 240. 1938.] Procumbens Group. Hornibrook's description is too uncertain to identify this with any form I know. Pending identification from an old specimen of unquestionable origin this form must be regarded as lost to cultivation.

- –'**Fastigiata**' [*T. baccata stricta* Lawson, Agric. Man. 398. 1836; *T. hibernica* Loddiges Nurs. Cat. 39. 1820; *T. fastigiate* Lindley, Syn. Brit. Fl. 241. 1829; var. *fastigiata* Loud. Arb. Frut. Brit. 2066. 1838; *T. communis erecta* Nels. Pin. 172. 1866.] As will be seen from the selective synonymy given, numerous attempts have been made to deal with the nomenclature of the fastigiate forms and no doubt a case can be argued for retention of each resulting name. Loudon tells us that his var. *erecta* was a seedling from the Florence Court yew whose history he records so well, and it is possible that that plant is (like Eve) the 'mother of all living' fastigiate Yews. But even excluding this possibility, there seems no case for retention botanically of more than one *forma,* since the only divergence from normal is common to all the forms and only varies marginally in degree from plant to plant. The epithet *stricta* was used in a rather obscure publication two years before the more commonly used *fastigiata* so as a botanical category f. *stricta* has priority.

The fastigiate character comes more or less true from seed, but bearing in mind that each form in cultivation is a vegetatively propagated clone of a selected seedling, with one or more fastigiate branches doing duty for the leader that propagands of *T. baccata* seem unable to develop, I feel we are on safe ground in treating them all here as cultivars. We are horticulturally at liberty to preserve established usage as best we may and this we do by choosing FASTIGIATA for the Group name and retaining 'Fastigiata' as a cultivar name for the Florence Court yew.

'Fastigiata', then, is the well known Irish yew. This and its colour variants **'Fastigiata Aurea', 'Fastigiata Aureo-marginata'** and **'Fastigiata Aureovariegata'** become too large in time to be regarded as dwarf forms, but in their early years they are very slow-growing and strictly columnar and are very useful for their architectural qualities. (Illustration 410).

– –'Fowle' New name [*T. baccata* 'Adpressa Fowle' Wyman, Arnoldia 29: 7. 1969.] ADPRESSA GROUP. A compact, hardy, fruiting clone of f. *adpressa* which originated on the Frederick S. Moseley estate in Newburyport, Massachusetts. Growth is dense, with small dark green leaves, 8 mm × 2½ mm. Named in honour of the late Herbert Fowle who first distributed it. There is no need for the word 'Adpressa' to be included in the cultivar name. (Illustration 411). The mother plant in the Arnold Arboretum is now 2.5 m high by 4.5 m broad.

– –'Gracilis Pendula' Dallm. [Holly Yew & Box. 202. 1908.] See 'Pendula'.

– –'Horizontalis' [*T. baccata horizontalis* (Pepin) Carr. Traité, 518. 1855; R. Smith, Pl. Fir Tribe, 48. 1862.] PROCUMBENS GROUP. Richard Smith records of this variety 'It is furnished with whorls of branches at the terminal growths of the main shoots, and sometimes so regularly as to look like grotesque copies of the frame of an expanded umbrella'. This should make this clone easy to recognise if still in cultivation, but several arboreal forms with noticeably horizontal branching seem to have been introduced into cultivation, and any of them, as H. G. Hillier says [Dw. Con. 60. 1964], can be grown as 'a horizontally spreading bush' so this can only be a rather loose term, not for use in any clonal sense.

– –'Kadett' [*T. baccata* 'Nissen's Kadett' Nissen, Nurs. Cat. 20. 1957/58.] This is the second of the Nissen selections referred to under 'Corona'. This form is a broadly pyramidal form without a leader but with upright branches and thin, dark green foliage.

– –'Knirps' Moll ex Krussm. [Nadel. 260. 1955.] NANA GROUP. A dwarf, compact, broad shrub, irregular in outline, very slow-growing; branchlets dark brown; leaves 8-15 mm long, 2-3 mm broad, dark green. Originated in the nursery of Peter Moll, Heisterrbacherrott, Germany, before 1935. Twenty year old plants are only 30-50 cm high.

– –'Nana' [*T. baccata nana* Knight, Syn. Conif. 52. 1850 (Fox's Dwarf yew); Carr. Traité, 519. 1855; *Foxii* Knight ex Gord. Pin. Ed. 2, 391. 1875; NON *nana* Paul ex Gord. Pin. Ed. 2, 392. 1875; NON *nana* Dallm. Holly Yew & Box. 203. 1908.] This is a very old form which is very seldom seen. It forms a slow-growing and rather open bush with an irregular branching system and dark green, very glossy leaves which are sometimes large and curved away from the shoot (up to 20 mm long by 2 mm broad) sometimes much smaller, straighter and held forward and sometimes minute. This irregularity and the open habit make this not one of the most attractive of garden forms. **'Miniata'** [Carr. Traité. Ed. 2, 736. 1867] a form with similar irregular foliage but fastigiate habit, and **'Monstrosa'** [Carr. Traité, 519. 1855] if not in fact the same, were two occupants of the NANA GROUP that we must regard as lost to cultivation.

– –**'Nutans'** [*T. baccata nutans* Beissn. Mitt. d.d.d.G. **19**: 121. 1910; NON *T. baccata* var. *nutans* Hornb. Dw. Con. Ed. 2, 235. 1938.] NANA GROUP. This is another very diminutive form. It was distributed by H. den Ouden and Son, nurserymen of Boskoop, Holland, in 1910. It forms a rather upright or squat little bush with an ascending branch system and dense, radially held foliage which is dark green above with some sheen and pale green below, with the mid-rib faintly discernible above and below. The leaves are 8-10 mm long by 1 mm wide at the growing tip and point forward. The leaves near the base of the shoot are shorter, but leaves on two year old wood are much larger (to 20 mm × 2 mm) and are strongly recurved. (Illustration 412).

It is near to 'Nana', but young plants I have received from Messrs. Den Ouden do not display the irregularities described by Hornibrook and so I am of the opinion that Hornibrook's description was taken from a plant of 'Nana' Knight.

– –**'Page'** [*T. baccata* 'Nissens Page' Nissen, Nurs. Cat. 19. 1957/58.] NANA GROUP. This is the third of the selections referred to under 'Corona'. It is described as a neat, dense, bushy variety with light green foliage.

– –**'Parvula'** [*T. baccata parvula* Gibbs, Journ. Roy. Hort. Soc. **51**: 207. 1926; Dallm. Holly Yew & Box. 203. 1908; NON var. *expansa* Hornb. Dw. Con. 162. 1923.] NANA GROUP. This seems to have been a name cooked up by Hornibrook and Vicary Gibbs to help overcome the use previously of the epithet 'Nana' for several different forms by different authors. Beyond the fact that it formed a low, spreading bush, wider than high with horizontal spreading branches (which distinguishes it from any form I have ever seen) and that it is a female clone with leaves that according to Hornibrook were long, narrow, pointing forward at an acute angle and according to Dallimore were small and deep green, we have no information, so must regard this form as lost to cultivation.

– –**'Paulina'** [*T. baccata paulina* Gibbs, Journ. Roy Hort. Soc. **51**: 207. 1926; *nana* Paul, Proc. Hort. Soc. Lond. 493. 1861 and Gord. Pin. Ed. 2, 392. 1875; var. *cheshuntensis* Hornb. Dw. Con. 162. 1923 and var. *Paulina* Ed. 2, 237. 1938.] NANA GROUP. 'Paulina' forms a dense, compact, sometimes conical bush with dark green, glossy leaves, sometimes bronzing in winter. The branch system is ascending; the leaves are radially held and of varying length, 5-15 mm long by 1.5 mm wide, flat and dark green above and keeled, a light mid-green below, each leaf close to the shoot at its base but strongly decurved to 70-90° at its tip. This is the most prosperous looking of any plant in this group and should be better known.

– –**'Pendula'** [*T. baccata pendula* Nels. Pin. 172. 1866.] PROCUMBENS GROUP. On p. 339 I explain how it comes about that several pendulous forms are described in the conifer books as 'trees with a leader and spreading branch system, pendulous at the tips' yet are only found in cultivation (unless grafted on a tall stem) as low, spreading bushes. Into this category come '**Dovastoniana**' Carr., the Westfelton yew and its variegated counterpart '**Dovastonii Aurea**' (still well known in cultivation) and '**Jacksonii**' Paul ex Gord., '**Recurvata**' Carr., '**Expansa**' Carr., '**Horizontalis**' Carr. and others, all possibly now unidentifiable. Descriptions are too brief to identify the clones with us today, but there are several of which we have good photographs. Dallimore [Holly Yew & Box 194. 1908] and Vicary Gibbs [Journ. Roy. Hort. Soc. **51**: Fig. 52. 1926] have left us pictures of '**Gracilis Pendula**' (the latter of a specimen 'on a stem') and the characteristic growth of each of those plants identifies a form in cultivation today of which there are specimens in the Pygmy Pinetum. Dallimore describes 'Pendula' [p. 203] as 'very similar in appearance to *gracilis pendula*, but the habit is somewhat looser and the growth less robust'. By inference this sufficiently identifies a very similar form (indistinguishable except as to habit) also represented in the collection at Devizes. Alas, that I must confess my sins! These were wrongly identified in my previous book as 'Cavendishi' and 'Repandens' respectively. (Illustration 413).

– –'**Präsident**' [*T. baccata* 'Nissen's Präsident' Nissen, Nurs. Cat. 19. 1957–58.] This is the last of the Nissen selections (see under 'Corona' above). It is described as a strong-growing bush, much broader than high; leaves broad and dark green.

– –'**Procumbens**' [*T. procumbens* Loddiges Nurs. Cat. 39. 1820; *T. baccata* var. *procumbens* Loud. Arb. Frut. Brit. **4**: 2067. 1838; Kent in Veitch, Man. Ed. 2, 1900; Hornb. Dw. Con. 160. 1923; 'Procumbens' Welch, Dw. Con. 289. 1966.] Of all the early epithets chosen to describe the wide-spreading plants in cultivation this has clear priority and Loudon's description—'A low and somewhat trailing shrub'—is surely sufficiently umbraculiferous for it to serve us very well for our group name here. Unfortunately, subsequent writers have erroneously assumed that Loudon was equating his form with *T. canadensis*. What Loudon actually wrote was 'It appears to be nothing more than a stunted variety of the common yew and to be identical with the *T. canadensis* of Willdenow . . . but as we have only seen small plants . . . we have thought it worth while *to keep the latter separate for the present*'. Since Loudon had passed on five years later he may or may not have lived to see his doubts confirmed, but by 1900 Kent was clear enough as to the difference.

I have already referred (p. 16) to the inability of some vegetatively propagated plants to develop a true leader, a handicap found in other genera but seldom (perhaps never) overcome by the Yews. This has widespread effects. It means, for instance, that any 'Yew tree' with a trunk and normal crown must have been a seedling. It explains why there are no conical cultivars of Yew, but only fastigiate forms (from a fastigiate mother plant) or forms within the range 'upright-spreading' to 'prostrate' according to the *branching* habit of the mother plant. It follows that all cultivated plants are cultivariants. This means there is no botanical significance in their habit variations, so any attempts to give them botanical classification is absurd and the only real nomenclatural solution is to treat them as cultivars, for that is what they are.

This means we must search, this time not for the earliest name validly published for an identifiable class of plants, but for the earliest description capable of being identified with a clone in present cultivation.[1] This is a difficult task. In certain cases there is no such description, so unless an old plant whose recorded history identifies it with the name can be found we must treat the cultivar as lost to cultivation. 'Expansa' and 'Horizontalis' are cases of this kind. 'Cavendishii' and 'Repandens' were, I fear, wrongly identified by me in my earlier book so this mistake must be corrected. Hornibrook left us quite a good description of his 'Pseudo-procumbens' but I have not found a plant to correspond.   My previous descriptions of 'Procumbens' and 'Prostrata' being from living types, I leave them well alone here.

'Procumbens' then, is a low-growing, procumbent form with its branches spreading widely and with bright green leaves. There are several plants in the Taxus collection at the National Pinetum at Bedgebury, Kent, which I believe to be this form. They are all low-growing (to 50 cm high), very dense, prostrate shrubs irregularly branched, and densely clothed with foliage on the young shoots but having many of the main branches bare. The leaves are very variable in size, up to 15 mm long by 2 mm broad, parallel-sided, with a fairly abrupt taper ending in a fine and very sharp drawn out point. The young twigs and buds are green, the leaves are held up stiffly, often nearly vertically, and are green above, bronzing slightly in winter and light green below. The foliage has a somewhat wiry feel if brushed with the hand. Annual growth 50 mm.

– –'**Prostrata**' [*T. baccata* var. *prostrata* Bean, Trees. **2**: 581. 1914; 'Prostrata' Den Ouden and Boom, Man. 403. 1965 and Welch, Dw. Con. 289. 1966.] PROCUMBENS GROUP. This form is described as "a low, trailing form, lower and flatter than 'Procumbens' and other prostrate forms". In the Taxus collection in the National Pinetum is an old plant of a very low, spreading form which I have never seen elsewhere and which answers to the description. It is a very flat-topped plant 50 cm high by 1.5 m across with the habit of *Picea abies* 'Nidiformis' (including its nest-like formation). It has a very horizontal branching habit and it is densely and quite regularly clothed with semi-radial foliage. The leaves are 20 mm long by 2 mm wide, straight or nearly so, held up at ± 45°, a shiny dark green above with a prominent mid-rib, very light green below. Annual growth 6–8 cm; all growing tips are horizontal except at the edge of the plant where they tend to droop slightly.

– –'**Pseudo-procumbens**' [*T. baccata* var. *pseudo-procumbens* Hornb. Dw. Con. Ed. 2, 241. 1938; var. *procumbens* Ed. 1, 160. 1923.] PROCUMBENS GROUP. This form was described as a low-growing, regular bush with rounded top and pendulous elongated branches in thick layers. Leaves light green 12–30 mm long. Hornibrook described as a characteristic of this form the presence of two terminal buds, of which the stronger makes a shoot pointing downwards and the second a smaller shoot pointing upward. This should make this form quite distinctive, but if so I have never seen it.

– –'**Pumila Aurea**' [*T. baccata pumila aurea* Gibbs, Journ. Roy. Hort. Soc. **51**: 208. 1926.] Although from the brief descriptions given by Hornibrook (who had only

[1]This description may be a photographic illustration.

seen small plants) it is difficult to be sure, I think this must be the form represented by two very old plants at Bedgebury at the top of the bank. They are now flattish, irregularly globose plants 75 cm high by 1.5 m across, of dense growth and tapered leaves 20 mm long by 2 mm wide, densely set, arranged imperfectly radially and all pointing well forward and of a rich golden-yellow, almost orange in the general effect. The young shoots are yellow, the buds pinky-brown to yellow. It is an extremely attractive form, very slow-growing and outstanding for colour, and one that should be more widely planted.

– –'Pygmaea' [*T. baccata pygmaea* Beissn. Mitt. d.d.d.G. **19**: 120. 1910.] NANA GROUP. This is the last and probably the smallest form in this group. It is certainly the smallest of the three forms distributed by H. Den Ouden & Son. It forms a dense little ovoid or conical bush, with an upright branching habit and uniformly short (5-10 mm long by 1 mm wide) leaves which are thin and light green. It makes a dainty little plant of which Den Ouden and Boom [Man. 402. 1965] give a good illustration.

– –'Repandens' [*T. baccata* var. *repandens* Parsons & Sons, Nurs. Cat. 92. 1887; f. *repandens* (Parsons) Rehd. Bibl. 3. 1949 *; NON SENSU Welch, Dw. Con. 1966.] PROCUMBENS GROUP. There is much confusion in Europe over this form. Since it originated in America we must look there for clarification. Bailey [Cult. Everg. 187. 1923] tells us it is "a low form with long wide-spreading branches and dull, bluish-green, narrower and longer (i.e., than 'Procumbens') leaves, partly falcately curved upwards". He also (Plate XI) gives a good picture. Elsewhere he writes of its luxuriant, dark green foliage and mentions that this has a slight glaucous tinge. It is considered the hardiest of all the *T. baccata* forms in the United States, a quality that should assist with its identification.

The description of the clone grown under this name in the Secrest Arboretum tallies with Bailey, but Chadwick and Kenn add that their plant is a female clone with slightly flattened two-angled globose seeds, the aril exceeding the seed by one third, seeds being scattered and scarce. This agrees with a form grown at Devizes, but finality rests, I feel, with the selection of a venerable specimen in one of the Long Island estates connecting it with the old Parsons nursery to serve as a type.

– –'Repens Aurea' Hillier [Dw. Con. 61. 1964.] Despite the name, this is probably a cultivariant of the tall-growing variety 'Dovastonii Aurea'. It is a very attractive, prostrate plant with bright golden variegation. (Illustration 414). It would not surprise me if several cultivars described from the mother plant as 'pyramidal' have acquired a new name when the propagations developed only a bushy or spreading habit—a change bound to occur! The following cultivar, for example, might very well be this metamorphosis of **'Barronii'** [*T. baccata* 'Barronii Foemina' Barron, Nurs. Cat. 8.1875] at first described as a seedling from the old Golden Yew but much stronger-growing and brighter ... very symmetrical, a perfect pyramid (it may have been one seedling with a very loose attitude towards sex or two seedlings, since plants of each sex seem to have existed), but later [Gibbs, V., Journ. Roy. Hort. Soc. **51**: 198. 1926] referred to as having formed plants much wider than high, and now, apparently, no longer to be found.

– –'Semperaurea' [*T. baccata semperaurea* Dallm. Holly Yew & Box. 204. 1908] is by no means a dwarf form, but because of its colour and habit it is desirable as a young plant and being slow-growing can be made use of for some years. It makes a delightful specimen on a lawn, especially where it will be seen in sunlight against a background of dark evergreens or a shadow mass. It forms a spreading shrub to 1.5-2 m high by much more across with no trunk but its (eventually numerous) main branches ascending at a steep angle and with numerous, short, side branches. The leaves are 10-20 mm long by 2.5-3 mm broad, a bright golden-yellow, paler below, keeping their colour well for two years. (Illustration 415).

– –'**Standishii**' [*T. baccata fastigiata Standishii* Dallm. Holly Yew & Box. 201. 1908.] Fastigiata Group. This is a very slow-growing, fastigiate form with rich golden-yellow leaves 20-25 mm by 3.5-4 mm across with a raised mid-rib. A most desirable plant. A freely fruiting female clone.

Taxus cuspidata Sieb. and Zucc. The Japanese yew is a hardy, slow-growing species that thrives in North America, where innumerable clones have been selected and named. From the English yew it can be distinguished by the yellowish tinge of the under-surface of the leaves and by the longer, more oblong, winter buds with looser and more pointed scales. It has given us several dwarf forms which, although not particularly outstanding, are useful because of their extreme hardiness and adaptability.

– –'**Aurescens**' Den Ouden and Boom 1965 [*T. cuspidata* f. *aurescens* Rehd. Journ. Arn. Arb. **1**: 191. 1920.] This forms a compact but rather widespreading shrub. 'Aurescens' (meaning 'turning yellow') is somewhat of a misnomer, since the young foliage at first is a deep, golden yellow, turning to green the second year. It is a very beautiful plant. (Illustration 416).

– –'**Bobbink**' Wyman [*T. baccata* Bobbink, Amer. Nurs. **119, 1**: 89. 1964. (Note the date error on title page).] Described as a little known fruiting clone with small needles and a pyramidal, dense outline. It reaches 1.25 m at 20 years, so it seems reliably dwarf.

– –'**Densa**' [*T. cuspidata* var. *densa* Rehder ex Wilson, Conif. & Tax. Japan, 13. 1916; f. *densa* Rehd. ex Wilson Bibl. 3. 1949 *; Hornb. Dw. Con. Ed. 2, 243. 1938.] A dense, dwarf, low, spreading shrub usually pistillate, with short side branches, very dense and compact; leaves dark green. It is distinguishable from 'Nana' by being much lower-growing. It was introduced from Japan by the former Parsons Nursery, Flushing, Long Island, New York, U.S.A.

– –'**Minima**' [*T. cuspidata* f. *minima* Slavin, Rep. Conif. Conf. 142. 1932; Rehd. Bibl. 4. 1949.] A seedling form discovered by Bernard H. Slavin, then Superintendent of Parks, Rochester, New York. It is one of the smallest of hardy conifers. The branches are irregular, generally ascending, ramified and covered with small brown branchlets forming a small upright bush. The leaves are lanceolate-oblong to almost oblong, 4-12 mm long, and lustrous dark green. The annual growth is about 7-19 mm. A somewhat similar form '**Pygmaea**' recorded by Hornibrook [Dw. Con. 165. 1923] is lost to cultivation.

– –'**Nana**' [f. *nana* Rehd. in Bailey, Cycl. Amer. Hort. **4**: 1773. 1902; var. *compacta* Bean, Trees, **2**: 582. 1914; var. *brevifolia* Hort. Amer. (in part.)] This is the commonest form in cultivation but is scarcely a dwarf since it will form an irregularly spreading bush seldom over 3 m high but much more across. It has long spreading main branches usually well furnished with short branchlets carrying broad leaves (about 2 cm by 3 mm), glossy dark green above with a raised mid-rib, dull light green below with barely visible stomatic lines beneath, obtuse at the end with a tiny drawn out tip. The leaves are very densely borne and stand up stiffly all over the plant. Usually raised from seed, it shows considerable variation. (Illustration 417).

Taxus × media Rehd. A hybrid (*T. cuspidata × T. baccata*) with characteristics intermediate between the two parent species, of which a number of selections have been made and introduced to cultivation, especially in the United States, where it is hardy. Certain clones are widely used for hedges but most cultivars of this hybrid are too large for inclusion here.

– –'**Beanpole**' Vermeulen [Nurs. Cat. 33. 1970.] This is one of a number of fastigiate yews of mixed parentage selected by John Vermeulen of Neshanic Station, New Jersey, U.S.A. Most are too tall-growing for inclusion here, but 'Beanpole' is a real dwarf. It forms a very narrow, dense little columnar plant and fruits heavily. It is too slow for propagation from cuttings, so is usually grafted. It is a little gem.

Other Vermeulen selections, all rather large for inclusion here, are:

– –'**Flushing**' Verm. [Nurs. Cat. 2. 1952; *T. × media* 'Parade' Grootn. Dendroflora 4: 69. 1967, and Hort. Eur.] has large, sturdy, shiny dark green needles and bright red berries. Very slender and stately.

– –'**Pilaris**' Verm. [Nurs. Cat. 2, 1973; as *T. media* 'Viridis' Nurs. Cat. 2. 1947] forms a dense column with gracefully curled medium-green leaves.

– –'**Pyramidalis**' Verm. [Nurs. Cat. 4. 1946] makes, as the name suggests a robust, pyramidal plant. The leaves are mid-green and the berries are bright red.

– –'**Sentinalis**' Verm. [Nurs. Cat. 3. 1947/(Fall)] quickly grows into a slim sentinel-like plant with bright red berries and light green curled needles.

– –'**Viridis**' Verm. [Nurs. Cat. 4. 1948, and as 'Stricta Viridis' Nurs. Cat. 4. 1946.] This forms a very dense, upright plant with twisted, fresh green needles.

– –'**Hicksii**' Hicks [Home Landscapes (Nurs. Cat. ?) 1924. *T. cuspidata fastigiata* Andorra Nurs. Cat. 21. 1926; *T. media* f. *Hicksii* Rehd. Bibl. 4. 1949.] This upright and columnar form, according to C. E. Lewis [Amer. Nurs. **134, 10**: 101. 1971] was a seedling raised at the former Parsons Nursery (now Kissena Park, Flushing, Long Island, New York, where it was known as the 'Blue John Yew'), which was selected and introduced to the trade by Henry Hicks, nurseryman, also of Long Island. It has been planted widely in North America where it has been much used for hedges, but it is chiefly remarkable as the mother of many later selections. This would perhaps justify recognition of a botanical *forma* (with appropriate circumscription) but 'Hicksii' itself is a clone.

– –'**Kelseyi**' Verm. [Nurs. Cat. 1933.] This is another introduction from the Vermeulen Nursery, Neshanic Station, New Jersey, U.S.A., but this is a globose form with dark green leaves and usually a heavy crop of dark red berries. It was raised about 1915 and named after F. W. Kelsey of New York. This variety is said to fruit well when only four or five years old.

THUJA

The Thujas, first cousins of Chamaecyparis, differ from their relatives mainly in the cones, which are egg-shaped or rounded with flat, oblong and usually thin scales, quite unlike the top-like scales of that genus. The similarity in foliage, especially in the juvenile stage, can give us difficulty in identifying our treasures when (as is usual with our dwarf forms) we are restricted to the foliar characteristics.

Thuja koraiensis Nakai, like several other conifer species, forms either a pyramidal to fastigiate tree or a low-spreading, almost trailing bush. With the former we have nothing to do here, but the low-growing form is very useful and attractive where there is room for it to spread over a fairly large area of ground. The leaf spray is bright, dark green, flat and the underside very thickly coated with a white glaucous bloom which is not easily brushed off. The crushed foliage is less objectionable than in *Th. occidentalis,* it having a rather pleasant medicated smell which Alan Mitchell says 'gives a scent of rich fruit-cake with plenty of almonds'—doubtless just like mother used to make!

Thuja occidentalis L. The American Arborvitae is normally a tree of no particular attraction. The foliage is much flattened, the lateral pair folded and overlapping the facing pair which bear (usually prominently) a raised round to oval resin gland. The species can be usually recognized by the presence of this gland and even in abnormal foliage forms by the unpleasant acrid smell of the adult foliage when bruised. The species is found in nature mainly on marshy ground and does not thrive in dry soil, so presumably the dwarf forms will also do best in moist situations.

Th. occidentalis has given rise to numerous dwarf forms which are good garden plants, but mostly they share the habit of this species, and turn dull green or dirty brown in the winter.

The nomenclature of these dwarf forms is difficult because the original descriptions were very brief and inadequate and because dwarf seedlings can turn up at any time which are but little different or barely distinguishable from the existing clones. Several writers have attempted to get round this by describing such cultivars as they knew and picking on a likely variety to treat as a collective name to cover the remainder. This almost always leads to trouble. Beissner, in 'Compacta', lighted on a name which had already been used for a compact rather than a dwarf form. Hornibrook with 'Froebelii' fared little better, for it now seems certain, so far as certainty is possible, that 'Froebelii' is synonymous with 'Hoveyii', which he described separately and outside his 'Froebelii' group.

Mr. Hillier [Dw. Con. 1964] suggested some very wholesale lumpings together, but sympathetic as I am with his frustration with regard to the present confusion I cannot but help feeling he has over simplified matters, since within his synonymy he included clones which are quite discernibly distinct and in some cases different enough to have quite separate garden uses. I therefore give full descriptions of all the clones I have in the Pygmy Pinetum or know personally and have quoted other published names as synonyms of these whenever I could be reasonably sure of being right. In the case of other clones which I could not honestly fit in anywhere and do not myself know, I repeat earlier descriptions for what they are worth.

There are undoubtedly unnamed clones in cultivation arising from later seedlings that are more or less similar to those I have described. I suggest that the names I have treated here as synonyms be allowed to drop out of use and that nurserymen take the trouble to ascertain that their propagating material comes from true stock and not from any of these unnamed clones.

Several new clones have recently been introduced to cultivation. Since this means that true clonal material is being used it is all to the good, even when the new cultivars show little if any improvement over the older ones.

The dwarf forms lend themselves to a simple gardener's grouping, as under:

Juvenile Foliage Forms	*Globose Habit*	*Conical Habit*
'Ellwangerana Aurea'	'Danica'	'Cristata'
'Ericoides'	'Globosa'	'Cristata Aurea'
'Hetz Junior'	'Golden Globe'	'Ellwangerana Aurea'
'Ohlendorffii'	'Little Champion'	'Holmstrupensis'
'Rheingold'	'Little Gem'	'Hoveyi'
'Tetragona'	'Meinekes Zwerg'	'Lutea Nana'
	'Pumila'	'Pygmaea'
	'Recurva Nana'	'Spiralis'
	'Umbraculifera'	'Watnong Gold'
	'Wareana Globosa'	
	'Woodwardii'	

Bun-shaped Forms	*Colour Forms (Golden)*	*Abnormal Foliage Forms*
'Caespitosa'	'Cristata Aurea'	'Batemanii'
'Dumosa'	'Ellwangerana Aurea'	'Bodmeri'
'Pygmaea'	'Golden Globe'	'Filiformis'
'Recurva Nana'	'Lutea Nana'	'Ohlendorffii'
	'Rheingold'	'Tetragona'
	'Watnong Gold'	

Miniature Forms	*Colour Forms (Variegated)*
'Caespitosa'	'Globosa Variegata'
'Globosa Rheindiana'	'Meinekes Zwerg'
'Hetz Midget'	'Wansdyke Silver'
'Milleri'	
'Ohlendorffii'	
'Tiny Tim'	

‒ ‒'**Bodmeri**' [*Th. occidentalis bodmeri* Beissn. Handb. 42. 1891; *Th. occidentalis Batema-nii* Bailey, Cult Conif. 170. 1933 (pro syn.); *Th. occidentalis lycopodioides* Hort.]

forms a dense, conical shrub. It is a monstrous form with thick main and side branches. The normal leafspray is entirely missing, the leaves are more or less closely appressed to the stem and, being often folded or keeled, give a (sometimes exaggerated) tetragonal appearance to the shoot. The foliage is a rich, deep green, there being little or no differentiation between the facing and lateral pairs. This is an abnormal foliage form of the type that has cropped up in several of the Thuja and Chamaecyparis species, where it has frequently been given the name of 'Lycopodioides', so it is not surprising that our present variety is sometimes, quite incorrectly, so labelled. Bailey gives the following description: 'A monstrosity form with thick, clumpy growth due to shortened more or less curved branches and dense overlapping foliage, green beneath'. This description does not at all fit our plant as we know it in Europe but he adds "the plant known as **'Batemanii'** is said to be this variety". It may well be that his description was of that otherwise unrecorded variety, which I have not seen.

‒ ‒**'Boothii'** R. Smith [Pl. Fir Tribe, 44. 1867.] A globose, American form, in appearance like 'Wareana'; **'Ensata'** Sén. [Conif. 193. 1867] a monstrous form; **'Froebelii'** (Hort.) Beissn. [Handb. 43. 1891] a dense ovoid bush of yellow-green, near to 'Hoveyi'; **'Globularis'** Lamb u. Reiter [ex Beissn. l.c.; Welch, Dw. Con. 301. 1966] a globose form, looser than 'Globosa' and of a light green colour; **'Hugii'** Olbrich [Mitt. d.d.d.G. **25**: 226. 1917] a monstrous form found in Switzerland; **'Intermedia'** Rehd. [1803. 1902] a compact dwarf form; **'Monstrosa'** Nels. [Pin. 65. 1866] 'rustic-branched'; and **'Spihlmanii'** P. Smith [ex Beissn. l.c.; Welch, Dw. Con. 302. 1966] a globose form said to retain its fresh green colour all the year, are old forms lost to cultivation or difficult now to identify, so their propagation should be discontinued in favour of the new clones now available, about the identity of which no doubt should arise.

‒ ‒**'Caespitosa'** [*Th. occidentalis* var. *caespitosa* Hornb. Dw. Con. 174. 1923] is a very slow-growing plant which forms a low, hemispherical bun wider than high. The foliage is very congested and irregular. There is no flat leaf spray formation in the ordinary sense, but the leaves are either closely appressed around an almost cord-like shoot with the points of the lateral leaves free standing or they occur on shoots which are very much flattened out (to 2.5 mm). There are also occasional shoots bearing juvenile foliage. It is an attractive little plant, which should be better known. (Illustration 418).

‒ ‒**'Compacta'** [*Th. occidentalis compacta* Carr. Traité, 104. 1855; R. Smith, Pl. Fir Tribe, 44. 1867; f. *compacta* (Carr.) Rehd. Bibl. 46. 1949; NON *Th. plicata compacta* Knight ex Gord. Pin. 325. 1858; NON Nich. Dict. Gar. **4**: 33. 1888; NON Beissn. Handb. Ed. 2, 509. 1909.] The early descriptions agree that this was a conical form, compact rather than dwarf, so the use of the name for a globose form by Beissner and American writers following him has resulted in much confusion.

The name, rightly or wrongly, is in general use in this country for a compact form that forms an ovoid to conical bush much larger and looser in growth than the dwarf forms, but I mention it since it has appeared in earlier works on the dwarf conifers. It has a large flat spray with the branchlets parallel and with the ultimate shoots short and uniform in length so that the space is more or less filled up, without the overlapping that is characteristic of 'Umbraculifera', for a coarse, open specimen of which a young plant of 'Compacta' could be mistaken. The colour is deep green, developing a deep, glaucous bloom the second year. This gives the plant as a whole a much darker appearance.

– –'**Cristata**' [*Th. occidentalis cristata* Hort. ex Beissn. Handb. 43. 1891; Carr. Traité. Ed. 2, 111. 1867; Rehd. Bibl. 47. 1949 *.] The name, and the reference to the 'cock's comb-like branches' in the descriptions are apt to give the impression that this uncommon variety is more exciting than is really the case. I have only seen it in Holland as an upright, rounded bush, rather open and with narrow foliage finer than in 'Globosa' but not so fine as in 'Sphaerica', the sprays held at all angles and curved in a way which to me suggested inspiration for a designer of scroll ironwork rather than a cockscomb—certainly there was nothing cristate about it. The foliage developed mostly on only one side of the shoot. (Illustration 419). '**Cristata Aurea**' [*Th. occidentalis cristata aurea* Beissn. Mitt d.d.d.G. **13**: 133. 1904] is a variation in which the foliage is a dull yellowish-green, its stems orange. It is slower growing so forms a smaller plant.

– –'**Danica**' Jensen [Amer. Nurs. **129, 9**: 88. 1969.] This new form was found in a seed bed on the Jensens Nursery at Orting, Denmark, in 1948. It forms a slow-growing, compact, globose plant with dark green foliage in vertically held sprays which bronzes slightly in winter. In habit it is very similar to 'Wood-wardii' but it is much slower growing.

– –'**Dumosa**' Welch [Dw. Con. 297. 1966; *Th. dumosa* Gord. Pin. Suppl. 102. 1862, with *Th. occidentalis dumosa* Hort., *Th. o. nana* Hort., *Th. plicata Llaveana* Hort., *Th. p. dumosa* Hort., *Th. antarctica* Hort., *Th. minor* Paul; *Th. nana* Hort. (pro syn.); *Th. occidentalis plicata dumosa* Beissn. Handb. Ed. 2, 504, 1909; NON *Biota orientalis dumosa* Carr. Traité. ed. 2, 96. 1867.] This useful little plant has had difficulty in shaking off the effects of the confusion between the different Thuja species that was at one time current. Our plant is not plicate nor does it have any connection with *T. plicata,* so the simpler epithet is to be preferred. (Illustration 420.) It was described by Carrière as 'A spreading little bush, densely clothed with numerous short, tufted, flat, fan-shaped branches growing in all directions, thickly set with short, forked, two-edged (much flattened?) branchlets. Of a glossy light green above, much paler below'. To this description Gordon adds, 'This kind forms a dense, confused little bush, seldom growing more than 60-90 cm high, somewhat resembling in its branchlets the Nootka Sound Arborvitae (*Thuja plicata*) but of a much lighter colour'.

To these descriptions we may add that it differs from 'Recurva Nana' in that its foliage is less regularly recurved—some of the sprays indeed lying quite flat—and by the coarse vertical, cord-like shoots, up to 12 cm in annual growth which it frequently throws up and by which it increases in height.

– –'**Ellwangerana Aurea**' [*Th. occidentalis ellwangeriana aurea* Späth Nurs. Cat. 1895; Späth ex Beissn. Mitt. d.d.d.G. **28**. 1896 and Handb. Ed. 2, 503. 1909 (often offered as 'Rheingold' in the trade).] There is a lot of confusion between this plant and '**Rheingold**' [*Th. occidentalis ellwangeriana Rheingold* Vollert, Mitt. d.d.d.G. **10**. 1904 and 139: 1906; Beissn. Handb. Ed. 2, 503. 1909; "*Rheingold Compacta*" Hort. (in part).] The former is a slow-growing golden form which is ovoid when young but which eventually builds itself up into a pyramidal tree several metres high. Except as a very young plant it bears predominantly adult foliage with pinkish-brown shoots and golden-yellow foliage in flat sprays held at random angles, but even when large there can always be found a stray shoot or two near the ground bearing juvenile foliage. 'Rheingold' forms a dense, globose or ovoid bush, never over 1 m, always with the juvenile foliage predominant. (Illustrations 421, 422).

Although the differences are evident when you have mature plants before you, differentiation by description is very difficult indeed and recognition in young plants almost impossible. 'Rheingold' tends to have smaller sprays which curl away from and develop branchlets out of the plane of the spray (unlike 'Ellwangerana Aurea' where the sprays lie flat), holds its leaves slightly less appressed round the terminal buds, and always carries more juvenile foliage in which it will be found that the leaf is a little wider in proportion to its length and stands at a wider angle to the stem. But these differences are very small and the only constant feature is that 'Rheingold' is the dwarf form always retaining a good proportion of juvenile foliage.

Both are excellent garden plants, and as Mr. Hillier aptly remarks, 'Perhaps the richest piece of radiant old gold in the garden at the dead of winter'. They revel in the hardest weather and are indispensable for planting amongst winter flowering heathers.

– –'**Ericoides**' [*Th. occidentalis* var. *ericoides* Rinz. Nurs. Cat. 37. 1861; *Th. occidentalis* f. *ericoides* (Laws.) Beissn. ex Rehd. Bibl. 47. 1949 *; NON *Th. occidentalis ericoides*, R. Smith, Pl. Fir Tribe, 44. 1867.] This unfortunate plant is merely a form of the species with fixed juvenile foliage, but it has suffered almost unbelievable trouble from the coiners of names—You say it, someone has tried it—and all quite unnecessarily, because the earliest readily available description [Hoopes, Book Everg. 324. 1868] is accompanied by an excellent illustration of the foliage. It is the largest and strongest growing of the fixed juvenile forms amongst the different conifer species that have been saddled with this cultivar name. It forms a large, blowsy, ovoid to globose bush with erect, dense, twiggy growth densely clothed with very soft and flexible juvenile leaves of varying size (up to 8 mm by 1.5 mm), appressed near the growing tips, elsewhere held at an angle of up to 50°, each leaf almost invariably being incurved towards its tip. The colour is a soft, dull green in summer and changes to a medium brown—the colouring of walnut furniture—in winter. Whilst not an outstanding variety it is not unattractive even in its winter colouring, which avoids the half dead appearance of some cultivars of this species. Being easily damaged by snow it should not be planted in a situation where damage of this kind, by destroying its regular outline, would spoil the effect and it is probably most effective planted in an informal group. (Illustration 423).

The material in cultivation is uniform and appears to be clonal, but any plants allegedly '**Ericoides Glauca**' Hornb. [Dw. Con. Ed. 2, 249. 1938] which I have seen have turned out to be some *Chamaecyparis pisifera* 'Squarrosa' form. '**Hetz Junior**' Krüssm. [Handb. 323. 1972], a selection from the Fairview Nurseries, Fairview, Pennsylvania, U.S.A., is a form with similar foliage but slower growth.

– –'**Filiformis**' [*Th. occidentalis* f. *filiformis* (Beissn.) Rehd. Bibl. 46. 1949 *; *Th. occidentalis Douglasii* Rehd. Moll. Deutsche Gart.-Zeit. **16**: 357. 1901; NON *filicoides* Beissn. Handb. 43. 1891 (= 'Spiralis')] is a loose and rather open shrub, eventually a small tree, with long thread-like branches and few branchlets, these often pendulous at their tips. This cultivar can be distinguished from the (much less common) thread-like forms of *Thuja orientalis* by the prominence of the resin gland on the back of the leaves and by the fact that although the entire growth is threadlike, always a few of the terminal growths of this cultivar are flattened as though they had been neatly gone over with a flat iron. Also the leaves have the characteristic odour of the species when bruised. (Illustration 424).

It should not be confused with '**Pendula**' Gord. [Pin. Suppl. 103. 1862] which is a form of the species with normal foliage but pendulous habit, not by any standard a dwarf.

– –'**Globosa**' [*Th. occidentalis* f. *globosa* (Gord.) Beissn. in Rehd. Bibl. 46. 1949 (and syn. in part).] This is a popular form the identification of which has not been made any easier by Hornibrook looking unknowingly at a plant of 'Woodwardii' (or so it would appear) when he wrote up his description of 'Globosa'. 'Globosa', as he rightly remarks, forms a compact, globose bush up to about 1.25 m high and like many of the gardeners who plant it, it suffers from middle age spread. But the foliage is a light green, almost a grey-green, turning darker in winter. The sprays are flat and crowded, with much overlapping of the shoots, which are similar on both sides, irregularly glandular; flattened (rarely beyond 1.5 mm wide). The habit frequently seen with this species of developing the axial buds in the lower part of the year's growth only on one side of the shoot is well marked and it is not uncommon to find a shoot on which only the upper buds have developed shoots until almost at the end of the season's growth. The main branches are ascending but the leaf sprays are held at random angles, giving a very dense look to the plant. (Illustration 425).

– –'**Globosa Rheindiana**' Bergm. [Pl. and Gar. **21, 1**: 22. 1965.] Described as a globose to somewhat spreading mound with light green foliage differing from other globose forms in having the branchlets in little rounded tufts or clusters during the dormant season. A 1 m spread in about 10 years.

– –'**Globosa Variegata**' is the name under which a new form reached me from a continental nursery. It is, however, disappointing—the variegation, although bright in the spring, soon fades, and so far the plant has made an upright rather than globose bush. If it is retained in cultivation a fancy name will need to be found for it.

– –'**Golden Globe**' Grootn. [Dendroflora **2**: 48. 1965.] There are several reliable globose cultivars of this species. There are also brightly coloured golden forms which are quite upright or conical, but in 'Golden Globe' we now have that useful combination—a globose form which is a bright, golden-yellow. It was introduced by the Grootendorst nursery at Boskoop in Holland and Mr. Hermann J. Grootendorst informed me that it reached him from a customer in America who had picked up a plant at some small nursery whose name and location he could not recollect. From its habit of growth it could be a coloured sport from the cultivar 'Woodwardii', but I think it is much more likely to have come from seed. With such outstanding colour it is an extremely attractive plant, truly globose in habit and probably capable of reaching 1.25 m high. (Illustration 426).

– –'Hetz Midget' Hetz [Fairview Nurs. Cat. 1. 1942; Hetz ex Wyman Amer. Nurs. **113, 7**: 68. 1961; 'Minima' Hort. Amer. (in part)?] This is a very diminutive and slow-growing compact globe. Frank R. Hetz selected the mother plant from seedlings he had raised in the late 1920s or early 30s and it was introduced to the trade by the Fairview Nurseries, Fairview, Pennsylvania, U.S.A., in 1942. It is very hardy but since it has a distinctly vertical branching system and no central trunk it can suffer from snow unless tied together. The foliage is dark blue-green in rather open and lace-like sprays (to 10 cm across) regularly circular in outline and all downcupped so that all the growing tips are at ± 10°, shewing up as horizontal lines across the side of the plant, viewed from a short distance away.

– –'Holmstrup' Den Ouden and Boom 1965 [*Th. occidentalis holmstrupii* Jensen Nurs. Cat. 27. 1951; 'Holmstrupensis' Welch, Dw. Con. 302. 1966.] This is one of the few dwarf forms to give us a conical plant. It makes a slow-growing, dense cone of healthy looking foliage and the colour is a very rich, deep green, well maintained except in hard winters. The foliage is in dense, flat sprays very much overlapping, flattened (uniformly to 2 mm), carried in vertical planes which more or less radiate from the trunk.

Because of its colour and shape this will be much more planted when better known. With very little attention it could be kept to quite a symmetrical outline and so should be useful in small formal gardens. It would also make an excellent low hedge. (Illustration 427).

– –'Hoseri' [(Wrob.) Bugala, Int. Dend. Soc. Yearb. **1971**: 32. 1972.] A seedling found in the Kornik Arboretum in Poland by A. Wroblewskii in 1927 is a shrubby form with dense, dark green foliage in horizontal sprays. It slowly forms a congested, globose bush, at 20–30 years not over 50 cm.

– –'Hoveyi' [*Th. occidentalis Hoveyi* Hort. ex Hoopes, Everg. 322. 1868; f. *Hoveyii* (Hoopes) Beissn, in Rehd. Bibl. 46. 1949 *.] This form is a slow-growing variety which reaches 3 m in time and which forms a globose to squat-ovoid bush. The colour of the foliage is a light yellowish-green which is well maintained during the winter. The older twigs are a yellowish to medium brown. The sprays are flat, regular and open, noticeably glandular front and back, the young shoots much flattened (to 2 mm wide). The sprays are identical on both sides and are carried vertically in parallel planes, giving the bush a distinctly laminated appearance. As with so many of the forms which become large in time it grows slowly for a number of years and it may have been such a bush which led Hornibrook [Dw. Con. Ed. 2, 252. 1938] to write of it as 'a very compact, oval bushling'. There may well be a diminutive form of 'Hoveyi' but if so I have never seen it.

– –'Little Champion' [*Th. occidentalis Little Champion* McConnel Nurs., Cat. 4. 1956; Wyman in Amer. Nurs. **113, 7**: 69. 1961.] A form selected in the seed bed at the McConnel Nursery, Port Orwell, Ontario, Canada, in 1935, and introduced in

1956. It is a fairly slow-growing globose plant not unlike 'Woodwardii', with green foliage bronzing in winter. (Illustration 428).

– –'**Little Gem**' Beissn. [Handb. 44. 1891; NON *Th. occidentalis* f. *pumila* (Otto) Rehd. Bibl. 46. 1949; Hornb. Dw. Con. Ed. 2, 252. 1938.] Although one of the most easily recognised forms this cultivar is often confused with other globose forms. It shares with 'Pumila' the flattened globular shape of that variety when young, but there the similarity ceases. 'Little Gem' has glossy foliage of a deep, rich mid-green, darkening in winter. The foliage is conspicuously glandular on both sides (which are similar) and much flattened (to 3 mm) as though each little spray had been passed through a mangle, and the ultimate branchlets twist and curve out of the plane of the spray. This last is further obscured by the eruption of tiny shoots at all angles from second year and older wood. The sprays are held at all angles, mostly perhaps horizontal or nearly so, but the effect of all these divergent shoots all over the plant is to give it a very dense appearance which can be accentuated to any required extent by a little pruning. It is one of the best garden forms. (Illustration 429).

– –'**Lutea Nana**' [*Th. occidentalis lutea nana* Beissn. Handb. 41. 1891.] This is one of the most desirable forms. It could well be described as a dwarf form of cultivar 'Lutea' (better known in America as the George Peabody Arborvitae). It forms an upright pyramid to about 2 m with dense, yellow-green foliage which develops in winter into a rich, glowing golden-yellow which bears comparison with 'Ellwangerana Aurea'. It can be distinguished from that cultivar because the foliage is denser and wider (2 mm compared with the 1-1.5 mm of 'Ellwangerana Aurea') and lacks its graceful lace-like quality; also it never carries juvenile foliage. (Illustration 430).

It is a variety that should be made much more use of in gardens because of its winter glory and its upright, formal habit of growth.

– –'**Meinekes Zwerg**' [New cv.] A new, dense and very slow-growing globose form in which the whitish-yellow growing tips form an attractive contrast with the dark green of the older foliage. Hardy and smoke tolerant. Introduced by the Karl Meineke Baumschule at Harz in Germany, from a seedling found in the seed beds in 1955. The mother plant at 18 years is 60 cm high by 50 cm across.

– –'**Milleri**' [New cv.] This seems to be the correct name for another slow-growing dense, globose form which has circulated in the trade as 'Minima', a name in prior use for quite a different form. 'Milleri' has mid green foliage in rather long and narrow sprays which although lying in random directions are all held rather stiffly upright, so as to shew up as vertical lines at the side of the plant seen from a little distance away.

– –'**Minima**' Superlative adjectives invariably make bad names. This one was cited by Beissn. [Handb. 45. 1891] as a synonym of 'Pygmaea'. As "var. *minima*" it was used by Hornibrook [Dw. Con. 166. 1923] for a rather horrible sounding little bush that we seem well rid of, since I cannot trace it in cultivation.

– –'**Ohlendorffii**' [*Th. occidentalis Ohlendorfi* Beissn. Conif. Ben. 28. 1887; f. *Ohlendorffii* (Beissn.) Rehd. Bibl. 47. 1949 *; *Th. occidentalis späthii* P. Smith ex Späth, Nurs. Cat. 12. 1890.] This is quite a horticultural curiosity. Left to itself it will form a clump of vertical shoots with closely set, decussate, juvenile foliage with strongly decurved leaves (up to 10 mm by 1.5 mm), and arising therefrom a small number of strong, thick, sparingly branched, vertical shoots bearing tiny adult leaves, which being noticeably folded or keeled and appressed to the stem give it a more or less square cross-section. In summer the plant carries a pleasant two-tone effect, parts of the shoots being a dark green and parts a pinky-brown, but it lets itself down badly in winter. A related form is **'Tetragona'** Welch [Dw. Con. 304. 1966; *Thuja tetragona* Hort. ex Beissn. Handb. 39. 1891; *Th. occidentalis filiformis* Hort. Fr.] This is a distinct and much less common form which could roughly be described as a much coarser edition of 'Ohlendorffii'. It carries the same two types of foliage, but the few juvenile leaves are smaller and much less decurved, and the vertical shoots (which predominate) are much longer, thicker and more pronouncedly tetragonal (to 3 mm 'across the flats'). It forms a much larger bush or (if kept to a single stem) a small tree. Hornibrook was quite right in drawing attention to the persisting effect of selecting juvenile material of 'Ohlendorffii' for propagation, but I have no doubt whatever that these are two very different clones. (Illustration 431).

– –**'Pumila'** [*Th. occidentalis pumila* Otto. Hamb. Gart & Blum. **23**: 162. 1867; Hort ex Beissn. Handb. 44. 1891; *Th. occidentalis* f. *pumila* (Otto) Rehd. Bibl. 46. 1949 (excl. 'Little Gem' in synonymy).] The early descriptions of this cultivar all refer to it as a dense, dwarf form growing broader than high, but the pictures of my type plant on the Rock Garden at Glasnevin show that in time it can build itself up to a height of 2 m or more, although no doubt it would maintain its globose shape indefinitely if any strong upright growths were cut out as they appeared. The foliage is a deep, rich green above, lighter green beneath, in flat, regular, crowded sprays in which the angle of divergence of the branches and branchlets is noticeably less (40-50°) than in most forms, with each branchlet slightly twisted so that the leaflets do not touch each other, even when they overlap. The growth is flattened (1.5-2 mm). The sprays, in a mature plant, are very gracefully held in nearly horizontal planes, the habit being very clearly seen in Illustration 432. In colour it is not unlike 'Little Gem', but the foliage is narrower and very neat and regular, with no trace of the aberrant shoots of that variety.

– –**'Pygmaea'** [*Th. plicata pygmaea* Hort. (*Th. plicata minima* Hort., pro syn.) ex Beissn. Handb. 45. 1891 and as *Th. occidentalis plicata pygmaea* in Ed. 2, 504. 1909; *Th. occidentalis* var. *pygmaea* Hort. ex Bailey, Cult. Conif. 171. 1933.] This old variety forms a low, stunted bush with a very irregular branching system. The growth is in flat sprays, held at random, with a greatly reduced entre-noeud, so that the leaves are very densely crowded and overlapping, and as they are much flattened (to 3 mm) the spray is very dense, and there is much overlapping of the branchlets. The glands are prominent above and below, especially so as they are noticeably glossy. The flattening extends to the very tip of the shoot, giving a distinctly round-ended look and, as Hornibrook noticed, these tips are liable to some form of die-back. It is an attractive little plant with deep, blue-green foliage which contrasts nicely with the lighter green of the young growth in the summer. It seems to do much better in America than in Britain. (Illustration 433).

- -'**Recurva Nana**' [*Th. occidentalis recurva nana* Carr. Traité Ed. 2, 111. 1867; *Th. occidentalis* 'Robusta Recurva' Hillier, Dw. Con. 63. 1964.] This is an attractive form which is not by any means always found true. It begins as a low, squat plant, becoming conical later with rising main branches and uniform and very much flattened (from 2 to 3 mm wide) foliage in crowded sprays that are usually held nearly horizontally but with each growing tip recurved and twisted as though one held one's hand spread out at eye level, palm downward, bent all the fingers slightly and twisted the wrist a little. It lacks the upright cord-like shoots of 'Dumosa' which is often supplied in its place. (Illustration 434). '**Recurvata**' is a tall-growing form outside the scope of this book.
- -'**Rheingold**'. See above under 'Ellwangerana Aurea'.
- -'**Sphaerica**' [*Th. occidentalis* var. *sphaerica* Hornb. Dw. Con. Ed. 2, 253. 1938] is a dainty little plant represented in several collections in this country which should be popular when it becomes more available. It has tiny, lanceolate foliage quite the narrowest (1 mm or less) foliage of any *Thuja occidentalis* form I know and the sprays are all crimpled and curled in a most attractive manner. It is at first a globose little plant but in time becomes upright, to about 1.5 m.
- -'**Spiralis**' [*Th. occidentalis* 'Spiralis' Rehd. in Bailey. Cult. Everg. 224. 1923] is not a dwarf form but a narrowly columnar tree. Where a plant of a formal and architectural character is required it takes a lot of beating. It is a densely branched, narrowly pyramidal form with the ultimate branchlets short and regularly pinnately arranged, very much after the fashion of *Chamaecyparis obtusa* 'Filicoides' from which it can at once be distinguished by the smell of the crushed foliage. With a little systematic pruning back of the lateral shoots it can be induced to form a very narrow and dense plant indeed.
- -'**Tiny Tim**' Grootn. [Dendroflora **2**: 49. 1965.] This is a very slow-growing broadly globose form, in 8 to 10 years reaching only 40 cm broad and 30 cm high. Raised as a seedling at Little Tree Farm, London, Ontario, Canada, and introduced to the trade by the Bulk and Co. Nursery at Boskoop in Holland. It seems to be intermediate in vigour and rate of growth between 'Hetz Midget' and 'Globosa'.
- -'**Tom Thumb**' [*Th. occidentalis* var. Tom Thumb Beissn. Handb. Ed. 2, 305. 1909; NON Wilson Gard. Mag. 1920] is, despite the name, not a dwarf form. It is a synonym of 'Ellwangerana', the green equivalent of 'Ellwangerana Aurea' and a much stronger grower.
- -'**Umbraculifera**' [*Th. occidentalis* var. *umbraculifera* Beissn. Moll. Deutsche Gartn. **4**: 179. 1892.] 'Umbraculifera' is one of the best of the compact, rounded forms and is easy to identify since it has the bluest-green foliage of any. It usually has several upright main stems which later spread out to support the dense, dome-shaped crown which gives the plant the umbrella shape to which it owes its name. The twigs are conspicuously pinky-brown and the foliage is in flat sprays with the shoots irregularly flattened (to 2 mm, usually less) and daintily laid out and curved in the plane of the spray. It turns a dark bronzy-green in the winter. 'Umbraculifera' forms quite a large bush in time, but it is a bad transplanter so should be planted in a small size if possible. (Illustration 435).
- -'**Wansdyke Silver**' Welch [Dw. Con. 307. 1966.] This is a very slow-growing

and congested form in the Pygmy Pinetum which has light green foliage in short sprays liberally splashed with creamy-white, the colour being held all the year. The mother plant (the origin of which is not on record) is a columnar little plant about 1.5 m high which has not grown appreciably in five years, so that I do not think it can be any of the variegated forms of *Thuja occidentalis* that have been hitherto named. It is a very attractive form for those who like variegated plants and it keeps its colour well throughout the year. (Illustration 436). **'Beaufort'** has similar colouring but is a tall-growing variety.

– –**'Wareana Globosa'** [*Th. occidentalis Wareana globosa* Hort. Beissn. Handb. 41. 1891; *Th. occidentalis* 'Robusta Nana' Hillier, Dw. Con. 63. 1964.] This was described by Beissner as a congested, globose form of the arboreal 'Wareana Lutescens'—which is well known and distinctive in its foliage.

In 1964 H. G. Hillier suggested using this name and 'Robusta Recurva' as collective names for a number of forms which I separate here, but I notice he has restored them their autonomy in the *Manual* [1971.] I do not know Beissner's clone, but his description is precise enough for identification if it is still in cultivation.

– –**'Watnong Gold'** Hebb. [Arnoldia **33**: 208. 1973.] A sport of 'Ellwangerana Aurea' introduced by Watnong Nursery, Morris Plains, New Jersey, U.S.A. Don Smith tells me that it makes a tall, compact, slender column growing 30 cm annually, retaining the same good winter colour as the parent.

– –**'Woodwardii'** [Arborvitae 'Woodward' Manning Nurs. Cat. 2. 1874; *Th. occidentalis* f. *Woodwardii* (Späth) Rehd. Bibl. 46. 1949 *.] This is a strong-growing, globose form with rich green foliage in flat sprays which are held stiffly in vertical planes rather in the manner of some of the *Thuja orientalis* forms. The foliage is quite coarse and open, is very much flattened (to 3 mm) and is approximately the same colour on both sides of the spray. It was introduced by the Reading Nurseries, Massachusetts, and named by the proprietor Jacob Manning after his son J. Woodward Manning, a landscape architect, in 1872. It assumes a naturally globose shape without artificial training and whilst growing quite large eventually, it retains its globose shape in maturity. (Illustration 437).

Thuja orientalis L. This is normally a small tree to 10 m or a large globose bush. The species is easily distinguishable from all other Thujas and Cypresses by the fact that its branches are held erect or curving upwards and carrying the leaf sprays in a vertical plane, these being of the same colour and appearance on both sides of the spray. The leaves are small and closely set, overlapping, triangular and bluntly pointed. They are dotted with stomata, and the facing pair has a central groove. *Thuja orientalis* was at one time regarded as a distinct genus, *Biota*, and the name survives in the popular names of some of its forms, for instance "*Berckman's Golden Biota*", so well known in the United States, but if regarded as a distinct genus, the name having priority would be *Platycladus orientalis* (L.) Franco 1949.

The species can be clearly distinguished (in all adult forms) by the foliage and habit as given above, and by the strongly hooked cone scales. The dwarf forms can be grouped as follows:

Juvenile and semi-juvenile foliage	Golden foliage (Dwarf)	Golden foliage (Tall, conical)
'Decussata'	'Aurea Nana'	'Aurea'
(See 'Juniperoides')	'Berckman'	'Beverleyensis'
'Juniperoides'	'Bonita'	'Conspicua'
'Meldensis'	'Sieboldii'	'Elegantissima'
'Minima'	'Summer Cream'	'Hillieri'
'Rosedalis'		'Semperaurescens'
'Sanderi'		

Foliage variants

'Athrotaxoides'	'Filiformis Nana'	'Monstrosa'
'Filiformis Elegans'	'Flagelliformis'	'Tetragona'
'Filiformis Erecta'	'Intermedia'	'Triangularis'

– –'**Athrotaxoides**' *Th. orientalis athrotaxoides* (Carr.) Nich. Dict. Gar. **4**: 34. 1887; *Biota orientalis athrotaxoides* Carr. Rev. Hort. 229. 1861.] is an interesting, very rare and extremely slow-growing form with very thick branches and branchlets, these all being completely cupressoid, lacking any trace of the flat spray characteristic of the species and suggesting a very coarse edition of the foliage of *Chamaecyparis obtusa* 'Lycopodioides'. The only large plant I know is in the National Botanic Garden at Glasnevin, Dublin. This is probably the plant of which Hornibrook wrote in 1938 but it is now a flat-topped tree 2.5 m high by 3 m across. There is a plant in the Pygmy Pinetum at Devizes. (Illustration 438).

– – f. **aurea** (Carr.) Rehd. [Bibl. 48. 1949 *.] *Forms distinguished by the young foliage being at first a bright golden-yellow.* Note: All such forms gradually fade to the normal green.

A number of seedlings with this attractive peculiarity have turned up from time to time and there are probably many more clones in cultivation than we have names. The early loss of the lovely golden colour each year makes it a poor distinction for botanists and horticulturists alike, so here I list only the clones recognisable as cultivars. I must therefore disfavour '**Aurea**' as a cultivar epithet, since it cannot now be identified with any clone in cultivation. '**Aurea Compacta**' is equally unsatisfactory and there are other names of the kind to be found, all of which would be better dropped from use in favour of new registrations of desirable and identifiable clones.

– –'**Aurea Nana**' [*Biota orientalis aurea nana* Sén. Conif. 2. 1867; *Thuja orientalis* var. *aurea nana* Hornb. Dw. Con. Ed. 2, 263. 1938.] This is the one clearly distinguishable variety which is in easy supply and it is deservedly popular. It should be in every collection, however small. (Illustration 439). 'Aurea Nana' forms a round-topped, oval little bush, seldom over 60 cm high. The foliage is very dense and all the leaf sprays seem to be trying to lie in parallel planes, giving the plant a distinctly laminated appearance. This characteristic it shares with the much stronger growing and upright form '**Semperaurescens**' [*Biota orientalis semperaurescens* Lemoine ex Gord. Pin. Ed. 2, 422. 1875; *Th. orientalis* f. *semperaurescens* (Gord.) Schneid. in Rehd. Bibl. 48, 1949; 'Semperaurea' Welch, Dw. Con. 309.

1966] from which it is indistinguishable when they are small plants, both having the same rich golden-yellow colour in early summer and green for the rest of the year. 'Aurea Nana' roots readily from cuttings, but 'Semperaurescens' is a poor rooter.

Other golden and/or green forms that make upright plants that are slow-growing but too large for most situations (save, perhaps, to fill a prominent spot temporarily until a sufficiently large plant of a slower-growing and dwarfer form is available) are **'Elegantissima'** [*Biota orientalis elegantissima* (Rollisson) Gord. Pin. Suppl. 17. 1862; *Thuja orientalis* f. *elegantissima* (Gordon) Schneider in Rehd. Bibl. 48. 1949 *] (which turns pinkish-brown in the winter), **'Hillieri'** Hillier [Nurs. Cat. 201. 1930] (foliage at first yellow, soon turning green) and 'Semperaurescens' (See under 'Aurea Nana' above.)

– –'*Berckmans*' (Berckman's Golden Biota). See 'Conspicua'.

– –**'Beverleyensis'** [*Th. orientalis* f. *beverleyensis* (Rehd.) Rehd. Bibl. 48. 1949 *; 'Beverley Hills' Wyman, Amer. Nurs. **133, 7:** 70. 1961] is a tall-growing form which grows into a narrow column, not unlike 'Conspicua' (below). The foliage is a golden-yellow in the early summer, turning to green later. The leaf tips on this form are sharply pointed and less closely appressed than is usual in this species, giving the foliage a somewhat false appearance of prickliness. A form that originated in California, U.S.A.

– –**'Blijdenstein'** Den Ouden [Conif. 350. 1949.] A dense, conical form with thin, crowded, fastigiate branches, which originated as a seedling in the Blijdenstein Arboretum, Hilversum, Netherlands, in 1937.

– –**'Bonita'** [*Th. orientalis bonita* Slavin, Rep. Conif. Conf. 147. 1932.] This is an old American selection which is described as a broadly conical slow-growing form of regular, formal outline with young foliage at first golden-yellow, soon turning to a bright green.

– –**'Conspicua'** [*Th. orientalis* var. *conspicua* Berckmans Nurs. Cat. 54. 1915-1916; *Th. orientalis* f. *conspicua* (Rehd) Rehd. Bibl. 48. 1949 *.] As grown in Europe 'Conspicua', although by no means a dwarf, is in my opinion the best of the fastigiate golden forms—the usual bright gold in early summer, but retaining its colour better throughout the year than any. It is a strong grower, always finishing at the top of the plant with a few pale yellow, rather scrawny, twigs— I beg their pardon—I mean with a few leading growths with extended entre-noeud and lighter colour. According to Dallimore and Jackson, the form raised by Berckman was 'of dense, fastigiate habit' but the cultivar grown widely in America as Berckman's Golden Biota today is neither as fastigiate as 'Conspicua' nor as broadly ovoid as 'Aurea Nana' of European cultivation. The picture given by Kumlien [Friendly Evergreens. 220. 1946] is of a plant intermediate in habit and agrees well with plants shewn to me as Berckman's Golden Biota so we must accept its separate identity under the obvious epithet **'Berckman'** New name [Berckman's Golden Biota Hort. Amer.; *Th. orientalis* 'Aurea Nana' Hort. Amer. (in part); NON 'Conspicua' Hort. Europe.]

– –**'Densa Glauca'** [*Th. orientalis* var. *densa glauca* Hornb. Dw. Con. 180. 1923; *Biota orientalis densa glauca* Beissn. Nadel. Ed. 2, 326. 1909.] Material received from the collection at Rostrevor, County Down, Northern Ireland, which I think must be this form, answers well to Beissner's description, although I would hesitate about applying to it the adjective 'pretty'. It forms an upright-oval bush, rather looser than 'Sieboldii', blue-green in summer but turning the most atrocious deathly brown in winter. This seems characteristic of all the blue-green seedlings that turn up and precludes their achieving much popularity.

– –'Filiformis Erecta' [*Biota orientalis filiformis erecta* Sén. Conif. 43. 1867; f. *filiformis stricta* Beissn. Handb. 64. 1891; Hillier, Dw. Con. 64. 1964; NON *Th. filiformis* Loddiges, Nurs. Cat. 39. 1820] is a very distinct form in which the usual foliage in sprays is entirely absent, the whole plant consisting of tightly bunched shoots clothed with leaves (the facing and lateral pairs being of equal size) with only their pointed tips (1–3 mm long) free standing. The branching system is strongly vertical, save for a few straggling shoots at the sides and the plant forms an upright-ovoid bush seldom seen more than 1 m but capable of reaching twice that height. Leaves yellowish-green in summer, greenish-brown in winter, an interesting plant. (Illustration 440).

– –'Flagelliformis' [*Th. flagelliformis* Knight, Syn. Conif. 16. 1850; *Biota orientalis* var. *flagelliformis* Jacques ex Hoopes, Everg. 334. 1868 (and Illus.); *Th. orientalis* f. *flagelliformis* (Jacques) Rehd. Bibl. 48. 1949; *Th. pendula* D. Don in Lambert, Desc. Pin. **2**: 115. 1824; *Th. filiformis* Loddiges Nurs. Cat. 39. 1820; *Biota orientalis filiformis pendula* Sén. Conif. 44. 1867.] More or less monstrous forms with threadlike foliage have turned up from time to time and several attempts have been made to name them. Although no doubt each author had a particular clone in mind the early descriptions are very brief and it has been difficult to determine which names properly belong to the forms in cultivation.

A very good illustration of 'Flagelliformis' left to us by Hoopes [Book Everg. 335. 1868] enables us to identify a strong, upright-growing form with foliage similar to 'Filiformis Erecta' but with much larger leaves standing off at a wider angle (except near the growing tips, where they are folded so as to give a square cross section to the shoot). The growth is not so densely upright and is a light, yellowish-green in summer. This form is doubtfully hardy. There is a good specimen on the upper bank at the National Botanic Garden at Glasnevin, Dublin.

At Cliveden in Buckinghamshire, one of the beautiful gardens made available to the public through the National Trust, there is a large specimen of a strong growing thread-leaf form with dark green foliage very similar to *Chamaecyparis pisifera* 'Filifera', and with pendulous branchlets. This is certainly not the 'Flagelliformis' of Hoopes's illustration and I think it may be accepted as **'Filiformis Elegans'** Sén. [Conif. 43. 1867], described as having glaucous foliage. Other names in the literature are—**'Filiformis Nana'** Sén. [op. cit.], a very dwarf, congested bush; **'Intermedia'** Sén. [op. cit.], a vigorous form with few branches; **'Monstrosa'** Carr. ex Sén. [op. cit.], a monstrous form (possibly *Thujopsis dolabrata* 'Nana'); **'Tetragona'** Beissn. [Handb. Ed. 2, 528. 1909], an upright bush with branches tetragonal (how surprising!) and **'Triangularis'** Nich. [Dict. Gar. **4**: 34. 1887], a variety of unusual leaf arrangement. These are all impossible to identify with anything in cultivation today. Doubtless the way to sort out this group would be to use 'Flagelliformis' as a group name and register new cultivars, but they are not very attractive plants and so are of little or no garden value.

– –'**Juniperoides**' [*Thuja juniperoides* Knight, Syn. Conif. 16. 1850; *Th. orientalis* f. *juniperoides* (Carr.) Asch. and Graebn. in Rehd. Bibl. 48. 1949 *; *Biota orientalis* var. *decussata* Beissn. and Hochst. in Hochst. Conif. 76. 1882.] This is one of several fixed juvenile forms of *Th. orientalis* which all form rounded bushes growing to less than 1 m, all with very dense, decussate foliage with acicular leaves free standing for most of their length with the tips tending to recurve. They are all most desirable garden plants. 'Juniperoides' has large leaves (the free standing part up to 8 mm long, held at 60° to stem), light greyish-green in summer, turning a rich purplish-grey in the winter, the colour of the bloom on a ripe grape. Always the greyish look is due to a heavy glaucous coating which is easily rubbed off. This plant is the least hardy of the group and should be sheltered from keen winds. (Illustration 441).

– –'**Meldensis**' [*Biota meldensis* Lawson in Gord. Pin. 37. 1858; *Th. orientalis* f. *meldensis* (Laws.) Rehd. Bibl. 49. 1949 *.] This form has smaller leaves (5 mm long, noticeably decurved, to 70°), stiff, dull green in summer and dull purplish-brown in winter. The foliage has a *stiff and rough feel* when the bush is patted on the top with the hand. This form occasionally throws out a spray of adult foliage. This determines for us the specific allegiance of this form and may be retained for its botanical interest, provided the plant does not carry the process too far and begin to lose character. (Illustration 442).

– –'**Minima**' [*Biota orientalis glauca minima* R. Smith, Pl. Fir Tribe, 9. 1872; *Th. plicata minima* Nich. Dict. Gar. **4**: 34. 1887 (Corrected to *Th. orientalis minima* in Suppl. 702. 1900); *B. orientalis minima glauca* Beissn. Handb. 62. 1891; *Th. orientalis* var. *pygmaea* Kent in Veitch, Man. Ed. 2, 250. 1900; var. *minima glauca* Hornb. Dw. Con. 180. 1923.] 'Minima' is a very slow-growing form with very small and closely set semi-juvenile leaves which are very harsh to the touch. Unlike the wholly juvenile forms, the difference between the lateral and facing pairs of leaves is quite noticeable, the young shoots are distinctly thujoid and the adult growth pattern in flat sprays is discernible. The foliage changes from light yellow-green in early summer to dark green later and becomes a rather dirty brown in winter. This is a defect, for in cold weather the plant looks almost dead. (Illustration 443).

– –"*pumila argentea*". See 'Summer Cream', below.

– –'**Rosedalis**' Welch [Dw. Con. 313. 1966; *Th. orientalis* var. 'Rosedalis Compacta' Hornb. Dw. Con. 180. 1923] is perhaps the most popular of the fixed juvenile forms, with its soft, narrow leaves (up to 7 mm long, held at 45°) and its change of colour three times in the year. In summer it is a light green, in winter brown to plum-purple and in the spring it changes to a beautiful butter-yellow. It can be distinguished readily from 'Meldensis' by these colour changes, and at all seasons by the feel of the foliage, which is very *soft and yielding* to the touch. '**Rosedale**' [*T. orientalis* var. 'Rosedale' Mast. Journ. Roy. Hort. Soc. **25**: 98. 1901.] This variety, which originated in the Rosedale Nurseries, Washington County, Texas, U.S.A., having (doubtless quite unwittingly) given its name to the plant still with us, seems to have quietly disappeared from view, so there would

appear to be no case for retaining the more clumsy name suggested by Hornibrook. (Illustration 444).

– –'Sanderi' [*Juniperus Sanderi* Sander ex Mast. Gar. Chron. Ser. 3, **25**: 287. 1899; *C.
obtusa* f. *sanderi* (Sander) Rehd. Bibl. 54. 1949 *; *C. obtusa ericoides* Hort. Japan ex
Boehmer Nurs. Cat. 2. 1899; *Shishendenia ericoides* Makino, New Flora Japan. Ed.
of 1938.] This interesting plant will always be rare on account of its tenderness.
(Illustration 445). Numerous taxonomists in the past have attempted to establish
its identity. Most of them have agreed upon its being a fixed juvenile form of
some kind but have disagreed as to which species (and even which genus) is
concerned, and surely the depth of botanical irresponsibility was reached by the
invention of a new genus to place it in meanwhile until we could find out where
it did belong. L. J. Gough of the Polytechnic of the South Bank, London S. E. 1,
whose work on resin chemistry initiated the clearing up of the *Chamaecyparis
nootkatensis* 'Nidifera' conundrum has looked into this problem as well and he
now informs me that the chemistry of 'Sanderi' is so similar to the juvenile
forms of *Thuja orientalis* ('Meldensis', 'Rosedalis' and 'Juniperoides') and so
distinct from that of any other of the numerous genera and species suggested in
the past that he is satisfied that this is where it belongs. The tendency to carry a
small amount of ternate (i.e., in threes) foliage is common in all these forms, and
a similarity in the smell of the crushed foliage of 'Sanderi' and 'Meldensis' are
confirmatory, as is also a report by the Asakawa Forestry Research Establish-
ment in 1963 of an experiment in which a male flower produced by spraying
with Gibberellin showed the greatest kinship with *Th. orientalis*.

It is normally seen as a low, round bush and it bears juvenile foliage stouter
and stiffer than any of the other recorded juvenile forms. In summer its foliage
and branchlets are a wonderful glaucous sea green and in winter they take on
the bloom and colour of a blue plum. It should be given shelter from wind
during the winter.

A very complete summarization of the many attempts in the past to find a
nomenclatural home for this plant is given by the late Dr. R. Bayer of Bad
Homburg, West Germany, in Deutsche Baumschule. 258. 1970.

– –'Sieboldii' [*Biota orientalis* Sieboldii Endl. Syn. Con. 47. 1847; *Th. orientalis* f.
sieboldii (Endl.) Rehd. Bibl. 48. 1949 *] is a very old variety, often met with under
the names *"compacta"* and *"nana",* which forms a round-headed bush up to 2 m
high, with the usual vertical branching system and a dense habit of growth. The
foliage (which at first is golden-yellow) soon turns to and remains a bright mid-
green, is very fine, open and lace-like in flat sprays in which each side shoot
branches off at precisely 45°, and so evenly spaced out that there is little or no
overlapping of shoots on the spray. The final shoots are about 1 mm wide and
even three year old twigs are barely twice as thick. None of the plants I have
seen has had the extreme tips of the branchlet spray bent over and outwards, as
described by Hornibrook. It may be this is a seasonal phase of short duration.

– –'**Summer Cream**' New name [*Th. orientalis* var. *pumila argentea* Hornb. Dw. Con.
179. 1923.] I obtained stock of this attractive variety from Everton Nurseries
near Lymington, Hampshire, and they suggested the name 'Summer Cream'
under which, I see, they now catalogue it. So far as it can be pieced together, its

history goes back, through A. H. Nisbet of Gosport to the Dalrymple collection at Bartley, Southampton, whence many of Nisbet's plants came when the land there was ploughed up during the war. In view of the interest Hornibrook took in that collection the plant not improbably came from him. I have looked again at his description of *"pumila argentea"*. I feel that although it is probably our plant some doubt cannot be excluded and that the balance of advantage now lies in accepting the new cultivar name in general use. It is a very attractive form, slower growing than 'Aurea Nana' and with all the young growth a creamy-white. This later fades to the usual green.

Thuja plicata D. Don, the Western Red cedar is normally a tree to 50 m or more but it has given us several excellent dwarf forms. The foliage is more nearly like *Th. occidentalis* than any other species, but it differs in that the leaves are less conspicuously glandular and streaked with white on the underside; also the foliage has a less objectionable smell when bruised.

– –'Collyers Gold' [New cv.] I received this form from a nurseryman in Surrey, now deceased, and I have no record of its origin. It is very similar to 'Stoneham Gold' both in habit and colouring, except that both the yellow of the growing tips and the green of the older foliage are lighter in tone. It lacks the rich tonal contrast of 'Stoneham Gold', but it is nevertheless an attractive and hardy form.

– –'Cuprea' [*Th. plicata cuprea* Den Ouden, Naamlijst. 45. 1937; Conif. 353. 1949.] This forms a low, spreading shrub with golden-bronze foliage. Both this and 'Rogersii' were raised by Mr. Gardiner at the Red Lodge Nurseries, at that time at Southampton, from seed from a tree of *Th. plicata* 'Aurea'. The bronzy-yellow colour is the same, but 'Cuprea' is much more open in growth and makes a much larger bush.

– –'Gracilis' [*Th. gigantea gracilis* Hort. ex Beissn. Handb. Ed. 2, 514. 1909; *Th. plicata gracilis* Den Ouden, Naamlijst, 45. 1937; Conif. 353. 1949] is a form in which the foliage is much lighter and finer than in the type, with the leaves much smaller. It is described as forming a slow-growing and broadly conical plant. It is not a dwarf form, but **'Gracilis Aurea'** [*Th. plicata gracilis aurea* Hort. ex Den Ouden. Conif. 353. 1949] is more slow-growing and might come into this category with its dainty, lace-like foliage and colouring. It makes an attractive large bush or small tree, which, despite Dr. Boom's warning, I have found to be quite hardy in Wiltshire, England.

– –'Hillieri' [*Th. plicata* var. *Hillieri* Hornb. Dw. Con. 182. 1923.] A slow-growing, dense, rounded bush, seldom seen over 1 metre high by as much through. The rich green foliage is arranged in curious moss-like clusters on the tips of stout, stiff branchlets. The growth is irregular and the plant is often improved, especially when young, by the shortening of any long shoots that develop out of character. (Illustration 446).

– –'Pumila' [*Th. lobbii pumila* R. Smith, Pl. Fir Tribe, 44. 1867; *Th. plicata nana* David ex Sén. Conif. 195. 1867; *Th. gigantea* var. *pumila* Hort. ex Fitsch in Beissn. Handb. Ed. 3, 493. 1930.] This very dwarf form carries foliage not unlike 'Hillieri', but it forms a low, bun-shaped little plant, not more than 50 cm high by a little more across.

- –'**Rogersii**' [*Th. plicata* var. *aurea rogersii* Hornb. Dw. Con. Ed. 2, 269. 1938; as *rogersi aurea* Gar. Chron. 50. 1929.] This form has the same origin and shares the same golden-bronze colour of 'Cuprea' but it forms a much denser and more upright plant with very congested foliage which is dark green in the interior of the bush but a rich copper-bronze on all the exposed tips. It is slow to get going, but when well established it throws up strong vertical shoots by means of which the plant gains its upright shape. If these are cut away it can be kept as an extremely dense, ovoid or globose little bush which is a glowing spot of colour at all seasons. (Illustration 447).

I have noticed that the colour varies considerably, some plants in the nursery rows appearing a creamy-white, but I do not think this variation is sufficiently stable to fix as a distinct cultivar.

- –'**Stoneham Gold**' [*Th. plicata* 'Stoneham Gold' Rogers, Nurs. Cat. 1948.] Although it will reach to 2 m or more high in time this form is very slow-growing for several years, so it should be planted more widely than at present because of its wonderful colour. It forms an upright plant with dense growth of more or less typical foliage which is dark green—often almost black—in the interior of the plant but a rich orange-yellow on all the young shoots at its surface. This two-tone effect is very attractive and the golden colour is well maintained throughout the year on plants that are growing vigorously. Older plants would probably pay for hard pruning to induce strong new growth. (Illustration 448).

THUJOPSIS

Thujopsis dolabrata (L. fil.) Sieb. and Zucc. is the sole occupant of this genus, which at one time was included in Thuja. A practical if not very scholarly way to describe its foliage is to liken it to foliage of Thuja that has been put through a mangle, becoming thereby squashed out very thin and much wider. It has given us one hardy and useful, if not particularly exciting dwarf form.

- –'**Nana**' [*Th. dolabrata* f. *nana* Endl. Syn. Conif. 54. 1847; Rehd. Bibl. 44. 1949 *; var. *nana* Sieb. and Zucc. Fl. Jap. 34. 1855.] forms a wide-spreading bush, never more than 1 m high but often much more across, with smaller leaves and length of shoot than in the type. It seems indestructibly hardy and is very useful for a rough corner. I have noticed that the colour varies a good deal; at its best it is a nice, rich, grass green, but sometimes one sees it a dull yellowish-green, and all the forms are a poor colour in winter. (Illustrations 449, 450).

TORREYA

This is a small genus allied to Cephalotaxus, of which only one species, *T. nucifera*, has given us any recorded forms suitable for inclusion in this book.

Torreya nucifera Sieb. and Zucc. is a Japanese species with foliage very similar to *Cephalotaxus harringtonia* var. *drupacea* but differing therefrom by the long, gradually tapered leaves ending in a very fine, sharp tip, with no noticeable mid-rib above and with two well defined, narrow sunk bands of (sometimes pinkish) stomata beneath.

– –'**Prostrata**' [*T. nucifera* var. *prostrata* Hornb. Dw. Con. 183. 1923.] The plant mentioned by Hornibrook at Glasnevin has now become very large, as will be seen from the picture. Although he states that it was planted as a seedling I am of the opinion that its status is merely that of a cultivariant. It could very well have been a seedling that had accidentally lost its leader which has never been able to recover its normal habit. 'Prostrata' is a useful and attractive plant for ground cover in open woodland or wherever a large specimen not above 1 m is required. (Illustration 451).

TSUGA

The hemlocks form a genus of 10 species of trees of which several, when raised from cuttings, are slow-growing. The foliage is not unlike that of the Yews, but the terminal shoots are thinner and usually pendulous, giving these trees a more graceful appearance. The leaves are actually borne radially on short stems which are pressed to the shoots, but they are twisted so as to lie in a more or less clear double tier with the leaves in the lower tier longer than those above. The leaf stems spring from a cushion-like projection which at once distinguishes this genus from the leaf scar of Abies and the peg-like leaf base of Picea.

Tsuga canadensis (L) Carr. Although a tree to 30 m, this species is very variable from seed and has produced many dwarf forms including some of the smallest conifers known. A native of Canada and the eastern United States, the species was introduced to European cultivation at an early date and a number of variants were given names by Carrière, Loudon and other 19th century European writers, accompanied, alas, as was all too often the case in those days, by descriptions so inadequate that it is now impossible to identify the clones to which the descriptions relate.

The species has not been widely planted in Europe, where in many parts it does not prosper, but in its native haunts it is a very common tree and as a species is very variable. As a result of variants found in the wild and of others selected in nursery seed beds the number of cultivated forms increased greatly and in 1931 Charles F. Jenkins, a prosperous publisher of Philadelphia, Pennsylvania, U.S.A., established the Hemlock Arboretum in the grounds of his home 'Far Country' on the outskirts of Germantown, on a plateau overlooking the Wissahickon Valley. This enterprise gave rise to much interest (not confined to the United States) and by means of purchases and contributions from botanical gardens, nurserymen and collectors he gathered together a remarkable collection. In addition to this he produced a quarterly Bulletin at his own expense and distributed it freely to all who were sufficiently interested.[1] In this he chronicled

[1]Thanks to the U.S. National Arboretum, Washington D. C., a complete set of these bulletins is in the library of the Pygmy Pinetum at Devizes, Wiltshire.

the development of the Arboretum and recorded the results of his study of the genus and any interesting item of Hemlock lore that came to his notice. The Bulletin ran to 74 issues and publication ceased only on Jenkins's death in 1951. Thereafter, sad to relate, his work at the Arboretum was not continued. A few of the plants were given to the Scott Foundation, Swarthmore, Pennsylvania, some went to the Morris Arboretum of the University of Pennsylvania and others were distributed to private individuals and when I saw the collection in June 1974 most of the specimens that had been allowed to remain had grown almost out of recognition.

Although Jenkins himself made no claim to possessing any botanical training he realised the need for a scientific approach and in Bulletin No. 19 issued in July 1937, he appealed for some young graduate to take the mutations of *Tsuga canadensis* as his subject for post graduate study. In Bulletin No. 22, 9 months later, he was able to report that one John C. Swartley had taken up his challenge and that he was already enrolled in Cornell University. In September 1939 a thesis with the title "Canada Hemlock and its Variation" was duly submitted to the authorities at Cornell. The thesis ran to 380 pages and was illustrated by actual photographs. A list is therein given of 73 nurseries and botanical establishments visited by Swartley, who makes an acknowledgement of characteristic generosity on the part of Jenkins in making so much travel possible. The thesis certainly secured the degree it was aimed at—had I done as much work I should have wanted a Doctorate at the very least—but unfortunately it was not printed and published. Had the authorities at Cornell realised at the time that it was and would remain the only major study of this group of plants for 35 years they might have acted otherwise. Although a *Code of Botanical Nomenclature* was available to Swartley the need for a separate *Code of Nomenclature of Cultivated Plants* had not then been generally realised. In 1945, however, Swartley prepared a supplementary thesis to bring his nomenclature of cultivars into line with developing trends. This, also, has remained unpublished.

Here the matter may well have rested had I not heard of the existence of the 1939 thesis, of which the Cornell University offered to supply a photographic copy. This offer I was at that time[2] too impecunious to take advantage of but when Dr. B. K. Boom of Wageningen, Holland, was revising *Manual of Cultivated Conifers* for the press I was able to pass this information on to him. The Dutch Government being more in funds than I, a copy of the 1939 thesis was obtained from Cornell University and Boom obtained the loan of the 1945 Supplement from Swartley himself. Both papers were freely cited by Den Ouden and Boom in the book. Fortunately (or unfortunately in this case—if you prefer) the Rules governing valid publication are definite. Neither Swartley's Thesis of 1939 nor the Supplement of 1945 having been validly published prior to the citations in *Manual of Cultivated Conifers* [Den Ouden and Boom] any names proposed by him can only be regarded as having been validly published at the date of the *Manual*, i.e., 1965. Correct citation of any such name must therefore be—Swartley ex Den Ouden and Boom [Man. 1965 . . .] Simplicity and convenience *must give way to exactitude*.

[2] And ever since!

In 1949 Swartley started in business as a landscape nurseryman. From 1957 he was for ten years Chairman of the Department of Horticulture at Temple University. In 1963 he joined forces with another nurseryman and former student but four years later he sold his interest in the business. When I first met him in 1970 he had returned to his early love and had started the preparation of a monograph on the genus Tsuga. In order to help in this work I had sent all my own notes on the *Tsuga canadensis* forms to Swartley, so when I had to commence the present work my obvious course was to enlist his help. This has been freely forthcoming and the following descriptions have been either checked or supplied by him. But his forthcoming monograph will, of course, cover the whole subject far more thoroughly and should be consulted as soon as it is available.

A few of the dwarf forms have arisen from the propagation of bud mutations, i.e., witches' brooms, but the majority began life as seedling mutations found in the wild or selected in nursery seed beds. Unfortunately, seedlings often grow very slowly at first and this may give to a young plant a spurious appearance of dwarfness so names have been given to supposed dwarfs which in time have turned out to be nothing of the kind. It is true that such forms when propagated vegetatively will often grow very slowly for some years and so they can serve a useful purpose, but eventually they put out coarse growth and outgrow their welcome. Varieties in this category mentioned in my earlier book which, on Swartley's advice, I now omit are **'Albospicata'**, **'Aurea'**, **'Boulevard'**, **'Broughton'**, **'Dawsoniana'**, **'Fremdi'**, **'Kelseys Weeping'**, **'Microphylla'**, **'Nana'**, **'Pendula'**, **'Strangeri'**, **'Taxifolia'**. As a rough rule, no varieties are included here that will ever grow higher than eye-level.

The descriptive names *"albospica"* [Beissn. Zierg. Ed. 2, 445. 1884]; *"aurea"* [(Nels.) Beissn. Zierg. Ed. 2, 445, 1884]; *"compacta"* [Sén. Conif. 19. 1867]; *"compacta nana"* [Beissn. Handb. 402. 1891]; *"globosa"* [Beissn. Conif. Ben. 65. 1887]; *"gracilis"* [(Gord.) Carr. Traité. Ed. 2, 249. 1867]; *"latifolia"* [Sén. Conif. 19. 1867]; *"nana"* [Carr. Man. 4. 334. 1854]; *"parvifolia"* [(Veitch) P. Smith ex Beissn. Zierg. Ed. 2, 445. 1884]; *"pumila"* [Ordn. ex Beissn. Handb. Ed. 2, 89. 1909] and *"sparsifolia"* [Beissn. Handb. 402. 1891] are amongst those given by early writers to clones that can no longer be identified. Any attempt by later writers to invest these names with a pseudo-botanical status is here rejected, in accordance with the treatment throughout this book. What use to make of each of these names—whether to republish it under the *Botanical Code* with a valid circumscription or use it horticulturally as a group name I must leave to Swartley. Here they can only be listed as cultivars lost to cultivation.

– –'**Abbotts Dwarf**' Hillier [Dw. Con. 65. 1964; 'Abbott Weeping" Welch, Dw. Con. 318. 1966.] As seen at Kingsville Nurseries, Kingsville, Maryland, U.S.A., this was a slow-growing conical bush 75 cm × 50 cm, densely furnished right through the plant with tightly packed, dark green foliage and long (up to 15 mm) and wide leaves except just at the tip of the shoot and along its upper side, where short (to 5 mm) leaves lie forwards along the shoot at 10° and twisted so as to expose the white stomata lines, giving an interesting two-tone effect to the plant.

– –'**Abbotts Pigmy**' Jenkins, [Heml. Arb. Bull. **62**: 3. 1948 and **63**: 1. 1948, excluding references to var. *minuta;* 'Pygmaea' Welch, Dw. Con. 321. 1966.] Swartley has taken a great deal of trouble to sort out the confusion between this form and 'Minuta'. No doubt his findings will be given in full in his forthcoming monograph. Here it suffices to say that Teuscher's account in *New Flora & Sylva* is essentially accurate, but he omits to state that the finder of var. *minuta* was Daniel St. George of Charlotte, Vermont, who sold two of his findlings to George E. Ehrle. In the Hemlock Arboretum *Bulletin* No. 62, Jenkins records the finding of 'Abbots Pigmy' north of Richmond, Vermont, in 1933 by Frank L. Abbott in a spot at least 15 miles away from where St. George made his discoveries, but the then prevailing uncertainty as to the application of pseudo-botanical names to cultivars led him to confuse the two plants. In Teuscher's later article [Pl. and Gar. **5, 3:** 141. 1949] the heading relates to one plant, the sub-heading relates to the other and confusion between Daniel St. George and Frank L. Abbott turns it all into nonsense.

Treatment of each discovery as a separate cultivar clears up the difficulty. They are undoubtedly different, although very much alike. The leaves on 'Abbotts Pigmy' are shorter, and the annual growth is about half that of 'Minuta'.

– –'**Armistice**' Warner ex Spingarn [Amer. Hort. Mag. **44,2:** 9. 1965; 'Warners Armistice' Hort. Amer.] This is a very slow-growing form which forms a flat-topped bush with a noticeably horizontal branching system, so that the deep, glossy, green foliage is in tiers. Joel W. Spingarn states that his plant is 45 cm high × 75 cm across after 28 years and is one of the finest plants in his collection. It is not always found true to name, a pyramidal plant being sometimes supplied in its place.

– –'**Bacon Cristate**' Smith ex Hebb [Arnoldia **23:** 208. 1973.] A new diminutive form recently introduced by Watnong Nursery, Morris Plains, New Jersey. The original plant was discovered by Mr. Ralph Bacon in 1925 as a wild seedling growing in New Jersey. The plant resembles 'Nearing' but is much more cristate and dwarf. The foliage is dark green. It was originally listed as 'Bacon's No. 4'. (Illustration 452).

– – *'Bennett'.* See 'Minima', below.

– – *'Brookline'.* See below.

– – *'Callicoon'.* See 'Curtis Spreader' below.

– –'**Coles Prostrate**' Bergman [Pl. & Gar. **21: 1,** 42. 1965; 'Cole' Welch, Dw. Con. 319. 1966; *T. canadensis* var. *prostrata* Hort. Eng. (in part); NON SENSU Bean, Trees and Shrubs Ed. 7, **3:** 441. 1950.] This popular cultivar is an extremely dwarf form which, unless trained up or grafted on to a stem, grows as a completely prostrate plant. The flattened main branches are mostly bare of leaves at the center of the plant and appear to press themselves against the ground as though held there by suction. (Illustration 453).

The foliage lies in flat sprays. These are much branched and carry leaves roughly parallel-sided, round-ended, 10 × 1.5 mm at base of shoot where they lie flat and pectinate, reducing in length at the tip (where they are irregularly held closer to the shoot) to 5 mm or less. Although so heavily overlaid by later growth the earlier growth holds its foliage surprisingly well, so that the mat of foliage has a very dense appearance except at the areas where the thick old branches lie bare and exposed, forming a ready means of recognition. Well established plants do well in sun, but younger plants are usually best planted in a shaded spot, or shaded until they are well established. This plant was collected by H. R. Cole near the bottom of Mt. Madison, Coos County, New Hampshire, in 1929.

– –'**Curtis Ideal**' Swartley ex Den Ouden and Boom [Man. 453. 1965; Bergm. Pl. and Gar. **21, 1**: 42. 1965] forms an upright to globose bush of rather open and irregular habit with gracefully arching branches and all growing tips pendulous. Leaves to 15 mm by 2 mm but much less on growing shoots, light apple green, loosely appressed to the stems, giving a dainty look to the plant. Mrs. Bergman records a plant 1.25 m high by 1.75 m across at 20 to 25 years. A selection made at Curtis Nurseries, Callicoon, New York. (Illustration 454).

– –'**Curtis Spreader**' Curtis ex Lewis [Amer. Nurs. **114, 2**: 55. 1961; syn. 'Callicoon' Hort. Amer. (in part.)] This is a form in which the branches fan out horizontally with some tendency to weep; the foliage is near to the normal hemlock. Selected and distributed by the Curtis Nurseries, Callicoon, New York, and referred to by Swartley in the 1945 Supplement under the name 'Callicoon'. (Illustration 455).

– –'**Doran**' (Swartley) Bergm. [Pl. and Gar. **21, 1**: 42. 1965.] Described by Bergman as a compact and symmetrical cone, appearing as though sheared. Branches crowded, ascending, tips slightly pendulous. Leaves normal size (12 mm long) closely set, medium green. At 15 years 75 cm high by 90 cm wide. I have not seen it.

– –'**Dwarf White-Tip**' Swartley ex Bergm. [Pl. and Gar. **21, 1**: 42. 1965; 'Whitetip Dwarf' Hillier, Dw. Con. 67. 1964.] A graceful, broadly-conical dwarf, very slow-growing and chiefly remarkable for the colour of its foliage. This unfolds green, becoming white by the summer and turning to yellow in the autumn before returning to green the second year. The mother plant is in the Morris Arboretum, Philadelphia, Pennsylvania, its origin not being on record. (Illustration 456).

– –'**Elm City**' Swartley ex Den Ouden and Boom [Man. 454. 1965.] This is a semi-weeping, spreading bush with several main branches usually broader than high. It is a moderately fast grower, reaching to 3 m in 20 years, and makes a fine isolated specimen where it has room to develop.

– –'**Everitt Golden**' Swartley ex Den Ouden and Boom [Man. 454. 1965; var. *Aurea Everitt* Swartley ex Jenkins, Heml. Arb. Bull. **18**: 3. 1937.] This slowly forms a stiff, open bush or small tree with ascending branches and dense foliage, the leaves being light golden in spring, greenish-yellow through the summer and turning a bronzy-yellow in winter. Good colouring depends upon full exposure to the sun and is best in cold winters. At 20 years, Bergman's plant is 1.5 m high by 1 m across.

– –'**Fantana**' Swartley ex Den Ouden and Boom [Man. 454. 1965.] This attractive clone forms a plant twice as wide as high. The main branches rise steeply at first but arch over so that all growing tips are pendulous. The leaves, yellowish-green, held pectinately, continue of uniform length (to 12 mm) almost to the tip of the shoot. Stomatic lines very inconspicuous. Since the main branches are few but their ramification profuse, the bush tends to be built up of a group of wide, curved ostrich-plume-like sprays arranged gracefully relative to each other so as to produce a most pleasing overall effect suggesting the studied irregularity of a carefully arranged bowl of ferns or similar decorative foliage. Bergman says 'At 12 years, 60 cm high, 1 m wide.' (Illustration 457).

– –'Gable Weeping' Swartley ex Den Ouden and Boom [Man. 455. 1965.] As seen at Kingsville Nurseries 1970, this was a bush 1.5 m high by as much through, densely furnished with foliage, but with all the growing tips pendulous, the surface of the bush consisting of vigorous upright shoots arching over at their tips, and pendulous laterals. These give a graceful look to the plant and are of course its means of gaining height. Leaves are narrow and set noticeably close to the shoot, especially towards the tip, 12 mm maximum length, becoming very much less towards the growing tip where there is a cluster of small leaves rather like a child's paint brush. These, and the pendulous ends of every shoot give the plant a graceful appearance in spite of the solidity of the foliage. Selected in the nursery of Joseph B. Gable, Stewartstown, Pennsylvania, U.S.A. (Illustration 458).

– –'Gentsch Variegated' New name [*T. canadensis* '*Variegata Gentsch*' Spingarn, Amer. R. G. S. Bull. **27**: 88. 1969.] As seen in J. W. Spingarn's collection in 1970 this was a flattened globose bush 1.25 m across × 75 cm high, of very dense growth, with the young shoots everywhere radiating outwards from the centre of the plant. The annual growth averages 8 cm at the sides but is noticeably less at the crown of the plant.

The leaves for the basal quarter of the shoot are quite normal, tapered and round-tipped, up to 10 mm × 1.5 mm, but above that point in every shoot they change character completely, all the upper leaves being very small (averaging 5 mm × 0.75 mm) and creamy-white in colour. Leaves on main shoots are very widely spaced, on laterals they are closer and every growing tip terminates in a small cluster of appressed imbricate leaves. Because of this leaf arrangement the shoots are well exposed and being of a medium brown-red and very numerous, they are very conspicuous.

The tonal effect of the coloured shoots and the clusters of white leaves at their tips, being so numerous as only to leave a suggestion of the green foliage in the interior of the bush, give a most unusual and attractive appearance.

Spingarn says the white tone is most intense in the autumn. It was discovered by a nurseryman, Mr. Otto Gentsch of West Merrick, Long Island, New York.

– –'Green Cascade' Vermeulen [Nurs. Cat. 1972.] A promising new addition introduced by Vermeulen Nursery, Neshanic Station, New Jersey, U.S.A. The original plant, in a block of plants 1.5 to 2 m high, was 45 cm × 45 cm, very dense and having pendulous branches. The foliage is closely set and short. I have not seen it.

– –'Greenspray' Wyman [Arnoldia **23**: 92. 1963.] A seedling mutation of *Tsuga canadensis* first observed in 1942 by Henry J. Hohman in the Kingsville Nurseries, Kingsville, Maryland. This seedling was estimated to be about 20 years old. It has spray-like growths that overlap each growth beneath; the centre is open and shows plainly the development of each growth made, which is unlike the mounded forms of dwarf hemlocks. The effect is a development of green sprays.

– –'Greenwood Lake' Ehrle ex Jenkins [Heml. Arb. Bull. **15**: 3. 1936] is a very slow-growing, congested form with a crowded, irregular branch system. Leaves are 6 mm long by 1.25 mm wide, round at the ends, very irregularly held on the branches, giving a very stunted look to the plant. It is not unlike 'Hussii', but older plants are more compact. This variety originated in five identical plants collected in the wild near Greenwood Lake, New Jersey, and sold to Geo. L. Ehrle. Since one collected plant was carrying cones, a genetic origin is evident.

– –'Horsford Dwarf' Bergm. [Pl. and Gar. **21, 1**: 41. 1965; 'Horsford' Welch, Dw. Con. 320. 1966; (sometimes misspelt *"horosford"*)] makes a congested, squat little bushling with very short, obtuse, crowded leaves and branchlets recurving. The branching system is irregular and the growth is confused and variable. This form tends to put on much looser growth that is out of character, and this should be cut out as soon as it appears. (Illustration 459).

– –'Hussii' [*T. canadensis* var. *Hussi* Jenkins, Heml. Arb. **1**: 3. 1932; *T. canadensis* f. *Hussii* (Swartley) Rehd. Bibl. 648. 1949 *] is a very slow-growing, upright form with very thick, light brown branches and short, twiggy branchlets which frequently form no definite terminals. The short leaves (to 10 mm by 1.5 mm) are dark green above, bluish-white below and closely set. The growth is dense but irregular, so the little tree has a picturesque outline that is characteristic of this popular variety. Originated with a Mr. Huss, Superintendent of Parks, Hartford, Connecticut, U.S.A.

– –'Jacqueline Verkade' Wyman [Arnoldia **29, 4**: 8. 1969.] This is a diminutive form originating in the seed bed at Verkade's Nursery, Wayne, New Jersey, first observed in 1961. When seen in 1970 the mother plant was a small, upright, round-topped plant about 25 cm high, with vertical branching system and foliage reminiscent of *Thuja orientalis* 'Rosedalis'. (Illustration 460).

– –'Jeddeloh' Grootn. [Dendroflora **2**: 49. 1965.] This was a selected seedling on the Jeddeloh nursery, Oldenburg, West Germany. It forms a flattened-globose plant similar to the well known *Picea abies* 'Nidiformis'. It is being widely distributed in Europe, where it is quite hardy. Its ultimate shape and size is, of course, not yet known. (Illustration 461).

– –'Jervis'. See 'Nearing'.

– –'Minima' [*T. canadensis minima* Hesse Nurs. Cat. 1891; *T. canadensis* f. *minima* (Schelle) Rehd. Bibl. 648. 1949 *; 'Bennett' Swartley, Thesis Suppl. 5. 1945; 'Bennett's Minima' Hort. Amer.] Despite its name, this is by no means the smallest form in cultivation. It is a dainty, slow-growing form with ascending branches and branchlets arching over with their tops drooping to -10°. Leaves (up to 15 mm by 2 mm) are closely set on the shoots. It is suitable for a large rock garden as it will ultimately develop into a fair sized plant. (Illustration 462).

According to Den Ouden and Boom [Man. 460. 1965] 'Minima' was a clone raised by Herman A. Hesse, nurseryman of Weener-on Ems in Germany. Swartley traces the history of 'Bennett' to a plant purchased by one Ralph Lott,

Eatontown, New Jersey, from a one-time nurseryman named Bennett who received it in a consignment of 'Chinese' hemlocks ordered from Japan about 1920. He now writes "I am unable to separate 'Minima' and 'Bennett'." So it will need a bold man to say they differ and we can safely recognise but a single cultivar. The earlier European name has priority.

– –'**Minuta**' [*T. canadensis minuta* Teuscher, New Flora and Silva **7**: 274. 1935; *T. canadensis* f. *minuta* (Teuscher) Rehd. Bibl. 648. 1949 *; NON *T. canadensis minuta* Jenkins, Heml. Arb. Bull. **62**. 3. 1948; NON 'Abbotts Pigmy Hemlock' Teuscher, Pl. & Gar. **5, 3**; 141. 1949.] The different origins of and the confusion often found between this and 'Abbotts Pigmy' are given under that cultivar.

'Minuta' is so slow-growing that it can never become in good supply, so it is outstanding as a connoisseur's plant. It forms an exceedingly dwarf, congested little plant of quite irregular branching habit, usually about as broad as high and very slow-growing (annual growth about 2 cm) with crowded long-oval leaves, mostly supra-planate, with bluntly rounded tips, shorter and more crowded than normal hemlock and medium in colour. The statement sometimes made that it never makes enough growth to propagate from cuttings is nonsense.

– –'**Nearing**' Swartley ex Den Ouden and Boom [Man. 460. 1965; 'Jervis' Bergm. Pl. and Gar. **21, 1**: 43. 1965.] Similar to 'Hussii' but slower growing and more twiggy, maintaining a more compact habit as it grows older; branchlets crowded, irregularly arranged, terminal growth congested, winter buds thickened with a corkscrew effect. The original plant was discovered by G. G. Nearing in a wooded area between Port Jervis, Pennsylvania, and Montague, New Jersey. (Illustration 463).

– –'**Palomino**' Spingarn [Amer. R.G.S. Bull. **27**: 88. 1969.] This plant forms a very dwarf, compact, globose bushlet. The leaves are small and the branches and branchlets very thin and flexible. The buds are hairy. The parent plant is owned by Mr. Paul Palomino of Long Island who received it from Otto Gentsch. It is now 21 years old and measures 33 cm high and 55 cm across.

– – f. **pendula** (Beissn.) Rehd. [Bibl. 17. 1949 *.] *Forms of more or less normal arboreal habit but distinguished by having all their terminal growths markedly pendulous.*

A number of pendulous forms of tree-like dimensions have come into cultivation. Pendulous forms will turn up at any time in the seed beds, and these forms come fairly true from seed, so their number is legion, but only a few have been selected and named as cultivars. Although I have intentionally left proposals for any grouping of the cultivars to Swartley, the general plan of this book suggests acceptance of this botanical *forma* and the use of its name for the PENDULA GROUP.

In his second edition Hornibrook gives the history of four of such plants found near the summit of the Fishkill Mountains by General Joseph Howland about 1870 and in an article entitled 'The Four Fathers of the Sargent Hemlock' in the American trade journal *American Nurseryman* of the 15th December 1962, Alfred J. Fordham brings the account up to date. He gives an excellent picture of the plant which went to Charles Sprague Sargent of Brookline, Boston, Massachusetts (Hornibrook's plant No. 4). This he states is now about 9 m in diameter, well and thriving, and well cared for by its present owner Mrs. Roger

Ernst. It has developed a horizontal system of branches which has built up into the form of a broad mound, new growths following the contour of the branches underneath in a dense thatch of foliage.

Mr. Fordham also gives a picture of a tree in the Arnold Arboretum, grafted in 1881, which can be traced to the tree planted by General Howland in his own garden at Matteawan (Hornibrook's plant No. 1) and he tells me that the old Parsons Nursery which existed at Flushing, sent a propagator up to Matteawan to procure material from the original tree which was the only one to be widely propagated.

The Arnold Arboretum tree has developed into an open, multi-stemmed, umbrella-shaped tree 10 m in diameter and about 4.5 m tall on a framework of trunk and heavy branches arising at angles, giving more elevation and less density to this tree than in the Brookline form.

We can therefore deal with this group as follows:

– –'**Brookline**' Welch. [Dw. Con. 323. 1966] PENDULA GROUP. The form of which the original tree, Hornibrook's No. 4, is available as the type.

– –'**Sargentii**' [*T. canadensis sargentii* Parsons, Nurs. Cat. 59. 1896; var. *sargentiana* Kent in Veitch, Ed. 2, 465. 1900 (Desc. taken from a young plant); var. *Sargentii* Bean, Trees, **2**: 606. 1914.] PENDULA GROUP. The form represented by the Arnold Arboretum tree, above. (Hornibrook's Tree No. 1.) (Illustration 464).

– –'**Pendula**' [*T. canadensis* var. *pendula* Beissn. Zierg. Ed. 2, 445. 1884; Bean, Trees, **2**: 606. 1914; var. *prostrata* Bean, Trees. Ed. **7**, **3**: 441. 1950.] In *Trees and Shrubs Hardy in the British Isles* W. J. Bean uses the three names vars. *pendula, prostrata* and *sargentii*. All the plants that I have seen in this country answer to the description given by Bean to his var. *pendula*—'A very attractive bush or small tree forming a hemispherical mass of pendulous branches, completely hiding the interior' and as they answer to the description of neither the Brookline plant nor the Matteawan form they must be assumed to have originated in another seedling— whether one of Hornibrook's trees 2 and 3 already dead in 1937 or not will probably never be known. The English form needs training to form a leader to the required height and in the absence of such training would form a plant exactly answering to Bean's var. *prostrata,* which cannot therefore be viewed as a valid name. I consider that the material in Britain is sufficiently homogeneous to justify the retention of the name 'Pendula' cultivarwise. Any new selections should be registered under new cultivar names. Since the Group name is available there would be no need for any new cultivar names to include the descriptive word 'Pendula' or its equivalent. (Illustration 465).

– – *"prostrata"*. This is an unsatisfactory name which should no longer be used. Small plants I have seen in English nurseries were 'Coles Prostrate' and the plant referred to by Bean [Trees & Shrubs, Ed. **7**. **3**: 441. 1950] was probably a plant of 'Pendula' (i.e., not a dwarf) that had not been stem-trained when young.

– – *"pygmaea"*. See 'Abbotts Pigmy'.

– –'**Ruggs Washington Dwarf**' Hillier [Dw. Con. 66. 1964.] A dense globose to cushion-shaped plant with congested growth. Foliage bronzy-yellow, especially in spring. One of the best small garden forms, said to have been introduced by Ralph M. Warner of Milford, Connecticut, U.S.A.

– –'Starker' New name [*T. canadensis* 'Minuta Pendula' Bergm. Pl. & Gar. **21, 1:** 44. 1965; Spingarn, Amer. R.G.S. Bull. **27, 3:** 87. 1969; 'Starker's Pendula' and 'West Coast Creeper' Hort. Amer.] PENDULA GROUP. As seen at Kingsville Nurseries, Kingsville, Maryland, U.S.A., in 1970 this was a spreading variety of medium vigour with main branches standing up at 30°, terminals and main laterals arching over to -80°. Foliage is fairly vigorous with long leaves (to 15 mm × 1.5 mm) rounded or bluntly tipped at the end and covering all but the main branches. Branching system is in flat sprays with several short lateral shoots on the current year's growth up to 35 cm, usually much less. It was raised from seed by Carl Starker. (Illustration 466).

– –'Verkade Petite' Wyman [Arnoldia **29, 1:** 8. 1969.] This extremely diminutive form was found as a seedling and introduced by Verkades Nursery, Wayne, New Jersey, U.S.A. It forms a congested little globe of dense growth, reaching only 5 cm by 8 cm across in 16 years, with an annual growth of only a few millimetres. It is winter hardy but burns in full sunlight. With so slow a rate of growth it can never be anything but a collectors' item, but in spring when all its tiny buds open into pale green foliage it is very beautiful.

– –'Verkade Recurved' Wyman [Arnoldia. **29, 1:** 8. 1969.] This is another introduction by Verkades Nursery. It was originally received by them as a malformed plant, but has developed into an attractive specimen with recurved needles on its branches not at all resembling what is normal to the species.

– –'Von Helms' Bergm. Pl. & Gar. **21, 1:** 42. 1965; *T. canadensis* var. 'Von Helms Dwarf', Swartley, Thesis. 1939. 212 and Suppl. 40. 1945.] A dwarf form raised in the Wm. Von Helms Nursery, Monsey, New York, U.S.A. It forms a dense, somewhat irregular, blunt-topped cone. Branches ascending, the tips slightly pendulous. Branchlets very crowded. Leaves much longer and broader than normal, very dark green. At 20 years 90 cm high by as much wide.

– –'Warners Globe' Hillier [List conif. 13. 1970; as 'Warners globosa' Dw. Con. 67. 1964.] As seen at the Arnold Arboretum in September 1970, this was a plant 80 cm high by 50 cm diam., an upright-oval bush of rather irregular outline with a very irregular arrangement of main branches standing up at a steep angle with all the terminal growths lying at ± 5°, an arrangement which, together with the leaves, gives the bush a very much solider appearance looked at from above than seen from the side. Leaves are 15 mm × 2 mm, gradually tapering to a rounded end, dark green above and below, with two very narrow stomatic bands beneath, widely spaced (especially the row along the top of the shoot) and reducing in size towards the tip of the shoot, where the leaves, pointing forward, cover but do not hide the terminal bud cluster. The terminal shoots are thick, are a dark mahogany-brown and are very conspicuous. At the time the description was made, the plant had put out new (secondary) foliage here and there all over the bush which was light green and this, against the dark green of the older leaves and the brown of the shoots, together with the neat outline and denseness of the bush, made a very attractive garden form. (Illustration 467).

– –'Watnong Star' Hebb [Arnoldia **30, 6:** 260. 1970.] This was found as a chance seedling in the woods in New Hampshire by Robert Clark of Rochester, New York, in 1958 and registered by Watnong Nursery. When I saw it at the nursery the mother plant was a rounded bush 1 m high and as much across, very densely furnished with growths having all the tips radiating outwards, similar to *Picea mariana* 'Nana', disguising the flat shape of the one year sprays. The leaves are about 12 mm, tapering to a fairly sharp point, reducing in size towards the tips. But apart from the neat, round, densely furnished appearance of the plant (in itself distinctly attractive), Mr. Don Smith told me that its outstanding feature is the silvery-white colour of the young growths which has suggested the name. (Illustration 468).

Tsuga caroliniana Engel. Caroline hemlock. Normally a tall tree, distinct for its slender, dark green, spikey, blunt-ended leaves not very closely set and red-brown shoots and squat red-brown buds.

– – var. **compacta** Hornb. [Dw. Con. 186. 1923.] This name was used by Hornibrook for a particular clone that outgrew its claim to the description. It should now only be used (if at all) as a collective or group name for slow-growing seedlings of this variable species.

– –'**La Bar Weeping**' [New cv.] As shewn to me by Layne Ziegenfuss at Hillside Gardens, Lehighton, Pensylvania, in 1970, this was an interesting plant, 1.0 m across by 65 cm high, with dense foliage and a weeping habit similar to *Cedrus libani* 'Sargentii'. (Illustration 469).

Tsuga diversifolia (Maxim) Mast. Northern Japanese hemlock. This species, usually little more than a bush in cultivation, has short, broad and blunt leaves.

– –'**Gotelli**' [New cv.] Habit dense and irregular with annual growth less than 25 mm long. Leaves shorter than the typical *T. diversifolia*. An old plant in the Gotelli collection in the U. S. National Arboretum was 60 cm high and 90 cm broad. Mr. Gotelli received this plant from the Thompson Nurseries in New Zealand; it is supposedly close to 70 years old. It was mistakenly labelled *T. sieboldii nana*. (Illustration 470).

Tsuga heterophylla (Raf.) Sargent. Western hemlock. A tall, usually conical, strong-growing species with leaves in two sets, of different sizes along the shoot.

– –'**Iron Springs**' [New cv.] A bushy plant with wide-spreading branches that may grow more upright with age; leaves shorter than typical *T. heterophylla*, 5-12 mm long. According to a letter from Joseph Witt, Acting Director of the University of Washington Arboretum, the mother plant was about 50 cm in height and breadth in 1972. It was discovered by Mr. Ainsworth Bogg on the coast of Washington near Iron Springs.

Tsuga mertensiana (Bongard) Carrière. Mountain hemlock. Leaves at first giving the appearance of a cedar.

– –'**Cascade**' [New cv.] A slow-growing, very compact plant resembling a dwarf Alberta Spruce, discovered at the 4000 foot level in the Cascade Mountains in the headwaters of the North Umpqua River, Douglas County, Oregon. In the spring of 1973 the plant was 4 m high with a trunk diameter of 20 cm at the base.

The annual growth is 35 to 50 mm and the leaves are shorter and more densely set than typical *T. mertensiana*. The discoverer is J. D. Vertrees, Roseburg, Oregon.

– –'**Elizabeth**' [New cv.] A spreading plant, about twice as broad as high. According to a letter from Harold Epstein, January 20, 1972, the original plant was collected by Mrs. Elsie Frye's daughter, Elizabeth, on Mt. Rainier. Mr. James Caperci of the Rainier Mountain Nursery, Seattle, Washington, claims he has the original plant, 60 cm high and 1.25 m. wide in 1971. Don Smith, Morris Plains, New Jersey, supplied some of this information. 'Elizabeth' is the only recorded spreading variant of Mountain hemlock. It is an attractive plant.

– –'**Glauca**' [*T. mertensiana glauca* Hesse, Nurs. Cat. 33. 1950/51.] A form described by Boom as dwarf and very slow-growing; leaves radial, distinctly glaucous. It becomes a small tree in time.

– – "*nana*" [*T. mertensiana* 'Nana' Welch, Dw. Con. 323. 1966.] I introduced this into my previous book on the strength of a letter from Wm. T. Gotelli. Referring again to that letter I see Gotelli says that his plant is the only specimen he has ever seen, so it does not technically qualify for recognition as a cultivar, and as Swartley writes that he does not know any such form, the name is no longer worth retention. Cuttings from *T. mertensiana* are often very slow-growing and bushy, but they doubtless develop a leader and become arboreal sooner or later.

– –**Sherwood Compact**' [*T. mertensiana compacts* Sherwood, Amer. Nurs. **133, 2**: 65. 1971.] Robert Snodgrass of the Sherwood Nursery Company, Portland, Oregon, supplied some information in a letter of February 7, 1972. 'This is an extremely slow-growing, dense, irregular, very attractive hemlock. Grafted plants are about 60 cm high in 15 years. It is presumably the same clone that Andrew W. Sherwood reported finding in 1943 at timber line on Mt. Hood. [Hemlock Arboretum Bull. No. 17, 1943.] At this time, the original plant was 1.5 m high and wide'.

CHAPTER SIX
PESTS AND DISEASES

This chapter will fortunately be a short one because the pests and diseases associated with dwarf conifers are few and they are very simply controlled.

I have dealt in other chapters with the adverse action of frost, wind and strong sunlight, but in this very specialized book I cannot attempt to cover all the hazards of modern garden life with which our poor plants have to deal. Readers must turn elsewhere for information on how to deal with such things as slugs, ants, wood lice, human feet (of all sizes), careless reversing and so forth, but I ought perhaps to give a warning on the subject of cats and dogs. These, the latter especially, can soon do great damage to the foliage of conifers which quickly gets 'browned off' by their attentions. Dogs, in particular, once they have decided that a certain plant is a suitable substitute for a lamp post, return to it each time they are passing.

The remedy depends upon whether the animals in question belong to yourself or to your neighbours. If they are your own, the remedy is simple; give them away or have them put to sleep. If the offending animals are trespassers, the best remedy is a supply of pea gravel and a good catapult. Two or three direct hits at the psychological moment will soon persuade your friend of there being some connection between sudden pain and that particular bush, and he will learn to transfer his attentions elsewhere, none the worse for his lesson.

Whenever there is an attack by pest or disease, conifers always advertise their distress to a watchful eye, and any tree looking at all off colour or dull in appearance should at once be closely examined for the cause. Scale shows itself by the characteristic patches on the stems and I have found Taxus to be the most prone to attack. An invasion by aphis, red spider and mites of any kind, too small to see with the naked eye, will cause the foliage to look dull and lacking in the colour and rich lustre which is characteristic of a healthy conifer. This if unchecked leads to discoloration of the foliage and possibly the death of the tree. These pests will increase on a plant very rapidly during the spring and summer and quickly spread to other plants so a watch should be kept and as soon as any tree looks off colour a spray of some kind is indicated. A number of suitable compounds are available. In the nursery here I use a spray containing Demeton-Methyl, better known under its trade name Metasystox, but this is not available in small quantities to the public who can however obtain a somewhat similar product called Dimethoate, more usually known under its trade name as Rogor. (Both of these are Organo-phosphorus compounds, to be used—and stored— with a due sense of responsibility for the harm they can do if wrongly used.)

These are both what is known as systemic insecticides, which means that if any part of the plant is wetted by the spray the chemical is absorbed into the sap which kindly takes over the task of distributing it to all parts of the plant and aphis, red spider and any sucking insects are quickly killed. The effect is very rapid, insect life being destroyed within hours, but if the foliage has already become discolored it will never regain its healthy appearance: evidence of freedom from the pest must therefore be looked for in the new leaves at the growing tips. I have found the Junipers and the Spruces most liable to be affected, and as the latter hold their leaves for two seasons, two years must elapse before the results of an attack will have disappeared, even although the attack itself has been dealt with. It is a good plan to follow up with a second spraying a week or two later. This will deal with any pest that has survived the first treatment and dispose of any further infestation subsequently hatched out.

Other effective sprays are available containing one or other of the chemicals BHC, malathion or the well tried natural compound Derris, with or without Pyrethrum. These are of course sold under trade or brand names, but the active ingredient is usually disclosed or will be known by your chemist or other supplier.

There are dozens of species of these very small insects known to entomologists but as each of the above sprays seems to be effective in dealing with the lot, most gardeners will not be concerned with the identification in detail of their particular pest and so this is all the space that I really need to give to the subject, but having got this far I felt that I had not covered the subject very thoroughly. In particular I considered that any of the many diseases and pests of coniferous woodlands might possibly at any time descend to the attack of dwarf forms especially in any gardens situated near pine woods. I therefore consulted a plant pathologist friend of mine for advice as to standard textbooks to which I could refer my readers and I feel that I cannot do better than to pass on his recommendations.

The first was a book entitled *Pathology of Trees and Shrubs* by T. R. Peace. This book covers diseases of temperate forests and ornamental trees and shrubs including those caused by fungi, bacteria, viruses and non-living agencies such as frost and wind. It is not a book that I could recommend for a weekend, for it is 3 in. thick, but if you are prepared to take it away for your annual holiday and really stick at it for a fortnight, it should set you up for the rest of your lifetime as an accredited authority on these subjects amongst all your gardening acquaintances. One thing in particular that struck me very much in reading it was the large number of fungal diseases or rusts that spend part of their life cycle on this or that conifer and the rest of it on an entirely different host plant. This may be another conifer, or (according to the preference of the particular fungus) a poplar, currant, prunus, rhododendron, or even (of all things) groundsel. This only shows how much more important thorough weeding has been than we have ever believed or acted upon!

After having tackled this book, you will find *Insects of the British Woodlands* by R. Neil Chrystal, M.A., D.SC., relatively easy going, as this is a bare inch thick. It, too, deals very thoroughly with its subject and from it you should be able to identify any insect invasion you may experience, but it does not deal in any detail with the methods of control. If the insecticides already recommended do not do the trick help can doubtless be obtained in Britain, from your local County Council Agricultural Adviser, and about February of each year the Ministry of Agriculture, Fisheries and Food produce a *List of Approved Products for Farmers and Growers* under the *Agricultural Chemicals Approval Scheme* containing very full details of all the chemicals available under the Scheme, with their uses and limitations. This list, I understand, can always be consulted at any sub-office of the Ministry and a copy is in most Reference Libraries, and as the development of chemical insecticides is constantly on the change, readers of this book will by studying the current list be able to keep themselves up to date even should the recommendations in this chapter become obsolete.

Similar sources of advice doubtless are available in other countries throughout the conifer-speaking world.

SELECT BIBLIOGRAPHY

It would be impracticable to include full bibliographical references to every publication cited. Many of these are more or less rare or obscure works, only available in large botanic libraries (where the abbreviated citations given in Chapter V would be readily understood by the library staff.)

The following are the principal works used in preparing the present work that are likely to be readily available to the general reader. The language, where other than English, is given in parentheses.

Bailey, L H.   1923 The Cultivated Evergreens. (United States)
                      1933 The Cultivated Conifers of North America (and numerous other works.)

Bean, W. J.   1914 Trees & Shrubs Hardy in the British Isles. (and later editions.)

Bergman, Helene M.   1965 Article on 'Dwarf Conifers' in special issue of 'Plants & Gardens' (Handbooks issued by Brooklyn Botanic Garden, New York, U.S.A.)

Beissner, L.   1891 Handbuch der Nadelhölzkunde. (German)
                     1909 Handbuch der Nadelhölzkunde. (German) 2nd Edition
                     1930 Handbuch der Nadelhölzkunde. (German) 3rd Edition edited by W. Fitschen. (And several other works from 1883 onwards.)

Boom, B. K.   1942 Nederlandse Dendrologie, 2nd Edition. (Dutch) (See also under den Ouden & Boom.)

Carrière, E. A.   1855 Traité Générale des Conifères. (French)
                     1867 Traité Générale des Conifères. (French) 2nd Edition

Dallimore, W.   1908 Holly, Yew and Box.
Dallimore, W. and   1923 Handbook of Coniferae & Ginkgoaceae. (and
  Jackson, A. B.   later editions.)

Den Ouden, P.   1933 Naamlist van Coniferen. (Dutch)
                     1949 Coniferen, Ephedra, Ginkgo. (Dutch)
Den Ouden, P. and   1965 Manual of Cultivated Conifers.
  Boom, B. K.
Endlicher, S.   1847 Synopsis Coniferarum. (Latin)

Fitschen, W.	1930	See Beissner, L.
Gordon, G.	1858	The Pinetum. (Also 1862—Supplement.)
	1875	The Pinetum, 2nd Edition.
Hillier, H. G.	1964	Dwarf Conifers. (Report of Third International Rock Garden Conference, 1961.)
	1970	List of conifers in the Hillier collection at the time of the Royal Horticultural Society Conifer Conference.
	1971	Manual of Trees and Shrubs. (and later editions.)
Hoopes, J.	1868	The Book of Evergreens. (United States)
Hornibrook, M.	1923	Dwarf and Slow-growing Conifers.
	1938	Dwarf and Slow-growing Conifers. 2nd Edition.
	1932	See Royal Horticultural Society.
Jenkins, C. F.	1939-51	Hemlock Arboretum Bulletin. (United States)
Kent, A. H.	1900	Veitch's Manual of Coniferae, 2nd Edition.
Knight and Perry	1850	Synopsis of the Coniferous Plants
Kobayashi, Y. *et al.*	1975	Matsu-zukan. (Pines—Illustrated.) (Japanese)
Krüssman, G.	1960	Die Nadelgehölze. 2nd Edition. (German)
	1972	Handbuch der Nadelgehölze. (German)
Kumlien, K. K.	1946	The Friendly Evergreens. (United States)
Loudon, J. C.	1838	Arboretum et Fruticetum Brittanicum.
	1842	Encyclopedia of Trees & Shrubs.
Mayr, H.	1890	Monographie der Abietineen des Japanischen Reiches. (German)
Melle, P. J. van	1947	Review of Juniperus chinensis *et al.* (United States)
Nicholson, G.	1884-8	Illustrated Dictionary of Gardening (and Supplement 1900.)
Rehder, A.	1927	Manual of Trees & Shrubs. (United States)
	1940	Manual of Trees & Shrubs. (United States) 2nd Edition.
	1949	Bibliography of Cultivated Trees & Shrubs.
Royal Horticultural Society	1932	Conifers in Cultivation (Report of Conifer Conference 1931. *Editor:* Chittenden, B.)
	1972	Conifers in the British Isles (Report of Conifer Conference 1970. *Editor:* Napier, Miss E.)
Sénéclause, A.	1867	Les Conifères. (French)
Siebold & Zuccarini	1870	Flora Japonica. (Latin)
Silva Tarouca, E. G.	1913	Unsere Frieland Nadelhölzer. (German)
	1923	Unsere Frieland Nadelhölzer. (German) 2nd Edition.
Slavin, A. D.	1932	See Royal Horticultural Society.
Smith, Richard	1861	Plants of the Fir Tribe. *No copy known to Author.*
	1864	Plants of the Fir Tribe. 2nd Edition. Enlarged and revised (270).

1867 Plants of the Fir Tribe. 3rd Edition (423).
1872 Plants of the Fir Tribe. 4th Edition (451).
1874 Plants of the Fir Tribe. 5th Edition. *No copy known to Author.*

These were issued undated, the above dates being determined from external evidence. Each conifer described being serially numbered, the known editions can be 'dated' from the last numbered entry (given above in brackets.) The late Professor Rehder is known to have used the 4th edition in compiling his *Bibliography* (incorrectly dated.)

Will anyone knowing of the existence of either of the untraced editions please communicate with the present Author at the Wansdyke Nursery, Devizes, Wilts., England.

Veitch, J.   1881 Manual of Conifers (For 2nd Edition, see Kent)
Welch, H. J.   1966 Dwarf Conifers—A Complete Guide.
                    1969 Dwarf Conifers—A Complete Guide. 2nd Edition.
Wilson, H. J.   1916 Conifers and Taxads of Japan. (United States.)

In addition to the above, the following three books, although not claiming to be works of reference, are of great value and interest because of the numerous excellent illustrations of conifers in colour.

Bloom, Adrian. Conifers in your Garden (Floraprint, Nottingham) 1975;
Harrison, Charles R. Ornamental Conifers (David & Charles, Newton Abbot), 1975.
Proudley, Brian and Valerie, Garden Conifers in Colour (Blandford Press, Poole) 1976.

Finally, the *Codes of Nomenclature* must be mentioned. These are the *International Code of Botanical Nomenclature,* March 1972 published for the International Association for Plant Taxonomy, Utrecht, Netherlands and distributed by A. Oosthoek's Uitgeversmaatschappij N.V., Domstraat 5-13, Utrecht, Netherlands and by Stechert-Hafner Service Agency, 1866 Third Ave., New York, N.Y. 10022, U.S.A. and the *International Code* of *Nomenclature of Cultivated Plants* July 1969, obtainable from the International Bureau for Plant Taxonomy and Nomenclature, Tweede Transitorium, Uithof, Utrecht, Netherlands, The American Horticultural Society, 2401 Calvert Street, N.W., Washington D.C. 20008, U.S.A. and The Royal Horticultural Society, Vincent Square, London S.W.1, England.

PLANT PORTRAITS

101. *Abies amabilis* 'Spreading Star'. The mother plant at Blijdenstein Arboretum, Holland. 1.3 m high by 5 m across.

Cultivars of *Abies balsamea* var. *hudsonia*.

102. *Abies balsamea* 'Hudsonia'. 'Nana' forms a globose plant and bears radial foliage. The cultivar 'Hudsonia' has semi-radial foliage, and in 'Prostrata' the leaves are pectinate.

103. *Abies balsamea* 'Nana'.
104. *Abies cephalonica* 'Meyers Dwarf'. 1 m by 75 cm. It may double in size.

105. *Abies concolor* 'Compacta'. A mature plant about 1.5 m high.
106. *Abies concolor* 'Gables Weeping'. A true miniature, ideally suited to pot culture.

107. *Abies concolor* 'Green Globe'. A specimen 75 cm high in the Verkade Nursery, Wayne, New Jersey, U.S.A.
108. *Abies concolor* 'Pigglemee'. Already a little gem at 20 cm across.

109. *Abies homolepis* 'Prostrata'. An attractive specimen 5 m across. More than one clone is in cultivation.

110. *Abies koreana* 'Compact Dwarf'. 1.25 m by 1.0 m high.

111. *Abies koreana* 'Prostrata'. A plant 3 m across.
112. *Abies koreana* 'Starkers Dwarf'. A fine specimen 2.5 m across in the Joel W. Spingarn collection, Baldwin, Long Island, New York, U.S.A.

113. *Abies lasiocarpa* 'Arizonica Compacta'. This young specimen will reach 3 m in time.
114. *Abies procera* 'Prostrata'. A young specimen, capable of spreading to 3 m in time.

115. *Calocedrus decurrens* 'Intricata'. A plant at Hilliers Nursery, Jermyns Lane, Romsey, Hampshire, England. 1 m by 50 cm.

116. *Cedrus deodara* 'Nana'. A specimen 2 m across at Arboretum Les Barres, France.

117. *Cedrus deodara* 'Pygmy'. So slow-growing that this plant at 15 cm is a veteran.

118. *Cedrus libani* 'Nana'. A specimen 1 m by 1.5 m across. Often seen with a more upright habit.

119. *Cedrus libani* 'Sargentii'. A mature specimen about 2 m across. Height depends upon stem-training the young plant.

120. *Cephalotaxus harringtonia* 'Fastigiata'. Note the spreading branches—best cut out so as to secure a truly fastigiate plant.

121. *Cephalotaxus harringtonia* 'Prostrata'. A plant 1.5 m across, capable of doubling this size.

122. *Cephalotaxus harringtonia* 'Drupacea'. A specimen 4 m x 5 m across in the National Pinetum, Bedgebury, Kent, England.

123. *Chamaecyparis lawsoniana* 'Aurea Densa'. A mature plant 1 m x 50 cm, with the characteristic blunt top.
124. *Chamaecyparis lawsoniana* 'Minima Aurea'. Difficult to distinguish from 'Aurea Densa' when small.

125. *Chamaecyparis lawsoniana* 'Dows Gem'. This young plant will reach several metres in time.

126. *Chamaecyparis lawsoniana* 'Duncanii'. The original importation at Castlewellan, County Down, Northern Ireland. 5 m x 2 m.

127. *Chamaecyparis lawsoniana* 'Ellwoodii'. A specimen of this popular 'dwarf' conifer, now about 2 m tall and beginning to grow rapidly.

128. *Chamecyparis lawsoniana* 'Ellwoods Pygmy'. A very old plant in the Wansdyke Nursery, Devizes, Wiltshire. 75 cm x 1 m.

129. *Chamaecyparis lawsoniana* 'Filiformis Compacta'. A mature plant 1.5 m at the Royal Horticultural Society's garden at Wisley.

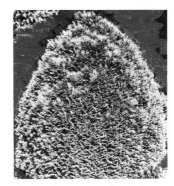

130. *Chamaecyparis lawsoniana* 'Forsteckensis'. A typical plant, about 50 cm. Anything tighter is usually the result of regular pruning.

131. *Chamaecyparis lawsoniana* 'Gimbornii'. Recognisable by its foliage and the dull mauve growth tips at certain seasons. 1.5 m.

132. *Chamaecyparis lawsoniana* 'Gnome'. The mother plant when at Warnham Court, Sussex, England. The matchbox gives the scale.

133. *Chamaecyparis lawsoniana* 'Lycopodioides'. Eventually of tree-like stature. It is of interest for its curious foliage.

134. *Chamaecyparis lawsoniana* 'Minima Glauca'. A well grown specimen about 1 m, of characteristic rounded crown.

135. *Chamaecyparis lawsoniana* 'Nana'. A plant 2 m at Hilliers Nursery, Jermyns Lane, Romsey, Hampshire.

136. *Chamaecyparis lawsoniana* 'Nana Albospica'. A young plant 75 cm.
137. *Chamaecyparis lawsoniana* 'Nidiformis'. A plant 2 m across.

138. *Chamaecyparis lawsoniana* 'Pygmaea Argentea'. A very fine old specimen. The growing tips are creamy-white. 1 m.
139. *Chamaecyparis lawsoniana* 'Tamariscifolia'. There are several clones in cultivation. This plant is at Grayswood Hill, Haslemere, Surrey, England.

140. *Chamaecyparis nootkatensis* 'Compacta'. 1.5 m × 1 m across.
141. *Chamaecyparis nootkatensis* 'Nidifera'. Note the foliage difference from *Chamaecyparis lawsoniana* 'Nidiformis'.

142. *Chamaecyparis obtusa* 'Caespitosa'. Rounded, blue-green foliage sprays.

143. *Chamaecyparis obtusa* 'Coralliformis'. Distinctive foliage. Seldom exceeds 1.5 m.
144. *Chamaecyparis obtusa* 'Chabo-yadori'. Specimens usually shew more patches of adult foliage, especially as they age.

145. *Chamaecyparis obtusa* 'Filicoides'. Usually seen as an open and rather straggling small tree.

146. *Chamaecyparis obtusa* 'Intermedia'. As its name suggests, intermediate in vigour. Foliage dark green.
147. *Chamaecyparis obtusa* 'Juniperoides'. Growth varies from year to year. To see any similarity to a juniper requires some imagination.
148. *Chamaecyparis obtusa* 'Juniperoides Compacta'. Another variable form, but always a little tighter than 'Juniperoides'.

149. *Chamaecyparis obtusa* 'Kosteri'. A well grown specimen 1.5 m high in the Arboretum Trompenburg, Rotterdam, Holland.
150. *Chamaecyparis obtusa* 'Lycopodioides'. 'Lycopodioides Aurea' differs only in colour, sharing the same coarse, bloated foliage.

151. *Chamaecyparis obtusa* 'Mariesii'. Seldom if ever seen over 1 m. All the growing tips are creamy-white.
152. *Chamaecyparis obtusa*. The mother plants of some of Joel W. Spingarn's seedlings, hardy in New York. 'Dainty Doll'. A conical plant 25 by 20 cm.

153. – –'Golden Sprite'. Now a golden bun 15 by 15 cm.
154. – –'Golden Filament'. 25 by 15 cm.

155. *Chamaecyparis obtusa* 'Minima'. Two mature, open ground specimens in the Royal Botanic Garden, Edinburgh.

156. *Chamaecyparis obtusa* 'Nana'. The true form is very slow-growing, a dull, dark green.

157. *Chamaecyparis obtusa* 'Nana Compacta'. More free-growing than 'Nana' and with foliage a bright, rich mid-green.

158. *Chamaecyparis obtusa* 'Nana Gracilis'. The well known popular form with dense foliage in twisted, glossy, deep green sprays.

159. *Chamaecyparis obtusa* 'Nana Lutea'. A plant 20 cm in the Arboretum Tempelhof, Holland.

160. *Chamaecyparis obtusa* 'Pygmaea'. A fine specimen 90 cm across at the Wansdyke Nursery, Devizes, Wiltshire.

161. *Chamaecyparis obtusa* 'Repens'. Another prostrate form, much more vigorous than 'Pygmaea'.

162. *Chamaecyparis obtusa* 'Tetragona Aurea'. The foliage is a rich old gold in full sunlight. A plant 1.5 m high.

163. *Chamaecyparis obtusa* 'Torulosa'. The foliage of this form is intermediate between 'Coralliformis' and 'Lycopodioides'.

164. *Chamaecyparis pisifera* 'Compacta Variegata'. Sometimes seen as a large bush. The variegation is in irregular patches of butter-yellow.

165. *Chamaecyparis pisifera* 'Filifera Nana'. The spreading habit distinguishes this form from its tall-growing counterpart 'Filifera'.

166. *Chamaecyparis pisifera* 'Nana'. Distinct from 'Compacta' only in vigour and leaf size.

167. *Chamaecyparis pisifera* 'Plumosa Aurea'. Several clones are in commercial cultivation. The best form keeps its golden-yellow colour through the winter.

168. *Chamaecyparis pisifera* 'Plumosa Aurea Compacta'. Has wholly juvenile foliage and always makes a round-topped plant, which breaks up as it ages. 'Plumosa Rogersii' with similar foliage always makes a conical little plant.

169. *Chamaecyparis pisifera* 'Plumosa Compressa'. A nice specimen 50 cm across in the Slieve Donard Nursery, County Down, Northern Ireland.

170. *Chamaecyparis pisifera* 'Plumosa Juniperoides'. Similar to, but distinct from 'Plumosa Compressa' in foliage, and making a taller plant.

171. *Chamaecyparis pisifera* 'Snow'. A fairly new introduction from Japan. When it is happy, the tiny white-tipped foliage is unmistakeable.

172. *Chamaecyparis pisifera* 'Squarrosa Dumosa'. The best dwarf of the 'Squarrosa' group. A plant 60 cm high at the Wansdyke Nursery, Devizes, Wiltshire.
173. *Chamaecyparis pisifera* 'Squarrosa Intermedia'. As it should appear. Badly reverted specimens are, however, not uncommon.

174. *Chamaecyparis pisifera* 'Squarrosa Sulphurea'. A tree 1.75 m high of characteristic shape. The colour in spring is well described by the name.
175. *Chamaecyparis thyoides* 'Andelyensis'. Rarely seen over 2 m high, but much larger plants are to be found.

176. *Chamaecyparis thyoides* 'Andelyensis Nana'. Distinctive by its shape and the absence of upright leader growth.
177. *Chamaecyparis thyoides* 'Ericoides'. A plant 85 cm high. Dark green foliage, plum-purple in autumn and winter.
178. *Cryptomeria japonica* 'Araucarioides'. A typical young plant showing the strong leader-growth characteristic of this form. It reaches tree-size in time.

179. *Cryptomeria japonica* 'Bandai-sugi'. Seldom seen over 1 m. The irregularity of growth is characteristic.

180. *Cryptomeria japonica* 'Cristata'. Not, of course, a dwarf form. The fasciations are sometimes as large as a man's hand.

181. *Cryptomeria japonica* 'Kilmacurragh'. Confused by Hornibrook with 'Cristata'. The two forms are quite distinct. Reaches to 5 m eventually.

182. *Cryptomeria japonica* 'Elegans Compacta'. Seldom seen over 2 m. The foliage is very soft to the touch. Plum-purple in winter.

183. *Cryptomeria japonica* 'Elegans Nana'. Quite distinct from 'Elegans Compacta'. The clusters of male flowers shew clearly.

184. *Cryptomeria japonica* 'Globosa Nana'. Not particularly well named. The foliage has (unlike 'Spiralis') no tendency to twist.
185. *Cryptomeria japonica* 'Jindai-sugi'. A large plant (2.5 m) in a garden at Boskoop, Holland.

186. *Cryptomeria japonica* 'Knaptonensis'. Unmistakeable by its glistening white-tipped congested foliage.
187. *Cryptomeria japonica* 'Monstrosa'. Always a much larger plant than 'Bandai-sugi', with much coarser foliage.

188. *Cryptomeria japonica* 'Nana'. An upright bush, seldom seen over 2 m, with light green foliage.
189. *Cryptomeria japonica* 'Spiralis'. The well known 'Granny's Ringlets'. Slow-growing, but it makes a large plant in the end.

190. *Cryptomeria japonica* 'Spiraliter Falcata'. Readily distinguishable from 'Spiralis'.
191. *Cryptomeria japonica* 'Vilmoriniana' is deservedly popular. It always makes a neat little plant, seldom reaching 75 cm.

192. *Cryptomeria japonica* 'Viminalis'. The clusters of foliage are characteristic.
193. *Cunninghamia lanceolata* 'Compacta'. The foliage is like the normal tree but smaller in every way.

194. *Cupressus glabra* 'Compacta'. A fine specimen nearly 1 m across in the Wansdyke Nursery at Devizes, Wiltshire.
195. *Cupressus macrocarpa* 'Golden Pillar'. This is the only golden macrocarpa to justify inclusion here.

196. *Cupressus macrocarpa* 'Minima'. The mother plant, now 1 m across, at the Wansdyke Nursery, Devizes, Wiltshire.
197. *Cupressus macrocarpa* 'Pygmaea'. Carries wholly adult foliage. 10 by 10 cm.

198. *Cupressus macrocarpa* 'Woking'. Carries juvenile foliage. 15 by 10 cm.
199. *Dacrydium laxifolium*. A specimen 15 cm across in the Royal Botanic Garden, Edinburgh.
200. *Juniperus chinensis* 'Echiniformis'. A well grown plant in Alpengarten Belvedere, Vienna, Austria. 25 cm.

201. The sub-form 'Belvedere' differs only in its hemispherical habit.

202. *Juniperus chinensis* 'Dropmore'. The mother plant at the Arnold Arboretum, Jamaica Plain, Massachusetts, U.S.A. 45 by 30 cm.

203. *Juniperus chinensis* 'Japonica'. A developing specimen 2 m high. Young plants are low, spreading bushes.
204. *Juniperus chinensis* 'Kaizuka'. The colour is a deep rich green.

205. *Juniperus chinensis* 'Maney'. A young plant 1 m by 1 m across.

206. *Juniperus chinensis* 'Monarch'. A group of three young plants 1.5 m high.
207. *Juniperus chinensis* 'Obelisk'. Two fine specimens in the Arboretum Trompenburg,
Rotterdam, Holland.

208. *Juniperus chinensis* 'Pyramidalis'. A fine specimen 3 m. (Note that the shape is not at
all pyramidal).
209. *Juniperus chinensis* 'Stricta'. A young plant, under 1 m. The conical shape is well
maintained even in maturity.

210. *Juniperus chinensis* 'San José'. This low-growing form will spread to several metres.
211. *Juniperus communis* var. *hemisphaerica*. Reproduced from Pallas, Flora Rossica 1. pt. 2. 12, t. 54. 1788.

212. *Juniperus communis* var. *montana*. Reproduced from Arboretum et Fruticetum Britannicum. Loudon. **4**. 2489. 1838.
213 *Juniperus communis* 'Berkshire'. A diminutive plant named by Alfred J. Fordham for the area where it was found in the wild.

214. *Juniperus communis* 'Compressa'. An old example of this diminutive gem 20 cm high. Specimens much larger than this are suspect.

215. *Juniperus communis* var. *depressa*. Canadian juniper—the form common in eastern North America.

216. *Juniperus communis* 'Aureospica'. The Golden Canadian juniper. A group in the University of Minnesota Botanic Garden, Minneapolis, Minnesota, U.S.A.

217. *Juniperus communis* 'Depressed Star'. A mature specimen in the Proefstation at Boskoop, Holland.

218. *Juniperus communis* 'Dumosa'. This specimen, now 95 cm high, will broaden with age.

219. *Juniperus communis* 'Hemisphaerica'. A plant 1 m across in the Wansdyke Nursery, Devizes, Wiltshire.

220. *Juniperus communis* 'Hornibrookii'. Use of the name should be restricted to wholly prostrate forms, of which several are in cultivation, varying only in vigour.

221. *Juniperus communis* 'Inverleith'. The mother plant in the Royal Botanic Garden, Edinburgh.

222. *Juniperus communis* 'Minima' ('Silver Lining'). A specimen in the Pygmy Pinetum, Devizes, Wiltshire.

223. *Juniperus communis* 'Nana Aurea'. The habit of growth and colour distinguish this form from 'Depressa Aurea'.

224. *Juniperus communis* 'Repanda'. The name is in use for a group of related clones. Some are noticeably more prostrate than the plant in the picture.

225. *Juniperus communis* 'Suecica Nana'. The rather blunt top is characteristic.
226. Coarse, reverting growth.

227. *Juniperus communis* 'Windsor Gem'. The mother plant in the Valley Gardens, Windsor Great Park, Berkshire, England.
228. *Juniperus communis* 'Zeal'. The mother plant, now over 2 m across.

229. *Juniperus conferta*. Will cover a large area in time.
230. *Juniperus davurica* 'Expansa'. A plant 1.5 m across on the Hillier Nursery.
231. *Juniperus horizontalis* f. *alpina*. The growth is quite uncharacteristic of the species.

232. *Juniperus horizontalis* 'Bar Harbor'. A plant in the U.S. National Arboretum at Washington D.C. There are probably more than the one clone in cultivation.
233. *Juniperus horizontalis* 'Douglasii'. The very fine foliage is grey-green, turning delicate mauve in autumn.

234. *Juniperus horizontalis* 'Glenmore'.
235. *Juniperus horizontalis* 'Hughes'.

236. *Juniperus horizontalis* 'Plumosa'. A wide spreading example at the Arboretum Tempelhof, then at Reeuwijk, Holland.

237. *Juniperus horizontalis* 'Plumosa Compacta'. Noticeably more compact in habit than 'Plumosa'. Several clones have been named.

238. *Juniperus horizontalis* 'Prostrata'. This is the clone usually supplied in Britain as *J. horizontalis*.

239. *Juniperus horizontalis* 'Wiltoni'. The 'Blue Rug' of the American nursery trade.

240. *Juniperus × media* 'Armstrongii'.

241. *Juniperus × media* 'Blaauw'. The colour is blue-grey.
242. *Juniperus × media* 'Hetzii'. A large plant at Herman J. Grootendorst's residence in Boskoop, Holland. 3 m.

243. *Juniperus × media* 'Kallays Compact'. Looking down on a young plant.
244. *Juniperus × media* 'Old Gold'. A stock plant (about 1.0 m) in the Grootendorst Nursery, Boskoop, Holland.

245. *Juniperus × media* 'Pfitzerana'. A plant already 4 m across and capable of considerable further growth.

246. *Juniperus* × *media* 'Pfitzerana Compacta'. (= 'Nicks Compact' Hort. Amer.) A plant 1.5 m across.

247 *Juniperus* × *media* 'Plumosa'. The colour is dark green. 'Globosa' is very similar in growth, but is light green.

248. *Juniperus* × *media* 'Plumosa Aurea'. The colour is a dull golden-yellow, brightest at the growing tips.

249. *Juniperus* × *media* 'Plumosa Albovariegata'. The variegation is creamy-white. 2 m by 1 m.

250. *Juniperus* × *media* 'Tremonia'. This differs from 'Plumosa Aurea' mainly in the more erect habit.

251. *Juniperus procumbens*.

252. *Juniperus procumbens* 'Nana'. Note the slight lifting of all the growing tips.

253. A large specimen at Wakehurst Place, Ardingly, Sussex, England.

254. *Juniperus recurva* 'Coxii'. This plant would be much improved by some drastic thinning out at the centre.
255. *Juniperus recurva* 'Densa'. Young plants are usually much lower and more spreading.

256. *Juniperus recurva* 'Embley Park'. Unmistakeable for its rich deep green colour. A young plant 20 by 25 cm.
257. *Juniperus sabina* 'Arcadia'.

258. *Juniperus sabina* 'Fastigiata'. A rare form, reputedly of this species. This plant is 8 m high in the Arboretum Schovenhorst at Putten, Holland.
259. *Juniperus sabina* 'Rockery Gem'. A very useful, slow-growing alternative to 'Tamariscifolia'.

260. *Juniperus sabina* 'Skandia'.
261. *Juniperus sabina* 'Tamariscifolia'. This old favorite is seldom now seen in a healthy state.

262. *Juniperus sargentii* 'Glauca'. This form is less prostrate than the typical species, but both can cover quite a large area.

263. *Juniperus scopulorum* 'Skyrocket'. Unmistakeable for its extreme slimness, but any non-conforming growth that occasionally develops should be removed.
264. *Juniperus squamata* 'Blue Star'. The blue colour is the same as 'Meyeri'.
265. *Juniperus squamata* 'Holger'. The young foliage is butter-yellow, turning to blue by autumn.

266. *Juniperus squamata* 'Loderi'. A mature plant at Castlewellan, County Down, Northern Ireland.

267. *Juniperus squamata* 'Meyeri'. This plant will reach to several metres in time. One of the bluest of conifers.

268. *Juniperus squamata* 'Pygmaea'. An old specimen, over 1 m across, in the Royal Botanic Garden, Edinburgh.

269. *Juniperus squamata* 'Wilsonii'. 1 m by 1.25 m across.
270. *Juniperus taxifolia* var. *lutchuensis*. The colour is a rich, mid-green.

271. *Juniperus virginiana* 'Blue Cloud'. A plant 3 m by 1.5 m in a garden at Boskoop, Holland.
272. *Juniperus virginiana* 'Globosa'. 1 m by 1.25 m across.

273. *Juniperus virginiana* 'Grey Owl'. A stock plant 1.5 m in a Dutch nursery.
274. *Juniperus virginiana* 'Nana Compacta'. Less regularly globose than 'Globosa'.

275. *Juniperus virginiana* 'Tripartita'. Will spread to several metres diameter.

276. *Microbiota decussata.* A specimen of this rare Siberian species in the Arboretum Trompenburg, Rotterdam, Holland. Photography by J. R. P. van Hoey Smith.
277. *Microcachrys tetragona.* A plant 75 cm across at Hilliers Nursery, Jermyns Lane, Romsey, Hampshire.

278. *Picea abies* 'Acrocona'. The terminal cones are unmistakeable.
279. *Picea abies* 'Beissneri'. The thick leaves, densely covering the terminal bud, are characteristic.

280. *Picea abies* 'Capitata'. The bud clusters distinguish this form from 'Beissneri'.
281. *Picea abies* 'Clanbrassiliana'. The original tree in Tollymore Park, Newcastle, County Down, Northern Ireland.

282. Detail of foliage. Note the variation in leaf size and vigour.
283. *Picea abies* 'Clanbrassiliana Stricta'. A young plant of the long-lost form.

284. *Picea abies* 'Diffusa'. 1 m by 1 m.
285. *Picea abies* 'Elegans'. An old plant 2.5 m across at Wakehurst Place, Ardingly, Sussex.

286. *Picea abies* 'Ellwangerana'. 1.25 m by 90 cm.

287. *Picea abies* 'Gregoryana'. 25 cm. *Picea abies* 'Echiniformis' is similar but with fewer and longer needles.
288. *Picea abies* 'Hornibrookii'. A plant 1 m high in the Dortmund Botanic Garden, West Germany.

289. *Picea abies* 'Humilis'. A very old specimen in Pinetum Schovenhorst, Putten, Holland.
290. *Picea abies* 'Inversa'. A specimen 5 m high at Bicton, Devon, England.

291. *Picea abies* 'Kamon'. The mother plant in Arboretum Kamoni, Szombathely, Hungary.

292. *Picea abies* 'Little Gem'. The mother plant 40 cm in the Grootendorst Nursery, Boskoop, Holland.

293. *Picea abies* 'Maxwellii'. A mature specimen 2 m across in the New York Botanic Garden, Bronx, New York, U.S.A.

294. *Picea abies* 'Merkii'. The type plant in the Dortmund Botanic Garden, West Germany.

295. *Picea abies* 'Microsperma'. A young plant 1 m by 1 m. The form known as 'Nana Compacta' is indistinguishable.
296. *Picea abies* 'Nana'. A very old specimen 2 m high and as much through.

297. *Picea abies* 'Nidiformis'. A specimen 1 m across, now losing its nest-like habit.

298. *Picea abies* 'Ohlendorffii'. Colour: Yellow-green, turning dark green later.
299. *Picea abies* 'Pachyphylla'. The plant at Glasnevin illustrated in Hornibrook's second edition.

300. *Picea abies* 'Procumbens'. An old specimen several metres across at Nymans, Handcross, Sussex, England.

301. *Picea abies* 'Pseudo-prostrata'. A plant 2 m across in the Wansdyke Nursery, Devizes, Wiltshire.

302. *Picea abies* 'Pumila'. A plant 1.5 m across at Grayswood Hill, Haslemere, Surrey, England.

303. *Picea abies* 'Pumila Nigra'. 2 m. Colour: Dark green.

304. *Picea abies* 'Pygmaea'. One of the plants at Leonardslee, Horsham, Sussex, England, mentioned by Hornibrook. Now over 2.5 m high.

305. *Picea abies* 'Reflexa'. A fine specimen in the late A. H. Nisbet's collection.

306. *Picea abies* 'Remontii'. An old plant 3 m in the H. A. Hesse Nursery at Weener, Ems, West Germany.

307. *Picea abies* 'Repens'. A fine specimen 2 m across in the National Botanic Garden, Glasnevin, Dublin.

308. *Picea abies* 'Sargentii'.

309. *Picea abies* 'Tabuliformis'. Many plants of this variety are completely prostrate. The specimen shown was probably trained up as a young plant.
310. *Picea bicolor* 'Howells Dwarf'. A plant 1.25 m at the Vermeulen Nursery, Neshanic Station, New Jersey, U.S.A.

311. *Picea glauca* 'Albertiana Conica'. The reversion growth is doubtless being left for its botanical interest on this otherwise normal specimen in the Arboretum Les Barres, France.
312. *Picea glauca* 'Alberta Globe'. A group of young plants on the Hoogeven Nursery in Holland.

313. *Picea glauca* 'Little Globe'. A plant 15 cm across in the Verkade Nursery, Wayne, New Jersey, U.S.A.
314. *Picea glauca* 'Echiniformis'. The colour is grey-green.

315. *Picea mariana* 'Beissneri Compacta'. A plant several metres high in the Alpengarten at Frohnleiten in Austria.
316. *Picea mariana* 'Ericoides'. Note the thin, wiry leaves standing off at nearly 90°.

317. *Picea mariana* 'Nana'. Note the forward angle of the leaves.
318. *Picea* × *mariorika* 'Gnom'. A specimen about 1.25 m high in the Jeddeloh Nursery, Oldenburg, West Germany.

319. *Picea × mariorika* 'Kobold'. A specimen 2 m across in the Jeddeloh Nursery, Oldenburg, West Germany.
320. *Picea × mariorika* 'Tremonia'. The mother plant in the Westfalen Park, Dortmund, West Germany.

321. *Picea omorika* 'Nana'. An old specimen 3 m high in the Dortmund Botanic Garden, West Germany.
322. *Picea orientalis* 'Gracilis'. A young plant—capable of reaching several metres in time.

323. *Picea orientalis* 'Nana'. The darker colour and the flatter leaf spray can be seen in the photograph.
324. *Picea pungens* 'Glauca Prostrata'. A reverting plant that has developed a true (but unwelcome) leader.

325. *Picea pungens* 'Glauca Prostrata'. This cultivariant will vary according to the clone from which the scion was taken.

326. *Picea pungens* 'Glauca Nana'. Colour: Grey. Usually seen as a flat-topped plant, wider than high.
327. *Picea pungens* 'Moll'. A specimen in the Jeddeloh Nursery, Oldenburg, West Germany.

328. *Picea pungens* 'Montgomery'. The mother plant in the New York Botanical Garden, Bronx, New York, U.S.A. Often offered by European nurseries as 'Glauca Globosa'.
329. *Picea sitchensis* 'Strypemonde'. A young plant 15 cm across in the Arboretum Trompenburg, Rotterdam, Holland. Photograph by J. R. P. van Hoey Smith.

330. *Pinus aristata.* This plant from mountain seed may well turn out to be *P. longaeva.*

A group of mother plants selected at the Arnold Arboretum, Jamaica Plain, Massachusetts, U.S.A.

331. *Pinus banksiana* 'Chippewa'.   **333.** *Pinus banksiana* 'Neponset'.
332. *Pinus banksiana* 'Manomet'.

334. *Pinus banksiana* 'Schoodic'.   **335.** *Pinus banksiana* 'Wisconsin'.

336. *Pinus banksiana* 'Uncle Fogy'. A prostrate specimen in the University of Minnesota Botanic Garden, Minneapolis, Minnesota, U.S.A. It should be stem-trained or 'top worked', to produce a pendulous tree.

337. *Pinus contorta* 'Spaans Dwarf'. A specimen 15 cm tall at the Pygmy Pinetum, Devizes, Wiltshire.
338. *Pinus densiflora* 'Alice Verkade'. The mother plant now 1 m across at Verkade's Nursery, Wayne, New Jersey, U.S.A.

339. *Pinus densiflora* 'Oculis Draconis'. The dragon's eye effect on this tree in the U.S. National Arboretum, Washington D.C., U.S.A., can be seen with a little imagination.

340. *Pinus densiflora* 'Oritsuru'. An old specimen in the Royal Botanic Garden, Edinburgh.

341. *Pinus densiflora* 'Pendula'. The trunk of this tree is on the right of the picture.
342. *Pinus densiflora* 'Tagyosho' ('Umbraculifera'). An old specimen in the Royal Botanic Garden, Edinburgh.

343. *Pinus flexilis* 'Pendula'. A specimen several metres across in the Vermeulen Nursery, Neshanic Station, New Jersey, U.S.A.

344. *Pinus leucodermis* 'Aureospicata'. The mother plant 4 m by 4 m in the H. A. Hesse Nursery at Weener, Ems, West Germany.

345. *Pinus leucodermis* 'Compact Gem'. A young plant about 15 cm, in the Wansdyke Nursery, Devizes, Wiltshire.

346. *Pinus leucodermis* 'Pygmy'. A small example in the Jeddeloh Nursery, Oldenburg, West Germany.

347 *Pinus leucodermis* 'Schmidtii'. The mother plant at the National Botanical Gardens, Pruhonice, Czechoslovakia.

348. A group of *Pinus mugo* at the Royal Botanic Garden, Kew.

349. *Pinus mugo* 'Gnom'. A fine specimen 1.25 m high on the den Ouden Nursery, Boskoop, Holland.

350. *Pinus mugo* 'Hesse'. The characteristic twisting of the leaves can be very clearly seen.

351. *Pinus mugo* 'Humpy'. The mother plant at the Draijer Nursery at Heemstede, Holland.

352. *Pinus Mugo* 'Kissen'. The mother plant now 75 cm across at the Jeddeloh Nursery, Oldenburg, West Germany.

353. *Pinus mugo* 'Knapenburg'. Another mother plant at Draijer Nursery, Heemstede, Holland.

354. *Pinus mugo* 'Mops'. A stock plant, about 1 m, at the den Ouden Nursery, Boskoop, Holland.

355. *Pinus mugo* 'Winter Gold'. A nice specimen, 80 cm across, in the Wansdyke Nursery, Devizes, Wiltshire.
356. *Pinus nigra* 'Globosa'. A specimen about 2.5 m in the U.S. National Arboretum, Washington D.C., U.S.A.

357. *Pinus nigra* 'Hornibrookiana'. A young plant in the Hillier Nursery, Jermyn's Lane, Romsey, Hampshire.
358. *Pinus nigra* 'Nana'. A young plant of an old variety, recently brought back into cultivation.

359. *Pinus nigra* 'Yaffle Hill'. This may turn out to be a synonym of 'Nana'.
360. *Pinus nigra* 'Strypemonde'. Stronger growing than 'Nana' and longer in the leaf.

361. *Pinus parviflora* 'Adcocks Dwarf'. The short leaves may belie the growth potential of this form

362. *Pinus parviflora* 'Bergman'. The mother plant at Raraflora, Feasterville, Pennsylvania, U.S.A.

363. *Pinus peuce* 'Arnold Dwarf'. A young plant at the Arnold Arboretum, Jamaica Plain, Massachusetts, U.S.A.
364. *Pinus pumila.* A species that itself is dwarf. The crimson flowers are an attraction.

365. *Pinus pumila* 'Draijers Dwarf'. The mother plant in the Draijer Nursery, Heemstede, Holland.
366. *Pinus pumila* 'Dwarf Blue'.

367. *Pinus pumila* 'Globe'. Appropriately named since it naturally assumes this shape.
368. *Pinus pumila* 'Pygmaea'. A form that spreads out wider than high. The twisted leaves are characteristic.

369. *Pinus pumila* 'Säntis'. A new selection on the Draijers nursery, Heemstede, Holland.
370. *Pinus resinosa.* Two attractive dwarf seedling selections at the Arnold Arboretum, Jamaica Plain, Massachusetts, U.S.A. 'Quinobequin'.

371. – –'Nobska'.
372. *Pinus strobus* 'Bloomers Dark Globe'. A compact, rather than dwarf form, outstanding for its dark blue colour. At Vermeulens Nursery, Neshanic Station, New Jersey, U.S.A.

373. *Pinus strobus* 'Jericho'.
374. *Pinus strobus* 'Macopin'.

375. *Pinus strobus* 'Merrimack'. Seedling selections at the Arnold Arboretum, Jamaica Plain, Massachusetts, U.S.A.

376. – –'Uncatena'.

377. *Pinus strobus* 'Prostrata'. A fine specimen in the Hillier Nursery at Jermyn's Lane, Romsey, Hampshire.

378. *Pinus strobus* 'Radiata'. A nice specimen, over 2 m across, in the Arboretum Trompenburg, Rotterdam, Holland.

379. *Pinus sylvestris* 'Argentea Compacta'. The mother plant of the true form in the H. A. Hesse Nursery at Weener, Ems, West Germany. Now 5 m by 5 m.

380. *Pinus sylvestris* 'Beuvronensis'.

381. *Pinus sylvestris* 'Doone Valley'. Differs from 'Beuvronensis' in habit and colour.

382. *Pinus sylvestris* 'Globosa'. A compact, rather than dwarf form. This specimen is in the Royal Horticultural Society's garden at Wisley.

383. *Pinus sylvestris* 'Globosa Viridis'. A young plant. It shows the 'Lammas growth' and the twisted needles clearly.

384. *Pinus sylvestris* 'Hibernia'.

385. *Pinus sylvestris* 'Nana'. This is the true form, a conical plant with blue-green leaves. Often confused with 'Pyramidalis Compacta' and 'Watereri'.

386. *Pinus sylvestris* 'Pygmaea'. This is the true form, wide spreading and flat-topped and very dense in growth.

387. *Pinus sylvestris* 'Repens'. A fine specimen in the Joel W. Spingarn collection at Baldwin, Long Island, New York, U.S.A.

388. *Pinus sylvestris* 'Inverleith'. The variegation is bright and clear. Becomes large in time.

389. *Pinus sylvestris* 'Watereri'. A young plant, typically conical at this stage.

390. The mother tree at the Knaphill Nursery, Woking, Surrey, England.

391. *Pinus virginiana.* Two of the seedling selections at the Arnold Arboretum, Jamaica Plain, Massachusetts, U.S.A. 'Nashawena'.

392. – –'Pocono'.

393. *Pinus wallichiana* 'Umbraculifera'. The kinked leaves are characteristic.
394. *Podocarpus acutifolius.*

395. *Podocarpus cunninghamia.*

396. *Podocarpus nivalis.*

397. *Podocarpus totara.* From *P. cunninghamia* it differs mainly in leaf size.
398. *Pseudotsuga menziesii* 'Densa'. Always a very dense, and usually a flat-topped plant.

399. *Pseudotsuga menziesii* 'Fletcheri'. A fine old plant in the one-time Nisbet collection at Gosport, Hampshire, England. 2.5 m.
400. *Pseudotsuga menziesii* 'Hillside Pride'. The mother plant in the Hillside Gardens nursery at Lehighton, Pennsylvania, U.S.A.

401. *Pseudotsuga menziesii* 'Tempelhof Compact'. A young plant (1 m) in the Wansdyke Nursery, Devizes, Wiltshire.

402. *Sequoia sempervirens* 'Adpressa'. One of the most beautiful of all dwarf conifers, when regularly and heavily pruned.

403. *Sequoia sempervirens* 'Nana Pendula'.

404. *Sequoia sempervirens* 'Prostrata'. A plant in the Wansdyke Nursery at Devizes, Wiltshire.

405. *Sequoiadendron giganteum* 'Pygmaeum'.

406. *Taxus baccata* 'Adpressa Variegata'. A rich golden-yellow with green centre to each leaf.

407. *Taxus baccata* 'Amersfoort'.
408. *Taxus baccata* 'Decora'. A stock plant in the Hillier Nursery, Jermyn's Lane, Romsey, Hampshire.

409. *Taxus baccata* 'Dwarf White'. A specimen 2 m across in the National Pinetum, Bedgebury, Kent.

410. *Taxus baccata* 'Fastigiata'. The well known Irish yew. Colour: Very dark green.
411. *Taxus baccata* 'Fowle'. The mother plant in the Arnold Arboretum, Jamaica Plain, Massachusetts, U.S.A.

412. *Taxus baccata* 'Nutans'.
413. *Taxus baccata* 'Gracilis Pendula'. More spreading than pendulous. The clone 'Pendula' differs mainly in the size and shape of its leaves.

414. *Taxus baccata* 'Repens Aurea'.

415. *Taxus baccata* 'Semperaurea'. A young plant. With age it will extend its main branches and become more irregular in outline.
416. *Taxus cuspidata* 'Aurescens'.

417. *Taxus cuspidata* 'Nana'.
418. *Thuja occidentalis* 'Caespitosa'.

419. *Thuja occidentalis* 'Cristata'.
420. *Thuja occidentalis* 'Dumosa'. Note the vertical cord-like shoots, absent in 'Recurva Nana'.

421. *Thuja occidentalis* 'Ellwangerana Aurea'.
422. *Thuja occidentalis* 'Rheingold'.

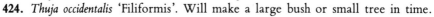

423. *Thuja occidentalis* 'Ericoides'. The fixed juvenile form. Mauve-brown in winter.
424. *Thuja occidentalis* 'Filiformis'. Will make a large bush or small tree in time.

425. *Thuja occidentalis* 'Globosa'. Colour: Light, grey-green all the year round.
426. *Thuja occidentalis* 'Golden Globe'. A stock plant in the Grootendorst Nursery in Boskoop, Holland.

427. *Thuja occidentalis* 'Holmstrup'. Often seen as a low, rounded bush. Colour: Dark green, blackish-bronze in winter.
428. *Thuja occidentalis* 'Little Champion'.

429. *Thuja occidentalis* 'Little Gem'. The colour is a rich, mid-green, bronzing in winter.
430. *Thuja occidentalis* 'Lutea Nana'. Colour: A rich, deep yellow.

431. *Thuja occidentalis* 'Ohlendorffii'. Distinctive by its dwarf habit and predominance of juvenile foliage. (Not to be confused with the vigorous 'Tetragona').
432. *Thuja occidentalis* 'Pumila'. Foliage very dense. Colour: Mid-green all the year.

433. *Thuja occidentalis* 'Pygmaea'.
434. *Thuja occidentalis* 'Recurva Nana'.

435. *Thuja occidentalis* 'Umbraculifera'. Will make a large dome-topped bush in time. The colour is a bluish-green, duller in winter.
436. *Thuja occidentalis* 'Wansdyke Silver'. The mother plant in the Pygmy Pinetum, Devizes, Wiltshire.

437. *Thuja occidentalis* 'Woodwardii'. Forms a large, globose bush. Note the parallel planes in which the foliage lies.
438. *Thuja orientalis* 'Athrotaxoides'. One of the rarest forms known.

439. *Thuja orientalis* 'Aurea Nana'.
440. *Thuja orientalis* 'Filiformis Erecta'.

441. *Thuja orientalis* 'Juniperoides' (syn. "*decussata*").
442. *Thuja orientalis* 'Meldensis'. Dull green throughout the year. Rough to the touch.

443. *Thuja orientalis* 'Minima'. (syn. *"minima glauca"*).
444. *Thuja orientalis* 'Rosedalis'. Cream in spring; green in summer; purple-brown in winter. Soft to the touch.

445. *Thuja orientalis* 'Sanderi'. The stiff, thick foliage is blue-green in summer, turning to a pale mauve in autumn. Long held to be a cultivar of *Chamaecyparis obtusa*.
446. *Thuja plicata* 'Hillieri'. A fine old plant 2 m across at Wakehurst Place, Ardingly, Sussex.

447. *Thuja plicata* 'Rogersii'. In time becomes an upright plant of looser growth.
448. *Thuja plicata* 'Stoneham Gold'. The two-tone effect of the dark green interior foliage and the orange-yellow growing tips is unmistakeably clear.

449. *Thujopsis dolabrata* 'Nana'. A fine specimen 1.5 m across in the National Pinetum, Bedgebury, Kent.
450. Foliage.

451. *Torreya nucifera* 'Prostrata'. A large specimen in the National Botanic Garden, Glasnevin, Dublin.
452. *Tsuga canadensis* 'Bacon Cristate'. Photograph by J. C. Swartley.

453. *Tsuga canadensis* 'Callicoon'. A plant 3 m across in Longwood Gardens, Kennett Square, Pennsylvania, U.S.A.

454. *Tsuga canadensis* 'Cole'. A specimen nearly 1 m across in the Joel W. Spingarn collection at Baldwin, Long Island, New York, U.S.A.
455. *Tsuga canadensis* 'Curtis Ideal'. A fine plant in the U.S. National Arboretum, Washington D.C., U.S.A.

456. *Tsuga canadensis* 'Dwarf White-tip'. A fine specimen 1.25 across in the Joel W. Spingarn collection at Baldwin, Long Island, New York, U.S.A.
457. *Tsuga canadensis* 'Fantana'. Another of Joel W. Spingarn's plants.

458. *Tsuga canadensis* 'Gable Weeping'. A plant 1.25 m high at H. J. Hohman's residence, Kingsville Nursery, Kingsville, Maryland, U.S.A.
459. *Tsuga canadensis* 'Horsford Dwarf'. Photograph by J. C. Swartley.

460 *Tsuga canadensis* 'Jacqueline Verkade'. The mother plant (50 cm) at the Verkade Nursery, Wayne, New Jersey, U.S.A.

461. *Tsuga canadensis* 'Jeddeloh'. A stock plant on the Jeddeloh Nursery, Oldenburg, West Germany.

462. *Tsuga canadensis* 'Minima'. A plant in the alpine house at the Royal Horticultural Society's garden at Wisley, Surrey.

463. *Tsuga canadensis* 'Nearing'. A nice specimen 1.5 high.

464. *Tsuga canadensis* 'Sargentii'. The specimen in the U.S. National Arboretum, Washington D.C., U.S.A.

465. *Tsuga canadensis* 'Pendula'. A plant over 4 m across. This is the clone that is grown widely in Europe under this name.

466. *Tsuga canadensis* 'Starker'. A plant over 2 m across at the Kingsville Nursery, Kingsville, Maryland, U.S.A.

467. *Tsuga canadensis* 'Warners Globe'. This plant, now about 20 cm high, is in the Arnold Arboretum, Jamaica Plain, Massachusetts, U.S.A.
468. *Tsuga canadensis* 'Watnong Star'. Photograph by J. C. Swartley.

469. *Tsuga caroliniana* 'La Bar Weeping'. A plant in the Ziegenfuss collection at Hillside Nursery, Lehighton, Pennsylvania, U.S.A.

470. *Tsuga diversifolia* 'Gotelli'. Photograph by J. C. Swartley.

INDEX*

*Key: References—roman; main description—bold; photograph—italics; identification plate—roman followed by IP.